APOSTLE *of* UNION

CIVIL WAR AMERICA

Peter S. Carmichael, Caroline E. Janney,
and Aaron Sheehan-Dean, editors

This landmark series interprets broadly the history and culture of the Civil War era
through the long nineteenth century and beyond. Drawing on diverse approaches
and methods, the series publishes historical works that explore all aspects of the war,
biographies of leading commanders, and tactical and campaign studies, along with
select editions of primary sources. Together, these books shed new light on an era
that remains central to our understanding of American and world history.

APOSTLE
of UNION

A Political Biography of
Edward Everett

MATTHEW MASON

The University of North Carolina Press CHAPEL HILL

*This book was published with the assistance of the
Thornton H. Brooks Fund of the University of North Carolina Press.*

© 2016 The University of North Carolina Press
All rights reserved

Designed and set in Bembo and Albertan types by Rebecca Evans
Manufactured in the United States of America

The University of North Carolina Press has been a member
of the Green Press Initiative since 2003.

Jacket illustration: portrait of Edward Everett by George P. A. Healy, ca. 1842–43.
Courtesy The Newberry Library, Chicago, Call # NL Artifact 20.

Library of Congress Cataloging-in-Publication Data
Names: Mason, Matthew, 1968–
Title: Apostle of Union : a political biography of Edward Everett / Matthew Mason.
Other titles: Civil War America (Series)
Description: Chapel Hill : The University of North Carolina Press, [2016] |
Series: Civil War America | Includes bibliographical references and index.
Identifiers: LCCN 2016000576 | ISBN 9781469628608 (cloth : alk. paper) |
ISBN 9781469628615 (ebook)
Subjects: LCSH: Everett, Edward, 1794–1865. | Legislators—United States—
Biography. | Statesmen—United States—Biography. | Governors—Massachusetts—
Biography. | United States. Congress—Biography. | United States—Politics and
government—1783–1865. | United States—History—Civil War, 1861–1865.
Classification: LCC E340.E8 M37 2016 | DDC 328.73092—dc23 LC record
available at http://lccn.loc.gov/2016000576

For Stacie, Emily, Hannah, and Rachel

Contents

Figures

Acknowledgments

In addition to gainful employment at Brigham Young University during the years of work on this book, I am grateful for those who have helped fund it. At BYU, those entities include the College of Family, Home, and Social Sciences; the Department of History; the David M. Kennedy Center for International Studies; and the General Education and Honors Programs. Further funding came from the Gilder Lehrman Institute of American History and the American Antiquarian Society. For help both financial and logistical in getting me access to Everett documents in Provo, I thank Paul Kerry as well as the Interlibrary Loan staff at Harold B. Lee Library at BYU.

For enormously helpful and encouraging readings of the whole manuscript, I am grateful to James Brewer Stewart, John Brooke, Michael Morrison, and Elise Peterson. For reading and making useful comments on parts of the manuscript, my thanks go to Michael E. Woods, Douglas Egerton, Nicholas Wood, Francois Furstenberg, Scott Heerman, Edward Rugemer, Corey Brooks, John Craig Hammond, Nicholas Mason, Jeffrey Kerr-Ritchie, Randall Miller, David Waldstreicher, Elizabeth Varon, Conrad Wright, Paul Kerry, Gary Gallagher, and Stacey Robertson. For helping me talk through earlier iterations of and issues with this book, I thank Fred Blue, Daniel Walker Howe, and Chuck Grench.

This book is dedicated to my wife and daughters, for whom I would willingly buckle a knapsack to my back and march anywhere.

APOSTLE *of* UNION

Introduction

In December 1859, with John Brown's raid on Harpers Ferry having shaken his beloved Union once again to its core, Edward Everett rose to address a mass meeting in his hometown of Boston. This audience knew Everett not only for his long career as a scholar and politician but also for his most recent career as a traveling orator for the Union. Throughout the late 1850s, Everett had journeyed to every section of the nation delivering an oration titled "The Character of Washington" to packed houses, donating the proceeds to save the first president's Mount Vernon estate as a shrine to the Union. Thus when he stepped to the podium of this meeting called to demonstrate Bostonians' attachment to the Union, the throng paid him "every demonstration of respect and enthusiasm." Everett's predominant purpose that day, as with his Mount Vernon activities, was "to inculcate the blessings of the Union," consecrated as they were by "the memory of our Fathers" who gave it to us: "Precious legacy of our fathers, it shall go down, honored and cherished to our children. Generations unborn shall enjoy its privileges as we have done, and if we leave them poor in all besides, we will transmit to them the boundless wealth of its blessings!" Such filial appeals had an electric effect. A newspaper reporter present remarked on "the close attention, the earnest feeling, which this vast crowd manifested," including "the frequent tears in the eyes and on the faces of multitudes touched by a common sympathy, as some patriotic emotion was awakened by the sentiments of the several speakers." Indeed, attendees' "hearts were swelling with pent-up emotions, longing to find adequate expression."[1]

A year and a half previous, he had taken this Unionist gospel into the belly of the secessionist beast, Charleston, South Carolina, and had received a similarly rapturous response. Reports of his performance of the oration in Augusta, Georgia, beat Everett to Charleston, and they described how his auditors in that town had "not yet recovered from the spell which was thrown around us by this mighty magician." Indeed, words failed when one attempted to convey "the impression which was made upon us by his magnificent oration upon the career and character of the *Pater Patrae*." Upon his arrival a committee of Charlestonians greeted Everett as the very "High Priest of the Union," come "to aid in perpetuating that Union in its whole constitutional integrity and sanctity, and in the spirit and wisdom of its immortal founder." A friendly newspaper editor who attended the speech the next night agreed with his Georgian counterpart that mere words could not capture the effect of the oration. But he did boldly declare that "an epoch in many memories will be dated from the happy privilege and experience" of hearing Everett expound upon Washington and the Union.[2]

Such public demonstrations of emotion in such apparently opposite and antagonistic places as Boston and Charleston on the eve of the Civil War cry out for exploration. They indicate both the strength of the Union and that this strength lay primarily in the hearts of antebellum Americans. As the content of Everett's speeches suggested, the Union packed such an emotive punch for most white antebellum Americans because of its connection to the revered Revolutionary Fathers and because it embodied the Revolution's legacy of political rights that were rare in the nineteenth-century world. Indeed, for them the term "Union" connoted a voluntary confederation rather than a nation cemented by force. Others might calculate the value of that compact and make decisions about slavery based on profit and loss considerations. But these patriots stood by a Union of the heart, not of the pocketbook.[3] Few if any Americans had done more to nurture this conviction than Edward Everett.[4]

Indeed, by then Everett had pursued an unusually long, complex, and high-profile career at the crossroads of slavery, a culture of reform, and nation-building in American politics. He had been much in the public eye as an orator, politician, scholar, and diplomat. His thinking, writing, and speaking about the nature and value of the American Union stretched from the death of George Washington to the presidency of Abraham Lincoln. The successes, failures, and evolution of his vision of how vexing political questions, including—but far from limited to—slavery, should interact with the sacred Union provide an unusually valuable window on the ebbs and flows of Unionism as a political force across this long period. The themes Everett's career illuminates dictate the parameters of this volume: it will have its hands full with presenting a political biography focused on the man's public life. His literary efforts and his private life will come in only as they shed light on that public career.[5]

Yet even well-informed general readers have only a vague recollection of Everett as the stodgy orator who rambled on for hours at Gettysburg before Abraham Lincoln took the stage. Most scholars of the early American Republic do not think much about, or of, Everett. They tend to dismiss him as a "doughface" (the derogatory contemporary term for Northern politicians who sided with the South in the sectional debates over slavery that led to the Civil War) and therefore craven and unpopular. Those who attend more closely to Everett's career caricature him as an academic out of his depth in the rough-and-tumble of Jacksonian-era American politics. As it stands, his fullest biography is almost ninety years old. The most extensive scholarly treatments of Everett are appreciative studies of his oratory by professors of communication studies, in which the political history of Everett's times forms only a backdrop. Given these works' publication in venues that do not reach historians, no wonder historians do not know Everett.[6]

It was not always so. At his death in 1865, Everett was a household name throughout the Union (and the Confederacy). Then for much of the late nineteenth century, scholars and the public ranked him high among antebellum orators, statesmen, and men of letters. Admirers most often mentioned him in connection with Lincoln, or with his close antebellum ally Daniel Webster, esteeming him as proverbial for patriotism.[7]

Everett's declining reputation is in large part a function of historiographical trends in recent decades. On the one hand, this study of Everett adds to a growing willingness among historians to take sectional moderates seriously. But on the other, recent historical literature remains disproportionately focused on Americans who espoused extreme proslavery and (especially) antislavery views. Either directly or by omission, the standard narratives of the era dismiss sectional moderates as irrelevant to the story of polarization that led to secession and war. Passionate Unionists like Everett and his audience have no role to play in such interpretations other than to stand on the shore, helpless against the rising antislavery tide in the North and the secessionist tide in the South.[8]

Those who have studied Everett have outdone this portrait by painting him as so out of touch that he should never have been in politics in the first place. Many cast him in a one-dimensional, static role as a typical doughface, insufficiently supplied with a moral compass or a backbone to resist the march of Southern slavery.[9] But beyond that, scholars universally treat Everett as a bookish fish out of water in the popular politics of his day. Constitutionally allergic to conflict, "he lacked . . . both taste and talent for the contentiousness, vulgarity, and violence endemic to the rapid democratization of American politics."[10] Such studies are not calculated to spark political historians' interest in Everett.

But to neglect or dismiss Edward Everett is to misperceive both Everett's political savvy and the popular appeal of the emotional brand of Unionism he represented. To be sure, Everett hated sectional conflicts so much that it sometimes harmed his physical health to be caught up in them. Contemporaries often found him "grave and prosaic to a fault." Especially after he left his Senate seat in the mid-1850s, he was ambivalent about whether what he was doing was political. And when it benefited him politically, he pleaded that his early career did not prepare him for what he disdained as "the low game of politics."[11] But he was not tone-deaf to the imperatives of popular politics. He vigorously resisted efforts to brand him an aristocrat, worked closely with newspaper editors to hone the printed versions of his speeches, and was so concerned about his public image that he asked correspondents to return copies of letters he had sent them![12] He understood politics well enough to serve in both houses of Congress, as governor of Massachusetts, as ambassador to Great Britain, and as secretary of state and to receive a vice-presidential nomination in arguably the most important presidential election in American history.

One key thing Everett understood about politics that historians have only recently begun to fully recapture is how deeply it was intertwined with both high and popular American culture. Decades ago, in what is today an unjustly neglected work, scholar George Forgie treated Everett's late antebellum popularity as evidence of Americans' "sentimental regression from politics to domesticity" in the crisis decade of the 1850s.[13] But Everett and his many fellow travelers would have scratched their heads at this attempt to separate the cultural and the political. They embraced this cause with unbounded sentimentalism, but theirs was no escapism. At all ranks they articulated a targeted political purpose: saving the Union. To be fair, Forgie wrote before the waves of recent scholarship elucidating the intersections between politics and culture in the early Republic and those between nationalism and the politics of historical memory.[14] For this reason among others, the time seems right, as historian Irving Bartlett put it over fifteen years ago, "for a reevaluation of one of our most visible, versatile, and productive Americans, whose life extended from Washington's administration to the year of Lincoln's assassination."[15]

There were numerous Americans toiling in varying ways to build national loyalty in the new and fractious Republic, and Everett's long career brought many of them together. Builders of the early American nation faced long odds. They encountered potent regional identities as well as tricky questions, like how much of their British heritage to include in the national autobiography. They also lacked most of the standard building materials of nationhood, such as a strong centralized state or a common religion or language or ethnicity.[16] But Americans' nation-building project was never going to fail for lack of trying. Some worked with the tools of highbrow literature, while others worked at the grass roots to develop the voluntary associations that marked a distinctively American civil society. Many emphasized American identity in opposition to a variety of "Others," ranging from foreigners to domestic racial minorities. Still others produced nationalist histories, memorials, and music meant to serve as the texts, shrines, and liturgy of a distinctively American civil religion. Their efforts clustered around commemorations of American military history, especially the American Revolution. That made the Fourth of July the premiere occasion on which to stoke the nationalist fire and venerate Washington as the preeminent national saint.[17] This active culture of historical celebration made powerful use of one of the primary building blocks of national identity in the modern world. It gave American nationalists, like those curating national memory elsewhere, a sense both of deep roots in a common history and of the nation's historical destiny.[18] Everett brought many of these nationalist tools to his long hours on the national work site. He worked with his pen, and he contributed money and organizational skill to efforts to memorialize American history.

But first and foremost he deployed oratory. It was an implement of enormous force. Early Americans valued rhetorical skill as the king of literary accomplishments, indispensable to the workings of a political system based on securing the consent of citizens. Individual orators such as Webster and Everett inspired awe that flirted with worship, in part because their art by design worked on the sentiments as well as on the reason of their audiences.[19] The particular topics Everett subjected to his oratorical treatment also drew on almost the full range of nationalist shibboleths. He repeatedly marshaled North America's history, and its military history in particular, to create a national biography for the United States and elevate it to at least equal importance with those of European nations. He appealed to the Constitution and Washington's Farewell Address as his civil religion's sacred texts; to the Founding Fathers, preeminently Washington, as its patron saints; and to historically significant sites, preeminently Mount Vernon, as its places of pilgrimage.

Although unity was the goal, contemporaries' reactions to Everett's exertions highlight the passions on all sides of the contest between sectionalism and nationalism. Most historians associate intensity of feeling exclusively with sectional extremists. While Everett and his fellow laborers made no effort to disguise the nation-building end of their mythmaking, they opposed as illegitimate sectionalists' equally instrumental usages of such symbols and language. Those on the other side likewise saw sectional moderates as traitors to the national heritage. The increasing intensity of these memory wars shows that neither side was especially "moderate" and helps explain the volume (in both senses of the term) of antebellum Americans' appeals to tradition.[20]

Indeed, more than any other problem in American life, slavery confounded both Everett and the nationalist project to which he dedicated himself. Everett's confusion on how to deal with American slavery was profound, and his public stances on the issue were situational rather than consistent. At one extreme, in his initial speech in the U.S. House of Representatives, he denied that slavery was wrong and pledged to strap on his knapsack and help the white South put down any slave rebellion in its midst. At another point in his congressional career he even (privately) pondered purchasing a plantation in Louisiana. At the other extreme, Everett as governor of Massachusetts gave public responses to abolitionists' election-year queries about candidates' stances on the key issues surrounding slavery that satisfied those abolitionists and panicked Southern slaveholders. More than two decades later a secretary in Lincoln's cabinet consulted Everett in advance of the publication of the Emancipation Proclamation.

It is difficult to discern a pattern in such swings, but to discount Everett as a rudderless opportunist would be to lose key insights into the twists and turns of American slavery politics from the 1820s through the 1860s at the state, national, and international levels. Indeed, a biographical treatment of such a long career allows us to watch how the key historical elements of place and time impact an individual's shifting priorities. The fact that Everett, one of the brightest minds of his generation, was so confused over how to address slavery helps us see the complexity of the issue for the antebellum generations as it interacted with all other contemporary issues. Everett sought the middle of the road on the slavery issue, but that road was a winding one.

To dismiss compromisers on the slavery issue is easy to do but impoverishes our understanding of a vast swath of antebellum American political culture. Philosophers and other theorists who have contemplated compromise as a concept have illuminated its complexity. Throughout their history most Americans have agreed that compromise is necessary to the workings of a democratic politics and society, as well as a historic basis for union. But most people also believe that a compromise between good and evil lies outside the just limits of compromise, so they can accept a compromise only when it involves two morally legitimate sides.[21] It is hard for modern observers when encountering historical compromises over slavery to imagine them as anything but a compromise between ultimate good (freedom) and evil (slavery) and Northern conciliators as anything but morally flawed. But excellent recent scholarship has recognized that as starkly immoral as slavery was, opposition to it encompassed a range of antislavery beliefs and actions rather than stark dichotomies between heroes and goats. As Caleb McDaniel has aptly noted, this literature focuses "attention less on stable *boundaries* between groups and more on unstable *bonds* that drew antislavery individuals together at particular moments in time."[22]

Instability certainly characterized Everett's relationship with abolitionists and antislavery politicians across his long career, and attention to that changing relationship illuminates the dynamics of his orbit within the antislavery solar system.

An insight from David Potter also helps us comprehend the popularity and persistence of compromises and compromisers by seeing them from the inside. Historians' recognition that "slavery, in one aspect or another, pervaded all of the aspects of sectionalism," Potter noted, has left them content to ask "a simple question: Did the people of the North *really* oppose slavery? rather than a complex one: What was the rank of antislavery in the hierarchy of northern values?" The complex version should help us perceive how the antislavery sentiment of the vast majority of Northerners conflicted with their love of a Union and Constitution that manifestly protected slavery. Thus the question became for them "not a choice of alternatives—antislavery or proslavery—but a ranking of values. . . . The difference between 'antislavery men' and 'conciliationists' in the North was not a question of what they thought about slavery alone, but of how they ranked these priorities." Such complexities should give us pause even in the terms we apply to people and positions, for "those who were 'moderate' about slavery were 'extreme' about the Union, quite as much as those who were 'moderate' about the Union were 'extreme' about slavery. When there are two reference points—the Union and slavery—it is purely arbitrary to make one, rather than the other, the measure of extremism."[23] From his emotional embrace of the Union to his shifts on the emphasis and tone with which he addressed slavery, Everett's career gives flesh-and-blood illustration to Potter's incisive points.

Revealingly, biography has proven the best route to illustrating the range of what was possible along a spectrum of antislavery belief and action. Biography done right can trace change and continuity across time and show an issue like slavery interacting with other issues that demanded the subject's attention and loyalty. Everett usually occupied places on this spectrum at several removes from radical abolitionists, but he was closer to antislavery icons like John Quincy Adams and Abraham Lincoln than one would at first suspect. Judicious biographical treatments of these and other antislavery heroes have shown that every one of them took changing positions on the issue because they dealt with slavery in the context of other commitments. Imperatives such as party loyalty or nationalism at times encouraged emancipationist sentiment and action, while at other times they could impede them. The same is true for this biography of Everett. It will show Everett "in motion" on slavery, as Eric Foner phrased his treatment of Lincoln, but it will not show Everett moving in one direction or in a predictable way.[24] Still, Everett's movement along the antislavery spectrum took place within limits. His antislavery principles dictated that there were bounds beyond which his conservatism could not go; his nationalism and respect for law and order also set boundaries around his antislavery for much of his career.[25]

Everett's dedication to moral reform was also part of what kept him from traveling to anti-abolitionist extremes. His devotion to the Whiggish ethic of improvement meant he would always be far less bitter toward abolitionists and antislavery politicians than doughfaced Democrats tended to be. All anti-abolitionists decried zealotry, but most Democratic doughfaces feared and loathed everyone who injected moral questions into the political arena. Everett recoiled from fanaticism but could better understand the antislavery reform impulse, for he was an ardent supporter of the range of humanitarian reform movements in the nineteenth-century Atlantic world that scholars have dubbed the Benevolent Empire. Histories of this culture of benevolent reform have emphasized the evangelical roots thereof, and recent studies have situated within this culture radical abolitionists like one of John Brown's Secret Six of supporters, the Bostonian Samuel G. Howe. Everett was neither evangelical nor abolitionist, but his commitment to the Benevolent Empire was indisputable. "Heaven knows I am no enemy to progress," Everett pled in a classic statement of the Whig brand of reformism. "In my humble measure I have longed for it, and toiled for it; in reference to some deep questions, I have wept and prayed for it; but let it really be progress." That Everett and Howe could have both emerged from this same culture underscores how broad and powerful this reform impulse was, and is worth explaining through the medium of biography.[26]

Everett's career with slavery was so complex in large part because he had pledged allegiance at once to nationalism, law and order, and reform. The oscillating vortex of slavery as it interacted with other issues encouraged him to emphasize one or the other of these commitments, depending on time and place. His career thus nicely illuminates the complexities of slavery and related issues for reform-minded antebellum Americans. The fact that Everett failed abolitionists' purity tests made his life more rather than less representative of his times.

Antislavery activists and politicians themselves obscured their closeness to people like Everett by pouring out some of their worst scorn on the "dough-faces" and "Cotton Whigs" as weak-kneed, craven traitors to the cause of freedom, and most recent historians have adopted that viewpoint as their own. But taking sectional moderates like Everett seriously involves understanding their self-image rather than accepting their enemies' view at face value. Sectional conservatives probably prolonged the torturous life of slavery in the United States by helping Southern slaveholders achieve the dominant power in the federal government that was so necessary to preserving slavery. But the moderates insisted that whatever their votes' and speeches' effects on slavery, that was collateral to their central and noble goal of preserving the Union. And they insisted that their willingness to compromise and conciliate while taking heat from their constituents meant they embodied the antebellum ideals of restrained manhood and political moderation.[27]

Studies of sectional moderates need not substitute that self-image for the abolitionists' view. Instead, in this book I purpose to build on the rich scholarship on abolitionists and antislavery politicians by putting Everett and his antagonists into dialogue. Furthermore, given that proslavery Southerners also repeatedly numbered among his opponents, attending closely to all participants in the debates swirling around Everett yields an important insight about the antebellum sectional controversy. While most studies of that conflict portray it as a two-way struggle between North and South, it was in fact even in its barest outlines a three-way contest between Northern sectionalists, Southern sectionalists, and committed Unionists. It was in truth more than three-sided because that latter team was riven by its own sectional and partisan differences, and African American stances on these issues rarely comported with many among any of the white teams. But consistently seeing this battle as three-sided would be a step forward for our understanding of the era. Contemplating it in this way across several decades also allows us to see the ebbs and flows in who had the upper hand in this combat at any given time.

As suggested earlier in this introduction, Unionism and Unionists were a force to be reckoned with, even when the sectionalists had the momentum and initiative. Elizabeth Varon has shown that even as disunion rhetoric and programs became more commonplace in the 1850s, attacking one's enemies as disunionists remained a winning political tactic. Again there is the case of John Brown. The national resonance of his deeds in both Kansas and western Virginia showed how a small band of antislavery zealots could drive the political agenda and put moderates of various stripes on the defensive. But when Brown's disciples met in 1858 to adopt the "Provisional Constitution and Ordinances of the People of the United States," they hotly debated an article that insisted that this constitution's articles "look to no dissolution of the Union, but simply to Amendment and Repeal." "Our flag," they added, "shall be the same that our Fathers fought under in the Revolution."[28] Their violent attempt to implement this constitution put Unionists once again into a reactive posture. But the throngs attending the Union meetings and the ideological power of the Unionism they represented made them a key audience for even the most radical of sectionalists.

And in a landmark recent study of the Civil War, Gary Gallagher has built a convincing case based on overwhelming evidence from a variety of sources that throughout that costly conflict, preserving the Union was the primary motivation for the vast majority of Union soldiers and civilians. Even after 1863, for most Unionists emancipation constituted a means toward the original end of saving the Union. President Lincoln repeatedly argued for this way of seeing emancipation, whereas his most determined Democratic opponents charged that the war aims had changed with the Emancipation Proclamation. Thus, "without an appreciation of why the loyal citizenry went to great lengths to restore the Union," Gallagher boldly but rightly proclaims "no accurate understanding of the era is possible."[29]

It takes some doing to explain to a modern audience, Gallagher muses, why the cause of Union "once resonated so powerfully." "A war to end slavery seems more compelling" to twenty-first-century Americans and far less abstract than a war for union. He explains this by noting that recent popular culture has rejected the idea of "nationalism as a motivating force." Moreover, while Civil War–era scholarship's focus in recent decades on race and emancipation has obviously paid enormous dividends, it "sometimes suggests the war had scant meaning apart from these issues—and especially that the Union victory had little or no value without emancipation." As if to prove Gallagher's point, James Oakes's own outstanding recent study of the war decries the idea that "an ethically dubious nationalism" motivated the Union war effort. "It would indeed be difficult to excuse so much bloodshed," Oakes posits, "if it served no purpose other than the restoration of the Union." So by making it clear that for Republicans it was also an antislavery war from the beginning, Oakes believes he is rescuing some purity for the war. The work of scholars who have shown how postbellum Americans marshaled the idea that the Civil War was about union to achieve North-South reconciliation for whites only has likely contributed to the souring of professional historians on what Gallagher calls the Union Cause. But as Gallagher demonstrates, wartime Unionism was far from abstract or meaningless to loyal Americans.[30]

The passionate connection to Union that prompted loyal citizens' enormous and sustained wartime sacrifices did not spring up ex nihilo in 1861. It was in large part the result of the cultural work done by Everett and his fellow laborers in the antebellum nationalist vineyard. The willingness to fight rather than allow secession, the at once high-minded and visceral attachment to union that sustained the war effort, and the wartime wielding (often by women) of historical symbols of American nationalism in organized prowar efforts all had antecedents illustrated by the prewar career of Edward Everett.[31] The searing politics of slavery that confounded Everett for decades and led to the election of 1860 and secession put him and his fellow Unionists almost entirely on the defensive. But the Civil War itself illustrated how they had helped order the priorities of most Northerners and many Southerners, such that they were willing to fight and die for the sacred American Union.[32]

1

Scholar, Preacher, and Paper Warrior

On 11 April 1794, Oliver and Lucy Everett welcomed their fourth child, Edward, into their home in the Boston suburb of Dorchester. Oliver, who came from a long-standing but rather undistinguished Massachusetts family, had raised his economic and social position by earning an education from Harvard and the post as minister of Boston's New South Church. In 1792 he lost this pastorate due to chronic health problems, and the family moved to Dorchester to regain Oliver's strength. His source of livelihood is murky until 1799, when he became a judge in the county Court of Common Pleas. While the family was headed by a man respected in Dorchester for his mental powers, then, Edward and his siblings were raised in lower-middling material circumstances at best.[1]

Both his father's example and the family's economic situation pointed young Edward's feet to education as the path of upward mobility. Dorchester was a propitious place to enter such a path, for the school took second place only to the church in its residents' hearts. Proud to lay claim to the first taxpayer-supported public school in America (dating from 1639), Dorchesterites hired an unusually long run of excellent Harvard-trained teachers. It was in the town's new brick schoolhouse that Edward attracted the earnest tutelage of not only his instructors but also the Reverend Thaddeus Mason Harris, the respected pastor of the First Church. Four decades later, Everett, by then the governor of Massachusetts, looked back on "the Boston schools" as "the friends of my friendless youth and poverty," gratefully gushing that they "gave me a better education than I had the means of getting any other way."[2] While "poverty" may have been a bit strong, this reminiscence is a key to understanding Edward's self-image as a success story made possible by education.

Edward's first political memory—in fact, many key personal firsts for him—came in connection with George Washington's death in December 1799, which touched off a months-long spell of national mourning in which citizens elaborately staged their grief. Though it came in the midst of bitter partisan divisions, this process of grieving eschewed party politics in favor of national unity. As one historian has put it, these public memorials for Washington "were significant events in advancing the development of an American civil religion," as clergymen eulogists "fused the symbol of Washington with Christianity" and a providential vision of American destiny. Women's heavy participation in the public mourning ceremonies helped cement the notion that it was all above the sordidness of partisanship.[3] Children also participated in these rituals. Edward's contemporary and future fast friend George Ticknor remembered seeing his father come home speechless with emotion; "my mother was alarmed to see him in such a state, until he recovered enough to tell her the sad news." He recalled that children joined in wearing black crepe on their arm during the period of mourning. Such vivid memories were part and parcel of an early national political culture in Massachusetts that centered on reverence for the Revolution and its heroes. Ruled by surviving patriots, surrounded by places full of associations with the Revolution, and indoctrinated by ceremonies commemorating its glories and heritage, young Bay Staters grew up very much in the shadow of the American Revolution.[4]

Though not yet six years old, Edward experienced Washington's death in an indelible way. Six decades later, he recounted vivid memories from that period. A song whose refrain was "Huzza for Washington" had stuck with him all that time. He remembered his father placing around his neck a black ribbon whose medal bore the inscription "He is in glory, the world is in tears." In school, "his first little declamation was the familiar elegy, beginning—'From Vernon's Mount behold the hero rise; / Resplendent forms attend him to the skies.'" Perhaps most memorably, Dorchester's leading citizens chose Oliver Everett for the distinct honor of delivering the town's official eulogy of Washington on the departed demigod's birthday, 22 February 1800. In the 1850s, Edward recalled in vivid detail his father's preparations to deliver the oration, the only writing of Oliver's ever published. "I seem even now," he added, to hear Dorchester's town bell calling the town's citizens to attend his father's speech. In another first, this was the first public secular discourse that Edward ever heard.[5]

In that eulogy, Oliver attributed Washington's "undeviating course of right actions" to his possession of a "combination of shining virtues." His general course was to "illustrate the character of General WASHINGTON" and to place him within a providential history of the march of that "civil freedom," "order and justice," which flourished in America and which WASHINGTON (always in caps) defended in war and peace. Americans must now emulate his selfless patriotic devotion by defending the nation he had founded. Although this Federalist saw that country menaced by "treacherous citizens" and "designing foreigners," he submitted that "by far the greatest portion of our citizens, it is believed, are friends to order and our excellent constitution" and if called forth by a crisis "will take their beloved offspring by the hand, and march towards the tomb of WASHINGTON." Rallying at this shrine, these patriots would swear "to preserve from ruin their beloved country; and to perpetuate those national blessings which it enjoyed, under the patronage of its departed SAVIOUR." Oliver made no attempt to hide the political benefits of such an imagined gathering, whose "effect shall be wonderful. Patriotism shall revive; . . . faction shall vanish. Order shall return. Righteousness shall reign."[6] In all of these unforgettable aspects of this moment were themes that would shape key parts of Edward's own future career of public Washington worship: unrestrained praise for the civic saint; the focus on his character and on how emulating it would save the imperiled Union from internal threat; the stakes involved in saving such a Union; and a vivid vision of Washington's tomb as a physical embodiment of and rallying point for Americans' devotion to a constitutional union of law and order. It is notable that this speech and all the other emotional connections to Washington and union far predated Edward Everett's exposure to slavery and other questions that would engross his attention in later years.

Such memories as these would become all the more poignant when Oliver died in 1802, whereupon Lucy moved her young family to Boston. Edward thrived there as well and in the process formed his friendship with Daniel Webster when the latter served as a substitute schoolmaster over Edward's school. In 1807, at the tender age of thirteen, the bright young scholar entered Harvard University, where he succeeded in every subject and graduated as valedictorian. In later years he remembered his experience at Harvard in great detail. In his reminiscences he admitted that ambition had driven most of his efforts, which went far beyond what was required to succeed in his studies. He also formed another relationship that would powerfully shape his career when he took classes from the first Boylston Professor of Rhetoric and Oratory, John Quincy Adams, which left an indelible impression on him.[7]

During his senior year, Everett joined with some classmates to found a literary journal for which he served as editor and contributor-in-chief, the *Harvard Lyceum*. The content as well as the endeavor itself was a preview of coming attractions from Everett. In the inaugural edition, the "Address of the Editors" pledged a journal that would attend to the widest range of Harvard students' intellectual interests in typical fashion for a "literary review," but "the subject of American literature will receive our particular attention. This ought to be the theme of the reflection and inquiry of all, whose reputation as Americans is involved in the result." There followed a long, defensive lead editorial granting but explaining away American literature's inferiority to European. One article did lament Americans' current mode of celebrating the Fourth of July, however, where the "feeble triteness" of the orations sent revelers away "without improving their minds, their patriotism, or their virtue." Another regretted some Americans' unnecessarily angry tone and unfair reverse criticisms in responding to their British critics.[8] At sixteen years of age, then, Everett enunciated a nationalist viewpoint on literature, balanced by a budding Anglophilia. He also perceived the largely untapped potential of public occasions such as Fourth of July celebrations to elevate citizens' hearts and minds to achieve political ends, including vindicating America in the Atlantic republic of letters.

Other articles Everett either contributed to or included in this sheet offered further glimpses into his forming ideologies relative to slavery and other leading political themes. One enthused that "every native of this happy land, taught to dread slavery as the severest curse, can well appreciate his privileges" and would never hesitate to fight in their defense. Another piece arguing against the tendency to disparage modern civilization and worship the ancient pointed out that "in the most refined periods of antiquity," the "state of society" was such that "more than nine tenths" of the lower orders of the population were "doomed to miserable servitude" despite all the leading citizens' paeans to Athenian liberty and denunciations of "usurpation and tyranny abroad."[9] Such reflections were imprecise predictors of how the young man would approach American slavery; they might have underwritten either a complacent attitude toward slavery based on its antiquity or on America's alleged freedom from its curse, or a vigorous opposition to Americans' appalling emulation of Athenian hypocrisy. Reflections on other political and social issues included one titled "Essay on Government" observing that "it seems to be necessary to the preservation of the human race on earth, that subordination of various kinds should exist in society." This conservatism was balanced by an article called "Enthusiasm," which took a charitable attitude toward this much-abused trait. It should be channeled and prudently managed but not extinguished because it had beneficial effects on the sensibilities of a man, even with all its excesses.[10] Judging by these articles, he was a budding conservative but no reactionary, committed to rational reform and hesitant on the painful issue of slavery.

These predilections reflected in large measure the influence of Everett's mentors. One influence that Everett himself cited was Benjamin Franklin. In 1855, he vividly recalled reading Franklin's famous autobiography while at Harvard. "Few books that I have ever read," he declared, "have had a greater influence over me than this little volume." From it he gleaned a respect for the kind of "industry, perseverance, and method" that earned him the nickname

"Ever-at-it" among his Harvard peers. This volume also helped lay the foundation for his trademark conciliatory interpersonal and public-speaking style: "I learned from it the superiority of a modest intimation of opinion over dogmatic assertion, and the propriety of speaking with diffidence on controverted points." As scholar Alan Houston has shown, Franklin committed himself to "a host of social and political reforms," moved by an ethic of "improvement." Everett showed across several decades how deeply he had imbibed that ethic.[11]

Among the living, he emulated foremost the Unitarian minister of Boston's Brattle Street Church, Joseph Stevens Buckminster. Everett's family had attended the hugely respected cleric's congregation for some years, and Everett regarded Buckminster as the very model of a clergyman and a scholar. While at Harvard Everett visited Buckminster weekly to discuss matters theological and literary. Buckminster taught that the spheres of church, state, and letters should interrelate and that men of letters should seek to influence the other realms. As such, Everett's career would epitomize Buckminster's legacy.[12] Among Buckminster's sermons that enunciated political and social themes was a Thanksgiving sermon celebrating the circumstances in the United States "which are favorable to great moral and religious eminence." All of these conditions were in contrast with, and at a providential distance from, the decayed, stratified, unfree, and warlike Old World. While Buckminster encouraged his protégés Everett and Ticknor to travel to Europe to continue their studies, such counsels were tempered by this nationalist vision of the United States.[13] Another running theme in his sermons was a reverence for the apostle Paul, whom he painted as zealous but not fanatical or delusional. Indeed, Buckminster offered a paean to self-mastery, which he contrasted with "the spirit of the times" with all its "state of passions in constant turmoil."[14]

This call for Christian zeal tempered by moderation shone through a discourse touching on slavery in Paul's—and by extension in Buckminster's—time. In an undated discourse on the New Testament book of Philemon, Buckminster argued that the main lesson of this short book was what we can learn about "the character of the writer Paul," and hence about "the nature and spirit of Christianity." In Paul's letter to Philemon urging him to take back his runaway Christian slave Onesimus as a brother in Christ, the careful reader "would see the distinctions of master and slave, of the chief apostle and his meanest convert, vanishing in their common relation to Jesus and his gospel." But the honest reader would also "find, that Christianity made no alterations in the civil or political relations of the converts, for Paul demands not the emancipation of the slave, but, on the contrary, returns him to the service of his master." "How generous," Buckminster concluded, "how disinterested, and yet how practicable is all this! How conformable to the preaching of Jesus of Nazareth, and how unlike the customs and the spirit of modern society!" He who failed to understand this example of true, practicable benevolence "understands not the nature of Christianity. He has not imbibed that spirit of charity, without which the most confident faith and the most burning zeal are but a hypocritical show, or a ruinous delusion."[15] In this sermon Buckminster embodied the Massachusetts Unitarianism that historian Daniel Walker Howe has helpfully depicted as torn between optimism about humans' ability to solve worldly problems by the application of rational moral sense, and commitment to hierarchy and order. "Religious liberals and social conservatives, at once optimistic and apprehensive," Unitarians like Buckminster were "reformers who feared change," especially as achieved by "aggressive debate."[16] In this sermon as elsewhere, Everett's mentor advocated truly reaching out to the less fortunate, but not by means of a divisive radical spirit.

———

After graduating, Everett conformed his public expressions to this spirit of reconciliation. Yielding to Buckminster's and others' advice, Everett stayed at Harvard to prepare for a career as a minister. In 1812 Buckminster died suddenly, and in 1813 the Brattle Street parishioners invited his pupil Everett to take his place. Leading one of the preeminent churches in Boston confirmed Everett's meteoric rise into the city's intellectual and social elite. He may have been foolhardy to take up such a task at the tender age of nineteen. Be that as it may, he hewed closely to Buckminster's legacy, devoting himself more to literary matters than to theology. Invited to deliver the prestigious Phi Beta Kappa poem at Harvard in 1812, Everett's offering pondered the literary potential for American poets in "patriot topicks," starting with the Pilgrims in 1620 and moving through events like Bunker Hill.[17]

Amid the deeply divisive War of 1812, Everett continued to preach broad patriotism and partisan moderation. Indeed, in June 1814, at the height of New England Federalists' opposition to the war and after two years of radical Federalist preachers branding the war a visitation upon America's national sins, Everett declared from the Brattle Street pulpit that "I do not enquire" into the "right or wrong" of the war. And the next month, with Philippians 4:5 — "Let your moderation be known unto all men"—as his text, Everett enthused that Christianity "could not be founded in fanaticism and enthusiasm, but was indeed divine." As such it not only was "a rational and practical religion" but was also "calculated for man in his present condition." For unlike the enthusiast, "the man of moderate views . . . builds his hopes upon foundations least likely to fail, and strives for objects most certain to be secured." Moderation, he disclaimed, "gives no excuse to those, who are ever shrinking from the effort of improvement" of self or society. But it did teach "that difference of opinion or diversity of interest" was never "a sufficient reason for cutting off the ties of common charity." It was not for Everett to emulate the Massachusetts Federalist preachers who upbraided Republican warmongers in the harshest language, for he had set out to be such a man as he described in this sermon.[18] His youth and brilliance did at times draw him into controversy, notably a five-hundred-page, often personal as well as theological rebuttal of a doubter of Christianity's authenticity. He earned great praise for himself and helped establish Unitarians' Christian credentials by means of this book.[19] But this demonstrates that he saved the brashness natural to a young academic for academic disputation, eschewing political strife.

His labors in his parish, however, proved far from moderate, and within a year of taking up the pastorate, Everett was on the verge of a nervous breakdown. He projected a trip to the Washington, D.C., area to realize a respite. Armed with letters of introduction from Massachusetts luminaries such as Harrison Gray Otis and John Adams — the latter of whom introduced him to Thomas Jefferson as "probably the first literary character of his age and State" — Everett set off in the fall of 1814.[20] Heretofore reluctant to comment on slavery in the partisan wartime context and uncertain in his abstract ponderings on the institution, Everett on this journey observed slavery up close for the first time. Interacting largely with respectable Upper South slaveholders, he reached conclusions that fell considerably short of abolitionism. And a sojourn at Mount Vernon reinforced his already strong Unionism.

Everett responded philosophically to the plight of slaves. "From what I could observe on various occasions" interacting with the slaves of the area surrounding Washington, he recorded, "these poor wretches do not feel the debasement of their condition, and are as much resigned to their slavery, as servants here to their servitude." While praying with a family in Alexandria, he spied a slave secretly kneeling on the stairs. This reverential act struck him as proof that even the most debased and unenlightened in all countries "have yet that common spark of spirituality, in them, which under happier auspices would have kindled into Sensibility, Improvement, and Bliss." It was enough to make him yearn for the future Judgment Day, "when the ills and privations they suffer here will be repaid." Moreover, "while this poor creature was kneeling and listening to my prayer, I could not help reflecting how differently God sees from man. Tho' sunk in our eyes, out of the circle of humanity, and not entitled to a word except of command or censure, 'tis likely that not one joined the petitions, with greater acceptance, to God, than this poor slave."[21] Of a piece with the philosophy of Buckminster's Philemon sermon, this response was consistent with both a benevolent Christian view of individual slaves and a resignation to their temporal lot within God's time frame.

In the here and now, Everett agonized over what course true humanity should take concerning American slavery. On the one hand, he was impressed that his elite hosts treated the "several generations of slaves" they owned "with the greatest kindness." They struck him as eminently reasonable, cautious opponents to slavery in principle; this impression laid the foundation for decades of cooperation with just such Upper South moderates.[22] But on the other hand, he fretted that "the moral influence of slavery upon the virtue of" slaveholders "is deplorable," arising from an intimate familiarity with their body servants that "made me shudder." He quoted Jefferson on how the commerce between master and slave turned the former into petty despots. "But what can be done?" he despaired in a lengthy diary entry. "To emancipate the slaves, is to exchange a great evil, for a greater," given that freed blacks "have almost universally proved vicious mischievous and miserable." Even the slaves famously freed by George Washington's will had found that "the gift was a gilded curse: humanity itself can hardly wish the example to be followed." Therefore, "it would be most desperate madness, or rather an impossibility, to emancipate them all at once." Given all these countervailing aspects of the question, the problem of slavery in the South "is the greatest political problem I have met, and one which I fear will never be solved, till it is done at a future day, in terrible convulsions; and the subversion of the countries where this deplorable system prevails." Mass slave rebellion would lead to "a horrible conflict" whose outcome would be either that the few surviving slave rebels would be reenslaved, or, what "I fear is more likely, that a desolating success would be the consequence of their attempt, which would drench the State in its best blood [and] strew it with the ruins of its noblest fortunes." The black conquerors "would probably soon be invaded from" other American states, "hemmed in," and reduced to a guerrilla force "driven to the ridge to harass the country, for a few generations, till they gradually disappear like the Indian tribes. The soil would thus be restored to the whites, who would as likely as not, cover it in ten years, with another population of Slaves."[23]

This priceless passage foreshadowed and helps explain Everett's decades-long perplexity over Southern slavery. As a truly humane man encountering what seemed an intractable political and social problem, he feared that immediate emancipation would prove calamitous for everyone of both races. Haunted as he was and would remain with the specter of the Haitian Revolution, because of the geography and demographics of the United States he seems to have expected a massive slave revolt there to be even worse than in Haiti, as well as ultimately fruitless. Although not ultimately proslavery, these ruminations contained impressions of American slavery's mildness that would surface later. And so strong was Everett's rejection of rapid emancipation in America that in this, as with nothing else, he was willing to broach the heretical notion that Washington had made a mistake.

Everett's good standing in the Unionist church was never in doubt, however, and he bolstered his faith by a pilgrimage to Mount Vernon in a critical hour for the Union. In 1814, New England town meetings and legislatures had called for a convention to discuss revising or disbanding the Union in order to prevent future calamities akin to the War of 1812. Aggrieved Federalist leaders would meet in the Hartford Convention beginning in December 1814, and as this movement went forward in that season, lovers of constitutional union everywhere were deeply alarmed. In late November 1814, Everett visited Washington's estate and enjoyed illustrious company, including the family of Washington's heir Bushrod Washington. At dinner one evening, the table talk dwelled "principally upon the supposed determination of Eastern federalists to sever the Union." When they called on Everett for a toast, he pointedly offered "the 'Union of the U.S.'" The next day he more extensively surveyed the mansion and grounds and "brought a few geranium leaves and orange leaves, as relicks from Mt. Vernon, but they all withered and decayed, like the good impressions we carry from a church." He remarked that "the evergreen" of a grove of cedar trees, "waving over the General's tomb, amidst the surrounding desolation of the vegetable world, seemed like the tradition of the hero's own virtues, still cherished amidst the corruption of the political community. I broke a branch of cedar from one of the trees." He wished he could have visited Mount Vernon alone, in which case "I should have seen and felt a thousand things, becoming the veneration one should cherish for a spot like this," and would have taken away "feelings that would have lasted me all my life." But his companions' familiarity with Mount Vernon led them to take it for granted, and most of their conversation during the visit was disappointingly commonplace.[24] Although hoping for a more moving religious experience, Everett the pilgrim did the best he could. And there is something poignant about this Bostonian of Federalist leanings toasting the Union at its emotional epicenter at one of its times of crisis.

Everett's opportunities to travel and glean new light on American nationhood and American slavery would continue after his return from this Southern itinerary. In yet another incredible opening for the brilliant young scholar, Harvard invited him to accept a new chair in Greek literature endowed by wealthy Bostonian Samuel Eliot. The offer included two years of sabbatical up front, during which he could pursue advanced studies in Europe, making it an offer he could not refuse. One day after turning twenty-one, Everett officially left his congregation and took up his professorship. Four days later, in a group that included Ticknor, he sailed for Europe for what ended up being four years rather than two. During that span he earned his Ph.D.—the first American to earn this degree—from Gottingen University and traveled extensively across Britain and the Continent.[25]

The young American felt all the ambivalence that other provincial republicans felt when they traveled in cultured, aristocratic Europe.[26] He understood keenly that Europeans set a standard of scholarship and literature that Americans could only hope to approximate after their most arduous efforts. He was proud, therefore, to mingle with the European intelligentsia and gratified that in these circles he had "met with kindness and cordiality." The budding Anglophile found to his pleasure that "the idolatrous veneration with which I once regarded the English, has been succeeded, not as is too often the case by jealousy and hatred, but by a grateful and sincere respect." Upon returning to the United States, he confided to his older brother Alexander that "I fear I shall have to prepare myself for the day of small things."[27] Yet amid the splendor of European civilization, Everett hardly lost interest in America. Conservative that he was, he professed no love of hereditary aristocracy while inspecting it. Keen to understand American history within the context of world and European history, he "thought a good deal" about a projected statue of Washington while visiting the ruins of Rome. Also while in Rome, he composed a hundred-page sermon examining the advantages America enjoyed over Europe in "some of the commonly supposed constituents of National happiness."[28]

In this context of exploring Europe and comparing it to America, Everett's years abroad also further informed his evolving thoughts on slavery. Like friend and traveling companion Ticknor, Everett had long revered the British abolitionist statesman William Wilberforce, and they both relished the opportunity to meet him in England. He rhapsodized in his journals about the great good that such moral reformers did in the world.[29] Wilberforce's model of incremental legislative progress against slavery stood for Everett as a wise, humane alternative to the Haitian Revolution's model of abolition. Despite this reformist streak, he was rather matter-of-fact in his response to relics of ancient slavery he encountered in Rome, and the tens of thousands of sturdy beggars he witnessed in Naples only confirmed his fatalistic resignation to the existence of poverty in human societies. By contrast, however, he was shocked by the squalor he often witnessed in his travels on the Continent—especially in the German states, where he took dire poverty to be the default situation of the peasantry. This made him all the more grateful for the relative prosperity Americans of every class and color enjoyed.[30] As his European tour neared its end he could say that he had "theorized a good deal" about American slavery, presumably in light of such a range of European contacts and observations. Indeed, he invited Alexander to contribute to "a clever duodecimo treatise" he contemplated preparing on the subject.[31] As no such treatise seems to be extant, it would appear that Everett applied his European reflections on the subject principally to future public declarations on American slavery and its abolition.

His return to America with the novel doctoral degree in hand ensured numerous and eager audiences for his reflections on social and political questions. In the early 1820s, he helped produce English translations of Greek grammar and literature that became staples of college curricula around the country for the next three decades. This was just the beginning of his influence on Hellenism in American art, oratory, and public life more generally.[32] He also returned to a Harvard student body eager to hang on and mimic his every word. Witness after witness testified that "he seemed to express and embody our dreams of an accomplished scholar and a finished man," so much so that Everett helped inordinately to create "the classic New England diction" emerging in this era. One student from Virginia kept his notes from Everett's classes to the day he died. Ralph Waldo Emerson captured Everett's impact in a much later lecture titled "Historic Notes of Life and Letters in New England." The novelty of his German learning, Emerson remembered, together with the "natural grace and the splendor of his rhetoric," meant that "there was an influence on the young people from the genius of Everett which was almost comparable to that of Pericles in Athens." And more than young people fell under this spell, for the restless genius could not be confined to the Harvard classroom. He delivered several sermons as an itinerant preacher throughout New England and the Mid-Atlantic. He also gave a series of lectures that Emerson recalled being "largely and fashionably attended for two winters in Boston." As a net result, "the word that he spoke, in the manner in which he spoke it, became current and classical in New England." "All his speech," Emerson continued in what would become a theme in describing Everett's oratory, "was music, and with such variety and invention that the ear was never tired."[33]

The words that became so "classical in New England" included refinements of his thoughts on social inequality and on the American Union. An 1819 sermon thanked God for his goodness to America, which was best appreciated when compared with the plight of Europe. From that vantage point Everett saw "a thousand civil & political details, which would illustrate the happy state of our land." All those details testified that it was "the design of God, to build up a most free & happy People here." He warned against a spirit of "indifference" to such unexampled blessings and against wasting "our tho'ts & cares on the little imperfections, which our human nature mingles up even in this almost perfect system." His audience's "momentous charge" was to preserve these blessings. Should they fail they would dash the hopes, "I will not say of our Country or of our Age, but of the World & of Mankind."[34] This would be the tack Everett the nationalist and Unionist would pursue throughout his life: there was nothing wrong with this providentially designed nation (or at least the flaws were comparatively minor), so nineteenth-century Americans' only task was of conservation. And the stakes involved with this task were enormous.

In a sermon delivered in various places in Massachusetts and New York in 1820 and 1821, Everett continued his spoken meditations on the biblical teaching that God is no respecter of persons. Everett recognized as real and natural the distinctions in society resulting from men's differing opportunities and stations. A society without differentiated roles would be "nothing but a barbarous horde of individuals, each vainly endeavouring to dispense with the help of his fellows." But social distinctions, he pursued, "have no moral merit," being socially constructed and temporary. To balance a proper sense of "true, moral, eternal Equality" with "all these outside distinctions," one needed to understand "the doctrine" that "there is no respect of persons with God—there is no connection between these natural distinctions, & the moral condition of men." "This," Everett exhorted, "is the great solution of the hard problem of human fortune, at which we are so apt to repine, and which will reconcile us, if any thing will to whatever inferiority we may labor under. Unfortunately for the peace and happiness of the world," too few had understood these principles and had even fought "cruel wars" to vindicate "an imaginary & fantastic equality." Other lessons he derived from these doctrines included the need for society's superiors to learn humility and for everyone to strive for spiritual improvement in anticipation of that true superiority being rewarded in heaven.[35] Consistent with Buckminster's Philemon doctrines, this sermon called for moral reform rather than anxious revolution in the name of equality. While some individual passages could have been read as reactionary resignation to worldly injustice, read whole it was yet another manifesto of a tenderhearted conservative in a revolutionary age.

Everett the unattached Unitarian preacher was perfectly free to develop his own social and political conclusions, and his scholarly authority and rhetorical manner generated enormous interest that transcended the various antagonisms non-Unitarians harbored toward the growing sect. Aside from a rejection of the Trinitarian view of God, Unitarianism was a big tent for a variety of views on almost every doctrine. This helps to account for how Unitarians could have produced both radical reformers and law-and-order conservatives. Unitarians in nineteenth-century Massachusetts faced an increasingly bitter foe in orthodox Congregationalists alarmed by Unitarians' rapidly growing ascendancy in Massachusetts's intellectual and spiritual life.[36] As Massachusetts became proverbial for driving the sectional tensions of the early Republic, Unitarians' growing dominance of the Bay State set other Americans against them. The young Everett, however, seemed to glide unusually easily across all these divides. On an 1820 speaking tour in the Mid-Atlantic, Everett's triumphant speeches even helped break down "the local & geographical prejudices" of anti-Unitarians in Baltimore. When John Quincy Adams heard him preach in Washington, he noted that New Englanders in the congregation were much more enthusiastic than were Southerners. But Adams himself proclaimed Everett a "genius" and his sermon "the most splendid composition as a sermon that I ever heard delivered." Even an English auditor of this sermon, who reacted violently to a nationalist passage therein, agreed that "his voice, bewitchingly melodious, yet manly, filled the house, and made every word tell." So telling were his preachments in Washington that he finished third in all six ballots in a November 1820 election for the chaplain of the Senate, despite making it clear that he did not want the office.[37]

––––––––––

While Everett shied away from the chaplain's job, he was being drawn increasingly away from the pulpit and the classroom and toward politics. He took a step in that direction by a distinguished career focused on political-cum-literary writing and editing. This proved a halfway house on the way to a political career in earnest.

In 1820 Everett chose to pour most of his boundless talent and ambition into productions of the pen when he accepted the editorship of the *North American Review* (*NAR*). Founded in 1815 by Boston men of letters with a Federalist bent, this was a modestly influential literary journal when Everett took it over. Despite his endless complaints about the nature of the editorship, he was a rousing success in the position, increasing its circulation fivefold and extending its nationwide reach before he quit the post in 1823.[38] As an editor and writer during this period, Everett engaged in illuminating ways with the issue of slavery both during the Missouri Crisis and the Literary War, or Paper War, with Great Britain.

When Everett visited Washington in February 1820, Congress was in the grips of a protracted and bitter debate over whether to restrict slavery in Missouri as a condition for admitting it as a state. It was a complicated debate touching on constitutional, political, and social issues of the most sensitive kind, and when Everett dined with Secretary of State John Quincy Adams and leading members of Massachusetts's congressional representation in Georgetown, he found the group divided over what Congress should do. Letters to Everett from Washington also sent mixed signals, ranging from bemused wonderment that Northerners would care about slavery at so great a distance to calls for Massachusetts men to defend the North against the South's relentless pursuit of power.[39] Everett was inclined to follow the lead of Daniel Webster, who at this phase of his career was a moderate but confirmed New England sectionalist of the Federalist stripe. He and Webster, for instance, both applauded the vigorous antislavery speeches of Rufus King, the New York Founding Father who was the most ardent restrictionist in the Senate.[40]

It was in a review of King's two most famous antislavery speeches from the debate that the conservative antislavery position of Everett's *NAR* gained a literary entrée into the debate. Reviewer Lemuel Shaw, a Federalist lawyer and politician, decried slavery as "a great and acknowledged evil" but quickly added that it "must be regarded, to a certain extent, as a necessary one, too deeply interwoven in the texture of society to be wholly or speedily eradicated." Thus the subject "should be approached with . . . that sober and discriminating benevolence" that aimed at "attainable good" and "the practicable means of arriving at it" rather than with cheap demagoguery. Slavery could not be eradicated suddenly where it was "long established" without producing "greater evils than the continuance of slavery," including the danger of racial violence, so its future should be left to the local people. None of these concerns about the rootedness of slavery pertained to Missouri, however, and for Congress to sanction its spread there would be a gratuitous abandonment of its past practice of containing the evil institution.[41] While restrictionist in policy, this line of argument laid the foundation for a position of accommodation to slavery where it existed.

Everett seems also to have contributed to a series of conservative restrictionist essays in the eminently Federalist *Boston Daily Advertiser*. This series had pursued much the same line as the *NAR* article had, including granting that Southern slavery was a necessary evil but arguing that extending it to Missouri would violate the nation's founding principles.[42] The essay that was most likely from Everett's pen was written in early March 1820, with the crucial vote approaching in Congress. He worried that the New England public had deserted "the Gentlemen in Congress, who with unwearied perseverance are there defending the cause of the Free States." He scolded that "we of the northern and middle States," who "claim and shall ever claim to have taken such a lead in the original councils for freedom" in the Revolution "as forever to entitle us to a full and respected voice in deciding the destinies" of the nation, had for too long allowed united and cunning Virginians to rule over the fractious North. He therefore hoped this controversy would "bind the free states heart to heart, man to man," and that their representatives would resist the Virginia siren song of "a *treacherous compromise*."[43] This disdain of compromise was remarkable coming from Everett. In later days he would also reject the very idea that congressmen should be representatives of the free states rather than of the whole Union. But by early 1820, Massachusetts conservatives had come to believe that their core values of protecting the Constitution and the Union recommended restriction rather than compromise on slavery in Missouri.

As complex and absorbing as the Missouri controversy was, it was not the only consideration setting the context in which Everett as writer and editor groped for a middle ground on slavery. Although a brash young academic, Everett's native caution and practicality kept him from considering and expressing himself on slavery simply from an abstract point of view. So there was for him, as for his contemporaries, a seemingly endless set of pragmatic concerns that shaped his response to slavery and often made it seem contradictory.

One powerful consideration was Everett's appreciation of the power of racism in American life. In a July 1820 article for his own journal, Everett hoped that bringing in German immigrants to replace black slaves colonized out of the United States would prove "the means of gradually rooting out negro slavery from among us." For one "great difficulty in abolishing negro slavery, is the colour. You can do nothing with the man when you have emancipated him." Such a passage suggested that Everett was neither unusually progressive nor viciously racist. Like many other Americans in his day, he seems not to have probed issues of race very deeply and was content to defer to Jefferson's authority in asserting "the intellectual inferiority of the blacks."[44]

Everett devoted much more thought to the prospects and potentially noble impact of the *NAR*, and that also shaped what he published relative to slavery. In October 1820, Everett went over young author Caleb Cushing's article on Haiti "with care" and toned down some of the more antislavery passages—not, he assured Cushing, "as containing any thing I disapproved, but as being more than the public (w'h is mighty squeamish) would bear." He could understand how Cushing, "fresh from the perusal of the annals of ye Haytian Revolution," wrote with a certain "warmth of feeling." But he sought to impress on his younger protégé that "it is the cool tranquil manner that cuts deepest." While as editor Everett was willing to allow Cushing a wide latitude of content and tone even on such touchy issues as abolishing capital punishment, slavery was different. Everett would not have his magazine "suspected of meaning to whip the Southern Planters, over the shoulders" of Haiti's vicious slaveholding class, so he deleted certain sections that were "too strong for the Southern Stomach." He assured Cushing that this submission to the "servitude of public opinion" would be temporary. "Should the North American Review acquire a decisive authority & popularity in the Country," he pledged, "Slavery shall be one of the things on which its battery shall oftenest be played, while I have any concern in it: but by beginning too soon, we sh'd defeat our own efforts."[45] This was yet another revealing episode for Everett. While he posed as in advance of public opinion, that public included the South, in the very midst of the Missouri Crisis as well as of Everett's efforts to build up his journal's national influence. His caution in this instance was also a function of Cushing's article's subject matter, the Haitian Revolution, emblem in Everett's mind of a worst-case slave rebellion. It is probably too easy in light of Everett's later career to read as hypocritical his promise to train his guns on slavery when prudential considerations were done away with. For while some of the particular restraints changed over time, they never went away for him, at least until 1861.

In his tenure as editor, however, even the weighty matters of Missouri, race, and a hoped-for Southern readership combined could not surpass the ever-present literary conflict raging with Britons. In the decade following the War of 1812, and in particular in the early 1820s, the so-called Paper War between Britain and America featured writers of literary reviews, travel accounts, and pamphlets savaging each other's institutions. Americans fought mostly on the defensive, repelling the caustic criticisms of British travelers and editors. Everett stepped squarely to the forefront of America's defenders, so that both American and British writers recognized the *NAR* as preeminent on the American side. British recognition of the *NAR* and its editor, however, came clothed in robes of condescension toward the "bad, boyish temper" of its responses to British attacks and accompanied by blanket statements that the United States had no scholars worthy of the name. Indeed, American men of letters were haunted and goaded for decades by Sydney Smith's infamous taunt in the enormously influential *Edinburgh Review* that urged American readers not to believe their "orators and newspaper scribblers" who assured them "that they are the greatest, the most refined, the most enlightened, and the most moral people upon earth." For "in the four quarters of the globe, who reads an American book?"[46] As historian Sam Haynes has shown, to appreciate the impact of such words we must learn to "think of the early republic as a developing nation" full of people who "remained inordinately sensitive to the opinion of Great Britain." Given the severely unequal power relationship in the early nineteenth century, the Anglophobic outbursts of American mobs, politicians, and writers "drew their energy from a sense of powerlessness." For no group was the relationship more fraught, however, than for the Eastern intellectual elite, who sought to reconcile their Anglophilia with their drive to reduce the new Republic's cultural reliance on Great Britain. British criticism deeply stung these men who aspired (for themselves and their nation) to membership in a transatlantic republic of letters, even as they sought to build up American nationalism.[47]

British critics did more than read the Americans out of this club, however; highlighting American slavery, they ultimately read them out of the rank of humane and civilized nations. The published accounts of the veritable postwar army of British travelers in the United States fixated on the horrors of African American slavery, and magazine editors used reviews of these narratives as occasions to pile on. No one in the world, such writers maintained, should be "duped by fine speeches and lofty pretensions in the cause of humanity" from Americans, who were far too willing to downplay or pass over "the great disgrace and danger of America—the existence of slavery." Enemies to the United States' republican system of government asked, "Under which of the old tyrannical governments of Europe is every sixth man a Slave, whom his fellow-creatures may buy and sell and torture?" The question and its answer embarrassed British friends to democratic reform, who worried that the continued existence of slavery would not only harm America's exemplary force for reform but also ultimately ruin the young nation itself. All this might have been reasonable criticism, and indeed the sort of thing Everett and his kind had said themselves during the Missouri debates. And some Americans used Paper War critiques of slavery to advance their own antislavery agenda rather than circle the nationalist wagons.[48]

But for Everett, the British source was what mattered most in these criticisms, pushing him decidedly against fulfilling his vow to Cushing to attack American slavery. In April 1820, reviewing Robert Walsh's prominent book-length refutation of British calumnies, Everett maintained his restrictionist stance from the Missouri Crisis on the world stage even as he granted nothing to the British. He lamented certain Britons' "pitiless pelting" of the United States and commended Walsh for taking a vigorous part in the high-stakes Paper War. "A few facts," Everett added, "will show with what justice America is reproached by England, on the score of negro slavery." Among those facts was how Great Britain was currently "as deeply involved in it as America; her colonies being all stocked with slaves" whose treatment was "no better, if as good, as in America." He also parroted the standard American line that British merchants had foisted slaves on unwilling colonists in the first place, but he did regret that the Missouri Compromise, passed "by a bare majority" of feckless politicians, deprived Americans "of some of the consolations" of casting blame fully on the British. So as much as he personally respected some of the Northern compromisers, he wailed that "every American should have felt an impulse within him to resist the progress of slavery" rather than deepen their country's "shame."[49]

However, as the Missouri Crisis ebbed from his consciousness and the Paper War dragged on, Everett's already mild sectionalist stance became confused and ultimately faded away. He could never embrace the anti-restrictionists' knee-jerk rejection of all reformers as dangerous do-gooders.[50] But by July 1820, he wrote for true American nationality and against "local prejudice" and sectional parties. When in Paper War mode, unlike during the height of the Missouri Crisis, Everett found national unity much more attractive than sectionalism.[51] A year later, English reviewers had responded negatively to Everett's review of Walsh; so had Southern editors unhappy with his criticism of the extension of slavery. Everett responded to both by clarifying his position as no defender of slavery but as a take-no-prisoners nationalist. He claimed that his earlier review "had no further object, than to deplore the decision of the Missouri question, . . . remarks, for which we were duly censured, in the journals of the Southern States." So his editorial "we" was exasperated "to be accused as the champions of slavery" in England. If those English critics wished to be thought "candid men," they must "contrive a reasonable, practicable plan of eradicating negro slavery from this country, or any country where it exists. If they can devise no such plan, and the evil is without remedy," then they should cease upbraiding Americans for failing to do so. "We should be glad to see," Everett flourished in conclusion, "if slavery is stamped deeper and blacker on a bale of cotton or a hogshead of tobacco, than on a puncheon of rum or a box of sugar" coming from Britain's own slaveholding colonies. "If providence should enter into judgment with the civilized world for this offence, we would fain know whether Bristol or Liverpool would be last visited" and if Britain's long domination of the African slave trade "would stand lowest on the accusing angel's book." Until Great Britain abolished slavery throughout its empire in 1833, these were effective counterpunches.[52] By July 1823 Everett would not admit a German writer's claim that slavery contradicted American freedom. "We certainly have no call to defend the institution of domestic slavery," he disclaimed, "but, if it deprive America of the right to be called free, what becomes of Greece and Rome," with all their slaves in antiquity? And boasts of

Germanic traditions of freedom overlooked serfdom, which still persisted "in some parts of Germany."[53]

Everett tried to maintain the standing of a fair-minded, candid nationalist in this fray. He corrected a friend of America's assertion that no new state had allowed slavery; the Missouri Compromise still bothered him in part because it made such statements unfortunately untrue.[54] But in later years he could see how "an exaggerated nationality" drove both the writings and the orations from this time in his life.[55] He repeatedly repelled suggestions that he was a defender of slavery, but his disclaimers of that sort became briefer as the Paper War persisted, and with each new defense of America's version of slavery he moved to the edges of sanctioning it. As he marshaled classical authority and his observations of European poverty to defend against European criticisms of slavery, he put himself on the road to his 1826 congressional speech.

Everett's mix of personal and patriotic motives for combat with British critics was exemplified when he became deeply involved in a hot controversy surrounding the travel narrative of William Faux. This British Tory's account of life in America included assaults on American slavery that were severe even by Paper War standards. Among his catalog of horrors was his allegation that while in South Carolina he had heard reliable testimony of a local master whipping his slave to death. The reviewer in London's Tory *Quarterly Review* implicitly trusted Faux's honesty as a reporter and repeatedly cited Faux's "horrid detail" concerning the cruelties of American slavery and racism. Even a review in the *Westminster Review*, a reform periodical, praised Faux for his "courage" in exposing "the horrible and degrading effects" of slavery.[56]

Carolina slaveholders cooperated with Everett, they to defend the honor of their state and he the honor of his nation. Everett asked Samuel Gilman of Charleston for the facts of the slave whipping case, and Gilman told him that the local authorities had been prompt and vigorous in investigating Faux's allegations. Especially after South Carolina's new U.S. senator Robert Y. Hayne had read the *Westminster Review* treatment of Faux, he happily corresponded with Everett to put him in possession of helpful facts as the latter prepared the *NAR*'s own review. Hayne passed along from his local informant the relevant facts of the slave murder case, including that Faux made his snap judgment while the case was still being investigated. He insisted that slave murders were both "more rare than almost any other" crime and always prosecuted and punished as a capital crime in South Carolina.[57] The fact that in 1824 Everett was corresponding with proslavery Carolinians rather than with restrictionists as in 1820 was in one way natural given the focus of Faux's allegations. But in

fund-raising circular of September argued that the dwindling presence of the "few revolutionary patriots and heroes among us" was "a sight, which this generation ought not to behold without emotion." Enjoying "every thing, which can make a people happy," these heroes' grateful posterity could not "refuse to bestow a trifle" on the projected monument on the sacred battlefield. Indeed, "the general propriety and expediency of erecting public monuments of the kind proposed are acknowledged by all," in part because such works "have the happiest influence in exciting and nourishing the national and patriotic sentiment." The young Republic's government was essentially "a government of *opinion*; but it is one of *sentiment* still more," depending for its perpetuity on "a strong, deep-seated, inborn sentiment; a feeling, a passion for liberty," and "the glorious tradition of our national emancipation."[70] The agitators of such overt emotionalism never hid their political agenda of attaching people to the sentimental Union. In their political culture in which emotional filiopietism for the Founders was a given, the political incentives were all on the side of open claims to impeccable Unionism.

Armed with a growing reputation rooted in such consensus themes and a bipartisan appeal, Everett found his first congressional race remarkably easy. Everett's moderate, nonpartisan career to that point came in handy in his Middlesex congressional district, which encompassed both traditionally Republican and Federalist strongholds.[71] Everett's reverence for the Republicans' patron saint Jefferson was genuine as well as politically helpful. The two carried on an occasional correspondence between 1822 and Jefferson's 1826 death, and in one letter Everett enthused to Jefferson about his hopes of visiting the University of Virginia and "at the same time making my Pilgrimage to its Patron & Founder."[72] Everett's wide appeal made him a difficult target even for the Boston *Statesman*. This paper had been founded to oppose just such conservatives as Everett in Massachusetts politics and supported William Crawford for president against Everett's ally John Quincy Adams. But the paper only halfheartedly supported Everett's opponent John Keyes, and editor Nathaniel Greene, normally a fierce partisan, even apologized for running a mild attack on the manner in which Everett's supporters had nominated him. In the months following Everett's election, all the while full of sour grapes over Adams's election, Greene published glowing praise from Boston and New York papers for Everett's superlative orations.[73]

Since this passed as opposition to Everett, he and his supporters gladly took the high road all the way to Congress. The National Republican organ the Boston *Patriot* refused to criticize Keyes, emphasizing instead the rare opportunity to elect a candidate of Everett's unusual stature. Once he consented to run, one supporter stated matter-of-factly, "A strong desire has been expressed, not only in this State, but in the country at large, that he might be elected."[74] When Everett demolished Keyes by a margin of 1,529 to 603, then, both sides' reportage of the result had a decided ho-hum quality.[75] This sort of election where he and his had the luxury of staying above any hint of a fray was surely to Everett's taste. It must also have been heartening to him as evidence that at least in New England, conspicuous intellectual attainments did not rule out political prosperity.[76] But this electoral cakewalk, and the comparative love feast that followed, was no preparation for the firestorm his first speech in Congress caused.

2

The House

DOUGHFACE

Edward Everett served his district in the House of Representatives for a full decade, engaging with a wide variety of issues. But his first speech in Congress, with its controversial expressions on slavery, would become by far the best known part of that career. It and others of his congressional expressions provided the sizable kernels of truth to those then and thereafter who branded him a doughface entirely too eager to placate Southern slaveholders. He had his reasons derived from other issues and commitments, but these could never be disentangled from slavery.

Everett entered the House of Representatives loaded with high hopes from his supporters. Due to the peculiarities of the early Republic's political calendar, he had to wait until the Nineteenth Congress convened in December 1825 to take his seat. But in the intervening year his regional and national stature had only grown, in large part due to a speech he delivered in that interval period. On 22 December 1824, he was the featured speaker at the formal opening of Pilgrim Hall in Plymouth, Massachusetts. Speaking in front of a mural version of Henry Sargent's *Landing of the Fathers*, Everett delivered an oration that both contemporaries and subsequent scholars have ranked with a famous 1820 Plymouth oration by Daniel Webster as preeminent articulations of the Pilgrims as the founders of American liberty.[1] Especially in the glow of this performance, no one contested one contemporary's encomium on Everett's "profound learning and persuasive eloquence." All that his political opponents in Boston could muster was a weary parody of his hyperinflated reputation as "the great northern light."[2]

But Everett's smooth ascent to Congress was an anomaly in the toxic political atmosphere that greeted him on arrival in Washington. The four-way presidential contest of 1824 had produced no candidate with a majority in the electoral college, and only after weeks of wrangling did John Quincy Adams emerge with the majority of votes in the House of Representatives necessary to make him president. Most of Henry Clay's supporters backed Adams, which led Andrew Jackson's supporters to denounce what they termed a "corrupt bargain" when Clay accepted the position of secretary of state in the new administration. Adams's first annual message to Congress in December 1825 further outraged the Jacksonians by holding forth a vision of a relatively activist federal government committed to the improvement of the United States' physical and human infrastructure. Much of this partisanship savored of sectionalism. The 1824 campaign proceeded under the shadow not only of the Missouri Crisis but of several significant explosions in the intervening years. The cumulative effect of the sectional politics of the early 1820s rendered Southern whites, particularly in the Lower South, hypervigilant against threats to slavery.

The most clear and present danger, they thought, came in the form of Northern do-gooders seeking to turn the federal government into a meddlesome agent of emancipation. In the summer of 1822, South Carolina slaves told their masters of a plot to overthrow slavery led by free African American Denmark Vesey. Interrogators of the alleged conspirators learned that they had taken courage in part from reading the strident antislavery speeches of the likes of Rufus King during the Missouri debates. This was proof positive, one South Carolina newspaper editor fumed in a threatening letter to King, that "the late diabolical plot against our lives" was the product of "those who, during the agitation of the Missouri Question, labored together in the humane vocation of rendering the slave discontented with his situation." Another Carolinian wailed that Northerners' "whining, canting, sickly kind of humanity" had induced them to send a "swarm of MISSIONARIES, white and *black*," to preach sedition to Southern slaves. Thus they had produced the South's "hour of peril and danger" when they should have been the "first to assist us."[3] As part of their effort to repel such influences, the southeastern states passed laws, known as Negro Seamen Acts, detaining all black sailors while their ships were in their docks. Federal courts ruled these laws unconstitutional, but Southern states defiantly continued to enforce them. Ohio's legislature raised the sectional tension further in 1824 when it passed resolves calling for national action to gradually emancipate America's slaves, "predicated upon the principle that the evil of slavery is a national one." State officials circulated these resolutions to Congress and other state legislatures, and by June 1825, eight other Northern legislatures—including the one in Everett's Massachusetts—had endorsed the Ohio plan. The legislatures of six Southern states vehemently rejected it as the latest and worst in a series of "officious and impertinent intermeddlings with our domestic concerns."[4]

The Lower South's politicians responded out of their bunker with violent rhetoric aimed in particular at the federal government. In December 1824, South Carolina's governor called for fellow white Southerners to manifest "a firm determination to resist, at the threshold, every invasion of our domestic tranquillity," lest they become either "victims of a successful rebellion, or the slaves of a great consolidated Government."[5] Southern vitriol only increased when Adams took office and enunciated his agenda for the federal government. In 1825, Whitemarsh Seabrook published a scathing pamphlet exposing Northern newspapers' casual disregard for Southern interests and security concerns. Whether these Northern editors were writing of an expansive federal government or more directly about general emancipation, he warned, "slavery, slavery, slavery is there." Fellow Carolinian Robert Turnbull felt no better about the Northern press by 1827 and in this besieged state asked, "What can preserve us but constant jealousy" of the North and of Congress? "There is a point," he warned darkly, "beyond which, we never can endure the oppression of Congress." The most outrageous usurpation of Congress, of course, was when it presumed to discuss slavery "in any way," for even the barest "discussion will be equivalent to an act of emancipation, for it will universally inspire amongst the slaves, that hope." Northern "enthusiasts" who thought it "a trifling matter" to stir up slave insurrections in this way were "the worst of enemies."[6]

In contrast with this Southern image of him, Adams as president was hardly itching for a fight with the South over slavery. He hoped to serve as what he called a "statesman of the Union." With Adams the only Northern candidate in the 1824 election, much of the rhetoric of his supporters was bound to be sectional. But Adams himself repeatedly pledged to "be the President not of a section, or of a faction, but of the whole Union." Upon taking office, he was painfully aware that he had not been elected president "by the unequivocal suffrages of a majority of the people," and he bent over backwards to assuage especially Southern fears. In November 1825 he was favorable to the idea of a presidential proclamation of a Thanksgiving for the District of Columbia. But his cabinet opposed it "as liable to imputations of political purposes, of introducing New England manners," and Adams "acquiesced in these opinions." That same solicitude to avoid needless collisions with Southerners led President Adams to push Great Britain for a convention for the return from Canada of American fugitive slaves. There were limits to his willingness to accommodate Southern cranks, to be sure. When he was preparing his first message to Congress, Secretary of War James Barbour quoted a South Carolina congressman as wishing "that something conciliatory to the South might be said in the message, to calm their inquietudes concerning their slaves." Adams told Barbour that South Carolina's persistence in enforcing its Negro Seamen's Act despite a Supreme Court justice from South Carolina ruling it unconstitutional "had put it out of my power to say anything soothing to the South on that subject." Instead, he decided to say nothing on the Negro Seamen's Acts. "To be silent," he reminded Barbour, "is not to interfere with any State rights."[7]

Adams and his allies watched in perplexed horror when such caution failed to keep his opponents from injecting slavery into national politics. The most formidable opposition to Adams surrounding slavery arose in early 1826. When the Senate debated the administration's proposal to send a delegate to a conference in Panama of all the newly independent nations in the Western Hemisphere, the politicians coalescing around Jackson and against Adams sought to make opposition to this proposal a key ingredient in the glue for their nascent party. Three decades later, Missouri Jacksonian Thomas Hart Benton remembered this unusually weighty and sharp conflict as "a master subject on the political theatre during its day." During the Senate's secret debate, Southerners' anxiousness to protect slavery overtly mixed with concerns about national neutrality and sovereignty. An Ohio Adamsite warned that the Jacksonians had "touched the question of Slavery with great indiscretion," not anticipating the backlash it would cause in the North. But Northern Jacksonians joined their Southern brethren under the anti-Panama-mission banner. They included Pennsylvania's James Buchanan, who warned that meeting with Latin American nations that had "always marched under the standard of universal emancipation" would lead inexorably to the visiting of "the dreadful scenes" of the Haitian Revolution upon American shores. As bad as slavery was, this would be to introduce "evils infinitely greater."[8] Because it went well beyond a few Carolina extremists, this was the most alarming injection of slavery into the partisan atmosphere early in Adams's presidency. Anyone who could help deflect these poisonous missiles would have the thanks of a president who wished to govern above party and section.

Everett fit this bill by inclination as well as by party loyalty. Like the president, Everett was puzzled by men who went to irrational extremes to defend state rights and a strict construction of the Constitution but preferred to conciliate rather than unnecessarily provoke them. As he gathered impressions on his journey to Washington in November 1825, he learned that Rufus King's extreme positions against slavery during the Missouri debates were still haunting him, proving the one serious obstacle to his confirmation as Adams's minister to Great Britain. In early 1826 he heard from a correspondent calling for the establishment of a national university. Although as an Adams supporter and an academic he sympathized, he pointed out that "a large class of our politicians deny the Constitutional power of Congress to found any university." He had already learned from his few months in Washington that "there are points on which it is in vain, here to reason; this I should fear was one." Everett's nationalist streak reinforced this observation. The *Massachusetts Journal*, a Boston paper he helped found, took as its motto "Our Country, Our Whole Country."[9] Everett was thus a logical choice to help Adams combat the charges of rampant abolitionism in the administration's foreign policy, and the president did consult Everett about joining the debate. But Everett spoke only briefly during the Panama mission debates.[10]

It would be in another, lesser debate that Everett made his long-awaited debut speech. South Carolina Jacksonian George McDuffie introduced a constitutional amendment meant to avoid a repeat of the House having decided the election of 1824. Among its other features was a district system for presidential elections rather than the electoral college. Although subsidiary to the contemporaneous Panama debate, McDuffie's amendment touched off a long and heated controversy that became, as Andrew Burstein has put it, "a lightning rod for the considerable tension that Adams's election had generated." By this means Jacksonians positioned themselves further as defenders of the voice of a people wronged by the corrupt bargain of 1824. As one editor jabbed, the Adamsites could be counted on to oppose anything that would "enlarge the powers of the people." Meanwhile, administration men (also known as National Republicans) stood behind reverence for the Constitution's established procedures for electing a president.[11]

Everett sat through these debates with mounting anxiety as to how to make his maiden speech. He had told friends that he intended to do so during the Panama debate. He himself hoped his first speech in Congress would not be "a set speech previously prepared," but no one saw his extemporaneous intervention on Panama in early February as a true debut. He received conflicting advice from powerful friends in Washington and Boston as to whether he should venture into the McDuffie minefield. "The uncertainty" about whether to give a formal speech in this debate, he recounted to his brother Alexander, "weighed on my spirits; till I found I had better try & fail than be haunted with the ghost of that uncertainty." After two days seeking to gain the floor of the House, he obtained the Speaker's permission to speak on Thursday, 9 March 1826. But Everett's inexperience in such parliamentary struggles "gave me such a headache as I never had & threw me into a high fever." He spent a sleepless night and could eat no breakfast Thursday morning. He went to the House and begged McDuffie to allow the debate to be postponed a day but in vain. Unwilling to scramble for the floor yet again and believing that "if I flinched then I was done for life," he rather grandly told Alexander that he determined then and there "to speak if I died on [the] spot. I accordingly took the floor with my ears ringing & little specks of light dancing before my eyes, & for 2 or 3 minutes did not hear my own voice." This indisposition was the more unfortunate for him given a congressional culture that strongly discouraged the reading of speeches; congressmen routinely prepared their remarks but never read them. But in short order he had gained possession of himself and delivered a three-hour effort before going home and collapsing into bed.[12]

This speech, one of the most important of Everett's life both short- and long-term, began as a spirited defense of the Constitution's integrity. Adopting McDuffie's amendment, he argued, would be "essentially to change" the frame of government that was Americans' political "life and soul." Although the Constitution was imperfect, Everett thundered that he "would sooner lay down this right hand, to be cut off, than I would hold it up to vote for any essential change in this form of Government." He warned that if Congress proved willing to "disturb that curious, that happy adjustment of powers, which is now our life and our peace, . . . all will be lost" not only for Americans but also "abroad," where the Constitution stood as "an exemplar to the discouraged nations of that long desired union of liberty and law."[13] Thus far the speech was a good sum of the constitutionalist conservative's creed at the heart of the National Republican response to McDuffie. It added a sense of the stakes involved in preserving the United States' constitutional union that would be a hallmark of Everett's public career at all its stages.

But this address would be memorable for its handling of slavery. Everett first injected this volatile substance into the speech to demolish the Jacksonians' much-ballyhooed claim to be restoring the right of choice to the people. As a result of the Constitution's clause counting three-fifths of slaves for representation in the House and the electoral college, Everett jabbed, the would-be amenders erred in "treating this subject, not as a constitutional question, resting solely on the terms of the compact, but as one of abstract popular right." Not that Everett would do away with or even complain about that part of the constitutional compact, "but when we come to talk of popularity, that is another thing; and I cannot permit it to be calculated by the ratio of the three-fifths."[14] This line of argument had served previous generations of Northern Federalists as an effective retort to Southern politicians' claims to be leading the party of the people. It also had the advantage of being true. In the election of 1824, Jackson received 99 electoral votes to Adams's 84; but without the three-fifths clause, Adams would have outdistanced Jackson 83–77.[15] But as tempting as it was to twist this knife, Everett did not mean to play the sectionalist amid the fraught sectional-cum-partisan fissures of 1826.

The most sensational segments of the speech then went well beyond what was necessary to defend his—and by extension the administration's—Unionist credentials. John Forsyth of Georgia had recently groused in writing that there were many Northerners "who would think it immoral or irreligious to join in putting down a servile insurrection at the South." From the late 1810s, Forsyth had become convinced that too few men outside the Deep South shared his sense of urgency on matters relevant to the safety of slaveholders. In the 1820s, seeing Adamsite policies like a protective tariff as a menace to slavery, he held the North's shocking disregard for the South's interests and even safety responsible for a "critical state of the relations between" Northern and Southern states.[16]

Everett sought to disabuse Forsyth and those he represented of this vision of wild-eyed Yankee abolitionists, or at least to distance himself and the administration from it. Reiterating that he would never seek "to disturb the compromise contained in the Constitution" on the three-fifths clause, he continued that "neither am I one of those citizens of the North" who would refuse to put down a slave insurrection.

> I am no soldier, sir: my habits and education are very unmilitary; but there is no cause in which I would sooner buckle a knapsack to my back, and put a musket on my shoulder, than that. I would cede the whole continent to any one who would take it—to England, to France, to Spain: I would see it sunk in the bottom of the Ocean, before I would see any part of this fair America converted into a Continental Hayti, by that awful process of bloodshed and desolation, by which alone such a catastrophe could be brought on.[17]

As infamous as this passage would become—and as comical as was the picture of the scholarly Everett marching in any army—had he stopped there this passage would have resonated with almost every white American both North and South. New England newspapers in 1826, for instance, carried several depressing accounts of the political and economic situation in Haiti that underscored Everett's point: the Haitian Revolution's numerous horrors seemed to have done no ultimate good for anyone.[18] It was an eloquent statement of his preference for order and constitutional obligations over chaos and race war, a widely shared preference in the United States in 1826.

But Forsyth had struck Everett's sensitive conservative nerve, and that carried the scholar and erstwhile preacher into a startling passage. "The great relation of servitude," it began, "is inseparable from our nature." "Domestic slavery"—the slavery carried on in Southern households—may not be the most beneficial form of servitude for either master or servant, but it "is not, in my judgment, to be set down as an immoral and irreligious relation." Therefore, he could not believe that the voice of "Religion" told slaves, "'Rise against your Master.' No, sir, the New Testament says, 'Slaves obey your Masters.'" To be sure, Everett's understanding of European history taught him that through "the benignant operation of Christianity, which gathered master and slave around the same communion table, this unfortunate institution disappeared in Europe." But that could not mean "that, while it subsists, and where it subsists, its duties are not pre-supposed and sanctioned by religion." Piling his scholarly authority onto this clerical pronouncement, he insisted that "at the meridian of the refinement of Greece," one of that great civilization's "instruments of improvement" was "domestic slavery, which delivered the free citizens from all the cares of gaining a livelihood." And as for slavery in the South, Everett asserted that "the slaves in this country are better clothed and fed, and less hardly worked, than the peasantry of some of the most prosperous states of the continent of Europe." Why else would the slave population grow faster even than the white population? "These," he added, "are opinions I have long entertained, and long since publicly professed on this subject." Presumably this referred to his stance during the Paper War, but this vigorous defense of American slavery and fumbling foray into a defense of slavery in the abstract went beyond the ground he had taken then. Perhaps sensing that this passage was gratuitous, he admitted that its inclusion had been provoked by the charges against the North and then circled back to his original objection to the Jacksonians' talk of the popular will.[19]

What would have convinced Everett to go to such lengths on such an explosive issue that was also strictly tangential to the subject at hand? To some degree this speech was but an extension of earlier thoughts, as he claimed it was. His horrified fascination with slave revolt and race war was a constant, in private as well as in public speeches. Expressed first in his 1814 journal entry on emancipation in the United States, it echoed in his later reaction in 1829 on learning that during the War of 1812 the British had schemed "to send black emissaries in, among the slaves to excite them to revolt." During a stint in the late 1820s as guest editor of the *North American Review*, Everett published a review by friend Caleb Cushing of two reports that painted the standard picture of decline in civilization and prosperity in Haiti "as compared with what it was previous to the insurrection of the blacks." Such alarming reports, Cushing pointedly noted, "have a bearing upon the questions now in agitation" about whether Great

Britain would and should abolish slavery in its West Indian colonies. Hardly a proslavery rant, such a piece was consistent with Everett's anti-abolitionist caution and illustrated a key foundation for that attitude.[20]

But Everett had been pondering issues surrounding slavery about the time he gave this speech, and it bore the marks of that study. He did not cite his brother Alexander's influence, but when he pointed to the growth of the Southern slave population as evidence of the benefits of the institution, this echoed Alexander's book-length refutation of English political economists. "The increase of population," Alexander insisted, "was a symptom and a cause of public prosperity," as well as a symptom and cause of true civilization. One corollary of this theory was that Americans need only point to the census to refute European allegations that Americans were "an indolent, immoral, and irreligious people."[21] Published in 1826, this was an interesting parallel to Edward's congressional argument that Southern slavery could not be "immoral and irreligious" for similar reasons.

A note in Everett's journal provides as close to a smoking gun as can be hoped for concerning what he was reading relative to slavery when he gave this discourse. This note, while undated, is in the diary that covers the years 1825–27. Headed "Slavery see," it unsurprisingly refers to Joseph Stevens Buckminster's sermon on Philemon. Buckminster's analysis clearly continued to inform his vision of how true Christian humanity toward slaves and masters did not consist in intervening in their relationship from the outside. The note also vaguely refers to the English poet and essayist Samuel Taylor Coleridge and to "Canning's Speech."[22]

Everett's citation to Coleridge is cryptic, but there are some plausible sources. The most likely is a series of lectures Coleridge gave in 1818 and 1819 on the history of philosophy. In one of these lectures, Coleridge lauded the early Christians for refusing to intervene in the master-slave relationship. This was strong evidence "of the wisdom of the first founders of Christianity, and especially so as an instance of the benevolence and the temperance with which Christianity was taught." Less likely chronologically but similar thematically was an 1800 essay Coleridge wrote praising George Washington's manumission of his slaves in his will as an act that balanced "the deep and weighty feeling of the general principle of universal liberty" with "the wise veneration of those fixed laws in society, without which that universal liberty must for ever remain impossible." Unlike the extremists of the French Revolution, Coleridge concluded, "Washington was no 'architect of ruin'!" But whether Everett drew from these specific essays or from a personal interaction with the literary lion while in England, his diary note manifestly referred to the conservatism that was the hallmark of Coleridge's stance on slavery after his abolitionist effusions of the 1790s. The nineteenth-century Coleridge believed increasingly in reform rather than revolution as the humane vehicle for social change.[23]

Everett's engagement with "Canning's Speech" also reinforced the notion that emancipation should happen peacefully and very gradually. In 1823, British foreign secretary George Canning responded in the House of Commons to Thomas Fowell Buxton's motion to adopt the gradual emancipation of the slaves in the British Empire. In keeping with his Tory conservatism, Canning warned that the system of colonial slavery, "with all its roots which had been growing for ages . . . ought to be touched with a light and delicate hand." In another passage that bore a curious and telling resemblance to Everett's reaction to the "immoral and irreligious" phrase, Canning took umbrage at Buxton's declaration that "slavery was repugnant to the principles of the British constitution and the Christian religion." To the contrary, history showed that while the spirit of Christianity corrected all manner of injustices, it did so very gradually "by the mild diffusion of its light and influence." It had first ameliorated and then almost imperceptibly removed ancient slavery, "and that influence would gradually produce the same happy effect in the present day." In 1824, presenting the government's own plan for the amelioration of slavery, Canning argued that by very gradual emancipation, the slave in Britain's colonies might not only be set free but also "lifted from a level with the beast of the field." And by gradual Canning meant neither that nor the next generation of slaves, lest freedom come "before the Negro was prepared for the enjoyment of well-regulated liberty." "If we are to do good," he summed, "it is not to be done by sudden and violent measures." Thus His Majesty's Government would pursue "a middle course" between antislavery and proslavery extremes.[24] Whether Everett studied the 1823 or 1824 speech or both, his natural conservatism and Buckminster's influence would have been reinforced by these powerful articulations of the (very) gradual emancipationist point of view.

But while these sources help illuminate the content of Everett's speech, they fail to answer the question of why he would have broached slavery at all in a debate that ostensibly did not require engaging with it. The political setting, as I have suggested above, surely had much to do with it. But it is also important to remember that the Everett who delivered this infamous speech was a young, ambitious, and brilliant academic stepping onto the national political stage for the first time. In the 1820s, many knew Everett as "an ambitious, proud, and successful loner" whose writings had "contained 'new and strange things,' which he asserted with an air of superiority and condescension."[25] The thirty-one-year-old newcomer had something of the brash young buck in him, reinforced

Portrait of Edward Everett, attributed to Anson Dickinson, 1828. This portrait captures something of the brash young hotshot Everett could be early in his congressional career. Courtesy of the American Antiquarian Society, Worcester, Mass.

by the academic's eagerness to score debating points and display his learning with an unconventional disquisition on the history of slavery and Christianity.

———————

The response to his speech taught Everett the virtues of discretion, especially on such a touchy subject as slavery in the tense arena of national politics. Members of the House responded incredulously to Everett's bombshell. Southern Jacksonians steered clear of the slavery passage; they found plenty else in his speech to assault and generally posed as men of the people in contrast to the elitist Everett.[26] Northern National Republicans reveled in Everett's use of the three-fifths clause to rebuke Southern claims to populism but ran away from his defense of slavery. Ichabod Bartlett of New Hampshire, for instance, followed Everett's general line of reasoning in opposing McDuffie's amendment. But he hastened to add that "if the language used" by Everett "was intended, as some do understand it, to vindicate the *principle* of slavery, and to say, Christianity sanctions the practice, however great my confidence in his opinions, in this I cannot hesitate to dissent from its correctness, totally, unqualifiedly." The Founders' true position, likewise, was to tolerate—even to the point of putting down slave rebellions—but not defend slavery.[27] Other Northern representatives joined Bartlett in chiding Everett for having left the true moderate position and ranged himself with proslavery zealots like the notorious John Randolph of Virginia. Thomas R. Whipple Jr. of New Hampshire granted that Americans "must endure" slavery, but he could not agree with Everett "that *involuntary servitude* is either founded in, or sanctioned by, the *law of nature*." In the midst of the Panama debate, James Buchanan vowed that if the Adams administration's wild-eyed foreign policy led to a slave revolt, "I would, without hesitation, buckle on my knapsack, and march in company with my friend from Massachusetts (Mr. Everett)" to put it down. But as for slavery itself, "I believe it to be a great political, and a great moral evil."[28] Such rejoinders illustrated that Everett's speech would have maintained truly moderate ground had it stopped short of discussing slavery itself.

The true fireworks, however, came in an exchange between New York Jacksonian Churchill Cambreleng and Everett during the Panama debate. On 20 April 1826, Cambreleng voiced his opposition to the Panama mission but specifically listed reasons for which he did not oppose it, including the Latin American nations' policy of "universal emancipation." Cambreleng's eyes, it was clear, fairly lit up with the chance to distinguish true moderation (so often abused in the North as "doughface-ism") from proslavery and to vindicate it as in keeping with good old American doctrines on slavery and freedom with the European-educated Everett as foil. "My doctrines, sir, on the subject of slavery, are the doctrines of our ancestors," who left slavery "in the political condition in which they found it." Thus, while he agreed with much of Everett's practical stance on slavery within the Union, in terms of slavery's morality "the gentleman has gone too far—he has expressed opinions which ought not to escape without animadversion. I heard them with equal surprise and regret." Cambreleng jabbed that if he had, "amidst the wild visions of German philosophy, . . . persuaded myself to adopt a political maxim so hostile to liberal institutions and the rights of mankind—I would have locked it up forever in the darkest chamber of my mind" rather than make such "singularly extravagant" statements on the floor of the House of Representatives.[29]

When Cambreleng's assault had finished, Everett immediately rose to reply that the critics had either misconstrued or misrepresented his knapsack speech. "In all that I said upon the topic in question," Everett claimed, "I think it no more than fair that I should be understood as carrying out the proposition with which I began; which was, 'that I did not deem it immoral nor irreligious to join in suppressing a servile war.'" It was "to justify this disclaimer, (and not otherwise can it be justified) I said, that slavery was sanctioned by religion, morality, and law." Because anything but "an exceedingly gradual process" of emancipation would result in race war in America, "slavery, like the other institutions of society, was sanctioned by the laws of religion and morality." Finally, he resented Cambreleng and others insinuating that he had changed his speech for the published version, and ascribed Cambreleng's unfairness to wounded feelings over a jest Everett had previously made at his expense.[30] On one level Everett's studied rejoinder was standard fare for a politician claiming to have been misrepresented by people who had it in for him. But on another it was a substantive attempt to reclaim solid conservative ground by channeling Canning's "exceedingly gradual" emancipationism and connecting American slavery to all settled institutions. His reply failed, however, to walk back the proslavery passages or to explain why reverence for the Constitution was not sufficient motive for him to pick up his knapsack to prevent Haiti in America.

Certainly it failed to avert a blizzard of reaction in the partisan press. As one editor remarked, Everett's speech "called forth the particular notice and remarks of many of the editors of newspapers throughout the country."[31] Southern editors, especially beleaguered National Republicans, rejoiced. They of course especially valued its "compliment to" slaveholders, "which is the more honorable and gratifying, as Mr. E. comes from a State (Massachusetts) of all others the most illiberal to the South." Other Southern National Republicans framed the speech to their liking by branding it simply "Mr. Everett's Speech in defence of the Constitution."[32]

But the fiercest party combat surrounding and using the speech took place in New England. After years of abuse as doughfaces dating at least from the Missouri debates, the region's Jacksonian editors gleefully put the shoe on the other foot in the North's bruising politics of slavery. Throughout the summer and fall of 1826, the leading Jacksonian paper in Boston, the *American Statesman*, launched a full frontal attack on Everett's willingness "to alter the word of God, and for such a detestable and inhuman purpose as the justification of slavery." "What inducement could he have," one writer puzzled, "gratuitously to proclaim the justification of a practice known to be revolting to the feelings of his constituents," other than to seek for himself and the administration "southern influence, and to conciliate southern favour"?[33] A Maine editor newspaper crowed that Everett had made it impossible for National Republicans to argue that the Jacksonian senators from Maine had opposed the Panama mission because they "had necessarily become the opposers of *emancipation*." It was Everett, not they, who had lined up with "Mr. Randolph's eccentricities."[34]

All this put New England's National Republican editors in rather an awkward position that they dealt with in a variety of ways. Everett's friends at the *Boston Patriot* decided to go over the top with praise of Everett and his speech, quoting an account gushing that it "was as great an effort of the human mind, as we have witnessed on the floor of Congress." They offered no apology for "Mr. Everett's remarks on slavery," which, far from containing anything "to condemn," constituted "a judicious attempt to allay" Southern fears of the North. They commented wryly on how incongruous it seemed for the *American Statesman* to have so suddenly "discovered a warm zeal against what it calls 'the crime and curse of slavery.'" Still, they preferred to avoid this issue and instead traffic in ad hominem defenses; in their final analysis, any criticism of the brilliant young congressman must proceed out of hearts burning with "envy and hate towards the man whose mental, moral, literary, and political superiority they cannot reach."[35] A leading administration organ in Maine wriggled from declaring Everett's position "singular and perhaps not strictly defensible," to refusing to "defend Mr. EVERETT for his ill advised and mortifying declaration," to differing outright with his "unrequired and regretted position . . . in defense of slavery" And a National Republican editor in Vermont praised Everett's eloquence to the skies but deeply regretted his slavery passage as not having "been warranted, either by the occasion, or by a proper regard to the dictates of humanity." As a conservative he would join Everett in discouraging slave rebellion, but it was in fact "an immoral and irreligious act in the master to hold a fellow-being in undeserved slavery."[36]

American abolitionists responded less equivocally. Antislavery colonizationist Ralph Randolph Gurley of Washington worried that Everett's eloquence would bolster the wrong side of the "great battle to be fought . . . in our republic, in the cause of justice." The Reverend Leonard Bacon was moved in part by Everett's "novel apparition of an apology for slavery" when he gave a 4 July sermon at New Haven denouncing slavery as a national evil and calling for a national effort to abolish it. Bacon also obliquely attacked "the man who dares to stand up in Congress and, presuming on the forbearance of those who sent him, attempts to purchase popularity by defending the principle of slavery."[37] Abolitionist Benjamin Lundy clinched his newspaper's demolition of Everett's scriptural defense of slavery by pointing out that the slaveholders' nervousness about their safety — the very nervousness that had prompted Everett's offending passages — showed that they "do not believe that slavery is to be justified by the commands of the Supreme Being." Lundy's columns repeatedly drove home the idea that by his outlandish speech, Everett had fallen in with the very small band of proslavery cranks in the South epitomized by Randolph. But antislavery would march undaunted past these throwbacks. The influential Everett might enlist as chief of "the Slavites," but "there is not a human being upon the face of the globe, of ordinary moral perceptions whose conscience does not tell him that he has no right to enslave his fellow man."[38] If Everett was aware of such abolitionist critiques, he might have welcomed them given that he had set out in his speech to distance himself and most Northerners from these radicals. Still, Lundy's repeated drumming of himself—the learned, humane reformer—out of the bounds of civilization would have hurt.

Two of the voices of enlightened Western civilization that Everett prized the most also expressed their disapprobation of his expressions on slavery, in this case directly to him. Thanking Everett for sending him his "very able and eloquent speech," Thomas Jefferson noted gently that he differed with Everett "on the question of the lawfulness of slavery, that is, of the right of one man to appropriate to himself the faculties of another without his consent." He claimed never to have changed his "early opinions" that slavery was unjust in principle. He added, however, that they were "probably nearer together" on the question of the right "of 3d persons to interfere between the parties." Anti-abolitionism held the men together in a moderate persuasion on antislavery politics, but on slavery itself Everett had gone past where even Jefferson, after a considerable and long-term accommodation to slavery, was willing to follow.[39] Everett had also sent a copy to Lafayette, who responded with nothing but praise when he commented directly on the speech. But he proceeded to offer a masterfully mild, indirect rebuke via a passage on what he knew Everett cared deeply about, the global struggle for rational liberty. After many reflections on the sad state of Europe, Lafayette celebrated the American example but lamented that "there is but one blot" on it, that of slavery. "This is a most lamentable calamity," he pressed, both to the South and as "the greatest obstacle to the diffusion of American principles throughout this hemisphere." Indeed, "here to the lovers of America it is a daily torment."[40]

Everett responded to these letters' cherished writers in revealing ways. To Lafayette's indirect rebuke he offered indirection of his own, dwelling on their shared passion for the advance of liberty in Europe and South America rather than on the divisive plight of Southern slaves.[41] Jefferson's reproof elicited as apologetic a statement on his knapsack speech as Everett offered in the 1820s—that is to say, a halfway apologetic statement. "On the subject of slavery," he sought to clarify, "I do not mean to maintain that *in the abstract*, one man has a right 'to appropriate to himself the faculties of another without his consent.' But it is another question, whether, taking things as they are, the kind and merciful master . . . has not a right" to the obedience of his slaves, "in a state of society, where a general Emancipation is allowed to be impracticable." For all his attempts to walk back and qualify this passage, he admitted to the Sage of Monticello, it had proven "exceedingly distasteful at home. Nearly all, of all parties, have united to condemn me." This torrent of criticism had convinced him "that if I have not failed in doctrine, I have in prudence." He thought Jefferson of all people might understand this from experience, for his impression was that "such strong expressions as you use in your Notes on Virginia" to decry slavery had proven "offensive to the citizens of the Slave-holding States" when published. Everett added his surmise that had Jefferson written after the Haitian Revolution had changed the landscape of revolution and slavery, "you might not have expressed yourself as you did."[42] It is a remarkable letter. Even as chastened—and clearly he was chastened at least politically—by the outcry, Everett had the temerity to lecture Jefferson that his early revolutionary enthusiasm should be sobered by Haiti. It would seem that a conservative's craving for order was what pushed Everett out in front of Jefferson in the proslavery camp in this exchange. Moreover, the narrative of chastening is a heroic one, in which Everett compared himself to Jefferson breasting the winds of public opinion.

This was not the only hint of Everett's heroic self-image surrounding this speech. Indeed, he refused to run from or go beyond his apology to Jefferson for any part of the address, preferring instead to spin it. He leaned on the editors of the official register of congressional debates to include his corrected version, but once he had edited it to his satisfaction he never omitted it from copies of the speech he sent out. When confiding in his brother Alexander, Everett took some measure of sibling pride in having been attacked more roundly than Alexander ever had and admitted only that his remarks on slavery had been imprudent—not incorrect.[43]

Part of why he felt no reason to retreat from his notorious speech was that in the long term as well as in the short term, it did him no great harm with people who counted to him. Indeed, he received effusive praise for it from people of importance both political and personal. His wife, Charlotte, watching anxiously from the gallery, convinced herself that the speech was "the most perfect success & seemed entirely to put down his opponent by his arguments," while Everett boasted to his sister that McDuffie himself had "congratulated me very handsomely." Charlotte did worry about the slavery passage but was sure he would come out all right, especially since so many of the ladies in Washington fawned over the speech and the speaker. "I keep hearing from all quarters," she reported jovially, "that they wish he was not married—& they wonder who the *second* Mrs. Everett will be." From her perspective, "Husband's Speech has had all the success that he could have wished."[44] Some of the luminaries of national and local politics expressed to Everett their assent to the speech's "general and leading doctrines," which they construed as a "successful defence of Free institutions" as embodied in the sacrosanct Constitution.[45] His father-in-law, Brooks, sustained the entire speech, including the sentiments on slavery. Caleb Cushing's congratulations, which reminded Everett of some conversations they had had about slavery since their antislavery posing in 1820, convinced him that Cushing would have given the same speech in Everett's position, and that was a real solace to him. Michigan politician Lewis Cass lauded Everett for vindicating a moderate position on a subject that "excited too much sensation." Importantly, President Adams told Everett privately that his "doctrine" on slavery "was sound." Another friend waxed philosophical about the firestorm the speech caused, given that "Slavery is the last thing upon which this country"—whether North or South—"will be brought to *reason*, as well as the last upon which it will cease to *feel*."[46] Such votes of confidence from such sources surely helped him dismiss his critics. "Had I not made the Remarks I did on Slavery," he told his sister a month after the speech, "something else would have been found to cavil at" by his opponents.[47]

But much as he wished to dismiss them, Everett worried about these critics as his reelection campaign neared. In light of the *Statesman*'s abuse of him using the speech, Everett sensed as early as August 1826 that "if I am opposed at the next election, it will be chiefly on the pretence of holding unsound opinions on that subject." That worried him, he wrote candidly to Cushing, for "tho' I have pretty firm nerves & have been tolerably well steeled by some experience of the rough & tumble of the world, I should willingly slide into Congress without the process of a contest." Thus if he could, "by any honorable means, neutralize the Statesman, I would gladly do it." He would prefer, he hinted to Cushing, to do so on "general grounds"—meaning the sort of plaudits for his overall eminence and attainments that had gotten him elected in the first place.[48]

Everett got his wish when by early October it was clear that the Jacksonians in his district had failed to organize an opposing campaign. Massachusetts party chieftain Daniel Webster, like others, was relieved that Everett would return to Congress, "notwithstanding his one *heresy*."[49] This allowed Everett's supporters the luxury of staying above the fray. The *American Traveller*, a Boston paper of which Everett was a part owner, offered only a brief notice of his controversial speech on a back page, describing it as "the successful effort of a distinguished scholar and gentleman."[50] The *Massachusetts Journal*, another Boston paper in which Everett had a share of ownership, editorialized on Everett's candidacy only once, and in the most general of terms. The *Boston Patriot*, in its desultory attention to this non-campaign, continued its ad hominem contrasts between Everett—who had earned the respect of both his constituents and his congressional colleagues "from every section of the Union"—and the hacks assaulting him in the pages of the *Statesman*.[51] Everett proved prickly about campaign attacks on his knapsack speech, particularly because one rather mild one appeared in the *Yeoman's Gazette*, a paper that had been very friendly to Everett up to that point. But ultimately he of course shared the National Republicans' overall relief that he faced no rival for reelection. He also read that reelection primarily as vindication of his course as representative rather than as a comment on how pathetic the Jacksonian forces were in his district.[52]

But despite his reelection, and even the quick disappearance of the McDuffie debate from the American political scene, Everett's speech would not go away. On 1 April 1826, the House voted 138–52 in favor of the principle of McDuffie's amendment, but by 18 May its implementation had died in a hopelessly deadlocked committee.[53] That did not keep other congressmen from dredging up Everett's speech, and not just in the Panama debate. In January 1828, for instance, the very avatar of the South's proslavery stance, John Randolph, declaimed that "that man has a hard heart, or at least a narrow understanding—yes, and a narrow heart, too, who would justify slavery in the abstract." Everett sat quietly through this allusion, not eager to remind people that he had been just such a man in 1826.[54] And the speech haunted his congressional career well beyond the walls of the House. In 1827, when rumors that the party leadership was considering nominating Everett to be a United States senator, the *Statesman* argued that Everett's "political principles, his opinions on the subject of Slavery, his youth and want of political experience, will put him entirely out of the question."[55]

In 1828 Everett did face a Jacksonian opponent, L. M. Parker, and the knapsack speech popped up in this campaign. A Parker supporter anonymously spread handbills smearing Everett as "the candidate of the Aristocracy, . . . and as the Advocate and Apologist of Slavery." This prompted a vigorous defense of Everett in a Lowell, Massachusetts, newspaper. Its editor, J. S. C. Knowlton, reminded people of the context in which Everett thought it necessary to assure the nation that all Northerners were not wild-eyed abolitionists cheering on slave insurrections and proceeded to declare that Everett "admitted the necessity of the existence of Slavery in the present order of things, but no where advocated it." Still, Knowlton felt the need to protest that the speech's "sentiments on the subject of slavery, though they may not harmonize with those most prevalent in the community, are entitled to respect as coinciding with opinions cherished by many men of liberal minds and humane feelings. That Slavery is an evil Mr Everett is ever ready to admit"—he only opposed any talk of its "immediate removal."[56] It was a skillful effort to spin Everett's stance as gradual emancipationism rather than proslavery, and Everett welcomed this editor's effort. But perhaps because of Knowlton's logical slip—Everett was a humane antislavery conservative, but his sentiments on slavery were out of step with his constituents'—he thought it "might have been made still more strong, in my favor, with perfect truth."[57]

———————

By 1828, however, Everett himself had provided his enemies with further material with which to paint him as "the Advocate and Apologist of Slavery." In January 1828, the House endured a protracted and heated debate over whether the federal government should consider slaves as property. This was but one of several congressional debates in the early nineteenth century that addressed themselves to this question, but it was divisive even by the standards of this topic. The occasion was the claim of a Louisiana slaveholder, Marigny D'Auterive, to compensation for medical services for one of his slaves who had been pressed into military service for the defense of New Orleans during the War of 1812. The Committee on Claims had filed a recommendation against reimbursing D'Auterive for this part of his claim, because slaves were "not put on the footing of property, and paid for, when lost to the owner in the public service." Most Northerners in Congress, alarmed by what had morphed from a $239 claim into a philosophical dispute over the very legitimacy of slavery, sought for some middle ground on the question. But enough Northern representatives openly denied property in man in the debate to compound Southern representatives' outrage over the committee report's language. As Randolph put it with his accustomed bluntness, the debate was further evidence that "the Missouri question never has been settled."[58]

Two weeks into this debate, Everett rose to support D'Auterive's full claim. Pointing to the Constitution's guarantee that the federal government would not take property without compensation, he contended that to vote against this part of the claim would be effectively to amend the Constitution by adding "the qualification 'excepting slaves.'" The Constitution, he assured his audience, would never have been ratified with such a qualification. Furthermore, the only true analogy for such a stance that occurred to Everett was to "suppose an act of the Government emancipating the slaves, and enabling them to enlist in the army" without compensating their owners. Such an act was unthinkable to Everett, for it "would indicate a tyranny, as absolute as any that ever oppressed a people."[59] Unlike in his ill-fated knapsack speech, here Everett sought to narrow the wide-ranging debate to a strict consideration that slaves were property under the Constitution. Framed this way, it was the most natural thing in the world for a National Republican to stick up for the rights of property.

But as the debate unfolded, Everett found his position to be better aligned with that of Southerners than with that of Northern National Republicans. Southern Representatives applauded Everett, insisting that slaveholders' property rights in their slaves must be "sacred in every State." Southern editors echoed the tone of dire alarm if Congress voted down D'Auterive's claim. As one Louisiana editor put it, common sense dictated that "*if they are not property, they are not slaves.*" "Establish the first proposition," he warned, and "the second inevitably follows, and will soon be carried into effect."[60] But Henry Martindale, a National Republican from New York, rebutted Everett by proclaiming that under the Constitution, masters had property in the labor but not in the persons of their slaves, whereas Everett had fallen into the "fallacy" of "putting the services of slaves for slaves themselves." Martindale countered Everett's history of ratification by doubting whether any amendment or clause declaring slaves different from apprentices or minors "on account of the inviolable and sacred nature of this kind of property" would have been ratified. He also offered the former professor a history lesson by pointing out that Northern states had emancipated slaves without compensation to their masters, which "event has been our boast, our pride." For his part, Charles Miner of Pennsylvania asked whether Everett's "ingenious argument" had indeed gone "to the root of the matter." He thought Everett had tried in vain to evade the real question, which was whether the federal government should consider slaves as property or as persons with duties to that government. Although recognizing how "delicate" this question was, he had no doubt that the Constitution treated slaves "as persons, and not merely as property."[61] By such reckonings from his fellow conservatives, Everett's speech had been unworthy of a statesman and had put him at odds with the Founders.

Another Northerner wondered whether Everett had not further inflamed the debate, which gave Everett the opportunity to affirm his desire to quiet it. Tristam Burges, a Rhode Island representative of no certain partisan affiliation, rose five days after Everett's speech to assure everyone that no Northern Representative had the slightest intent to deprive slaveholders of their slaves by congressional action. Thus Everett's cries about the effectual amendment of the Constitution and the tyranny of forced emancipation were "peculiarly of a kind to produce, either here or elsewhere, some degree of excitement," giving Southerners a very wrong idea of most Northerners' true principles. The idea that he, rather than the claim's opponents, was troubling the waters brought Everett to his feet. He declared with some emphasis that he had never stated that opponents of the claim wished to amend the Constitution but rather that that would be the result of their votes.[62] While Everett was lecturing the claim's opponents on the unintended consequences of their actions, Burges had turned the tables by arguing that Everett's uncalled-for vehemence disqualified him as a true friend to conciliation.

When a crucial vote in favor of D'Auterive's slave claim came on 23 January, the editors of the *National Intelligencer* earnestly hoped that would settle the issue. With those rose-colored glasses on, they rejoiced that the final vote "was marked by neither geographical nor party lines."[63] They were half right. The measure passed by a 96–92 vote, and the roll call revealed the absence of any party discipline on this issue. National Republicans voted 19–15 against the measure, while Democrats voted 53–46 for it. But the vote was starkly "geographical": Southerners voted 76–7 in favor, while Northerners voted 85–20 against. It was typical for the North to be more divided than the South, but most of the yea votes from the North came from either Northern Democrats (11) or Northerners with no clear party allegiance (7). Still, most Northern Democrats clearly were not prepared to make their stand alongside their Southern brethren (who voted 43–3 in favor of the claim) on this issue, particularly in an election year; 43 of them voted against the claim. Among Northern parties, the Adams supporters showed the strongest inclination to vote against D'Auterive's claim, by a margin of 17–2. Despite the fact that the *Daily National Journal*, a leading Adamsite organ in Washington, proclaimed that no "reflecting man" could "entertain a moment's doubt" that slaves were property, only Everett and the political nonentity Thomas H. Blake of Indiana voted for the claim. A Democratic editor in Louisiana was thus selective but accurate when he cried that "most of the friends of Mr. Adams in Congress" had denied that slaves were property.[64] If Everett thought he was carrying the water of sectional conservatism for the Adams administration in the face of such attacks, he was carrying much more than his fair share.

That eagerness to advance a conservative position on slavery provoked further vilification of Everett. A Rhode Island editor groaned that Everett's was "the most conspicuous" of "the 'dough faces' exhibited" in the D'Auterive dispute. "This gentleman goes always with the south," he added.[65] Calling the D'Auterive debate the most important since Missouri, Benjamin Lundy devoted reams of column space to recording it, beginning in January and not ending until August 1828, five months after D'Auterive's claim had died in congressional committee. He thundered that "the sentiments advanced by the advocates of slavery, in the course of the discussion, are richly deserving of record, as we are enabled, by their perusal, to unveil the very crater of burning despotism, engendering in this republic." While Lundy's fulminations on this issue set their sights largely on Northern Jacksonians and Southerners, he did quote a New York editor lamenting that "Mr. Everett has not changed his sentiments, since he tried to vindicate slavery on the floor of Congress" in 1826.[66]

Everett was fully aware of such criticisms. He responded to them in private and his surrogates responded in public. In August 1828, he expressed to abolitionist acquaintance Samuel Whitcomb his surprise at Lundy's recent attacks on him, for previously the only ones who had sought "to represent me as a friend to Slavery" were "political partizans." But passing over his stance in the D'Auterive case, he insisted that the only "two propositions I advanced, on the subject, were that Religion did not call on slaves to massacre their masters, & that" a particular Greek word "means *slave*." Given that he had no reason to believe Lundy "hostile to me," he was at a loss as to why "he should ascribe to me sentiments, which I have openly disclaimed on the floor of Congress" (in his response to Cambreleng during the Panama debate). Everett somehow thought he knew the antislavery community better than Lundy did, for he lectured him via this intermediary that no "portion of the community, who are sincere friends of Benevolent Efforts to diminish or wholly remove the Evil of Slavery, will be gratified at an attempt to hold me up as the friend of Slavery." All he had ever done, he pled in a later letter, was "to confirm the sentiment, that C[hristiani]ty did not require religious persons, to refuse aid in suppressing a servile revolt." So framed, he pledged to stand by this interpretation of scripture from both a scholarly and a political viewpoint.[67]

While Everett dodged the D'Auterive debate in all these pleadings, the editor of the Everett organ the *Massachusetts Journal* tried to spin it in a way that made Everett's vote look pregnant with antislavery possibilities. Reporting that Congress had voted for the claim, he warned that "this decision, in our view, is full of danger to slaveholders," because it sanctioned General Jackson's act of impressing slaves by providing compensation to their masters. "Suppose some other Chieftain" in the future, inspired by this example, "should impress negroes under the pretext of public necessity, and the sanction of this decision; what will prevent his so doing to the destruction of slave-owners themselves and of the liberties of the country?" This was a shrewd end run around the idea that Everett had voted for slaves being property. It kept the focus on the favorite National Republican theme of Jackson as a military chieftain setting precedents dangerous to liberty while also spinning Everett's vote as somehow antislavery in implication. Not that the paper named Everett as having voted in the debate, however. Indeed, the paper's Washington correspondent—who could have been Everett himself—downplayed the debate as a waste of time because no "principle is likely to be settled."[68]

Everett was able to get away with such weak answers because unlike his knapsack speech, his D'Auterive speech and vote did not become a partisan tool against him. The Jacksonian presses were uncharacteristically reticent to attack Everett on this score, probably because so many Northern Democrats had voted alongside him. In his 1828 reelection campaign it was the knapsack speech, not D'Auterive, that Massachusetts Democrats used to try to paint Everett as an ambitious and aristocratic pol out of touch with his constituents. And at any rate, Everett won a crushing reelection victory despite a secret handbill campaign trying to confuse voters. The National Republican press in his district seemed most concerned about how a low turnout in the uncompetitive race would not reflect his constituents' esteem for Everett. Triumphing over new dirty tricks and the old proslavery cry vindicated his paper's boast that "we have no fears for this District. Mr. Everett can no more be shaken than Bunker Hill Monument."[69]

Everett's responses to his critics, as with so much else in his fumbling career with slavery during his years in the House, illuminate much about the politics of slavery in the 1820s. As Donald Ratcliffe has provocatively argued, the common image of that decade as a quiet prelude to the escalation of slavery controversy does not ring true. As Everett had found to his disquiet and admitted in his first Whitcomb letter, the fluidity of parties in this period encouraged Northern partisans in the press and even in Congress to adopt a strident antislavery posture that party discipline would soon discourage.[70] In that setting, it was a species of wishful thinking on his part to think that his obscure disclaimer in response to Cambreleng, and these much later learned parsings of his meaning, would have as much political weight as that first disastrous speech.

Yet for all that, Everett's attempt to warn off Whitcomb from dividing the Whiggish benevolent reform community suggests that he thought his conservative hopes for slavery reform best represented that community. Other aspects of his career while in the House provided the factual foundation for this self-image as a benevolent reformer. And those aspects ran alongside the stances discussed in this chapter, both chronologically and in his own mind.

3

The House

WHIG NATIONALIST

For all the considerable shadow which his D'Auterive and knapsack efforts cast, Everett's congressional career was multifaceted and complex. More than any other thing, he was an ardent party and nation builder through this period of sectional turmoil, and those roles sent him careening in more than one direction on the sectionalist spectrum. During his years in Congress, he helped his political allies transition from the National Republican Party, which combated the Jacksonians during Adams's administration and Jackson's first presidential term, to the Whig Party, which arose to combat Jackson's second administration.[1] Along the way, his fervent opposition to Indian Removal and nullification, together with his commitment to his party's success at the polls and in policy, led him into sectionalist territory. At other times his connections with Southern party brethren led him back in the opposite direction. While this meandering course left him open to being labeled both a sectionalist firebrand and a dough-face, Everett wanted to dedicate his congressional years not to a proslavery or antislavery position nor to a Northern or Southern position. Instead, his priorities were the solidification of national unity and the advancement of the Whig agenda of improvement. While those two goals were mutually reinforcing, sectional strife would threaten both.

The single cause to which Everett was perhaps most committed throughout his congressional term was resisting Indian Removal. The controversy began when state officials in Georgia removed the Cherokee and other Native American tribes from their boundaries and handed the land over by lottery to white settlers. Amid much debate in the cabinet, the Adams administration cautiously hewed a line that put it in conflict with Georgia's government, including issuing an injunction against Georgia surveying the land in dispute. Georgia's governor responded by framing the issue as a zero-sum struggle over sovereignty, and the standoff continued throughout Adams's term.[2] When Andrew Jackson took office in 1829, he prioritized facilitating the removal of the Southeastern Indians to territory west of the Mississippi. His submission to Congress in December 1829 of a proposal to do just that sparked an enormous conflagration, but he and his supporters were determined to see it through. "Indian Removal held the place in Jackson's vision," Daniel Walker Howe has written, "that internal improvements occupied in that of John Quincy Adams: the key to national development." At the core of this vision was both "American sovereignty" and especially "white supremacy." Howe and other scholars have pointed to this debate as the great sifter of partisan loyalty early in Jackson's term.[3]

But Jackson's policy touched off a sectional and cultural explosion as well as a partisan squabble. As much recent scholarship has shown, the encounter between whites and Indians touched an emotional chord in the Northeast. Only one Massachusetts member of Congress voted for the Removal Act. The Democratic press in the Northeast was largely at a loss for arguments to defend the Removal policy. Years later, Martin Van Buren remembered Northern Democrats being "brought to death's door" politically for supporting Removal. Unlike in the South or the West, Indians no longer posed a threat or occupied prime real estate in the Northeast. Northeastern men and especially women pored over dozens of novels that sentimentalized Indians. More significantly, the Removal policy outraged the army of men and women who were card-carrying members of the Benevolent Empire, a loose Anglo-American organization of zealous Christian reform organizations. Viewing Removal in the context of this project of national and international moral reform, they believed the issue raised fundamental questions about the American national character. Many women's charitable institutions in particular placed a high priority on sponsoring missions to American Indians, and their members became personally attached both to the missionaries and to their Indian charges.[4]

These women's mass participation would make this a novel kind of congressional debate. To be sure, for most petitioners, resisting Removal belonged to women's sphere because it was benevolence, not politics. But "popular opposition to Jackson's Removal bill overwhelmed traditional forms of political participation," as historian Mary Hershberger has put it. A petition campaign organized by Catherine Beecher, for instance, was "the first national petition drive by women," one that "succeeded in deluging Congress with women's petitions." And these women's participation in politics had a partisan tinge. As excellent recent works by Amy Greenberg and Elizabeth Varon show, the National Republicans and later Whigs were far more likely than the Jacksonians and later Democrats to appeal to the ladies. The Whig persuasion's norms of manliness tended to be more comfortable with sentimental devotion to benevolent reform efforts.[5]

Everett involved himself in the Indians' cause early and often. Even before taking his seat in the House, he met with Indians and military men fresh from the scene in Georgia. These meetings, together with correspondence with Georgians in the know, informed his activist's worldview, which had white Georgians clearly in the wrong. Then when Adams took office, Everett advised him on the Removal issue. Thus it came as no surprise in 1827 when the Speaker of the House made Everett chair of a select committee dealing with Removal.[6] Presenting his committee's report to the House in March 1827, Everett blamed Georgia officials for creating this "unhappy subject" and "so unpleasant a controversy" and yearned for its "amicable adjustment." As if to prove his point about the subject's explosive potential, a debate erupted over whether to even print the select committee's report.[7] Everett did not relish such sectional controversy but found himself squarely in the middle of this one.

Three years later, Everett reluctantly but fully participated in the donnybrook provoked by Jackson's drive for a Removal Act. On 19 May 1830, deep into the debate, Everett rose to plead for "this friendless, unrepresented people." He demanded in his loftiest tone to know whether there are "two kinds of rights, rights of the strong, which you respect because you must; and rights of the weak, on which you trample, because you dare?" Everett had never hesitated to use Native Americans in the abstract as a foil for civilization, or even to celebrate their westward retreat. But the tribes in question "are essentially a civilized people." To this firm believer in improvement and progress, they are "so much the more interesting, as they present the experiment of a people rising from barbarity into civilization." Yet the current bill would drive them back to barbarity by making these, "our civilized red brethren," go out and fight for survival against the "wild savages of the desert."[8]

For all his solicitude for these tribes, the core of his complaint against the bill was what it would do to the United States, especially on the world stage. His "great objection to the removal" was "that it is compulsory." Forced removal produced the strange spectacle of Indians seeking "protection against the law," which was instead supposed to protect all. This derogation of the rule of law was a "fatal mischief" and meant that the bill "is all unmingled, unmitigated evil." And "the evil, sir, is enormous; the violence is extreme; the breach of public faith deplorable; the inevitable suffering incalculable." The erstwhile Paper Warrior Everett also knew the harm it would inflict on "the fair fame of the country" before "the severe judgment of enlightened Europe. Our friends there will view this measure with sorrow, and our enemies alone with joy."[9] In short, the Removal bill would provide congressional sanction to a vigilante brand of injustice that would harm the cause of human liberty throughout the Atlantic.

Such speeches and actions in Congress put Everett squarely into the Removal issue's crossfire of philanthropy and politics. Some, such as a Cincinnati man, claimed that "thousands" in his region revered Everett as "the champion of a race more outrageously abused than any other recorded in history." A leading National Republican editor proclaimed that Everett "merits the gratitude of all good citizens for his exertions." And one of his speeches moved Cherokee leaders in the House gallery to tears.[10] Given such reactions, Northern National Republicans thought resistance to Removal a winning issue for them. Everett's allies in Boston happily trumpeted his doings as chair of the select committee in 1827. In 1830, national party editors printed Everett's "deservedly celebrated speech on the Indian Bill" in its entirety. And in 1832 the National Republican Convention's Address to the People, drafted by a committee headed by Everett, complained against Removal under the heading of Jackson's overall disregard for "*the sacred authority of law.*"[11] For other Northerners, to lavish philanthropy on the Indians was a function of a falsely romantic notion of the Indians. In the Cherokees, Western antislavery advocate Timothy Flint charged, Everett was defending little more than a "nation consisting of some 25 scoundrel-quarteroon-aristocrat-negro-holders."[12] Clearly, the ever-shifting race and philanthropy cards could be played on both sides of this debate. Nevertheless, Removal's overall unpopularity in the North benefited both Everett and his party.

If Flint distinguished between philanthropy for African Americans and for slaveholding Native Americans, white Southerners lumped both kinds of do-gooders together as one common threat. As soon as Removal became an issue in the 1820s, sectional moderates like Missouri senator Thomas Hart Benton fretted that the policy's opponents "might awake the slavery question, hardly got to sleep after the alarming agitations of the Missouri controversy." But ironically, Southern spokesmen were the ones most likely to inject slavery into the contest. Southern advocates of Removal were wont to castigate expressions against the policy as "the *canting phrase of a puritan.*" South Carolinian William Gilmore Simms spoke even more bluntly than this. He lauded as inevitable and just the federal government's policy of Indian Removal and groused that "this removal has been resisted in various quarters, and chiefly by the instrumentality of those universal philanthropists, who are now known as abolitionists." But they were pseudo-philanthropists at best, given that their policy would lead to "more serious evils" for the Indians than they sought to avert.[13] Georgia's own Wilson Lumpkin railed even more hysterically against "the Northern fanatics, male and female," who had gotten up petitions slandering "my own beloved Georgia as the headquarters of all that was vile and wicked in her intercourse with Indians; and to finish the picture, in these petitions we were denounced as slaveholders." Their movement was the essence of ambition under the guise of false humanity, "the fruit of *cant and fanaticism*, emanating from . . . the boasted progeny of the Pilgrims and Puritans." For Georgia to yield to either these petitions or those against slavery would be "to abandon our rights." Finally, it was these men and women who "are engaged in the unholy works of discord" that "weaken the bonds of Union" by alienating the South.[14]

It was clear that no matter his stance on slavery itself, Everett's opposition to Removal meant the likes of Lumpkin and Simms would number him with their enemies. As early as 1825, when Everett inquired of a friend in Savannah as to "what insuperable obstacles, in public opinion, exist against incorporating the Creeks with the state and making citizens of them," Southerners publicly branded his letter "an *impertinent interference*." Everett's friend defended him in a public letter, but the image of Everett as the armchair philanthropist stuck.[15] An Alabama congressman mocked that Everett's 1830 speech "reminded him of an old maid of his acquaintance, who pitied a goose because it had to go barefoot in winter." In 1831, Charles Haynes of Georgia told the House that he detected in Everett's course on Removal an essentially political brand of humanity. Given that Everett had previously celebrated the Pilgrims' displacement of their local Indians, he was clearly practicing a sectional double standard. Moreover, his willingness to override state sovereignty threatened the Constitution and the Union far more than Removal ever did.[16] By 1832, irritated Southern congressmen flared at Everett and other "political missionaries against the State of Georgia" for impairing "the character of Congress" as well as of Georgia by their "dark insinuations and mysterious inuendoes [*sic*]" against the workings of Removal.[17] And in 1833, when Adams joined Everett in complaining that Removal altered the Constitution, Augustin Clayton of Georgia was incredulous. "There is something so amusing," he fumed, "in these grave arguments about the violation of the constitution, used by gentlemen who have stretched it in every possible shape which such a pliant instrument could assume."[18]

If the conservative Everett shuddered to be cast as a Yankee in league with abolitionists, it did not show on this issue. He was in this cause for the long haul and served it unflinchingly as a political manager and informational clearing-house. Far from the amateurish scholar lost in political combat, he lined up newspaper support in advance of introducing the topic in Congress; cultivated the cultural sphere by encouraging the authors of studies of Indian life; and continually gathered information about the situation of the threatened Indians, both for his own and for allies' speeches and publications. He was effective enough in all such activities that in 1832 party leaders asked him to be their point man on the issue. And when delegations from the beleaguered tribes visited Washington, they sought out Everett for help.[19] He got so worked up about this issue that he suggested to National Republican leaders that Jackson deserved to be impeached for Indian Removal (among other crimes). Indeed, in a reversal of future roles on the slavery issue, when Indian Removal was the cause, Everett earnestly encouraged the influential Unitarian divine William Ellery Channing to lend his public support, while Channing hesitated to publicly back this particular reform cause.[20]

Everett also played the bulldog on the House floor on the Removal issue. In February 1831, assured of the backing of the Massachusetts legislature, he introduced and advocated a petition from his constituents to repeal the Removal Act passed the previous session. He revived this delicate controversy because Removal threatened "the Union itself" by undermining "the undisputed paramount operation, through all the States, of those functions with which the Government is clothed by the constitution. When that operation is resisted, the Union is in fact dissolved." The Jacksonians' support for Georgia's course thus constituted "the commencement of that convulsion of these United States, to which the friends of liberty throughout the world look forward with apprehension, as a fatal blow to their cause." This hit Everett—as one who cared passionately for the Union and Constitution as the vanguard of the global cause of liberty—where he lived. So, "disagreeable as the consequence may be to one who loves strife as little as I, I cannot keep silence" while witnessing "the constitution invaded; the honor of the country tarnished; the Union impaired." The overall burden of his two-day speech was disbelief that Congress could sanction this inhumane twin to South Carolina's contemporaneous drive for nullification.[21] Compelled by such motives, Everett returned to the issue in January 1832 and then again in January 1835. These motions and speeches provoked sharp exchanges in which Southerners painted Everett as overeager to stir this pot for political gain. Everett of course denied such charges, insisting that his was the stance of the principled statesman.[22]

Much as he protested his distaste for political altercation in such speeches, Everett seems to have taken some pride in pushing forward in this cause no matter the opposition. In January 1831, he asked Pennsylvania Jacksonian William Ramsey to be the one to reintroduce the issue on the House floor, which would have neutralized some of the partisan sting. But Ramsey "declined on the ground that it w'd get him into a hornet's nest." So Everett charged into that nest himself, brushing off the "great efforts" his opponents made against him in a way he never did when slavery was the direct issue.[23] "None is more willing" than himself "to meet the responsibility of the Crisis," Everett boasted to one correspondent. Especially if supported by constituents, he swaggered, "the floodgates of abuse" may open against him "without giving me any uneasiness." As he pondered reintroducing Removal in January 1831, he acknowledged to his wife, Charlotte, that "it is a subject that will kindle the worst passions; & my illness at the beginning of the session has left a languor on me, that I cannot shake off." But while he seems already to have noticed the pattern that his fragile health did not improve in the midst of serious political conflict, on Removal he would not skirt the fray. "Perhaps the necessity of making a strenuous effort will start me," he surmised. His health and his enemies notwithstanding, he pledged to his damsel at home, "I am not afraid of the subject, nor of my ability to handle it." At one point in the debate, he regaled her, "the Administration folks . . . endeavored, in every way, by leaving their places & talking loud behind the bar to confuse me; but in this they mistook their man." By the end of the session he did assert that he was "sick of Washington, sick of politics, sick of speaking, writing, & printing[,] sick of the vanities of this world." But otherwise his letters to Charlotte indicated that as aggravating as was this renewed fight over Removal, unlike slavery this was not an uncomfortable topic for him or one that he lacked confidence in handling. Indeed, the assaults he had taken as too pliant on slavery may well have helped stiffen his spine on Removal.[24]

Another reason this was a comfortable subject for Everett is that it fit neatly with his wide-ranging, irrepressible interest in reform and benevolence. One newspaper account of an exchange between Everett and a Southern congressman during the Removal debate trumpeted it as evidence of Everett's superior "moral sense," and Everett would (modestly) have agreed. On one typical day, he met with representatives of both the Society for Suppressing Intemperance and the Humane Society. On another, he corresponded with a like-minded constituent about both Indian Removal and how he "lost no time in presenting to the House of Representatives" a memorial against mail service "on the Sabbath." Other diary entries and correspondence attest to his involvement in everything from poor relief to the reform of hospitals and insane asylums. He publicly attacked imprisonment for debt as part of his overall support for prison reform. He summed up his Whiggish principles well in an address to the New York Institute in 1831, asserting that national prosperity was to be achieved "by free institutions of government,—laws affording security to property,—and the diffusion of education and useful knowledge."[25] Fighting Indian Removal fit naturally within this constellation of concerns.

In 1835, when English abolitionist and über-reformer Harriet Martineau visited Washington, she socialized frequently with Everett. In one way, this would seem an unlikely friendship; while Everett's first political notoriety came from his 1826 knapsack speech, Martineau had burst on the Anglo-American literary scene in 1832 with a staunchly antislavery novel. "I am a radical" on slavery and other questions, Harriet proclaimed, "and am known to be so, wherever I go." But they were not so far apart as this would suggest, for they both had a Unitarian background that nurtured their shared commitment to rational, modernizing benevolent reform stretching across a wide variety of causes. When she visited Richmond and debated slavery with her hosts, she reported to him that "some gentlemen adverted to you & a speech of yours in Congress, as sanctioning the institution. Of course, I disbelieve this, after what passed between us; but, if you write to me, will you tell me what it was you did say, that I may be prepared against the next time I hear you so quoted?" Everett's infamous speech clearly seemed out of character for the citizen of the Benevolent Empire whom Martineau knew Everett to be. Whatever he replied to this request did not cool their relationship, for they continued a friendly and mutually admiring correspondence for months and years thereafter.[26]

Whether fighting against Indian Removal or for a panoply of humane causes, Everett was not one to be daunted by Southerners and Democrats flailing away at what they called false philanthropy. Indeed, when it came to Indian Removal, Everett talked of "dough faces" in the third person. In a fascinating letter to a supporter in January 1831, he looked back on the epic 1830 battle over Removal. "Last winter," he recalled, "supported by the memorials poured in from various quarters, we made a stand on the Indian question, & very nearly triumphed. We broke the ranks of an iron party phalanx" by peeling off some Northern Democrats, "& but for our own dough faces should have defeated the bill."[27] No Northern politician called himself a doughface, but this aspersion on politicians who proved untrue to their section in a crucial vote meant that Everett was even more unlikely than most to have recognized himself among the doughface ranks.

But for all that, Everett was never a radical on any question, and Removal and like causes hardly set his path toward abolitionism. Many scholars have recently drawn links between anti-Removal petitioning in the early 1830s and antislavery petitioning later in that decade, especially for the women involved in both causes. Seeing anti-removalism as the natural precursor to abolitionism, they have struggled to understand how anyone could oppose Removal but also support colonizing freed blacks (something radical abolitionists came to oppose).[28] Alisse Portnoy, however, has argued that "most antiremovalists actively embraced African colonization" rather than immediate abolitionism as the best antislavery corollary to their work for the Indians. Indian Removal was to their minds "oppressive" and African American colonization voluntary and "benevolent, 'a subject of almost romantic interest.'"[29]

Likewise, despite Southern attempts to lump him in with abolitionists, Everett saw the American Colonization Society (ACS) rather than radical abolitionism as the appropriate companion to Indian Removal. Indeed, as early as 1825 when he wrote a Georgia friend for facts on the Indians there, he assured him that "I entertain none of the views on Negroes or Indians" that Georgia's "zealous" governor had ascribed too broadly to all Northern opponents of Removal.[30] He would make his conservative views on "Negroes" plain in his 1826 speech, of course, but he buttressed that by frequent contacts with ACS officials and attendance at ACS meetings (including serving formally as a delegate from Massachusetts) at all stages of his congressional career.[31] An English correspondent saw eye to eye with Everett when he evinced his interest in "the cause of your Indians" while also rejoicing at news of "the continued prosperity of Liberia," the ACS settlement on the coast of Africa.[32]

Convinced of the rightness and political orthodoxy of the colonization cause, Everett also delivered what he thought to be an important address at an ACS meeting. He lavished his usual care on preparing to deliver and publish this speech, to supplement his ongoing gathering of relevant facts across a period of years.[33] On 16 January 1832, at the ACS gathering in the hall of the House of Representatives, he offered a resolution "that the colonization of the coast of Africa is the most efficient mode of suppressing the slave trade, and of civilizing the African continent." Noting the "depressed" state of and high degree of criminality among the free black community in the North, he did not ascribe these "to any superior proneness of the colored population, as such, to crime. But I think it proves that as a class they are ignorant and needy." He urged that this was "an evil of momentous character to the peace and welfare of the Union." He gushed that the objects referred to in his resolution were "universally interesting to the philanthropist and friend of humanity." He also professed to be entirely confident in the prospects of both abolishing the slave trade and civilizing Africans, specifically contending against those who "said that it is impossible to civilize Africa" based on the progress Europe had made from its barbarous past. His stature as a scholar of ancient civilization increased the potency of this argument. "Sir," he perorated, "when men have a great, benevolent, and holy object in view, of permanent interest, *obstacles are nothing.*"[34]

Everett was supremely confident that the ACS was both a benevolent and a mainstream organization. To be sure, even within Everett's natural constituency of New England Whiggish reformer types, there were fine shades of opinion on the proper approach to slavery. One observer, for instance, dismissed both radical abolitionists and the ACS, the latter because "slavery is too great an evil to be trifled with. Nothing should be done which may increase it," as the removal of free blacks seemed to him calculated to do.[35] But trusted friends lauded his 1832 speech. And the rather more authoritative voice of more than ten state legislatures supported federal aid for the ACS's Liberia project. Even more to the point, in 1831 the Massachusetts legislature requested members of its congressional delegation to exert themselves in favor of the ACS.[36] Historian John Brooke has calculated that when Everett delivered his speech in 1832, the ACS had 98 auxiliaries in the free states (one auxiliary per 71,518 in free population) and 127 in the slave states (one auxiliary per 29,958 in free population). The Upper South region, from South Central Virginia up to Maryland, was a particular stronghold for the ACS.[37] That cross-sectional support would have been enormously encouraging to a nationalist like Everett. The ACS also had powerful friends like Henry Clay and Daniel Webster, whose support only compounded its impact on their multiple followers from all regions. All this contributed to make the ACS, as Eric Burin has demonstrated, one of the great success stories of nineteenth-century American politics.[38]

Everett perceived that support for the ACS would (safely, moderately) burnish his rather dubious antislavery credentials. Throughout the late 1820s, when not abusing Everett as a doughface, Benjamin Lundy followed the transatlantic activities of the ACS from something like a neutral point of view, alongside reporting on abolitionist societies throughout the Union.[39] Deep Southerners certainly thought they saw antislavery activity when they looked at what Carolina hothead Robert Turnbull called the "Colonization, or Insurrection Society." The increasing calls on Congress to fund the ACS were an especially alarming federal usurpation, Turnbull raged. "Do these enthusiasts think it a trifling matter to hold out to our slave population prospects which never can be realized" when they passed resolutions supporting the liberation and colonization of America's slaves? "Are they to scatter firebrands, and say they mean well"? The legislatures of South Carolina, Georgia, and Missouri threatened to leave the Union rather than see the ACS receive federal aid. Georgia's legislators resolved themselves "ready and willing to make any sacrifice, rather than submit longer to such ruinous interference."[40] For all their hysterics, Deep Southerners might be forgiven for seeing the ACS as part of the phalanx of antislavery interests ranged against them. While it functioned as a big tent hosting several slave-holders interested in making the United States safer for slavery by removing free blacks, that big tent did include several moderate reformers who lodged at various points along the antislavery humanitarian spectrum. Although historians have sought to draw clear, bright lines for the 1820s and 1830s between various Northern antislavery persuasions, Beverly Tomek's recent research has shown that, "in Pennsylvania at least, they were actually quite blurry." Too many historians, she persuasively argues, have followed the Garrisonian abolitionists' attacks on the ACS and thus left it "out of the antislavery picture entirely."[41]

Everett was thus entirely sincere and by his own lights justified in 1828 when he protested to Samuel Whitcomb in response to Lundy's assaults that "I am as great a foe to slavery as you or any one else" and offered as evidence that "to the colony on the coast of Africa, I am a decided friend." He did acknowledge that his antislavery might be difficult to detect outside of his support for the ACS. "But in times like these," he pled, "when it is impossible to take a step, to utter a word, to enter a house, without being dogged about the streets, misrepresented & vilified I must ask to be excused from entering on this subject in any way"—aside from the safe engagement with the ACS, it would appear. Were he to be more public in active opposition to slavery, he asserted, that would not help the cause. "I have not the least doubt, that were I to hold a conversation for 5 minutes with friend or foe, on the subject," within two weeks at the most the partisan press would be alive with rumors that "Mr. E., a friend of the Adm[inistration] & a warm friend of Slavery was now trying to get up an anti-slavery society, with a view to the ruin of the Southern States."[42] This was on one hand a classic doughfaced plea to cover inaction. It was also a typical (if perceptive) conservative assessment of how proslavery, antislavery, and partisan zealots both pressed for absolute consistency on the slavery issue and painted a moderate politician's minor turns on the issue as wild and damning swings. His time in Washington had certainly made him worldly-wise when it came to the intersection of slavery with partisan politics. But in the days when abolitionists like Whitcomb recruited opinion makers on an ecumenical basis and could consort with colonizationists like Everett, Everett thought it natural to talk of the antislavery community in the first person despite his overall conservatism and inaction on the issue.

More than the backlash against his 1826 speech had produced Everett's change of tone, slight though that shift was. His continuous and accelerating activity in opposing Indian Removal had reinforced his natural inclination to full participation in the Benevolent Empire. Furthermore, other key partisan efforts for most of his time in Washington put him in opposition to powerful Southerners of various stripes. He continued to seek to anchor his party on solid conservative ground, but on many issues beyond Removal, that ground tilted northward.

In the service of Adams's reelection campaign in 1828, for instance, Everett edged toward a sectionalist stance, albeit one of an undeniably conservative sort. He had learned by then that slavery had to be accounted for in the national political calculus, mixed in as it was with other issues. In March, he confided in a correspondent that he took deadly seriously long-standing talk from Southerners, notably John Randolph, that the Southern policy was to divide New England and thus rule the nation and "drive us to the wall." He dreaded a Jackson presidency as the day when "the yoke is fixed on us" in New England. He let slip such sentiments in a widely reprinted speech in Faneuil Hall in June 1828. Adams should be reelected, he argued, in part because the South had "already had its full share in the Administration of the Government, and that a monopoly of it is inconsistent with the rights of the other members of the confederacy, and with the spirit of the Constitution." This rhetoric was consistent with the limited embrace of defensive sectionalism manifest in the Adams press in Boston during this campaign. In this theme, the likes of Adams, Webster, and Everett embodied true Unionism by standing up for New England against Southern assaults, while Jacksonians enabled Southern sectional selfishness and nullification. In this light, Unionism and New England regionalism could be seen as compatible.[43]

But such statements remained aberrations for Everett even in 1828, uttered in moments of prospective electoral frustration. For most of the long reelection campaign, he played his more familiar role of crafting a public narrative in which Adams was a national, not a sectional, man. In the spring of 1827, Everett asked President Adams to clarify, obviously for public consumption, what his stance had been during the Missouri controversy. That gave Adams the chance to emphasize that he had thought the proposed restriction of slavery in Missouri unconstitutional, which was a very selective and Southern-friendly rendering of his private thoughts on the matter in 1819–21. Everett used this statement to tell Southern correspondents that they could very easily defend Adams in the South as a sectional moderate.[44]

A set of issues that drove Everett in a more consistently northerly direction was support for a protective federal tariff and resistance to South Carolina politicians' attempts to nullify that tariff. This national struggle, which ranged from the mid-1820s through the early 1830s, involved conflicting worldviews on political economy. The debate was yet another example of sharp sectional politics in this era, with the Southeast lined up against a tariff to benefit American manufacturing and the Northeast lined up in favor. Carried on almost simultaneously with the Indian Removal battle, the effort to nullify the tariff was also inextricably linked to anxiety about slavery's future among slaveholders in the Lower South. In this as in the Removal debate, those Southeastern politicians characterized the Union as a loose confederacy of "independent sovereignties."[45]

Although it was easy for Massachusetts's National Republican leadership to know how to respond to such a paltry conception of the Union, at first other aspects of the controversy were not so clear. This was a time of continuing partisan realignment in the state, and it was unclear how the politics of the tariff would impact the nascent two-party competition between National Republicans and Jacksonians. By the very late 1820s, however, Bay State National Republicans perceived that supporting the tariff and opposing nullification would cast the Boston political elite as both "a defender of regional interests" and as protector of the Union. The National Republicans could—and did—attack anti-tariff Jacksonians in Massachusetts as "dough-faces." So triumphant was this twin issue that in the spring of 1831, National Republican stalwart John Davis boasted that "in Truth, we have no Jacksonism in Massachusetts."[46]

Everett made significant contributions to his state party's efforts to prosecute this debate. His views on political economy aligned with his party's "American System," in which tariffs were part of an overall program of government-encouraged improvement. Nullification outraged him as a vitiation of the Union at least as much as Indian Removal did. And he was puzzled and alarmed to see "the insidious course taken by some of the Southern gentlemen" in combating the tariff, namely in early and often and "gratuitously connecting it with Slavery."[47]

Everett was slow to address the issue but did so decidedly once his oar was in. His first major speech came on 7–8 May 1830, deep into a sharply sectional congressional debate. He defended New Englanders from South Carolinians' charges of sectional selfishness. And as slavery had already been introduced, he thought it not inappropriate to turn on its head the charge that the North benefited disproportionately from protective legislation. "The southern States," he observed, "have a monopoly of a species of property, increasing in numbers, and which would, under other circumstances, decrease in value: I mean their slaves." Federal tariff protection of Louisiana's booming sugar sector, he explained, drove up the value of slaves sold through the vast domestic slave trade, which he calculated added $12 million annually to the value of all slave property throughout the South. No benefit that the North might derive from the tariff could compare with this staggering sum. He protested that he did not mean to defame the South, which "is generous, liberal, high-minded," but to defend New England, for "all that I have or hope, I owe to her noble institutions." He ended by chiding the Carolinians for their "tone of fierce denunciation," calling instead for "a conciliating language" to enter the debate.[48] Everett's sugar-bonus argument struck South Carolinian William Drayton as "an extraordinary one," for cotton planters had been in the habit of seeing the sugar tariff as a wealth transfer from cotton to sugar cultivators.[49] At any rate, Everett's speech was certainly a potent mix of defensive New England chauvinism, conciliatory Unionism, and cold-eyed amorality in dealing with the explosive issue of slavery.

In June 1832, Everett's old nemesis Churchill Cambreleng turned his sugar tariff appeal back on him. A Democrat leery of National Republicans who so habitually injected moral concerns into politics, he challenged the so-called philanthropists of the North to think about their own logic in this case. Were they prepared to tell their Yankee constituents that they had "voted for a duty on foreign sugar, the effect of which is to encourage" what these do-gooders lambasted, "the domestic slave trade"? He had mistaken his mark to some degree in Everett, who was a colonizationist and philanthropist overall in politics but who did not see slavery simply as a moral issue. But Cambreleng had effectively exposed a tension in this argument coming from a Northern National Republican and made Everett wriggle. Forgetting that he had raised this argument in 1830, Everett professed himself "sorry to hear this topic introduced" by Cambreleng, noting, "It is scarcely possible to touch it, without offence, one side or the other." Everett's rejoinder hinged on the idea that if Americans did not buy sugar from Louisiana, they would from Cuba. That would encourage "not the domestic slave trade, but the African slave trade, with all the horrors of 'the middle passage.'"[50] It was a sloppy affair on both sides, as both Cambreleng and Everett were seeking not consistency in a debate about the relevant slave trades but rather to score points by introducing slavery and the slave trades into the tariff dispute.

While Everett was always apologetic about his deployments of slavery in this debate, that never stopped him. In his 1832 speech, he refuted Carolinians' wailings "that the tariff is a withering curse to South Carolina" by charging that the inefficiency of slave labor was the real cause of their economic distress. He paused to protest that "it is not for me to read a lecture to gentlemen on the evils of slavery" and that "I desire to treat it without offence." But he pressed on, citing for support the recent debates in the Virginia legislature about the future of the peculiar institution in that state. He quoted at some length "a representative of a county in Eastern Virginia" who objected to slavery "because it is ruinous to the whites; retards improvement; roots out an industrious population," and so forth.[51] This was pretty bold stuff for Congressman Everett, although he still sought a middle ground where he was neither proslavery nor an abolitionist but rather one with enlightened Southerners.

Ultimately, however, Everett gave his best efforts in and out of Congress to defending the Union, not the tariff. For all his rhetorical sorties against the South on the House floor, behind the scenes Everett put his growing political muscle behind finding a Union-saving compromise on the tariff. In a meeting of National Republican chieftains at his house in December 1831, Everett, "comparing himself to the devil's advocate at the canonization of saints," asked his colleagues whether persisting in support for a provocatively protective tariff "was not setting the South at defiance." Adams agreed with him that it would be neither wise nor politically advantageous to defy not only the South but the entire Jackson administration. Interestingly, it was Henry Clay who responded that he preferred to "defy the South, the President, and the devil" if that was what it would take to secure his American System.[52] After another year of Union-menacing brinkmanship, however, Everett presumably had Clay's blessing when he led a visit to his old adversary McDuffie to seek a compromise. And in February 1833 he and colleagues Webster and Davis sought to maintain a middle ground after Clay had fluctuated to proposing tariff reductions, which they adjudged too rapid and deep.[53]

There could be no quarter for the heinous doctrine of nullification, however. In the peroration of his 1832 speech in the House, Everett declared the topic of nullification, "if possible, more important than that of the expediency or utility of the tariff." For the assertion of the right to nullify a federal law clothed "what is, in reality, rebellion, under an alleged constitutional form," and had made "resistance to the laws" acceptable to far too many people. And where would it end if this rebellion stood in 1832? Pennsylvania, for instance, could nullify South Carolina's repeal of the tariff, and this doctrine could spread to an endless variety of locally unpopular laws. So nullification not only was unconstitutional—one state was not competent under the Constitution to determine a law's legitimacy—but also would create "the greatest misfortune which could befall the Union," namely "a scene of civil discord . . . , for which the history of the world has no parallel." Such a civil war "would end in military despotism," so "the State which secedes from this Union bids farewell to republican Government forever." He implored Carolinians and their sympathizers "not to deprive" their posterity of the "happy birthright" received in common from the Founding Fathers.[54] This defense of the rule of law and painting disunion as a nightmare scenario would become central themes in Everett's career.

He contributed more than his own speeches to the cause of the imperiled Union during the nullification crisis. Some of his most signal offerings came again behind the scenes, in collaboration with two living legends. In April 1830, while working in his usual meticulous, scholarly way on an article for the *North American Review*, Everett enlisted James Madison to help him demolish nullification's claim to the legacy of the Founders. Senator Robert Y. Hayne, for one, had appealed to the Virginia and Kentucky Resolves of 1798 as a precedent for state resistance to unjust federal law. Everett was but one of many who called on the surviving Founder to clarify his views. But the *NAR* would provide him a medium of unrivaled influence, so Madison responded quickly with a very long letter contrasting the multistate approach he and Jefferson took in 1798 with the single-state heresy of South Carolina. This initiated a months-long exchange of views and documents in which Madison further developed his position against nullification. Everett treasured this correspondence and used Madison as his final authority in the article that framed nullification as an unconstitutional attempted revolution.[55] He sent the article and a speech he delivered on the subject to the Sage of Montpelier. Madison approved of both, hoping Everett's efforts would help Americans appreciate "a constitution which has brought such a happy order out of so gloomy a chaos" into which the nullifiers would return Americans. Everett was grateful not only for this praise but also for Madison's indispensable aid in assembling his all-important historical arguments.[56]

The making of this article underscores how thoroughly and systematically Everett thought about the nature and binding power of the Union. He buttressed his own careful ratiocination by collaborating with the highest recognized authorities on the subject. He continually refined and candidly stated his reliance on historical appeals to further magnify the impact of his Unionism. And it worked; this article told. Chief Justice John Marshall commended Everett for framing the true issue as between union and disunion. For rather different reasons, nullifier John C. Calhoun asked Everett to lend him a copy and inquired pointedly as to who authored it. Even brother-in-law Charles Francis Adams, who had an intense dislike of Everett, declared it "a Masterly Essay." Over two decades later, Thomas Hart Benton remembered Madison's letter to Everett published in the *NAR* as a linchpin in dismantling nullification's legitimacy.[57]

Everett also helped a statesman of the next generation, Daniel Webster, formulate and publicize his pronouncements on the perpetuity of the Union. Their friendship and partnership blossomed during Everett's time in Washington, despite portents of the rough patches Everett would endure in this relationship. In November 1823, Webster asked Everett for source references for a contemplated speech in Congress. Using Everett for his own purposes would become a theme in this partnership (as with many others in Webster's life). Everett's willingness to play second fiddle to Webster was on display in 1827, when Everett ended his close-to-the-vest campaign for Massachusetts's vacancy in the Senate upon learning of Webster's interest in the seat.[58] He revealed why this deference was his habit in 1832 when he confided to Cushing that he had experienced not only Webster's kindness but also "other times & occasions when I have thought I had great reason to complain of him. But I have never allowed this to make the least change in my conduct or language to or concerning him as a public man."[59] And as biographer Irving Bartlett has pointed out, Everett joined multitudes of other people in their extravagant attachment to Webster. At a time of dislocating material change and threats to the Union, Webster "represented for them the majesty and strength of the United States. He gave them a sense of safety." Everett phrased it this exact way as early as 1821. "When he is among us," Everett confided to a friend, "I feel as if we could not be run off with, by the dogs."[60]

The need for such a defender only increased during the perilous days of the nullification crisis. As a result so did Everett's collaboration with Webster, based on their shared sense that "the question of paramount importance in our affairs is likely to be, for some time to come, *the preservation of the Union, or its dissolution.*"[61] They combined forces most fruitfully in 1830, when Hayne brilliantly encapsulated Southern radicals' doctrines on the Union and attacks on New England during a tense debate surrounding federal lands. Webster's epic speeches in reply to Hayne, particularly their peroration in which he invoked "liberty and Union, one and inseparable, now and forever," became Unionist scripture in both the short and the long terms. Everett made his contribution to this iconic moment of Unionist triumph when he helped Webster edit the speeches for publication. At one crucial moment, he pointed out the unseemly similarity between Webster's reference to "the standard of Union" and the language John Milton had used to describe Satan's ensign. Webster wisely decided the phrase "the gorgeous ensign of the republic" would go over better in the published version. And that publication had enormous reach throughout the nation, so that historian Merrill Peterson has concluded that "no speech in the English language, perhaps no speech in modern times, had ever been as widely diffused and widely read as the Reply to Hayne."[62] This statement may partake of biographers' tendency to overstate their subjects' importance, but not by much. Webster, probably more than any single antebellum person, and his Second Reply to Hayne, more than any other text, had elevated Unionism to sacred status. And Everett's care in helping him craft the canonical published version, as well as Webster's responsiveness to his suggestions, spoke to the need to get things just right in propagating the Unionist gospel.

For Everett, securing partisan advantage was clearly subordinate to saving the Union. That was just as well for much of the nullification controversy, because both Jacksonians and National Republicans sought to ensure that their opponents would not profit politically from the alarms for union touched off by nullification. The editor of the president's official organ, the Washington *Globe*, speculated that warmed-over Federalists like Webster and Everett were encouraging the South to leave the Union so the North could have more weight within it. While this outlandish statement bespoke the lengths to which partisan hacks would go, Everett gave as good as he got in this phase of the struggle. He realized from growing experience that to make a "lofty appeal on the union" was to occupy "a broad & popular ground." But he regretted that that ground "has been almost monopolized by" Jackson. So the National Republican Party's 1832 election address charged that "the whole tone of the Administration is against the Union."[63]

But after Jackson's December 1832 proclamation that he would enforce the tariff by force if necessary, hard-core state rights men in his party started to desert him, and he considered allying with Northern Unionists of both parties. Everett for one was open to the president's overtures. The depth of the crisis had convinced him that "the South does not love the Union," so it would take "almost a miracle" to save it. In such a situation, he saw "no use" in scoring political points against Jackson while he stood against nullification. So in June 1833, when Jackson traveled to Boston for consciously bipartisan events, Everett invited Jackson "to make my house your home, for yourself & the gentlemen of your suite, while you are in the town." He was an active participant in the committee in charge of hosting Jackson. His duties included formally addressing the president at Bunker Hill on 26 June. He presented Jackson with relics from the Battles of Bunker Hill and New Orleans, a connection between Revolutionary and more recent history that was very favorable to Jackson as the hero of the latter battle. Everett ended his speech with an expression of "UNANIMOUS approbation of the firm, resolute, and patriotic stand which you assumed" against nullification "in order to preserve that happy union under one constitutional head,—for the establishment of which . . . this hill was drenched in blood." The exchange between Everett and Jackson gained wide and approving attention.[64]

There was no one better suited than Everett to take an active part in this high point of bipartisan Unionism, as one who had already repeatedly argued for that Union as the great object and fruit of the Revolution.

The nullification crisis, however, did subtly change Everett's thought regarding the Union. At its height in December 1832, he reflected to a friend that "if this Union is to be preserved, it can only be in virtue of a strength inherent in it, to put down disaffection." Were nullifiers to win their stare-down with the federal government, "the fairest opportunity of establishing the Sovereignty of the Law" and the supremacy of the Union, "which could ever be presented, will have been thrown away." He believed the nullifiers should be "put to the bar, with an indictment three yards long;—couched in the plain-spoken formalities of the Old Common Law against treason; and after a fair trial & conviction, have them pardoned."[65] This fell far short of what others proposed, but it did show that Everett imagined a coercive strength in the Union that he normally talked about as tied together by sentiment and history.

The idea of a fusion Unionist party reached its apex in the summer of 1833, after which the renewal of economic issues revitalized traditional partisanship. When party strife returned, Everett proved himself a dedicated and shrewd partisan for the cause now identified as that of the Whig Party. He hosted several strategy sessions for the Whigs in his Washington home and became Clay's chief Massachusetts correspondent when they were away from Washington. He played an integral role in efforts to build the Whig Party not only in Massachusetts but also throughout New England. He demonstrated a full understanding of the power of the mass media of his day to shaping both his and his party's career. Throughout his terms in Congress, he exercised vigilance to ensure that published versions of his speeches, toasts, and other effusions were correct, especially in party organs with a national reach. He understood the populist nature of Jacksonian-era politics well enough to never let the charge that he was a patrician go uncontested. In December 1831, Everett received two votes for Speaker of the House. And in December 1833, when the Twenty-Third Congress organized itself, Everett took third place in the voting for Speaker of the House. It was a distant third, to be sure—15 votes to winner Andrew Stevenson's 142—but all this undercuts the notion that Everett was a fish out of water in Washington politics.[66]

Such activity earned Everett the reputation of being a leader of the Northern branch of the nascent Whig Party. This led some observers to mistake him for an ardent Northern sectionalist. A Massachusetts voter, for one, mourned deeply over Everett's "defection" when he supported a compromise tariff. He could not see Everett for what he was, a Unionist alarmed as well as offended by nullification. For his part, an Ohio editor celebrated one of Everett's speeches for casting into the shade all the arguments against the tariff offered by "the statesmen of the *slave States*" and their very few Northern "*co-adjutors and apologists.*" Apparently, Everett no longer belonged in that latter category. Rather more predictably, anti-tariff Southern newspapers abused Everett, Webster, and the like for manifesting "mean selfishness" on behalf of their region. And in July 1828, a crowd in Columbia, South Carolina, burned the tariff bill together with effigies of Clay, Webster, Everett, and other perceived enemies of the state. Such attacks irritated Everett, going to the heart of his self-image as a national statesman.[67] On the other hand, when Everett spoke in favor of keeping a tariff on imported cotton as a generous gesture to the South, Representative Samuel Vinton of Ohio responded that he could "not consent to hold up the shield of protection to those who persisted in dealing out blows upon his constituents." The North should act in "self-defence" rather than rely on "the magnanimity of others."[68] Being upbraided as something of a doughface by Vinton and as a wild-eyed Northern radical by others likely convinced Everett that he had found the middle road on this issue.

———————

For all his dedication to the Whig cause and cumulative bitter experiences with Southern extremists, however, Everett remained devoted above all to the Union. As such he hated both the partisan and the sectional bitterness all too prevalent during this time in Washington. In his debut speech in 1826, he had declared that "party of all kinds, in its excess, is certainly the bane of our institutions. . . . The evil of geographical parties is, that they tend to sever the Union. The evil of domestic parties is, that they render the Union not worth having" by encouraging all the bitterness of "personal and private enmity." And he had long felt that "it is a matter of great grief that political differences sh'd be allowed to break in upon personal attachments." He was thus horrified when he visited the Senate chamber and witnessed "a furious altercation in the Senate between Mr. Benton & Mr. Clay. The personalities were the most violent I ever witnessed."[69] And he knew this was no isolated affray but rather a sign of the times.

Everett's response was not to despair but to work to maintain the warm personal relationships that would model how to cement the Union. After the Clay-Benton fracas, he boldly lectured Clay "not to let it go further." "For myself," he told Democrat and fellow scholar George Bancroft, "I must by force of natural constitution be a moderate partizan, as far as I am a party man at all." He publicly lauded Benjamin Franklin's "habit of expressing himself with diffidence; never using terms of positive affirmation, like *certainly*, and *undoubtedly*; but such as, *I conceive*, or *I apprehend*." This practice "would be worth considering by those engaged at the present day in religious and political controversy." Vilifying opponents "is too much the practice of many of our sects and parties." This was not just cant for Everett. In addition to serving as a unifier within National Republican and Whig ranks, even in the bitterest times of partisan strife he managed to maintain cordial relations with men of very different political principles, including Jackson, Calhoun, and Van Buren.[70]

Given the sectionalism that plagued national politics throughout his time in Washington, it is not surprising that Everett specifically sought to cultivate friendships across the Mason-Dixon Line. He carried on a friendly correspondence with Southern men of letters as well as with politicians. In late 1831 and early 1832, he followed news of Nat Turner's slave insurrection in Virginia, and the debate it touched off in Virginia's legislature about the future of slavery in the state, with great interest. The legislative debate seems likely to have convinced him that at least the Upper South men could be open, democratic, and reasonable on this question.[71] Everett's strong sense of the threats to the Union convinced him, like other nation builders, to work at Union-saving on several fronts simultaneously, both personally and politically.

The personal and the political combined nicely in April through June 1829, when Everett set out to explore the South and especially the West. This was a chance to see these hotbeds of American democracy and growth for himself, as well as to preach the Unionist gospel to friendly crowds there. After sixteen days of travel he arrived in New Orleans, where he stayed about two weeks. He sojourned in Natchez, Nashville, and Lexington for a few days each on his return trip. In his diary observations, slavery was an unremarkable part of the scenery and was certainly no obstacle to enjoying the sociability and adventure of this trip. And throughout, he mingled with kindred spirits in the Whiggish elite of Mississippi valley society. His itinerary thus set this up to be a more pleasant experience in the South than he would have had in, say, South Carolina or Georgia. And the consciously bipartisan, bisectional nature of the public dinners given in his honor gave him the perfect stage on which to preach the Union of fellow feeling. In a speech at Nashville, he relished his hosts' eagerness to promote "that mutual good will, which," he waxed bold enough to declare, "is more important for the perpetuity of the Union than all the forms of the constitution." At Lexington, Everett summed up one key purpose for the whole trip when he declared that "in a popular government, where every thing is ultimately referred to the will of the citizens, mutual good will between them is all-important." Therefore, in an era of increasing polarization, "to remove these prejudices, to establish kind feelings, to promote good will between the different members of the political family, appears to me, without exception, the most important object at which a patriotic citizen, in any portion of the country, can aim."[72] While countenancing the idea of coercion during the nullification crisis, Everett's clear hope and preference was for this voluntary affective Union.

Many observers beyond Everett himself understood the political aspect to all this sociability. The public dinners given for Everett featured toasts that spoke eloquently (as toasts went) to the union of feeling that Everett's trip was meant to cultivate. The toasts in Lexington included "*the Union of these States*—Monarchs form alliances—Republics form leagues—but here, behold a band of brothers." In his report of Everett's visit, a Nashville editor adopted the very terms Everett used to describe his journey. "The reciprocal intercourse and mutual hospitality of distinguished men, in the different sections of this great Republic," he enthused, "may even be regarded as essential to the perpetuity and perfection of our National Union." Influential Baltimore editor Hezekiah Niles agreed that Everett was showing how mingling between the respectable people of all sections "would tend to do away many bitter prejudices."[73]

This journey showed Everett just how well labor in the vineyard of Unionism paid. Years later when composing his memoir, he recounted his trip in 1829 to the South and West as "a very agreeable journey" on which he "was treated with great kindness, wherever I went." And newspaper notices of the public events during his sojourn were both overwhelmingly positive and widely circulated. Something about the eminent European traveler and Eastern man of letters showing an interest in these "remote" sections of the Union seemed to have captured many editors' imaginations. His Unionist speeches and the accompanying toasts also inspired. His speech in Lexington, waxed the editors of the *National Intelligencer*, soared above partisanship and sectionalism "into the purer element of a disinterested patriotism. . . . If Mr. EVERETT had never done any thing else to entitle him to the respect of his countrymen, the benign tendency and irresistible influence of these addresses of his would entitle him to the gratitude of the nation, and to the admiration and respect of all sincere lovers of their country." A correspondent from Alabama wrote Everett to say that he had long thought "that too few visits of this kind were paid us by our northern friends." Unless Southerners saw more of the likes of Everett outside of the gladiatorial combat of Washington, they would remain "wholly ignorant of your true *national* character."[74] Looking back, it is easy to see these encomiums on his Unionist activities and speeches as pointing out the road to Edward Everett's ultimate influence.

But not long after this Southern tour, one of his Southern friendships, combined with perceived financial necessity, almost took Everett out of the center range of the slavery spectrum and into the ranks of the slaveholders. Everett's relationship with his father-in-law, Peter C. Brooks, both contributed to this scheme and helped avert it. Marrying Brooks's daughter Charlotte ensured that Everett would have money behind him, but his pride and notions of manhood dictated that he find a way to earn his own living. Unfortunately for Everett as for so many of his colleagues, the $8 per diem paid to congressmen was insufficient for his needs. His financial shortages meant, among other things, that he could not afford to bring his family with him to Washington for most congressional sessions. So he pursued or contemplated a variety of moneymaking projects during his time in office. He and his brother Alexander looked into purchasing the *NAR*, but instead Edward guest-edited the journal from late 1827 through early 1829, earning $250 per issue. Money was a consistent enough concern that in 1833 he mournfully sold his land in his hometown of Dorchester, and money matters contributed to a rift between him and Alexander in the early 1830s.[75] Such material circumstances surely seemed to Everett a humiliating contrast to his political eminence.

In 1832, Everett thought he might be able to leverage another relationship to salvage the situation, this one with Louisiana congressman Josiah Stoddard Johnston. Everett and Johnston had long enjoyed a close friendship. Ten years Everett's senior, Johnston was born in Connecticut and moved to Louisiana in 1805 to begin his prosperous career in law, politics, and sugar planting. A conciliator amid contentiousness as well as an ardent proponent of Clay's American System, he was a natural Everett ally temperamentally and politically. They were messmates while in Washington, when their wives were in Washington in 1829 the two couples sought out lodgings near each other, and Everett stayed with the Johnstons in their Philadelphia residence on the way to and from sessions of Congress. They carried on an extensive political and personal correspondence when they were apart. The Everetts looked after Johnston's teenage son William when he came to Massachusetts to study in the late 1820s. When Josiah was killed in a steamboat explosion in 1833, Everett mourned deeply. He took some solace from the fact that William had survived that accident, but within a few short years William died young. When the Everetts had a son in 1839, they named him William after their recently deceased young friend.[76]

Johnston accompanied him on almost all of his private visits and public occasions during his time in Louisiana in 1829. During that visit Everett also toured at least one sugar plantation, looking at it with the eye of a potential investor (and nationalist interested in this key industry) more than of a moralist, recording precisely its annual income and expenses. In the midst of financial travail in late 1832, Everett cast his mind back on what he had learned and entered discussions with Johnston about purchasing a sugar plantation in Louisiana, possibly in Johnston's name to keep it quiet. So attractive was this idea—and so much was it strictly a matter of profit and loss—that Everett seems to have preferred it even to a revived scheme with Alexander to purchase the good old *NAR*. On 9 December, he wrote to Brooks in the strictest confidence to ask his advice.[77]

Brooks's reply followed the tone of Everett's inquiry in that neither dwelled on the morality of slaveholding except as it related to Northern public opinion. "Nothing could have surprised me more" than to learn of this plan, Brooks began. And "nothing would be more mortifying to me, my son, than to be told that you are the owner of a plantation and slaves." For the Southerner Johnston to own slaves "does not affect his good name in the least," but for Everett, "as a public man, in the north, I think it would ruin you." He doubted doing this transaction "in the name of Mr. Johnston" would help, for "it would be known and flourished oft in our papers in less than a month. Nothing of this kind could be kept secret a moment," whether long- or short-term. It was also far from certain that Everett serving as an absentee master would prove profitable. Likewise, at the height of the nullification crisis, "every thing in the South seems to be thrown into uncertainty," which worried the prudent businessman Brooks.[78] This stern advice killed the arrangement with Johnston. "As I expected," Everett reported to Johnston, Brooks "disapproves it altogether, . . . and on grounds which are pretty strong." Everett had enormous regard for the man to whom he referred in his diary as "my much honored & beloved Father-in-Law." And he was manifestly convinced by Brooks's political calculus.[79]

His financial dependence on Brooks remained unchanged as a result. In April 1833, Brooks promised to pay a particular bill for Everett but admonished him for having let himself be bound to the obligation in question. As late as 1837, while Everett was governor, Brooks purchased a house for him and Charlotte. From the 1820s through the 1840s, Brooks gave the Everetts an ever-increasing quarterly sum and even after that had to bail them out of pressing financial difficulties. Along with the necessary funds, Brooks sent a chiding letter about the pecuniary prudence to which he had always exhorted his "children."[80] This was precisely the sort of paternalism Everett had sought to escape with the Johnston and other star-crossed schemes for financial independence. But Brooks had undoubtedly saved the Massachusetts base for his career in politics.

———

From that base during his time in Congress, Everett appealed, albeit in a New England accent, to his fellow citizens throughout the country to preserve the precious Union by communing with their common Revolutionary past. He did this with deeds as well as with words. He continued his work with the Bunker Hill Monument Association throughout his congressional terms. He also joined the Washington Monument Association, which worked to bring a suitable statue of George Washington to Boston, and one of his first acts in Congress was to offer a motion inquiring into a bill allowing this association to bring that sculpture into Boston free of import duties. Also early in his first term, he appealed for better funding for Revolutionary War veterans' pensions. Later he was active in the House's efforts to purchase a portrait of Washington for its hall and a statue of Washington for the rotunda. He never missed a celebration of Washington's birthday, happily dispensed advice to all who approached him with projects commemorating Washington, and listened raptly to those who shared with him any and all fun facts relative to the hero. Beginning in 1830, Everett became a founding and active member of the group of Boston-area gentlemen proposing to purchase property in Cambridge and make it a garden cemetery. Modeled after London's pioneering and fashionable Highgate Cemetery, this became Mount Auburn Cemetery, itself fashionable and a pioneer in the American movement for garden cemeteries. In an 1832 address to the public, Everett suggested that "its summit may be consecrated to Washington, by a cenotaph inscribed with his name. Public sentiment will often delight in these tributes of respect," Everett assured the public. The trustees did not move to create the current observatory tower at the summit of Mount Auburn or dedicate it to Washington until the 1850s, but Everett had planted the seed.[81]

As always with Everett, he also thought out his oratory on this subject very carefully. American nationalism, mingled in complex ways with slavery, race, and Indian Removal, was a key theme in the selections attributed to Everett in Caleb Bingham's 1832 edition of his enormously influential textbook *The Columbian Orator*. This would have associated Everett's name with these themes in the minds of a very broad audience of schoolchildren across the nation.[82] He also prepared several speeches not only for Congress but also for occasions that naturally lent themselves to historical commemoration. These occasions included not only invitations to address the Fourth of July and other anniversary festivals but also the opportunity to eulogize Thomas Jefferson and John Adams together in 1826 and Lafayette in 1834. In all these venues and more, he was able to articulate his vision of how connecting Americans to their common Revolutionary heritage would bind them emotionally to the Union.

Everett was never shy about proclaiming the instrumental purposes of such commemoration. It helped the sincerity of these appeals that he felt these sentiments himself; in 1832, for instance, when a veteran of Bunker Hill died, he thought it worthy of two diary entries. But he repeatedly and openly declared commemoration to be a means to the larger end of emotional nationalism. In the *NAR*, he proclaimed that the Fourth of July and other memorial occasions were opportunities to promote "common feelings to citizens of a common, but immensely extensive country." Given the stakes involved, "everything, that tends to promote such a sympathy, everything that carries us back to objects of common pride, . . . is worth another Louisiana purchase to the country." "The Union," he admitted, would perhaps always be a "metaphysical and theoretical thing" compared to state and local loyalties, so statesmen were needed who could bolster that theory with sentiment. In the nullification-ridden year of 1832, when some members of the House rather surprisingly suggested that the nation could rally around Adams, Everett advocated a more populist, emotional vision for what would hold the nation together. "I rely for the preservation of the Union," he declared, "on the intelligence and the patriotism of the people at large, who enjoy its blessings." At a time when South Carolinians were openly calculating the economic value alone of the Union, the religiously charged word "blessings" was not an accidental choice.[83]

Nothing aroused Americans' gratitude for the blessings of the sacred Union, Everett believed, like the memory of George Washington. In a February 1832 congressional debate about removing Washington's remains to the nation's capital, speaker after speaker vied to be most lavish in their praise of Washington, even as they contested the political usages of his memory. But none could outdo Everett in such a debate. He gushed that if the motion carried, "such a procession would be formed, such a feeling would be excited, such an effect would be produced on the minds of all, old and young, who might witness the solemnity, as was unparralelled [*sic*] in the whole range of history. The moral emotions which would spring from such a spectacle, would operate for good upon the human mind." And it would not do to remove his remains to Richmond, either, as some Virginians proposed in their alarm at losing this relic. The whole point of this exercise would be to underscore that "the sacred remains are . . . a treasure of which every part of this blood-cemented Union has a right to claim its share."[84]

In an 1833 address at Faneuil Hall, Everett merged many of these lines of argument to urge continued exertions to erect a Bunker Hill monument. He extolled the perpetuation of "generous and patriotic sentiments, sentiments which prepare us to serve our country, to live for our country, to die for our country." To those who argued that history books would be sufficient, he replied that "history alone, without sensible monuments," would be insufficient. For "there is an original element in our natures, — a connection between the senses, the mind, and the heart, — implanted by the Creator for pure and noble purposes, which cannot be reasoned away." Thus one might not be moved properly by reading history, but "you cannot set your foot upon the spot where some great and memorable exploit was achieved, especially by those with whom you claim kindred, but your heart swells within you . . . and you are ready to put off the shoes from off your feet, for the place whereon you stand is holy ground." Because of his faith in the power of such feelings, Everett was sure that patriots commemorating their Revolutionary heritage could conquer sectional and partisan divisions. In fact, he asserted that "it is scarcely possible for men who have just united in an act of patriotic commemoration . . . to go away and engage with unmitigated rancor in the work of party defamation."[85]

Many of the occasions on which Congressman Everett offered orations commemorated specifically Massachusetts anniversaries. This and the politics of the era led him at times into New England-centric reflections potentially in tension with this capacious Unionism. In his early addresses, Everett's vision commonly focused on New England's history as the part of American history worth celebrating, it being "the spot where the first successful foundations of the great American republic were laid." In an address to the Massachusetts Historical Society in 1833, Everett baldly stated that an "interest in the lives, characters, and exploits of our ancestors forms no small part of the sentiment of patriotism. It is natural, generous, and unselfish. It is not only pardonable, but it is our duty to indulge it." Keenly aware that patriotism must be sentimental, Everett was never one to apologize for local attachment. Provided it was of the appropriate rather than the exclusive kind, it could and should underwrite rather than threaten national patriotism. Of course, what made one American's local attachments divisive and another's appropriate was very much in the eye of the beholder.[86] But taken all in all, Everett's reflections on an American nationalism resting on selective historical commemoration were systematic and sophisticated.

Part of why he devoted his considerable intellect and prodigious energies to the problem of American nationalism was that he thought the stakes involved were enormously high. Across his entire congressional career, his Unionist vision extended to the United States' example to the whole world. As he noted on 4 July 1826, as Latin American states gained their independence, "we learn the importance of the post which Providence has assigned us in the world." Likewise in 1835, he pronounced that "if this great experiment of rational liberty should here be permitted to fail, I know not where or when among the sons of Adam it will ever be resumed." Only by demonstrating that men could govern themselves in amicable union could Americans fulfill "our destiny in the world." Fortunately, the Revolutionary fathers had set the example for their patriotic sons to follow. In his 1826 eulogy on Adams and Jefferson, he drew inspiration from their rapprochement late in life after years of estrangement. "Shall we not rejoice," he effervesced, "that we are taught, in the lives of Adams and Jefferson, that the most imbittered contentions which as yet have divided us furnish no ground for lasting disunion?"[87]

In the glare of his triumphalist nationalism, however, American slavery had a way of fading into Everett's blind spot. Speaking in Concord, Massachusetts, on the fiftieth anniversary of the great Revolutionary battle there, the classical scholar Everett adjudged the American narrative more inspiring than ancient history. For while the exploits of Greek soldiers were admirable, "we cannot forget that the tenth part of the number were slaves, unchained from the work-shops and doorposts of their masters, to go and fight the battles of freedom." In the American case, the blood of the fathers "calls to us from the soil which we tread . . . in the thrilling words of one of the first victims in the cause, 'My sons, scorn to be slaves.'" Thus, "should the foot of a tyrant, or of a slave, approach these venerated spots, the noble hearts that bled at Lexington and Concord . . . would beat beneath the sod with indignation." It was a breathtaking example of reading slaves out of the history of the United States, which Everett presented as the history of Lexington and Concord writ large. As Everett observed the material and civilizational progress of the United States from his New England perch, the country did not look half-slave and half-free. Indeed, he saw the South's cultivation of the cotton processed in New England's textile mills not as a moral stain but as further evidence of the progressive state of the new nation's political economy. He would carry this reluctance to recognize the American experiment as defective from these early speeches all the way through to his address at Gettysburg.[88]

As consciously political as his Unionist historical commemoration was, Congressman Everett received valued praise and very little censure for his activities in this sphere. Luminaries like Marshall and Adams praised him for elevating both the new nation and its standard of oratory, as did prominent men of letters and even political opponents. His eulogies to departed Revolutionary heroes were particular triumphs. Everett's twin eulogy of Adams and Jefferson, for instance, almost instantly popularized the phrase "Jefferson survives" as Adams's canonical last words. A Boston critic offered grudging praise for that speech, adding that "if all his speeches had been equal to this eulogy, we should never have indulged in any sarcasms against his pretensions." His local political enemies inadvertently conceded the power of his appeals when they accused him of playing politics with Revolutionary memory in election years.[89] It is not easy to account for this broad assent to Everett's nation-building efforts. But as excellent recent scholarship has shown us, the vitriol of the politics of race and slavery in the late 1820s and early 1830s alarmed many observers. In this era of threatened and actual racial violence in both North and South, nullification, Indian Removal, and rising militant abolitionism, sectional moderates spoke to many Americans' yearnings for peace. And no one spoke more clearly to that desire than Everett.[90]

It was an uncomfortable fact for the conciliatory Everett that his first decade in political life would be spent in such an atmosphere. But the dislocations and unpredictability of this era also seem to account both for why Everett's stances on slavery and sectionalism oscillated so wildly and for why he could get away with that. He drew the ire of antislavery men and women for his knapsack speech and of proslavery men and women for his visible opposition to Indian Removal and nullification. But he also earned enough votes to be reelected four times and enough political credibility to rise to second-tier leadership in both the National Republican and Whig Parties. In private, he could both explore an abortive scheme to purchase a Louisiana plantation and approach Massachusetts abolitionists for help placing two young Louisiana boys with "a slight admixture of African blood" in schools where they might escape the prejudices prevailing against "our unfortunate brethren" of color.[91]

Part of how he could do and say all these contradictory things was that the National Republican and Whig Parties accommodated a wide variety of points of view, especially when they were in opposition rather than in power. They were in many ways the conservative parties, and Everett fit that bill. But within the ranks of these parties and the reformist culture they embodied, he associated on persistently friendly terms with antislavery heroes like Martineau and Adams. In fact, during Everett's time in Congress he and Adams had exactly the same record on the issue that would later make Adams an antislavery icon: the right of abolitionists to petition Congress. In 1835 when Southerners and their allies sought to permanently table such petitions so as never to receive them again, neither Adams nor Everett led the Northern response, but both voted against the innovation. Historians have long argued that representing a Massachusetts district rather than the whole Union as president freed Adams to pursue an antislavery political career. Everett of course represented just his district the whole time. But his most notorious flirtation with proslavery conservatism came in 1826, in large part to defend the president against charges of abolitionism that could damage his desire to be reelected as president of the entire Union. It is notable and perhaps not coincidental that Everett took a much more Northern-friendly line later in his congressional career, when his party was in opposition to President Jackson.[92]

If Everett knew that he had been charged with meandering on slavery, he would probably argue that his stances were actually a function of his consistent support of the Union. He could rightly claim that whether in his knapsack speech or in utterances relative to Removal or nullification, he had set out to stand up not for or against slavery but for the Constitution and Union. In a remarkable letter in 1830, he tied his stance on Removal to the logic of his knapsack speech when he asked what prevented the nightmare of mass emancipation. "The faith of the compact with the Southern States" in the North, which is what he meant to vindicate in his knapsack speech, was the answer. Southern proponents of Removal were thus playing with fire with their loose attitude toward sacred compacts — in their case the United States' treaties with the relevant Indian tribes.[93] With Removal, the Georgians and Jacksonians had violated true conservatism and would pay a price that these Northern conservatives did not want them and the Union to pay. In 1826, Union and the antislavery manifestation of Everett's commitment to reform were competing priorities; in opposing Removal and nullification, they became complementary. For similar reasons, much of his season as governor of Massachusetts would echo the later rather than the initial years of Everett's congressional terms.

4

The Governor and the Abolitionists

Massachusetts voters elected Edward Everett as their governor in 1835 and re-elected him every year until he left office in 1840 after a narrow defeat. Had he had his way Everett would have focused entirely on his Whig improvement agenda, but one of the defining themes of Everett's gubernatorial years was his complex and very public interaction with politically assertive abolitionists. After a spectacularly negative early confrontation, Everett and the abolitionists developed friendly relations that Everett saw as both politically necessary and consistent with his commitment to reform. Everett would never be one of them. But he veered in sometimes surprisingly antislavery directions, both in private and in public, during the years in which his political context was a state whose public opinion was also becoming friendlier to abolitionism. These shifts in his stance on slavery made his gubernatorial years a pivotal era in his career.

———

Everett found neither leaving Congress nor running for the governorship to be easy decisions. Approached as early as 1833 by representatives of the nascent Antimasonic Party seeking to run him for governor, he firmly declined. Weary of his labors in the House, he was contemplating leaving public life altogether, and in August 1834 he declared that he would not stand for reelection that next fall. Then in December 1834, Daniel Webster approached him with a scheme to have Governor John Davis run for Massachusetts's vacant U.S. Senate seat and Everett run to replace him as governor. This changed Everett's thinking. He relished the popular approval that he had achieved in his congressional district and thus felt a continued pull from public life, but serving close to home as governor would be more congenial than the onerous service in Washington. Webster's proposal, unlike the Antimasons' request, also meant he would not need to run against his partisan brother-in-arms Davis.[1] Everett remained ambivalent about a career in politics even after deciding to run for the governorship. "I think I can say with truth" that "I do not *much* care" about the outcome, he told one correspondent, given that he had "pursuits, & taste, & duties, which will furnish me employment, & I trust happiness, in private life." He candidly admitted, however, that "having been nominated, I should like to be spared the mortification of a defeat."[2]

Everett's anxiety about the possibility of defeat stemmed from the complex, unpredictable stew of issues and loyalties that consumed Bay State politics in the mid-1830s. As the state's economy industrialized, conflicts between labor and capital, native and immigrant, protectionist and free trader mingled with the politics of gender and race to destabilize the two-party system at its very inception. In this setting, both Democrats and Whigs had to appeal to single-issue groups as potential swing votes in close elections. The disruptive effect of such splinter groups was all the greater in gubernatorial elections, for in 1831 Massachusetts amended its constitution to require successful candidates for governor to secure an outright majority of votes cast.[3]

Candidate Everett certainly encountered all the complications of such a volatile climate in his first statewide campaign. For instance, he found it necessary to repeatedly defend against accusations that he was an elitist foe to the common man. "If I am such a dangerous aristocrat as is alleged," he wrote testily to a newspaper editor, "it is somewhat remarkable that I should have been five times elected to Congress, by very great majorities," in a district that had been heavily Jeffersonian.[4] His opponents also made liberal use of his 1826 knapsack speech to tar him as an advocate of slavery, and that image stuck in the minds of many voters. In a letter to another editor, Everett declared that the "insinuation . . . that I am 'in favor of perpetuating Slavery,' is as groundless, as it is absurd." He emphasized that that speech was addressed only to whether "the People of the North would look with favor on a servile war," leaving aside his gratuitous passages on slavery itself. He added the disclaimer that "no man more than myself, deplores the existence of slavery, or would more cheerfully contribute to its extinction, in any mode suggested by the dictates of Humanity & Religion, & not inconsistent with the Constitution & the Law of the Land." As evidence of this sentiment, he sent the editor a copy of his speech to the American Colonization Society.[5]

But the politics of class and slavery were sideshows in this election compared to Everett's successful tightrope walk between the Whig and Antimasonic Parties. Born in western New York in the mid-1820s, the Antimasonic movement had convinced multitudes, especially in New England, that members of the Masonic fraternity held themselves above the law and threatened the very basis of republican government and Christianity. By the early 1830s this grassroots movement had mobilized enough new voters that it demanded the attention of the two major parties. While in Massachusetts, Antimasonry constituted a rebellion against the Whig ascendancy, that did not necessarily lead to a mass exodus to the Democrats. It had a populist style but also comprised mostly the middle-class religious traditionalists who were the Whigs' natural constituency, and its emphasis on law was a potentially good fit with the Whig worldview. Whig leaders thus divided over whether to seek to put down or coopt the Antimasonic Party.[6]

Those who favored coalition found their man in Everett. In 1833 John Quincy Adams had failed to attract voters from both parties for a gubernatorial run. But Everett, alongside his brother Alexander and Webster, persisted in orchestrating this delicate dance in Massachusetts and surrounding states. Everett publicly opposed Masonry in very Whig terms as a violation of the supreme loyalty citizens should give to their country and its laws. Given the usual close margin in statewide elections, he lectured Whig leaders, it was "extremely indiscreet" of them "to urge the irreconcilable hostility of National Republicanism & Antimasonry." Such preaching won him the suspicion of many Whigs, but he was sure this would add far more voters to the Whig column than it would alienate. His candidacy put that to the test, as in March 1835 he became the first Massachusetts gubernatorial candidate to accept the nominations of both parties. His political advisers admonished him that he would need all his talent for conciliation to appeal to enough in both parties to win the election. The election results proved both that Everett was right about coalition and that he was a better politician than most gave (or give) him credit for. He secured 37,555 votes, versus 25,227 for his nearest challenger, Democrat Marcus Morton.[7]

It proved a short-lived triumph for the Antimasons. Reading the election returns convinced Everett that the Antimasons had proven more loyal to him than had the Whigs in Boston. Everett's brother-in-law Charles Francis Adams read the election returns similarly, sure that "the Antimasons will now be daily coming in" to the corridors of state power. Such was the Antimasonic euphoria over the election that a leading party paper in Pennsylvania nominated Everett for the presidency. But Everett proved a disappointment to the Antimasons, governing from a position of indifference to Antimasonic priorities. Everett had deserted the Antimasonic part of his base because he clearly judged, as has a historian of Antimasonry, that by 1836 Antimasonry was spent as an independent force. With national issues surrounding banking rising to preeminence over local issues, the Antimasons largely scattered into the two major parties. Most Antimasons, however, campaigned bitterly against Everett in 1836.[8]

The return of the rivalry between the two national parties to center stage suited Everett just fine, for he was in his heart of hearts the quintessential Whig. Everett remained the consummate party insider. He exerted his influence within the party mostly in the service of Webster, especially as a key manager of Webster's 1836 presidential campaign. On one occasion he declared that no matter Webster's presidential prospects, "I had rather sink with him than rise without him."[9]

Everett also committed his governorship to an ambitious agenda of Whiggish reform. His basic humanity made him sensitive to "what has been done & suffered in the world," and he devoted his energy and political capital to alleviating it. He disagreed with an article by Harriet Martineau warning that a worldwide political revolution was imminent because he believed that "a political revolution is insufficient." "A new dispensation of religion is needed," he declared, "& is not an unlikely event." As this suggests, Everett thought globally about benevolent reform, such as when he carefully followed British debates over the Poor Law system or debated a pacifist visitor over the merits of a congress of nations to achieve world peace.[10] But his position gave him power to act locally. Some reforms he felt powerless to achieve: he confessed to having "scruples on the subject of capital punishment," for instance, but his Whig notions of his role as governor taught him that "so long as the law enjoins it, it is my duty to enforce the law." But he could use proclamations as a bully pulpit, such as one for a day of public fasting in which he suggested that citizens pray that God "would give success to all efforts for the relief of suffering, the reformation of vice, and the diffusion of knowledge, and especially to those great enterprizes of Christian philanthropy, which form the chief glory of the age in which we live." And he of course had his annual address to the legislature and used this forum to recommend such policies as humane prison reform. Championing this cause attracted attention to him beyond Massachusetts. As governor he also had direct oversight over state-sponsored hospitals and asylums for the blind and insane, and he took his visitations to these seriously and evinced a real compassion for their inmates.[11]

Governor Everett also distinguished himself by his deep commitment to the Whig ideal of improvement, both of the physical and human infrastructure of his state. He saw internal improvements like roads, canals, and railroads as the essence of advancing civilization. Moreover, innovations in transportation were among the technological wonders of the age that had fascinated him since he was a child. "Never did I sign my name with greater alacrity in my life," he affirmed, than when signing a bill investing state funds in the Western Railroad. So committed was he to internal improvements that he addressed a celebration of the Warren Bridge in Charlestown becoming a free rather than a toll bridge, even though that offended family members like father-in-law Brooks who opposed the change. He also passionately championed education to help all citizens soberly meet the responsibilities of citizenship in a republic.[12]

These themes dominated all his messages to the legislature. In his inaugural message, he claimed the legacy of the Founders when he encouraged legislators "to imitate our forefathers, in the great trait of their characters, — the courage of reform." The reforms he recommended were rationalizing the state's legal code, militia, and banking regulations; striking down "monopoly in every form" and "all secret association"; humanizing the state's penal statutes and prisons; and above all funding internal improvements and education ("the solid basis of true equality"). In his second message to the legislature in January 1837, with the state treasury flush with funds in part due to an unexpected windfall from the federal government, he made these twin preferences crystal clear. His top priority for these funds was helping to pay for the Western Railroad, the completion of which "appears to me of paramount importance to the prosperity of this Commonwealth." His second priority was furthering "the intellectual improvement of the People" by expanding the public school system. "I can imagine no worthier use" of the federal funds than this, for "good schools are a treasure, a thousand fold more precious, than all the gold and silver of Mexico and Peru."[13] Then the Panic of 1837 forced him to pare back this lofty rhetoric and policy program, making retrenchment the order of the day. Only the less expensive reform causes such as hospitals and asylums maintained their original momentum for the second half of Everett's time as governor. Nevertheless, Everett was able to achieve education reforms that had a far-reaching impact in Massachusetts and confirmed his status as something of a national sage on the subject.[14]

———

Serving as one state's governor shrunk neither Everett's nationalist vision nor his reputation as a preeminent nationalist orator and historical commemorator. Even as the Whig Party purposely ran different candidates for president in different sections in 1836, Everett hoped Webster's campaign would transcend that parochial orientation. When a young Edgar Allan Poe solicited Everett's support for the fledgling *Southern Literary Messenger*, Everett responded with support for this as for other Southern literary endeavors, not only to further the cause of letters in the South but also to strengthen the intersectional ties of union. He declared hostility to not only sectional threats to the nation but also captious foreign critics.[15]

As before, during his gubernatorial years Everett found perfectly adequate vents for his nationalism in both commemorative orations and historical writing. In an era in which the public memory of the Revolution in particular was hotly contested in Massachusetts politics, public celebrations of historical events were undeniably important to his and his party's political prospects.[16] Yet Everett managed to persuade himself that historical commemorations were nonpartisan events and thus appropriate to address whether as candidate or incumbent. Many celebrated the founding of various Massachusetts towns, which gave him the opportunity to laud the Puritan Fathers as the embodiment of the true spirit of liberty and equality. At Barnstable's bicentennial, Everett remarked that "I regard all these historical celebrations as highly interesting and important," for thoughtful commemoration would help Americans understand that theirs had been "a chosen land" ever since the Pilgrims initiated and defended "the first written constitution of popular government." It was up to the present generation, he remarked on another occasion, to preserve the balance of liberty and order enshrined in America's founding. "To no people since the world began," he exhorted, "was such an amount of blessings and privileges ever given in trust." Even in a local Massachusetts setting, Everett remained a preeminent expounder of the transnational stakes involved with preserving the nation intact.[17]

Commemorating the American Revolution, in particular, allowed him to slip the bonds of any Massachusetts-centric version of his nationalism and dwell upon his favorite character, George Washington. At Boston's 4 July fete at Faneuil Hall in 1838, Everett confessed himself "desirous, on the highest public grounds, to perpetuate the tradition of his personal influence." Washington comprised "the *best portion* of our political inheritance," Everett maintained, because "while man remains as he is, example is the great teacher. It is in vain for books to proclaim that ambition ought to be sacrificed to patriotism" when contemporary events seemed to belie such pieties. "But when a character like Washington arises, truth is vindicated, and patriotism is personified."[18] Everett always had time to continue gathering hagiographical details about Washington and the other Founding Fathers, no matter the press of public business while governor. He found this work instructive personally, consciously taking Washington—"the perfection of the Prudent man"—as his model for a chief executive. But he never tried to hide the "public grounds" he knew would be served if other Americans followed the Founders' example. So, whether in private conversation or correspondence with fellow men of letters, Everett did his part as curator of the national archive. In 1835, for instance, he approached James Madison with an offer to help him publish his records of the Constitutional Convention and other documents that would shed light on the political and constitutional history of the country. Engaged to write a magazine essay on Washington, Everett spent months gathering materials that would establish Providence's role in raising up Washington as an American icon. In the process, one of Washington's relatives sent him a play dramatizing a famous "Indian Prophecy" from the 1750s that Washington would rise to greatness, and Everett contacted a Boston playhouse owner in hopes he would stage the production.[19]

Such efforts kept Everett's fame rising before a public both within and well beyond the state he served. Early in his terms as governor, Everett had his first volume of patriotic orations published. The glowing reviews of this collection came out during his first reelection campaign, adding force to the perks of incumbency that included invitations to speak at public celebrations. John Quincy Adams declared the speeches "among the best ever delivered in this country." His eloquence, Adams told his diary, had raised both the standard of oratory in America and Everett's own political career. More publicly, Everett's published orations gained him acclaim from all the leading literary magazines of the country. Newspapers in all quarters of the nation lauded Everett as one who never failed to offer "apt, eloquent, and chaste" remarks at the high occasions that called for nationalist oratory.[20]

Everett understood that his reputation as a statesman and man of letters was key to his public image and electoral successes. So he recorded in his diary instances of public and private praise for his oratory and then contested in the public prints critiques of his style and manner. When Martineau, who continued in Everett's friendly company for much of the summer and fall of 1835, criticized his oratory in her widely circulated travel account, he felt betrayed on both personal and public grounds. Martineau singled out Everett's speech at Bloody Brook celebrating New Englanders' triumph in King Philip's War as an example of the "vain-glorious . . . patriotic boasting," done "for electioneering objects," that was all too common in American oratory. This imputation of impurity to what he believed was above politics grated on Everett, and he could only ascribe it to "the extreme *maledicence* of Miss Martineau." His repeated reelection and growing national reputation certainly salved that wound. And he might have taken consolation in another passage in Martineau's volume that bore unwitting testimony to the cultural work the likes of Everett had been accomplishing. To many Americans she met, she recorded, "the Union has long been more than a matter of high utility. It has been idealised into an object of love and veneration."[21]

Deeply committed to ideals including law and order, nationalism, and reform and improvement, Everett as governor would have preferred to pursue all of these equally at all times. But as with so many other times in his public career, the insistent agitation of the issue of slavery forced him to choose which of these loyalties he would emphasize at any given time. In his gubernatorial years his interactions with his state's dedicated and increasingly influential abolitionists pushed him in a winding path that trended in an antislavery direction. While in those years he gave priority to order and union, by 1837 electoral pressures and his dedication to reform led him to accentuate the antislavery element in his worldview.

The months between Everett's departure from Congress in the spring of 1835 and his inauguration in January 1836 roiled with the most stunning antiabolitionist violence in his home state's history. Radical abolitionists headquartered in Boston, led by William Lloyd Garrison, had spent the 1830s provoking ire in both the South and the North with their assaults on slavery and the ACS. In 1835 they flooded Congress with petitions for emancipation in the District of Columbia and inundated Southern post offices with abolitionist tracts. The mid-1830s also witnessed a more general upsurge of riotous violence throughout the country. Anti-abolitionist furor thus found a natural outlet not only in public indignation meetings but also in mobbings of abolitionists in Northern cities and towns. Citizens of Massachusetts fell in many places along a broad spectrum of opinion on abolitionism, but in the mid-1830s most Bay Staters seem to have blamed the abolitionists for this disturbing flare-up of violence. In the middle of 1835, Garrisonians threw a spark into this combustible atmosphere by promoting the public speaking tour of British abolitionist George Thompson. In August leading anti-abolitionists fulminated against Garrison, Thompson, and others at a public meeting in Faneuil Hall. Most disturbing to opponents of slavery and lovers of tranquillity alike, in October a menacing throng roamed the streets of Boston seeking to lay violent hands on Thompson. They settled for Garrison, leading him through the city with a rope around his neck before some mobbers took pity on him and delivered him to jail for his protection. Thus opened what abolitionists forever dubbed "the Reign of Terror" for their movement in the North.[22]

One prominent Bostonian who found himself outraged by such doings in his city was the Unitarian preacher and reform maven William Ellery Channing. Previously merely a private enemy of slavery, he found his antislavery fervor stoked by the mob. The result was his pamphlet *Slavery*, which combined an uncompromising moral stance against slavery with a reluctance to force emancipation on the South from outside. But while abolitionists had "done wrong" in speaking to slaveholders in a "fierce, bitter, and abusive" manner and speaking directly to the slaves themselves, "there is a worse evil than Abolitionism, and that is the suppression of it by lawless force." The government rather than mobs should be the one to take effective action to suppress any sedition abolitionists might commit by plotting slave insurrections.[23] These arguments bore many similarities to a less-publicized pamphlet published in Boston the year previous. But Channing's almost incalculable moral authority and aura of respectability meant that men and women who would never have looked at Garrison's flagship paper the *Liberator* would read this pamphlet.[24]

Channing's production also provoked a fierce pamphlet skirmish in 1835–36. One of Channing's parishioners, James Trecothick Austin, led those disgruntled by their pastor's stance. Austin had served as Massachusetts's attorney general since 1832, a post he would hold until 1843. He wrote a pamphlet response accusing Channing of stirring up slave insurrection by his radical attacks on slavery and blaming anti-abolitionist riots on the abolitionists' provocations.[25] The attorney general's diatribe was just the opening salvo in a flurry of pamphlets in which Austin and his coadjutors reiterated their disdain for Channing and the abolitionists and charged them with seeking unnatural racial equality and ultimately race war. Although ambivalent about the legitimacy of anti-abolitionist mobs, these writers evinced an absolute certainty about the preeminent claims of the Union. At one point one writer even declared that "we are *married* to" Southerners, "and they to us."[26] Writers on the other side of the debate depicted their opponents' arguments as thinly veiled proslavery pleading and rebuked their "spirit of skepticism with regard to moral means of influence." Austin and his crowd would set back the whole cause of reform if they prevailed.[27]

In the heat of this contest Austin had articulated arguments that might well have made his boss Everett squirm. While the governor shared his attorney general's horror of race war and desire to preserve civilization, he also shared the other side's concerns about anyone who would exclude morality from politics. Moreover, for Austin's side to flash such fury at the abolitionists and employ patently racist appeals evinced more of the Democratic style of anti-abolitionism than Everett ever would.

However, this Boston debate surrounding Channing's pamphlet took place in a larger national context that would demand that Everett take a stern stance against abolitionism. The petitions and mails campaigns of 1835 increased both federal and Southern state officials' determination to suppress abolitionism. The House of Representatives adopted a ban on antislavery petitions that would be known as the Gag Rule. President Jackson connived at the suppression of the abolitionist mails, and in his December message to Congress he accused abolitionists of fomenting slave revolt. Given the need to preserve the Union, he hoped that if mobs failed to silence abolitionism, the Northern states "will be prompt to exercise their authority in suppressing so far as in them lies whatever is calculated to produce this evil." Meanwhile, horrified Southern governors asked their legislatures to pass resolutions demanding that the Northern state governments crack down on abolitionists. Missouri's legislature even called for a convention of slaveholding states to determine how to meet the threat, "peaceably if they can, forcibly if they must."[28]

But this legislature's resolutions and Jackson's presidential screed were the essence of calm compared to the annual message of Everett's old nemesis in the House, South Carolina's governor George McDuffie. Railing against "the wanton, officious, and incendiary proceedings" of the abolitionists, he pronounced *"my deliberate opinion, that the laws of every community should punish this species of interference* BY DEATH WITHOUT BENEFIT OF CLERGY, *regarding the authors of it as enemies of the human race."* Therefore, he urged the legislature to appeal "to those great principles of international law which still exist, in all their primitive force, among the sovereign states of this confederacy," to demand that the free states disclaim any power in Congress or their state governments "to interfere in any manner whatever, with the institution of domestic slavery in South Carolina," and further that they pass "penal laws" enacting "such punishments as will speedily and for ever suppress their machinations against our peace and safety."[29] This bloodthirsty message smacked of the nullification doctrine by treating American as well as British abolitionists as foreign emissaries and underlining the sovereignty of the states. But to an incoming governor like Everett who cherished the maintenance of the Union, it—together with the chorus of like-minded messages and memorials from state legislatures and governors and the president—demanded serious attention.

How Everett would respond was no foregone conclusion. Although invited, neither Everett nor his crony Webster attended the Faneuil Hall anti-abolitionist meeting. Neither did he sign the public letter calling the meeting, although hundreds of other respectable Bostonians did so. Typical of Everett, the only meeting he recorded attending in that hall in August 1835 was the annual benefit dinner for the public schools. He noted the October mob in his diary but without comment. He clearly had no relish for the maelstrom of anti-abolitionist politics, preferring Whig causes like education to what he called "the knotty subject of Slavery." The absence of evidence on Everett's stance nurtured cautious optimism in some antislavery advocates. After reading Everett's Bloody Brook oration, especially the passage "in which he pictured the fate of King Philip's wife and son, sold into slavery under the burning sun of the tropics," one stretched this shred far enough to interpret Everett as expressing "bitter scorn and detestation . . . for slavery." Wishing Everett had been in the Faneuil Hall meeting to rebuke the doughfaces with such rhetoric, this writer announced, "Hereafter we claim Mr. Everett an anti-slavery man."[30]

Everett, however, was not nearly so much an antislavery man as a Whig, and the mainstream of Massachusetts Whiggery was staunchly anti-abolitionist in 1835. Throughout the latter half of the year, the two leading Whig papers in the state, the *Boston Daily Advertiser* (edited by Everett's brother-in-law Nathan Hale) and the *Boston Atlas*, cast the abolitionists, particularly Thompson, in the worst light possible. Led by *Atlas* editor Richard Haughton, both papers championed the August Faneuil Hall anti-abolitionist meeting, hoping that such Northern Unionist expressions would calm Southern minds. Hale downplayed the actual violence of the October mob but worried enough about future violent disorder that he urged "the officers of the law to step in, and preserve the public peace." Haughton argued that both abolitionists and the fomenters of mobs should be held accountable for their "lawless violence" by "a trial, conviction and punishment of both classes of offenders." Haughton's paper was especially fruitful in electioneering attempts to brand the Democratic, not the Whig, Party as most likely to harbor abolitionists.[31] Anyone reading these pages, as Everett did, would have struggled to avoid the conclusion that anti-abolitionism was a grassroots movement of enormous popular appeal whose fervor needed the channeling or restraint that law should provide. Had he read Democratic sheets like the *Boston Statesman*, he would have seen even further evidence for the popularity of anti-abolitionism in the efforts of its editor to monopolize that popularity for Northern Democrats.[32]

Everett's inaugural message to the legislature walked a middle line that veered toward anti-abolitionist preferences. He devoted his usual painstaking care to its preparation, although December and early January were one of the darkest periods in his life, dominated by the illness and death of his eight-year-old daughter Grace Webster Everett. Delivered on 15 January amid pomp and ceremony that did not entirely take his mind off his private grief, the inaugural message comprised almost entirely a ringing statement of Everett's Whig reform and improvement agenda and a celebration of the blessings of the American Union.[33]

But a passage of about two pages in this thirty-three-page-long message was destined to provoke a firestorm of controversy. "The country has been greatly agitated during the past year in relation to slavery," he began, "and acts of illegal violence and outrage have grown out of the excitement kindled on this subject, in different parts of the Union, which cannot be too strongly deplored nor too severely censured." Then, as was his wont, he offered a history lesson on how the free states had at the founding of the Constitution entered into a compact that "expressly recognizes the existence of slavery; and concedes to the States where it prevails the most important rights and privileges connected with it." "Our fathers" had thus set an example "of forbearance and toleration on this subject" that their sons would be wise to heed. Abolitionist agitation was thus "at war with" the spirit of the Constitution and might also stir up "an insurrection among the slaves." As such, it "has been held by highly respectable legal authority, an offence against the peace of this commonwealth, which may be prosecuted as a misdemeanor at common law." But Everett would prefer that no such laws need even be considered. For "as the genius of our institutions and the character of our people are entirely repugnant to laws impairing the liberty of speech and of the press, even for the sake of repressing its abuses," it would be far better if "the patriotism of all classes of citizens" induced them "to abstain from a discussion, which, . . . if not abandoned, there is great reason to fear, will prove the rock on which the Union will split." Such a silencing of abolitionism "would leave this whole painful subject where the Constitution leaves it, with the states where it exists, and in the hands of an all wise Providence, who in his own good time, is able to cause it to disappear, like the slavery of the ancient world, under the gradual operation of the gentle spirit of Christianity."[34]

Everett by this message sought to balance plaintive rebukes of abolitionism with a shorter but stern reproof of anti-abolitionist mobs; hints at the desirability of repressive legislation with ardent hopes that such would prove unnecessary; and an overall emphasis on preserving the Union with a dream of very gradual and peaceful emancipation. While the message obviously leaned against abolitionism, it had not thrown red meat to the sternest anti-abolitionists by demanding punitive legislation. It also showed that he had learned various lessons from his previous career. On the positive side, he had become unrivaled in marshaling the Founders' legacy behind his positions. And on the negative side, he had learned ten years previous that he should not even hint at defending slavery in principle, even (perhaps especially) in a message whose policy thrust might lead to a positive response to Southern demands. The moral he drew from the story of ancient slavery in 1836 was that Christianity's benevolent influence had almost imperceptibly and with the spirit of love abolished slavery. This reached back to the teachings of Joseph Stevens Buckminster from his youth but differed from the moral he had drawn in 1826. This careful, moderate tone, he surely hoped, might keep this unavoidable wade into the turbulent waters of slavery politics from sinking his newly launched raft of state.

He also had reason to think that this passage had been firmly anchored in the mainstream of Northern and national slavery politics in early 1836. He had read Channing's influential pamphlet while preparing his message. Its ceding of final control over slavery to the South, as well as its preference for governmental rather than popular suppression of abolitionists if they had truly crossed the line, would have helped convince Everett that his recommendation occupied moderate, majority ground on the issue.[35] After close advisers had read the message, they also assured him that "the People would sustain the doctrines therein set forth." After reading a draft, Brooks "could see nothing for a practical man to object to, and much to commend." Political heroes Webster and Madison lauded it. One solidly antislavery Massachusetts editor extolled the message for its "purely democratic" and Antimasonic political principles and said nothing about the abolitionist passage. A New York paper "heartily" approved Everett's rebuke of the troublemakers, and a Vermont sheet believed that sentiment would be echoed by everyone who understood and wished to perpetuate "our institutions." Such voices would have assured Everett that he had distilled the quintessence of Whig patriotism.[36]

But Massachusetts's most antislavery citizens perceived the message not as the voice of reason but as an existential threat that they needed to counter. In a letter to a newspaper, "CONSISTENCY" perceptively probed the contradictions in Everett's speech. When it came to slavery, Everett had urged that the Founders' compact meant that individuals must do nothing to combat slavery but instead await God's inscrutable timing. But while advocating every other reform, Everett found that the Founders' legacy encouraged direct human rather than divine agency. For his or her part, "P. J." thought Everett's message aimed "a deadly blow at the liberty of speech and the press" and lamented that "any respectable authority in New-England" would have joined "the advocates for slavery" who willfully twisted the Constitution into a blanket protection of slavery.[37] Unsurprisingly, the pages of Garrison's *Liberator* also put Everett back in the ranks of the "advocates for slavery" where Benjamin Lundy had cast him early in his congressional career. After the "painful shock" of Everett's knapsack speech, Garrison recounted, Everett had lain low enough on the issue as to cause some doubt of where he stood. But Garrison saw his 1836 message as the fruition, not the contradiction, of that 1826 expression, making Everett's plea that he hated the mobs ring just as hollow as his plea that he hated slavery. Even worse was "how great an amount of mischief" Everett had done by throwing his indubitable authority as "the every-day eulogist of our revolutionary fathers, *the orator on Lexington plains*," behind abolitionism's worst enemies.[38] The Quaker abolitionist poet John Greenleaf Whittier stepped up to challenge Everett's appeal to the founding. While all Bay Staters granted that "the Constitution recognizes Slavery," abolitionists saw the Constitution properly construed as "their guardian." Not only did the Founders set slavery up to "die of consumption," but "the blow which shall compel them to 'abstain from discussion' must reach them through the very heart of the Constitution," which was "its guaranty of free discussion and the right of the people" to assemble and petition. "Is it in Massachusetts over the graves of Adams and Warren and Hancock and Otis," he demanded, "that the spirit of free investigation is to be arrested and stricken dumb?" Here was an abolitionist willing to contain the damage Everett could do to the cause by challenging him on his own grounds, interpreting the Founders' bequests on the vital issues at stake in this dispute. And this was but the most effective stroke in the drumbeat of criticism Everett's message produced in Garrison's sheet for much of 1836.[39]

By March 1836, however, the main stage of this conflict had moved to the state legislature more than to the press. The drama was a face-off between anti-abolitionist legislators and the embattled activists manning the headquarters of New England abolitionism. The state legislature had assigned to a committee chaired by Senator George Lunt the task of responding to Everett's and the Southern states' recommendations relative to abolitionism. Fearing that this committee might produce the penal legislation Southerners demanded, in February the Massachusetts Anti-Slavery Society requested that its agents be allowed to testify in a hearing. On 4 March, Lunt grudgingly allowed this hearing to proceed, and it quickly turned into a debacle. The witnesses—who were the leading lights of Massachusetts abolitionism—had spent hours sketching out a shrewd plan of attack in which they stressed that the issue involved was not so much abolitionists' rights as the broader right of free speech. By such arguments, the abolitionists painted Everett and his fellow Whigs, not the abolitionists, as the dangerous innovators misreading American history and threatening the Constitution and the rule of law. As the hearing wore on, Lunt increasingly interrupted the abolitionists' speeches, and the day ended in confusion and bitterness. The showdown resumed on 8 March, as did Lunt's eagerness with his gavel. After a series of contentious interchanges in which Lunt asserted the authority of the committee and parried accusations of encouraging mobs, this hearing also broke up in disorder.[40]

Irritating and menacing as it was to abolitionists on 4 and 8 March, Lunt's imperious behavior helped to elevate their cause and sink his own reputation. The backlash against Lunt began within his own committee and continued on the floor of both houses of the legislature. The debates over Lunt's committee's doings turned sharp, illustrating how deeply legislators felt about free speech, on the side of Lunt's critics, and about abolitionists, on the side of his defenders. Lunt's committee's final report, which offered a sternly anti-abolitionist account of the proceedings, failed in both houses.[41] The whole episode had changed the issue from union (as Lunt and his allies preferred to frame it) to threats to the rights of Massachusetts citizens (as abolitionists framed it). Under headlines "Despotism" and "Application of the Gag Law," items in the *Liberator* detailed Lunt's committee's "trampling on the Bill of Rights, on freedom of discussion and petition." By the end of its session the legislature was fielding the reverse of the committee's recommendations: abolitionist petitions for the legislature to call on Southern states to repeal their laws "which operate to the injury of the citizens of Massachusetts." Sensing an opportunity to strike at a Whig leader in Lunt, the Democratic press criticized his procedure while protesting its own anti-abolitionism. There were not too many obvious opportunities to gain partisan advantage from such a fraught issue as slavery and abolition, but Lunt had provided one.[42]

But Lunt did not feel he had blundered, and Everett felt the need to distance himself from Lunt's unrepentant zeal for vigorous anti-abolitionism. Deep into the 1860s, Lunt railed in print that "it was unfortunate that appeals were not made to the criminal tribunals" to stamp out the abolitionists and thus preserve sectional calm. From that vantage point he remembered his role in the infamous committee hearings as defending true freedom of speech against "that license which the more ardent abolitionists mistook for it" in their disregard for "the ordinary rules of civility, or of the recognized deference due to constituted authorities."[43] For his part, Everett had so little relish for this whole affair that he made no mention of the Lunt committee hearings in his diary. By April 1836, Everett passed along anti-abolitionist resolutions from Mississippi and Kentucky without comment. In November 1836, when the state Whig leadership decided not to nominate Lunt for reelection to his state senate seat, Everett declined to appoint him to another post. In an 1838 letter discussing candidates for a militia commission, political adviser Robert C. Winthrop raised many names, including Lunt's, but commented that Lunt "is rather impracticable, & of Anti Abolition notoriety." It was the last mention of Lunt as Everett and Winthrop discussed these appointments. Lunt's bullying brand of anti-abolition savored of the Democracy and of mobocracy, none of which would fly for a Whig governor appointing someone to keep the peace. To be sure, Everett kept Austin on as attorney general. But retaining a long-standing official was a different matter than appointing a new one.[44]

Such gradations along the anti-abolitionist spectrum were lost on the abolitionists, for whom the persecutions of the mid-1830s constituted a transformative experience. Before this "Reign of Terror," most Boston abolitionists had Southern slaveholders squarely in their sights, and doughfaces only obliquely.[45] But the trauma of what Martineau called the "Martyr Age" of American abolitionism focused their moral suasion increasingly on Northern consciences. Everett and his influence encapsulated how much work remained to be done even in New England. At the 1836 convention of the New England Anti-Slavery Society, Samuel May marveled that Everett's speech "did not raise universal indignation throughout New England." Another delegate warned of the insidiousness of Everett's smooth-toned anti-abolitionism. "Give me an open enemy," he cried, "rather than a secret foe, who . . ., pretending to be the friend of liberty, counsels the worst of slavery, and calls it *patriotism*; who gives us soft words, and at the same time, fetters our limbs, and palsies our tongues." An 1836 report of the Boston Female Anti-Slavery Society likewise noted with disillusionment that the Boston mob included "men who have repeatedly said they were 'as much anti slavery as we were,' that 'our principles were righteous,' and that they only objected to the rashness of upholding them." The Reign of Terror had revealed the doughface soul to be but a whited sepulcher, and New England's abolitionists devoted themselves to cleansing the inner vessel.[46]

In the longer term, many abolitionists forgot neither the Reign of Terror nor Everett's role therein. Frederick Douglass alluded bitterly to both in a speech in England in 1860. Henry Wilson's influential post–Civil War multivolume abolitionist history of antebellum politics recorded Everett and Lunt's committee combining to produce "a dark and trying hour for the friends of the slave," who "had reason to be alarmed at these demands for penal legislation." When May set down his recollections of the abolitionist movement in 1869, a minutely detailed account of the Reign of Terror stood at the heart of his narrative. But he also remembered the new accessions to the cause and the defeat of its enemies that followed, including that "at the very next election" Everett "was beaten by the opposing candidate, whose sentiments on slavery were thought to be more correct than his."[47]

Although May's mind preserved the details of the persecution in pristine condition, his memory of Everett's fate in the 1836 gubernatorial election proved faulty. This was not for lack of trying by Massachusetts abolitionists. Although Garrison had forsworn voting, the *Liberator* nevertheless functioned as a clearinghouse for abolitionist politics, and its columns campaigned vigorously against Everett in 1836. Garrison repeatedly decreed that "all true, uncompromising abolitionists, who go to the polls in this State, will consistently vote in opposition to MARTIN VAN BUREN and EDWARD EVERETT." When some readers asked whether other candidates were preferable to Van Buren, Garrison granted that true abolitionists might well opt out of the presidential ballot; but there was no doubt that they should vote against Everett. Sensing that many abolitionists felt the pull of loyalty to the Whig Party, Garrison via a pseudonymous letter writer hectored, "Christians, republicans, citizens of Massachusetts, by your love of Truth, and Freedom, and Honor, fail not to record your votes against the man who has sacrificed all these to Falsehood, and Slavery, and Infamy." Clearly, at election time and for electioneering purposes the supposedly apolitical Garrison was alive to the fact that people faced conflicting loyalties rather than stark black and white choices. This was all the more reason he and his kind urged the binary language of slavery versus freedom to clarify the situation to their advantage. But for all that, Everett handily secured reelection, albeit by a diminished margin from 1835. Running as he always would against Morton, he won 42,160 votes to Morton's 35,992.[48]

Although Everett won the November election round, the abolitionists won the next few throughout the North. The maltreatment of abolitionists — culminating with the murder of Illinois abolitionist Elijah Parish Lovejoy in 1837 — won several new and vital converts to their cause. Moreover, Northerners who never joined an antislavery society signaled their sympathy for abolitionists' rights of free expression by opposing the Gag Rule. Northern sectionalism also coalesced around opposition to the proposed annexation of Texas to the United States, which would add untold power to the South's balance in the national scale. As historian Corey Brooks has written, "no other antislavery rhetoric was as compelling" as the growing cry against the "Slave Power," with its "claim that slaveholders wielded disproportionate power and threatened the liberties of northern whites." The reaction was so strong that no Northern legislature could bring itself to pass the laws restricting abolitionists that the South had requested in 1835. By 1838, an organ of the American Anti-Slavery Society treated Everett's and Lunt's 1836 antics as relics of what "was *then* the unpopularity of abolitionism."[49]

Massachusetts public opinion mirrored this Northern trend. It had its limits, as Massachusetts abolitionists found in 1838 and 1839 when they petitioned the state legislature in vain to repeal its ban on interracial marriage. But the state's Whigs divided more over whether to stress legal or moral considerations on the Texas issue than over whether to oppose annexation. As early as fall 1836, caucuses and conventions of Massachusetts Whigs passed platform planks opposing the Gag Rule and Texas annexation. In January 1837, less than a year after abolitionists' confrontation with Lunt's committee, the Massachusetts

Anti-Slavery Society won permission from the state House of Representatives to meet in its chamber. While groping for conservative ground, party leaders like Webster had to recognize that "the Anti Slavery feeling is growing stronger & stronger every day." Northern Whigs, Webster continued, must pay more attention to the "friendship & support of those great masses of good men, who are interested in the Anti Slavery cause," than to "conciliating those whom we never can conciliate" in the South. So in 1838, Webster broke with Henry Clay over his anti-abolitionist resolutions in Congress.[50]

But antislavery politics also divided the Massachusetts Whig Party in the late 1830s. In the pages of the *Daily Advertiser*, Hale maintained his anti-abolitionist stance. He reveled in any evidence of abolitionist opposition to Everett as proof that Everett was right. He opposed the Gag Rule but ultimately blamed the abolitionists for calling it forth in the first place. In March 1837, when the Massachusetts legislature debated resolutions against the Gag Rule, Hale published a furious editorial titled "The Abolition Phrenzy," denouncing legislators for "entering the vortex of the slavery discussion." It ought "to be palpable to the dullest man's comprehension," he fumed, that this agitation would weaken "past remedy the bonds of the Union."[51] Hale's personally insulting language provoked a response from Haughton in the *Atlas* that turned into a war of words between the two Whig organs. Deep into this controversy, Haughton summed up the distinction between his movement on the issue along with the majority in the legislature and Hale's inflexible anti-abolitionism. "The trouble with the *Advertiser*," he jabbed, "is, that it is, as usual, just about two years behind the times." Stuck in an anti-abolitionist siege mentality more appropriate to 1835, Hale had missed that the legislature and the *Atlas* meant only to defend the rights of the North, not to invade those of the South.[52] This newspaper duel captured how the rise of antislavery politics in the late 1830s challenged Whigs to consider just what constituted true conservatism—as opposed to radicalism on the one hand and a reactionary position on the other—on this issue.

In his own typically moderate way, after 1836 Governor Everett tended to side more with Haughton's than with Hale's point of view. He was never in danger of becoming an abolitionist himself. He praised Martin Van Buren's March 1837 inaugural address—in which the new president declared himself "the inflexible and uncompromising opponent" of anyone who would offer "the slightest interference" with slavery—as "a temperate & judicious document in which particularly the difficult topic of Slavery is treated with great discretion."[53] But that same week Everett privately rebuked Hale for his "Abolition Phrenzy" editorial, "because I fear that such a title & some of the language used in the article are calculated rather to irritate than to persuade" and to give sanction to some of the South's anti-abolitionist excesses. Knowing that the public saw this paper as a mouthpiece for Everett, and "believing as I do, that the Union is on the verge of dissolution," Everett instructed Hale that he was "deeply anxious to avoid every thing, which can feed the angry feelings, & add bitterness to passions already too much excited."[54]

Everett also quietly sided with Channing in disputes with his attorney general, Austin, as well as with his party chieftain, Clay. In December 1837, at a Faneuil Hall meeting organized by antislavery leaders (including Channing) to protest the murder of Lovejoy, Austin made a memorable scene. He rose to protest against the protest, provocatively casting the Illinois mob rather than Lovejoy as the legatees of the Boston Tea Party. The audience demonstrated how divisive such a harangue could be when some cheered and others shook their fists with rage. This hijacking of the Revolution's legacy so outraged Wendell Phillips that he felt compelled to rise and deliver his first public abolitionist speech as a rejoinder.[55] Everett tried to remain on good terms with both Channing and Austin, but his relationship with Channing was more cordial and lasted until the preacher's death in 1844.[56]

The governor also expressed deep alarm when Clay gave a much-publicized anti-abolitionist Senate speech in February 1839. Clay vigorously defended exclusive Southern control over slavery and referred repeatedly to "the insurmountable obstacles" in the way of abolition in the United States that made slavery's continued existence an "inexorable necessity." Talk of impossibilities came strangely from the lips of the great Whig improver and eternal optimist Clay. More to the point, the speech delegitimized anyone who petitioned Congress to act against slavery in any way. Soon after reading reports of Clay's speech, Everett implored Webster to help "to throw off from Massachusetts the burden of doctrines like Mr. Clay's;—a burden which it would be hard to carry to the polls next fall." Channing responded to this speech with an equally widely publicized pamphlet, which he sent to Everett. While unconvinced by Channing's argument that it was impossible for the law to make people into property, otherwise Everett found Channing's open letter to Clay "very able" and persuasive. And while Austin continued his vendetta against Channing with a pamphlet calumniating Channing's response to Clay, Everett made no mention of reading this polemic. In the aftermath of his 1839 speech, Clay convinced himself that only antislavery "Ultra's" found it offensive, but Channing was closer than was Clay or Austin to Everett's new brand of moderation.[57]

Everett remained, as always, keen to find the Whig Unionist's truly moderate path, but after his first weeks in office that path went in an antislavery direction. He explained this shift in his beliefs in a candid letter to Winthrop in 1837. After offering comments to help his protégé frame a speech against Texas annexation, Everett admitted that "there was a time, & that not long ago, when I should have doubted the expediency of expressing" even the mildly antislavery views he saw in Winthrop's draft. "But the South has labored hard to drive all moderate men from their ground, & has herself to thank, in no small degree, for the spread of Abolitionism.—I remain of opinion, that the Union will split on this rock; but I am less clear, than I once was, that it is our duty, as honest men or patriots, to struggle against it."[58]

———

Everett also grasped toward rapprochement with abolitionists in more formal and public ways than these rather passive manifestations. As both governor and candidate he had the opportunity to go officially on record relative to the Gag Rule and Texas annexation. He had privately encouraged the state's members of Congress who fought against the Gag Rule. But in 1837 the Massachusetts legislature received dozens of petitions from thousands of constituents vindicating the right of petition and advocating the abolition of slavery and the slave trade in D.C. Overwhelming majorities in both houses responded by passing carefully crafted resolutions and distributing them widely.[59] Asserting that no right was "more indispensable to the enjoyment of freedom" than the right of petition, these resolves declared that the Gag Rule was "injurious to the cause of freedom and free institutions." As for the subject of the petitions in question, they resolved "that Congress, having exclusive legislation in the District of Columbia, possess the right to abolish slavery in the said District, and that its exercise should only be restrained by a regard to the common good."[60] While Everett did not initiate these resolutions, he did assent to them and sent them to the state's representatives in Congress. And when running for reelection later that year, a pamphlet written for his campaign declared that Bay State Whigs (unlike the Democrats) would sanction no additions to the Union "which have either for their design or their effect, to extend or perpetuate the institution of slavery."[61]

It was in such reelection contests that both Everett and the abolitionists showed concretely how much they had changed since their 1836 face-off. In the aftermath of the Reign of Terror, some abolitionists decided to break with the nonvoting Garrisonians and make their growing political power felt in elections for both Congress and state offices. In the fluid state of Massachusetts party politics, they saw the potential to make both Democrats and Whigs earn what could be an abolitionist swing vote. Morton's narrowing of the electoral gap between his 1835 and 1836 runs against Everett, together with growing divisions within the Whig Party, gave them hope of influencing future gubernatorial contests. Playing defense in the 1837 campaign against the aggressive and persistent Morton, Everett might need to pacify the abolitionists much in the same way as he had done with the Antimasons two years previous. Well into 1837 Everett remained a byword for doughface-ism among abolitionists, but as the head of the state's majority party he could do them real harm unless he turned against anti-abolitionism. In this campaign, therefore, abolitionists sent public questionnaires to the two parties' candidates and published their responses (or failure to respond). If no candidate answered acceptably, they would instruct followers to scatter their votes among write-in candidates.[62]

The common perception when the abolitionists began their questionnaire campaign was that it would benefit Morton, but the story between the 1837 and 1839 gubernatorial elections turned out to be much more complex and interesting than that. In the 1837 trial run, the abolitionists nodded to the strong pull of partisan loyalty by having Democratic-leaning activists query Morton and Whig-leaning ones query Everett. William Jackson's public letter to Everett picked no partisan quarrel with the governor but claimed that many voters thought opposition to slavery was "a much greater and more noble object" than any party agenda. He asked Everett whether America's slaves should be emancipated and whether Congress should abolish slavery in D.C. and bar Texas from the Union. Winthrop Atwill, Whig-leaning editor of the *Northampton Courier*, wrote to give Everett a chance to defend himself from accusations that he was a friend of slavery and would imprison abolitionists. Believing that these repugnant ideas could not have been the import of the 1826 and 1836 speeches cited so often against him, Atwill wrote "respectfully to inquire, whether you have changed or modified the opinions you once held, with many other eminent northern gentlemen, on the subject of slavery since its agitation at the north by the friends of immediate emancipation." On one level this query slyly offered Everett the trap of admitting to having changed his mind in response to the abolitionists, but overall it seemed to have been a good-faith offer of an opportunity to clarify.[63]

Everett contemplated his responses carefully. When he first learned of the abolitionists' drive for antislavery purity in candidates, he suspected this tactic would both aid the Democrats and destroy the Union. But when he received actual inquiries, the political realities dictated answering rather than discountenancing them. After drafting a part of his letter, he read it to Webster and Winthrop. Everett trusted that Winthrop, a well-connected rising star in Massachusetts politics, had his finger on the pulse of Massachusetts Whiggery. But in a move that embodied his changing relationship with abolitionism, he also consulted with William Jackson's brother Edmund.[64]

Everett could have confined himself to the constitutional and foreign policy questions implicit in these queries, but he realized that would do nothing to burnish his antislavery credentials so he rose to the bait. Beginning by acknowledging the subject of slavery to be "vast in extent & importance," he answered Jackson first by stating that because slavery was "a social, political, & moral evil of the first magnitude, it is required by justice, humanity, & sound policy that the slaves should be emancipated, by those having the power constitutionally to effect that object, as soon as it can be done peacefully, and in a manner to better the condition of the emancipated." This answer, with its important qualification that Southerners should in due process of time be the ones to emancipate, fell far short of the Garrisonian line. But it was a thoroughly mainstream answer in Massachusetts in 1837. As for abolition in D.C., he expressed full approbation of the legislature's resolutions the previous winter, adding that he had voted against a proto–Gag Rule in Congress in 1834. On Texas, he emphasized that its annexation as one or more slave states would completely undermine American pretensions to merely be tolerating slavery, constituting "a voluntary extension of Slavery" across an "almost boundless" extent of new American territory. He also shrewdly aligned himself with Channing by citing and lauding his discussion of the Texas issue "in his recent letter to Mr. Clay." He finished by adding that if, at the very moment Great Britain had set an "example" on the world stage by abolishing slavery in its empire, the United States "should rush into a policy of giving an indefinite extension to Slavery over a vast region, incorporated into their Union, we should stand condemned before the civilized world."[65]

While his epistle to Jackson was the most widely circulated of the two, his response to Atwill was also telling and far from private. In the latter he once again sought to limit the implications of the slavery passage in his knapsack speech. All he had meant to say, he sighed, was that where slavery exists it was so "sanctioned by morality and religion, that we look to the benignant operation of Christianity, and not to *violence* and *bloodshed,* for its disappearance. — The charge of being friendly to slavery, made by political opponents, was *instantly denied* by me" in congressional debate. His response to the charge that he was an eager abolitionist hunter was more persuasive. He admitted to having, "in the mildest language, deprecated such an agitation of the subject, as was calculated to *inflame* the angry passions" surrounding slavery. Although partisan myth posited that his 1836 message countenanced a legal crackdown on abolitionists, he rightly claimed to actually have "said, that all restraint on discussion must be the voluntary dictate of the patriotism of the individual." Moreover, he had since upheld the right of petition and Congress's power to abolish slavery in D.C. He went back to a shakier account of his record when he claimed to have always regarded slavery "as a *social, political,* and *moral evil* of the *first magnitude*; whose removal, as soon as it can be constitutionally and peacefully effected," was eminently desirable. This evil's "proposed indefinite extension, by the annexation of Texas, I should regard as the *greatest evil,* that could possibly befall the Union."[66] The two letters added up to a unified, moderately antislavery stance. He had traveled a fair distance between January 1836 and October 1837.

These letters also came in handy when other abolitionist groups approached him with similar queries. While Atwill and especially Jackson had written well enough in advance of the election for Everett to consider his response, less friendly inquisitors did so on short notice before the election, perhaps hoping to trip up the candidate if he proved slow to respond. So it was vital to Everett to be seen to respond quickly. When a committee of black abolitionists from New Bedford, a white committee from Danvers, and his old correspondent Samuel Whitcomb interrogated him separately in early November, he sent them his letters to Jackson and Atwill, together with the legislature's resolutions on the Gag Rule and Texas "which were approved & signed by me on the 12th April last."[67]

In 1839 the process was similar.[68] Nathaniel Borden accepted the assignment from the Massachusetts Anti-Slavery Society to question Everett. Borden worried that too leading a questionnaire would aid Morton and thus Van Buren, but after working through some drafts with fellow activist Francis Jackson he was ready to send it. Its queries numbered only two: whether Everett favored "the immediate abolition, by law," of slavery in D.C. and of the interstate slave trade; and whether he was "opposed to the admission into the Union of any new State the Constitution and Government of which tolerates domestic Slavery."[69] Upon receiving Borden's inquiry, Everett consulted, as before, with Winthrop, now Speaker of the state house, but he was surer of his response than he was in 1837. He had a better antislavery track record by then, although he still leaned heavily on his support of the 1837 legislative resolutions. Although believing that those resolves "cover the whole ground of your two interrogatories," he forthrightly added that "I respond to both your inquiries in the affirmative."[70] In this direct and unequivocal reply, Everett rather astoundingly but confidently posed as a thoroughgoing antislavery politician of long standing.

Everett's entente with antislavery activists, however, remained a work in progress on their side for much of his time as governor. In 1837, abolitionists approved of Everett's replies but still entertained distrust of the governor. "Mr. E's letter to Jackson I like pretty well," wrote one. But as Election Day neared, he still anguished over which candidate "is worthy of the honest vote of an honest Abolitionist." The Bristol County Anti-Slavery Society resolved its approbation of Everett's letters, which encouraged local Whigs. But that county society did not have nearly the power of Garrison, who in his issue of the *Liberator* just prior to the election dedicated no fewer than eleven separate articles to Everett and slavery. Most of those articles cast doubt on this would-be friend to the cause in light of his past record. "As he has played the *parasite* to the SOUTH in 1826," swiped one piece, he now sought to "play the *parasite* to the ABOLITIONISTS." In an editorial directly addressing the question "FOR WHOM SHALL ABOLITIONISTS VOTE," Garrison argued that they should vote for neither Morton—and "thus serve to strengthen the power of Martin Van Buren, the modern Pharoah [*sic*]"—nor "Mr. Everett, in view of all that he has said and done against them and their cause." They should administer a principled rebuke to both candidates by scattering their votes.[71]

In 1839 abolitionists seemed much more willing to be convinced by Everett's communications. Francis Jackson assured Everett that Garrison and "all the friends of the Slave whom I have seen" united "in denominating your Excellency's letter to Mr. Borden, as 'frank & satisfactory.'" A relieved Everett recorded all such manifestations in his diary, although he may well have waited to read it in the *Liberator* to believe it. What he read was Garrison rebuking Hale for declining to publish "the Governor's commendable letter in favor of immediate emancipation" in the *Daily Advertiser*. "Edward Everett now speaks the language of a patriot, a republican, and a christian," Garrison proclaimed. Moreover, "we believe it is the real language of his soul." The same Garrison who for years had pounded Everett now pledged "to obliterate all that has gone before, and to commend him for his present honorable course. To refer invidiously to what he said when public sentiment was deeply corrupt, would be ungenerous; to charge him with being insincere at the present time, would be unjust." Especially because Morton had evaded the issue that year, Governor Everett "ought to receive the undivided support of the anti-slavery voters of this Commonwealth; nay, they are pledged to give him their support."[72] That Everett received the outright endorsement of Garrison while his brother-in-law distanced his paper from him showed how much had changed since 1836.

———

While on the face of it abolitionists rather abruptly abandoned their suspicions of Everett's motives and commitment in 1839, this change had been a long time coming. After his apparent willingness to buckle to Southern demands in 1836, he had built up a track record of antislavery action in his interactions with Southern states. Everett was governor in a time of increasing tension between slave- and free-state governments over the illicit movement of African Americans across their borders, from runaway slaves to the kidnapping of free black citizens. Everett occasionally dealt with such issues throughout his terms, although looking back after he left office he felt relieved that he had not had to deal with the truly contentious cases then brewing between Maine and Georgia and New York and Virginia. He was able to avoid major clashes with slave states yet effectively to safeguard the rights of black Massachusetts citizens by working solidly within the law and deploying his diplomatic demeanor and personal contacts with Southern politicians. While not one to challenge the South's runaway laws, he was able to protect some citizens of his state from their abuse and other abuses of the slave system.[73]

In the winter of 1836, not long after his notorious anti-abolitionist message, he worked with the unlikely combination of abolitionist lawyer Samuel E. Sewall and Attorney General Austin to secure the liberty of a woman named Mary Smith. Sewall's activities as an abolitionist lawyer were conspicuous enough that in 1836 he received death threats from Southerners and was even physically assaulted in his office by one aggrieved slaveholder. But that image dissuaded Everett no more than the threats deterred Sewall. Smith, a mixed-race native of Massachusetts, had been held in slavery after being shipwrecked on the coast of North Carolina. After gathering facts and crafting his message with help from Austin and especially Sewall, Everett appealed to North Carolina's governor to free Smith. He trusted that his Southern counterpart would agree that nothing deserved his intervention more than "rescuing a free citizen of a sister State, reduced to a condition of perpetual bondage, in the peculiarly disastrous manner" this case exhibited. He also urged secrecy for the whole transaction, not only because the kidnapper might sell her farther south if it became public but also because this should be a straightforward humanitarian case that should not become complicated by sectional politics. Everett's desire to help in this case was clearly not perfunctory, and he stayed in close touch with Sewall on the matter until and even after Smith gained her freedom in June. Smith appeared at an abolitionist meeting in Boston soon after her return from bondage, and this meeting did not begrudge acknowledging Everett's role in aiding her.[74]

Everett's other major kidnapping case came as his terms were coming to a close in 1839. In September he learned of two mulatto boys kidnapped from Massachusetts into slavery in Virginia. Interviews with Sewall and others in the know taught Everett that the perpetrators of this outrage were the operators of a big-time Virginia kidnapping ring. In short order he wrote to Virginia's governor seeking both the return of the children and the felons' extradition to Massachusetts to be tried for this "atrocious offence." Because most of the accused were already on trial in Virginia for kidnapping, Everett was able to bring only one of them to his state for trial. But this interstate cooperation brought the victims back home, and their families and Boston's abolitionist press expressed gratitude to Everett.[75]

Another way by which Everett mended fences with abolitionists was his public reaction to British emancipation. In 1833, Parliament abolished slavery in all of the British Empire's direct dependencies, effective 1 August 1834. The act compensated slaveholders for their freed human property and gave colonies leeway as to whether to immediately liberate their slaves or to move them through a halfway house to freedom known as the apprenticeship system. In 1838 Parliament moved to strike down the apprenticeship scheme in all colonies. This seismic shift in the history of New World slavery became one of the most important events in the history of slavery in the United States. Scholar Edward Rugemer has shown that the debate over the meaning of Parliament's act for American slavery was "a national phenomenon," which is not terribly surprising given the centrality of Britain to the early Republic's postcolonial culture and the centrality of slavery to its politics.[76]

The cosmopolitan Everett, in the midst of his awkward dance with abolitionists at home, was not about to ignore this epochal event or leave its implications for his own country unexplored. As late as 1837 his constitutionalism and caution overshadowed his penchant for reform. In two letters to Conservative British statesman Sir Robert Peel, Everett explained that the impetus to abolish slavery in the South encountered "innumerable difficulties" not present in the British Empire. The danger of sectional political conflict and "the stipulations of the federal Constitution which recognize its existence" were among these peculiarly American obstacles. But he also regretted that these facts put the United States in conflict with the antislavery direction of the opinion of "the civilized world." In the face of this quandary, he could only "hope that Providence will guide us to an adjustment of the question such as humanity demands, without the sacrifice of the peace of the Union."[77] These letters were consistent with his long-standing search for the balance between humanity and union and with his perception of obstructions rather than opportunities when he contemplated an American emancipation.

But then Everett read glowing reports of the British experiment with freedom from sources he trusted. In the spring of 1838, Edmund Quincy gave the governor a copy of American abolitionists James Thome and Horace Kimball's account of their travels in the post-emancipation West Indies, as part of a campaign by the American Anti-Slavery Society to distribute this book to American opinion leaders. Everett made it a priority in his busy schedule to pore over this lengthy work and immediately judged it "a very interesting & important volume." It riveted him so that he lent it to Winthrop, who in return called Everett's attention to a recent article in the *Edinburgh Review* that gave "even a better & more encouraging account of the success of" the experiment. Everett immediately devoured not only this article but also some recent parliamentary debates about the possible repeal of the apprenticeship system. In 1839 British abolitionist Joseph Sturge sent him his own account of conditions in the West Indies, which had proven instrumental in abolishing the apprenticeship system. While Everett might have been inclined to look askance at the abolitionist authors as biased activists, Quincy was just the right man to introduce their writings to Everett: he was Harvard-educated, well connected to men of letters, and the grandson of Federalist icon Josiah Quincy. As for the other sources of this information, Winthrop was an increasingly trusted friend, and Everett was naturally inclined to respect British statesmen and literary men. And to top it all off, he learned encouraging things about the state of the West Indies from a visitor to Boston whom Everett described as "a gentleman of fortune & education" from Edinburgh, hotbed of the Enlightenment.[78]

What he read spoke with one voice that British emancipation had been a rousing success worthy of emulation throughout the world. All the evidence, Thome and Kimball boldly told their American audience, pointed to an orderly, religious, prosperous state of society that benefited both freed people and planters and "conclusively proved" the success of abolition in the West Indies. Abolitionists were now the acknowledged benefactors of their country, for emancipation had removed "the fear of insurrection" that had stalked the slave societies. Slavery, not abolition as so many had feared, had been "emphatically 'the reign of terror.'" Sturge's work made many of the same arguments, echoing other testimony that Antigua was far better off for having embraced immediate abolition than Jamaica was with its apprenticeship regime. So much for Everett's dread of race war that had for so long made him a quintessential gradualist on emancipation.[79] The author of the *Edinburgh Review* essay positioned himself as a sober, fair observer standing between the wild-eyed abolitionists and the stubborn critics of emancipation. From that Everett-esque point of view, he declared Britain's experiment in applied benevolence to have been "the greatest work which has been done in these times, and at the noblest sacrifice." For whether in terms of profits or of civilization and social order, "nothing as yet has gone backward." And, he reminded readers, Parliament had accomplished all this without any attempt "to dictate the terms" whereon the colonial legislatures chose to give practical application to the decreed emancipation.[80] It was as if this article were written specifically for Everett. It like the others assuaged his fears of black insurrection and appealed to his desire for practicality. It also addressed his reservations about the British model of dictatorial central government by denying the premise.

These arguments and the sources from whence they came to Everett furthered his antislavery momentum. In April 1838, he and Quincy had long and amiable talks about Thome and Kimball's book and abolition more generally. In December 1838, Everett noted in his diary that the abolition of apprenticeship in Jamaica seemed to be producing "favorable" results. "God grant it may succeed," he prayed. In 1839, he thanked Sturge for the receipt of his "very able volume" on what was "unquestionably the most important event of the Age." Sturge's and others' testimony "has gone far to remove a very prevailing impression that African Slavery once established was a remediless evil. It has convinced many persons in the Northern States who doubted the practicability of emancipation without disastrous convulsions." He even boldly ventured that it would obviate the "Constitutional difficulties" in the way of American emancipation by convincing "reflecting men in the Slaveholding region," thereby proving "under Providence the means of uniting all hearts in the Country in the same work."[81] Peaceful, orderly British emancipation was the model Everett had been waiting for since his ruminations on abolition in the 1810s, and he cheered it on with his whole soul. He was of course unduly sanguine that Southern slaveholders would emulate the British, but he had been convinced so it was easy to imagine his reasonable friends there would be as well.

These private thoughts became public in late April 1838. In a letter to Quincy endorsing Thome and Kimball's tome, Everett averred that "from the moment of the passage" of Britain's abolition law, "I have looked with the deepest solicitude for tidings of its operation." His solicitude stemmed from his belief that "the success of the measure" in the West Indies "would afford a better hope than had before existed, that a like blessing might be enjoyed by those portions of the United States where slavery prevails." Most defenders of American slavery still pointed to it as a necessary evil, but "the emancipation of nearly a million of slaves in the British colonies" brought "this momentous question to the decisive test of experience. *If the result proved satisfactory, I have never doubted that it would seal the fate of slavery throughout the civilized world.*" Thus it was "most gratifying" to read Thome and Kimball's book, which "appears to place beyond a doubt" that Antigua's "experiment of immediate emancipation . . . has fully succeeded." In short, all this evidence "*has given me new views of the practicability of emancipation*," which it now appeared could be achieved "not merely *without danger* to the master, but without any sacrifice of his *interest*." He thus expected the book to persuade readers in both the North and the South.[82] This letter would open Everett to suspicions of closet abolitionism. One would have thought the conservative Everett would have preferred Jamaica's apprenticeship system to the immediate emancipation of Antigua, but even on that score he followed Thome and Kimball.

When Everett first gave Quincy his letter he requested that he not publish it, lest he be identified as "a flaming abolitionist." But Quincy earnestly entreated Everett to change his mind. After another consultation with Winthrop, and then a thorough correction of the draft, the governor consented to its publication. He did instruct Quincy to frame it as a private letter rather than as somehow the property of the American Anti-Slavery Society "to be communicated to the Society as they think fit." While Everett ascribed this request to a desire "to creep inoffensively into retirement," this was nonetheless good politics in Massachusetts in 1838. It got his antislavery message out to the public while avoiding the impression of being the tool of the abolitionists.[83]

Publication of the letter also offered potentially large benefits to the antislavery cause. As a moderate moving in an antislavery direction, Everett was one of the few public men who were open to being convinced by the reported evidence from the West Indies. Most American commentators had reacted negatively to West Indian emancipation. After Everett's letter appeared, for instance, Nathan Hale laid out the many reasons that "expectations of the abolition of Slavery in the United States, founded on what has been done or may be done in the West Indies, are altogether fallacious." Everett's endorsement of Thome and Kimball might prove valuable in refuting these criticisms for the undecided.[84] Abolitionists themselves were still undecided about Everett in the spring of 1838, and many of them wondered in print about the motives for and permanence of his apparent "conversion." But an antislavery citizen of Quincy, Massachusetts, thought the time was right for his town to have an abolitionist Fourth of July oration addressed by "Ex-President Adams, or Gov. Everett, (as it seems the governor has recently received some new light on the subject)." So antislavery operatives took full advantage of his letter's potential by securing it a wide distribution. They published it in their periodicals and cited it in letters hectoring national leaders to get on board the abolition train. The letter also made it into the mainstream party press and was reprinted as far afield as Cleveland, Ohio. No wonder when the famous Quaker abolitionist

Lucretia Mott met Everett on a steamboat in the summer of 1838, she thanked him for his testimonial.[85] She would of course have thanked him for very little just two years previous.

————

The electoral impact of these interchanges is difficult to determine, in part because all parties concerned seemed unsure of how to play the politics of abolition in gubernatorial races. In 1837, the abolitionist vote-scattering effort failed to keep Everett from crushing Morton by a margin of 50,565 votes to 32,987, which Everett proudly claimed was "the largest majority ever given in Massachusetts at a contested election." Yet in 1839 Garrison endorsed Everett but Morton won election for the first time. Such results led political abolitionists to rethink the whole questionnaire tactic and debate alternate strategies, such as establishing a third party.[86] The Massachusetts Democratic press walked a fine line in the late 1830s, seeking to both distance itself from and appeal to abolitionists, sometimes in the same editorial. In 1839, the Democratic press printed nary a word about Everett's response to Borden or Morton's lack of response to abolitionist queries, hammering instead on themes of aristocracy versus democracy and exhorting that victory was within reach if the Democrats could get out the vote.[87] Meanwhile, Boston's Whig press, led by Haughton's *Atlas*, hoped the Democrats would not fool "the honest Abolitionists of the North" into joining their ranks but did not call for them to join the Whig ranks either. In both 1837 and 1839, Haughton pounced on Morton's apparent evasions of abolitionist queries as evidence that Morton was playing a double game: placating abolitionists in Massachusetts but avoiding offending his pro-slavery national party leaders. But in neither campaign did Haughton cast this as a major issue.[88]

The issue that more than any other brought Everett's time as governor to an end was not slavery but temperance. To be sure, Everett's public correspondence with the abolitionists would be the strongest long-term legacy of his time in office. And the tensions between him and Hale in 1837 and 1839 emblematized divisions within the Whig Party as a whole over how to respond to the rising relevance of antislavery politics. Furthermore, understanding shifts in the electorate for the nineteenth century is an even less exact science than it is for today. But the vast majority of observers, including Everett himself, chalked up his defeat in 1839 to the unpopularity of the Whigs' law banning the sale of alcohol in quantities less than fifteen gallons. Its passage gratified a powerful and long-running urge for temperance reform within New England's reform culture and Whig Party coalition. But while the fifteen-gallon provision was meant to discourage taverns from selling drinks, its opponents had little difficulty painting it as an elitist measure that favored wealthy purchasers of alcohol.[89]

Everett only very reluctantly signed the bill into law and subsequently implored legislators to alter it. As with antislavery agitation, he had sympathy for the temperance cause, but as a hard-core moderate he could not embrace the proscriptive spirit of its zealots. By 1834, he had become convinced that it would be best if he as a member of the social elite abstained from wine so as to set a temperate example. He was also convinced that abstaining from alcohol would help his always-precarious health. So when at home, he drank only water. But in true Everett fashion, he did not wish to offend when in company; thus, "when I dine abroad, habit, & sympathy have led me to conform to the practice of those around me, & share the decanter as it passes." Thus, he thought "the attempt to discountenance & discard entirely the use of wine & beer, as well as spirits . . . a species of rigorism that can only be kept up by the members of a small society or sect."[90] After signing the bill in 1838, Everett fretted that it would divide Whigs and energize Democrats, helping Morton make a sizable dent in Everett's previous margin of victory. His concerns proved correct when Morton gained almost nine thousand votes over his 1837 total and narrowed Everett's margin to fewer than ten thousand votes. He thus ended his January 1839 message by urging legislators to consider altering the fifteen-gallon law, which had been "the subject of much division of opinion among the people of the Commonwealth." The lack of popular "approbation," he forecast, would not allow it to "go into successful operation." But instead it did go into operation with a vengeance, as reform-minded law officials enforced it with vigor and the temperance lobby in the state house showed no disposition to water down their great accomplishment. Everett's recommendation to modify the bill became controversial itself within the Whig Party, and in 1839 he contemplated resigning as a result. "I wish I could give you a little better account of the good old Bay-State," he summarized to Webster in Washington, "but the Temperance fever continues to burn."[91]

That fever burned Everett out of office. Whig leaders tried to arouse their rank and file in defense of their party's core principles and their statesmanlike governor, but such bland appeals could not blunt the impact of the liquor law. Election Day on 11 November began a period of agonizing uncertainty for Everett. It was plain that Morton had secured more votes than Everett, but what remained to be seen was whether he had won an outright majority; if he had not, the election would go to the state legislature and Everett would stand an excellent chance of reelection by that means. In late December Everett even began preparing another inaugural address, although he believed it "very doubtful" that he would actually deliver it. Finally, on 9 January 1840, Everett learned that Morton had won a majority by only two votes. The final tally was 51,034 for Morton, 50,725 for Everett, with enough scattered votes that Morton had needed 51,033 votes to win a majority. Everett had lost fewer than a thousand votes from his column since 1838, but new antitemperance voters increased Morton's total by almost 10,000 since 1838.[92] In election postmortems, Everett mused that Morton's victory constituted an aberration directly traceable to Democrats' successful politicization of the temperance issue. He regretted that there were so many special interest groups within the Whig coalition "who attach more importance to some one or two questions in no way connected with" the true political principles at stake between Whigs and Democrats "than they do to those principles." This made it so that no governor could "hope to please all." It is hard to argue with this conclusion when so many other political analysts then and since have agreed.[93]

Everett was not quite sure how to react to his defeat. He had long both privately and publicly professed his personal preference to leave politics. And while public life obviously had its pull over him across his career, his scholarly inclinations, and his own and his wife's chronically unpredictable health, meant that these were more than the usual platitudes from a nineteenth-century American politician. Still, he had long prided himself on the fact that he had never experienced defeat in an election, and this rebuke stung. He noted in his diary instances of personal betrayal in the election, most egregiously when his own secretary of state did not even bother to vote. He also recorded losing a great deal of sleep during the weeks of suspense. But when a joint legislative committee investigated several local Whigs' remonstrances against the legitimacy of their towns' returns in the gubernatorial election, Everett hoped it would not pursue the matter. A nasty fight in the house would represent all that put him off about contemporary politics, so he was relieved when the idea of contesting the election petered out. Perhaps only looking back did he fully realize the pain of this loss. When he learned that Davis had soundly beaten Morton in 1840, Everett confided in his friend Winthrop that this news was "balm to my wounded spirit; for I rather think I was more grieved at the result of the election in Nov. 1839, than I was willing to shew. The loss of the office *per se* I cared nothing for," he persisted, but he had been discouraged by the Whigs' divisions and lack of effort for his candidacy.[94]

One thing that seems to have soothed the pain of defeat was that Everett rather quickly turned his thoughts to travel, and perhaps a diplomatic post, in Europe. As for most Americans, England and Europe were never far from his thoughts. But receiving letters from his friend Webster about his voyages in Europe in 1839 made Everett wistful. He remembered his time there fondly but wished he had been mature enough to take full advantage. Even as he read avidly of American history and politics, his mind wandered more and more to European, and especially English, affairs. Soon after learning of Morton's election, Everett weighed in his journal the possibilities of what was next— replacing Webster in the Senate, or perhaps a foreign post if presumptive Whig presidential candidate William Henry Harrison were elected. While what he would do was up in the air, what he would not do became clear in the early spring of 1840, when he refused Whig efforts to nominate him to run again for governor. He declared this "an important step in my life," and he was right; it took him out of the orbit of Massachusetts politics.[95] What would follow became clearer later in the spring when he decided to take his family to Europe for an indefinite period. He ended up accepting the contemplated foreign post, but not under the president or by means of the nomination process he had expected.

5

Good Cop

MINISTER TO GREAT BRITAIN

Everett and his family spent over five years in Europe, embarking from New York to France in June 1840, going to represent their country in London beginning in late 1841, and arriving in Boston from Liverpool in September 1845. Despite both personal and professional adversity during his nearly four years as American minister to Great Britain, Everett would always look back fondly on this stint in Europe. His absence did not ease his fears that the sectional politics of slavery posed a mortal threat to the Union. Indeed, in London he had constant reminders of how American slavery complicated American foreign policy and vitiated the nation's world standing. Contemplating slavery in the headquarters of the Benevolent Empire only encouraged his embrace of reformist antislavery priorities that had begun while he was governor. In his official capacity as a representative of the slaveholding republic, Everett showed far more vigor and initiative in defending his country's sovereignty than in advocating the interests of its slaveholders, as difficult as those were to separate. This approach helped put him at odds with the proslavery secretaries of state under whom he served in the latter part of his time in Britain. He proved an effective minister with a strong working and personal relationship with leading British officials, but his superiors in Washington increasingly suspected rather than valued his brand of diplomacy.

————

Arriving in Havre, France, on 2 July 1840, Everett exulted at being back in the Old World. He reveled in revisiting and showing his family Western Europe's "lovely hill sides, noble castles, venerable ruins, prosperous villages, ancient towns, feudal recollections." He was proud to have left as a young student and returned as a reasonably well-known American statesman and orator. Residing principally in Paris and Naples, Everett mingled easily with the leading literary, social, and political lights of Europe. He happily devoted himself to scholarly pursuits when not sightseeing and socializing.[1] But he could not refrain from responding positively when his political friends back home suggested that he return to public life. Specifically, he made the case through Robert C. Winthrop that "if I am fit for anything, it is a diplomatic employment." Submitting as evidence his decade on the House Committee on Foreign Affairs, his many ("many, I mean, for an American") well-placed contacts in Europe, and his ability "to converse & do business" in "the principal continental languages," he expressed his hopes to serve his country at London, Paris, or Vienna should the Whigs win the presidency in 1840.[2]

Everett would have to wait a full year after William Henry Harrison's victory in November 1840 to learn whether he would get this wish. Harrison's death in early April 1841 delayed all nominations, and his replacement, John Tyler, contemplated other candidates before Everett's name came up for London. Important Northern voices demanded that in light of the ongoing dispute over the United States' northeastern boundary with Canada, the president appoint a New England man, but they did not mention Everett. As late as June, his own correspondents suggested that Paris might be his destination.[3] The leading candidate to be Harrison's secretary of state, Daniel Webster, hesitated to accept that position in part because he also wanted the London post. After Webster accepted the position at state in February 1841, Everett's congratulatory correspondence included a candid admission (protesting all the while that he was not fishing for office) that he would prefer London, Paris, or Vienna—in that order. After inquiring of Everett's father-in-law, Peter C. Brooks, whether his family situation would conduce to service in London, Webster prevailed on Tyler to nominate Everett for the London post.[4]

While being at the whim of Webster was nothing new for Everett, the greeting his nomination received in the Senate and the press was something completely different. On 16 July 1841, Tyler nominated Everett to be the U.S. minister to Great Britain. The Senate debated Everett's nomination in executive sessions, which debate dragged on intermittently until it confirmed Everett's appointment by a 23–19 vote on 13 September, the last day of this special session of Congress. The Senate's executive sessions were secret, but as the delay grew protracted, word leaked out that Southern senators opposed Everett's appointment because they considered him a dangerous abolitionist. The resulting press furor in the South and especially the North produced talk of retaliation and ultimately disunion.[5]

While the opposition to Everett would draw on his career in Massachusetts politics, it was driven by the intersection of the sectional, national partisan, and international politics of slavery. Both sectional and partisan conflict poisoned the atmosphere in which the first session of the Twenty-Seventh Congress would deliberate Everett's fate. That Congress was plagued by searing debates, including those over political economy touched off by the new president's betrayal of the Whig Party platform on which he came to power as vice president. Moreover, the opening of this session, much like the sessions preceding it, had been racked with sectional conflict over whether to continue the Gag Rule.[6] Held in this highly charged atmosphere, this session of Congress featured sharp, if brief, sectional clashes over the alleged abolitionism of nominees for positions including the Speaker of the House, committee chairs, cabinet officials, and even a midlevel Indian agent. In August 1841, Missouri's Thomas Hart Benton served notice to the Senate that the diplomatic corps would not be exempt from screening for "Federalists [Whigs] and Abolitionists." "The Abolitionists," he complained, "have their share of all appointments" as a result of Whig misrule.[7]

Although clearly every position was touchy in such a situation, the appointment of a minister to Great Britain was even more sensitive than the norm. A wide range of stubborn and contentious issues had by the early 1840s brought the United States and Great Britain into serious conflict, but two of them led the catalog. First was a decades-long dispute over the northeastern U.S. boundary with Canada, which provided many spectacular cross-border incidents that captured headlines in both countries. Second was the clash between Britain's antislavery foreign policy and Americans' desire to protect slavery, their sovereignty, or both. Britain's pressure on the United States to cooperate with its efforts to suppress the illicit Atlantic slave trade continued in full force, met on the other side by deep suspicions that any treaty would grant British sailors the right to board and inspect ships flying the American flag. Such controversies both rallied Americans to defend their sovereignty against the encroachments of the mighty British Empire and divided them along sectional lines as to which sort of Anglo-American controversy was most pressing. New Englanders obviously assigned the northeastern boundary highest priority. Southerners saw British officials' quest for the right to search vessels as the prime threat, being of a piece with their openly avowed antislavery foreign policy. The fate of American runaway slaves who crossed into Canada was one of the hot topics that inflamed that border. When in the late 1830s British colonial officials liberated American slaves when ships trafficking them from one American port to another ended up instead in British West Indian ports, this confirmed Southerners' image of Britons as powerful people who would stop at nothing to destroy slavery the world over. In another August 1841 Senate speech, Benton accused the British government of supporting "the organized attempts now made in London to excite a negro insurrection in our Southern States" and argued that the Senate should lead the American protest against such an outrageous policy.[8]

If Tyler and Webster had calculated that Everett, with his Northern base and mixed record on slavery, might give both North and South a mix of reassurance and alarm, they miscalculated for the Southern Democrats in particular. There had been minor rumblings of concern in the South when Everett pursued an antislavery line as governor. Scattered Southern Democratic sheets painted the Whig Party as the party of abolition based in part on Everett's 1839 letter to Nathaniel Borden. Even a Whig paper in Richmond ruefully held up Everett's antislavery electioneering tactics as sad evidence of the progress of abolitionist principles in the North. Everett's election-year letters came as no surprise to John C. Calhoun. As early as 1836, this maven of Southern rights had admonished his fellow Southerners that their apparent friends would prove unreliable so long as they were tied to the two-party system, because the abolitionists would prove a decisive swing vote in closely contested elections that Northern party men would always placate.[9] Everett had proven alarming confirmation of Calhoun's dark prophecy.

But the Southern response to Everett's swing toward antislavery was tepid and isolated while he was governor compared to when Tyler nominated him for the London post. At first slaveholders expressed their concerns privately. In early August, Southern rights sentinel Abel P. Upshur groaned in a letter to a fellow Virginian that there could be "no excuse" for Tyler's "abominable" appointment of Everett. "The present condition of the country," he preached to this choir member, "imperiously requires that a Southern man and slaveholder should represent us at that court. . . . And yet a Boston man is appointed, half school-master, half priest, & whole abolitionist!" Later in the month, Upshur reiterated privately that he hoped to rally a state rights party in the South behind "that appointment to the Court of St. James," which constituted "an insult to the whole slave holding country."[10] With this sort of determination to use this foreign policy appointment to further a Southern domestic agenda, it was no wonder that Southern Democrats and other Southern proslavery politicians came out against Everett in the Senate.

As those Senate debates were private, it was up to leading Southern Democratic newspapers to lay out the full case against Everett. That case rested first and foremost on the stakes involved in this particular appointment. Sending someone like the former governor, who "stands fully and publicly committed" to an antislavery position on domestic issues "while a Crusade is proceeding in that country against our Domestic Institutions," would be unacceptable. British abolitionists had hosted the inaugural World Anti-Slavery Convention in

London in 1840, and influential Southern Democratic editor Thomas Ritchie asked that in the event of another such convention, "who will guarantee that the Resident Minister will not co-operate with it, perhaps take his seat at the foot of Prince Albert?" Put such a way, few slaveholders could contemplate Everett taking his place in London without a shudder. It was disturbing enough to William Rufus King of Alabama that he told the Senate in debate that "the Union would be dissolved" if it confirmed a man "holding views in opposition to the South" to this particular post.[11] There was deep irony in this picture of Everett encouraging slave revolts given how his Northern opponents had used his 1826 knapsack speech against him, but Southern Anglophobia ran roughshod over such nuance.

Southern party politics also helped fuel the controversy. The Whigs, Southern Democrats gleefully charged, were so desperate that they were "ready to kiss the hand that is raised to shed their blood."[12] Southern Whigs were not about to let such characterizations of their party go unchallenged. One part of the twin Southern Whig strategy in this debate was to deny that Everett was a dangerous abolitionist, usually by shifting the focus to Everett's congressional career.[13] Other Southern Whigs, however, standing on the logic of national parties and the desirability of preserving the Union, argued that the Southern Democrats' course was reckless in the extreme. In the Senate, Henry Clay was reported to have upbraided Southern Democrats for their "selfish and suicidal course." Gesturing dramatically to King of Alabama, Clay warned that if this opposition to this candidate for this reason prevailed, "*we have no longer any Union to dissolve!*"[14] The *Richmond Whig* led this charge outside of Congress, hectoring its fellow party sheets in the South not to "play into the hands of the Locos" and the abolitionists with "this fresh firebrand, which may ignite the fabric of Union."[15]

Northern Whigs' reaction to the Southern Senators' delay of Everett's nomination was actually angrier even than this Southern debate. Everett's own camp, quite naturally, was agitated by the controversy. Everett's friend and Massachusetts Whig operative J. H. Clifford told Winthrop that on a recent visit to Boston "[I] had my ears filled and my heart made heavy with rumor and confidential communications from Washington" about Everett's imminent rejection, among other matters. Clifford himself could not "think of it with any patience," at once for party, patriotic, and personal reasons.[16] But more than the Bostonians Clifford conversed with found themselves outraged by the whole affair. Private citizens and politicians throughout the North registered their indignation.[17] Northern Whig newspaper editors, however, loudly led the charge. Shocked that the eminently qualified and nationalistic Everett would prove obnoxious as an alleged abolitionist, they warned that Everett's rejection would constitute an affront to the entire North.[18] Some Northern Whig writers were sufficiently embittered by the prospect of the nomination's demise that they welcomed the sectional confrontation. A Boston editor warned darkly that "the FREE states may begin *now* to do what the SLAVE states professed to do some years ago — viz.: *to calculate the value of the Union.*" A widely reprinted New York editorial agreed that the central issue here was similar to that involved with the Gag Rule: Northerners should have "all the rights and privileges of citizens," and the Senate was depriving Everett of his with its litmus test. "Beware, we say, of making such an issue with the North," for if they did, "we trust it will be met as FREEMEN ought to meet it."[19]

Few Northern Democrats evinced much eagerness for this fight. The idea of a Whig nominee suffering delay or rejection was desirable in the abstract, but to see this turn into a sectional controversy in which their own party acted visibly for slavery could turn disastrous. When dealing with the Everett issue, most emphasized partisan rather than sectional reasons to oppose him.[20] Other Northern Democratic editors dipped a toe into the troubled waters of antislavery politics by insisting that Everett was receiving his just deserts for dabbling with abolitionists. Still others sought to deny Everett antislavery martyrdom by highlighting his anti-abolitionist record. One editor managed to survey both sides of Everett's treatments of slavery, in order to pan his "inconsistent course" on the issue.[21] This range of depictions showed how complex and dangerous this issue could be for Northern partisans. It was hard for most Northern Democrats to see how they could win, no matter how the Everett affair turned out.

Abolitionists themselves were of a divided mind about the whole issue. Some had never trusted Everett and thus gloated that he was getting what he deserved from his quondam Southern friends. This echoed another abolitionist refrain: that this was the sort of treatment abolitionists had long warned Northerners that they could expect from their Southern allies. Despite Northerners' mobocratic efforts to show "our *loyalty* to the South," William Lloyd Garrison gloated, when they nominated a qualified candidate like Everett, "*our* Southern task-masters cannot grant us even *this reasonable* indulgence." But beyond saying "we told you so," abolitionists encouraged the sectionalist response to this debate. Garrison enthused that Southerners "may find, when it is too late, that they have . . . waked up the wrong passenger."[22]

The battle over Everett ended with a whimper when the Senate confirmed Everett's nomination, but it took some doing by Whigs in Congress to make that happen. The fact that Tyler stood behind Everett's nomination, and especially that Clay led the Senate fight for it, helped the cause greatly. As late as 12 September, a straw poll suggested senators were split 24–24, so Whigs delayed the vote to the next day, the last day of the session. The result of this and other maneuvering was a largely partisan, rather than a sectional, vote.[23]

A crisis that never reached full crisis stage, the Everett nomination fight nevertheless revealed much about the antebellum politics of slavery. It also foreshadowed the tensions he would experience with the Tyler administration once confirmed. To the watchdogs of Southern slavery, concerns for slavery's future were real rather than contrived, which was why they were so politically useful. So while Northerners might lodge largely private protests that the northeastern boundary controversy meant their interests would best be served by sending a Northern man to the Court of St. James, even this persistent and sharp regional issue paled in comparison with the long-standing fervor with which Southern slaveholders defended slavery. And in formulating that defense, they saw the state, national, and international levels of American politics as one seamless web that might entrap slavery. The threat to slavery posed by the feared British juggernaut only raised the stakes for defensive Southern slaveholders. In this context, as in others throughout his career, the plight of the moderate was to be deeply suspected by both antislavery and proslavery extremists. Many Southern Whigs had resisted this logic during the nomination fight, but they were not the brand of Southerners under which Everett would serve in London. Accordingly, his nomination fight served as a prologue to the ways in which the Southern practitioners of domestic-cum-international politics of slavery would scrutinize his every action and even his tone as ambassador.

———

All that was in the future, however, and what Everett experienced for much of 1841 was a protracted uncertainty over whether this mortifying opposition would prevent him from the plum post. When apprising him of the nomination, those in Everett's inner circle advised him to expect an easy confirmation, with opposition only from the most factious of Democrats.[24] But Everett's realism about his record spared him from the shock they experienced. Upon receiving word of his nomination, he repeatedly registered his skepticism that he would be confirmed. More precisely, he wrote that he "should not be surprized if some opposition—perhaps successful—should be made to it from the South." He was unsure enough of confirmation that he planned his travels as if he were not going to London anytime soon.[25] He tried to see benefits in his expected rejection, listing in his diary the political minefield and financial sinkhole he would avoid by being denied the job. Likewise, his friends back home submitted that the sympathy for him aroused by the opposition might do him long-term political good. But he ultimately bought neither of these weak attempts to spin the ordeal as a positive thing. "The mortification is severe" from a personal point of view, he admitted. He lamented the idea that any Southern Whig would join others in a course that "blasts my political prospects forever." He and his wife both grumbled that this proved that "the career of a states-man is a thankless one."[26] The stakes were clearly high for him personally and politically: either vindication and occupying the prized position in London, or personal humiliation and political ruin.

When Everett received authoritative word of his confirmation in mid-October, his relief and gratitude were palpable. He left Naples for London the day after receiving reliable (if not yet official) word. His subsequent letters also expressed genuine appreciation for Whig allies who had worked so vigorously to defend him in a "battle" that had been so full of "peril." As late as 1844, Everett clipped out of the newspaper a piece trumpeting details of Clay's successful defense of Everett in the Senate. Everett especially took heart when he learned through Webster of President Tyler's unwavering support.[27]

The eager new minister threw himself immediately into his new position. Arriving in London exhausted late at night on 18 November, he was greeted by a table "covered with letters—parcels—& papers, the accumulation of the month which had elapsed" since his predecessor had left London. He also lacked the assistance of a secretary. But aided by "a cup of strong tea," he read through that entire pile that night. When he finally went to bed, "[I] threw myself on my knees, & prayed for strength to support the great burden. That night I slept but little," he recalled in later years. But "at 6 o'clock the next morning I was in the office; by 12 every thing was filed away & put in train; several of the letters answered; & a note despatched to Lord Aberdeen, that I was ready to present my credentials."[28] This was classic Everett: especially when he felt a sense of mission, his work ethic was indomitable.

The day after sending his note to British foreign secretary Lord Aberdeen, the two had a meeting that got their relationship off to a flying start. In this conversation on Aberdeen's turf at the Foreign Office, Aberdeen won Everett over when he "received me with great ease and courtesy & placed me at once at my own ease." In the course of the interview Aberdeen expressed his friend-liness to America and its ministers and his desire to adjust Anglo-American difficulties and to respect American sovereignty. For his part, Aberdeen had been informed of Everett's "mild, calm & conciliating manner & temper" even before he had arrived in London. Prepared for an amicable beginning, he was not disappointed.[29]

The immediate warmth between Everett and Aberdeen mirrored an over-all change in personnel in both London and Washington that could not have been more fortuitous for Anglo-American rapprochement. In Washington, Tyler continued the recent history of Anglophobic presidents, but Webster had recently traveled in England and came to office convinced that the serious issues dividing the two countries could be solved rather quickly by "men of sense." In London, a new Tory ministry led by Sir Robert Peel had taken power in September 1841. Peel ceded full control over foreign policy to Aberdeen, who quickly determined that a special mission to the United States would be necessary to resolve Anglo-American controversies. He sent to Washington Lord Ashburton, whose personal and financial relationships with Americans predisposed him to a pacific stance. As important as the new personnel was the group they replaced. In the late 1830s London had become a scene of repeated clashes between Foreign Secretary Lord Palmerston and the American minister Andrew Stevenson, a Democrat from Virginia, both of whom were avatars of a hard-line policy to the rival power. So frayed had this relationship become that Palmerston hesitated before allowing Stevenson the standard exit audience with the Queen.[30]

Everett in particular would prove a breath of fresh air to Britons after Steven-son's antics. Arriving in 1836 after four years in which the United States had gone unrepresented by an official ambassador in London, Stevenson's pugnacious style left open the question of whether his presence was better than no minister at all. Soon after Everett arrived in London, an acquaintance informed him that neither the legation's secretarial staff nor the administration had felt they could leave Stevenson to act on his own initiative, "for fear he would commit some indiscretion." Their fears were not groundless. Reports of his activities between 1836 and 1841 featured such soothing items as Stevenson challenging Irish statesman Daniel O'Connell to a duel. When O'Connell publicly vented his disgust at the United States' "vile union of republicanism and slavery" and painted Stevenson himself as "a slave breeder" and thus "a disgrace to human nature," Stevenson impulsively dashed off a challenge. O'Connell deflected it but refused to apologize for his remarks, and the bitter exchange played itself out in the press in both Britain and the United States. Only those who shared Stevenson's Southern machismo lauded him for standing his ground.[31] Indeed, throughout his time in London Stevenson struck his most strident poses in defense of slavery. His lectures to British ministers about American sovereignty on the high seas and his insistence on indemnity for American slaves freed in the West Indies took a consistently bellicose tone.[32]

Especially in matters of style Everett set out to be what came most naturally

Portrait of Edward Everett by George P. A. Healy, c. 1842–43. This depiction from his London years captures the amiableness of the middle-aged Everett. Courtesy of Newberry Library, Chicago.

to him: the anti-Stevenson. Even before being nominated for London, Everett had determined that the "functionary" Stevenson "ought, in my humble opinion, to have been long ago removed, for entire incompetency to discharge the most important duties devolving on him." So both in writing and in person, Everett assured both Aberdeen and Peel that "my confidence" in their administration "is unlimited & entire." Beyond Aberdeen, he cultivated friendships with leading intellectual and political figures in Britain, for whom his London residence became a center of convivial meetings. The impression made by his repeated visits to Queen Victoria and Prince Albert at their royal residences was clearly mutual. Everett's fulsome depictions in both diary and letters evinced how much he reveled in these sojourns with the royals. Meanwhile, Albert appreciated Everett's ability and willingness to converse about things German in German. Everett and his family spent Christmas holiday seasons at the country estates of the likes of elite writer and reformer Sydney Smith or Lord and Lady Ashburton.[33] Especially in Stevenson's wake and at this fraught period in Anglo-American relations, style mattered enormously, and Everett's effectiveness as ambassador soared as a result. Lady Ashburton spoke for many an elite Briton when she gushed to Webster in an unveiled contrast to Stevenson that Everett "is in every respect calculated to sustain the high opinion *now* entertained of American Statesmen."[34]

The love fest between Everett and Britain transpired in public as well as in salons and diplomatic offices. Even during the 1820s, Everett's public speeches had managed to strike a balance between American nationalism and deep filial "tenderness" and "reverence" for England. "It seems to me a classic, yea, a holy land," he had gone so far as to say, for the exact same ideological reason as why he loved the United States: England was "the only part of Europe, where, for any length of time, constitutional liberty can be said to have a stable existence." At agricultural fairs and scientific and literary gatherings in Britain, he wooed his audiences with heartfelt gratitude that he found himself in "another native country, if I may so call it,—the country of my fathers." He stressed the common ground between two nations "ardently, passionately attached to liberty" as "enshrined in constitutions, and organized by laws."[35] Britain's public men—including the editor of the *Edinburgh Review*—responded with similar pieties, and Everett was feted and heaped with honorary degrees from Manchester to Cambridge to Dublin.[36] This public coziness opened Everett to the gibes of Democrats back home, but these proved mild, and friendly editors parried them rather easily. They annoyed Everett, who did worry about his image at home, but hardly dissuaded him from his charm offensive.[37] Both Everett and certain key Britons had come a long way since the Literary War.

As the setting for these love feasts suggests, the reformer Everett found himself very much at home in this, the seat of the Benevolent Empire. He conceived of the United States and Britain as together in the van of "the advancing civilization of the present century," bound by literary ties and scientific efforts in the cause of improvement. At every opportunity, Everett went to see the British version of the spirit of improvement up close. He found enormous moral grandeur and even beauty in what he saw, whether a model school or an electric telegraph. His diary musings on moral quandaries multiplied during his time in London, and by his own admission his commitment to the whole project of reform likewise increased in this clime. "In my youthful days," he confessed to his diary in 1845, he had "exceedingly opposed" the Benevolent Empire's "missionary operations[,] deeming them at best wholly useless." But now "I hear nothing but good of them all over the world . . . not in the way of gaining converts to any particular theological opinions but in scattering the seeds of general civilization, establishing schools, and teaching the elements of human knowledge." He was also taken in by the spirit of economic and technical improvement he saw in the home of the Industrial Revolution, at one point enthusing that the steam engine allowed for such progress "without the crimes and woes of slavery." What is more, he found in British-style reform the mirror image of the American Whig ethic of improvement and respect for law and order. Both political persuasions aligned with his preference for "moral improvement by gentle means, in distinction from sudden changes under violent influences."[38]

If Victorian Britain's moral loftiness and spirit of progress stirred Everett's heart, however, the harsh realities of its class system tore at it. His feelings were so tender that he could not bring himself to approve of fishing as a sport, and the yawning social gap in Britain gave him much more than aquatic distresses over which to brood. During a cold snap, he worried that "the sufferings of the houseless poor must be extreme. The problem presented by the frightful inequality of conditions in all parts of the world & particularly in this country, where the extremes are so fearfully contrasted, is that which most tasks the human mind." He doubted whether "such an enormous disparity [was] necessary" as the price of "the high State of civilization which prevails" in England. British reformers of various social stations thus saw in Everett a fellow laborer in the good cause. For them, if Stevenson had been the Ugly American in every way, Everett was the Good American presenting a liberal, humane face.[39]

This meeting of the minds extended to slavery, on which Everett's thoughts continued to harmonize with the moderate brand of British antislavery thought. As with reform questions in general, Everett's private ruminations on slavery and abolition proliferated during his European residence. While in Paris Everett read Gustave de Beaumont's recently published book *Marie*, which was meant to be a novelistic sociological study of racism in the United States. When finished with it Everett faulted Beaumont for shedding no light "on the great practical question, what is the remedy for the existing evil of Slavery." On that question, Everett still believed "that the emancipation of the Slaves in the West India Islands will do very much to promote the abolition of Slavery in the United States," in this case "by holding out a convenient place of refuge for the free negro," whom Beaumont had shown to be so persecuted.[40] While in London his commitment to British-style emancipation did not flag. Pondering how little the world had embraced true religion, he listed slavery in the catalog of "crimes, & sorrows which seem to call to heaven for a remedy." He marveled that white Southerners could not "perceive that this institution is too shocking an anomaly to exist much longer." That faith in slavery's ultimate demise, however, was part of what kept Everett from agitating the issue himself. In 1844, when learning of a Louisiana planter who allowed his slaves to work for their freedom, he thought that "such a measure can hardly be called generous" because it took these people fifteen years to save enough. But unlike "the

Abolitionists" who rebuked this planter, Everett considered that "as the world goes it is not to be denounced." He found himself somewhere between the parsimonious planter and the punctilious purists on the antislavery spectrum.[41]

Evidence of the distance he had traveled on that spectrum from his knapsack days emerged in a remarkable extended interchange with British colonial secretary Lord Stanley in November 1842. Stanley had begun with many other British statesmen to fear for the stability and prosperity of the great experiment in free labor ongoing in the post-emancipation British West Indies. He approached Everett with a scheme to encourage free blacks from the United States to immigrate to British Caribbean islands to help solve the chronic labor shortage there. The operation of this project would require a strong and visible administrative presence from the British government, meant both to protect the immigrants against entering into "a qualified slavery" in their plantation destinations and to prevent American slaves from taking advantage of the program to illicitly gain their freedom. That would mean posting British officials to key ports, such as Baltimore and Charleston, to certify the freedom and regulate the labor contracts of would-be immigrants. Stanley rightly judged that this might "excite jealousy, or be deemed objectionable," in many an American mind, which is why he approached Everett for advice.[42]

Everett's response showed how far removed he was from Southern sensibilities. He agreed with Stanley that the scheme would not require formal approval from the U.S. government to go forward and "thought that the plan might safely be put in operation at Baltimore, Charleston, and New Orleans." The only prudential consideration he urged with any force was "that it would be wise to avoid making a great parade of drawing Labourers from the United States." But on the whole, "he expressed himself friendly to the removal, and said he looked upon the British West Indies as the natural resort of the coloured Population of the United States" since the Americans' own experiment in Liberia seemed to be failing. For Everett, this proposal promised to help rescue two causes that had been dear to his heart for varying lengths of time: the colonization of free African Americans, and the British emancipation experiment. Whether oblivious to or ignoring Southern anxieties, he did not detect a problem in this plan for British emissaries to interact with African Americans in key Southern ports (two in the Deep South), unless a slave ever escaped as a result. This was almost incredibly obtuse in the context of Anglo-American slavery politics in the 1840s, which had conditioned almost all white Southerners to reflexively distrust all British actions in advance. Ironically, it was left to Lord Aberdeen to point out the political realities to both Stanley and Everett. Stanley's recommendation to put the scheme into operation without securing the official sanction of the U.S. government, beginning "with Orders in Council, and publick acts in the Colonies," would "not improbably render the American Govt hostile to the whole project."[43] The project went nowhere, but Aberdeen had not improbably averted an Anglo-American flashpoint of Stanley's making and Everett's acquiescence.

———

This episode was all the more curious because Everett so often demonstrated jealousy for his country's sovereignty and reputation throughout his time in London. If anything, his travels through Europe had made him a stauncher republican than ever. Though proud of the number of royals and aristocrats with whom he mingled, he came away convinced that "the average character of our elective American rulers is altogether superior to that of their heredi- tary contemporaries in Europe." His reverence for the only chief elective ruler whom he had not personally met, George Washington, continued in full force. In 1840 he stayed with Lafayette's family in France, marveling at relics of the Revolutionary icon and reveling in his connection to Washington. He also spread the gospel of Washington abroad, if less often and more subtly than in his public orations at home. He kept a portrait of his hero in his London office, which became a conversation starter with visiting dignitaries. In exchange for portraits of the royal family, he gave Victoria and Albert—boldly enough, given that she was a relative of George III!—what Albert called an "interesting relic of the illustrious Washington."[44]

His time in Europe also confirmed his views of the paramount importance of preserving the Union. From this vantage point he came to a keener appreciation of how Anglo-American controversy helped feed "the violence of our domestic feuds"; peace on one front would help secure peace on the other. Moreover, mingling with European liberal reformers only convinced him further of the transatlantic stakes involved in the American experiment in self-government. They, like he, grieved at the partisan and sectional dangers to the Union, which represented "the best hopes of human happiness and freedom."[45] To be sure, he made certain that his home audience knew him as an American nationalist rather than a weak-kneed Anglophile. But Everett's American nationalism was undoubtedly as sincere as it had ever been. He took umbrage at how the Brit- ish press put "the worst interpretation" on all American actions and overrated the superiority of British society. He did not take much solace in the fact that "on all public & private occasions I find the greatest cordiality of reception." The well-disposed Britons' treatment of him did not fully make up for the fact that "the entire press is more or less hostile" to his country.[46] As both an

Anglophile and a committed American nationalist, such national insults bit at least as harshly as they had during the Paper War. So he exulted when American sculptor Hiram Powers's statue of a Greek slave became a sensation in London in 1845. On the other hand, he fretted from afar at the progress both abolitionism and proslavery seemed to be making in American politics, "in which lies the germ of much future difficulty,—perhaps separation of the Union & Civil War."[47] He looked on this possibility with as much terror from his European vantage point as he had at home.

In London as in Boston or Washington before it, then, Everett's commitments to reform, the Union, and the global cause of liberty constituted a complex stew in which various flavors asserted themselves more strongly at times than at others. His occupational loyalty to the Tyler administration likewise contended with his commitments to Anglo-American comity and to personal amity with British officials. During his time as ambassador, a full range of slavery-related Anglo-American conflicts mingled so thoroughly with questions of American sovereignty that Everett's task proved delicate in the extreme. He proved a good soldier for the most part in advocating his slaveholding republic's policy on slavery-related issues, but his heart was in it only when he felt its sovereignty and reputation were the crux of the particular matter. His superiors in Washington were prone to exaggerate his ambivalence, but his hints to Aberdeen and others that he was a reluctant soldier on these matters were real.[48]

Everett found to his chagrin that questions that appeared minor gained incredible staying power and significance from even the most tenuous connection to slavery. Throughout his term, for instance, he carried on what was to both him and Aberdeen a wearisome negotiation concerning the British duties on imported American rough rice. Specifically, the British government levied a higher tariff on imports of the grain from America than from West Africa, because slave labor produced the former but not the latter. The early 1840s proved a high point in the partisan use of slavery in British politics, as Palmerston's Whigs and Aberdeen's Tories repeatedly sought to put the other on the low ground on this issue. In this period even more than in others, scholar Richard Huzzey has written, opposition leaders took "an opportunistic attitude" toward any potential "anti-slavery crises"; "in government, therefore, a defensive posture was essential." Moreover, in this era of British politics all duties became intertwined with raging debates over repealing Britain's Corn Laws. In these debates, free traders reviled protectionists for placing an antislavery tariff on New World sugar but not on American cotton. So the rough rice duties would shore up the Peel ministry's claims to antislavery consistency. This policy, of course, offended Southerners in Washington and beyond, confirming their hatred of British antislavery foreign policy. The Tyler administration therefore pushed constantly for Everett to combat this tax.[49] Both Everett and Aberdeen played good cop on this issue and made other officials in their respective governments out to be bad cops. On rough rice as on cases of American ships seized off the coast of Africa, Aberdeen assured Everett privately that he would adjust British policy to meet American demands if he could but that the Treasury tied his hands. Everett powered through the multiple remonstrances on this issue his job required of him but once back in America joked with Aberdeen "that you will open a note from me with some satisfaction, now that you are sure it is not about 'Rough Rice'" or other such pesky affairs.[50]

Less surprising to Everett and of more obvious significance was the ongoing Anglo-American feud over cooperation to abolish the slave trade and the concomitant question of the right of search. Everett found his approach to this problem in accord with Webster's but at variance with those of other diplomats in Europe and of other administration officials. He and Webster's view scored a temporary victory in 1842 with the Treaty of Washington, but in the longer term Everett had to accede to the rival position.[51]

At stake for both governments were questions of national security and morality that would prove difficult to compromise. Driven in large part by the domestic politics of slavery in Britain, the early 1840s marked a high point in Britain's commitment of money and diplomatic energy to suppressing the transatlantic slave trade. The diplomatic initiative focused on securing the cooperation of the five major European maritime powers against the trade, and in a perfect world for any British administration it could secure the United States' consent to such a scheme as well. The politics were also difficult in Britain because most Britons saw the ability to impress British-born sailors—no matter whose flag they were found sailing under—into the Royal Navy as a bulwark of their empire. Thus in the 1830s successive governments proved impervious to British reformers' efforts to abolish the practice. As Aberdeen told Everett, his government had "no expectation" of exercising the practice of impressment, but it was "difficult to renounce it" as a right.[52] For decades, American officials and public opinion had responded with spread-eagle nationalist hostility to all British proposals for slave trade cooperation that involved the right to board and search vessels flying the American flag.[53] This stance proved so popular that even American diplomats not serving in England weighed in on the issue during Everett's tenure. Henry Wheaton, U.S. ambassador to Berlin and an authority on international law, and Lewis Cass, U.S. ambassador to Paris and aspiring Democratic presidential candidate, both published pamphlets encouraging American and French resistance to the British abolition scheme. In their narratives, Britain's drive for slave trade abolition was a thinly veiled adjunct to its imperial drive for power, and the United States wanted only to defend its sovereignty. Cass publicly attacked his boss Webster as too soft on this issue and gave it as his reason for resigning in 1842. Press coverage of these pamphlets praised their defense of America against the machinations of the jealous, "arrogant" British superpower. "Whenever Great Britain shall decide to have a war with this country," thundered one Whig reviewer, "she has only to attempt" to exercise the right of search.[54]

Meanwhile, Webster proved willing to think outside this box. Ashburton shook the secretary of state by pressing him on "whether America could remain in the position of refusing all remedy against crimes which they had been the most vehement to denounce." Furthermore, as one committed to Anglo-American peace, Webster hoped to "escape all future collision, or disputes, about the right of search." While hunkered down with Ashburton seeking a solution to this knotty problem, Webster fended off Cass. He did so by assuring him that President Tyler approved of his zeal for American sovereignty but rebuffing his interference by highlighting other considerations, including the United States' international duties as a maritime power, and by apprising him that "the whole subject is now before us here," where negotiations belonged.[55]

Webster proved more receptive to Everett's pleas on the other side of the debate. Within a month of arriving in London, Everett informed Webster that "Lord Aberdeen disclaims, in a more distinct manner than it has ever been done, all right to search, detain, or in any manner interfere with American Vessels, whether engaged in the Slave Trade or not." He was sanguine that this tack would remove "this subject of irritation" from Anglo-American affairs. The likes of Cass would have seen this as far too trusting in British good faith. But Everett also verified this disposition in Aberdeen and hoped to further it by pressing hard for compensation for American ships wrongfully seized off the coast of Africa. He saw this as a matter of respect for American sovereignty, which was as important to him as preserving America's good name as an opponent of the slave trade.[56] In light of Aberdeen's attitude, he pushed Webster to consider, "is it out of the question for the United States to come into the agreement with the Five Powers?" It would certainly redound to America's "honor" to make "common cause with them" before the "tribunal" of "the whole civilized world." Surely Webster and Ashburton could find a formula for cooperation that would not harm "our interests," he thought.[57]

Everett was deeply gratified when he saw how the Webster-Ashburton

Treaty dealt with this question. Article 8 of the treaty provided for the American and British navies to conduct joint operations off the coast of Africa, obviating the specter of British officers boarding American ships, which even a joint right of search would have raised. Aberdeen told Everett that he would be attacked in the British papers for conceding this unusual method of cooperation to the Americans. Everett assured Aberdeen that this was the only workable solution, for while "I individually was not hostile to such a qualified mutual right of search," Americans in general "could not bear their [British] officers in our ships." He congratulated Webster that the treaty's "mode of disposing of the African question is capital," although adding that Congress should go further by passing "a law forbidding the building and equipping ships for the Slave-trade."[58]

In reality, however, the treaty had dodged the question of whether British officers might visit ships flying the American flag, and President Tyler's interpretation of that issue triumphed over Webster's and Everett's. Senate Democrats, led by Missouri's Thomas Hart Benton, pressed the administration on whether the proposed treaty would by implication allow this right to board. Tyler responded by interpreting Article 8 as a British renunciation of any right of visit. Although he had to accept the joint naval scheme as part of the treaty, he would construe it as narrowly as possible. Everett, Webster, Ashburton, and Aberdeen all would have preferred to gloss over this question in the interests of securing the treaty's ratification in both Congress and Parliament.[59] But the president's position was bound to prevail on the American side of the equation, and when Webster resigned in 1843, he appointed a new secretary of state, Abel P. Upshur of Virginia, who shared Tyler's attitude toward Article 8. As secretary of the navy, Upshur had made a clear statement of his and the administration's priorities in instructions to the commanders of the African squadron. "While the United States sincerely desire the Suppression of the Slave Trade," he averred, "they are not prepared to sacrifice to it any of their rights as an independent nation." Under Upshur's leadership as secretary of state, Everett had the disagreeable duty to tell Aberdeen that the United States would not even sign any "*joint* note of remonstrance to foreign powers against the admission of Slaves," despite Article 9 of the Treaty of Washington having stipulated that the two powers would indeed sign such a note.[60]

The American politics of slavery also thrust Everett into the role of reluctant warrior for the administration position on cases of American slaves freed by British West Indian officials, none more explosive than the case of the *Creole*. On 25 October 1841, this brig had left Richmond bound for New Orleans to sell tobacco and the 135 slaves on board. On 7 November on the high seas, 19 of them rose in revolt, killing some of the crew in the process. The majority of the slaves on board knew Virginia slaves who had gained their freedom on the British island of Nassau when their own slave ship had wrecked there the previous year, so the mutineers decided to sail there. Upon the ship's arrival, British colonial officials took the 19 into custody but otherwise charged forward in favor of freedom, allowing the other slaves to leave the ship. The American consul's reports to Webster painted the British officials as active rather than passive in this liberation, while the British government's own statements and rulings found that "it does not appear that the slaves were liberated by any act of British authority; but that being within the limits of British Territory, within which limits the consideration of slavery is not recognized by law . . . , there was no legal power to detain them."[61]

Either way, white Southerners' response to this nightmare scenario of black-on-white violence encouraged by officious Britons was predictable. Southern state legislatures passed thunderous resolutions in its aftermath, and while some demanded only financial restitution from Britain, others cried out that the administration must insist on "the restitution of the slave property . . . to their rightful owner or owners" and that "such demand should be enforced at all hazards." Led by Calhoun, Southerners in the U.S. Senate likewise clamored for strong action from the Tyler administration. By February 1842, Calhoun had lost all patience, railing that Webster's "apparent indifference" would only encourage British delay and calling for the Committee on Foreign Affairs to investigate the administration's dilatory course. Southern newspapers piled on, arraigning Everett and Representative John Quincy Adams alongside Webster for apathy at best toward Southern rights. "With an Abolition Secretary of State, an Abolition Chairman of the Committee of Foreign Affairs, and an Abolition Minister to England," groused an editor in Alabama, "the South stands but a poor chance of protection or regard."[62]

While the Tyler administration never called for the return of the actual mutineers, otherwise it pursued a vigorous course that would confound these Southern critics. Webster himself did feel a distinct lack of urgency in the *Creole* case, admitting in private letters to Everett that it was mostly Southern pressure—and in particular Calhoun's resolutions in the Senate—that called his full attention to it. It severely complicated his overall negotiations with Ashburton, in part because the British government had refused compensation for previous parallel cases. But while Ashburton had almost no wiggle room within British law, he also found that American politicians, in particular Tyler, proved extraordinarily obstinate on this case. Getting nowhere on this issue, the negotiators decided to punt by including only a very general agreement on the extradition of criminals as Article 10 of the treaty.[63]

That left London as the scene for the ongoing discussions of this issue, and Webster's 29 January 1842 instructions to Everett on the *Creole* case took center stage. In this role Webster branded the British assertion that the rebellious slaves were simply asserting their natural rights an "absolutely ferocious" doctrine that privileged loose notions of general humanity over considerations of law and international comity. Viewed from the latter perspective, he wrote to Everett, this was a "perfectly lawful" voyage whose human cargo was "recognized as property by the Constitution of the United States, in those States in which slavery exists." This and the "outrages" committed by the rebels meant that British officials should have restored the crew to command and sent the ship back on its way to New Orleans rather than liberated the slaves. "One can not conceive," Webster maintained, "how any other course" could be consistent with "the code regulating the intercourse of friendly States," which intercourse was at the heart of how "civilization has made progress in the world." Webster was frustrated by British politicians' apparently willful misinterpretation of the American position as asking for the return of the actual people involved rather than monetary remuneration, but in other respects he had made the administration's views unmistakably clear.[64]

The domestic political response to Webster's letter to Everett was as swift and divided as one might expect. Antislavery politicians and editors cried that Webster had inverted the natural order and disgraced his nation by seeking to make slavery protected nationally rather than only locally. In his diary, Adams lambasted Webster as "a heartless traitor to the cause of human liberty." Rather more publicly, Adams's ally Joshua Giddings resolved in the House of Representatives that the administration's policy was unconstitutional as well as "incompatible with national honor." The wrangling over these resolutions led to Giddings's resignation from the House.[65] The Northern public sphere outside of Congress likewise teemed with denunciations of Webster's doctrine. A group of Massachusetts abolitionists resolved that Webster "has betrayed the sacred cause of Liberty, and the interests of our country, . . . and forfeited the respect and confidence . . . of the friends of impartial liberty throughout the world." William Ellery Channing published a pamphlet decrying Webster's dispatch for committing "the free states to the defence and support of slavery." The letter "openly arrays us as a people against the cause of human freedom," he continued, ceding the moral high ground to antislavery Britain. Garrison's *Liberator* hammered Webster but also pointed out that the federal government's pledge "to protect slavery" everywhere made it impossible to talk about slavery as "a mere municipal institution — a local interest" with which Northerners had no right to interfere.[66]

Webster's defenders included Southerners of both parties and some Northern Whigs. His missive to Everett managed what had seemed almost impossible: it quieted even his sternest Southern critics. Southern Whigs crowed that Webster's able letter "shows how unjust" those critics were to question "the soundness of his views on the subject of our *peculiar* domestic institutions." But Southern Democrats confessed that the spirit of that letter "has most agreeably disappointed our expectations." And Calhoun even granted that such a letter would do all the more good because it had come from a Northern man.[67] Webster's rather uncomfortable Northern champions reminded readers that he served not as the defender of slavery or abolition but rather as "the representative of the whole country" to be governed by constitutional and international law. "Every true American in the north," they scolded, would realize that American sovereignty, not American slavery, formed the heart of this case. More plausibly, others characterized Webster's line as moderate and statesmanlike given that he demanded only compensation for the slaves in question.[68]

Webster's critics failed to train their fire on the recipient of his infamous dispatch. In fact, they hoped in light of Everett's growing antislavery reputation that he would refuse to convey Webster's shameful message to the British government.[69] He would disappoint them, beginning with his letter to Aberdeen upon receiving Webster's instructions. Framing his plea along Webster's lines of American slaveholders' property rights, he followed his boss into the murky logic of declaring the mutineers both property and Americans. While stressing above all American sovereignty and international comity, Everett added the conservative credo that in such matters "it is always necessary to proceed with extreme caution." He urged that such caution was in keeping with the spirit of the 1833 British emancipation law, with its gradualism and compensation for masters. If the British government had compensated its own subjects for the loss of their slave property, surely it should do so for American slaveholders.[70] Similar cases arose after Webster and Ashburton ducked the *Creole* question in their negotiations, such as in late 1843 when seven runaway Florida slaves made their way to freedom in Nassau, killing and robbing as they went. Everett faithfully followed Upshur's and Calhoun's instructions to continue to press the British to instruct West Indian colonial officials to respect American sovereignty and slave property, although he did filter especially Calhoun's proslavery effusions out of what he passed along to Aberdeen.[71]

Everett's Southern critics, however, would not have been reassured had they read his diary and other private writings relative to the *Creole* affair. In the winter and spring of 1842, at the height of tension over this issue, his notices of it lacked the passion he reserved for the cause of Anglo-American peace. He admitted that he kept strictly within the letter of Webster's instructions on the case. Only when contemplating the *Creole*'s bearing on American sovereignty did he show much initiative. He perceived a disparity in national respect, for instance, when noting that the British freed American slaves but not a group of Russian serf seamen recently arrived in London. Everett's accounts of his conversations with British officials about these cases of liberated American slaves did not record himself responding very energetically to their antislavery arguments. Some of those arguments proved quite telling, such as when Aberdeen twitted Everett for failing to apply the supposedly "self-evident truth" of the Declaration of Independence to the *Creole* rebels.[72] Everett also communicated his reluctance to pursue these cases in a revealing letter to Winthrop. When Winthrop complained of the heat Northern Whigs were taking for Webster's "ultra Slave paper" to Everett, Everett responded with a cogent and rueful statement of what was required of him as the representative of the slaveholding republic. "Is not the ultraism in the relation of Slavery itself?" he pushed back. If American law recognized slavery "at all, it must be recognized in all its incidents," so Webster really had no choice but to uphold this claim to property in his policy. "God grant," he concluded, "that this millstone may be taken from the neck of the country, in some peaceful & Constitutional way." Likewise, after drafting a report of his conversation with Aberdeen on the Florida case, he exclaimed in his diary, "Would to God Slavery were abolished."[73]

The Tyler administration's drive to annex Texas to the United States also caused Everett personal discomfiture in London and political harm back home. The fate of the new republic involved a complex mix of issues that had engrossed the attention of diplomats in Mexico, the United States, and Europe as well as in Texas since it had declared its independence in 1836. But from the Tyler administration's point of view, a prime reason to annex Texas was to protect it—and therefore the United States—from British meddling to abolish slavery there. Masses of Americans, mostly white Southerners and Democrats, shared this fear of British abolitionism in Texas. Although pursuing this anti-abolitionist foreign policy toward Texas risked raising the antislavery hackles of Mexico as well as of Britain, the Tyler administration pressed forward.[74]

Webster had dragged his feet on Texas in passive resistance to Tyler's wishes, but with Upshur and then Calhoun as his secretaries of state, Tyler had found men who shared his vision. That vision began with the strong conviction that Great Britain plotted for the abolition of slavery in the United States not for the stated philanthropic reasons but to hinder the Republic's rise to rival Britain on the world stage. Tyler dispatched the proslavery, Anglophobic newspaper editor Duff Green to London in 1843, and in a steady stream of letters to Upshur and Calhoun, Green fed their fears of British abolitionist schemings in concert with the British government. Green also went public with a passionate, somewhat rambling screed threatening war if British officials pursued their reckless abolitionist foreign policy in Texas—a war for which Upshur had been preparing since his days as Tyler's secretary of the navy.[75] British officials repeatedly disclaimed participation in any scheme to increase their influence, abolitionist or otherwise, in Texas. But in the spring of 1843 annexationists got valuable ammunition when it emerged publicly that Charles Elliott, the British envoy in Galveston, had been urging his superiors to use Britain's financial leverage to abolish both slavery and racial discrimination in Texas. Moreover, in December 1843 Aberdeen had avowed in a letter to the British minister in Washington (a letter he surely knew would go public) that "Great Britain desires, and is constantly exerting herself to procure the general abolition of Slavery throughout the World." He denied only that there was anything secretive about this foreign policy toward Texas or anywhere else. This was all more than enough to convince Tyler and both of his Southern secretaries of state that Texas "is, emphatically, *the* question of the day."[76]

Throngs of other Americans, mostly Northerners and Whigs, agreed with this assessment of Texas's significance but were alarmed by the prospect of annexation rather than by any antislavery British plot. Anti-annexation sentiment had risen in prominence in Everett's home state's politics since he had left. The state legislature passed a series of resolutions that influenced other states' statements. Everett's friend and U.S. senator from Massachusetts Rufus Choate delivered a scathing speech in which he declared that any man looking at Texas annexation "as a patriot, a Unionist, a statesman, a Christian, a lover of his kind" would reject it. A large Faneuil Hall meeting, which gathered everyone from conservative Whigs to abolitionists, decried both Tyler's proslavery intent and his unconstitutional means in pursuing annexation. "We know not," their resolutions thundered, "on what occasion bad objects have been more emphatically pursued by bad means." Once Webster left Tyler's cabinet he fought vigorously against the annexation project, hoping "all the North, will rise up, like one man, to oppose this abominable project." He advised Everett that if Tyler persisted in his Texas policy, it would unify especially Massachusetts, where the antislavery "Liberty party is constantly encreasing."[77]

Undecided on the merits of Texas annexation and caught politically between his home state and the administration he served, Everett felt true ambivalence on the issue while in London. Upshur and then Calhoun of course instructed Everett repeatedly on how to advance American claims in Texas and rebuff British ambitions there. This correspondence included Calhoun's April 1844 letter to British minister Richard Pakenham, which became notorious for its unabashedly proslavery rendering of American policy toward Texas. Everett conveyed these positions to Aberdeen, but his reports back to Upshur and Calhoun of these conversations were entirely devoid of commentary, and he was wont to speak in the third person about those who feared British motives and actions.[78] In late 1843, when Ashbel Smith, a Texas diplomat in London, confronted Everett with a report of Aberdeen stating that his government would guarantee only "the interest of a loan wh' should be raised & applied to the abolition of Slavery in Texas," Everett was predictably much slower to believe Texas backers' paranoia than Aberdeen's assurances.[79] Like other moderate Northern Whigs, however, Everett was unsure whether "the question of Annexing Texas is one of extending Slavery," given that slavery might thrive in Texas whether in or out of the United States. And the American nationalist in him bristled when Aberdeen suggested the complete illegitimacy of any surrender of Texas's sovereignty to the American Union.[80] Everett's attitude on his government's Texas policy, then, proved just as torn between competing preferences and allegiances as did his attitude on the full range of Anglo-American slavery issues during his time in London.

———

But the Tyler administration harbored no appreciation for infirmity of purpose on such issues. So especially when Webster left the State Department, Everett's relationship with his superiors was fraught with tension. Everett served under Webster until Webster's resignation in May 1843, then under Upshur from late July 1843 through Upshur's sudden death at the end of February 1844, then under Calhoun from 1 April 1844 through the end of the Tyler administration in March 1845.[81] While during Webster's tenure Everett obviously had a powerful ally and kindred spirit in Washington, even on Webster's watch President Tyler's suspicion of Everett began to increase. The veil over the administration's hostility to Everett grew thinner during Upshur's term and was practically nonexistent in Calhoun's.

The first sign of Tyler's distrust came in 1841 when Tyler sent the peripatetic Southern Jacksonian newspaper editor Duff Green on two missions to London as a quasi-official American counterspokesman to Everett. In 1843 Green returned in a similar guise to represent the administration's views on Texas and report back on British machinations. Much as the president valued the Webster-

Everett team's contributions to averting a war for which the United States was unprepared, he never lost the dread that Britain stood as an implacable obstacle to America's national destiny. So he sent Green under cover of seeking capital for Green's business ventures, apparently even keeping Webster in the dark about Green's true purpose. But soon after arriving in London, Green blew that cover by engaging in Stevenson-style proslavery anti-diplomacy.[82] Everett's diary and correspondence brimmed with animus toward Green. He feared the results of Green's rash proslavery political agenda and resented Green's indiscreet revelations of his status as a semi-official alternative American ambassador. Everett went so far as to aid his friend Sydney Smith in shaping his arguments in a press skirmish with Green.[83]

Nothing about Everett's course in London had disabused Upshur of the grave doubts about Everett's reliability on slavery he had entertained since the former's nomination. As he rose through the ranks of Virginia and national politics beginning in the early 1830s, Upshur had distinguished himself as a defender of slavery "as a great positive good, to be carefully protected and preserved." He had joined the Whig ranks to protest President Jackson's stern resistance to nullification. A true believer in Green's gospel of a British abolitionist conspiracy, he was a natural choice to succeed Webster and further Tyler's Texas project. Thus, while Green gave Upshur plenty of suggestions for direct commands to give Everett, Upshur needed little prompting to control Everett in this way.[84] In the fall of 1843, Upshur breathed his skepticism about Everett to political allies. "Mr. Everett I fear," he plainly told his political mentor Calhoun, "is from the wrong side of Mason & Dixon." America's ambassador in Britain should be "some one who understands domestic slavery as it exists among us, & who can properly appreciate its bearing, upon other great interests of the U States." "In the present condition of our affairs," he wrote to his Virginia crony Nathaniel Beverley Tucker, "Southern men ought to be at" both Paris and London, "particularly the latter."[85] He was slightly more subtle in his dispatches to Everett, hinting that the U.S. government must not look "with indifference" on the powerful antislavery British menace. He parroted many of Green's conspiracy theories and appeared to worry lest Everett be taken in by the ludicrous idea "that England is actuated in this matter by a mere feeling of philanthropy." He lectured Everett that "the question is not sectional" but rather "a national question" about which all Americans should care deeply.[86]

When Everett learned that a freak naval accident killed Upshur, he graciously expressed not only his condolences to President Tyler but also his support for Calhoun as the rumored replacement. But Everett had very little chance of working amicably with Calhoun, who like Upshur had vigorously opposed his nomination to London in the first place. Moreover, Calhoun had made a blend of Anglophobia and proslavery dogmatism the cornerstone of his political career. What is more, his framing of annexation as a proslavery measure brought his ongoing clash with antislavery Northern Whigs (with whom he associated Everett), as scholar John Ashworth has put it, "to crisis proportions."[87] While working under Calhoun, Everett continued to emphasize the Peel administration's good-faith efforts to preserve the peace. He granted that British public opinion against slavery "is powerful and unanimous to a degree perhaps unexampled" but believed Aberdeen could be trusted to balance that with "prudent" statesmanship so long as the United States did not pick unnecessary fights on "this important and delicate question."[88] Calhoun cared very little about the delicacy of the question from the British point of view, so such missives would have struck him as hopelessly milquetoast.

Both Calhoun and a legion of his political correspondents therefore grew in their conviction that Everett was unsuited to his position. A local politico from upstate New York counseled Calhoun that Everett was not the man to resist the sinister designs of the "Anti Slavery League in Europe." Though "a Gentleman of handsome literary acquirements," he lacked the necessary skill in the Machiavellian world of European diplomacy. Southern Calhounites, quite naturally, minced even fewer words. Remembering that Calhoun himself had called Everett "an unfit representative of this Country to Great Britain," an Alabama crony growled that "his tone is at best nothing more than apologetic on the Slave Question whilst all his secret *sympathies* are against us."[89]

Neither Calhoun nor Tyler seem to have considered removing Everett,[90] but the secretary of state did repeatedly attempt to yoke the diplomat to the task as Calhoun saw it. He worded his dispatches to Everett in tones of imperative command. "It is hoped," went one typical instruction, that "you will not fail to avail yourself" of a favorable moment "for pressing" the rough rice issue with Aberdeen. Doubting that Everett was properly exercised by Anglo-American slavery questions, he provided him with arguments with which to advocate the administration viewpoint. Such epistles, he confided to a South Carolina ally, were "calculated to make a strong impression" on the recipient. Calhoun did not hesitate to nag Everett about delays in negotiations, or even to declare his conversations with Aberdeen "very unsatisfactory." After reading one such report, he bade Everett "to urge a speedy decision, in strong and earnest language."[91]

Everett had his pride, and he chafed under such treatment. After Webster's departure, he rarely felt secure in his post, sure that Southern office seekers would convince Tyler to oust him. And some of Upshur's instructions to Everett on Texas made him want to quit before he was fired. But then, he confided in

Winthrop, he contemplated "what sort of a successor . . . this Administration" would send, and "how much mischief" he would do. So he decided to stay as long as he could do his job "without compromising my principles . . . on this most difficult of subjects." Even on a personal level, he complained to his diary, Upshur had treated him "in the most illiberal manner," including in restricting Treasury reimbursement for expenses that his predecessors had received without incident. Months after Everett's return to the United States, ongoing wrestling with the Treasury on this point caused him to remember his service under Upshur as "a yoke as mean & debasing as it is heavy."[92] Calhoun's term was no easier, of course. Everett's correspondence only thinly concealed his irritation at Calhoun's and his newspapers' questioning of Everett's dedication to the position. That forced him to defend his work via more friendly Whig papers in Washington. Soon after Calhoun's advent, Everett exploded in his diary that "to be the American minister at present is not the most enviable thing in the world," in part because he was "the representative of a Country little respected & a government not at all:—faithfully & laboriously serving an administration who so far from thanking and encouraging me, are vexed at my very fidelity & assiduity which leave them no decent reason to recal [sic] me."[93]

Everett found it hard to keep his resentment from taking on a sectional flavor, or even to keep it from bursting out in the most inconvenient circumstances. He still had staunch allies among Southern Whigs such as William C. Rives of Virginia, who advocated Webster's and Everett's policies in the Senate and whose son rendered valuable assistance to Everett as a secretary. But Everett gravely distrusted Calhoun's commitment to the Union. And under Upshur's regime he indulged in a deviance from his normal discretion in a remarkable conversation with Aberdeen. He told his friend that "I felt my situation here to [be] precarious in consequence of my not sharing fully the views of the present government in reference to Slavery." From a personal point of view, he confided, he would not mind being released from such a position, but "I feared I should have a successor less disposed than myself to maintain a good understanding between the two countries" if Tyler and Upshur were to install a man of their choosing.[94]

Everett had mixed feelings of a personal as well as a professional nature about staying in his London post. On the one hand, he loved London life, reveling in the intellectual as well as the social riches that London could uniquely provide. But as is often the case with sojourners in a foreign land, his most fulsome expressions of affection for Britain came upon his return home to America. In a note to Charles Sumner in 1846, for instance, he reminisced on one particular social gathering in England as "perhaps the most joyous occasion

I ever witnessed." And he gushed to Aberdeen that in contemplating his twenty years since running for Congress, the period "on which I dwell with the great satisfaction, is the time I passed in England; & I regard the friendships I there formed with wise & good men, as the best fruit of my public life."[95] But Everett's nostalgia filtered out substantial personal as well as professional adversity, for the later London years witnessed a terrible tragedy for the family in the death of twenty-year-old daughter Anne Gorham Everett in October 1843. "I have lost in her more than a dutiful & affectionate child," Everett confided to a correspondent, "for she has been for years, — young as she was, — my companion & friend." The loss of this child with which Everett had an unusually strong bond plunged him into deep and lasting despair.[96]

Everett's mind and heart were fully divided, then, during the drawn-out end game to his time as ambassador. Back in the spring of 1843, when Webster openly contemplated sending Everett to serve as the first U.S. minister to China so he could take his place in London after resigning as secretary of state, the proposed change had made Everett "perfectly sick at heart." He managed to rebuff Webster's maneuver without breaking with his friend and patron.[97] But by 1844, when confronting a change in the U.S. presidency, Everett's thoughts became less decided. In the spring, anticipating Henry Clay's election, Everett said he would "be very happy to continue in Europe" under the new president despite having realized "by experience, how little there is in a public career, in our Country, to gratify a generous ambition or reward honest service."[98]

When Democratic dark horse James K. Polk instead defeated Clay in November, that sealed Everett's eagerness to return to private life in Boston — sort of. Everett knew that even were Polk inclined to keep him on, the tension between him and the Tennessee Democrat's administration would be even worse than it had been with Tyler's. Friends in both Britain and America dissuaded him from resigning outright, but he told them he hoped to be recalled.[99] That recall was a long time coming, as Polk and his secretary of state, James Buchanan, approached four candidates before Louis McLane accepted the nomination in mid-June 1845. Not knowing anything of these difficulties, Everett took offense as well as suspense from the wait — "how shabbily they treat me," he whined in his diary. As the end drew so hesitantly near, he focused more and more on the burdens of the office. But his eagerness for a final resolution that would send him back home mixed with a flickering hope that Polk would have the wisdom to retain him because he was not a partisan hack seeking to advance his political career and because his "three years' experience . . . enables me to get along much better now than I did" when first arriving in London. When he finally received authoritative word of McLane's appointment in late

June, however, he expressed relief given McLane's well-known moderation and experience as a diplomat.[100] Everett and his remaining family spent weeks taking leave of friends in England and performing the material preparations to depart—including arranging for Anne's body to be shipped home with them—and then embarked from Liverpool on 4 September 1845.

It had been an eventful and revealing four years as U.S. ambassador for Everett. He prided himself on serving his country without reference to "the spirit of party" and still very much thought of himself as "a Northern man of moderate views" on slavery. But at least as much as when he was governor of Massachusetts, from his position in London that moderation took on a decidedly antislavery tinge. The nature of his service under Tyler, Upshur, and Calhoun hardly improved his opinion of Southern politicians. In fact, in 1845 he made the blanket statement that "the extreme opinions they all entertain carry them immediately to impracticable lengths, and prevent their confining themselves within the limits of the law of nations." As a result, he left office convinced that in advocating many of the Tyler administration's positions to Peel's administration, he had been doing "the business of the South" rather than simply the business of the nation.[101]

6

Harvard President and Semi-Private Citizen

Perhaps in no period of Edward Everett's life did the antislavery reformer and the conservative Unionist sides of him compete so equally than between his return from England and late 1852. Everett held no political office during these years, but he did not experience that fact as anything like a luxury. While he had very little power to directly shape political events, his opinion remained valuable public property, so he could never completely escape scrutiny. These years of struggle left Everett no more decided between these competing imperatives than he had ever been, illustrating yet again that his movement was rarely decisive, unidirectional, or predictable.

———

Anticipating Everett's return from England, his American friends and acquaintances pressed him to take up the presidency of Harvard College. The aged Federalist lion Josiah Quincy's time as college president was clearly winding down, and Harvard's trustees had long thought Everett eminently suited for this position of national prominence. But Everett took serious persuading. He had no stomach for either the theological controversies besetting Harvard or "the constant recurrence of acts of insubordination" for which its students (as indeed all students at the universities of the early Republic) were proverbial. "Controversy of all kinds," he reflected, "I have ever disliked; the older I grow the less I like it," so he feared that the twin forms of discord at Harvard would "make me wretched." But the powerful friends urging him to take the post were not to be trifled with. Though he had been contemplating this offer for months, weeks after returning to Massachusetts he remained "perfectly paralyzed" by indecision. Finally in late November 1845 he accepted the offer, and in February 1846 Harvard's Overseers made his appointment official.[1] One of the tragic patterns of Everett's life was that he detested controversy but repeatedly placed himself in the middle of some of the great Massachusetts, American, and Anglo-American controversies of his lifetime. While he had learned that was a recipe for misery, he had a very hard time turning down positions of prominence.

In none of the offices Everett accepted was he more miserable than as president of Harvard. The office's difficulties were of the petty, harassing variety and had none of the compensations of the cares of great statesmen. He found the state of discipline among the students and even the faculty far beneath his standards and spent almost all his time in the thankless task of trying to raise it. After passing one morning in the "hateful duties" of disciplining unruly students, he despaired in his diary, "Is this all I am fit for?" A typical diary entry described "another soul-killing day." In August 1846 "the care-worn expression" of a portrait of him struck him as apt, for "the period during which I have been sitting" for it "has been the least happy & joyous of my life." As he put it to his nephew, he had "undergone a complete intellectual paralysis, since I came here," thanks to the minutiae and grind of administrative life.[2] He felt the full length of the fall from dining with Queen Victoria to disciplining refractory young adults.

Such duties not only proved tedious but also involved Everett in painful conversations and correspondence with disappointed parents and provoked an unremitting attitude of confrontation from the student body.[3] His very inaugural ceremonies only confirmed that Everett would not be the students' president. The crowd of dignitaries was so great that students could not get into the inauguration dinner as they normally had. And Everett's inaugural address itself spoke more of Harvard's obligations to "the community in which we live" and even "the country" than of those to its students. This demonstrated Everett's keen understanding of Harvard's many constituencies, and as president he was sufficiently adept with the wealthier members of those groups to secure a new president's residence (courtesy of a donation from father-in-law Peter C. Brooks) and the founding of the Lawrence Scientific School (courtesy of manufacturing mogul Abbott Lawrence).[4] But none of that helped his relationship with students. They targeted him for pranks ranging from minor shenanigans—igniting firecrackers outside his home office, posting a caricature of Everett speaking—to rather more threatening acts, such as when someone ignited a large bundle of straw in the doorway of his house. As much as the persnickety president was asking for some of this, it is hard (at least for this university faculty member) not to sympathize with him. These attacks and other incidents of campus disorder routinely robbed him of a precious night's sleep. All this was even more exasperating because, as he confided in his nephew, "it was to get out of a life of constant tension & conflict, that I left politics, in the expectation of having things here in my own way. This," he concluded in a grand understatement, "proved too sanguine a calculation."[5] This post, then, proved the inverse of his time in London: instead of a glorious overall experience punctuated by adversity, it was an unhappy overall experience punctuated only occasionally by relief.

At its peak, Everett's dissatisfaction took the form of talk of resigning. In April, June, and July 1847, then again in the summer of 1848, he threatened to step down after particularly egregious episodes of student misconduct. He decided to stay on in the tenuous hope that he could make a difference to an institution that, after all, he did revere. But then in late November 1848, he made good on the threat. At the end of his last day as president on 11 January 1849, he experienced a flood of relief, only partially mingled with a limited sense of accomplishment. The whole ordeal had taken a severe toll on his health, as serious conflicts always would. So it was less than histrionics when he remarked in 1850, "That I ever consented to be President is a marvel to me. That I escaped with my life still more so."[6]

Quitting the presidency without any definite career prospects, Everett found his inclination to retire from public life reinforced by inheriting a large sum of money when Brooks died on the first day of 1849. Freed from his perceived need to find gainful employment, he could pursue the life of literary leisure for which he had long pined, and he indulged himself by building an ornate library in his new Boston home. But he also resented being forced away from "more active pursuits" by chronic health complaints. At the age of fifty-five, he found it hard to reconcile himself to the prospect of accelerating mental and physical decline. "I want cheerful stimulus," he moaned in his diary, and as he grew restless his standard ambivalence toward political participation increased rather than dissipated. "Can a good citizen be justified in refusing public life," he mused in early 1852, "in consequence of the dangers & disgusts which attend it? Socrates did so." His desire to have it both ways reached a new height in a letter to Daniel Webster in October 1850. "I am in no degree in the confidence of" Whig managers in Boston, he groused, who had not even approached Everett about taking the seat in the U.S. Senate that Webster had vacated when he again became secretary of state. "I could not & should not have accepted it," mind you, "but it ought . . . to have been offered to me."[7] Everett's long-anticipated semiretirement from public affairs into the literary life proved a blessing that was hard for him to take.

Coming into independent wealth expanded Everett's native philanthropic bent. He spent much of his now-free time by serving as an officer for a wide range of benevolent and scholarly organizations. He also felt a sense of moral steward-ship over his new wealth. In 1850 he consulted with the enormously popular singer Jenny Lind on how to dispose of the funds raised by her charity concert in Boston. He was inspired by her stated scheme of accumulating a fortune via her celebrity in order to donate it to charity. He took an active part in good works such as endowing a public library for Boston and gave generously to an increasing stream of visitors asking for donations for their particular causes.[8] Resisting meaningless platitudes in favor of organized work for change, he aided a host of causes that fell under the capacious umbrella of the Benevolent Empire. He was also open to persuasion by some of the more vigorous advocates of pacifism, vegetarianism, and the abolition of the death penalty.[9]

In true Everett fashion, he rejected what he judged to be extreme manifesta-tions of the reform spirit, even as he was willing to live a reformer's life when he did believe in a position. He lauded anti-abolitionist George Lunt's 1851 poem "The Dove and the Eagle," which attacked the restless spirit of monomaniacal do-gooders, as conveying "a moral of great importance." And in a conversation with a temperance advocate, Everett "was obliged to speak discouragingly of legislation in temperance matters," despite the other man's support for such laws. He reminded him of how politically toxic and counterproductive Massachu-setts's temperance law had been while he was governor.[10] But in his inaugural address at Harvard, Everett had praised "the divine law of temperance," and the fact that no alcohol was served at the post-inaugural festivities made national news. And in 1847 he quit a social club that provided him some of his only relaxation in Cambridge because "the weight of my precept & example, on the subject of Temperance is diminished by belonging to" a club "which once a fortnight has an elaborate supper with wine of five kinds." Rather than achieve reform through the force of law, Everett continued to search for the "means of producing moral improvement by gentle influences."[11]

Wrestling with student rascality at Harvard threatened to disillusion Everett with the whole cause of moral reform. He believed strongly in higher education as the pinnacle and vessel of civilization, but life as Harvard president seemed very far from those ideals. He worked endlessly to promote better conduct from the students and faculty by encouraging religious devotion among them. But half a year into this project, he had so little to show for it that he found himself "painfully agitated in mind all day as to the possibility of producing any deep effect on the conduct especially of the young by rational views of religion. — My experiences & observation scarcely allow me to hope for it." A few months later, he confided in his diary that "my opinion of human nature has been lowered the last twelvemonth." Although religion as practiced in New England was clearly not doing the trick, he held out hope that "some new Dispensation" of religion would reinvigorate Christianity there and beyond. And after six weeks' separation from the presidency, his spirits had rallied enough to conclude that "one good & great man is sometimes enough to redeem an age."[12]

What he witnessed in the world beyond campus also challenged but did not completely break Everett's optimism. Like so many other Americans, he followed with intense interest the rise and fall of revolutions in Europe beginning in 1848. But unlike most early American observers, Everett was skeptical of the outcome from the beginning and thus was not surprised at recurring reports of turbulence and popular injustice. Although his friend George Bancroft wrote to Everett from London in the spring of 1848 of his high hopes for Europe creating stable republics, Everett cautioned that if people tried to achieve "a safe practical liberty" by "abrupt revolutions the operation is almost sure to be bloody, fluctuating, & for the time disastrous." Even the American Revolution was no exception to this rule, given that political instability had plagued the early national period and had returned in the late 1840s. His was not a reactionary response, however; he only wished to counsel "the anxious friends of liberty in Europe" not to "be too sanguine nor too easily discouraged." He deplored in equal measure the social and political evils that had produced the revolutions and the wild course of those revolutions when "the mob which usurps the name of People" took over. "The remedy is worse than the disease" of contemporary Europe, he summed, "while the disease is intolerable." Everett's yearning for reforms rather than for revolution to redress real suffering resonated with a broad transatlantic group of reformers. He believed both Old and New England, with their common tradition of gradual legislative change and strong religious morality, had a role to play in stabilizing Europe. He stated flatly to an English friend that as he pondered the questions of political reform agitating in Europe, "were I an English subject, I should with my present feelings lean to" the "moderate conservatism" of the Whigs rather than to the reactionary stance of the Tories.[13]

Everett's Whiggish enthusiasm for the modern spirit of improvement kept him from a complete descent into crotchetiness. Although fretting occasionally that communications and transportation innovations made mid-nineteenth-century life more hurried, on the whole he evinced real eagerness for these advances. Before the advent of the telegraph, he gushed, "to transmit intelligence in an inappreciable space of time" had been "one of the attributes which we ascribe[d] to higher Spirits." Fascinated with the miracle of anesthesia, he pronounced it "the greatest discovery of the age; perhaps of any age." Moreover, "we have every reason to suppose that our arts & improvements brilliant as they are, are but child's play to those which will be made by our successors." And that was encouraging, for internal improvements not only "annihilated time and space" but also worked to bind the Union together.[14]

In short, in the late 1840s and early 1850s Everett may have seemed ready to veer off into old fogy-ism, but ultimately he sought and preached a balanced approach to questions of reform and improvement. In his public speeches, he argued that "the conservative element is as important in our natures and in all our relations as the progressive element. A wise, practical philosophy combines the two." "Heaven knows I am no enemy to progress," he intoned. "In my humble measure I have longed for it, and toiled for it; in reference to some deep questions, I have wept and prayed for it; but let it really be progress," which was "thoughtful, hopeful, serene, religious, onward, and upward." It was only by "the union of the two great principles of STABILITY and PROGRESS" that "the great designs of Providence in reference to our beloved country can be fulfilled."[15]

––––––––

Everett's search for a moderate position on the great reform questions of the day contributed to continued complexity in his views on racial equality. When contemplating racial equality in the abstract, Everett's views were decidedly mixed. He rejected the theories of inherent racial incapacities gaining greater currency in that era but also still considered the project of colonizing free African Americans to Africa "one of the noblest of the age." When confronted with actual free black people of manifest talent and character, Everett saw their humanity more than abstractions. As a congressman in 1828, for instance, he had found himself much impressed by the celebrated erstwhile African prince and freed slave Abd al-Rahman Ibrahima. In 1848, when the African American editor of the Albany, New York, newspaper the *North Star and Freemen's Advocate* asked Everett for a contribution, Everett sent a glowing biographical portrait of Ibrahima. He also offered to send sketches of other remarkable black men. The moral of stories like Ibrahima's, he taught, was that whites should learn "to respect the African race, as one whose best specimens will not suffer in comparison with our own."[16]

Everett put this meritocratic notion into practice while president of Harvard in the case of Beverly Williams. Beverly Garnett Williams had been born a slave but by some unknown process got his freedom and became the ward of an antislavery Baptist minister in Cambridge. That minister enrolled Williams in the Hopkins Classical School, a private school devoted to preparing boys for Harvard. Williams distinguished himself as the best Latin scholar at Hopkins and attracted Everett's attention in 1846 by performing unusually well at an examination Everett helped oversee. Everett was impressed enough that he employed Williams as a Latin and arithmetic tutor for his son William. When noting this in his account of William's intellectual development, Everett made no mention of the tutor's race, seeming to think it was irrelevant. In 1847, Williams applied for admission to Harvard, encouraged by his white friends at Hopkins.[17] Had Everett's administration admitted Williams, it would have made history. As with so many other American colleges with colonial roots, Harvard's history had long been intertwined with slavery and the slave trade. Slaves had performed a significant part of the college's menial labor in the eighteenth century, and in the mid-nineteenth century "scouts," who served as sort of all-purpose personal servants to the wealthy students, made up the entire African American presence on campus.[18]

Everett dealt with the prospect of Williams applying neither as a radical racial egalitarian nor as a defender of white supremacy. Accounts of Everett staring down white protesters in Cambridge, vowing to devote the whole resources of the college to Williams if all the white students boycotted, seem to be apocryphal.[19] But he did have a very real, if muted and distant, confrontation with a critic as a result of Williams's application. The son of a Georgia planter, apparently to deflect attention away from his failure to pass the Harvard entrance exam after two tries, wrote to his father about how "a negro-boy" would be entering the class of 1851. The father wrote Everett in some alarm to ascertain the truth of this report, in part because "I have two other sons to send to College." This letter reached Everett right after the burning straw incident, and he was in no mood to countenance an entitled and inept prospective student at the expense of someone as upstanding and able as Williams. So he replied curtly to the Georgian that Williams "is a boy of very good capacity, studious habits and excellent character." He was unsure whether Williams would actually apply for admission, but "should he be offered, as he will be very well suited, I know of no reason why he should not be admitted. He associates on terms of perfect equality with the boys of his school, among whom are sons of several of our Professors, — a son of my own, — and two young men from Georgia." The problem was not with Williams but with this meddling racist father and his unfortunate son.[20]

For Everett this was a case of how meritocracy should prevail over pigmentocracy. While not necessarily spoiling for a fight, Everett was hardly relieved when he learned that Williams had died in July 1847, just two months shy of his eighteenth birthday. He lamented his absence at the examination of Hopkins students later that month. And when it became his duty as chairman of the Hopkins School's Board of Visitors to pen Williams's obituary, he held up the young man's scholarly career as a model of excellence conquering racial prejudice. Not only was the young man "well fitted for the university," Everett argued, but he also had "wholly overcome the prejudice against his color & was a universal favorite" among his peers. Everett almost certainly exaggerated the racial openness of these students, and Harvard would not admit its first black student until after the Civil War. But the Beverly Williams lightning flash had illuminated Everett's commitment to racial equality of opportunity in education.[21]

————

While Everett's racial attitudes and actions tended to the liberal side, his views on slavery remained thoroughly in the Northern Whig mainstream. Like almost all his partisan fellows, he diagnosed the Polk administration's war against Mexico as a land grab for slavery. He concurred with a Whig state legislator who argued that the extension of slavery to any new territory violated the constitutional compact between the free and slave states. He resented Southern political power enough to grumble that if Webster were a Southerner, he would have easily gained the presidency. Southern extremists, from John C. Calhoun down to Harvard students pining for Dixie, put him off. Unlike in March 1826, in 1845 he had no patience for defenses "from reason & scripture" for slavery, concluding that slavery could be justified and maintained only by force. And in 1850, rereading an official account of Denmark Vesey's conspiracy that he had read in 1822, he found himself "amazed to think that I then thought favorably of the conduct of the Magistrates. — They hung 33 persons & banished 35" on very flimsy evidence.[22]

But Everett had traveled only so far along the antislavery spectrum. For him, moderate British commentators on slavery still possessed far more moral authority than American immediatist abolitionists. He rejoiced to read two American travel accounts by the British geologist Sir Charles Lyell, for instance. Lyell depicted American slavery as a paternalist institution, if an inefficient form of labor and marred by the aberrant cruelties of the domestic slave trade. Lyell raised serious doubts about whether the agitation by Anglo-American abolitionists for immediate emancipation would improve the slaves' situation. The burden of his accounts was that emancipation would be beneficial in America only in a very gradual form, although slavery was destined to lose out to free labor in the long run.[23] Everett applauded Lyell's work both in his diary and as part of an ongoing correspondence with the author. He thought Lyell treated "the subject of Slavery with discretion & moderation making statements which are well calculated to open the eyes of the blindest to the evils of the system; but without kindling their bad passions." The idea that any British observer's commentary on American slavery would encourage Southerners to embrace emancipation was clearly quixotic on Everett's part. And it is far from clear how Lyell's gauzy portrait of Southern slavery highlighted "the evils of the system." But his faith in the inevitable, if imperceptible, natural process of emancipation echoed Everett's own. Everett continued to contemplate human bondage on a global scale, and his researches only confirmed his belief that slavery was a "stupendous anomaly in human affairs." "It may last the rest of this century," he reasoned, "but I think not longer."[24]

Lyell's conciliatory tone toward Southerners also resonated with Everett. For all his irritation with Southern extremists, Everett retained faith in moderate Southern men and women and strongly believed any emancipation should come with their consent. He paid close attention to the state of white Southern opinion on the future of slavery and retained hope for Virginia in particular. That attitude came in handy in 1850 when Everett's daughter Charlotte married Henry Augustus Wise, whose prominent Virginia family included cousin Henry Alexander Wise, later governor of the Old Dominion.[25] This sanguine attitude regarding some Southerners led Everett to believe abolitionist agitators' insulting tone toward Southerners was uncharitable. While he granted that it might have a place in stirring the North's antislavery conscience, he cringed when he saw honest white Southerners subjected to it. So when a Harvard club's parade featured a student "upon a sofa with a negro fanning him," Everett determined to suppress such "indecorum & impropriety." He objected to abolitionist sermons delivered in the campus chapel as "unfair," given that "the Sons of Slave-holders" were required to attend these services. Everett also deemed intemperate affronts to Southerners counterproductive to the antislavery cause. A Virginia woman, for instance, told him that in the 1820s, "Virginia was on the eve of emancipating the Slaves." But beginning in the 1830s, "the violence of the agitators at the north had produced such a change of feeling, that a man would now be in danger of being lynched, who should utter language" that in the 1820s had been "boldly & freely used."[26]

For all these reasons and more, the heart of Everett's objection to immediatist abolitionism lay in his view that it was utterly impractical. He believed abolitionists to be "generally honest & sincere" but could not abide how they set aside "all considerations not merely of prudence and expediency but of common sense & practicability. They are purely *destructive*; they admit that their agitation looks only to unconstitutional emancipation, without any thought of *how, when,* or *what next.*" Everett also believed that most abolitionists were highly overrated as true friends of African Americans. In the late 1840s and early 1850s, a steady stream of black people made their way to his door to solicit donations for causes ranging from building black schools and churches in the North to buying family members' freedom. He consistently gave generously, especially to those seeking the freedom and reunification of families. He could not help noticing that "I see none of the reputed Abolitionists among" the subscribers to one black man's project. Most abolitionists' "friendship for the blacks ends where it begins," he jabbed on another occasion: "in agitation." All this confirmed his self-image as a practical antislavery man, in contrast with the armchair philanthropists in the abolitionist ranks.[27]

It did not help Everett's relationship with abolitionists and stridently antislavery politicians that they abused him in public, and their reaction to his eulogy of John Quincy Adams only hardened his suspicions of especially the politicians. In late February 1848, the Whig icon whose congressional career in the late 1830s and 1840s had also made him the elder statesman of the fight against slavery's power in national affairs died. When the state legislature asked Everett to deliver Massachusetts's official eulogy for Adams, he felt he had no choice but to accept this opportunity to honor his relative and longtime political ally, despite being in the midst of a busy time in the academic calendar. Everett struggled not only to master the relevant facts of Adams's long and distinguished life but also "to narrate his political course truly, without espousing party controversies one side or the other." The fallen hero's son (and Everett's brother-in-law) Charles Francis Adams sustained Everett in trying to walk that balance. While his father's jousts against the Gag Rule and slavery expansion formed "the most brilliant portion of my father's career," to lay inordinate stress upon that phase "might give rise to dispute," so it would probably "not be proper to walk upon such hot cinders in a Eulogy," he advised.[28]

On 15 April 1848, a heavily female crowd jammed into Faneuil Hall to hear Everett's oration. In it, Everett disclaimed that because Adams was being mourned "by good men and patriots of every party name," he would avoid "present or past controversies." He devoted very brief attention to his presidency and remembered Adams, like Washington, as resisting "an intimate and exclusive union with any party." While he did not dodge Adams's fight against the Gag Rule, he argued that his antislavery career, like Britain's act of emancipation, evinced a spirit of "caution inspired by a profound sense of" the subject's "difficulty and delicacy." This manner during the debates made it "impossible not to respect the fearless, conscientious, unparalleled old man."[29]

But Everett failed to rally consensus behind his depiction of Adams. He had tried to align Adams's career with his own and portray both as the mainstream of antislavery Whig statesmanship, but neither the nation, the Whig Party, the North, nor Massachusetts enjoyed anything approaching consensus on slavery. Everett thought he had pulled it off well, and there was no shortage of public and private praise for the eulogy. But even on the day itself, Everett noticed that the audience was "very attentive but very cold" and unreceptive compared to other audiences. Abolitionist preacher Theodore Parker judged that that was because the speech itself was "*poor—heartless* and *cold*," and others lampooned it for its "cat-like timidity."[30] Everett tried to be philosophical about such criticisms. "I endeavored to do justice to Mr. Adams' exertions in reference to Slavery," he insisted to one abolitionist, "but in alluding to subjects, on which extreme opinions are entertained on both sides, the man 'of moderate counsels' is too apt to please neither." And it helped when rising antislavery star Charles Sumner assured Everett that he had placed "Mr. Adams's Anti-Slavery character . . . in its proper relief." But the criticism stung and convinced him that political abolitionists "have so accustomed themselves to extravagant overstatements . . . that nothing suits them but caricature & exaggeration."[31]

He had not needed much convincing to dislike and distrust the Free Soil Party, the prime political channel of antislavery agitation in the late 1840s. From the late 1830s to the mid-1840s, conservative Whigs like Webster and Everett had entered warily into cooperation with Whigs who prioritized antislavery action. But their differences came more fully into view beginning in 1845, when the latter sought to undo the annexation of Texas and the former argued that this futile endeavor would only split the national party. The antislavery activists took to calling themselves the "Conscience Whigs" and their intraparty foes the "Cotton Whigs" to emphasize their alleged subservience to the South. They were so able to frame the debate that even traditionally consensus Massachusetts Whig national priorities, like a protective tariff, came to be seen by many "Conscience Whigs" as traitorous to New England's true interests. Later in the decade, "Conscience Whigs" who gave up hope for control of their party joined with disaffected Democrats to form the Free Soil Party, whose platform's central plank was to pass the Wilmot Proviso's proposed congressional ban on slavery from all territory taken from Mexico.[32]

Neither the battle for the soul of the Whig Party nor the rivalry between Whigs and Free Soilers featured much rhetorical restraint, and Everett took the verbal warfare hard. In part because of exaggerated attacks on his own record, he judged Free Soilers, like abolitionists, "indifferent to truth." When one Free Soil paper wrongly attributed a bloodthirsty anti-abolitionist sentiment to

Everett, he railed in his diary that "one of the instruments of the free soil agitation is unfounded defamation of all who refuse to join it." The way Everett saw it, "in the proper sense of the word, a large majority in the non-slaveholding States" supported true antislavery positions, "that is are sincerely desirous of preventing the extension & hastening the disappearance of Slavery." But the labels the antislavery agitators applied to themselves ("Conscience Whigs" and "Free Soilers") and to their intrasectional enemies ("Cotton Whigs") sought to wrest the antislavery high ground from those like himself who were more practically seeking the same end.[33] This was certainly the burden of a letter he wrote for the *Boston Daily Advertiser* in 1849. The abolitionists and Free Soilers who pushed for a dissolution of the Union, he charged, not only shrugged at the devastating civil war that would follow but also turned a blind eye to the plain fact that disunion and a Southern confederacy "would tend, more than any other conceivable event, to perpetuate Slavery." He thus rejected union versus abolition as a false choice and adopted as his pseudonym the rather wordy but telling "A FRIEND OF THE UNION, AND AN ENEMY OF SLAVERY."[34]

Such chicanery as this could not have proceeded from a pure source, Everett was convinced. So when Free Soilers formed a partnership with the state's Democrats to try to take control of Massachusetts politics, that only confirmed Everett's suspicion that this movement was a stalking horse for the Democrats both locally and nationally. Their association with previously doughfaced Democrats also convinced him that "few of them are the enthusiasts they pretend to be." He harbored no doubts that only "Bribery & Corruption" could hold together such a "profligate coalition." As one attuned to a multiplicity of reform causes, he found it fishy that preachers influenced by Free Soil sentiment ignored "all the wrongs, crimes, and abuses" available to rebuke in New England, shooting instead "at a mark 500 miles off." By the early 1850s, Everett had become so disgusted with growing Free Soiler influence in Massachusetts that he ascribed all manner of social and religious maladies to this "contagion."[35]

Complaints like these carried a personal tone because this was in large part personal. The life path of "Conscience" man turned Free Soiler John Gorham Palfrey, for instance, had been remarkably similar to Everett's. Born in 1796, his bright career as a student gave way to following Everett as pastor at Brattle Street Church, then to a teaching career at Harvard, and then into politics. Palfrey even had a son in the same Harvard class as Beverly Williams and introduced the likelihood of Williams's admission into Harvard as evidence of African American equality in an 1848 congressional debate. Palfrey himself had long felt overshadowed by Everett—indeed, both had courted Charlotte Brooks! So the personal and the political were always intertwined in this relationship, and their familiarity and similarity had bred a complex mix of emotions in Palfrey about Everett. But Everett also felt Palfrey's defection from the Whigs as something of a personal loss and found painful at least one conversation where they tried but failed to see eye to eye politically. Similarly, Everett had sponsored the early career of Samuel G. Howe, encouraging and even funding his 1820s activities in favor of Greek independence, and they shared many of the same causes and friends throughout their lives. Such deep personal backstories help explain Everett's irritation when the likes of Howe and Palfrey claimed "Conscience" for themselves and branded other Whigs the abject lapdogs of "Cotton" interests (even as Palfrey advanced Everett's prospective admission of Williams to prove Massachusetts's enlightened racial attitudes).[36]

But this interplay between the personal and the political seems to have been thorniest for Everett when it came to Charles Sumner. Sumner had that effect on people. In 1848, he famously ascribed the Whig nomination of Louisiana slaveholder Zachary Taylor for president to "an unhallowed union, conspiracy let it be called, . . . between the lords of the lash and the lords of the loom." One of those manufacturing loom lords, Bay State textile magnate Nathan Appleton, took exception and initiated a correspondence with Sumner whose venom derived from much personal history as well as political disagreement between the two.[37] For his part, Everett saw in the younger Sumner "a man of great & various accomplishment & no ordinary talent." But as Sumner strayed into the Free Soil ranks, Everett feared his young friend was playing "a dangerous game of ambition for himself & the country." Everett let his knee-jerk reaction to Free Soilers lead him into behavior behind Sumner's back that he knew was unworthy of himself. For instance, when Robert C. Winthrop consulted Everett about publishing an essay assaulting Sumner, Everett rather casuistically "told him I should like to see it printed; but would not advise" Winthrop outright on whether to print it. And one night in 1852, Everett wrote regretfully in his journal that he "got into a foolish argument" with a Sumner supporter "about Slavery" and about Sumner's course in the Senate.[38] But perhaps because neither was an active, open persecutor of the other, these two (unlike Sumner and Appleton) were able to maintain a friendly correspondence from the 1840s through the 1860s. Their letters and conversations about slavery convinced Everett that the question of means constituted "the only thing of importance on which we differ." "Could I emancipate the slaves in America by an act of my will," he protested to his friend, "I could cheerfully sacrifice ease, property, & life itself." But antislavery fomentation, "especially in connection with party politics," would "obstruct and postpone the operation of all the mild influences, which, under divine Providence, are at work to effect the eventual abolition of Slavery." Thus "I cannot sympathize with you in reference to" this one question, although he was enough of a reformer at heart that "I am not, at times, without misgivings that you & the friends who act with you may be in the right, & I in the wrong." "Pardon my freedom," he asked, and Sumner did pardon it, perhaps in part because of the rather remarkable uncertainty about his position that Everett's letter betrayed.[39]

Indeed, Sumner harbored enough hope for his friend that he became the instrument in one of the real surprises of Everett's unpredictable career in slavery politics: an offer to become the vice presidential nomination of the Free Soil Party in 1848. The Whig nomination of Taylor pushed most "Conscience Whigs" out of the party, and they quickly entered into partnership with Liberty Party leaders and Democratic supporters of the Wilmot Proviso to create the Free Soil Party. But this alliance proved shaky from the start due to previous, deeply held partisan allegiances, and the first task of party managers working toward the party's August convention in Buffalo, New York, was to assemble a presidential ticket that could unite the fledgling party. Martin Van Buren stood as one of the leaders of the dissident Democrats, and momentum built to put him at the top of the ticket. But Van Buren raised serious opposition especially among the former Whigs, who had long hated him as both a doughface and a Democrat. "To ask a Whig," thundered a Detroit newspaper, "to vote for Martin Van Buren is an insult." Securing someone with strong Whig antecedents for the bottom of the ticket was imperative, but the leadership's first choice, Supreme Court justice John McLean, refused.[40]

Thus, on the last day of July 1848, Sumner reached out to gauge Everett's interest in the vice presidential slot. He apprised Everett of the movement for a Van Buren–McLean ticket in hopes of forging "a powerful combination between seceders from both the great parties." In light of McLean's delay in responding, Sumner told Everett candidly, "several persons interested in the movement have turned their thoughts upon you" as their prime second choice to unify the party and "impart to our movement more of that character which we desire to impress upon it." "I have no reason to believe," Sumner ventured, that Everett would have any objection "to mingle in our movement." Therefore, Sumner concluded, "I have made bold to seek your permission to use your name."[41] Sumner was neither the first nor the last to believe he and his party could shape Everett's moderate, meandering career on slavery into almost any image they wanted. Clearly in this case, Sumner and other Free Soilers banked on Everett's reputation for a conservative and fundamentally Whig brand of antislavery.

But the would-be nominee gave zero thought to accepting. Everett received

Sumner's inquiry on 3 August and responded the next day. He led by assuring Sumner that he "deeply sympathize[d]" with "the avowed object of the Buffalo Convention," namely to prevent slavery's extension. "If I thought my accepting their nomination would promote that object, I would not hesitate a moment" to accept. But while he claimed a bit disingenuously to Sumner to have no doubts of the Free Soil leaders' "honesty & pure intentions," he did not believe this third-party effort would achieve its stated goal. He spoke "from my political experience" (such as with Antimasons and with the temperance agitators who cost him reelection in 1839) when he denounced the disruptive effects of "*third* parties, formed from the two leading parties, to advance some single principle." Moreover, "I have ever . . . acted as a Whig" and had "received from them the highest honors and trusts they had to bestow; and nothing but a clear and most imperative call of duty would I think justify me in separating myself from true & faithful friends. — I was willing to fall with them, & do not wish to rise without them." Furthermore, when voting for president, "we are bound, — bound in conscience, to consult the practical result of the vote we give. I think no one expects that the nominees of the Buffalo Convention will be chosen." Therefore, the only practical choice was between Taylor and the Democratic nominee Lewis Cass, and "I do not see how any Whig of whatever stamp can hesitate in that alternative." He closed by reiterating his personal regard for Sumner and by praying "that I may live to see the day, when all good citizens, — North & South, — will unite in wiping out" slavery, "this dreadful blot upon the fair fame of our Country."[42] As if to underscore how personal all this was, after Everett's refusal the Free Soilers placed his far less conflicted brother-in-law Charles Francis Adams at the bottom of their ticket.

Everett's tactful but direct response captured not only his moderate antislavery principles but also the full extent of his ambivalence about party politics. Historians of partisan identity and loyalty have debated whether by the mid-nineteenth century, American voters were deeply committed to the two-party system and particularly their own party's rectitude, desperate for stable party identity in a period of near-constant third-party challenges, or conflicted in their attitude toward a system of party rivalry that was an undeniable fact of political life but was practiced by unsavory party hacks.[43] As his letter to Sumner illustrates, it is no cop-out to say that for Everett, the answer to that question was "yes." He found overly strong party identity suspect, but he also detested third-party action because of the harm he had seen it do to his Whig Party. As for antislavery third parties, he held the Liberty Party largely responsible for Henry Clay's defeat in 1844 (and thus his recall from his cherished post in London) and believed the Free Soilers would likewise benefit only the Democracy.

Better (not only politically but "in conscience") by far to battle from within for the antislavery soul of the great national Whig Party. So for all his sincere desire to float far above the low arts of party maneuver, he consistently voted the straight Whig ticket throughout this chapter of his life and energetically encouraged others to follow his example. Attached as he was to Webster, when the Whig Party again passed up Webster for its presidential nomination, Everett blasted as hopelessly impractical his "overzealous friends" who contemplated a third-party run for their hero.[44]

———

The ultimate test of the zeal of Everett's loyalty to Webster, however, would come surrounding the debates leading to the Compromise of 1850. Through the late 1840s, their political partnership and personal friendship appeared unshakable, even by the stress Webster's behavior sometimes put on them. Webster's self-serving approach to this as to so many other relationships came into sharp focus when he paraded into Everett's installation as Harvard president fashionably late, making his grand entrance right as Everett began his oration. Symptomatic of his patience with his exasperating and great friend and patron, Everett simply sat down until Webster was seated and the gawkers returned their attention to the pulpit. Beginning in 1847, Everett willingly served at Webster's request as his prime literary executor, expending tedious mental labor on editing and introducing published volumes of his political and diplomatic correspondence. As editor and introducer he consistently put Webster in the best light. For instance, Everett's introduction to the 1848 publication of select diplomatic papers argued that Webster's heroic efforts for peace with Britain alone rendered his term as secretary of state "as beneficial to the country as any of which the memory is preserved in her annals." He also adeptly used subject headings to put slavery at the front or back of the stage as it suited Webster's reputation, framing the Treaty of Washington as achieving the "Suppression of the Slave Trade" and the *Creole* case as involving "Maritime Rights." One could only hope for so good a friend and spin doctor as Edward Everett.[45]

But for much of 1850, Everett found himself troublingly at odds with Webster on the politics of slavery. Congresses convening from 1848 forward found themselves both roiled and paralyzed by debates centering on the Wilmot Proviso but also ranging to serious new issues like the border between the New Mexico Territory and the slave state of Texas. In this situation, older issues took on new life as abolitionists continued their crusade against slavery and the slave trade in the District of Columbia and as citizens and politicians from especially the Upper South demanded a more stringent law than the federal Fugitive Slave

Act of 1793. Sectional divisions even kept the House of Representatives from appointing a Speaker—and thus moving forward on any business—for weeks in December 1849. As one historian has aptly phrased it, both the disorderliness of the debate and the legislative paralysis raised the specter of the United States as "a failed state, a nation no longer capable of governing itself." President Taylor's creative plan for resolving this impasse involved immediately admitting as free states California and New Mexico, thus evading a congressional debate over their status as free or slave territories. But this scheme, on top of other provocations, only added fuel to the fire of Southern sectionalism, and in response to fire-breathing state legislative calls for a convention, representatives from many Southern states met in Nashville in 1850 to discuss secession.[46]

Alarmed especially by the Nashville Convention, Unionist lions like Webster and Clay sought to reprise the formula of compromise that had saved the Union before. Clay threw his enormous political capital into a scheme more acceptable to many Southerners than the president's pro-Northern program. At the dawn of 1850, convinced that the menace to the Union was dire, Webster decided to support Clay's rather than Taylor's approach. In letters to supporters, he tried out arguments for compromise and declared his intention "to make a *Union* speech, and," he pointedly added in anticipating of being called a "Cotton Whig," "discharge a clear conscience." Webster pushed his lieutenants in Boston to assemble a meeting at Faneuil Hall to support compromise in advance of his speech. But when the would-be organizers asked Everett to speak at such a rally, he demurred on grounds that such a meeting would be premature while developments in Washington remained so obscure. From his position in Washington, Winthrop agreed that any Whig rally should react to rather than lead out for a speech from Webster. Until "the *oracle* has spoken," Northern Whigs' course would remain uncertain.[47]

On 7 March, Webster rose to deliver his much-anticipated pronouncement. Speaking "out of a solicitous and anxious heart" for "the preservation of the Union," he lectured that Northerners must recognize that the South's "whole interests" were bound up with slavery. He did scold "the extremists in both parts of this country," but the North's abolitionists came in for most of his blame. He devoted his fiery peroration to elaborating on the "pain, and anguish, and distress" with which he heard talk of secession. "Peaceable secession!" he cried. "Sir, your eyes and mine are never destined to see that miracle." Americans both past and future "would cry out shame upon us, if we of this generation should" walk willfully down the road to civil war.[48] From most sectional moderates' point of view, this was the most memorable thrust of Webster's speech, speaking so powerfully for their passionate commitment to the Union. The entire congressional debate had revealed how emotional the Unionists were and how adamant they were that theirs was a principled position. It had become a protracted debate precisely because all three sides' attachment to their positions was proving adamant.[49]

But other passages proved harder for many Northerners to swallow. In one, Webster admitted that he had previously opposed the annexation of Texas with slavery but insisted that now the United States was bound to honor the pledges it made to Texas with annexation. In what would become the most controversial passage, Webster defended the more stringent Fugitive Slave Act (FSA) proposed by Calhoun disciple Senator James Mason of Virginia, which would pay informers who brought fugitives to court, deprive accused slaves of the right to testify, and set up a police force in every Northern county to enforce the law. Webster decreed that in light of Northern efforts to frustrate the existing fugitive law, "the South is right and the North is wrong" on this issue. He purposely framed it in such moralistic terms, pleading for the assent "of all conscientious men in the North" to his position on this "question of morals and . . . of conscience" as well as of constitutional duty.[50]

Abolitionists and Free Soilers disagreed vehemently with this assessment of where conscience led. They turned on Webster with the fury of politicians scorned, for throughout the late 1840s they had harbored cautious hopes for bringing him in line with the Wilmot Proviso. John Greenleaf Whittier mourned Webster's apostasy much as John Milton had lamented the fall of Satan. Webster had proven

> A bright soul driven,
> Fiend-goaded, down the endless dark,
> From hope and heaven!

Their ire produced other memorable lines, such as when black abolitionist Samuel Ringgold Ward declared that Northern supporters of the FSA "lick up the spittle of the slavocrats, and swear it is delicious." "The man who can read" the FSA "without having the blood boil in his veins," Massachusetts Free Soiler Horace Mann marveled, "has a power of refrigeration that would cool the tropics." Ralph Waldo Emerson added to this stock of quotable phrases when he grumbled that "the word *liberty* in the mouth of Mr Webster sounds like the word *love* in the mouth of a courtezan." Still furious a full year after Webster's speech, a group including Palfrey and Whittier called for a convention to discuss how to resist the federal government in its purpose "of *forcing* every citizen to become an instrument to fasten slavery upon the country" by means of the FSA.[51]

Free Soilers and abolitionists naturally bristled at any suggestion that Webster's position enjoyed any substantial measure of public support, and influential contemporary historians have followed suit. They have emphasized the popular reaction against the FSA and its Northern supporters. The least nuanced of these interpretations argue that since FSA backers could only have been "aggressively pro-slavery," "Webster had become a pariah in the North" after his "Seventh of March" speech and "had lost almost all credibility with his constituents." Scholars of this persuasion ascribe any Northern support for compromise with the South to the economic self-interest of Boston and New York merchants and manufacturers.[52]

But other historians and much evidence from the primary sources illustrate that this is a simplistic picture of the political fortunes of Webster and the FSA in the early 1850s. Historian Stanley Campbell's close study of Northern public opinion found that most Northerners privileged their desire to preserve the Union and obey the laws over their very real discomfort with the FSA. Only later in the 1850s, as antislavery sectionalism surged in politics due to territorial issues, did the tide of public opinion turn in favor of resisting the law. Certainly Webster's mailbox refuted the idea that he was a pariah, teeming as it was with letters of support from groups and individuals throughout the North and the South.[53] Fewer people voted for Sumner as a Free Soil candidate for Congress in 1850 than attended some individual cities' public rallies for Webster's battle for compromise and signed individual congratulatory letters to him. So desirable was the Unionist high ground that Massachusetts Whigs and Democrats jockeyed to claim it for themselves alone. Accounts of a July 1852 Boston rally for Webster describe how the popular "outpouring of devotion and respect" reached such a pitch that it was "as though the people were professing a religious faith."[54] If we accept the abolitionist portrait of Northern Unionists, we are left to wonder how many cotton merchants there really were in the North![55]

But in truth, these masses had more than cotton profits in their souls. Especially in light of the failure of the European revolutions of 1848, many Americans understood the global stakes involved should their republican Union fail. Men like Webster were thus in complete earnest when they insisted they were appealing to the public's highest ideals. The very title of an 1850 pamphlet from Webster supporter Moses Stuart, *Conscience and the Constitution*, appealed to both. All the antislavery men staking proprietary claims to conscience, Stuart charged, in reality violated the "peaceful spirit" of the gospel, which guided "those who love their country, love peace, love their neighbor." Compromise, wrote one Boston editor, was not only necessary in this case but also "an eternal principle lying at the foundation of all republics." The statesmen who supported it, wrote another, simply had the "moral courage" to "find out what is *right*, and then say that and do that."[56]

The fullest picture of Northern and Massachusetts public opinion on the Compromise of 1850 would capture how both sides evinced confidence in their respective position, even as they also manifested defensiveness for different reasons. Both Mann and Webster, for instance, took a defensive tone in a public exchange in the summer of 1850, Mann insisting he loved the Constitution and the Union just as Webster protested he was no advocate of slavery. Likewise, in early 1851, Sumner complained that the Whigs had "started against me, & used with effect, the calumny that I am a Disunionist." As late as June 1852, one observer remarked on the mutual "hate" on both sides of the great slavery divide in Massachusetts politics. And when Theodore Parker rose to savage Webster after the latter's death, he described his target as a revered statesman who "for the last two years . . . has had a vast influence on the opinion of the North." With large numbers of both politicians and voters dug in on both sides, one scholar of Bay State politics in this period has astutely described the state as "a center of both free soilism and conservative unionism."[57]

Everett found himself torn by such fiercely competing viewpoints early in this struggle. Nothing would have been less surprising than for Everett to have upheld Webster's position in this fracas. Indeed, in July 1850 when Webster accepted the position of secretary of state, an abolitionist newspaper carped that Everett would be the perfect replacement for Webster, for "no doughface could have been more servile" than Everett had been in his previous congressional stint.[58] But both the prediction that Everett would go into the Senate and the assumption that he aligned fully with Webster proved premature.

Gathering as much information as he could from his semiprivate position, Everett expressed unequivocal fear for the Union's survival but an uncertainty over which section's extremists were most to blame for this peril. Especially when the stormy Congress met starting in December 1849, Everett felt a relentless wave of fear for the beloved Union. "I have never known the political horizon so dark as at the present day," he moaned in one diary entry, and that was saying something.[59] But Everett could not decide who was responsible for this state of affairs. It had become second nature for Everett to argue that antislavery agitation "tends directly to disunion, civil war, & a murderous struggle between the races." At times he seemed eager to grasp at any evidence of Southerners' commitment to the Union and overall reasonableness.[60] But Everett more often chalked the threat up to a Southern plot to dissolve the Union. "I have for a long time been coming to the conclusion," he wrote to Appleton in February 1850, "that some leading men at the South desire a separation," out of a range of motives including "ambition" and "a conviction, sincere but most erroneous, that separation would diminish the annoyance of antislavery agitation."[61] At other times he blamed both sides about equally. On one occasion he rhapsodized that if the members of Congress could learn "to think other people are as good puppies as themselves, the world in general & Congress in particular would get along better." But he thought that unlikely in the present conflict. As he told a close English friend, the United States' slavery question equaled "any & every plague combined that afflicts the rest of Christendom." This was how "the Sin of Slavery" visited "its own punishment" on the whole nation.[62]

Such wavering carried over into wrenching indecision over whether to back Webster's support of the compromise measures, especially the FSA.[63] When he received an incomplete early version of the speech, he felt he could support its overall tenor. On 11 March, he recorded in his diary that it was "an exposition of great ability, well calculated if moderate counsels prevail to pilot the country through the broken & stormy sea:—but _____."[64] The dissent that Everett could not bring himself to register even in his diary emerged slowly. On 12 March, Everett dashed off a note assuring Webster that all "reasonable men will be satisfied" with it. The next day he followed up with a letter opining that a revised FSA would stand on firm constitutional ground. "Should your views be questioned" on scriptural grounds "in reference to the surrender of fugitives," he volunteered, "it would be worth your while to cast your eye over Mr. Buckminster's sermon on the epistle to Philemon."[65] Buckminster's homily clearly exerted great influence on Everett's thinking about slavery almost four decades later, and those views made room for at least the principle of returning fugitive slaves to their legal owners.

But then he read a fuller version and was mortified by the passages on Texas, slavery in the territories, and especially Mason's particular fugitive bill. To oppose Webster was no small step, so he initiated a confidential correspondence with Winthrop in Washington to talk through how to deal with the matter. "My deference to Mr. W's judgement has become so habitual," Winthrop responded, that "I always support him at the expense of my own, when my conscience will allow me." But this was not such an occasion, in part because the FSA was so gratuitously pro-Southern that Northern Whigs "shall all have hard work to sustain ourselves under it." Everett responded that his own reaction had been precisely the same: "habitual deference" to Webster's "authority" coming face to face with massive qualms especially about the FSA. The old law had been "against the feeling of the People," and this new one was even worse. "I could not vote for it, were I a member of Congress; nor as a citizen would I perform the duty which it devolves 'on all good citizens.'"[66] By 22 March,

Everett decided he had to send Webster a modified retraction of his assent to the speech. He admired it so much in general, and had been so accustomed to agreeing with Webster, he admitted, "that I did not stop to scrutinize details." He had since found the details on Texas and the territories inconsistent with the moderate antislavery tack to which both he and Webster had committed themselves as candidates and officeholders since the late 1830s. More significantly, he had "misgivings" about the new FSA because runaway slave renditions were "the incident of Slavery . . . which is most repugnant to the Public Sentiment of the Free States." In this and a follow-up letter in April, Everett wished "it were possible to arrange some extradition bill that would be less likely to excite the North" than Mason's. "Southern gentlemen, who wish the Union preserved, must make that allowance for Northern feeling, which they claim for Southern feeling."[67]

Because the FSA did this sort of violence to the voluntary bonds of feeling that were essential to the Union, Everett severely doubted whether it would be the Union-saving measure its proponents advertised. "It is out of the question," he informed a British friend, "to awaken any *feeling* in favor of such a law" in the Northern citizenry. It was thus the height of political madness for the South to demand the enforcement of a law that was sure "to make every man, woman & child in the Free States ready for Separation" of the Union. He agreed with Winthrop that the FSA "more resembles in some of its details" the draconian laws of ancient civilizations "than any American or European Code."[68] The FSA's political inefficacy would be inseparable from its inhumanity. While "the constitution & the law" favored the rendition of fugitives in the abstract, "natural feeling & human sympathy" were ranged against this particular bill. "I asked myself this question" on reading the Seventh of March speech, he confided in Winthrop: "'could you as a good citizen assist in carrying out such a law as Mason's. If you heard the hue & cry after a runaway slave, would you run out of your house & help catch him?' This question I answered to myself in the negative, & so I fancy would Mr. W. himself." When a Georgia politician's wife told him she would look the other way rather than return a neighbor's fugitive slave, it would have convinced him further that the FSA was an affront to basic, not just Northern, humanity.[69]

Everett marked all his misgivings about Webster's course "Private" or "Confidential" for a reason. He had no desire to align with Webster's public assailants, who were overwhelmingly abolitionists and Free Soilers. Their known political prejudices, he believed, meant their "denunciations will rather aid than impair the effect of the speech with the Conservative portion of the community." "It is one thing to differ from him," Winthrop agreed, and quite "another thing to assail him." While Winthrop had disagreed with Webster in a congressional speech, he continued, "I hope that I have done it kindly." "I really feel myself," he said in another sentence to which Everett would have agreed, "to be about half way between Webster & Horace Mann." But neither of them were close enough to Mann's position to embrace the Free Soiler's style of attack on Webster.[70]

Even in semi-retirement, however, Everett found it impossible to keep his divergence from Webster's position private. "If you can conscientiously defend my Speech," Webster entreated him even before Everett had had a chance to read the whole speech, "I beg of you to go to Faneuil Hall, & do so." And as early as 20 March, the redoubtable Boston conservative George Curtis visited Everett beseeching him to sign a letter commending Webster's address. Everett declined because he could not honestly sign a memorial "expressive of entire concurrence in his [Webster's] opinions." But that did not stop others from accosting Everett on the street over a week later, urging that the memorial was Webster's own idea. Eight hundred Massachusetts worthies signed it, but not Everett. In early May, Everett shook his head sadly when the august guests at a dinner party all agreed that Webster had been wrong to support Mason's FSA, "& yet every one but Mr. Gray & myself had signed the letter declaring a full concurrence with Mr. W." A week after this incident, Webster and his friends seemed highly solicitous to see Everett attend a private dinner in Webster's honor, but Everett again begged off. He finally and grudgingly agreed to sign a generic pro-compromise letter to Massachusetts's congressional delegation in June 1850, in part to get the petitioners off his back.[71] His silence was probably damaging in light of his well-known closeness to Webster. But it was also true that Everett's moderately antislavery reputation might provide antislavery cover for Webster just as it would have given the Free Soilers conservative credibility in 1848.

The whole break with Webster, however, caused enough pain as to be unsustainable. In May, Winthrop sighed to Everett that the past two months had "been a trying time" for all moderate Northern Whigs in Washington. That echoed Everett's earlier revelation to Winthrop that "the affair of Mr. Webster's speech has quite troubled me." Knowing he would be called on to defend it but knowing he could not do so fully, "such was the state of my own mind at the end of six or eight days from the time I got the speech" that "I saw scarce any one & expressed an opinion to no one." Being forced to take a stand even by means of silence was thus what he described to another friend as "a severe trial to me."[72]

By the summer and fall of 1850, with Webster and his enemies refusing to budge from their positions, the likes of Everett and Winthrop had to decide whose side they were on. Unsurprisingly, they chose Webster. In July 1850, when President Taylor died and Millard Fillmore took his place, the new president nominated Webster to be his secretary of state. This was a key signal that Fillmore supported the compromise measures rather than Taylor's plan, and it gave Webster more sway to push for the compromise. On hearing of Fillmore's intentions toward Webster, Winthrop wrote Everett on 19 July to signal that he thought Webster was "the man for the emergency." By 13 September, when Everett learned of Congress's passage of the compromise measures, he wrote Webster to congratulate him on an achievement that "is mainly the consequence of your wisdom & courage." He hoped the compromise would save the Union by removing "the material of" antislavery agitation and offered his help in steering the Whig Party toward support of Webster's position. Webster happily took him up on the offer, urging Everett to do all he could to remove abolitionism and all "other *isms*" from the party. "I am out of patience with the littleness, the bigotry, the stupidity" of his opponents, Webster raged, and hoped Everett could help to "*nationalize* the Whig Party" again. Everett by his own account "lost no time" in testing key state party leaders for their Unionist orthodoxy. From the fall of 1850 through the fall of 1851, Everett became a valuable source of intelligence for Webster on the progress of their battle for the soul of the party.[73]

This was part of a complicated and gradual reconciliation between Everett and Webster. In November 1850 Everett was not yet ready to speak at a public rally for Webster. By April 1851, Everett himself had lost patience with stubborn antislavery agitators who refused to get behind the Union. A Fast Day preacher who "said though we condemn their course 'we ought to honor their conscientiousness'" miffed Everett to no end. "When the flames of civil war are lighted throughout the continent," he exploded in his diary, "the conscientiousness of the fanatics & intriguers, who are now working the abolition excitement for the most profligate purposes, will be very precious to the Country!" In April 1851 he again declined an invitation to speak at a Webster rally but this time sent a public letter arguing that all good citizens owed Webster their "confidence and gratitude" for his Union-saving efforts. "I have not in every instance agreed with him as to individual opinions and measures," he candidly confessed. "But I have never differed from him without some distrust of my own judgment."[74]

As that letter suggested, Everett became increasingly willing to publicly embrace Webster's position. In September 1851, he informed a correspondent that standing in the good graces of "Mr. Webster's friends" was such a priority that "that consideration is decisive with me." Also in 1851, Everett attached his name as editor and introducer to a much-anticipated six-volume publication of Webster's speeches. His introduction staked out for Webster the position of an unrivaled authority on the Constitution and defender of the Union. His whole career, Everett argued, walked the thorny path of statesmanship in order "to confirm and perpetuate the great work of the constitutional fathers of the last generation." As editor Everett made sure to include all of Webster's major speeches defending the Compromise of 1850, and he introduced his Seventh of March effort as "a speech for 'the Constitution and the Union,'" rather than with the original published title that had advertised the speech as being "upon the subject of slavery."[75]

Everett also came to play a prominent role in Webster's political schemes in 1851 (pushing for a Unionist coalition of Whigs and Democrats) and 1852 (once again seeking the Whig presidential nomination). By November 1851, Everett was such a prominent supporter of the Unionist merger that at least one newspaper suggested he would be an excellent vice presidential nominee in 1852 for this projected new party. Instead, he followed Webster's lead when he abandoned that endeavor and worked hard to secure Webster the Whig nomination.[76] In the final analysis, Everett sided with the Unionist part of himself and thus with Webster. Looking back in January 1852, he was relieved that "things were not carried to worse extremes than they were, at the South." That happy escape "must I think fairly be ascribed, in a good degree, to Mr. W's course."[77]

———

But that confidence about Webster and the Union's prospects had been a long time coming, and in the midst of the prolonged crisis Everett had become shockingly cavalier about the prospect of secession. It is jarring to read him repeatedly thinking in pragmatic terms about making disunion work, heretical as that was against both the Seventh of March speech and Everett's career-long and earnest Unionism. Secessionists would be taught the ultimate lesson by being allowed to leave and see how much they missed the Union, he vowed more than once. They needed to learn somehow that seceding would not protect their property in slaves from Northern agitation, just as Northern agitators had to learn that slavery would not be abolished as a result of disunion. He could imagine such instruction as temporary because he believed South Carolina would be alone in seceding. "It would be wrong," he granted, "to abandon the loyal minority," who were "entitled to be protected in their attachment to the Union."[78] But "a separation would probably be a less evil," he offered, "than a continued Struggle & antagonism under the name of Union." And saving even the shell of national unity seemed increasingly out of reach anyway. "A deadly arrow is in the body of the victim," he despaired in November 1850, yet "to extract it is almost certain death."[79] He therefore devoted much thought and ink to privately probing the practicalities of an amicable national divorce. In one letter he mused that "dividing the territory between the separating parties" would prove an "impossibility." But more often, he thought it might not be completely unworkable. The federal government might appoint commissioners to negotiate terms of separation with representatives from South Carolina. And in whatever administrative form, he believed, "the proper course to be pursued by the North" was to warn Southerners "that the dissolution of the Union would be the worst thing imaginable both for North & South,—but we see you are determined to have it." "Reasonable men" should thus work to "draw up a plan of a peaceful separation;—not rush blindly upon it, & leave the *mode* of bringing about this great event to chance, which is nearly the same as insuring a civil war."[80] Trying to be hardheaded, Everett fell victim in this case to fuzzy thinking; if disunion were truly "the worst thing imaginable," why let it happen under any scenario?

In the early 1850s, then, even the redoubtable Unionist Everett's position was a far cry from hardcore, unconditional Unionism. Indeed, he believed it was possible "to push what we may call the 'Union agitation' too far," alienating by one's own intemperance those who were precariously in the Unionist camp because they were put off by proslavery and/or antislavery zealots. By May 1851, all Everett could say was that secession rested ultimately on the right of revolution, in which "it is the right, in a case of extreme & hopeless oppression, to rebel." But "no government can ever admit the exercise of this right, because that would be to admit itself to be intolerably & hopelessly oppressive."[81] But failing to believe any administration would allow secession was not to dismiss outright the legitimacy of secession. To study Everett during this crisis is to understand how much cultural work he and others had to do to create a mass of Americans committed enough to fight for the Union—starting with himself.[82]

As these reflections suggest, Everett at times even lost faith in the ability of historical commemoration to bind the Union together through patriotic emotion. In 1848, Everett's belief in this cause had been strong enough that he jumped at the invitation to address the New England Society in New York, sure that "expounding & unfolding the principles on which New England was founded & prospered" was just what the country needed. His friend Winthrop had just given an oration at the 4 July cornerstone ceremony for the Washington Monument in the nation's capital, and Everett was very encouraged by its sentiments and reception. At that hopeful moment early in Europe's revolutionary year, Winthrop intoned that this was the time "to hold up afresh to the admiration and imitation of mankind the character and example of George

Washington." But the sectional crisis as well as the course of European revolution would severely test such hopes, making many leading Americans wonder whether they could rescue a consensus view of the Revolutionary heritage. They also feared that younger generations had lost their sense of connection to the Revolutionary generation.[83]

For Everett himself, the virulence of sectionalism in 1850 suggested that perhaps unifying works of historical commemoration were as much the fruits of as the means toward national harmony. So throughout 1850, he wondered whether the atmosphere was just too poisonous for orators to make a difference. Patriotic emotions in which he had previously put so much stock came to seem to him mere "vague & sentimental exclamations." He rejected speaking invitations that he likely previously would have accepted and vacillated even after receiving offers he really could not refuse—such as to give a high-profile speech on the seventy-fifth anniversary of the Battle of Bunker Hill. That was partly on account of his health, but "our community too is so wretchedly torn to pieces, on the great questions which would force themselves into a patriotic address, that I hardly dare undertake to deliver one." Even after accepting this invitation, he fretted that "there is no longer any patriotic feeling in the country. All interest in every other topic" seemed to be "eaten up" by the slavery question. For Everett to fuss about the size and attentiveness of his audience was not new, but for him to speak of "hardly dar[ing]" to address these themes was. To another invitation to speak on a commemorative occasion, he responded that while he retained a strong "desire to make an appeal to the Public, in favor of the Union of the States," "I want courage to make up my mind to do it."[84]

For the conflict-averse Everett, this deficit of daring flowed from the rising stridency of those who would contest his version of American history. Southern sectionalists protested his speeches' tendency to treat the North and South evenhandedly and declared literary independence from Yankee productions like Everett's. The *Southern Quarterly Review*, while extolling the oratorical style of Everett's speech at Bunker Hill, differed widely with its message. While Everett had argued that the Union should trump any local interests, this Southern reviewer retorted that union with abolitionists led to dangerous discord and the threat of national authority trampling Southern rights. In the Senate, Calhoun argued vociferously that legislation protecting those rights, not "eulogies on the Union," was what would save that Union. And he warned that Southerners like himself found nothing in the Revolutionary Fathers' history "to deter us from seceding from the Union, should it fail to fulfil the objects for which it was instituted."[85]

More important for Everett, Massachusetts abolitionists and Free Soilers escalated their claims to the founding legacy during the late 1840s and early 1850s. In 1851, for instance, as authorities marched Thomas Sims back to slavery under the provisions of the FSA, abolitionists pointed with shame to "the holy spot[s]" of Revolutionary history the procession passed. Mann called on the state's young men to live up to "the noble lineage of the Pilgrims" by rejecting the Compromise of 1850's "base desertion" of New England and American founding principles. Parker placed abolitionists' provocative activism within the tradition of troublemaking begun by the "troublesome commonwealth of Puritans" and carried on by the American and other revolutions. Sumner, however, proved the most effective expounder of this subversive reading as he worked to identify the principles of the Free Soil Party with those of the Founding Fathers. Seeking to parry those who continually quoted Washington's Farewell Address against the very existence of his party, he countered that it was slaveholders and their allies who had subverted the Founders' original intent and practice. In fact, he maintained, by dint of "constantly avowing his sentiments in favor of the abolition of Slavery, Washington is properly called an Abolitionist." In speech after speech, he attacked compromising pols as unworthy of the cherished Pilgrim and Revolutionary inheritances.[86]

Everett's narrative of American history had never been uncontested, but such competitors as Sumner put Everett on the defensive like never before. Even while mired in doubt, he considered that it would be unpatriotic to leave this field entirely to the Sumners of the world. In June 1850, Everett assured his close friend and erstwhile London physician Henry Holland that there was no avoiding the American Revolution in contemporary American culture. "All the important events connected with it," he informed Holland, "have acquired & possess that interest for us" with which all nations endowed their "most signal national occurrences. Whatever Marathon, or Thermopylae, or Salamis was to the Greeks, Bunker Hill & the Fourth of July are to us." Given that fact, "the only question is by whom shall the commemoration be conducted and in what spirit?" If "moderate & conservative" men did not take the stand on such occasions, "it will fall into the hands of a different class," namely "our radical party."[87]

Everett waded back into these waters in 1850 in part through letters to be read at public meetings to which he had declined to speak. "It is shocking to reflect," he wrote for a New England Society meeting, that the "labors & sufferings" of both Pilgrims and Founding Fathers would be wasted on their posterity "unless a better feeling can be made to prevail between North & South."[88] He did address the citizens of Concord on the seventy-fifth anniversary of that town's Revolutionary battle. He used the occasion to extol the Revolution for giving Americans the constitutional Union as their birthright. "Blessed by the wisdom of our forefathers with such a safeguard against anarchy and wars," he exhorted, if the present generation "should rashly cast it away, what words of condemnation will adequately describe our folly?"[89]

Everett also continued his work behind the scenes to preserve and maximize the political impact of relics of American Revolutionary history. He labored to acquire for Harvard's library some volumes that had once belonged to Washington and to transcribe the sainted man's marginal notations in these books. This was just one of many Revolutionary relics he acquired and carefully conserved in these years. During a visit to the nation's capital in 1851, he and some traveling companions persevered through "uninviting" weather to perform a pilgrimage to Mount Vernon. He reveled in and when necessary defended Washington's spotless international reputation.[90] Throughout 1849 and 1850, he did yeoman's work for the Bunker Hill Monument Association, including directing endless meetings trying to get assorted details of the monument just right.[91] Everett was far from alone in seeking to leverage patriotic relics for Unionist purposes during this era. Early in the congressional debates that led to the Compromise of 1850, Clay moved that Congress buy a manuscript copy of the Farewell Address, given that "some tangible, palpable object, always addresses itself to our hearts and to our feelings." Later in the debate Clay brandished what he called "a fragment of the coffin of Washington" as a voice from the grave for compromise and Union.[92]

In late 1850, Everett corresponded with Winthrop and others in Washington seeking congressional funding for a statue of Bunker Hill hero General Joseph Warren for Faneuil Hall. He and the committee for which he wrote hoped this would be but the beginning of a whole federally funded "system of commemorative works of art." They had the political acumen to also approach a representative from Virginia for support in pairing the money for Warren with some to erect a statue to a Virginia hero of the Revolution in that state.[93] Nor did this committee neglect private sources of funding, circulating a subscription book to Boston's elite to marshal peer pressure for the cause. Everett made no effort to hide the political purposes that would be served by this statue to the fallen hero. Given America's sectional impasse, he wrote in December 1850, "we ought to employ all honorable means to strengthen the feeling of patriotic attachment to the Union; & few things are better calculated to promote this end, than a recurrence to the services of the great men to whose efforts & sacrifices we owe the Union." "A marble statue of a revolutionary worthy in Faneuil Hall," he argued, "would plead as strongly for the Union, as the most eloquent living man that ever opened his lips there."[94] These were pressure sales tactics, to be sure, but the Warren statue campaign gave Everett the opportunity to reflect on the efficacy of such efforts at a crucial time. Didactic commemorative work might not save the Union, Everett seems to have concluded, but nothing else would.

Everett's first truly prominent oratorical effort in this troubled period was his Bunker Hill address on 17 June 1850. He prepared diligently to address the dignitaries and enormous throng who gathered in a huge ship house in the Navy Yard in Charlestown. Given the expected crowd and the gigantic stakes for such an address at such a time in the nation's history, he recorded that "I have never felt so much anxiety for the result" of a speech.[95] When his time to speak came, he asserted that the battle's importance "rests mainly" in how it "affected the cause of liberty and the condition of man for ages," for his review of Western history convinced him that the American Revolution was "a mighty step forward in the march of humanity; an all-important portion of the great plan which regulates the fortunes of our race." Part of that impact was in how the Revolutionaries embodied "unsuspected disinterestedness." This was especially true of Washington, whose character was a veritable "dispensation of public virtue." "Oh," he cried, "that the contemplation of their bright example and pure fame might elevate our minds above the selfish passions, the fierce contentions, and the dark forebodings of the day!" He emphasized that the true "fulfilment of the destiny of the American revolution" was the creation of the Union. Those who would break up said Union would "commit a folly for which the language we speak has no name," in part because Europe's beleaguered reformers "are looking anxiously to us for lessons of practical freedom." All the material progress in the world would be hollow, he concluded, unless "public spirit and love of country catch from heart to heart."[96] This speech announced that Everett was back. Situating American history within both the global history and the contemporary fortunes of human liberty, he countered those who argued that slavery impaired America's example by asserting that disunion would more surely achieve that catastrophe. While Providence had a plan for freedom, Americans must choose to participate in that design by giving their hearts to the sacred Union.[97] And it must have been encouraging to Everett to receive significant support for this effusion from important sources. Webster, for one, sent a letter to be read at this event. And papers including a Southern Whig sheet lauded Everett's Bunker Hill oration for its "brilliant" exhortation to Unionism.[98]

He built on the momentum from this speech when he addressed a throng of like-minded souls in New York City at a dinner celebrating Washington's birthday on 22 February 1851. Washington's life, he pronounced, was "a subject of which an American audience can never tire," for "I might almost say, but for the sacrifice of human life that would be occasioned by it, that one would rather that half the continent should sink, than that we should lose his memory and character." Americans in 1851 needed his example so badly because his great Farewell Address emphasized above all else "ADHERENCE TO THE UNION." For Everett had reluctantly "come to the conclusion that the Union is in great danger." He rebuked those who thought disunion would lead to two peaceable neighboring nations, warning that disunion would lead to civil war. Thus "there will not be two confederacies, nor eventually any confederacies, but as many despotic governments as, in the chances of conquest and reconquest, military chieftains may be able and willing to establish." Thus, only "when we have turned a deaf ear to the voice of Washington, and Adams, and Jefferson, and Franklin, the Moses and the prophets of our political dispensation," would Americans be so foolish as to tear asunder "this family of States."[99] The dangers of the times that had once dispirited Everett now urged him to even more effusive Unionist rhetoric. In this speech he elaborated perhaps like never before the dystopia of disunion and escalated his familial rhetoric as applied to the Union.

Especially once this speech was published, Everett had reason to believe that it had been a Unionist triumph. As he had done on the Bunker Hill occasion, Webster had sent a letter to be read at the New York dinner, preaching the relevance of Washington's Farewell Address. Everett proceeded from New York to visit his daughter Charlotte in Washington. During this sojourn, various friendly Washington dignitaries lavished "extravagant" praise on the oration. He reflected that when it came to the impact speeches have, "much depends on circumstances of the time: the feeling of the audience & of the speaker."[100] The man and the hour had met, and Everett had risen to the challenge.

Everett aspired to more than transient influence, however, so he paid increasing attention to his published legacy in the early 1850s. On Christmas Day in 1850, paralyzed by "low spirits & ill health," he tried to be philosophical about the resulting lack of opportunity to "do something for the benefit of society & my own reputation." Jesus Christ, he reminded himself, had "died a cruel death at the age of 30" but had wrought a "mighty change in the world by a few spoken words." In the nineteenth century, however, the printing press exerted the broadest and most permanent sway. Surely influenced by working on Webster's published writings, he set about putting his own papers in order so that he would have control over their message. He also worked to ensure that newspaper accounts of his orations approximated accuracy.[101]

He jealously guarded his sterling reputation as a nationalist orator in other less subtle ways. In an 1849 didactic work for the young men of America, Cincinnatian Elias Magoon urged his audience to emulate Everett's "acute sensibility to patriotic associations" as well as his careful dedication to his craft. Everett appreciated "the friendly spirit" of this unsolicited treatment by Magoon but was not above orchestrating friendly reviews. He published a second volume of orations and speeches in 1850. When he read a letter in Richmond's *Southern Literary Messenger*, the flagship Southern literary review, lamenting that he had wasted his talents on such "ephemeral productions" as orations, Everett responded to the editor with a point-by-point refutation of these criticisms.[102] The editor, John Thompson, replied quickly that if he had his way, both volumes of Everett's orations would be "favorably noticed" in his journal. In fact, Thompson preferred the review to be "done by some literary friend of" Everett's. Everett promptly approached fellow Whig Charles Wentworth Upham with an invitation to write this review as an act of "friendship." At Upham's request Everett offered suggestions on themes and speeches he wanted emphasized and even agreed with Upham's suggestion that Everett inspect the essay and then be the one to send it to Thompson! At the same time Everett and Thompson were jointly engineering a gushing commentary on his volumes, Everett was working to achieve Thompson's bid to travel as an American representative to the London Exhibition in 1851. Neither, it appears, had any qualms about mingling these two items in their correspondence.[103]

More than his own reputation was at stake, of course; his Christmas diary entry had also named "the benefit of society." And that society had no more pressing political problem, Everett reflected in April 1850, than that "the immense extent of the Country & its division into separate States destroys its political unity." Congress was no unifier, bringing together representatives of state and sectional rather than national interests. He thus hoped that nationalist orators could obtain "a legitimate general influence throughout the country." He would thus have been thrilled to read the *North American Review* essay on volume 2 of his orations. Because reviewer C. C. Felton hoped "the counsels of a wise moderation" would prevail in America in 1850, Everett's new volume "could not have come out in a better time, or more seasonably for the state of the public mind." For what tied together the apparently disparate speeches in the volume was a certain "Americanism of feeling," a "pervading patriotic purpose."[104] There is no evidence that Everett directly procured this particular review, but it could not have captured his speaking and publishing career's goals better if he had.

If Everett in the early 1850s had reembraced that career with new vigor, as he and the country moved toward the mid-1850s he would have opportunities to augment it with a return to the national political stage proper. The crucial turning point was the late 1852 death of Webster, the friend and mentor who had overshadowed Everett in politics and even oratory.[105] The events that followed not only opened up new contests over memory with abolitionists and Free Soilers but also placed Everett back on a promising political trajectory.

7

Shooting Star in Washington

SECRETARY OF STATE AND SENATOR

After the relative obscurity of the early 1850s, from late 1852 to the end of 1853 Edward Everett saw his political star rise to dizzying heights, including widespread talk of an 1856 presidential nomination. This political prominence was very much a function of that brief period's atmosphere of sectional and partisan entente, as well as of Everett's political acumen as secretary of state. That political moment also allowed him the space in which to synthesize and promulgate his mature judgments on questions ranging from slavery, race, and reform to the American nation's standing in history and on the world stage. But in phases over the first half of 1854, his star fizzled out, ending with another retreat from the national political stage in May of that year. This precipitous tailing off had everything to do with the Kansas-Nebraska Act and Everett's response to it in the Senate. Everett thus had abundant personal as well as political reasons to decry the existence and authors of that fateful bill.

––––––

Daniel Webster's death on 24 October 1852 would do for Everett's political arc what the death of another patron and mentor, Peter C. Brooks, had done for his financial prospects. In the short term Everett's primary task was to properly preserve and present the statesman's public legacy. Knowing that that legacy would be safe in Everett's hands, Webster in his will had appointed him chief among his literary executors. Everett also served as an adviser to various community efforts to commission memorial portraits and statues of the fallen hero. He had plenty of company both in publicly lamenting Webster's death and in tending his posthumous image. George Ticknor, another of Webster's literary executors, bore witness to "the sincerity and extent of the sorrow" in Boston at the loss of the statesman. He hoped he discerned "a touch of repentance in it for the injustice that has been done him" when alive.[1]

Webster's abolitionist and Free Soiler critics ensured that his decease touched off not consensus but another bruising debate. Abolitionist Wendell Phillips attacked Conscience Whigs for even attending Webster's public funeral in Boston; this was no time to apply the standard deference to the dead. Charles Sumner decided to remain silent and abstain from attending the memorial services.[2] Theodore Parker, for his part, did not hesitate to speak ill of the dead. New Englanders and Americans, he charged, revered Webster as great only because of their moral adolescence. In fact, Webster had lacked "both moral principle and intellectual ideas, political ethics and political economy," as revealed by corrupt productions such as his *Creole* letter and Seventh of March speech. He railed that Webster had rechristened 7 March the "day of St. Judas," for on that day in 1850 "Mr. Webster became the ally of the worst of men, . . . the advocate of slavery," and "the assassin of Liberty." In fact, "the Anglo-Saxon race never knew such a terrible and calamitous ruin" as Webster's, in part because "he enticed the nation in his fall. Shame on us!" Parker continued such assaults in future years. In 1854, for instance, he decried fund-raising by Everett's committee for a statue of Webster near the State House in Boston. Revolutionary heroes like John Hancock, Samuel Adams, and John Adams had no such memorials, because "the homage of the people is their epitaph." Webster, meanwhile, "had his monument" when the federal government forced the return of a fugitive slave to Virginia.[3]

Everett rose to meet this challenge. Everett's first assessment of Webster's career, offered privately to his son-in-law Henry Wise on the day he learned of Webster's demise, featured qualification and nuance. "It might upon the whole," he ventured, "be admitted that Mr. W. was in many respects the first of American Statesmen."[4] But Everett knew that this tepid stuff would not do in the contested public arena. The previous July, Henry Clay's funeral procession from Washington to Kentucky had allowed for an enormous outpouring of Unionist sentiment, and both Webster and the nation deserved the same in relation to his death.[5] Everett presided over Boston's public memorial service on 27 October 1852, at which Webster's statesmanlike devotion to Union was the dominant theme. In his speech, Everett argued that Webster's career was one long effort "to strengthen the pillars of the Union." This was why, he submitted, the nation's grief in 1852 was comparable to the 1799 mourning over Washington.[6] A few days later he publicly appealed for Whigs to rally around Webster's grave and support the regular party ticket in the imminent election. Everett also heartily joined an August 1853 celebration of Plymouth's Pilgrim heritage, which abounded with grassroots tributes to Webster, Washington, and other symbols of the Union as a vital part of that heritage. What the Pilgrims brought to the New World, Everett chimed, was a "political code" uniting "religion and liberty, morals and law" in balance, just as he and Webster had advocated.[7]

Everett agreed to replace Webster as secretary of state, in fact, in part to perpetuate a friendly version of Webster's memory. Webster himself had made clear to President Fillmore his wishes that Everett succeed him. The president wasted no time, telegraphing Everett with the offer on the day word reached him of Webster's death. Five days later, Everett decided that his family situation would allow it and accepted the nomination. "It has not been the least of the motives that have influenced me," he confided in a friend a few days later, "that the Department should pass into the hands of a devoted personal friend" of Webster's. He physically took up the office on 6 November, four days after the election of Franklin Pierce had officially made the Fillmore administration a lame duck. He found the State Department in some disarray due to Webster's long illness and immediately went about the one task of bringing his hero and friend's work to an orderly conclusion.[8]

But Everett made sense as the secretary, and gladly accepted the post, for more reasons than his association with Webster. He had remained earnestly engaged in the international sphere ever since his return from his diplomatic tour of Britain. He had pushed the ideal of the finished English gentleman on the students during his time at Harvard and remained proud of his ongoing British connections and international reputation. Years after his return to America he wished he had spent fewer hours corresponding with friends in Europe, but on the other hand, "I enjoy a great deal of pleasure in this epistolary intercourse." Furthermore, "I think a friendly correspondence between Europe & America not without beneficial effects of a wider kind, than personal gratification." Indeed, he had harbored hopes of returning to the post at St. James, which he thought "the most desirable under the government," when Taylor was elected president in 1848. Short of that, his correspondence with policymakers on both sides of the Atlantic sought to further amicable Anglo-American relations.[9]

Everett had not confined his interest and expertise to Britain when out of diplomatic office. Fillmore respected his authority on international matters and was especially grateful for Everett's support for his administration's refusal to intervene in the revolutions in Europe.[10] That was only natural given that Everett had helped shape the public articulation of that policy. Both in Britain and America in the early 1850s, appeals by Hungarian revolutionaries such as Louis Kossuth for intervention against the Austrian Empire's domination of their homeland created sensational enthusiasm. But this issue also exacerbated partisan and sectional divisions in the United States. Webster and Fillmore wanted no part of a movement that raised such a specter of disunity in the tense aftermath of the Compromise of 1850. Conservative Whigs also deeply resented Kossuth's public dismissals of George Washington's farewell plea for a noninterventionist American foreign policy. So the administration rebuffed both Kossuth's demands for intervention on his side and Austrian ambassador Johann Georg Hulsemann's complaints that the United States had already done too much to support the Hungarian movement.[11]

In late 1850, Webster asked Everett to help him craft a public response to Hulsemann. Everett had long had no use for the Kossuth mania, which in any event could never compare to the authority of Washington's Farewell Address as a guide. So he responded with a draft emphasizing that this was no time to abandon the United States' traditional nonintervention policy. Webster added rhetorical flights to the final Hulsemann letter about America's greatness and destiny, which were gratuitous from a foreign policy perspective but served his larger goal of preserving national unity. "I wished to write a paper," he confessed to Ticknor in January 1851, "which should touch the national pride, and make a man feel *sheepish* and look *silly* who should speak of disunion." For his part, Everett followed the publication and reception of the letter with mild irritation that his help never became public knowledge. The tone of the final letter also bothered him slightly. He had long believed that "our politics in every department are poisoned by electioneering & demagoguery." So while he shared Webster's hope that rallying behind George Washington would cement national unity, he thought Webster's additions to his draft "too fierce & bitter," catering "to the American appetite for highly spiced statements."[12]

But for all of Everett's suspicion of electioneering foreign policy, his time at the State Department provided irresistible temptations to advance a political agenda. For starters, he clearly had the ear of the president, as witnessed by how he helped shape Fillmore's final message to Congress in December 1852. Noting that Queen Victoria's recent speech to Parliament had paid tribute to the late Duke of Wellington, Everett suggested that Fillmore do the same for Webster. Fillmore, almost as solicitous for Webster's legacy as Everett was, readily agreed. Fillmore also submitted drafts of his message to Everett and asked him to pay close attention to passages on slavery and on "progress." The final version of the latter passage bore Everett's imprint in its call for "conservatism and progress" to "blend their harmonious action." But Everett, along with Postmaster General John J. Crittenden of Kentucky, strongly advised Fillmore to studiously avoid the no-win topic of slavery. Although they were outnumbered in the cabinet, Fillmore deleted the slavery section. What is more, the message disavowed an interest in annexing Cuba specifically because "it might revive those conflicts of opinion between the different sections of the country which lately shook the Union to its center, and which have been so happily compromised."[13]

Everett's and Crittenden's advice triumphed for much the same reason that Everett's star was on the ascendant in late 1852: it was a period in which most American citizens and politicians wished to let sleeping sectional dogs lie. Unlike his sectionally fraught nomination fight in 1841, Everett's nomination as secretary of state sailed through the Senate with nary a whisper of protest either there or in the press. Within a matter of days of this confirmation, Americans went to the polls. Democrat Franklin Pierce won nearly 51 percent of the popular vote, Whig Winfield Scott 44 percent. The only major candidate who did not endorse as final the Compromise of 1850, John P. Hale of the Free Soil Party, managed only half as many votes as Van Buren had received in 1848, including only 6.6 percent of the overall Northern vote. Democrats also had enormous momentum in House elections in the North in 1852 and 1853. Despite low turnout, it is hard to avoid reading all this as an overwhelming endorsement of the compromise by those who did vote.[14] It would prove tempting to Everett to use foreign policy to further American politics' trend toward national unity.

The prime political opportunity of Everett's secretaryship came from the French and British ministers in Washington in relation to Cuba. As Spanish power in the New World ebbed in the second quarter of the nineteenth century, American policymakers grew concerned that the enslaved sugar island might fall under the sway of Great Britain. Both they and their constituents were divided on the idea of the United States annexing Cuba, however, in part because that would inevitably stir up sectional controversy. Ardent American expansionists including aggressive slaveholders and the Young America movement within the Democratic Party swelled the chorus for annexation in the early 1850s, but caution still ruled the day with policymakers. In 1852, the French and British governments, alarmed by the prospect of yet another American annexation of a strategically placed slave territory, invited Webster to join them in forswearing the incorporation of Cuba into any of their expanding empires. Webster and Fillmore seem to have hesitantly supported this scheme but decided it would be rash to act with the presidential election still looming.[15] These ministers pressed the issue on Everett within days of his arrival in Washington. After consultation with the cabinet reinforced Everett's own resistance to this "entangling alliance," he retired to his room at Willard's Hotel and tossed off a response that became the official letter with very little alteration. This missive went to the two ministers on 1 December 1852. Everett preserved his self-image as a nonpolitical secretary by declining Fillmore's suggestion that he send this epistle to Congress as part of the documents accompanying the president's message. But he also immediately pronounced it "my great Cuban Manifesto" and understood that it would have significant political impact once it became public.[16]

Everett's letter deflected the proposed convention in a way that deftly balanced conservatism with Young American–style nationalist rhetoric. All past American territorial expansions, he argued vigorously, "have been brought about by the operation of natural causes, and without any disturbance of the international relations of the principal States." However, there would be something alarming to the United States, and nothing natural, about the transfer of Cuba from Spain to another European power. Thus, the Fillmore administration "considers the condition of Cuba as mainly an American question. The proposed convention," by contrast, "assumes that the United States have no other or greater interest in the question than France or England; whereas it is necessary only to cast one's eye on the map" to see the folly of such an assumption. "For domestic reasons," he delicately hinted, "on which, in a communication of this kind, it might not be proper to dwell," the administration believed it would be "hazardous" to annex Cuba. Still, it seemed very likely that Cuba would come into the Union at some point anyway, for territorial expansion was "the undoubted operation of the law of our political existence." Therefore, to sign this treaty would not only break with one of "the oldest traditions of the federal government," namely the "aversion to political alliances with European powers" enjoined by Washington and other Founders. It would also be unwise to disable all future generations of Americans "from making an acquisition which might take place . . . in the natural order of things." In sum, the proposed convention rested on European notions that were "not applicable to America," whose history was characterized by "the law of progress, which is as organic and vital in the youth of states as of individual men."[17] It was a remarkable nod to the Young American idea of Manifest Destiny for this Northern Whig to cast the annexation of Texas and even the Mexican War acquisitions as the benign working out of the law of American progress. But this epistle also placed the refusal in context of the long traditions of American foreign policy stretching back to the sainted Washington.

A politically important epilogue to this December 1852 exchange stretched well beyond Everett's time as secretary. British foreign secretary Lord John Russell took umbrage with Everett's response to the tripartite scheme, and his rebuttal in a February 1853 dispatch to the British minister in Washington went public. Russell contested the idea "that the United States have an interest in Cuba, to which Great Britain and France cannot pretend," pointing to the proximity of their colonial possessions. He ended by lecturing all Americans that they should not be "insensible to the value of those eternal laws of right and wrong, of peace and friendship, and of duty to our neighbors, which ought to guide every Christian nation." In September 1853, after ascertaining that the new secretary of state had no objection to his publishing a response, Everett did just that. His open letter refuted Russell's claims to have an equal interest in Cuba. But mostly he remonstrated against Russell's hectoring tone, which echoed that of the European press that abused Americans "as a nation of land-pirates." That was precisely why his original letter set out "to show that our growth had been a natural growth." As a clincher, Everett asked readers to consider "the recent antecedents of the powers that invite us to disable ourselves to the end of time from the acquisition in any way of this natural appendage to our Continent." France had engaged in imperial conquest under all of its recent regimes. "England, not to mention her other numerous recent acquisitions in every part of the globe, has, even since" Russell's letter "was written, annexed half of the Burman empire to her overgrown Indian possessions," on dubious grounds. In short, while Everett was "not led to think that the United States have reached the final limits of their growth," he found it unreasonable and disrespectful for "England and France, while they are daily extending themselves on every shore and in every sea, and pushing their dominions, by new conquests, to the uttermost ends of the earth, to call upon the United States" to forswear forever annexing "an island which lies at their doors, and commands the entrance into the interior of their continent."[18] Russell had obviously touched a nerve with Everett, the same one that had been exposed during the Literary War and at times when he served in London, by manifesting the insufferable condescension too many Europeans displayed toward the United States. Given the global as well as personal stakes involved, such snobs should be summarily removed from their high horse.

Everett earned almost universal plaudits for such jousting with the European powers. The process of his seminal original letter going public began in late December 1852 when James Mason, chair of the Foreign Affairs committee, read it and moved for it to be communicated to Congress. Over Everett's weak protests, by January it had made it into the newspapers. The reaction underscored that Everett had found the rare consensus position on a complex international-cum-sectional issue. All congressmen and their wives who approached Everett after reading the letter offered high praise.[19] Everett's exegesis of the Monroe Doctrine shaped the Cuba policy of all subsequent administrations down to the 1890s.[20] Press coverage of both of Everett's letters was fulsome. Some Democratic sheets offered the tepid critique that Everett should have left to the sitting secretary of state the task of responding to Russell. But on the whole editors in both parties and all regions declared Everett's defenses of America's honor unanswerable. They also remarked on its balance; "it is at once," gushed one typical editor, "a noble vindication of American progress and independence, and a conservative, statesmanlike survey of our foreign and domestic policy." A Southern writer noted that one of the chief attractions of Everett's correspondence on Cuba was "the absence of all sectional spirit in a question which, in some aspects, presented great sectional difficulties."[21] Everett's diary entries reveal that he happily absorbed all this praise and easily deflected the weak criticism.[22]

Everett rode this sudden wave of national popularity into the U.S. Senate even before his term as secretary of state had concluded. Whigs in the Massachusetts legislature nominated him for the seat in late January 1853, and his foreign policy acumen and the consensus behind it were chief among the reasons that all observers considered his election a certainty. That election took place on 2 February. On 18 February, Senator John Davis presented Everett's credentials as his replacement, effective when his term as secretary expired. He took his seat in the Senate on 4 March, just minutes after concluding business at the State Department. Despite qualms about his and his wife's health holding out for six years, Everett relished this whirlwind transition from one important national government position to another. He had also recently taken the unusual step of purchasing a home in Washington and could look forward to owning rather than renting in the capital. Not only was a place in the Senate "perhaps the most respectable under the government," but his election signaled the indefinite extension of his unexpected second lease on national political life.[23]

The Everett wave was so strong in 1853 that numerous observers prognosticated that it would carry him well beyond the Senate to the presidency. Multiple politicians and editors of both parties conversed with and wrote to him about his prospects for 1856.[24] Newspapers of various partisan tints recognized his sudden rise, many of which sought to further this boomlet. The pseudonymous writer "Cotton Plant," in a piece originally in the Baltimore Times but widely reprinted, celebrated "EVERETT'S PROGRESS," for he represented all that was patriotic as well as the blessings of peace with the world. "Everett would teach us to surround our homes with comfort and our firesides with cheerfulness," "Cotton Plant" effused. "Everett's is the progress of men acting under the impulse of their noblest qualities—his opponent's, the progress of men with every baser passion aroused." That unnamed opponent—surely the Young American faction within the Democracy—"seeks to gain an extensive domain saturated with blood; the other, to spread over what we have, the pleasant verdure of rural culture and waving harvests." Everett's vision was best suited to this "age of benevolence," so "*his* progress is true progress, and it will be well if the American people listen to his voice."[25] For his part, a Southern Democratic writer differed with his party brethren who would impede Everett's progress. Democrats would rally better against a worthy opponent like Everett, he argued. "We trust that he *will* be the nominee of the whigs," he forecast, "and that we shall beat him, through an equal, and a gentleman—one with worth and education, and ability, like his own."[26]

One of the more curious negative responses, and the one that drew Everett's attention the most, came not from a Democrat but from New York Whig power Thurlow Weed. In August 1853, at the very peak of Everett-for-president talk, Weed's *Albany Evening Journal* ran an editorial that on its face sought merely to deny Clay the credit for saving Everett's nomination as minister to Britain. Instead, his story went, two other Southern Whigs in cooperation with Weed himself had assured Everett's confirmation. His account rehearsed the accusations against Everett from Southerners but pronounced them "unfounded" and the opposition to him "wanton and intolerant."[27] Everett was convinced that this seemingly harmless story was Weed's cunning way to damage his popularity in the South and thus clear away a rival to fellow New York Whig William Seward's rise to the presidency. Even such a subtle introduction of the slavery issue into the discussion of Everett for president was anathema to the would-be candidate, eroding the very ground on which he stood.[28] And black abolitionist Frederick Douglass's published reaction to Weed's story illustrated precisely why Everett could derive no benefit from the injection of this issue. Weed's account of how Southern Whigs secured his confirmation took any potential "anti-slavery wind out of the sails of Mr. Everett," Douglass averred. "The great representatives of slavery in the Senate" had supporting his confirmation because they were convinced he "was sound on all subjects relating to Southern interests." And they were right, for "the only position he has been known to occupy, is that of the most desperate enmity to human rights."[29]

On the other hand, rival New York Whig editors sensed that Weed was trying to damage Everett by associating him with abolitionism while also staking a Union-saving claim for Seward's clique. James Gordon Bennett, in the powerful *New York Herald*, proclaimed plainly that "the object of Mr. Thurlow Weed, in this exposé of his concerning Mr. Everett's confirmation to England, was to cripple him in the South, and among the Union whigs of the North, in reference to the next presidential campaign." It had "become manifest, within the short interval of half a year, that there is not a man in the country . . . in any way more acceptable to the Union compromise men of the late whig party, than Edward Everett." He had as secretary and senator proven himself "as the fit successor of Daniel Webster in enlightened, liberal, national and truly American statesmanship. If the administration of Mr. Fillmore went out in an unexpected 'blaze of glory,' it was due to" Everett's tripartite letter. And Everett continued to guide the country's foreign affairs in the Senate. But more to the point, because "Mr. Everett is not a free-soiler" he had "become obnoxious to W. H. Seward, Weed and Company, in the inverse ratio of his popularity with the Union compromise and progressive whigs of the whole country; and unless the stigma of abolition or free soil antecedents can be fastened upon him, there is some danger that he may become too strong for the Seward disorganizers in 1856."[30]

Everett's response to all this presidential talk was a mixture of pride, guarded optimism, and genuine surprise given that just months previously he had come out of relative obscurity to finish Webster's work. He assured a New York editor that until the dawn of 1853 "I had no more idea of being thought of for the Presidency than for the throne of China." But while he had not originally designed this rise to presidential prominence, "it would be absurd in me to say that the idea" of a nomination had not "occurred to me because in that time, I have received a great many letters & newspapers from all parts of the Union" trumpeting his name. He reveled in his newfound celebrity, and in his year-in-review diary entry on his fifty-ninth birthday he ventured that his acceptance of two prominent national positions gave "a complexion . . . perhaps to all the remaining days of my life." He confided to Wise that he would be "willing to do the hard work required for a candidate." But in the same letter, he half-jokingly and astutely estimated that only if he were several years younger, a Democrat, "& the owner of 100 Slaves" would he "stand a chance" for the presidency. And in other letters, he downplayed his real chances in light of the ongoing importance of "party machinery" and his Whig identity as that party's future faced serious uncertainty.[31] But the very uncertainty of party alignment, together with relative calm in the sectional politics of slavery, was what more than anything else drove the Everett boom.

To be sure, his reputation in the spheres of conservative reform and especially foreign policy were solid bases for his popular appeal. That was the reason, the *New York Times* enthused, that "Mr. Everett, in the course of a few months, has taken his stand in the front rank of those statesmen of whom our country has most reason to be proud, and from which she has the most to hope."[32] Everett understood this well enough that he even flirted with publicly taking credit for authoring the Hulsemann letter by arranging for the printing of a pamphlet putting his draft and the final document side by side. But his friends advised against diminishing Webster's reputation in this way, and he pulled the plug on publication.[33] Likewise, Everett still believed in Whig-style reform and improvement, and also that this ethic would triumph over the niggling small-government ideas of the Democrats. He took a particular interest in technological advances and the benefits he believed the new Boston Public Library would provide. When he took his seat in the Senate he pushed petitions and bills that would reward inventors and otherwise advance this agenda. And he gave and had published a 4 July address reiterating his ideas on "Stability and Progress." This was all not only right but good politics, he believed.[34]

While these issues arguably increased the momentum of Everett's star, the atmosphere through which it rocketed was rendered hospitable by the tenuous promise of partisan and sectional peace. The first several months of Pierce's presidency built so strongly on the voters' desire for political calm that many observers considered it a latter-day Era of Good Feelings. Pierce was unusually popular personally in Washington circles, and 1853 brought official Washington's usual culture of friendly sociability to new heights. He and outgoing president Fillmore staged occasions, including an elaborate state dinner at the White House, to make conspicuous the cordiality of the transition in administrations. Pierce also cultivated a cooperative relationship with Everett, seeking both his advice and his company. Pierce understood that perpetuating the honeymoon atmosphere of his ascension would take such work and much more. He struck a cautiously sanguine note in his inaugural message, offering that "I fervently hope that the [slavery] question is at rest, and that no sectional or fanatical excitement may again threaten the durability of our institutions."[35]

Everett was the man for such an hour. Bipartisanship and cordial personal relations across political differences came naturally to him. In the waning days of the Fillmore administration he had counseled the president to create the necessary office of assistant secretary of state, even though this would "increase the patronage of our successors." He served as a peacemaker among the hostile factions within the Massachusetts congressional delegation. He valued his friendships with colleagues as politically diverse as James Buchanan and Charles Sumner, and his personal cordiality with the likes of Stephen A. Douglas never waned despite bitter disagreements over foreign and domestic policy.[36] Unlike many congressmen who kept their bipartisan and cross-sectional Washington friendships behind the scenes lest constituents think them soft, Everett consciously and publicly embraced conciliation. In one debate, he joined Douglas in rebuking a Southern senator for "the somewhat sectional aspect of" his remarks. And when Pierce's vice president, William R. King, died in December 1853, Everett took the Senate floor to laud the fallen Alabama Democrat for "the rare and the highly important talent of controlling, with impartiality, the storm of debate, and moderating between mighty spirits, whose ardent conflicts at times seemed to threaten the stability of the republic." He included this speech in his published orations, which he also studiously kept free of anything partisan.[37]

And of course, Everett thought of occasional and historical speeches as the best opportunity to "powerfully influence the public mind" toward domestic peace. In this period of increasing fame he had to reject many invitations to speak, but when doing so he sent a Unionist toast to be read in his absence. And he made no bones about how his particular political purpose for such speeches and toasts was the only legitimate one. For instance, he rejected an invitation to address an anti-immigrant group on Washington's birthday, considering their cause divisive and their appeal to Washington's legacy a distortion. And he lectured Sumner for using one such occasion to deliver "a free soil speech," admonishing that "our patriotic celebrations will be broken up & we shall get all to hate each other . . . if we turn every occasion into a party channel."[38] Sumner might well have protested this selective diagnosis of "a party channel," but it would have fallen on deaf ears.

Fostering his image as peacemaker paid off for Everett in 1853. A late 1853 speech in Faneuil Hall had the desired effect at least on one auditor, who enthused that "nothing abusive or dictated by party prejudices fell from his lips. He spoke like a man who has the real interests of his nation at heart, and . . . with the dignity of a statesman." Newspaper plaudits also stressed Everett's bipartisan and national appeal as underlying his growing reputation. After reading one of his occasional speeches, the editors of the *Daily National Intelligencer* sighed that it was "so refreshing to turn" away "from the arid fields of party politics" to contemplate Everett's "graceful and instructive effusions." A North Carolina admirer proclaimed him the man of the hour in part because "even his political opponents must respect his character, admire his talents, and do justice to his integrity." "Cotton Plant" piled on by asserting that Clay's and Webster's mantle had fallen on Everett. "His future is full of significance" precisely because "as a man, patriot and republican, Edward Everett has a hold upon the hearts of his countrymen, which even party animosity cannot destroy." And in truth, only abolitionists publicly dissented from his soaring patriotic speeches, accusing him of callous indifference to the monstrosity of slavery when he sang America's praises.[39]

Even a speech in favor of African American colonization struck an unusually responsive chord for Everett in this golden year. When the American Colonization Society invited him to address its national meeting in January 1853, Everett felt the labor required to advocate "this great work of Christian Benevolence" would be well spent and even skipped church at least once to prepare the discourse. He delivered it to an attentive audience packing a Washington church and thought "I never spoke to better effect."[40] In it, he asked those who argued that free blacks should stay in America and fight their way through discrimination whether, if people had told the Europeans who had immigrated to America the same thing, "would that have been true friendship, would it have been kindness, would it have been humanity?" Moreover, he asserted, the ACS colony of Liberia had materially aided the fight against the African slave trade, and "I ask, what earthly object of this kind more meritorious than this can be named?" But the ultimate reason to support the ACS was how it would aid "the civilization of Africa." Africa seemed so far from civilized that observers had questioned whether the African "does not labor under some incurable, natural inferiority," but "of this, for myself, I have no belief whatever." It was not only history that proved it was "unphilosophical" to attribute "essential incapacity" to Africans but also enlightened black men whom Everett himself had observed, including Ibrahima and Beverly Williams. Finally, Everett was convinced that black American emigrants would be the "chosen agents" of "august Providence" for this grand mission.[41] In the 1850s even more urgently than in the 1830s when he first advocated the ACS project, it proffered both a panacea for America's race problem and a big tent for sectional cooperation. And Everett's speech won him what he called "the most extravagant compliments" from friends, acquaintances, and newspaper editors from all sections and parties. Again, only committed abolitionists seem to have dissented in a major way. "The cause of African Colonization," Everett inferred later that year, "never — I think — stood more favorably before the public in the United States, than at the present day."[42]

But this speech's strong partisan shadings also typified Everett's stance during this Era of Good Feelings. His view of the ACS embodied the Whiggish vision of improvement on a transcontinental scale, but unreasoning racial prejudice would strangle it at its inception, so he offered a vigorous critique of racism that very few Democrats could have mustered. Likewise on other issues, his amiability and pursuit of bipartisanship never led Everett to agnosticism on the superiority of the Unionist Whig persuasion. So in December 1853, in a meeting dividing up committee assignments between Whigs and Democrats for the Thirty-Third Congress, Everett declared that he "could not consent to" Charles Sumner "being regarded as a whig" — indeed, as a professed Free Soiler, "it is what he would himself disclaim." Everett's objection, which became public knowledge, only exacerbated the frustrations Sumner experienced as he took his Senate seat in this Unionist heyday, and he took it personally. This led to an anomalous personal breach between the two senators, and although Everett led out (as prodded by Washington social broker Julia Fish) in reconciling with

Sumner personally, he never surrendered the political point at issue.[43] And Everett believed President Pierce's efforts to preserve the Democratic Party's unity doomed to fail because of the strength of its discordant Free Soil and Southern rights factions. He hoped that in the event of a breakup of the Democracy, its sectional moderates would ally with those from the Whig Party, thus solidifying Whig moderates' recent gains. In short, Everett believed, the blurring of old party lines might be inevitable under the new political conditions, but the last boundary that should be broken down was the one between sectional moderates and sectional extremists. For Everett as for many other conservative Whigs, this should be an Era of Good Feelings for Unionists only.[44] The political benefits for Everett of that epoch had been considerable.

————

But then came the Kansas-Nebraska Act. This bill began as the brainchild of Illinois Democrat Stephen A. Douglas, who was in a position as the well-known champion of the West and the long-standing chair of the Senate Committee on Territories to accomplish his goal of organizing the vast region within the Louisiana Purchase known as Nebraska. Although the Missouri Compromise of 1820 had outlawed slavery in this region, Douglas had long objected to that prohibition as a violation of Western settlers' right to self-determination and as a standing insult to his Southern allies. Douglas was no grand political philosopher, however, and his Nebraska bill's pragmatic first version simply applied this so-called popular sovereignty formula to the would-be territory, remaining mum on the Missouri Compromise. Only under repeated behind-the-scenes pressure from Southern congressmen who distrusted this sort of vagueness did Douglas import language specifically repudiating the Missouri Compromise. The later bill also divided the territory into the Kansas and Nebraska Territories. While key Northern Democrats warned Pierce of the sectional firestorm that would follow such a bill's introduction, a delegation of Southern spokesmen convinced the president to throw his support behind this version. As scholar Sarah Paulus has recently demonstrated, Douglas and other advocates of this bill had decided to jettison Clay's time-honored formula of "compromise by fair negotiation," which accommodated deeply held sectional positions, demanding instead a commitment to "the inherently moderate doctrine of popular sovereignty." Ironies abounded, for they had thus blundered into a tragic betrayal of their own cherished dreams of national and party unity by sponsoring legislation that shattered the fragile sectional peace that had so benefited fellow moderates like Everett.[45]

The bill first came to Everett's attention at a meeting of the Committee on

Territories, on which he was the lone New Englander. In early January 1854, he alone objected to the bill, chiefly due to his certainty that "the anti-slavery agitation of 1850 would be re-opened" thereby. He was particularly horrified by Douglas's abandonment of his earlier assurance in their committee meetings that "no man was so wild as to think of repealing the Missouri Compromise." But Everett was very much in a reactive position and his dissent was fruitless; in both ways these early committee discussions proved prophetic. Nevertheless, foreseeing the sectional clash this bill would provoke, he set about gathering advice from trusted conservative Northerners on the course he should take when the bill reached the Senate floor.[46]

As their advice suggested, Everett nurtured a forlorn hope to control and moderate the Northern reaction to the bill. Everett remained in a conservative antislavery position, seeking practical ways to advance the abolition of slavery and racial prejudice but distrusting Free Soilers' and political abolitionists' sincerity and reprobating their confrontational tactics.[47] Coming from this point of view as well as that of passionate Unionism, he and his friends hoped against hope that they could mute the Free Soil voice in favor of their own. Nathan Hale's *Boston Daily Advertiser*, after hesitating, confined its early response to the bill to protesting the repeal of the Missouri Compromise and the gratuitous revival of slavery agitation. Robert C. Winthrop repeatedly urged from Boston that letting the likes of Sumner be the face of opposition to the bill would materially damage that cause. Fillmore chorused that conservative Whigs "should take the lead" against the bill rather than follow "the lead of known and avowed *abolitionists*." Rufus Choate informed Everett in early February that all his Boston conservative friends "feel the deepest solicitude that you should not be drawn into a position which can impair your large prospects" nationally. Thus, he implored, Everett must find a way to oppose the Kansas-Nebraska bill "by reasonings that will not lose you one American heart or judgment anywhere." Likewise, a Southern colleague in Washington hinted "that one great object for which" the Kansas-Nebraska bill "was brought forward was 'to put [Everett] to the test.'" Such assessments of how the bill would impact his presidential hopes appealed to Everett's own now-exaggerated but understandable sense of his own significance. This was the context in which Everett debated with other Massachusetts Whigs in Congress whether it were better for the state legislature to say nothing on the bill to avoid saying something extreme, or to have conservatives in that body beat the radicals to the punch (Everett advocated the latter).[48]

It was in such a frame of mind that Everett prepared and delivered his first full-dress response to the bill on the Senate floor. On 7 February 1854, Douglas as committee chair proposed amended language declaring "the principles of non-intervention by Congress with slavery in the States and Territories" to be the heart of the bill. Everett quickly rose to ask for more time to prepare a speech explaining why "I have found myself unable, both as a member of the Committee on Territories and as a member of this body, to give my support to the bill" in all its permutations. These "grave questions" were not to be dealt with "on the spur of the moment." Douglas disingenuously insisted he was in no hurry, and the Senate voted to delay debate until the next day. That night Everett wrote in his diary that one more day was "very inadequate" time to prepare, so "it happens unfortunately, that I am called to speak on the most important Subject & the most critical occasion of my life, with less premeditation than almost ever before." That difficulty was compounded by the unexpected arrival of family visitors that evening, so after sitting with them for an hour or two, his preparations kept him up late into the night.[49] Fortunately for Everett, he had decided on the overall course this speech would take, so his preparation could focus on details (which, granted, were always of surpassing importance in his mind). "The grounds I should think it prudent to take," he wrote to a friend on 6 February, would decidedly not include "general denunciations of Slavery."[50]

Everett delivered his 8 February speech to a packed chamber and gallery, eager to hear the noted orator's opening salvo in his showdown with the Democrats' rising star Douglas. He took about an hour and a half, the full time allotted to the bill in the Senate that day.[51] He led with process concerns, including not only the efforts of the bill's sponsors to rush it through Congress but also his fear that unduly hastening territorial status for such a sparsely settled region would give inordinate power to the very few settlers then on the ground. He also objected to its trampling on agreements with Indian tribes there, some of whom had already been removed more than once by the federal government.[52] This was good, solid Whiggery, pointing up the sham in cries of popular sovereignty and harking back to the Indian Removal debates. But these were preliminaries.

His peroration got closer to the heart of the matter, affirming his creed in relation to slavery and its extension. He advocated "the ancient, the universal, the traditional opinion and feeling of the non-slaveholding States, which forbid a citizen of those States to do anything voluntarily, or except under a case of the sternest compulsion, such as preserving the union of these States—and really I would do almost anything to effect that object—to acquiesce in carrying slavery into a Territory where it did not previously exist." This was the opinion that had been "universal throughout the land" in the Revolutionary generation and that had produced the Missouri Compromise. The current bill innovated against this long-held American and Northern tradition, not least by denying Congress any right to intervene with slavery in the territories. "Why, sir," he cried, "from the first enactment of 1789, down to the bill before us, there is no such principle in our legislation." What was worse, the repeal of the Missouri Compromise — "which has been a platform of conciliation and of peace" for thirty-four years — was gratuitous, for "I believe it is admitted that there is no great material interest at stake" given that no one "supposed that this is to become a slaveholding region." "With reference to the great question of slavery — that terrible question — the only one on which the North and the South of this great Republic differ irreconcilably," he would say only that "I rejoiced to hear" a senator from Kentucky "utter the opinion that a wise and gracious Providence, in his own good time, will find the ways and the channels to remove from the land what I consider this great evil." He did suggest that colonization might be that providential means. But Everett believed "in my conscience" that "systematic agitation of the subject . . . powerfully repressed and discouraged" that proper antislavery feeling, because it produced a "recoil of the conservative mind of the non-slaveholding States from this harassing and disastrous agitation." So he would use "no other words on that subject than those of moderation, conciliation, and harmony between the two great sections of the country." Any other course (such as this bill itself) was dangerous in the extreme, for "I believe the union of these States is the greatest possible blessing — that it comprises within itself all other blessings, political, national, and social."[53] This closing creed was equal parts conservative and antislavery, in about the same balance that had obtained in his mind since his days as governor. This part of his speech must therefore have cost him very little of that late-night preparation time.

But the main thrust of his speech was to raise doubts about how truthful Kansas-Nebraska's sponsors could be when they asserted that the Compromise of 1850 had set the precedent for their bill, for they must have known better. In making this case he stood on his authority "as a friend and supporter of the compromises of 1850" and as Webster's literary executor — and thus, he implied, the semi-official historian of that compromise. But more powerfully, he dismantled this argument by showing from the history that no grand principle of popular sovereignty was asserted in 1850 for Utah and New Mexico, let alone a principle written into that compromise that applied beyond them. "I adhere" to the Compromise of 1850, he summed, "for many reasons. One is respect for the memory of the great men who were" its authors. "I would not so soon, if it were in my power, undo their work. . . . But beyond this, I am one of those — I am not ashamed to avow it — who believed at that time, and who still believe, that at that period the union of these States was in great danger" and that "the healing effect of the measures" was still needed. But the Kansas–Nebraska bill's sponsors did "not strengthen them, you do not show your respect for them, by giving them an application which they were never intended to bear."[54]

This speech thus opened a fascinating contest over the memory of the compromise and the legacy of Webster between Douglas and Everett, Democrats and Whigs. That battle continued in the Senate almost a month later in an exchange between Everett and Douglas in which both once again laid claim to that legacy.[55] Douglas's revisionist history was breathtaking in its scope and boldness. To be sure, in 1850 and 1851 some Deep Southern defenders of the compromise argued that its defeat of the Wilmot Proviso had by implication replaced the Missouri Compromise with all the dishonor to the South that its line had supposed. But that was not an argument that occurred to many other people in 1850. And no one cared more about the meaning of Webster's iconic speech than Everett and his cadre. Much as modern Christians ask what Jesus would do, the likes of Winthrop had grown accustomed to asking, "What says the 7th of March?"[56] However, Everett indulged in some of his own revisionism by depriving Douglas of authorship of the compromise measures. That was key to casting him instead as the destroyer thereof, but it did not ring true to Douglas's central parliamentary role in 1850.

Responses to this speech were generally politely positive. Naturally, Everett's allies in Boston approved the ground he had occupied. "Nothing could be more effective than your Speech," Winthrop said, "from one standing at your point of view." Notices from friendly newspapers described it as a "calm, logical, and conclusive speech" and hoped that such a rational approach might sway some Southerners to oppose the bill. Everett had no reason to expect that his speech would be attacked as too soft on slavery. In a moment that Everett would long remember, Sumner crossed the Senate floor at the conclusion of the address and congratulated him for having "dealt the monster a blow between the eyes." In fact, some Northern Democratic sheets groused that it was a thinly veiled Free Soil manifesto. And even William Lloyd Garrison published without comment a description of Everett's "common sense" speech.[57] While Everett purposefully had not provided red meat for abolitionists and Free Soilers, he had delivered a devastating exposé of the logical, historical, and legislative flaws in this bill, and that was a real contribution to the cause.

————

Such glimmers of optimism, however, only temporarily punctuated the overall gloom of a period in which he saw the initiative passing to other, less moderate hands. That change of drivers began in January when the Free Soilers published their "Appeal of the Independent Democrats," which set the terrain of the debate as sectional rather than partisan by charging that the bill was the product of Douglas's and the administration's knavish submission to the Slave Power. That, together with a rather naive level of surprise at the bitterness of Northern opposition to the bill, activated Douglas's and his allies' knee-jerk loathing of abolitionism. While Everett thought the intemperate "Appeal" had given "some provocation" to Douglas, he also recoiled at the "great vehemence & affected passion" of Douglas's responses in the Senate. While his position was somewhere between Douglas and Sumner, his sympathies were with neither.[58] Sumner revealed his stance perfectly when he proclaimed Kansas-Nebraska "the best bill which Congress ever acted; *for it annuls all past compromises with Slavery, and makes any future compromises impossible.* Thus it puts Freedom and Slavery face to face, and bids them grapple," leading inevitably to the day when "there will really be a North, and the Slave Power will be broken." Everett could never agree to such a statement, of course, but by late February he moaned to Winthrop that "the ultraism of the South leaves no middle ground to stand upon." Therefore, "I am thrown in spite of myself into co-operation with men"—like Sumner—"whose general course on this subject, I generally disapprove." On the two days previous to writing this letter, he and Sumner had in fact risen at the same time from their Senate seats to defend Massachusetts against Southern slanders.[59] Being in this position of hapless follower was a far cry from Everett's high-water mark just a few weeks previous.

Finding himself in a passive role contributed to a sinking feeling that for all his efforts, the Kansas-Nebraska Act would inevitably prove fatal to his and all other moderates' political hopes, and therefore to the Union. He truly hated, both for their sake and his own, to disappoint his Southern Whig friends who hoped Northern Whigs would support the bill. "I am not insensible," he confided in a correspondent, that opposing Kansas-Nebraska "will cost me all the little favor I seemed to possess at the South." But Douglas and his accomplices had crafted such a disastrous bill that "I see no alternative." It added insult to injury that the bill's sponsors paraded as moderates, for they had in fact betrayed and travestied sectional moderation. In a letter to his Democratic friend Buchanan, Everett railed that the bill had "unnecessarily . . . plunged the Country into a new Slavery discussion" and that its effect was "to discredit conservative opinions & moderate Counsels, and to strengthen extremists." Many other Northern Whigs shared his frustration, for just weeks before, in the words of Fillmore, they "had fondly hoped that this question was at rest, for a time at least."[60] That pervading pessimism and powerlessness would prove predictive of coming events for Everett.

The first and most politically calamitous of such events was missing the Senate vote on the Kansas-Nebraska bill. As the debate of 3 March raged into the wee hours of 4 March, Everett passed in and out of the Senate chamber due to the length and offensive tone (fueled in part by "evident excess in liquor") of both sides. Sensing that a vote might be nearing, Everett was careful on that evening to "pair off" with Kansas-Nebraska supporter Lewis Cass; both of them leaving the chamber would neutralize the effect of either of them possibly missing the vote. None of this was unusual, as it was quite common for congressmen to come and go during stretched-out debates and for the conscientious ones to "pair off" when doing so. But Everett's health had been heading south for some time, and at about 3:30 A.M. the "exhausted & ill" senator decided to call it a night. The Senate finally voted at 5:00, passing the bill by a margin of 37 to 14. Everett was one of multiple senators not left standing at that hour, and he calculated that "had all been present the vote would have stood 40 to 20."[61]

Despite the fact that it was clear to all observers in early March that Everett was quite ill, he was mortified to have missed arguably the most important vote of his political career. His diary contains enough protests that he was not malingering to reveal his defensiveness on this subject. He also hastened to control the damage in public. On 4 March he wrote to brother-in-law Nathan Hale to provide material that the Boston Daily Advertiser would use in his defense, such as information about his health and a plea that his absence made no difference in the outcome. After Seward's organ the New York Tribune assailed Everett for his absence, Everett remonstrated with Seward himself. That produced a statement for the press from Seward and other Whigs certifying that Everett's health, not some desire to dodge the vote, had been responsible.[62] Everett also acted in his own defense on the Senate floor on 7 March, when he asked for consent to belatedly record his vote. "As is well known to my friends," he pled, "my general state of health" had rendered him "utterly unable to remain" in the Senate at the absurdly late hour of his retirement. "I suppose it cannot be a matter of doubt," he submitted, that he would have voted against the bill, but "as it is a matter of very great consequence and interest," he wanted to register that vote officially. Delaware senator John M. Clayton asked if he could do the same, but the chair ruled that Senate regulations against retroactive voting could be overturned only by unanimous consent. Various senators spoke against opening the floodgates by setting this precedent, whereupon Everett and Clayton withdrew their request.[63]

This episode remained a sore spot in the Everett family for decades. In Nathan's son Edward Everett Hale's 1859 story "My Double, and How He Undid Me," the narrator wished that "every member of Congress might have a double to sit through those deadly sessions and answer to roll-calls and do the legitimate party-voting, which appears stereotyped" anyway. "As things stand, the saddest State prison I ever visit is that Representatives' Chamber in Washington. If a man leaves for an hour, twenty 'correspondents' may be howling, 'Where was Mr[.] Pendergrast when the Oregon bill passed?' And if poor Pendergrast stays there! Certainly the worst use you can make of a man is to put him in prison!" Everett's own son William, who was fourteen years old in March 1854, offered a particularly vigorous defense of his father's absence in a 1908 memoir of his father, attributing it to "a misinformation as to the time of taking the vote."[64]

An episode in itself less damning but adding to an unflattering cumulative portrait of Everett's Kansas-Nebraska performance followed just days after his missed vote. As he took his seat in the Senate chamber on 14 March, he was called to the door to meet a Reverend Mr. Dexter, who bore a memorial from 3,050 New England clergymen (more than three-quarters of all of the region's ministers) against the Kansas-Nebraska bill. Everett had presented several previous anti-Kansas-Nebraska petitions, so he was a natural choice to take charge of this one. Due to its prodigious size, without reading it he asked Senate officials to take it straight over to the clerk's table. Everett introduced it without fanfare. Its imposing physical size, however, attracted the Senate's attention. And Douglas was not disposed to overlook its fierce rhetoric branding the Kansas-Nebraska bill "a great moral wrong" and "a breach of faith." In a speech breathing forth his anticlerical as well as anti-abolitionist animus, he declared the memorial "not respectful to the Senate." Everett had moved that the memorial be tabled as per standard practice, but in an echo of the Gag Rule decades before, Southern Senators called for it to be turned away entirely. Taken aback by the unexpected fury of this exchange, Everett apologized that he had not read it carefully enough to know whether it was respectful. He did, however, dispute Douglas's charges that the ministers had illegitimately stepped "from their sacred profession into the arena of party politics," for their opposition to the bill represented a consensus position in New England. He ended by regretting that this whole debate had occurred but suggesting that the petition should receive the usual treatment. His position prevailed in the vote, but that did not make him feel better. That night writing in his diary, he confessed that it was "particularly distasteful to me" that his motion had provoked such a "stormy debate." "The language of the memorial was objectionable," and it was embarrassing to him to have been "unwittingly" but unavoidably associated with such a document.[65]

Everett's failure to more vigorously support the clergymen, added to his failure to vote, called down a torrent of censure from Free Soilers and abolitionists. Given the enormous stakes involved—as Ohio abolitionist politician Salmon Chase put it, "our American Experiment will fail" if Kansas-Nebraska prevailed—such an uneven performance was intolerable.[66] Sumner "was burning to say something" after Everett's apologies during the clergy petition debate but hesitated on personal and political grounds to place "myself in unkind contrast with him." Sumner's friend and correspondent Theodore Parker felt no such compunctions. In an address to the New York Anti-Slavery Society, Parker charged that "that denomination which is called 'doughfaces,' are only overseers for the owner of the slave. Mr. Douglas is a great overseer; Mr. Everett is a little overseer, very little." As he had done for Webster two years earlier, he asked his audience to "pause with me and drop a tear over the ruin of Edward Everett, a man of large talents" whose long career "yet comes to such an end." Such a man, "when he falls, he falls like Lucifer, never to hope again!" In another 1854 speech, Parker lamented that "Southern slavery is an institution which is in earnest. Northern freedom is an institution that" had not been "in earnest" since the Revolutionary War. Thus no one—especially "none who knew his antecedents" such as his knapsack speech—should have been surprised at Everett's weakness on Kansas-Nebraska.[67] Other commentators made uncharitable allusions to Everett's health. Kidney stones were among the ailments that caused him to miss the vote, and Boston wits gibed that someone "with so much gravel" had proven to be "without grit." A New York editor, meanwhile, diagnosed Everett's real health problem as a weak backbone, suggesting that "a sojourn of six months among his constituents would be of more service to his vertebral column than anything he could possibly do."[68]

Given Everett's long and oft-tortured relationship with abolitionists and Free Soilers, as well as how thoroughly Kansas-Nebraska had aroused them, he should not have been surprised at this response. But its ferocity did take him aback. His surprise began when Free Soilers criticized him for asserting in his February speech that the climate would not suit slavery in the new territories, despite his having drawn that argument from a Free Soil publication. The ferocity of the Free Soil–leaning press also startled him in part because he retained such good personal and political relations with leading antislavery lights like Sumner and Seward. The latter even professed to Everett a hope that Everett's moderate means of resisting the bill would prove effective.[69] "I have been a good deal wounded," he confessed to Winthrop, "at the readiness manifested to suspect me of 'dodging.'" Everett more fully vented his amazement and resentment in an extraordinarily candid letter to Wise in April. He had still been riding high after his 8 February speech, he recounted, for "it gave great satisfaction north & south, & for immediate effect, I never did better." Indeed,

American citizens had subscribed for over thirty thousand printed copies of the address. But this was not to last long, for "with the progress of anti-slavery excitement at the north, my speech was found to be below the war-fever." Upon missing the vote, "the whole free-soil press of the north opened upon me." Then came the clergymen's petition incident, and although he had defended the petitioners "as far as I could consistently defend them," his performance had failed "to satisfy the excited popular feeling of the north, & still less political enemies who do not wish to be satisfied." "All these things," he confided in his son-in-law, "worry me. I am not *pachydermatous* enough. You will think at my age, — I am 60 tomorrow, — I ought to be callous, but I am not so, & the very suspicion of having done wrong makes me uneasy."[70] It was a narrative of going from a position of mastery, where he delivered prepared speeches that satisfied all the right people in both sections, to reacting out of fear to extremists in control of the agenda.

Everett searched for comfort and distractions to help him deal with this painful turn of events. For consolation, he feebly tried the time-honored refuge that his speeches and actions had been misreported. More useful as well as more accurate was a sense that he had done his best to maintain his style of national statesmanship in a crisis that had rendered the atmosphere too poisonous for that style to thrive. Especially in such times, he wrote to an admirer, "it is usually the fate of public men, who pursue moderate counsels, to fall below the tone of one party, too often of both. It will be my consolation, in the dark days of civil discord, which I fear . . . I may yet live to see, that I have done & said nothing, to inflame the angry feelings agst each other of the opposite sections of the Union." It was all the more welcome, then, to meet his devotee Elias Magoon on one of his springtime steamboat journeys home. When Magoon told him that "my addresses — when he was young — first awoke in his mind a desire for literary excellence," Everett remembered having heard that from others. That thought, he told his diary, "consoles me under the barbarity of the free soil & abolition press & orators."[71] For distractions, he focused on other less distressing issues. He tried to get an essay he had written on the importance of the Bible published and started another on the global issues of inequality and civilizational progress, which had preoccupied him in happier times. He studied ancient history and languages, and he confessed to a friend that although he found therein no guide to contemporary "social and political problems," he did like those subjects "much better than Nebraska."[72]

Ultimately none of these palliatives worked well enough to keep him in the Senate. Everett's health, as usual for him, suffered progressively in this contentious environment. His wife Charlotte's health, always fragile in the 1850s, was poor enough in 1854 that she could neither live at their house in Washington nor manage their house while living in Boston, so Everett shouldered that twin load of worry and household management as well. He may also have been aware of rumors circulating in Washington and elsewhere that Charlotte's real affliction was alcoholism, in which case shame would have compounded his trials.[73] But while all these very real personal hardships may have become more acute in the spring of 1854, none of them were new to that period. He had faced many of them while secretary of state and in that period reported an improvement in his physical health as well as a satisfaction with his work. He likewise expressed only slight worries about his and Charlotte's health when taking the Senate seat.[74] Everett seems not to have been quite a hypochondriac, but when social and political amiability reigned, he had enough incentives of ambition and political usefulness that he could brush aside personal burdens as minor and find his health improving with work.

But beginning with the bout of illness that was both cause and consequence of his missing the Kansas-Nebraska vote in early March, Everett's health worsened, and he began to think that his political and personal ordeals made it not worth sticking it out in the Senate. Given his growing political feebleness and "the disposition to cavil at all I do & say," he began to think "that I made a sad mistake in returning to public life" and "that my paramount duties are at home." He went home in mid-March to gauge the situation there and confer with friends. While the latter counseled him to stay at his post, continued political criticism and the advice of his doctor kept him on the verge of resigning through April and into May. "I wish, intensely, to be at rest," he divulged to a friend in early May, "to cut wholly loose from the corruption of Washington,—its toil and conflict, and live at home." He hesitated only because he sensed that quitting under such circumstances would make it "a final retirement from public life."[75] A visit home in early May pushed him off the fence. He was so badly off that he could scarcely go up and down stairs. Moreover, Charlotte had "one of her worst turns," alternately convulsing in bed and racing wildly around her room. "I was in the next room & saw it all," Everett reported to their daughter, "& a more terrific sight I never saw." Less than a week after this horrifying event he advised Governor Emory Washburn of his intention to resign so this fellow Whig politician could seek out a suitable replacement. When he informed his political friends of this step, they implored him to reconsider but to no avail. On 17 May he submitted his resignation, effective 1 June. The Senate heard this letter read on 22 May.[76]

Everett felt the need to defend his reasons for this abrupt and unfortunate end to his once-promising national political career. Most newspapers simply reported his resignation without comment, leaving his resignation letter with its emphasis on his health and personal crises to speak for itself. Critics thought they discerned some "stratagem" still in pursuit of the presidency on Everett's part, but they were rather easily dismissed.[77] But Everett was hypersensitive to even the slightest questions about his true reasons. So when he determined he would not be able to return to Washington to fill out his term, he wrote to Sumner to ask for a favor in case of a new Senate vote on another version of the bill in his absence. He asked Sumner to arrange for a Georgia senator to "pair off" with him, and failing that "to state that I am prevented by ill health from attending the Senate, & that had I been present I should vote in the negative on the passage of any bill repealing or declaring inoperative the Missouri Compromise." He also dashed off a series of private letters to refute the expected flood of "invidious comment" on his retirement. Deep into the summer he was protesting, including to entirely sympathetic friends, that he was no malingerer. "I naturally struggled against" resigning the Senate seat "as long as I could," he insisted.[78]

This largely unnecessary defensive exercise bespoke just how excruciating the unceremonious fizzling out of his political star had been for Everett. But otherwise Everett proved adept at analyzing his own demise. "I do no good, I gain no credit, I have no future," he moaned to a confidant on the day he decided to resign. "The Country is given over to ultraism on both sides, and moderate counsels are despised alike at the South and the North." To those who asked whether he should have expected that result, "I answer *No*. It was all different" in 1853 when he had crossed in glory from the executive branch to the Senate. "The Country reposed in quiet under the adjustment of 1850, and there was every prospect of an indefinite period of tranquil prosperity."[79] At the end of July he offered a fitting epitaph for "the first half of 1854; six laborious, anxious, eventful months, which have produced a material change in my mode of life & prospects."[80] The particular shape that change would take would be very slow in revealing itself.

8

Saving Mount Vernon

After a year in the political wilderness, in the second half of the 1850s Edward Everett emerged into perhaps the most significant and enjoyable era of his varied career. He threw enormous newfound energy into the deeply political but consciously nonpartisan effort to purchase Mount Vernon for, and thereby help save, the Union. Everett willingly narrowed his field of vision to this endeavor, and put himself through the inconveniences and labor involved in nationwide travel, because he considered it a holy cause. The sectional conflict of the era shadowed and at times paralyzed this campaign as sectionalists north and south sought to turn its attractiveness to their own ends. But such efforts of appropriation, together with the sensational popular response to Everett and his cause, illustrate how deeply ingrained this emotional Unionism was in the political culture of the late antebellum United States.

———

After Everett left the Senate, over a year of almost unbroken personal and political gloom awaited him in Boston. Even before his resignation went into effect, the political hurricane that was Kansas-Nebraska gathered yet more strength due to the federal government's show of force on the Massachusetts capital's streets to return the fugitive slave Anthony Burns to Virginian bondage. This further embittered the state's existing debate over whether the rule of law or personal liberty should prevail. The conservatives lost so thoroughly — due in part to defections from their ranks — that by the spring of 1855 the state legislature resolved that the Fugitive Slave Act was unconstitutional. The Bay State's destabilized political scene saw the abrupt entrance of not only the Republican Party with its sectional appeal but also the American, or Know-Nothing, Party with its anti-immigrant populist appeal.[1] Everett was of course horrified by the political paralysis of sectional conservatism in the North. He lamented the Burns affair as "terrible," though more for how it had "crushed out" Boston's "conservative feeling" than for what it had done to Burns himself. He knew as well as anyone that the issue of slavery, "once agitated, defies compromise." He feared that the triumph of sectional parties and disunion would soon follow the twin boosts this agitation had received in 1854.[2]

For the rest of 1854 and most of 1855, Everett struggled to find any productive public role for himself. He now had time for scholarly pursuits, but as an earlier biographer perceptively noted, "he was constantly thinking that he wanted leisure to write, and yet discontented when the leisure came." He claimed to be "thankful" to be "out of the turmoil" and pledged himself "determined to make my retirement from political life final." But these seem to have been personal pep talks to resist his self-diagnosed "specimens of weakness" for returning "to official life."[3] These new depths of ambivalence about political participation led him to inconsistencies, such as declining invitations to deliver historical addresses while writing political editorials during a fall 1854 stint substituting for brother-in-law Nathan Hale at the Boston Daily Advertiser. He did, however, maintain consistency in feeling sorry for himself, grumbling about the fickleness of public favor and whimpering that "justice I suppose will one day be done me."[4]

While this double-mindedness about political life was an intensification of an earlier theme in Everett's career, for the first time in his adult life he had no obvious partisan home in the late 1850s. The Northern and Southern wings of his Whig Party had taken such divergent positions on the Kansas-Nebraska issue that it could not survive this final test. Everett knew from painful experience that any attempt to assemble a Unionist coalition around remnants of Whig conservatism was at the mercy of the reckless politicians who had brought America the Kansas-Nebraska Act.[5] As he looked back in anger on the Washington political scene from his den in Boston, Everett damned its denizens as corrupt as well as reckless. Such was the country's political degeneracy that "small men of no distinguished talent intriguing for places . . . & utterly regardless of the public service" were in the ascendancy. "There is really not one man of eminent character at Washington at the present day," he concluded. This bitter broth was made up of more than Everett's sour grapes, for multitudes of Americans shared his unease with the corruption of politics in the 1850s.[6]

Many aimless ex-Whigs found refuge in the Democratic or Know-Nothing Parties, but Everett could fully embrace neither in the long term. The Know-Nothings had undeniable momentum in Massachusetts in the mid-1850s, and the likes of Millard Fillmore asked Everett to see this movement as sectionally conservative. When Fillmore garnered the Know-Nothing nomination in 1856, Everett rather tepidly supported him despite serious qualms about the nativist bigotry and secrecy of the Know-Nothings.[7] When Everett's friend James Buchanan remonstrated with him for failing to support his own Democratic candidacy, Everett explained that he thought Fillmore's campaign offered the better chance to prevent a Republican victory throughout the North.[8] But he would never forgive the Democracy for Kansas-Nebraska. When his friend Rufus Choate argued that "it is idle or worse to enquire which of the two great parties is to blame for producing" the fire burning throughout the Union, Everett dissented from that "sophism." Given that "the democratic party has by the repeal of the Missouri Compromise thrown the country into its present state of combustion" and stood by that disastrous law in the election of 1856, "surely we must not call upon the incendiary who has just kindle[d] the fire to go & put it out. . . . What will he do but pour oil not water on the flames." So for instance in 1856, he voted for Fillmore for president but could not support the Know-Nothing candidate for Congress because he had been a longtime supporter of Kansas-Nebraska. And in 1857, for the first time since he began voting in the 1820s, Everett abstained from voting. He would do the same in 1858 and 1859, assigning the same reason: no choice of evils.[9]

Everett's relationship with political antislavery had deteriorated to the point that he never considered supporting the new Republican Party. He still held conservative antislavery beliefs but emphasized the first word in that phrase, while the Republicans tended to emphasize the second. Everett continued to donate to and mingle with free blacks on various occasions and went to some lengths to help a former servant in his household purchase her daughter's freedom. He also put his money and influence behind making Kansas a free territory, including by investing in shares in the Emigrant Aid Association, which funded antislavery settlers there. He differed widely from Southerners whose "extreme opinions on the Slavery question" embraced it as a blessing. "I regard it as a great evil," he told South Carolina friend William H. Trescot, "though permitted by Providence for a season." To be beneficial, however, emancipation must be peaceful and would most likely "be the work of generations, perhaps of ages."[10] He maintained his moral and material support for the American Colonization Society. And as he interacted with leading Southerners in the late 1850s, he avoided discussing the issue of slavery.[11]

Everett also continued in his reform commitments, but they took up less of his time and thought than in previous periods. He still advocated "a liberal conservatism" that would balance "stability and progress." His fund-raising and activism focused largely on helping to found the Boston Public Library and on a benefit oration for poor relief, which he repeated several times throughout the country.[12] But in this defensive phase of Everett's career, his vision had narrowed, from an Atlantic or even global Benevolent Empire to preserving the American nation-state. And although the ethic of "improvement" still undergirded that nationalism, he believed more than ever that reform must be pursued with caution. He thought the efforts of recent French reformers well intentioned but undermined by an "insane warfare against the existing institutions of society." And in 1859, he resisted an invitation to endorse or preside at a Faneuil Hall meeting to protect the Indians. "I do feel a deep sympathy with the Indians," he noted, but he was put off by the organizer's spiritualist extravagances, as well as by his "impudence" in listing Wendell Phillips with Everett as leading supporters. He would not appear with or support a cause in conjunction with "a man who for 20 years has made it a main object to libel me in the most abominable manner."[13]

This objection to Phillips got to another core reason for his growing hatred of Republicans and abolitionists: their attacks on him did not abate once he left the Senate. He filled his diary in these years with swipes at the antislavery agitators, very often provoked by their own swipes at him. It galled him in particular to be branded weak and cowardly by men who now went with the sectionalist tide that he swam so boldly against. During his editorial run at the *Daily Advertiser*, he lumped Republicans and abolitionists together as "par eminence, the intolerant, persecuting & abusive party." Antislavery agitators had a method to their madness, but Everett became increasingly unwilling to see any justification for their rank intolerance (especially toward him). Worse than devoid of manners, they had no "view to principle" and thus were capable of all manner of nefariousness. And just as Republicans and abolitionists failed to perceive his commitment to antislavery, he failed to perceive the Republicans' commitment to the Union. He thus seemed genuinely confused when a staunch Massachusetts Unionist "went over to the black republicans." Intriguingly, he found them all the more threatening because they wielded a perverted version of the good cause of antislavery. "The South and the North are equally wrongheaded," he apprised the British man of letters Thomas B. Macauley, but Northern "ultraism" was "the more dangerous, inasmuch as it is founded, in truth and justice."[14]

————

Giving up on mainstream politics and politicians for all these reasons, Everett eventually hoped to provide light in this darkness by means of historical commemoration on an unprecedented scale. By late 1855 he had decided that rather than throw up his hands and retire from the nation, he would put his faith in the persuasive power of his oratory and the emotional power of America's common history, properly understood. There was a new breadth and intensity in his efforts of these kinds in the late 1850s. Bay Staters eager to memorialize their Puritan past sought Everett's advice and sanction.[15] He also cultivated and marshaled the political legacies of recently departed friends. He paused in a memoir of Peter C. Brooks to descant on the economic benefits of the Union. He pointedly lauded Choate for rejecting the low demagoguery of party politics.[16] He sent $100 to a group building a statue for Clay in Lexington, Kentucky, which remembered the Great Compromiser as an "illustrious Statesman and Patriot."[17] For similar reasons, Daniel Webster's devotees, among them Everett, continued their passionate loyalty to his Unionist memory. They organized feasts to celebrate his birthday, commissioned a statue for the State House grounds, and even organized an 1858 "pilgrimage" to his tomb in Marshfield, Massachusetts. At an 1856 birthday fete, Everett submitted "there never was a battle fought whose consequences were more important to humanity" than the ones Webster fought for "the maintenance or overthrow of that constitutional Union which, in the language of Washington, 'makes us one people.'" To "loud cheers," George S. Hillard toasted Everett at this celebration as "the statesman, the orator, the patriot, the Elisha upon whom the mantle of our departed Elijah has fallen." Everett was also the featured speaker at the dedication of the Webster statue in 1859. Besides Washington, he insisted, no one had rendered "greater service" to "the true principles of the Constitution" than Webster. "Reverence" for the Union was "the central idea of his political system." Everett might seem like a Unionist Elisha to his toasters, but he himself could not help wishing that Webster's statue "would descend from its pedestal, to stand in the front rank of the peril" of the nation, "and the bronze lips repeat the cry of the living voice, — 'Liberty and Union, now and forever, one and inseparable!'"[18]

Everett's commemorative work still centered, however, on the American Revolution. One of his first public appearances after his retirement from the Senate was as featured speaker at a 4 July festival in his hometown of Dorchester in 1855. Addressing the theme "Dorchester in 1630, 1776, and 1855," he dwelt most fully on the middle year. He painted the Revolution as "the consummation of three centuries," an event "which will be felt in its consequences to ourselves and the family of nations, till the seventh seal is broken from the apocalyptic volume of the history of empires."[19] He also worked with Robert C. Winthrop and others to honor Revolutionary heroes at Mount Auburn Cemetery. Under their watch, this garden cemetery in Cambridge would receive three statues of those icons in its chapel, as well as an imposing observation tower built in honor of George Washington.[20] He devoted countless hours in these years to the memory of Benjamin Franklin, including organizational work toward erecting a statue of the hero in Boston. Winthrop's speech at the statue's dedication stressed Franklin's role in establishing the Union and his statesmanlike fealty to the Constitution. Everett's Franklin activities culminated with an oration on Franklin's connections to Boston, delivered first in January 1859 in Boston and later repeated throughout New England and the Mid-Atlantic states. Franklin may have been Boston-born, went the burden of this speech, but "the memories which cluster round" relics of his early life "are interwoven with the inmost life" of the entire "American Union." Franklin's motto devised to promote intercolonial unity in the 1750s, "Join or Die," proved useful to Everett in this period, of course.[21]

And Everett never doubted the political as well as cultural usefulness of all this memory work. Though some contemporaries and historians have seen him and his audience as seeking escape in the past from the traumas of the 1850s, he was determined to use the past to shape the present.[22] Still facing doubts among literary men about how substantial his career of giving occasional speeches could be, Everett had come to believe more firmly than ever that it united literary interest with vital public service. And that civic service had a very particular point, as he revealed by making everything from lighthouses to the career of Washington Irving serve as "a symbol of [the] Union's duration and solidity."[23] But nothing was better calculated to bind the nation, both at the time and going forward, than memorializing its history, whether in word or physical monuments. In his 1855 Dorchester oration, Everett granted that there was something indefinable and even "mysterious" in the process of making and preserving a nation out of diverse human elements. But "I believe in monuments," he told the audience at the dedication of an equestrian statue of Washington in Richmond. Such a marker "embodies patriotism, truth, and faith; it gives form and expression to the best feelings of our nature." And as long as this massive sculpture of Washington stood, "that rigid arm shall point the unerring road to the welfare of the country more surely than any arm of living flesh; and a fiercer thunder than that of the elements shall clothe the neck of the monumental war-horse, and strike terror to the hearts of the enemies of the constitution and the union." "What parent," he asked at the dedication of the Webster statue, "as he conducts his son to Mount Auburn or to Bunker Hill, will not, as he pauses before their monumental statues, seek to heighten his reverence for virtue, for patriotism"?[24] It was thus no coincidence that a multitude of impressive memorials to Revolutionary heroes, many of them overseen by Everett and his cronies over years of planning, came to fruition in the late 1850s when the Union needed their didactic and emotional force.[25]

For all these multifarious commemorative activities, Everett's supreme effort to combine passionate oratory with the cultivation of physical shrines and relics in order to bind heartstrings to the Union came in the form of a campaign to purchase Mount Vernon. Unionist patriots had long imagined Mount Vernon as a haven from sectional turmoil and invited their countrymen to "come to this hallowed spot, and, around this sacred sarcophagus, promise to live together like brothers, for he was the Father of you *all*." Inasmuch as Washington had always embodied the Union more than any other figure, the hope was that reverence for this hero in general, and pilgrimages to Mount Vernon in particular, would convince Americans that disunion meant apostasy as well as folly. But those pilgrims tended to help themselves to relics from Mount Vernon, and the resultant material decline of the estate had become intolerable to many observers by the 1850s. Proposals that the Virginia or federal government purchase the estate from John A. Washington Jr. failed amid sectional and constitutional squabbles that typified how Americans used Washington as a club as much as a shield.[26]

A group of women stepped into the breach, determined in this age of rising partisan and sectional furor to play a more old-fashioned women's role. Some Northern women in the 1850s quite visibly translated their antislavery activism into campaigning for the Republican Party. But a growing bisectional group of ladies, very much in the tradition of Jacksonian-era reform movements, conspicuously shunned the sordid self-interest and the violent passions that dominated the masculine political sphere, even as they worked alongside like-minded men to achieve a political objective. In December 1853, two women of South Carolina's planter class, Louisa Bird Cunningham and her daughter Ann Pamela Cunningham, launched a ladies' fund-raising campaign. It was a natural fit for women seeking to reinsert the domestic virtues into American public life to raise funds to purchase the private home of the Father of His Country. Alarmed at a rumor that "a company of Northern capitalists" had determined to buy the property, they began by appealing to "the daughters of the South." Women from especially the Upper South would long be a dominant force in the organization. But the group very quickly expanded to become a national body and religiously excluded parochial sectionalism from its vision and rhetoric. Indeed, after going through a variety of early monikers, in 1858 it changed its name to the Mount Vernon Ladies Association of the Union (hereinafter MVLAU). The name captured members' effort to harness the considerable power of the cults of domesticity and of Washington. It also embodied their driving dream to leverage Unionist sentiment to save Mount Vernon, while leveraging Washington to save the Union.[27]

By late 1855, it occurred both to the Cunninghams and to Everett that theirs would be a natural and mutually beneficial partnership. In 1853 Everett had agreed with one projector that "Mount Vernon ought to become Public property" in some way. In February 1854, at one of the worst moments of the Kansas-Nebraska debate, Everett had gone out of his way to Arlington, Virginia, to visit George Washington Parke Custis, grandson of Martha Washington, and see his collection of Washington relics.[28] On 17 July 1855, still deep in his personal and political funk, Everett received a request to speak at the inauguration of the new headquarters of Boston's Mercantile Library Association. In perhaps a fateful coincidence, that same day George Lunt approached him on Boston Common and imparted two anecdotes of Washington's visits to New England, which Everett recorded in detail in his diary. He also read from Washington's diary while contemplating the invitation, and by October he agreed to speak to the group on Washington's next birthday. Since the young men of the Mercantile Library Association—knowing their man—had informed him that their purpose was not only "to celebrate the Birthday of the Father of his Country" but also to fund the decoration of their new hall with "portraits of revolutionary & other distinguished characters," he could not refuse. That goal was "so commendable and so well calculated to strengthen the foundations of an enlightened patriotism, that I feel as I should do wrong to withhold my participation."[29]

He had decided to address these young men with an oration of over two hours, titled "The Character of Washington." Its political point would not be subtle. During the weeks he spent preparing the address, he confided in his publisher that given "that the disunion feeling is steadily gaining ground in this part of the Country," "I regard the Union Sentiment" of the emerging speech "as of paramount importance." But from his long study of the basis of Unionism and practice of the art of oratory, Everett knew that just addressing that theme guaranteed no dramatic effect without an "impressive" performance appealing to hearts as well as minds.[30] So he carefully crafted what would be his magnum opus, achieving success in stirring up that "Union Sentiment" with a power and to a vast audience that Everett could not have imagined at the outset.

Everett's thesis in the discourse was that to study Washington's career and attributes was to watch as "the august plan of Providence ripens" in "the greatest man of our own or of any age." Indeed, a large part of the oration examined other noted characters in Western history and contemporary American politicians, only to find them sorely wanting in comparison. Washington was, in short, "a man whose word you would respect as an uninspired scripture; . . . a man toward whom affection rises into reverence, and reverence melts back into childish, tearful love." In evangelical tones, he bore witness that "I believe, as I do in my existence, that it was an important part of the design of Providence in raising him up," to give Americans "a living example" of the sort of public and private virtues that could save the Union. One aspect of that example was the balance and harmony of his character, for while he was not flashy, the "sublime adjustment of powers and virtues in the character of Washington . . . puts him in harmony with more than human greatness." For "ineffable harmony rules the heavens."

Everett was not done with the rhetoric of civic religion. "O," cried Everett as if he were revisiting his days as a preacher, that Washington's "pure example, his potent influence, his parting counsels," or ideally his voice "from the heavens to which he has ascended," could unite Americans again in "one bond of constitutional Union!" But short of actual intervention from its patron saint, Everett's church of Washington did have a mecca in Mount Vernon, and "while it stands the latest generations of the grateful children of America will make this pilgrimage to it as to a shrine." Everett also proposed that this sect "make a national festival and holiday of his birthday," which would unite congregants as they realized that their "fellow-citizens on the Hudson, on the Potomac, from the Southern plains to the Western lakes, are engaged in the same offices of gratitude and love." Finally, this cult of Washington had a sacred text in the Farewell Address, to which parishioners must give "practical deference" by "the preservation of the Union of these States." Should Americans forget the Farewell, boats on "the Potomac may toll their bells with new significance as they pass Mount Vernon; they will strike the requiem of constitutional liberty for us, —for all nations. But it cannot, it shall not be. . . . No, by the sacred dust enshrined at Mount Vernon; no, by the dear immortal memory of Washington,—that sorrow and shame shall never be."[31]

The effect of the delivery of such rhetoric would prove electric, but even before he pronounced the oration, the buzz surrounding it was considerable. In late 1855, as he received numerous letters from places as far-flung as Cincinnati and Richmond importuning him to speak in their cities, a lightbulb switched on in Everett's mind. He had recently learned from Charles Sumner that Phillips was earning as much as $100 per appearance on urban America's burgeoning lecture circuit. "The delivery of lectures," he started to sense, "is destined to become the most brilliant, lucrative & influential of the professions." But he would go his nemesis Phillips one better by delivering his lecture not for sordid gain but for a patriotic purpose. He would decline to provide even a sketch of the talk to the press as he had done with other efforts, so that he could repeat it as many times as possible and have it be fresh for the hearers. In early November, Everett proposed to his friend John R. Thompson that if he were to accept the invitation to repeat his Washington speech in Richmond, "it would be very proper to apply the proceeds of the sale of tickets of admission, to the increase of the fund, now raising by the Ladies of Virginia, for the purchase of Mount Vernon." Everett's suddenly jaunty correspondence revealed that he was reinvigorated at the mere prospect. His life would be once again filled with purpose, and purpose reflecting his highest priorities.[32]

After addressing his initial audience in Boston on 22 February 1856, Everett immediately embarked on a triumphant tour of the Mid-Atlantic region in which certain themes emerged that would persist throughout his Mount Vernon crusade. He visited every large urban center and many a lesser town between New York and Richmond, speaking thirteen times between early March and early April. Halls both small and "immense" filled to capacity with auditors who received his address with unbridled enthusiasm. The postal service tracked him down in such places with earnest pleas from leading citizens in a multitude of other places. The drain of politely answering this flood of correspondence would eventually force Everett to get form-letter responses printed and then finally to hire a private secretary. By the time this expedition and an intensive spring tour of New England had concluded, he had raised in excess of $15,000. He invested the funds in bonds and eventually set up his own Mount Vernon Trust, complete with officers broken into subcommittees.[33]

While that sort of audience demand for and reaction to the speech itself was enormously important to Everett,[34] some of the significance of the campaign would also lie in incidents and interactions he experienced outside of the lecture halls. A poignant moment on this inaugural journey came when his boat passed Mount Vernon and "the bell tolled. This is the universal practice of all vessels which ascend & descend the river: a beautiful custom." As he passed through Philadelphia on his maiden Mount Vernon itinerary, he first met Ann Pamela Cunningham, who impressed him with how much she had already accomplished in this effort despite obstacles including her poor health. That only increased his own commitment.[35] He was routinely thronged by distinguished visitors both before and after his performances. Although the ad hoc receptions were less agreeable than the formal dinners, he usually gladly accepted that imposition as part of the job. Indeed, part of what attracted Everett to the MVLAU was the fact that it bid fair to unify sympathizers "in every part of the land." His oration travels allowed him to cultivate contacts with dignitaries—who offered him fulsome welcomes both in private and when introducing his oration—in all parts of the Union and confirm them in the faith. His amicable interactions with Southerners proved especially gratifying and politically significant, given his Northern origins. For both the speaker and his hosts, Everett's travels helped give their Unionism the coherence and concreteness of a social network.[36]

The nationwide circuit Everett undertook in this effort involved undeniable inconvenience and labor for a man in his early sixties. Although he marveled at the relative speed of train travel, his far-flung journeys could be tedious and long. And once he arrived, preparing to repeat the oration involved serious, concentrated mental effort for him, often interrupted by social calls. Moreover, his personal finances suffered following the Panic of 1857, making him wonder whether he could afford to give numerous orations from which he personally profited nothing. At times when he felt his age and relative financial straits, he indulged in feeling "almost tired of laboring gratuitously for the public."[37]

But he never went beyond that "almost" for long and derived far more psychic benefits than aggravation from this work. It did not hurt that valued friends and literary reviewers pronounced his "Character of Washington" an oratorical "masterpiece."[38] Furthermore, being on the road was also a relief from the forlorn scene at home. There, he faced trouble with household servants and especially the drawn-out trauma of Charlotte's failing health; she died in July 1859 after months of decline and weeks of serious crisis. Staying in the welcoming homes of local elites, and particularly in the Everett House, a New York City luxury hotel (appropriately located adjoining Union Square) named after himself, was preferable in every way psychologically.[39] A particularly gratifying moment came in Richmond in February 1858, when the MVLAU treated Everett and fellow orator William Lowndes Yancey as guests of honor at a celebration of the progress of the cause. Along with fulsome rhetoric, the ladies gifted Everett with a cane that had once been in the possession of Washington himself. Everett was genuinely touched by the whole ceremony and candidly recounted to the crowd how after his resignation from the Senate he had found "in these inoffensive pursuits, into which I have been drawn, consecrated to patriotism and benevolence, a more congenial occupation for my waning years." He loved being "engaged in a pure and honorable work," seeking to "soften the asperity of sectional feeling, by holding up to the admiration of all parts of the country, that great exemplar which all alike respect and love."[40] For decades Everett had put much stock in the power of patriotic oratory, and this campaign saw that faith vindicated.

As that little speech suggested, Everett's gratification was political as well as personal. "This is the time," he exhorted an Independence Day gathering at Faneuil Hall in 1858, "the accepted time, when the voice of the Father of his Country cries aloud to us from the sods of Mount Vernon, and calls upon us, east and west, north and south, as the brethren of one great household, to be faithful to the dear-bought inheritance which he did so much to secure to us." He was greatly encouraged "to find, amidst all the bitter dissensions of the day, that this one grand sentiment, veneration for the name of Washington, is buried—no, planted—down in the very depths of the American heart." Everywhere he had traveled he found that Americans "have their sectional loves and hatreds, but before the dear name of Washington they are all absorbed and forgotten." True, certain elements in American politics treated "'Union-saving,' as it is derisively called, . . . with real or affected contempt." But he had reason to hope that the momentum to save Mount Vernon would carry over to other hallowed places, until "all the cherished traditions of every part of the country may be woven and twisted into a bright cord of mutual good-will, to which every honored name, and every sacred spot, and every memorable deed shall add its golden and silver thread."[41]

The effect on his health was predictable. Despite the labors and inconveniences of his rigorous travel schedule, he found himself in far better physical condition than he had during past periods of intense political strife. "I am uncommonly bright," he wrote to his daughter Charlotte in a typically chipper report from the road. His friends seconded his self-diagnosis. William Hickling Prescott, for one, pronounced him "in good trim" in 1858, concluding that "his Washington address, with its concomitants, has done as much for him as for the Monument, by building him up." Everett himself suggested the strong link between his physical well-being, his mental state, and his political satisfaction in a fascinating diary entry in 1859, at the age of sixty-five. "Strange as it sounds I continually encourage myself to support" the "unseasonable hours & fatiguing journies [sic]" he endured in the Mount Vernon cause by comparing them to military men's campaigns. "My power of physical endurance is probably as great as" some of the great commanders in history, he wrote, "& I have only to add the will" to match their exploits. This was a revealing statement, for the same Everett whose endurance had been so calamitously limited during the Kansas-Nebraska debates did have the will to push himself on speaking expeditions ranging as far afield as St. Louis.[42]

For all its popular acclaim, the Mount Vernon campaign hardly experienced smooth political sailing. While it tapped a widespread instinct for consensus-building in response to growing sectional strife, it met with serious attacks from sectional extremists in both North and South. These challenges were all the more threatening to Everett and his cause because the challengers did not reject the appeal to the founding past; instead, they contested the moral

Everett and his kind drew from that origins story. The American Revolution and George Washington provided antebellum Americans with common ground that transcended local historical antecedents, but they used it more as a point of departure than a destination amid the slavery debates. Many historians have explored this antebellum battle over the legacy of the Revolution, but they have almost uniformly cast it as a two-sided struggle. Adding the experience of Everett and the MVLAU to this narrative helps us see this as a bitter three-way brawl. As Everett himself took blows from two different directions, he was certainly left with no lack of clarity on either the bitterness or the three-way nature of this melee.[43]

Everett and the MVLAU felt those blows most keenly and often from abolitionists and Republicans. In 1858, Elizabeth Cady Stanton enthused abolitionists by refusing an invitation to become a manager of an MVLAU branch, declaring her energies better spent aligning American life with the ideals of the Revolution by abolishing slavery. Frederick Douglass held up alternative heroes to Americans' gaze, such as in his 1853 novella celebrating the *Creole* mutineers as the true Virginia exponents of "the principles of 1776."[44] People from this end of the political spectrum also specifically targeted Everett. In the lead-up to his 4 July performance in Dorchester, a group of abolitionists circulated a handbill protesting his appearance, making sure to send one to the speaker himself. Trotting out Everett's greatest hits of betrayal to the antislavery cause from 1826, 1836, and 1854, the handbill's authors argued that "Mr. Everett has bowed too low and too often in vassalage to the Slave Power" to be counted on to properly celebrate the Fourth. Webster's antislavery enemies, of course, hated Everett's hagiographical treatments of this villain.[45] Some abolitionists dismissed Everett's Mount Vernon effort as a forlorn attempt to secure the presidency or a cabinet position for himself. Other hostile observers shrugged off Everett as one who "delights to forget the present in the memory of the more glorious past."[46]

Other abolitionists and Republicans, however, formed a more accurate estimate of the cultural potency of Everett's emotional Unionist appeal. Knowing that Everett's agenda was far from an escape into a dead past, they determined to redirect its present power into channels of their choosing. Their basic argument was that Everett, in his timidity in the cause of freedom, had dangerously censored the most valuable part of the story of Washington's relationship with slavery by omitting mention of his antislavery protests and will emancipating his slaves. In 1858, at an upstate New York celebration of the anniversary of British emancipation, Douglass railed at Everett for his "cowardly suppression of the most significant feature of the moral portrait of Washington, lest the exhibition of it should give offence to slaveholder." Everett, Douglass was sure, knew like Washington did "that Slavery is the mistake, is the curse, the crime, the disgrace, and the shame of America," but he shrank from bearing that witness. He and his fellow travelers "love the Union, but not the objects for which the Union was formed. They quote the great words of the fathers, but only to excuse the sins of their children. They would preserve the form, but murder the spirit of Liberty."[47] An influential Republican paper in Albany lambasted Everett's "Character of Washington" as guilty "of a falsification of the likeness of the grand man whose portraiture he undertook." "Washington's central and vital characteristic," this editorial lectured, "was love of Liberty and veneration of Man. Were he alive now, he would be in as sharp antagonism to the huge slavery-perpetuating, slavery-extending, slavery-apologizing organization which exists in" the whole of American politics "as he was in fiery and unconquerable antagonism to the despotism of Britain over the American Colonies."[48] New York Republican powerhouse Horace Greeley's *New York Tribune* summed up this critique this way: "We reproach Mr. Everett, not with building Washington's tomb, but with mutilating and disfiguring his character, by leaving out the testimony borne in his letters and will to the wrong and mischief of human slavery."[49]

As galling as were these attacks from New Yorkers, challenges from Sumner, Phillips, and Theodore Parker were more significant to Everett because they argued from the same Bostonian premises. As historian James Brewer Stewart has demonstrated in his outstanding biography of Phillips, that abolitionist firebrand emerged from the same upper-class Boston culture and republican ideological tradition as did Everett. Indeed, Phillips attacked the likes of Everett all the more rancorously because of his sense that they had betrayed this shared understanding of liberty, law, and order. "Foul perversion had been made of Boston's republican traditions" by slavery's allies there and elsewhere, he believed, so it came naturally to him to appeal to the Revolutionary legacy for his cause and against the enemies in this cousins' quarrel. For him as for Everett, the project of inculcating in both minds and hearts the proper morals of the national stories was deadly earnest. Also like Everett, in the late 1850s Phillips devoted increasing time and energy to delivering lectures that expanded his influence, rather than to traditional politics. Working from "premises which we all grant to be true," he appealed for the abolitionist interpretation of those "old and established principles." That was true for the Puritan heritage as well as the Revolutionary, for he maintained that "the true blood of the" Puritan Fathers "crops out in some fanatical abolitionist." In an 1859 lecture titled "Idols," Phillips railed against Everett's speech dedicating the Webster monument. His "silence" on Webster's "great treason" to America's true principles on the Seventh of March, he warned, was not simply an indication of the orator's native pusillanimity. "Monuments, anniversaries, statues, are schools," he agreed with Everett and Webster themselves, "whose lesson sink deep. Is this man's life a lesson which the State can commend to her sons?" Weeks after rebuking Everett thus, Phillips even made his own sort of pilgrimage, to abolitionist martyr John Brown's farm in New York, and gathered relics while there.[50] The sound and fury of this clash came at least as much from the striking similarities as from the profound differences between Everett and Phillips.

Everett's other Boston antagonists fought him just as vigorously. Throughout the late 1850s, Sumner vociferously argued that the Republican Party platform embodied the tradition of the Pilgrim and Revolutionary Fathers. He therefore set out to dispute Everett's exclusive claim to that inheritance—and even to the mantle of true conservatism—at the very commencement of his Mount Vernon campaign. In a public letter to the Boston Mercantile Library Association, Sumner thanked the organizers for the invitation to join them for the occasion on which Everett would deliver his "Character of Washington" for the first time. Washington's "great name," Sumner counseled, "should now be employed for the suppression of that Slave Power" whose tyrannical provocations threatened the Union he had founded. "It will not be enough to quote his paternal words for Union," he pointedly observed. "His example must be arrayed against the gigantic wrong which now disturbs this Union to its centre." To portray Washington "without his testimony against" slavery was the equivalent of staging Shakespeare's Othello "without the part of Othello" himself. In short, only if "the young men of Boston" were taught Washington's antislavery utterances and actions in such a way as to take them "to heart" would the great man's example "exert its just conservative influence over the country."[51] In 1858, determined to counteract Everett's influential distortions, Parker delivered four lectures giving his own spin on Founding Fathers Washington, Franklin, Adams, and Jefferson. He prefaced his homily on Washington by jabbing that Washington's unparalleled authority in American culture had led "the most selfish and deceitful of politicians" to "use his name as the stalking-horse behind which they creep when they seek to deceive and 'exploiter' the People." To set the record straight, Parker asserted that Washington's real moral virtue lay "in his relation to the Nation's greatest crime," for he hated slavery and did all he could to eradicate it. But alas, "the American rhetoricians" of the Everett school "do not dare tell half his excellence."[52]

Southern fire-eaters had no less an appreciation for their Revolutionary heritage, and many of them saw Everett's crusade as a more dangerous attempted theft of that birthright than what their open enemies offered because it was subtler. For one thing, intersectional nationalist efforts of this kind distracted politicians and voters from the real issue, the threat of Northern control of the federal government. Yet Southern rights men and women, like the Republicans and abolitionists, knew that the MVLAU appeal was too strong to simply dismiss or ignore, so they sought to co-opt it. Southern sectionalists, headed by the Alabama arch-secessionist William Lowndes Yancey, thought they might be able to steer the MVLAU bandwagon into their territory by painting Washington as the quintessential Southern slaveholder and secessionist. In the spring of 1857, Yancey, like Everett a renowned orator, decided to give his own speech on Washington to raise funds for the MVLAU. He identified his real audience by confining his speaking tours to the Southwest. His message was that Washington's life "served as the supreme example of determination and sacrifice to protect the rights of the oppressed against tyranny." His leadership of the colonies' secession from the British Empire, therefore, was the most salient part of his legacy. He and Everett, then, shared the MVLAU label and the stage at the impressive Richmond celebration in 1858, but they shared nothing else.[53] Everett privately worried about the harm Yancey was doing to the MVLAU brand. And when the leaders of the Southern rights festival that was the Southern Commercial Convention in Knoxville invited Everett to address them in 1857, he wisely declined.[54] At the next year's Southern Commercial Convention, Yancey expressed his distrust of just such supposed statesmen as Everett claimed to be. "A man who knew no North, South, East or West," Yancey warned, "but was for the Union, was for the spoils without reference to the rights of the people."[55]

No less discouraging for Everett and his allies were heated Southern retorts to Republican and abolitionist abuse of the MVLAU and its leading man. A North Carolina editor boiled with rage at "the scoundrel Abolitionists of New England" who charged Everett's speaking tours with giving "'aid and comfort to the slaveholding oligarchy!' What dogs! What hyenas! What traitors to their country!—No—not *their* country;—such disorganizers can have no country." Northern sectionalism thus marked a woeful declension from the days of the Revolution, when "there *was* union" because "Patriotism was in the ascendant, and Fanaticism had not begun its hellish work of heart-burnings, alienation and all uncharitableness."[56] Given that Everett's whole purpose was to transcend and minimize sectionalist rhetoric, seeing it crop up even among his allies and in his defense was disheartening.

Everett's inability to exclude sectional irruptions into his MVLAU paradise came into disturbing focus in the weeks and months following Preston Brooks's assault on Charles Sumner in May 1856. On 19–20 May in the Senate, Sumner delivered a blistering verbal attack on the South and its doings in Kansas, and soon thereafter South Carolina congressman Brooks beat him senseless with a cane on the Senate floor. Word of the outrage reached Everett on 23 May, and although he was mildly surprised that Sumner would have pronounced such a provocative speech, he claimed to his diary that "I have long foreseen an occurrence of this kind, which is likely to prove 'the beginning of the end.'" The next day, the organizers of Boston's "indignation meeting" importuned Everett to attend and sit on the platform at Faneuil Hall. As historian Michael Woods has shown, this was one of many such gatherings called throughout the North to give organized form to the community's reaction to the beating, and their uniform aspiration was to present that reaction as unanimous. Furthermore, in antebellum American culture indignation was a politically acceptable emotion, righteous and rational and not necessarily calculated—unlike anger—to disturb the harmony of the Union. The need to distinguish between indignation and rabble-rousing anger can be seen in indignation meetings' eagerness to report respectable men and ladies present. All of these imperatives explain the organizers' desire for Everett to be seen at the meeting. Everett "told them that I condemned as much as any one the outrage on Mr. Sumner," a protestation belied by many diary entries and letters blaming the affray at least in part on the imprudence of Sumner's rhetoric. But at any rate, he claimed, he "had definitely retired from political life" so he would not attend.[57]

Everett's real troubles began when reports that he had refused to attend circulated in newspapers. Lashing editorials from his left on the Northern antislavery spectrum were a predictable result, but then the Connecticut legislature rescinded its invitation to Everett to deliver his "Character of Washington" in New Haven. Everett's immediate response via the *Daily Advertiser* was to skewer Sumner's allies for railing at Brooks's assault on free speech in the Senate while depriving Everett of his "right *to be silent*," a right that the phrase free speech "implies." He circulated this statement to other editors in hopes it would contain the backlash to the Connecticut legislature. But the less-than-capacity crowd greeting his appearance in Taunton, Massachusetts, on 30 May underscored that the stakes involved now included the fate of the MVLAU campaign, so he decided to deliver a more extensive, forceful response.[58] In his prefatory remarks to his oration in Taunton that night, Everett spoke of his "irrepressible sadness" at the "civil war . . . carried on, without the slightest provocation, against the infant settlements of our brethren" in Kansas, as well as at "the worse than civil war which has for months raged unrebuked at the capital of the Union." The latter conflict had now, "by an act of lawless violence of which I know no parallel in the history of Constitutional Government, stained the floor of the Senate Chamber with the blood of an unarmed, defenceless man, and he a Senator of Massachusetts." "My friends," he groaned, "these are events, which for the good name, the peace, the safety, of the country; for the cause of free institutions throughout the world; it were worth all the gold of California to blot from the record of the past week." These events thus "fill me with sorrow 'too deep for tears,'" and only his hope "that there is a healing influence in the name of Washington" had induced him to carry on with his oration that evening.[59]

Everett had chosen his words carefully in the service of the delicate work of steering public emotion into proper channels. "The community," he perceived, "is divided between two sentiments" in the aftermath of the caning: "the fiercest wrath & the deepest melancholy." He not only felt the latter emotion more keenly but also believed—correctly, as Woods's work demonstrates—that wrath would only help the Republicans. So he clarified repeatedly that his Taunton remarks "were made in sorrow & not in anger, & were intended to chasten & not irritate the public mind. They have, for that reason, been caviled at by the extremists of the north." He knew that emoting sadness while others demanded rage would not please them, but he hoped to instruct rather than to follow them.[60]

The "extremists" north and south took the lead, however, when the Taunton introduction resounded throughout the Union. Everett's Northern defenders maintained that "nothing that Theodore Parker or Wendell Phillips uttered at the meeting which Mr. Everett declined to attend, was more direct or half as weighty in condemnation of the violence by which the course of our Pro-Slavery Administration is marked" than Everett's Taunton preface. The Connecticut legislature reconsidered its reconsideration and reinvited Everett to speak in New Haven, and that act convinced other Northern doubters.[61] But that only made Everett's Southern friends wonder how to defend him when unfriendly Southern editors seized on his Taunton remarks to call for the MVLAU to disassociate itself from this notorious man. "To preface a eulogy on the Father of his Country with a *whining cry* of sympathy with an infamous traitor," a Richmond editor exclaimed, "*is just like Edward Everett. He has no sincerity*, and no power of resistance to the frenzy of the moment." To another Richmond newspaper, his Taunton remarks underscored what the South had known since at least 1841: "throughout life, Mr. Edward Everett has been a consistent Abolitionist." It strained credulity, therefore, to see him "imported to Richmond to teach Virginia how to admire Washington!" The South in her "folly" thereby "warms the viper in her bosom" even "after she has felt the poison of the fang." While an Alabama editor demurred that "we shall ever admire the patriotic efforts of the Southern ladies," he felt compelled after Taunton to "enter our solemn protest against the admission of that man into our native State, whose eyes were bedewed with tears of sympathy when the *dastardly Sumner* fell by the hands of *the gallant Brooks,* and whose heart, to-day, *is cankered by the undying hatred it bears against the South, and Southern institutions.*" It was the worst of travesties to contemplate this "*abolition emissary*" eulogizing Washington in the Southland.[62] Then when Southern editors defended Everett as sound on slavery, abolitionists crowed that this proved that they had been right all along about this doughface.[63] Reading all this made Everett wonder whether his MVLAU effort was not about to be hopelessly squeezed in the sectional vise. "If welcomed" in the South, he mused, "in the existing state of excitement, I should be in a false position at home."[64]

For all that, the ordeal was over for Everett no more than it was for Sumner himself. A new chapter began on the evening of 3 June, when Carlos Pierce from Boston's Mercantile Library Association asked for Everett to sign a subscription for the purchase of a plate to present to the wounded Sumner on his return home. Predictably enough given Everett's luck with such matters, Pierce returned to gather his signature the next morning, after Everett had had a bad night's sleep despite taking chloric ether as a sleep aid. Still under the effects of the ether and not having yet dressed for the day when a servant brought the subscription roll to his room, Everett unrolled it only partially and, satisfied by seeing reliable men's signatures on the document, affixed his name. But then that afternoon, he read in the newspaper that this testimonial expressed "unqualified approbation" for Sumner's speech and applied rather violent language to Brooks and his supporters. A mortified and ill Everett summoned Pierce to his home, where he remonstrated "that I signed the paper without reading it & could not have signed it, if I had first read it." But the deed was done, and friends counseled him that there was no good way for him to remove his signature. He drafted an explanation of "the 'Testimonial' affair" and gave it to Nathan Hale, but Hale pocketed it rather than published it.[65]

But the subscription controversy would not go away. Richmond editor Roger A. Pryor seems to have aired it for the first time in February 1858, when in protesting the MVLAU's plans to honor Everett in that city he asked whether Washington's cane would be "worthily bestowed" on such a man. After Sumner's caning, he recounted, "a few of the fanatical citizens of Boston united for a testimonial of regard and sympathy for their scurrilous Senator.—Among them was EDWARD EVERETT," who donated money for and signed the tribute to Sumner and his speech. Everett's friends' "apology for him," that he was sick when he signed it, made him look all the more like a dupe of the abolitionists.

Everett, Pryor noted, had yet to distance himself from the Sumner subscription, and "his friends" had mounted a "whisper" campaign of disavowal only now that he was headed "South to peddle his rhetorical platitudes." Such noncommittalism would no longer fly.[66] Moved by such taunts, Everett decided that he could not withhold an explanation of this mess. In May 1858, the editors of the friendly *National Intelligencer* published Everett's account of the affair, and indeed of his whole political course since the advent of Kansas-Nebraska. "The ground on which I have endeavored to stand," he summed, was "that of conciliation, in the spirit of the Constitution." It followed that he was no apologist "for the manner in which the existing sectional agitation is carried on at the North, one feature of which has been a most violent and unrelenting warfare against myself."[67] Sectionalists remained unconvinced by this explanation. Phillips and Parker doubted even the facts of Everett's story, and the latter ascribed such "baseness" and "wickedness" to Everett's desire for the presidency. Massachusetts Republican chieftain Henry Wilson publicly jabbed Everett over the subscription episode in November 1858.[68]

Feeling paralyzed politically as a result of the Brooks-Sumner episode, Everett's health predictably continued on a downward path. He came to believe that the whole "dreadful explosion may make it impossible" for him ever to return to the South to repeat his oration. Deep into the winter of 1856–57, he diagnosed himself as "incapable of any strenuous exertion" and petulantly eschewed all public appearances because they would "only give new matter of cavil to the papers that abused me with equal virulence & meanness." "All I wanted," he whimpered when declining Pierce's invitation to attend Sumner's reception in Boston, "was to be allowed to pass the few remaining years of my life in peace." As if his own health were a barometer of that of the Union, he despaired anew of its survival and believed peaceful disunion might be preferable to "this eternal quarrelling." He visited Sumner in December, but they avoided the irritating subject of politics. He was even apt to talk of his MVLAU activities in the past tense. "I take some comfort in the reflection," he sighed to a major MVLAU supporter in June 1856, "that tho' I have not done what I intended, I have accomplished something."[69]

Everett's responses to the totality of these challenges alternated between self-pitying evasion and insightfulness. By far his weakest response was to dismiss his adversaries with ad hominem arguments. He set down his detractors as plagued with a variety of character flaws ranging from practical atheism to envy of his popularity.[70] Similarly paltry were his protests that he was out of politics and thus that hostile, self-serving pols were gratuitously politicizing Washington's appeal. In a letter to Southern friend R. M. T. Hunter in late 1857, he regretted that the likes of Pryor "play into the hands of Horace Greeley & Wendell Phillips who lose no opportunity of flying at my throat & barking at my heels; & who enjoy their greatest triumph, when a northern conservative is abused at the South." This abuse from both sides was all the harder to take because "this is a voluntary & private errand, proposed by ladies, appealing to the kind feelings of the community, of a patriotic but not a political character." He hoped Hunter would help protect "a person now in retirement, whose public life has perhaps been marked by nothing so much, as the unrelenting hostility of the enemies of the Constitution & the Union in the Northern States."[71] With his keen understanding of the political import of all his memory work, Everett knew better. He made these meager attempts to pose as outside politics because he knew that if the "notion gets abroad" that his MVLAU activities were partisan or meant to advance his own political career, "I shall have to stay home."[72]

Everett's retorts proved more rational when he directly contested his opponents' claims to the legacy of the Fathers. The likes of Phillips, he argued, were counterfeit heirs to the Pilgrims. True, the original Puritans like the Republicans and abolitionists offered "a striking example of the proneness of new parties, organized on moral principles to run to extremes." But, he jabbed, "I believe the Puritans never entered into coalition with the Stuarts" as had the Free Soilers with the Democrats and the Republicans with the Know-Nothings. Worse than these sham appeals to the Puritan legacy, he fretted, it had become too common for Americans (especially Bay Staters resisting the Fugitive Slave Act) to cite the Revolution as a precedent for "lawlessness." Under the headline of "Dangerous Doctrines," Everett led an editorial for the *Daily Advertiser* by noting how "a very zealous and active party at the North are constantly appealing to the example of the revolutionary fathers, and taunting the friends of the Constitution with having degenerated from the spirit of 'Seventy-Six.'" This view was both "fallacious" and "dangerous in its tendency" because "our revolutionary fathers" revolted only when their government became truly intolerable in the eyes of "the real people, the sober and reflecting portion of the community." Moreover, the people's own representatives in Congress, not some distant Parliament, had made the laws complained of now. A better historical analogy for what the agitators were truly launching would be "the internecine contests which have cursed continental Europe from Time immemorial."[73]

Everett was even more incisive when he warned his antagonists of just how malleable Washington's legacy could be. Everett recognized his own selective reading of Washington's career but defended it as fairer than the sectionalists'. To those who complained he did not highlight Washington's emancipatory will, he submitted that "it was not a particularly *characteristic* act." Slavery was "a subject . . . not mentioned by himself in any official communication, particularly not in" the canonical Farewell Address — which did, of course, preach the Unionist gospel. In an 1857 letter providing talking points for a defender of the MVLAU cause, Everett cautioned that "those who reproach me with suppressing his testimony against Slavery should remember, that it is a point on which much may be said on the other side, which if the subject were mentioned at all" in his oration, "it would not have been honest to suppress." In fact, the points to support a Southern-friendly interpretation of Washington might be stronger and were certainly more numerous. So to raise the issue of slavery and treat it fairly would not only hijack a speech that was about Washington's contributions to union but also result "in nothing favorable to the views of those who reproach me." "If we claim Washington as an abolitionist," Everett put it more succinctly in another letter, "the South will claim him as a Slaveholder; a signer of the Fugitive Slave Law; — and as having endeavored to procure the arrest of one of his own slaves under it. — What is gained by dragging him into the controversy in this way?"[74] Nothing, of course, would be gained and everything would be lost. The whole MVLAU effort to change the subject would be frustrated and the nation's wounds exacerbated rather than healed. Much as the sectionalists wanted to drag Washington into a two-sided contest, Everett insisted that it had three sides and determined to make his side the strongest.

Ultimately, building up that third side would not come from scoring debating points against the other two but rather by continuing his appeal above the heads of the politicians and agitators to the hearts of the American people. A sense of the hopelessness of party politics was reinforced by the outcome of the presidential election of 1856. While Everett's friend Buchanan won the election, the Republicans did spectacularly well, as their inaugural candidate John C. Frémont won nearly every Northern state. Neither Unionists nor Southern rights men found themselves very reassured by this outcome. Everett found that the only cure for his sense of paralysis in the aftermath of Brooks-Sumner and this election was to force himself back on the MVLAU trail by honoring previous commitments to repeat the Washington oration. That began at a Washington birthday celebration in Boston's Music Hall on 23 February 1857. Unsure of himself after a nine-month layoff, he found his confidence when he learned that the performance had sold out hours in advance and greeted the "immense audience" studded by "the *elite* of Boston." He returned home that night unsurprisingly "almost wholly free from my rheumatism." His MVLAU travels that spring and summer would take him as far afield as Missouri, and the repetitions of triumphs along the way would reignite his hope.[75]

And for all the contestations of and sectional encroachments on his MVLAU campaign, Everett had abundant reason for hope. The public response to his oration and other MVLAU activities proved overwhelmingly positive and at times extremely emotional. One fundamental indication of the success was that the MVLAU was able to raise enough money, despite a nationwide economic downturn in 1857 and constant competition from other fund-raisers, to pay John A. Washington in full and take possession of Mount Vernon in the fall of 1860. (The group raised about $200,000, and Everett's speaking and other fund-raising efforts had contributed about half of that total.)[76] Another basic measure of that response was in the sellout crowds—ranging from the dozens to the thousands, depending on the venue—which Everett attracted to almost all of the repetitions of the speech. These crowds paid either one dollar (the standard fee in the South) or fifty cents (the norm for the North) per ticket. Between February 1856 and April 1860, those repetitions numbered 131, delivered on 127 separate visits to cities (very few of them repeat visits) throughout the Northeast, Northwest, and Southeast of the United States. It would be easier, for one thing, to list the towns in Massachusetts and New York that he did not visit than the ones he did visit. Based on the number and crowdedness of these performances, one contemporary asserted plausibly that more people heard this oration than any other speech "since the beginning of time."[77] (For more, see appendix A.)

There were other more private actions that underscored the warm popular response to the speech. Railroad managers offered Everett free passage, or his audience reduced fares, on their trains as their contribution to the cause. Composers set their regard for Everett and Mount Vernon to music. A young woman in Virginia gushed in her diary after hearing Everett give his speech that "the *two* hours that he spoke, appeared scarcely so *many minutes*." Two years later when Everett delivered it at the University of Virginia, she eagerly anticipated hearing him again. "This is *my second* hearing, & I would not object to a *third*."[78] Other private citizens were devoted enough to the cause to do the hard, ground-level work necessary to prepare for an Everett appearance.[79]

Such efforts from a wide variety of civic organizations and individuals on the local level gave the MVLAU something of a grassroots movement culture. The MVLAU's own organ, *The Illustrated Mount Vernon Record*, quite naturally provided the fullest compendium of this cause's wide appeal. Its editors happily compiled a flurry of letters from local operatives and many other contributions

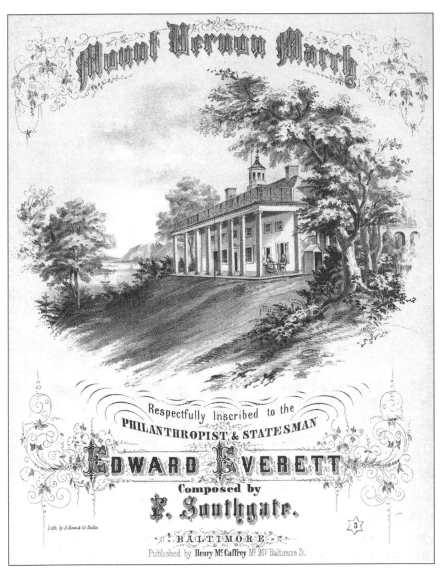

The cover of "Mount Vernon March," sheet music for piano composed
by F. Southgate and published in Baltimore by Henry McCaffrey, c. 1858.
Courtesy of the Albert and Shirley Small Special Collections Library,
University of Virginia, Charlottesville.

to the cult of Washington published in leading newspapers from around the country and even Britain. A Hartford, Connecticut, woman's poetic panegyric to Everett's MVLAU labors captured the spirit of these columns well, especially in this stanza:

> Learning and eloquence, and patriot zeal
> Move him, as from the buried Past he brings
> The living presence of our Nation's Sire;
> Touching like harp-string all those filial chords
> That thrilling thro' its mighty heart incite
> To union and fraternal harmony.[80]

She was not the only lady from whom Everett's campaign elicited lyrical lines.[81] And all this was more than the MVLAU party line. Reports describing "The Character of Washington" as a triumph that captivated its far-flung, standing-room-only audiences were the dominant theme in the coverage of a varied bevy of newspapers.[82]

The central trope in these press accounts was that this was truly an affair of the popular heart. Editors were apt to speak of Everett's oration as "calling up tears like grateful rain" and as leaving a "permanent impression" even on the most jaded of audiences. One admirer proposed erecting a bronze statue to the orator at a rescued Mount Vernon, given that he had himself become a national hero. "The emotion was so strong," read an account of a Brooklyn performance, "that it overleaped all restraint." One auditor's comparison of his experience to the apostles' at the Mount of Transfiguration certainly underscored such lack of restraint.[83] So did a Virginia newspaper's Richmond correspondent, who scribbled that "I might easily fill a quire of paper, searching for superlatives to express the beauty and grandeur of this admirable performance, but to what end? The description of a speech, is like the painting of a flower." But suffice it to say that "the day after his appearance in Richmond, the town was quite crazy—an absolute lunatic, with but one idea, a monomania." An elderly resident who had heard many of that generation's great orators exclaimed that he "never had listened to anything like this speech, and never expected to hear anything like it again. Another of the audience declared that it was an era in his life" to have been in Everett's audience. This correspondent heard the discourse in Petersburg, and from the very beginning "I do not think you could have failed to hear a pin drop for nearly two hours, if you will except the moments when the Hall shook with the thunder of applause, drawn forth by some exquisite image, some fine illustration, or some apostrophe to the mighty dead, which made the blood tingle in the frames of the audience, and their eyes fill with tears." Catching himself momentarily, he admitted to "writing what looks like extravagance— instead of extravagance however, I maintain that it is not even justice."[84]

None of these enthusiasts took any pains to hide the political upshot of this phenomenon—indeed, that was a core reason for their enthusiasm. The growing cult of Washington encouraged one literary reviewer because he imagined it would "fuse and mould into one pervasive emotion the divided hearts of the country, until . . . sectional animosity is awed into universal reverence." Likewise, for a Northern Unionist editor, Everett's visits to the South in particular promised to effect "a Patriotic Revolution" in that troubled region. Indeed, "he is the chosen Apostle of the Union, and his mission is as holy as that of St. Paul himself." A Philadelphia editor observed that it was precisely the MVLAU's political purpose "that has rendered Mr. Everett's progress through the country an event of unusual interest." Given that "disunion sentiments have, of late years, made much progress; that extremists of all sections are thoroughly disaffected; and that men now pause to count the value and blessings of the Union," it was vital to witness by means of the "response from the popular heart" to Everett that "the masses are strongly attached to" that Union for far better reasons than sordid gain.[85]

Such was the cultural power of Everett's "Character of Washington" that it attained the status of a Unionist shibboleth. It became a point of civic pride for cities to greet his appearances just as effusively as their citizens had read about other locales doing. A New York City editor, for instance, was keen to point out that the dominant presence of ladies at a packed repetition of the speech—Everett's third in the city by that point—gave "indubitable evidence that the ladies of New York share with their sisters in the other States the laudable desire to rescue the home and grave of Washington." The editor of the *Charleston Mercury*, either unaware or forgetful of how that sheet had treated Everett in the past, likewise protested that should Everett visit the South Carolina city, he would most certainly be "received with a warm and kindly welcome."[86] Neither did Everett's own scrupulous nonpartisanship keep parties and would-be parties from seeking to capitalize on his cause's good name. Everett's manifest popularity in this era even revived in some the hope that his name might be on a presidential ticket in 1860, rallying party-less ex-Whigs around his unparalleled "power to influence the Conservatives of the Union."[87] Meanwhile, a New Hampshire Republican sheet pointedly proffered that the predominantly Republican audience for an 1857 delivery of the oration "could join with Mr. Everett in the glowing apostrophe to" the Union "with which he closed." But such were "their patriotic desires" that they harbored righteous indignation in knowing "that the severest wounds which have been inflicted upon it were dealt in its madness by the Democratic party."[88] A New York essayist penned a perceptive analysis of this jockeying. "The popularity of Washington, at the present moment," was so "immense" that whenever one American party "makes much of Washington," its "rival parties, to show the world that they are just as 'American' as" their foes, strove "to out-do" them "in the frequency and fulsomeness of [their] adulations." The plaudits for Everett's oration multiplied accordingly.[89]

Everett cheerfully kept tabs on all this glowing press coverage,[90] and yet another evidence of his celebrity reached him in September 1858, when the entrepreneurial New Yorker Robert Bonner approached him with an extraordinary offer. Contemporaries knew Bonner, the editor of the mass-published *New York Ledger*, as "the mammoth advertiser of the age," in the same class as P. T. Barnum. Continually on the lookout for opportunities to expand his readership, by the late 1850s he had easily surpassed the threshold of 100,000 subscribers, which demarcated the largest-circulating papers in America. Realizing what a hot property Everett had become, Bonner offered to donate $10,000 to the MVLAU if Everett authored a year-long weekly series of essays for the *Ledger* on topics of Everett's choosing. Bonner's agents approached Everett in person with his proposal and proved very persistent, but Everett put them off while he consulted with his friends and the MVLAU's managers. He worried, he told the agents, about whether the workload and constant pace of this undertaking would interfere with his speaking tours.[91] What he did not tell them was that he also worried about whether he would be cheapening himself and his cause by appearing alongside authors with a reputation for appealing to the lowest common denominator. But he told himself that his essays would "rescue a portion of the paper from writers of that class; & I give the readers of the 'Ledger' some inoffensive reading." Moreover, across the weeks of consulting friends near and far, Everett came to believe that the actual readership he would reach with these essays would be somewhere in the neighborhood of a million people ("allowing four readers to each copy sold"). And Bonner's enormous payout for Mount Vernon proved the ultimate "temptation." When he signed on to the scheme in early November, he assigned the money as the "governing motive," followed by the huge audience he would reach.[92]

And while this essay series—titled "The Mount Vernon Papers"—was a true miscellany, Everett certainly did not shy away from preaching his Unionist gospel to this enormous readership. Amid this greater attention to writing, Everett agreed to write an article on Washington for the *Encyclopedia Britannica* that grew into a book-length biography of his hero. That also gave him a platform from which to expound on Washington's global significance, and he seized it. Within His larger scheme for human liberty, Everett argued, God had plainly raised up Washington—"THE GREATEST OF GOOD MEN AND THE BEST OF GREAT MEN"—to effect the founding of the American Union. And perhaps Washington's crowning achievement was his Farewell Address, with its prescient rebuke of sectionalism that spoke so directly to the 1850s. Not long after the popes had claimed infallibility, Everett claimed for the Farewell "marvellous discernment and unerring wisdom."[93]

Press reviews of these efforts were largely positive but mixed. Many papers guessed—accurately—that both Everett and Bonner had every reason to be satisfied with this arrangement: Bonner gave Everett a large and mostly new audience, while Everett elevated the dignity of Bonner's paper.[94] Everett's critics, meanwhile, found his collaboration with the sensationalist Bonner an easy target. Surely soon a famous promoter would offer Everett $20,000 "to travel with his circus in the capacity of a clown," one writer mocked.[95] And a few Americans believed Everett overexposed by the time his "Mount Vernon Papers" had run its course. "I am so sick of him," one woman told her sister in September 1859, "that I never think of reading what he says these days."[96] Such criticisms, unsurprisingly, bothered Everett, and complaining diary entries exaggerated them to the point that this trickle would seem to have been a flood of abuse.[97]

The real torrent, however, was of money in response to an appeal he made in "The Mount Vernon Papers." In his introductory essay in this series, dated 1 January 1859, Everett argued that gathering private contributions from around the nation would be the best mode of making Mount Vernon public property. Given that "it is not an extravagant calculation" that this series would reach one million Americans, "each one of whom venerates the character of Washington, and would gladly co-operate in rescuing his dwelling and his tomb from neglect and decay," he solicited a small donation from all of these readers. "The contribution of half a dollar each by the readers of the Ledger," he enthused, "would at once accomplish the object!" He offered to be the treasurer for this fund-raising campaign.[98]

Everett had received private donations separate from his oration before this essay, but that call greatly amplified the inflow of funds. The response came in such volume that Everett had his private secretary Edward Frothingham respond to almost all of the letters. Those letters dominate reels 16 and 17 of the microfilm edition of Everett's papers at the Massachusetts Historical Society. And a high volume of them dated from January to March 1859, illustrating the immediate response to Everett's plea. Everett kept a separate log for large donations—from $2 to $323—from wealthy individuals and from subscriptions by voluntary organizations (schools, fire companies, Masonic lodges, dramatic and debate clubs, and so forth). One notable subscription of $141 came from as far afield as Honolulu. Many of the subscriptions came from college campuses, and some of them resulted from benefit events, for which Washington's birthday in 1859 proved a natural occasion. But a strong majority of the contributions came from individuals and were a dollar or less. By mid-1860, Everett calculated that this fund drive had yielded almost $14,000. This was of course in addition to the money many thousands of Americans had laid out to hear his performances of "The Character of Washington."[99] (For more, see appendix B.)

Along with their money, many donors sent the effusions of full hearts. One donor spoke for many when he offered to both Everett and Washington "the homage of a patriotic heart, beating with deep emotion." "Oftimes while reading about the condition of the home of Washington," confessed another, "I would shed tears of sorrow." Everett had promised an autographed receipt to everyone who contributed in response to the "Mount Vernon Papers," and one donor gushed that that receipt "will be valued more than a hundred fold and cherished and preserved for our children and there's [sic] after them . . . , as their title to an interest in that sacred soil." One child who found a gold dollar in his Christmas presents sent that entire amount to Everett, adding that "Father says if I am a good boy and learn fast at school he will take me to Mount Vernon to see the Tomb of Washington as soon as he can."[100] Poor donors who wished they could do more spoke perhaps most eloquently. "I would like to give a much larger sum," one anguished, "but I am only a poor bookkeeper & cannot do it. Even this is much needed by dear ones, but I'll try to do without it." "Perhaps I ought to be ashamed to send so small a pittance" as $5 "for such an object," wrote a St. Louis man on behalf of his subscribers, "but we claim the right to contribute something."[101]

Pseudo-religious and outright religious rhetoric was not wanting in these missives. "As the widow's mite was Pleasing to the Lord," wrote a working-class Boston man, "I hope this Dollar will be acceptable to you Sir." A citizen of Newburyport, Massachusetts, enclosed with his donation "a small piece of yellow damask, . . . under which reposed the living form of our Washington, on the night" in 1789 when he visited that town. "If a virtue was imparted to the seamless garment of the Savior of the World, when He came among men," this donor waxed, "so that the multitude sought to touch Him,—is it too imaginative or profane a suggestion, that the invisible halo or moral atmosphere which surrounded & dignified the Savior of his Country, may have hallowed & blessed the draping which inclosed his animate body[?]"[102] Such a nationwide response, both in funds and in sentiments, surely reconfirmed for Everett both the wisdom of the Bonner scheme and the overall breadth of the Mount Vernon appeal. Everett's activities had given masses of his countrymen the opportunity to do something tangible to embody their nationalism.

———————

This outpouring of Unionist emotion and action, so counter to narratives of the thoroughgoing sectionalization of American politics in the 1850s, requires some investigation and explanation. One basic but powerful reason for it, explored by numerous scholars, was that George Washington resonated so powerfully in American culture. Decades of cultural work by patriotic commemorators like Everett had left its mark. In the 1840s America's restless culture strained against the yoke of the past, but the more sober 1850s saw a resurgence of reverence for the Fathers. Americans had deified Washington so thoroughly by the 1850s that one editor's complaint that "when you make him a demi-god you lift him out of human sympathy" was thoroughly countercultural. That power also rested in part on Washington's political malleability; as a symbol he was about equally available to all three sides in the national political and cultural contest of the 1850s.[103]

Still, while the MVLAU went from strength to strength, a contemporary effort to build a monument to Washington in the nation's capital languished until well past the turn of the twentieth century.[104] So clearly, the MVLAU had more than Washington going for it. One MVLAU asset was Everett himself, whose passion for the cause was contagious. Much as it suited his purposes to say so publicly, he also believed with growing fervor that Washington and the Union were both central to Providence's plan for human liberty. So he refused to be reimbursed by either the MVLAU or private donors for his expenses, pleading that "it would not only be unjust in me to take a dollar from the ladies' fund for the purchase of Mount Vernon, but it would destroy the real pleasure I now take in co-operating with" those ladies. Likewise, he offered inflexible opposition to those who sought to funnel the funds raised by his oration to some other source. He regretted those rare instances in which promoters charged less than fifty cents per ticket, not only for the lost revenue to the MLVAU but also because "it puts my Address & the object for which it is delivered on a level with traveling menageries & circuses." When the occasion required, he poured his energies into micromanaging the physical setting in which he would deliver his address. In 1857, a bloodied face as a result of a nasty fall at a Chicago train station did not dissuade him from speaking that same evening.[105] Nothing was going to break his stride in or distract him from this sacred work. And his consecrated labor took place very much in the public eye and was bound to have an effect. Certainly the officers of the MVLAU reveled publicly in having Everett as their not-so-secret weapon; as one put it, "his voice" had a way of speaking "the 'open sesame' to the purses of the people."[106]

Everett and his MVLAU colleagues put their minds as well as their hearts into it and proved skilled advocates. An enormous advantage they had over the Washington Monument projectors was that the efforts of women to preserve Washington's home linked to the cult of domesticity in ways that a male-dominated effort to build a marble obelisk never could. MVLAU officers both believed in and openly wielded the domestic ideal. "To woman," a 1857 fund-raising appeal confidently asserted, "on such a mission, no heart, no purse could be closed." An address of an MVLAU officer in Illinois, published in the organization's newspaper, argued that this cause "suggests, as nothing has ever before done, *the great responsibility of the women of a Republic.*" They would not seek to "transcend their heaven-appointed limits, and come forward to mingle in public affairs, which could only restrict their influence—but they should never forget that they are, and are to become, the mothers and educators of our rulers and statesmen" who might save the nation. Should not women, then, "re-light the pure flame of patriotism in the heart of the nation, as she rekindles once more, with filial care, the fire upon the cold hearth-stone of that nation's slumbering hero?" Another editorial rejoiced that Washington's remains had not been re-moved from their private dwelling place to a site in the nation's capital, for that form of honor "smacks too much of old-world glorification, to suit the senti-ment of this great and free confederation." Moreover, the hero himself would have resisted "the idea of being removed in death from the beloved scenes to which he was so much attached in life."[107] At Mount Vernon, Americans could celebrate Washington in a safely republican as well as domestic manner. It was a twin yearning widely held by conservatives in the 1850s, encapsulated well by Caleb Cushing in a newspaper article in 1859. Because of the exertions of "the ladies of America," he rejoiced, "Mount Vernon becomes a central shrine, a national temple, in which, by the sanctifying influences of the memory of Washington, to keep burning and bright forever the sacred fires of the love of home and of Country."[108]

A domestic Washington was also a more approachable Washington, and the MVLAU catered to Americans' yen for a personal connection to the sainted Founder. It manifested itself in the bevy of local legends of Washington's purported visits to a town or house or inn. For the same reason, antebellum entrepreneurs including but not limited to Washington relative Custis did a brisk business exhibiting or selling outright relics of the Father. At the upper end of this market, a wealthy American merchant paid $2,500 for an original manuscript of Washington's Farewell Address—which worked out, as Everett noted, to "very nearly a hundred dollars a page."[109] The MVLAU met the demand for tangible artifacts of the Mount Vernon cause in many ways. It traded on the idea of relics when it gave Everett and Yancey artifacts from Washington. It did so for its lesser supporters by thank-you gifts. For a $1 contribution they would send a "*Gold Mounted Washington Portrait*," and some $10 donors got an "Illuminated 'Farewell Address.'" The MVLAU also sold outright portraits of Everett and an "ILLUMINATED EDITION OF WASHINGTON'S FAREWELL ADDRESS TO THE PEOPLE OF THE UNITED STATES, INSCRIBED TO THE HON. EDWARD EVERETT." Various publishers saw the commercial opportunities and sold portraits of Washington and Everett, complete with the hard sell that "no American home should be without a good portrait of Washington."[110]

Everett also understood and adeptly played on this longing for intimate links to Washington. Sometimes at the expense of many hours of research, in multiple towns Everett prefaced the repetition of his oration with some authentic local connection to Washington or the Revolution. In Philadelphia, for instance, he eloquently urged the preservation of Independence Hall to "stand to the end of time, second only to Mount Vernon, as the sanctuary of American patriotism. Let generation on generation of those who taste the blessings of the great Declaration pay their homage at the shrine, and . . . kneel in gratitude to the Providence which guided and inspired the men who assembled therein" to achieve independence and Union.[111] Everett also became a one-man clearinghouse for Washington relics and expounder of their efficacy. In his travels, friends and new acquaintances repeatedly approached him to show or give him documents and other tangible remnants of Washington's time on Earth. This compulsion to show him these relics provides a personal glimpse into the political culture into which Everett was tapping. He distributed as well as collected. In 1860, Everett sent a copy of one of Washington's letters to a local leader to acknowledge her followers' contributions. He was sure she would be grateful for this thank-you gift, for the letter gave "insight into the affairs of one who" to Americans was "a sort of demi-god, lifted alike above human needs and passions."[112] Essays in the "Mount Vernon Papers" series urged the need to restore "paths, once pressed by feet which consecrated the soil on which they trod." Moreover, the restored Mount Vernon would house "a collection of all the personal relics and memorials of" the sainted Founder and would feature a mausoleum "to enshrine the sacred ashes of the First of Men." He invited his readers to "dwell upon" the scenes of the founding "in reverent contemplation" and rendered the dates of Washington's life with a level of detail reminiscent of biblical chronologies. For Everett every artifact or antiquarian detail connected with Washington constituted a holy relic in this civic religion.[113]

All of this reveals the earnestness of Unionist civic religion in this embattled age. What the whole MVLAU campaign highlighted about late antebellum American political culture was a deeply committed emotional strain of Unionism. Everett's speaking, writing, and fund-raising activities had helped to give tangible form to that political culture. It would remain to be seen between late 1859 and early 1861, however, what purchase that mobilized mass culture would have at the polls and with policymakers.

9

Last Ditches

UNION MEETINGS, THE ELECTION OF 1860, AND THE SECESSION CRISIS

As the sectional politics of slavery continued to put Everett and his kind on the defensive, they continued their creative search for ways to stay engaged in American political life. From December 1859 through November 1860, Everett and like-minded politicians ran an interim test of the political significance of affective Unionism. In response to John Brown's raid on Harpers Ferry, Unionists held rallies throughout the North and in parts of the Upper South to publicly flex their political muscles. The presidential election the next year offered the ultimate trial for how well the Unionist persuasion Everett had been mobilizing via the Mount Vernon campaign would translate to the ballot box. But the attempt to convince voters to support a pure-and-simple Unionist position fell well short, especially in the North. That was due in large part to the babel of voices offering their own Unionist accents as authentic. In particular, moderate Republicans successfully blurred the line between their stance and the Unionists'. Republican victory and the resultant secession of the Deep South led to a period of profound gloom and confusion for Unionists everywhere. But while once again reacting to rather than driving events, Everett and the mass political culture he represented remained a force to be reckoned with.

In October 1859, when John Brown led a small band of abolitionist zealots in a raid on the federal arsenal at Harpers Ferry, Virginia, he did no real damage to the short-term future of American slavery. But this event did give the peace and stability of the American Union a serious body blow, particularly when horrified white Southerners read of Northern abolitionists heaping praise on Brown. But another Northern response to Harpers Ferry was to call mass meetings to reassure Southern Unionists (and warn those abolitionists) that

Northerners would stand by the sacred Union. The number of Northerners responding to this call dwarfed those expressing overt sympathy for Brown, and they came from all political parties. Leading Unionists organized such assemblages in Bangor, Maine; Portsmouth, New Hampshire; Brighton, Lowell, and Barnstable, Massachusetts; Bridgeport, Hartford, and New Haven, Connecticut; Rochester, Albany, and Troy, New York; Newark and Morristown, New Jersey; Harrisburg, Pennsylvania; and Cincinnati, Ohio. Upper South Unionists conducted meetings in their own accent in Washington, D.C, and Knoxville, Tennessee. Published reports pointedly remarked on the enthusiasm as well as on the size of the Unionist throngs, asserting that they represented the vast silent majority.[1] Boston, New York, and Philadelphia hosted "Monster Meetings" whose turnout refuted the notion that old-school Unionism with its emotional appeals to Washington and the founding was limited to a few fossilized patricians and anxious merchants.[2]

These meetings tapped the public's deep emotional attachment to the Founding Fathers' Union. At the Philadelphia gathering, held 7 December 1859, a series of speakers lauded the Constitution as "our sovereign without mortal frailty." Its blessings should never be measured in crass material terms, for it was nothing less than "a divine revelation for the political regeneration of man." "Let the Union," urged one, "formed by the wisdom of sages and patriots, and sanctified by the breath and blood of sainted heroes, be guarded like the holy altar of the temple." And as if all these echoes of the Mount Vernon cause were not enough, a number of Philadelphia's ladies helped to consecrate the cause by sending a flag emblazoned with suitable Unionist sentiments to Virginia's governor.[3] The New York Unionists met in the Music Hall, whose owners traditionally prohibited political meetings but made an exception for this gathering as something higher and holier than mere politics. The crowd filled the massive hall and spilled out into the streets, and attendance estimates ranged from twenty thousand to forty thousand.[4] Speakers and letter writers repeatedly exhorted that "the voluntary affection and loyalty of the people" must be yielded to the Union not simply for its commercial benefits but as "the greatest political blessing ever conferred upon mankind." Such citizens would "ever resist the ruthless and sacrilegious efforts to rend asunder those grand communities which the great Architect of nations has so graciously joined together." This meeting was especially fruitful in such rhetoric equating the Union to the sacrament of marriage.[5] A banner on the hall's stage excerpted the Farewell Address, as did the last of the resolutions. One speaker pointed out that after a national separation, "the dividing line would take from us the grave of Washington" and leave only the "memory of John Brown in its place."[6]

These meetings amply illustrated the impact of the Mount Vernon campaign's melding of Washington's political principles with sentimentalism and domestic analogies to create a powerfully affecting Unionism.

As extravagant as these expressions were, they would not outdo the meeting that packed Faneuil Hall. Everett estimated the crowd as between five thousand and six thousand, and all reporters noted the earnest enthusiasm this throng manifested. From the opening prayer forward, the blessings of the Union were the central theme. The meeting resolved "that the advantages and privileges, through the blessing of Divine Providence, enjoyed by the people of this country, are unparalleled in the history of nations." Thus, the final resolution reiterated the Farewell Address's warning against sectionalism in tones of "the deepest emotions of veneration" for Washington. Those who could not attend but who sent letters participated fully in such histrionics, such as one who thanked "God we have Everett . . . and a host of others, fit priests to serve at altars, whose fires were lighted by pilgrim hands." Should someone strike up "a grand chorus to the tune of the 'Constitution and the Union,'" he continued, it would "find a response in more hearts than you dream of."[7] The memory of Washington may have been one of the few threads holding the Union together, but meetings like this testified that it was tied tightly to countless heartstrings.

Everett, one of the headline speakers, touched on that theme as well as on others he had been sounding throughout his political and oratorical career. He led by recounting his involvement in the "congenial" and "useful" work of the MVLAU, "seeking to rally the affections of my countrymen North and South, to that great name and precious memory which is left almost alone of all the numerous kindly associations, which once bound the different sections of the country together." He was thus gratified by "the favor with which these my humble labors are regarded by the great majority of my countrymen." All this success presented a stark contrast to partisan politics, where "I find no middle ground of practical usefulness, on which a friend of moderate counsels can stand," for "there is no place left in public life for those who love" both North and South. But Unionists could not afford to abandon public life or underestimate the seriousness of the threat to the Union and the sense of grievance in the South. Too many Northerners lacked true empathy for white Southerners facing Brown's attempt to "let loose the hell-hounds of a servile insurrection." Northerners should more vigorously shudder at this attempt to recreate the worst scenes of the Haitian Revolution at their own countrymen's firesides. In his travels in the South, he assured them that he had seen "touching manifestations of the kindest feelings" in the family circle, which bound together "all its members, high and low, master and servant." Invocations of order to ward off race war and a rosy southward glance took him back to 1826, but the main thrust of his speech was in keeping with his Mount Vernon period. Americans' sense of shared nationality, he pled, should also be nurtured by remembering at this crucial hour that the South had given America "some of the greatest and purest characters which adorn our history, — Washington, Jefferson, Madison, Monroe, Marshall." His predominant purpose here, as with the "Character of Washington" speech, was "to inculcate the blessings of the Union," consecrated as they were by "the memory of our Fathers," who had passed them to the next generations.[8]

These mobilizations of that Unionism were unequivocally political, but their relationship to partisan politics was muddier. Everett seems to have perceived speaking at the Union meeting as inching back into politics proper. But he included his Faneuil Hall speech in volume 4 of his published orations, which like its predecessors excluded strictly partisan material. Given the enormous stakes for the nation in the public response to Brown's raid, this rose far above partisan politics.[9] To maximize the Union meetings' political impact, organizers sought for and reporters emphasized bipartisanship. Brown admirer Amos A. Lawrence gave in to his Unionist sympathies and attended the Faneuil Hall meeting but refused to sit on the stand as a vice president "because I do not wish to help the Democrats." Organizers could not afford to lose many participants for such a reason, so they pressed men from all the major parties to make their attendance conspicuous. And in their official reports of the meetings, they trotted out all available evidences that "the heart of the people, irrespective of party, was in the movement."[10]

But some of the speeches given and letters read at these events took strikingly different tones, depending on the speaker's or author's party alignment. The ex-Whig lion Levi Lincoln offered the standard disclaimer of Northern moderates when he protested in the Boston meeting that "there is not a single pro-slavery man, in the opprobrious sense of that term, in all this vast assembly; no, not one." But a Democratic speaker in the New York gathering belied that claim when he defended slavery itself as "not unjust" and "benign."[11]

The central partisan difference, however, was over whom to hold responsible for the alarming state of the sectional crisis. Democrats blamed abolitionists and Republicans, reserving exceptional fury for the former. In a letter read at the New York rally, ex-president Franklin Pierce declared that a Union with only Yankees in it "would not be worth preserving." In his letter to the Boston meeting, Pierce warned that Brown's sympathizers, both open and (especially) secret, were "the most dangerous enemies of the Constitution and the Union." Good citizens' disapprobation of all such traitors, he hinted, should "be pronounced in tones so earnest that no man can mistake their import." In an anti-abolitionist stem-winder at the same meeting, Caleb Cushing put no veil over his threats. Though calling for "conciliation [and] mutual forbearance" between the sections, he offered no such things to abolitionists. Theirs was "a religion of hate, such as belongs only to the condemned devils in hell," manifesting all the "demoniac passions and . . . truculent ferocity of pretended philanthropy on the subject of slavery." If the Union broke apart, he glowered, there would be not only war between the sections but also "the more terrible and dismal spectacle of civil war upon our own soil in Massachusetts." For if antislavery men sought to carry out armed interference against slavery in the South, "are there not men enough here to seize the traitors by the throat . . . and say, 'You must walk over our bodies, you shall not otherwise engage in this fratricidal, suicidal, civil war with your fellow-citizens of other States!'"[12] Democratic anti-abolitionism had long been motivated in part by a passionate hatred for the intrusion of moralism into politics, a hatred not shared by Whigs. But such expressions confirmed other evidence that the anti-abolitionist rancor of people like Cushing and Pierce had reached new depths in the 1850s.[13]

No one articulated the very different Whiggish reading of the 1850s declension better than another ex-president, Millard Fillmore, in his letter to the New York gathering. In this narrative, the Compromise of 1850 had averted an earlier crisis of the Union, "and the government and the people for a time seemed to acquiesce in that *compromise* as a final settlement of this exciting question." But "in an evil hour" the Democrats, moved by "mistaken ambition," opened "this Pandora's box of Slavery" by the calamitous Kansas-Nebraska Act. "The flood of evils now swelling and threatening to overthrow the constitution, and sweep away the foundations of the Government itself and deluge this land with fraternal blood," Fillmore pronounced, "may all be traced to this unfortunate act." He closed with the standard consensus Unionist pieties, but various observers rightly remarked that there was a "wide difference in tone and spirit" between this letter and the Democrats' letters and speeches.[14] After some initial misgivings that must have related in part to Democrats' leading role as organizers, Everett had agreed to participate in the Boston meeting "partly to give—as far as my agency could do so—a salutary tone to" the meeting. And after the meeting, he guessed that his own speech "probably gave greater satisfaction to the reflecting part of the audience" than Cushing's had.[15]

Judging by press coverage, the public's satisfaction with the Union meetings was broad-based but as a rule encouraged the already converted. It was predictable that abolitionists, the target of so much abuse at these gatherings, would have responded in kind. In the *Liberator*, William Lloyd Garrison caricatured the New York rally as "characterised by every element of commercial selfishness, profligate demagoguism, unblushing pro-slavery, and promiscuous rascality." Wendell Phillips found Everett's raising of the specter of the Haitian Revolution libelous to its revolutionaries and offensive in general. From as far away as Rome, Theodore Parker panned Everett's Faneuil speech as "one of his most characteristic 'utterances' — so selfish, so cold, so sophistical."[16] While some Republicans publicly joined the Union meetings as part of their overall effort to distance themselves from Brown, others dismissed the whole effort as "quite unnecessary, if its object was merely to testify that the people of the North are still devoted to the Union." For, they protested, "none are more loyal to it than the very men, the 'Black Republicans' who are held up as disunionists by" some of the speeches at these rallies. Such abuse was misplaced, complained one editor, for "there is not one disunionist in the North to ten in the South." Abraham Lincoln agreed, declaring "the Union arrangements" a "humbug — they reverse the scriptural order, calling the righteous" antislavery men of the North "and not sinners" (Southern disunionists) "to repentance."[17] And even some conservative Northerners despaired of the Union meetings accomplishing much, given the basic fact that the political reins in key Northern states increasingly "belong to a sectional and revolutionary party."[18]

Most sectional moderates in the North, however, found the size, number, and spirit of the Union meetings heartening. They expected that the big cities' monster rallies would "have an important influence throughout the country . . . by kindling the flames of enthusiasm and suggesting similar meetings," and when that prediction came to pass they rejoiced. A Philadelphia editor cheered on these congregations, both for rebuking Northern fanatics and for showing Southern fire-eaters that they had "no justification whatever in talking of disunion, and blackening all our law-abiding, union-loving citizens with the imputation of sentiments held only by a few, and which the rest of us repudiate and loathe." They could not now deny that "the constitution and the laws — the faith and practice of our fathers — the sacred memories and blessed hopes of our Union, are enough for" the mass of Northerners.[19]

But much as in the North, in the South these meetings convinced few if any hostile observers. While the bipartisanship of these demonstrations was meant to reassure all onlookers, some Southern commentators found them unalterably tainted by the participation of "Black Republicans." Rather incongruously, others grumbled that the Union meetings had been "exclusively in the hands of" known friends to the South. Because they left out the Republicans, "the dominant party" in the North, Union meetings had proven to be "utterly ineffective and valueless as indications of Northern conservatism." A Mississippi editor chose to report and comment on the Rochester, New York, sample of "the recent 'glorious Union Meetings,' about which we hear so much talk now-a-days," because of its stern resolution warning Southerners not to break up the Union should they lose the presidential election. So much for so-called "Northern conservatism."[20] Everett rightly analyzed these Southern fire-eaters as men who did "not wish to be satisfied" with the Union meetings or any other evidence of Northern Unionism.[21]

Also as in the North, the Union meetings gave tangible evidence to support the hopes of Southern Unionists. "How my heart glowed within me," a Southern lady exclaimed in a letter to Cushing, "as I read your noble speech! The times, indeed, are dark and fearful, . . . but voices of the good and true come to us from the North" and "tell us that those who should be to us as brethren are not all turned away from us, . . . that good sense and patriotism still remain, enough, perhaps, to save the Union." A North Carolina Unionist editor judged the New York assemblage in particular "a most cheering event in the midst of the general gloom." And "the perpetuity of the Confederacy," he enthused, "would be secure did it depend upon the enthusiasm of the Union Meeting of the citizens of New Haven." Perhaps even more encouraging was abolitionist hostility to these events, which only underscored their potency.[22] However, a Georgia editor who had long supported the MVLAU and evinced a conditional devotion to the Union sounded a more cautious note. After a report on Philadelphia's Union meeting, he opined that "all this is very well; but the South to be re-assured, must have some effective demonstration of the conservatism of the North, and that must be made, not in talk, but in action; not in public meetings, but at the polls."[23]

———

Many conservative Unionists agreed with this editor's analysis and worked feverishly to capitalize in partisan politics on the Union meetings' momentum. Sectional moderates, especially in the Upper South, had long desired a Union party to provide a vehicle for their opposition to the Democrats. Leading light John J. Crittenden had worked with fellow conservatives to this end since 1858, and their organizational work in Washington was proceeding apace in late 1859. Well-wishers predicted that the contemporaneous Union meetings would help this cause by awakening "honest men everywhere" who would in future elections "frown down all attempts to sunder those whom a beneficent Providence has joined together." They would open "a new era in the political history of the country . . . by kindling the flames of enthusiasm" for a "conservative and Union ticket" as an alternative to the morally bankrupt Democratic and treasonable

Republican Parties. The new Constitutional Union Party (CUP) took full shape in January 1860. Successes that winter in local elections showed CUP supporters that the border states of the South would be their center of strength, although they harbored hopes for New York, New Jersey, and Pennsylvania.[24]

On 9 May 1860, CUP delegates gathered in Baltimore to craft their platform and nominate their presidential ticket. During the period of clandestine operations leading up to this convention, some party leaders had reached out to conservative Republicans such as Missouri's Edward Bates and, some evidence suggests, Abraham Lincoln. But it was a deal-breaker when these potential nominees adhered to the Republicans' platform on slavery. A platform taking a stand on the divisive issue of slavery was counter to the CUP's ideal of national unity. Indeed, on the first day in Baltimore, Leslie Coombs of Kentucky proposed that the CUP program consist only of "the Constitution of the United States as it is," which provoked hearty applause, "and the Union under it now and forever," which generated an even greater ovation. Despite the importance of platforms in nineteenth-century American party identity, another delegate asserted that the electorate was "heartsick and head-sick" of party platforms. So the convention resolved on a very brief sort of anti-platform whose heart was the assertion that "it is both the part of patriotism and of duty to *recognize* no political principle other than *the Constitution of the Country, the Union of the States, and the Enforcement of the Laws*."[25] The ticket remained an open question when the convention began, because the party's elder statesman Crittenden steadfastly and sincerely resisted all pre-convention attempts to nominate him for president. Various men had support for the nomination, but it was clear that the top spot must go to someone from the party's Upper South heartland. On the second day the convention settled on John Bell, a Tennessee Whig who had had a long career of moderate Unionism in Congress.[26]

Given his association with Washington and the Union, Everett was a natural choice for the vice presidential slot, so the convention nominated him by acclamation. Three hours' worth of fulsome speeches in praise of Everett and what he stood for intervened between the suggestion of his name and the unanimous voice vote nominating him. These speakers, standing beneath a full-length portrait of Washington on the wall, underscored that Everett's connection with Washington was a universally recognized Unionist talisman. Everett's selection thus proved a high point of an emotional meeting that repeatedly and loudly cheered every mention of party shibboleths. Speakers knew the Washington hagiography by heart and argued that to abandon the Union would be to "scatter the sacred dust of Washington ('Never,' 'never,'), teach your boys to forget his name, and never let the pilgrim's foot tread the consecrated groves of Mount

Vernon." As for Everett, one supporter recorded that his nomination "heaved the breast; it kindled the cheeks; it broke from the eyes in warm, gushing, irrepressible tears." His association with both Washington and the ladies was the touchstone for this response. Because Everett "has studied the character of Washington," a delegate from Mississippi enthused, his patriotism "is enough of itself to save the Union." Another Mississippian cracked that "the delegates were mostly married men, and must know very well that it was no use to oppose the ladies" with whom Everett was so popular, thanks to his MVLAU activities. A delegate from Tennessee assumed that ladies who had joined Everett "in that great work of redeeming the grave of Washington" were "to the last man, 'Everett men.'" More seriously, he continued, "if we have domestic discord and civil war, does it not visit the household? Does it not overspread the hearthstone?"[27]

With the MVLAU campaign as its crucial context, this part of the convention made it clear that as an avatar of domesticity, Everett epitomized both the nightmare of disunion and the virtues of the Union. Some historians have strained to understand Everett's appeal to the ladies, assigning it to good looks. But this assessment trivializes women's engagement with the substance of politics, as well as their symbolic role for male partisans.[28] For friends the idea that Everett was the ladies' candidate bespoke the enormous cultural power of emotional, disinterested Unionism. For foes it was a backhanded compliment at best, given that although women helped shape political culture, they did not vote. Everett as the ladies' candidate thus encapsulated both the cultural strength of Unionism and the limits of its appeal at the polls.

For all that, Everett proved torturously ambivalent about this nomination. He had given Boston editor George S. Hillard, his close friend and representative at the convention, clear and detailed instructions to oppose any party platform, but his directive was unclear as to any nomination that might come his way. Everett insisted on his retirement from public life but also suggested he would consider a nomination to the presidency. Neither Everett nor Hillard had anticipated a vice presidential nod. Moreover, the rush of support for Everett at the convention swept Hillard off his feet. He responded to the fulsome nominating speeches by gushing that "if my illustrious friend had been here and beheld your bright faces, heard the voices, and felt the enthusiasm which pervades this Convention at the mention of his name, he must be something more or less than human if he could hesitate to accept the nomination."[29]

But Everett had several reasons to at least toy with this species of inhumanity. He harbored almost no hope for the success of the ticket, which only reinforced his distaste for the scramble of partisan politics at this point of his life. He thus resented the degree to which "this terrible nomination" was a harassing distraction from his "ordinary pursuits."[30] Then there was his pride. He admitted to being "deeply touched with the cordiality of feeling, with which my name was received" at the convention. But he also candidly (if privately) stated that he took being the subordinate to the younger and less accomplished Bell—unlike if it had been Crittenden—as something like an insult. While this was a misreading of the inevitability of an Upper South man being the presidential nominee, contemporaries and subsequent historians have agreed that this was not merely Everett's ego talking. One editor dubbed the CUP's the "kangaroo ticket," having longer hind legs than front legs.[31] There was also still fund-raising work to do for repairs and other expenses now that the MVLAU owned Mount Vernon, and running for high office would seem to vindicate the Republican charge of "some selfish motive" for his MVLAU work. So he wondered whether "even in reference to the interests of the Union party, I render better service in repeating my oration on Washington . . . than I should do by going through this canvass."[32] Despite all these reasons to reject, his heart was sufficiently in the Union cause—and his friends gave him such conflicting advice—that for the rest of May 1860 he was painfully ambivalent.[33]

While Everett tried to keep his anguish over accepting the nomination private, his delay in deciding was very public, and damaging to the CUP. For this problem to crop up in its very infancy could prove fatal to its already slim hopes. Sober observers agreed that the best the CUP could hope for was to throw the election to the House of Representatives by preventing any other party from gaining a majority in the electoral college. But Everett's dithering threatened even this limited goal as it became widely known by word of mouth.[34] The party's General Executive Committee insistently urged him to accept, citing his ability to attract conservative voters and the election's high stakes. Everett declining, they lectured him, would be "disastrous" given that his nomination had "been received with the greatest satisfaction by *all* the conservative men of the country both South and North." His acceptance, on the other hand, would advance the party's efforts "to furnish a basis on which the patriotic and national and Union loving men of all parties could unite." Mustering such a band would result in "a great and permanent good to the country," even if the party did not win the election. "It was for these unselfish and important objects that the Union organization was formed," but Everett's refusal "would greatly impair if not destroy our chances of success and produce serious if not irremediable mischief . . . to the whole country." It was a powerful appeal to his "patriotism and sense of duty," hitting him where he lived.[35]

And it worked. On 29 May, Everett finally wrote a public letter accepting the nomination. He explained his delay by citing how the MVLAU had benefited from "my known and recognized disconnection from party politics." Rather than thinking he was "speaking one word for Mount Vernon and two for myself," his audience had given him "credit for having a single eye to that meritorious object." And there was still work to do, still parts of the country—he noted the Gulf states of the Deep South—to which to take the message. And "I feel as if I was doing more good, as far as I am able to do any good, and contributing more to revive the kindly feeling which once existed between North and South" by these labors than by entering into "the wretched scramble for office, which is one great source of the dangers that threaten the country." After diagnosing the many maladies of sectional politics, his prescription was that "a spirit of patriotic moderation must be called into action throughout the Union, or it will assuredly be broken up." The Union must be one of consent and harmony rather than force, and the spirit of one section seeking to dominate the other "comes loaded with the death smell from fields wet with brothers' blood."[36] It was a remarkable acceptance letter, yet another microcosm of the strengths and weaknesses of the CUP appeal. Affective Unionism was rhetorically powerful but had little hope of reaching its full political potential when its most effective proponent was so openly hesitant to put it to partisan purpose.

Most historians of the election of 1860 have emphasized the weaknesses rather than the strengths of the CUP. Distinguished scholars have taken the CUP and its political appeal seriously.[37] But to many other historians the CUP is a curious footnote in a campaign that was about the Republicans and the division of the Democratic Party into a Southern wing headed by sitting vice president John C. Breckinridge and a Northern wing led by Democratic mainstay Stephen A. Douglas. In an era characterized by sectional polarization, the CUP's evasive (non-)platform and reliance on the statesmanship of its candidates made it fatally old-school. As such the aged, ivory-towered Everett was a perfect choice for the bottom of the ticket. Especially in the North, only a few antiquated merchants could be counted on to support that ticket.[38]

The CUP, however, was hardly dead on arrival. Like most third parties in American history, it ran largely to prove a point. And it made that point forcefully. Party rallies and literature wielded the sword of sentiments associated with the Mount Vernon cause, and those sentiments attracted passionate support, especially but not only in the Upper South. The spelling in one supporter's letter alone refutes the notion that the CUP was an exclusively elite affair: "Thar is a grait stur about the Presadential Election," a North Carolinian wrote his brothers. "We go for the unin the constitunion & the in forsement of the law & Bel & Everit to cary them out." One young Baltimorean grew his whiskers in hopes of a Bell and Everett win. Other young men in Louisiana and elsewhere formed marching and singing groups like the Everett Guard and Everett's Rangers. And one Harvard alumnus recounted how "our crowd" vigorously supported the CUP ticket. He recalled that his coterie's "motto proud," which they proclaimed while "carry[ing] torches Sixty miles," was "Bell and the Belles."[39] On a larger scale, Bell was in Philadelphia when his nomination became public news, and a torchlight procession of around six thousand people serenaded him that night. Diarist George Templeton Strong recorded that on the day of the election in New York City, "the only signs of excitement and enthusiasm that I saw were in the crowd about the Bell and Everett headquarters."[40] Many of the CUP's mass meetings were emotional affairs laying direct claim to the legacy of Washington's Farewell Address's warning against sectionalism. At a CUP rally in Mississippi, when a speaker appealed to "our battle-fields, . . . our statesmen, and . . . the Father of his Country," it "warmed every heart and gave inspiration to those who have enlisted for the war." "Few could have failed to record a vow to Heaven that come weal come woe we will stand by the glorious Union of our fathers," the newspaper account concluded. Party faithful in North Carolina resolved that the principles that had been "approved and recommended by the illustrious Washington and his compeers, is National and broad enough for all true patriots."[41] The old-time religion was good enough for Washington, and therefore good enough for them.

Because "Mr. Everett's name is destined to be indissolubly connected with that of Washington," CUP leaders as well as the rank and file consistently linked Everett's MVLAU activities to his vice presidential candidacy. Indeed, it was largely for that reason that they took great pride in having Everett on their ticket. This pride was typified by their standard practice of referring (both in private and in public) to their ticket as the "Bell and Everett" ticket. By contrast, they directly mentioned rival presidential candidates but only very rarely rival vice presidential nominees.[42] Party publications highlighted how Everett's Mount Vernon endeavors gave both "popularity" and "nationality" to "his fame" and made him very well known and well loved by women. Everett's candidacy thus embodied all the disinterested patriotism associated with the ladies. But the party also claimed to embody "the courage and the manliness to stand firm" and defend the damsel in distress that was the Union. One of Everett's fans at the party convention got closer to this idea when he proclaimed that his state was "in love with Edward Everett."[43]

Everett himself was not about to run away from the Mount Vernon legacy in the midst of this election. He was the last man who would have violated the age's expectations that candidates refrain from stumping for votes, but he did give a few public speeches after accepting the nomination. In them he found every opportunity—no matter how much a stretch it might seem—to insert Washington's legacy and the Union into the proceedings. In a Fourth of July address in 1860, Everett noted that the Founders "are gone, but their work remains." Thus it was appropriate that Bostonians had "escaped from . . . the dissensions of party, from all that occupies and all that divides us, to celebrate, to *join* in celebrating, the birthday of the nation, with one heart and with one voice." His theme was the question of "whether the great design of Providence, with reference to our beloved country," was succeeding, or failing as British critics had recently asserted. He set out to vindicate American institutions, and his ultimate trump card was that Americans "may proudly boast of one example of Life and Character . . . , of which all the countries and all the ages may be searched in vain for a parallel." Washington's "peerless name," he added, "is stamped on your hearts, it glistens in your eyes, it is written on every page of your history, on the battle-fields of the Revolution, on the monuments of your Fathers, on the portals of your capitols. It is heard in every breeze that whispers over the fields of Independent America. And he was all our own."[44]

Aside from such speeches, however, Everett proved a terribly diffident candidate even by nineteenth-century standards. He received a succession of CUP dignitaries who wished to talk politics while visiting Boston. But seeming to believe that his apolitical image helped him politically, he took very little initiative himself. In October 1860, the last full month before the election, his work on Boston's committee to prepare to receive the Prince of Wales dominated his public activities. He channeled most of the arguments he wanted made in the campaign through Hillard rather than publish them himself. Indeed, he apparently had made it a stipulation of accepting the nomination that he would not bear the normal burden of correspondence for candidates in this era; that devolved upon Hillard as well. He made clear in a diary entry one powerful reason for his reluctance to lift a finger in this campaign. One full month after his nomination, he concluded that the breakup of the Democratic Party "reduces us to the Republican party which is exclusively sectional & to the elements as yet unconsolidated of a Union Party. It is extremely doubtful whether the latter can be formed" given the ascendancy of sectional agitation.[45] Among the misfortunes of the CUP was having a vice presidential candidate who was unsure that party had even fully formed!

That diary entry's characterization of Republicans as an unmitigated menace also predicted the times Everett would actually exert himself in this campaign. His political writing during this campaign consisted of occasional articles for Hillard's *Boston Courier* assaulting the Republicans as a sectionalist minority in the nation and urging undecided conservatives to resist their appeal.[46] This allocation of his political energy spoke volumes about his view of the Republicans. He remained as convinced as ever that Republicans' agitation of the slavery issue had inspired revolutionaries like John Brown and would prove counterproductive in combating slavery in the South. Worse, although the Republicans habitually disclaimed disunionism, that was for political effect—they knew their party benefited politically from sectionalism and secretly "wished to keep the sore open." At their state convention in Massachusetts they gave as good as they got from Everett, as the likes of Charles Sumner kept past battles with the CUP statesman alive.[47] Everett believed Republicans' professions of Unionism just about as much as they believed his professions of antislavery sentiment.

Although historians have tended to follow both sides' caricatures of the other—depicting Everett as hopelessly out of touch on slavery and the Republicans' victory as straightforward evidence of the sectionalization of Northern politics—each side had misread the other in fundamental ways.[48] For the Republican Party proved more adept at channeling Unionism than Everett expected and many accounts suggest. And the CUP's strength was perhaps most evident in other parties' campaigns, for the leaders of rival parties in 1860 knew they must grapple with the affective Unionism that the CUP sought to harness in the election.

The manifest fervor and statesmanlike nominations of the CUP convention emboldened William Henry Seward's opponents within the Republican Party. With his reputation as a radical, Seward would leave the Republicans vulnerable to the CUP in the Upper South and border regions of the North. In February 1860 the undecided New Yorker George Templeton Strong certainly thought so. Continual sectional irritants caused some, like him, to lean Republican. But "a cohesive feeling of nationality and Unionism gains strength silently both North and South," so that "the Republican party has lost and is daily losing many of the moderate men who were forced into it" by Kansas and the Sumner caning in 1856. Nominating a moderate therefore had the potential to unify the Republican Party and allow it to triangulate the CUP's one attractive issue. Furthermore, one-fifth of the delegates at the national Republican convention in Chicago represented Southern states.[49]

One of the men who had made himself most electable on this score was Abraham Lincoln. To be sure, he had real differences with the likes of Everett, such as when he laid primary stress on the Declaration of Independence or questioned the value and future of sectional compromises. But in the late 1850s he had repeatedly insisted on "the identity of" the Republican Party's stance on slavery "with the doctrines of the Fathers of the Republic" and with those of

Henry Clay. In this confidence, he would not cede the legacy of the Fathers to the conservative Unionists. In a February 1860 speech at New York's Cooper Institute that propelled him toward the Republican nomination, Lincoln went out of his way to address those who "delight to flaunt in our faces the warning against sectional parties given by Washington in his Farewell Address." Reminding his audience that the first president had signed legislation enforcing the Northwest Ordinance's ban on slavery, he asked, "could Washington himself speak" (as Everett had so often wished), "would he cast the blame of that sectionalism upon us, who sustain his policy, or upon you who repudiate it?" In his peroration he urged wavering Republicans to "be diverted by none of those" who besought "true Union men to yield to Disunionists" and "to unsay what Washington said, and undo what Washington did."[50]

Such rhetoric was the stuff with which to meet the CUP's appeal to conservatives both within and without the Republican Party. Thus, many delegates at Chicago seem to have believed that a Lincoln candidacy might blunt the CUP threat in the swing states of the border North. Furthermore, Lincoln received 20 southern votes on the first ballot, out of 102 total. On his winning third ballot, after Maryland transferred its vote from Edward Bates to Lincoln, he received 42 southern votes (18 percent of his overall vote). The choice of Lincoln as the nominee, as Douglas Egerton has astutely summed, "allowed the Chicago delegates to hold fast behind their party's core ideals while reaching out to northern moderates and winning over the states necessary to an electoral victory." By nominating Lincoln, historian James Huston has argued, the Republicans had "completely outfoxed the Constitutional Union Party managers." A contemporary Republican agreed, gloating that "the great Union Savers under the lead of Bell, Everett & Co. were about as badly surprised as any" by Lincoln's nomination, "and I think a great deal of wind has been taken out of their canvass." Lincoln himself crowed that his Southern support at Chicago should refute any attacks on him as a sectionalist, for "I had more votes from the Southern section at Chicago" than Douglas had in the convention that nominated him that summer.[51]

As Lincoln's jab suggests, both Douglas Democrats and Republicans repeatedly sought to steal the CUP's stance on the Union and thus chip away at the CUP's natural constituency in the contested border regions of both North and South.[52] The Republicans were particularly effective in pursuing this tactic. Bates, a former Whig from Missouri, dealt the CUP a blow by endorsing Lincoln as "*a sound, safe, national man. He could not be sectional if he tried.*" Other party stump speakers followed suit, arguing that they were the true conservatives, not the CUP men whose noncommittal stance would maintain the 1850s' violations of the Founders' original intent. Even the radical abolitionist Phillips sought to reassure conservatives worried about a Lincoln election. The conservative Everett's lionization of the rebel leader Washington demonstrated that what had once looked threatening would in time seem mainstream. "In 1760, what Boston rebel boys felt, James Otis spoke, George Washington achieved and Everett praises today. The same routine will go on" as Lincoln achieved what abolitionists had long felt and spoken.[53] As one frustrated CUP operative in New York reported, the widespread view that by nominating Lincoln the Republican Party "is becoming more conservative . . . operates upon many persons who are disposed to follow the current and take refuge in what they consider a strong and prosperous party."[54]

The CUP put the Breckinridge Democrats more on the defensive on the Union issue in the South than the Republicans were in the North. Breckinridge and his supporters insisted like others that their stance on slavery in the territories was truly national and in keeping with the principles of the Founders. In September, the candidate himself chose Clay's old seat of Ashland, Kentucky, to deliver a speech whose very subtitle, "Repelling the Charge of Disunion," addressed his rivals' charges against what he branded "The National Democracy." Breckinridge laid out his views and counterpunched that "if they are Constitutional, they are not sectional, for the Constitution covers the whole Union."[55] As this tepid response illustrated, Southern Democrats did better when they changed the subject. They countered the loaded charge that they plotted disunion with the even more explosive claim that the Republicans as abolitionists menaced the very safety of the South by stirring up slave insurrection.[56]

Indeed, while both the Republicans and Southern Democrats fought on the defensive on the Union issue, they both rather easily turned the tables on the CUP when it came to the burning issue of slavery. The campaign revealed the lack of a platform as the CUP's chief electoral flaw. Even as they triangulated the CUP's principles, all three rival parties dismissed that anti-platform as an evasion of the central issue — the expansion of slavery into the territories. As the CUP floundered to respond to these attacks and dismissals, its internal as well as electioneering weaknesses revealed themselves.

While Constitutional Unionists thought their strengths included eschewing a platform and nominating statesmen rather than politicians, their opponents worked to render both points liabilities. Its lack of a platform was an unmanly dodging of the defining issue of the day. Everett's image as a detached scholar played right into this line. Given that none of the parties rejected either Constitution or Union, a Republican editor spoke for many when he mocked that the CUP "might as well have taken the multiplication table and the Decalogue for its platform as the Constitution and the Union." Another Republican wit crafted a hypothetical conversation in which one man asked a CUP man, "'Why didn't you nominate Choate?' 'Choate! why, he is dead!' 'Oh, I know it; but he hasn't been dead a very long time.'" For his part, Frederick Douglass summarily dismissed the CUP, for "a party without any opinion need have no opinion expressed of it."[57] The Breckinridge Democrats lit into the CUP on slavery in their own regional accent. "The real issue of this canvass," they found it useful to hammer home, "is not union or disunion; but the effort on the part of the State Rights Democracy" to limit the power of the meddlesome Republicans. The South could not trust a slick pol (not statesman as he claimed to be) like Bell who had forever tried to play both sides of this good-and-evil issue.[58] Everett proved an especially easy target in light of his friendly gubernatorial correspondence with abolitionists. Given that Everett was notorious "as an Abolitionist" in 1841 and that there was more recent evidence of Everett's sympathies for rank abolitionists, one Breckinridge pamphlet pled, "Can any man point out the difference between Edward Everett and [the Republican vice presidential nominee] Hannibal Hamlin? And is this the man whom the Southern people would feel safe in supporting?"[59]

The CUP had little to offer in response to these criticisms besides reiterations. They were neither unmanly, they protested, nor fossilized relics from a bygone age. The eternal agitation of the slavery issue put the Union in mortal danger. The Republicans by their own admission (such as by removing the word "National" from their name at Chicago) and principles were a sectional, even a disunionist, party. The sectional breakup of the Democratic Party killed its claims to being national. George Washington would therefore embrace Bell and Everett's stance if alive in 1860. The CUP's large, enthusiastic rallies were evidence that it was becoming the great net gathering conservative men fleeing the breakup of the Democracy and the radicalism of the Republicans—indeed, the other parties were the unelectable ones. And make no mistake: "THE REAL ISSUE" was "UNION OR DISUNION." Or "THE TRUE ISSUE" was "BELL OR LINCOLN—PEACE OR STRIFE!"[60]

As unsatisfying as these bland and repetitive generalities were, however, they were the CUP's only chance to preserve unity as a national party. So effective were the Republicans' and Douglasites' claims to Unionism that Crittenden and other potential speakers declined invitations to stump for the ticket in New York and Pennsylvania, writing them off to the Republicans.[61] Such calculations led many CUP appeals to slant so southerly that they killed any attempt to regain the border North. The most prominent of these efforts came when a small group of Constitutional Unionists met in Selma, Alabama, and drew up their own platform pledging their determination that all territories be free for slavery expansion. The publication of this counter-platform led to the defection of many a Northern CUP man to the Republicans.[62]

This dilemma came into acute focus when it came to dealing with Southern Democrats' charge that Everett was an abolitionist. Desperate to refute the allegation, Southern Constitutional Unionists bombarded Everett with requests for clarifications that, if given, would have been bound to offend one whole bloc of voters either way. A Virginia man, writing on behalf of his friends, begged Everett to "say whether the sentiments imputed to you are *now* entertained by you; and if modified in any respect, please say to what extent and in what particular." He had high hopes for the CUP in his state but bluntly informed Everett that "to propound" the antislavery sentiments ascribed to Everett "as *our creed* would be fatal to our cause." "Unless you recant the doctrines attributed to you by" Breckinridge's supporters, another CUP man in Virginia lectured Everett, "or make some explanation satisfactory to the people of the South, I will owe it to myself—my section & the Union—to abandon the advocacy of you, & thousands in my state will do likewise."[63]

Everett was becoming a drag on the ticket in its Southern heartland, but if he assuaged such concerns too decidedly, he would kill whatever slim chances the party had in the North and abandon the CUP's guiding ethic. CUP papers countered Breckinridge Democrats' narrative of Everett's past by emphasizing the most sectionally moderate episodes in his varied career, preeminently his knapsack speech.[64] But when an Alabamian described to Everett how he defended him there, it only clarified the conundrum. When Alabama's Democrats, he wrote, "charge you with being an abolitionist I cut & slash in reply to the right and the left. Among many other things I tell them you left your own quiet happy home to travel thousands of miles to eulogize the memory of a slave holder [Washington] & toiled night & day to earn money to purchase slave territory [Mount Vernon] to present it to the wives & daughters of slave holders, when there was no slave holder willing or able to do the tenth part you did."[65] Everett was mortified to see this sectional spin on activities he had always seen as quintessentially nonsectional, necessary as such a spin was in Alabama.

Everett could have controlled this message by responding to these critiques and queries. But at first he resisted doing so. In July, an exasperated Everett confided to a comrade that "our Southern friends must understand that whatever is gained *there* is lost *here*, by demanding of me decidedly Southern principles: the very basis of our party is to unite the two sections." "What a mess we should make" if either Bell or Everett were to give in to either section's demands "for explanations!"[66] His logic was irrefutable, but it would not do to either ignore or wish away the sectionalism that drove the election of 1860. So by the time fall arrived, Everett drafted his own responses that he hoped stayed well within the narrow bounds of CUP orthodoxy. He told his Alabama inquisitor that "for the best reasons," the CUP (non-)platform very wisely avoided "every one, even of the most urgent political issues of the day." Thus it was "with extreme reluctance and only out of regard to the wishes of yourself and other valued personal friends" that he consented to defend himself against the misrepresentations of Southern Democrats. He led an open letter to the public by staking his just claim to "the entire confidence . . . of conservative men throughout the country." He wrapped himself in the mantle of Webster and Clay at every opportunity. Among the living, he cited evidence that both Breckinridge himself and Jefferson Davis had named him "as one of 'the noble band of northern conservatives.'" He explained away his antislavery expressions as governor by asserting that in the 1830s, "similar views were not only universal at the North, but they extensively prevailed at the South." He admitted to having opposed the Kansas-Nebraska Act but argued that he did so on eminently conservative ground: "we do not believe there is a candid man at the South of any party" who did not see that bill and its aftermath as "the Pandora's box of all the evils which now distract the country."[67] This Southern-friendly reply proved satisfactory to Constitutional Unionists in the Upper South, but the whole episode illustrated exquisitely well that, as a historian of the CUP has put it, "the slavery question simply would not be downed."[68]

Under assault from without and fissuring from within, the CUP's possible paths to the presidency seemed to narrow with every passing day. The CUP's travails led to a failure to reach many voters in its natural constituency of conservative Unionists. Conservative Philadelphian Sidney George Fisher, for instance, harbored serious reservations about the Republicans' sectionalist stance, and he had always hated the Democrats. He also approved of Bell and Everett personally as men of the highest respectability. But while the party claimed to uphold the Constitution, "as each party says the same thing, this assertion amounts to nothing." Slavery made up "the overwhelming and exciting subject now before the country," and "by its side all other issues are insignificant." "How," he wondered, "can a party which passes this question by hope for success"? Indeed, Fisher wrote, "it is common to hear men say they prefer Bell & Everett, but to vote for them would be useless." He abstained from voting rather than cast his ballot for the Republican ticket, but that mattered little to the CUP, which had lost his vote.[69] While the conservative Strong felt "much inclined to vote for anybody who promises to ignore" the tiresome subject of slavery, he ended up dismissing the CUP as "not of much practical importance" and voting for Lincoln. Edward Bates likewise wrote in his diary that "if they have really formed a *new party*, it is absolutely necessary to have a *platform*. . . . To say only they go for the Constitution and the enforcement of the laws, is only what every other party says." And Bell was no Andrew Jackson with the charisma to create a party without such a platform.[70] Others in the CUP base offered a simpler rationale for begging off: they thought the ticket unelectable. Fillmore probably swayed none of these when he vowed in a public letter to "vote for Bell and Everett, whether any one else does so or not." Even Everett's own sister, Sarah P. Everett Hale, confessed to one of her sons that she would have voted Republican![71]

In this dire scenario, one potential hope was for the CUP to coalesce with the Douglas Democrats to rally Northern Unionists. This became a key element in the CUP story in potential swing states New York, New Jersey, and Pennsylvania—and to a lesser degree in the Upper South. But actual fusions of this sort were short-lived, and many others were only rumored or dreamed of. Old partisan divisions plagued these attempts, with ex-Whigs chronically suspicious of Democrats and vice versa. And given how divided among themselves Democrats were in 1860, the Whig-Democrat divide was but one of many running through the fusion scene. Common hatred of the Republicans was simply not enough to overcome all of that.[72] The house divided that was conservative Unionism in 1860 was bound to fall.

Historians argue over whether the sectional moderates could have defeated Lincoln had they joined forces.[73] But what is certain is that in the absence of fusion, the CUP carried only 12.6 percent of the popular vote nationwide. Yet it was a power to be reckoned with in the South, especially the Upper South. By carrying Tennessee, Kentucky, and Virginia, it outdistanced Douglas in the electoral college with a total of thirty-nine votes. In the South as a whole, Breckinridge earned 44 percent of the popular vote, Bell 40 percent, and Douglas almost all of the other 16 percent. In the Upper South Bell garnered 43 percent of the vote and Breckinridge 40 percent.[74] CUP operatives in parts of the Deep South, to be sure, felt "almost alone, against a host of opponents." But deep into the contest, the size and enthusiasm of CUP rallies in the Upper South lent an air of plausibility to the standard partisan talk of assured success. The CUP appealed to the political culture of states like Kentucky, whose citizens felt a persistent optimism about the nation's future on the world stage and revered the Unionist hero Clay. Its stance also resonated with the independent spirit of Upper Southerners, which led them to resent the attempted dictation of disunionist hotheads from the Deep South. In the Upper South, CUP warnings of the dangers of disunion appealed not only to the positive love of Union but also to a more negative emotion: fear of a civil war being fought in that region. So central was the Upper South to CUP electoral calculus that party leaders pinned hopes of rallying "the conservative portion of the opposition" in key Northern states on the South delivering clear momentum for Bell and Everett.[75]

But its failure in the North was total. Even in Massachusetts, Bell and Everett polled only 13.1 percent of the overall vote. The party in Everett's home state had Everett but very little else—and certainly not a strong party organization—going for it. Only the Breckinridge Democrats were more marginal there.[76] In the North as a whole, Lincoln carried the vast majority of former Whigs to expand the Republican tally well beyond its 1856 total. Bell failed to achieve even a plurality of votes in any Northern county. Lincoln carried every county in New England, the only time anyone did that between 1832 and 1896. So beleaguered was the Friends of Bell and Everett Association in Philadelphia that the group was in constant search for a meeting place, since the owner of the building containing one of its rooms would not remove his Lincoln and Hamlin flag. Such a numerical nullity had the CUP become in the North that in later years, one Republican stalwart recalled the election of 1860 as a "three-cornered contest . . . between Lincoln, Douglas, and Breckinridge."[77]

If Northerners had voted like they supported the Mount Vernon cause and the Union meetings, the CUP showing in that region would have been far less anemic. But the other parties' triangulation of Unionism and the legacy of the Founders, aided by the CUP's own maddeningly nebulous non-platform, made Unionist voters' choices far from clear. Constitutional Unionists pictured Americans as torn between the angel of Unionism on one shoulder and the devil of sectionalism on the other. The Republicans' nomination of Lincoln, however, seems to have broken down the dichotomy between head and heart for multitudes of voters. The Republican campaign of 1860 offered them an escape from having to choose between their Unionism, their antislavery principles, and their desire for victory. For others, the Douglas branch of the Democracy struck a neater balance between Unionist moderation and standing up against Southern dictation than the CUP did.

Everett himself would have agreed with much of this analysis of the election. In his own postmortem, he astutely pointed to the bisectional sense of momentum that a national party desperately needed and the CUP had desperately lacked. Very few Northerners, he rued, knew prior to voting that vast numbers of Southern Unionists "manfully resisted" disunionists. That undercut Yankees' desire to throw their full voting weight behind a straight Union ticket. In turn, the CUP's inability to muster even "a very little show of real strength at the North" meant that the Breckinridge wing of "the democratic party at the South rapidly gained strength & the opposing elements (Douglas & Bell) lost confidence" in key Southern states. Disposed to give the Republicans as little credit for their victory as possible, he somewhat ludicrously charged that "the selfish views of the Republican leaders of the North" had led to this result. But he gave both them and the Breckinridge men unintentional credit for having achieved their objective when he fretted that "it is impossible under the conflicting statements of the newspapers to get at the truth" of whether Republican victory would mean Southern secession.[78]

When seven Deep South states did secede in response to Lincoln's election, it saddened—though it did not shock—Everett. He struggled to find the proper response to this development throughout the torturous months between this event and the beginning of the war. He vacillated between blaming abolitionists and Republicans, or Southern fire-eaters, for the breakup of the Union.[79] Upon learning of South Carolina's pioneering secession ordinance, he mused that the constitutionality of secession "may well be doubted" but concluded that whether secessionists justified it by reference to the Constitution or to the right of revolution "is a question of little practical consequences" in guiding the national government's response. Not quite two weeks later, already impatient at the lack of a response from lame-duck president James Buchanan and the lame-duck Congress, Everett speculated that the solution "would be for Congress, by a joint Resolution, to create General [Winfield] Scott dictator for six months." Although "there is not authority under the Constitution to create a dictator, it is an extreme remedy demanded by the extremity of the disease." While he appealed vaguely to Congress having clothed Washington "with dictatorial powers" at "a moment of extreme peril" in the Revolution, this suggestion was terribly uncharacteristic of Everett. Decades of rumination upon the nature of the Union under the Constitution failed to bestow much clarity in this new situation.[80]

In the absence of such clarity, Everett's instincts taught him that conciliation was far preferable to coercion in approaching the seceded states. While that stance in a way clashed with his love of the Union, ultimately he believed it would still be the best way to preserve that Union. In a letter he wrote to be read at a Faneuil Hall Union rally, he pled straightforwardly that "if our sister states are determined to separate from us for Heaven's sake let them go in peace." Those seven Deep South states would not be lost permanently if the rest of the South stayed in the Union, he reasoned both in this letter and in private writings. If secession could be contained, both antagonistic sections would eventually come to realize that secession had failed to achieve their particular aims. "The North will have done nothing for freedom" by pushing the Deep South out of the Union, while the seceded "South will have rendered slave-property far less secure" by cutting loose from the Union's protection. Given his long-standing conviction that the Union must be based on consent, he was convinced that it could be restored only "through moderate & healing counsels." What was more, he was sure that "if the border states are drawn into the Southern Confederacy . . . we shall plunge into the road to ruin" and the full horrors of civil war. "The idea of civil war accompanied as it would be by servile insurrection is too monstrous to be entertained for a moment."[81]

Everett thus had strong reasons to believe that while continued union would have been far preferable to peaceable secession, peaceable secession was preferable to the horrors of civil war. Some of his reasons were quite personal: the South was no abstraction to him as it was to many New Englanders. He had traveled widely throughout that region and made friends and allies, especially but not only on MVLAU business. "Greatly as I deplore the separation of the Southern States from the Union," he wrote to one of these in March 1861, "I should regret it, if possible, more deeply, if it was followed by a rupture of the kindly relations between individual friends, in different parts of the country." He hoped that at least in the short term, the Union and Confederacy would be able to live "in amicable & mutually beneficial relations, though not under the same federal government, & consequently not in the enjoyment of all the benefits flowing from such a government."[82]

For all the strength and consistency of such convictions, Everett's mood and behavior during the secession winter might be diagnosed as bipolar. He exhibited wild swings between feeling paralyzed by a sense of political marginality and hopeful bursts of creative thought and energetic action. Although he had not expended much energy psychically or otherwise to secure election in 1860, he could not help but feel isolated politically amid the swelling Republican tide in his home region.[83] While this was a passing feeling, his grief at the crisis of his beloved Union proved persistent and deep. "The prospect of any satisfactory solution of the present crisis is very dark," he wrote at one particularly low moment. "Some sanguine persons think they see the means of saving the Union. I do not." His by-now-standard protestation that "I have not the least inclination" to deliver public speeches—even for the Mount Vernon cause—thus rang less hollow in these months than it had in previous iterations. He offered passive support for efforts such as repealing Massachusetts's Personal Liberty Laws that had effectively nullified the Fugitive Slave Act but did not exert himself much in this cause because he feared "that these and all other healing measures will come too late."[84]

At other times in these same months, however—and at times in the same letters and diary entries cited above—Everett harbored tentative hopes that he might be able to nudge the national mood and national government toward conciliating the South. He was heartened by the reception of a speech in Rhode Island on the last day of 1860, noting that "the passages in my lecture in favor of Union were warmly applauded." Also encouraging was the invitation from thirty worthies in New York City to deliver his "Character of Washington" there yet again, on grounds that "at the present period in our history, we feel that the life and character of the 'Father of his Country' should be constantly held up for the reverence of the people." Other likeminded patriots implored him to bring his Washington address back to their region or to pen instructive histories of Revolutionary figures "which would now be so seasonable."[85] He earnestly threw his support behind Boston city officials' movement to invite Crittenden—who was the sponsor of the best-known congressional plan of sectional compromise in the secession winter—for a public visit to their city. Everett knew the importance of moderate Unionists sticking together across sectional lines in this crisis and of the visual of Boston publicly lauding Crittenden as the quintessence of true patriotism.[86]

Ultimately the appeal which moved Everett to action was from fellow Bostonians urging him to join the group traveling to Washington to present a mass pro-compromise petition. Various Washington politicians spent the secession winter desperately seeking to craft a compromise that would at the least placate the border slave states by settling outstanding issues surrounding slavery and its expansion. Instead of pinning their hopes on just one of these efforts, a committee of leading citizens gathered more than twenty-two thousand signatures in Boston to more generally endorse compromise as an approach or principle. Their petition urged "that such measures may be speedily adopted by Congress for the pacific settlement of our present difficulties, as will embrace substantially such a plan of Compromise as may be deemed expedient to restore tranquillity and peace to our now distracted country." This committee asked Everett to head up the delegation to Washington, in large part because he was "a person likely to have some influence on the Southern States. The affair, I fear, has gone too far for influence," he reflected in his diary, but "I do not feel at liberty to refuse." Surely the sheer magnitude of support for this petition—it was reckoned at one hundred yards long—helped rouse Everett from his torpor.[87]

The delegation—which included Everett, Robert C. Winthrop, conservative Republican Amos A. Lawrence, Charles L. Woodbury (son of New England Democratic icon Levi Woodbury), and president of the Boston Board of Trade Edward S. Tobey — left Boston on 23 January 1861. After staying overnight, appropriately enough, at the Everett House in New York, they arrived in Washington on 24 January and immediately started consultations with the Massachusetts delegation in Congress. They received little but hostility from the predominantly Republican Bay Staters in Congress, whose leader Sumner "pronounced the Petition mere *wind*, — nothing better than a penny-whistle in a tempest, & likely to produce only mischief." While they got a much friendlier reception during a week of mingling with other members of Congress and the executive branch, they found that hopelessness and irresolution about solving the country's crisis reigned among them. Unionist sentiment was as strong as ever, however, as they found when their lone supporter in the Massachusetts delegation, Republican Alexander Hamilton Rice, presented their petition to the House on 28 January. "When sent to the table, wrapped in the National Flag," Winthrop recorded, "it excited great applause." No measures were passed as a result, but it was good political theater.[88]

While in Washington, the earnest Everett also pursued other creative solutions to the national impasse. He called on some of the European diplomats to propose "a joint mediation of the three leading powers of Europe to prevent a rupture between the States." He stayed in Washington longer than other delegates in hopes of joining or observing the deliberations of the dignitaries from around the nation assembled at the Peace Conference but found that they had closed their meetings to the public. He finally left Washington on 7 February, but not before visiting with President Buchanan and supreme general Winfield Scott to urge the removal of Union troops from Fort Sumter in Charleston Harbor.[89] While the practical impact of all these efforts proved dubious, there could be no doubt of Everett's renewed dedication to the cause of sectional peace.

All of this put Everett squarely in the mainstream of the Northern experience of and approach toward the secession crisis. Local election returns, hundreds of Northern Union meetings calling for compromise, petitions like Boston's that helped prompt Congress's daily search for conciliatory measures, and the fact that twenty-one states sent representatives to the Peace Conference all suggested that pro-compromise citizens were the most vocal and organized Northerners. Advocates of letting the Deep South depart in peace as a way to save the rest of the Union were also far less marginal than we might expect in retrospect. Many Republicans had come to see compromise as a dirty word, but all Republicans had to reckon with the powerful public support for conciliation rather than coercion. The debate over what that meant in practice was loud and confusing; "the political barometer fluctuates violently from day to day," Henry

Adams observed from Washington. But one constant was the deep and broad reverence for and clamor to preserve the Union in some form. In a February conversation with Buchanan, Sumner captured his constituents' mood well when he "assured the President that the people of Massachusetts were attached to the Union; that real disunionists there might all be put in an omnibus; but Massachusetts could not be brought to sacrifice or abandon her principles" by supporting the Southern-friendly Crittenden Compromise measures.[90]

The central problem for all that Everett represented was that these sectional extremists were firmly in the driver's seat in late antebellum America. Republicans like Sumner who were hostile to particular compromises—not to mention Southern secessionists who had bidden farewell to the very notion of compromise—faced down proponents of some manner of compromise both within and outside their own party. They effectively blocked all compromise initiatives from success. Everett was entirely typical of the majority throughout the still-loyal states in his longing for conciliation. But his programmatic confusion among many alternative suggestions for preservation of the Union was also typical.[91]

For all these reasons, compromise failed during the secession winter. Thus the essential question for the United States became whether the majority of Northerners who had proved unwilling to vote for straight Unionism in 1860 would be willing to kill and die for that Union. For Everett the question became what role he would play in such a struggle.

10

Civil Warrior

The American Civil War that Edward Everett had tried so hard to prevent became in many ways his finest hour. The outbreak of open war clarified the confusions of the secession winter for Everett as it did for so many other Americans. As the length of the war grew and Everett's support for it continued, he resolved themes and priorities that had been in tension throughout his political career. By the end of his life he had achieved a full synthesis of his love of the Union, antipathy to slavery, and commitment to benevolent reform. His influence also may never have been greater. It certainly was less contested than ever, at least within the remaining Union states.

———

The beginning of the end of Everett's confusion came on 13 April 1861, when he received word while on a speaking tour in the West that Confederates had fired on Fort Sumter. By 17 April, Everett decided that while he had conscientiously disapproved of the Republicans' course, "I disapproved much more that of the secessionists." And at any rate that bombardment had fundamentally changed the central issue: "inasmuch as it is now an alternative between supporting the government and allowing the country to fall into a state of anarchy, & general confusion, I cannot hesitate as to the path of duty."[1] Given a few days to contemplate it, the firing on Fort Sumter had cut through what had been a tangle of painful questions and a thicket obscuring who bore responsibility for thrusting them on the country. Immediately upon return to Boston, he directed an official of the Boston Public Library "to have a Flag displayed." This was the same Everett who back in 1857 had discouraged other trustees of the library from mounting a portrait of Charles Sumner, seeing that as too political in the aftermath of his caning.[2]

But in a way it was not the same Everett. Within a month of Sumter, his historical researches centered on discerning the roots of secession in the stance of the likes of John C. Calhoun three decades previous. When he learned of a secessionist mob attacking Massachusetts soldiers marching to Washington in early May, he thought President Lincoln should not act "in the spirit of vindictiveness" but should calmly continue to march troops through Baltimore once order was restored, for "the streets of Baltimore are the streets of the United States, & must be fully used as such, at all hazards."[3] He now had nothing but contempt for traitors seeking by open secession and stealthy plots to overthrow the Fathers' Union. Addressing a group who serenaded him at his home in late April, he declared it nothing short of "barbarous . . . for fellow citizens, in the pretended exercise of a reserved right to break up the Union at pleasure, to seek by surprise to possess themselves of the Capital, or to lay in ashes the city that bears the sacred name of Washington." True, he was "too old to take the field, but nothing which I can do will be wanting to support the Government, to maintain the Union, & to vindicate the honor of the Nation's Flag." As an early Everett biographer aptly put it, such expressions make clear that "the attack on Sumter was like an attack on some dear and precious possession. It was as though his mother, or wife, or a member of his family had been struck!" And it convinced him that the war was a defensive one for the North.[4]

Everett's quick conversion to the war cause after Sumter was just as typical of the North as had been his confusion during the secession winter. As would become usual, President Lincoln articulated the way Sumter had boiled all preceding issues down to one. Before the war, he explained, when "freedom was in danger," he had spoken in its defense. But now that secessionists threatened the nation with violent dismemberment, "I speak single for the Union." The artillery fire at Sumter had shocked and alienated even the most pro–Southern Democrats in the North, violating their vision of peaceable secession. Thus source after source attests to nearly unanimous Northern support for the war for the rest of 1861.[5]

This startling unification came complete with some even more bracing admissions of error on both sides. In late April, Stephen A. Douglas confessed that Sumter had convinced him that he had done too much to placate Southerners. Like Everett, he came to believe that Southern fire-eaters had long been conspiring "against the government established by our fathers." "You do not know the dishonest purposes of those men as I do," the disillusioned doughface lectured Lincoln early in the war. Just as shocking was some abolitionists' willingness to admit that they might have caricatured such men as Everett and Douglas. "The only mistake that I have made," Wendell Phillips breathed after seeing the North's unity, "was in supposing Massachusetts wholly choked with cotton-dust and cankered with gold." By 1862 the erstwhile disunionist Phillips was even willing to admit that because a war for Union was necessary to destroy slavery, "I accept Webster's sentiment, 'Liberty and Union, now and forever, one and inseparable.'" He might not agree with Everett on everything, he told an audience in New York in 1862, but on this ground they had now converged.[6]

In his first public speeches of the war, Everett likewise offered a candid appraisal of how the Southern aggression at Charleston had disabused him of past notions and enabled him to unite with all other Northerners. At a flag-raising in Boston on 27 April, Everett rejoiced that "all former differences of opinion are swept away: we forget that we have ever been partisans; we remember only that we are Americans," united by "the deep patriotic sentiment of which that flag is the symbol and the expression." "I have been, through my public life, some of you have thought," overly friendly to the South. "To avert what seemed the impending danger of a general convulsion, I have been more willing than some of you to pursue, always, I hope through honorable paths, the policy of conciliation." In a May speech, he said that his audience knew by "my political course" that "I deprecate war, no man more so." "I have been pointed at for years as the friend of the South," but the South had "struck a parricidal blow at the heart of the Union; and to sustain her in this unnatural and unrighteous war is what my conscience forbids." In a July talk to soldiers, he admitted that he and his allies had spoken "the words of conciliation and peace, till they inspired nothing but contempt" from Southern hotheads. "Not upon us," therefore, rested "the dread responsibility of the unnatural conflict." In another July address, he urged those who believed peace with the Confederacy was still possible to join him in letting those scales fall from their eyes. Many people like him in the antebellum North "did believe in peace, fondly, credulously, believed that, cemented by the mild umpirage of the Federal Union, it might dwell forever beneath the folds of the Star-Spangled Banner, and the sacred shield of a common Nationality." But "from that dream we have been rudely startled by" Fort Sumter.[7]

With all the fury of a conservative scorned, Everett like Douglas indulged in far more bitter rhetoric than was his wont when describing the secessionists who had caused this war. Theirs was "the work of demons." If a murderer "is guilty of a crime," secession was worse: "history and after ages will consign to eternal infamy the traitors and conspirators . . . who aim a fatal blow at the life of the nation." Theirs was "an act of treason as flagrant as was ever perpetrated since the arch rebel revolted and 'drew after him one third part of Heaven's sons.'"[8] Such speeches expressed both a sense of having been misguided before the war and a sense of the strength that that stance gave his position now that war had begun.

There were limits to the capaciousness of the wartime political tent, however. A fortnight after Sumter, the Mexican War veteran and politician Caleb Cushing approached Massachusetts governor John A. Andrew offering his services in prosecuting the war. But Cushing had marked himself as extreme for pro-Southernism and anti-abolitionism even within the ranks of Northern Breckinridge Democrats, and Andrew rebuffed him. "Your frequently avowed opinions touching the ideas and sentiments of Massachusetts," he told him, "your intimacy of social, political, and sympathetic intercourse with the leading secessionists of the Rebel States," which he was not sure had been "discontinued, forbid my finding you any place in the Council or the Camp." He feared that "were I to accept your offer I should dishearten numerous good and loyal men, and tend to demoralize our military service."[9]

In the early weeks of the war Everett had reason to worry that potential "intimacy" with a secessionist would put him in Cushing's unenviable lot. The source of anxiety was son-in-law Henry Augustus Wise. While the naval officer Wise had sworn an oath of loyalty to the U.S. Navy, when his native state of Virginia seceded (urged on by relatives, including former governor Henry Alexander Wise) he felt seriously torn. Southerners in the American armed forces divided bitterly against each other during the secession winter on the question of resigning and found themselves scrutinized by devoted Yankees within and without the military.[10]

Everett anticipated both Wise's hesitancy and the suspicion that would bring on his whole family. So even before Virginia seceded in April he wrote to his daughter, Wise's wife, Charlotte, supplying arguments for staying with the Union navy. He also wrote forcefully to Wise himself that "if you resign, you will be supposed to act in some degree under my influence, in consequence of my known defence of Southern rights." Everett also advanced several principled arguments and was truly anxious for the immediate safety and long-term prospects of his daughter and grandchildren, but his solicitude for his own political situation was never far from the surface while Wise's "conflict of feelings" continued. During the agonizing wait for Wise to decide, Everett offered the house he still owned in the nation's capital to the federal government "at a moderate rent." But when he read newspaper accounts of how "other owners of houses in Washington had placed them at the disposal of the government rent free," he knew he could "not be behind my neighbors in patriotism," so he offered his house for free. He was therefore beyond relieved on 29 April when he learned of Wise's decision not to resign. Even better news for Everett (if surely personally painful for Wise) was that the navy sent him immediately to participate in the destruction of ships near his old home in Norfolk. Everett asked Charlotte for permission to mention Wise's participation in this important naval operation in an upcoming speech. "It will serve," he pled, "to correct a piece of venomous gossip, which is circulating here," that Wise was functioning as an informant to Jefferson Davis. "One cannot," he reminded Charlotte, "in these perilous times, be too careful" about refuting "the mischief-makers."[11] As self-serving as this all seems, Everett's reputation still hung by a thread that old enemies seemed eager to cut. The post-Sumter moment of rallying around the flag was indeed "perilous" for suspected secession sympathizers, and Everett did all he could to avoid unjustly falling under that cloud.

While Everett's public embrace of the war had undeniable benefits in his home region, it caused considerable consternation among his former friends in the South who joined the Confederate cause. Much as with the North, the outbreak of war forced Unionists in Bell and Everett country to determine their ultimate loyalties. The Upper South remained bitterly divided between Unionists and secessionists throughout the war. But the secession of North Carolina, Tennessee, and Virginia demonstrated that the Unionism of masses in these states had been conditional. They greeted Lincoln's call for troops to march south after Sumter with their own feeling of betrayal and shock. From Everett's perspective, an alarming number of Constitutional Unionists broke ranks, beginning at the top with John Bell. A very common scenario in the Upper South after Sumter was for staunchly Unionist fathers to see their sons in the generation born in the 1830s and 1840s embark on a dual rebellion by joining the Confederacy. But it was far from unheard of for older Southern Unionists to join their progeny in secession. A Georgia MVLAU supporter, who had pledged her sons "at the foot of Washington's statue" in Philadelphia "to support and defend the Union," assured them when their state seceded that "*that Union* has passed away and you are free from your mother's vow."[12]

These Confederates evidenced varied attitudes toward their Constitutional Unionist days. Much like Everett was doing on the Union side, some moderates-turned-Confederates claimed that their prewar stance actually increased their moral authority in embracing the war. "We glory in our course as a Constitutional Union man," wrote one editor in the royal pronoun. "The Union men, are, at least, 'guiltless of their country's blood.'" But others turned their back on what they had once held dear. The editor of a previously staunch MVLAU paper in Georgia, for instance, now rejected emotional appeals to the Union as "absurd." He mocked that it was "strange that 'sensible' men can find no evidence of the value of the Union, save a flag, a few graves and some facts of past history!"[13]

They also took disparate attitudes toward Everett himself, judging by their correspondence with him after the outbreak of the war. One young woman in Charleston sent a letter stamped with a secessionist flag, talking of how "I amuse myself moulding bullets" and making "provisions, for our soldiers." But she assured her "dear old friend" that "I don't think of you when I talk so." Similarly, MVLAU cofounder Ann Pamela Cunningham vigorously disapproved of Everett's support for the Union war effort but assured him that her personal regard for him remained.[14] Others proved less able or willing to separate Everett from the abstract category of hated Yankees. Three literary societies at the University of Virginia, who had hitherto awarded a prize for biographical essays out of funds raised at an 1859 benefit appearance he had made in Charlottesville, sent Everett a slap in the face in 1861. In a targeted part of the larger Confederate effort to achieve intellectual independence, they told him that they had "unanimously resolved that the 'Everett medal' should be forever abolished & the money *returned* to" Everett.[15]

The antagonism of former allies among Southern women proved especially virulent. One sent Everett a long screed in June 1861 in reaction to his prowar speeches. "You talk about the '*defensive* war of the north'" in order "to 'preserve the Union,'" but the war was really an enactment of the "malice and hatred which the abolition states have cherished against us for years." Finding the likes of Everett justifying this aggression, she concluded "that the voice of Justice was mute in the north, and there was nothing left" for Virginia but to defend herself in war. "We will cut our children's throats and our own," she pledged, "before we will consent to live under the same Government with the northerners again. No—you can never—*never* subdue us!" Her husband had "voted honestly for you last Fall, and made every effort consistent with manhood to keep peace, to the last." But she made plain that both he and she had come to a very different place than Everett when she lectured that George "Washington fought mainly for *Virginia's* independence." The Father thus would have been horrified "could he have imagined that *Massachusetts*—who helped so little about his Revolution—would one day rise up & demand to hold our beloved Virginia in chains."[16] Another Confederate lady who had been Everett's comrade in the MVLAU cause echoed the argument that the war had made a mockery of the old idea of a consensual Union. She pointedly addressed her missive to "Mr. Everett—tried to write 'dear Mr. Everett['] as formerly, but remembering the affliction you are helping to send upon us—*could* not." "You *must* know," she reasoned, "how useless, and without sense it is to talk or write about *Union* and *Constitution* now" that Union forces had invaded Virginia. "*We* can *never, never* be *forced* to live under the same government with your people again," she vowed. She hoped it was not too late for Everett to "prove yourself the worthy admirer of our noble Washington" by advocating an amicable separation of the

"Bell Traitor, Everett Patriot," engraved by Carpenter and Allen of Boston between 1861 and 1865. The divorce among former Constitutional Union Party men and women lent itself to such stark dichotomous terms as this image employed. Courtesy of the American Antiquarian Society, Worcester, Mass.

sections.[17] These erstwhile co-laborers in the Mount Vernon cause had clearly come to very different conclusions as to its legacy than had Everett and tried to shame him for his apostasy.

Everett sincerely mourned these personal-cum-political alienations but did not shrink from debating his former friends. Contemplating the manifest secessionist sympathies of people from Richmond to Savannah who had congenially hosted him on his triumphal MVLAU tours, Everett shook his head that they "would not probably now speak to me." "How sad," he cried, "the rupture of all these public & private ties!"[18] But he had room for anger alongside this sadness. "Our good friends at the South," he burst forth in a letter to Wise, were too blind to "comprehend that there are two sides to the question." In his direct replies to irate Southern correspondents—one of which became public—Everett reviewed how his long conciliatory course had even endured the secession winter. "But the wanton attack on Fort Sumter" and the organization of the Confederate government "have wholly changed the state of affairs." The Confederacy's "unprovoked war against the Government of the United States" had "made it the duty of every good citizen to rally to its support." "Must I, because I have been the steady friend of the South, sit still while he is battering my house about my ears?" The house in question, he clarified, included not only his cherished Union but also the Wise household residing in the nation's capital, which Confederates menaced. Southerners facing Yankee invasion, he pointed out, were not the only ones with a personal stake in the war, given that the promised Confederate bombardment of Washington "will not spare the house of my daughter & her little ones." Moreover, he lectured, it was "the Disunion Leaders of the Cotton States" who had "adroitly & selfishly managed to make the border States the seat of this most unprovoked & wicked war."[19] These recriminatory letters smacked of the rhetoric of divorce. In Everett's case, that feeling was reinforced by both gender and emotional factors, given that these correspondents were all women with whom he had worked devotedly for the sacred MVLAU cause.

Everett had no illusions that this divorce would be amicable, speedy, or painless. The day after learning of Fort Sumter, he admonished a friend that "my grandchildren may see the end of it, & envy me who lived so near the beginning." And as the evidence piled up around him of the determination for war in both North and South, he was surer than ever of the folly of the idea of a short, glorious war. When news of the Union defeat at Bull Run in July 1861 reached him, for instance, he reasoned that "it may be necessary that we should pass thro' this ordeal, in order to sober the minds of the People of the North, & prepare them for the tremendous struggle that awaits them."[20] These utterances echoed years' worth of prophecies from Everett about the horror of civil war in case of disunion. Many other sectional moderates in both North and South also warned of this nightmare scenario both before and after secession. Their testimony qualifies the common popular and scholarly wisdom that Americans rushed enthusiastically into the Civil War expecting triumph to come quickly and easily. The eager beavers are eminently quotable and may even have constituted a majority especially among younger generations but were not fully representative of either section.[21]

———————

Although Everett had dodged a political bullet in the Wise situation and felt himself in harmony with the Northern consensus in 1861, he wondered whether he would find a role of public influence in this new political world. Learning of the advance of U.S. forces into northern Virginia in May 1861, Everett worried about the symbolic as well as the physical damage this might cause. He feared that Union troops might do an "unintentional violence" while occupying the Arlington House mansion, where George Washington Parke Custis had stock-piled "many personal relics of Washington." Fearing that Confederates would violate either this mansion or Mount Vernon itself and seek "to throw the blame & odium on the troops of the U.S.," he solicited General Winfield Scott for a public order "that extra care should be taken for" the "preservation" and "protection of" these holy sites. Tramping armies, it seemed, might well physically accomplish as well as symbolize the displacement of the politics of memory in which Everett had thrived.[22] Everett also more than once heard ardent patriots declare "that the season for words has gone by, and that the time for deeds has come." "When the nation itself is struggling, gasping for the breath of its life," blustered one politician in earshot of Everett, "rhetoric, logic, eloquence, even, seem mean and paltry. Nothing, indeed, *is* eloquent but the roar of the cannon and the crack of the rifle."[23] Such sentiments raised the question of whether the war had rendered Everett and his kind obsolete.

It soon became apparent, however, that the time was hardly past for just such words as Everett was poised to deliver. Both sides waged the Civil War, which was rooted in ideological conflict, with pens and voices as well as with physical weapons. And while officials in both governments issued arguments for or against secession, private efforts to articulate the cause were the main thrust of the Union's war of words. Those speakers who could encapsulate previous constitutional arguments against secession and connect the Union struggle to the legacy of the Founders were in particular demand to boost and sustain civilians' as well as soldiers' morale.[24] By the summer of 1861, therefore, Everett found himself fully in demand to deliver both set-piece orations and impromptu remarks at rallies, dinners, and commemorative occasions. He also remained a hot commodity as an essayist, which the ever-perspicacious Robert Bonner indicated every year between 1861 and 1864 by paying him $200 each for monthly articles on the war for the *New York Ledger*'s enormous readership.[25]

In his wartime speeches, Everett took many of his traditional themes and applied them to the new wartime situation.[26] He continued his long study of the history and principles of the Constitution as they bore on the perpetuity of the Union.[27] That paid off in speeches and essays aimed at demolishing the constitutional pretensions of secessionists. In an early effort, he declared secession "still more unfounded" than the doctrine of nullification, "which was crushed, never to rise again, thirty years ago, by the iron mace of Webster in the Senate." Hoisting the pretended strict constructionists of the South by their own petard, he noted that "this monstrous pretended right of 'Secession,' though called a 'reserved right,' is notoriously nowhere *expressly* reserved in the Constitution." In later speeches he hinted that the South should not lock horns with a man who had corresponded with Madison himself on the unconstitutionality of nullification, for Madison's arguments on that occasion "defied refutation." Not being a constitutional right, therefore, secession must rest on the abstract right of revolution. But far from having any just claims to revolution, their reaction to Lincoln's election was as if to say, "if we succeed in this election, as we have in fifteen that have preceded it, well and good; . . . but we have no intention of acquiescing in any other result." He further reiterated and refined these arguments in a speech titled "The Causes and Conduct of the Civil War." The secessionists were revolting against a "transcendently beautiful system" of federal Union, and to boot were seeking to establish a horrible precedent. "Let no man," he urged, think "that, if the principle of secession is established, the process of disintegration will stop with the division into two confederacies." "This great prosperous Union" would in that event "be broken up into hundreds of contemptible principalities."[28]

Everett delivered his constitutional arguments with authority, but there is something revealing in the sheer number of times he felt the need to rehearse them. The normal trajectory of Union pamphleteering efforts was to rebut secessionism early in the war, then to focus more on current issues such as emancipation or civil liberties later in the conflict.[29] But Everett never seemed to consider the illegitimacy of secession settled. An April 1863 speech made it plain why he could never ignore or dismiss lightly the arguments for secession. They were being articulated, he stated forthrightly, by "some persons with whom I have usually acted, and whose judgment I greatly respect," but with whom he now fundamentally differed on the rightness of the Union war effort.[30] That group of friends and allies included antiwar Northerners but also the Southerners "with whom" he had "usually acted." Again as in a divorce, he could separate from those former close friends, but they would never truly be done with each other.

Everett was also far from done with his longtime effort to properly channel the legacy of the Founding Fathers. He set himself up as something of the Union's chief historian, ever ready to offer historical perspective on the vicissitudes of the war to people at all levels. In May and June 1862, with the Union army led by General George B. McClellan stalled fruitlessly outside Richmond, Everett sought to console people including McClellan's wife and President Lincoln by referring to the Revolutionary War. Washington himself, he pointed out, had faced just as much criticism during the darkest days of that war as Union leaders were facing now. Reaching even further back, he encouraged students at Yale in their support for the Union war by reminding them that Greek and Roman history taught that factions and local loyalties had destroyed those great nations.[31]

Everett also consciously delivered his Civil War speeches in the cool shade of the Revolution. He loved to point out that Washington had fought under the sacred American flag on sites his audiences could witness around them. Also, he noted that the rebels from the start of the war had menaced "the city baptized with the sacred name of the Father of his Country; the capital of the Union, . . . the depository of its archives, and as such the heart, if I may say so, of the body politic." The issue of the war was "nothing less, in a word, than whether the work of our noble Fathers of the Revolutionary and Constitutional age shall perish or endure." "The 'palladium of your political salvation,' as it was called by your sainted Washington, has descended from our fathers to us," and Providence had decreed that "it must, it shall go down from us to our children." An adjunct effort to these claims was to deny the Confederates the right to appeal to the Revolution for a precedent. Even Davis, he pointed out, had admitted that until very recently, they had lived "under the best form of government ever instituted by man." But when they lost control of that government for the first time they revolted. "What! a wonton rebellion like this to be compared with the righteous work of our sainted Fathers, of Washington and Franklin, and Jefferson and Adams, the heroes and sages of the Revolution!" If so, "then let all pretence of distinction between right and wrong, truth and falsehood, be abandoned."[32]

Initial public response to such intonations demonstrated that the war had hardly killed Everett's influence. Frank Moore, an important compiler of primary documents during the war, used one of Everett's discourses as the introductory address to his collection and sprinkled others liberally in it thereafter. There was also some demand for his speeches and other writings among Union troops.[33] From private conversations and correspondence, Everett gathered that his refutations of secession's constitutionality carried particular weight. A prominent New York conservative told Everett that he had been "somewhat doubtful how far it would do for conservative men to support the government," but reading one of Everett's orations "encouraged him to come out heartily."[34] Early press treatment of his speeches and his letters to disaffected Southerners was widespread and editorial comment from a variety of political perspectives luminous. Some abolitionists faulted him for offering patriotic platitudes rather than antislavery red meat, but other Northern editors judged that Everett had offered authoritative arguments that gave real encouragement to the Union war effort.[35]

The size, number, and enthusiasm of the audiences for Everett's talks also attested to his influence. As with his Mount Vernon speaking days, he found audiences raptly attentive, hosting dignitaries enthusiastic, and railroad operators solicitous. One such dignitary gushed that one of Everett's speeches "would

An envelope produced between 1861 and 1865.
This image bespoke the source of Everett's wartime influence.
Courtesy of the American Antiquarian Society, Worcester, Mass.

do as much good as any regiment Massts. had sent to the field," and one in Missouri asked for a thousand copies of the same speech "to distribute through the State, adding that they would do as much good as '2000 armed soldiers.'"[36] "The Causes and Conduct of the Civil War" became a latter-day "Character of Washington" for Everett, driving a nationwide speaking tour, albeit in a nation whose boundaries secession had reduced. Much as with the previous staple, Everett delivered this address first to the Mercantile Library Association of Boston, this one on 16 October 1861. He presented it sixty times between that date and June 1862, in fourteen states. Those numbers might have been greater had not a severe illness hampered many of Everett's activities between August 1862 and April 1863.[37]

As in previous chapters of his career, Everett's appeals carried this sort of power because of the passionate convictions that he shared with his audience. He certainly still believed deeply in the wisdom of the sainted Founders. "What a humiliating fact," he groused in his journal, "that the work of Washington, Franklin & Adams should be subverted by a creature like" the arch-secessionist William Lowndes Yancey. In early 1864, he threw himself into research and writing for an enlarged edition of his biography of Washington. One of the last letters he ever sent thanked correspondents for forwarding him a volume of American Revolutionary biographies, and despite his manifestly failing hand he offered two pages of comment on that book.[38]

Photograph of Everett from the Civil War years. This image illustrates how old Everett appeared in this stage of his career, which in turn underscores the dedication to the Union cause involved with his extensive speaking travels. In author's possession.

Everett's themes resonated strongly in the Union's wartime political culture. In his travels during the war, Everett found that Americans' patriotic reverence for Revolutionary relics had not waned. It was during the Civil War, for instance, that the new dome of the U.S. Capitol's rotunda, complete with the fresco *The Apotheosis of Washington*, was unveiled. Such veneration struck virtually no one as sacrilegious, given how the vast majority of religious Northerners saw the Union as quite literally sacred.[39] Pro-Union writers repeatedly offered similar arguments as Everett's, denying secession's claims to constitutional legitimacy and the Revolutionary heritage. Likewise, Democratic luminary Lewis Cass, much like Douglas as quoted above, urged a Detroit audience at the outbreak of the war to stand by "this glorious Union, acquired by the blood and sacrifices of our fathers." Washington's "ashes, I humbly trust, will ever continue to repose in the lowly tomb at Mt. Vernon," which would remain part of the territory of "the United States of America, (applause,) which he loved so well, and did so much to found and build up."[40]

One of the more remarkable popular effusions of this spirit gained Everett's seal of approval. On 24 June 1861, a Philadelphia newspaper published an article by a Wesley Bradshaw, claiming that on 4 July 1859, outside Independence Hall, an old man told him of hearing George Washington recount a vision of the future of the Union. At the vision's climactic moment, "a bright angel appeared, wearing a luminous crown emblazoned 'Union,' and slammed a flag bearing the words 'Remember, ye are brethren!' into the ground," whereupon contending armies of Americans threw down their arms and "united around the flag." The spirit guide's parting admonition to Washington was "let every child of the Republic learn to live for his God, his Land, and Union!" Washington took from this vision, the old veteran informed Bradshaw, the lesson that "in Union she will have her strength, in Disunion her destruction." This story garnered reprints in other Northern newspapers as late as spring 1862. When published in pamphlet form in 1864, its title page bore Everett's endorsement: "Washington's Vision Contains a highly important lesson to every true lover of his country."[41]

An even more influential fictional story of the Civil War years, penned by Edward Everett Hale, channeled Everett in ways that must have warmed the uncle's heart. Hale wrote *The Man without a Country* in 1863, with the goal of contributing to "the formation of a just and true national sentiment." The story's protagonist, Philip Nolan, unwittingly becomes a nationless man when he commits treason, sinning against the "idea" that was the United States. Many years later, during the Civil War when the repentant Nolan is dying, another character gets a look into his cabin and finds that "the stars and stripes were triced up above and around a picture of Washington, and he had painted a majestic eagle" on the wall. And the man who is with him when he dies tells him of as many incidents in American history since Nolan had gone away as he could, "but I could not make up my mouth to tell him a word about this infernal Rebellion!" In case readers somehow missed the moral, Hale's narrator says that he wrote it "as a warning to the young" traitors and would-be traitors "of today of what it is to throw away a country."[42] Hale echoed his uncle both in his unashamedly and unsubtly didactic style and in his rejection of the idea that the Confederate States of America was a new country. Confederates and their Northern sympathizers had thrown away the only country they ever had, and the rest must fight for its preservation.

The continuing force of Everett's brand of Unionism was also evident when Lincoln, first as president-elect and then as president, framed the issues of secession and war in terms reminiscent of the Mount Vernon cause and the Union meetings. On his way from Illinois to Washington, he complained that those who balked at forcibly upholding the Union treated the Union as nothing "like a regular marriage at all, but only as a sort of free-love arrangement." More soberly in his inaugural address, he again compared the Union to a marriage and appealed to disgruntled Southerners to consider not only the "benefits" but also the "memories" associated with the Union. "Though passion may have strained, it must not break our bonds of affection," he implored. "The mystic chords of memory, stretching from every battle-field, and patriot grave, to every living heart and hearthstone, all over this broad land, will yet swell the chorus of the Union, when again touched, as surely they will be, by the better angels of our nature." The whole passage channeled Everett for very much the same cause as Everett had channeled Washington.[43] Lincoln drew on Everett more clearly, if still indirectly, when preparing his inaugural address. One key document he reviewed to aid his argument that the Union was meant to be perpetual was Webster's replies to Robert Hayne from decades previous. Given Everett's crucial role in crafting and distributing the printed version of those speeches, Lincoln was consulting an Everett as well as a Webster production on this key occasion.[44]

When Northern soldiers marched south to prosecute the Civil War, they did so with this same holy zeal for preserving the Fathers' Union. Very early in the war, Wise reported to Everett that as his ship carrying troops "passed Mount Vernon, the colors were lowered, the bell tolled and the soldiers on board presented arms, while scarcely a man of us all could refrain from shedding tears."[45] Four years later, that sentiment had not changed for a group of Pennsylvania soldiers. In May 1865, one recounted, this group of hardened veterans stood "in front of the house in which lived and died the immortal Washington." They brought away pebbles from the hero's tomb "as mementoes," as well as some leaves and flowers. Entering the room where the Founder had perished, they uncovered their heads and felt "awed into silence, for we believe the place where we are standing to be holy."[46] In no sense did these veterans of Sherman's March feel rebuked by Washington's presence. If Edward Everett of all people had embraced their war to preserve the Union despite its bitter sectional violence, why should not they?

As this last example suggests and as historian James McPherson has illustrated, the "religious feeling, that this war is a crusade for the good of mankind" to be wrought by putting down "this hell-begotten conspiracy," was not just a fleeting sentiment at the start of the war; it sustained those who stayed through four bloody years of conflict.[47] Patriotic and political songs, which bore common citizens' as well as composers' imprint, also persisted in popularity throughout the conflict. In them, the rhetoric of a "union of hearts" sustaining the flag (the preeminent symbol of union) that "once covered Our Washington" predominated. Appeals to the founding heritage and to the ties between liberty and union proliferated so much in these songs that in March 1862, a *Vanity Fair* piece giving tongue-in-cheek advice on how to write a patriotic song suggested: "Here touch on Vernon's sacred tomb, / And bones of glorious

Washington." Union soldiers were more likely to talk both of the heritage of the founding generation and of transmitting it to future generations than they were of fighting for their own generation's interests or rights.[48] Union soldiers wrote letters on stationery featuring a variety of patriotic, Unionist slogans, including the CUP motto of "THE UNION, THE CONSTITUTION — AND THE ENFORCEMENT OF THE LAWS." "The Founders," Gary Gallagher has shown, "appeared on envelopes in various ways, most often in the person of George Washington." "Think of the Union [that Civil War soldiers] have helped to preserve," one of the regimental histories published soon after the war waxed, "with all its blessings, all its memories, and all its hopes."[49] Their use of such terms to describe why they were willing to fight for so long was in part a testament to the cultural work that people like Everett had done and were still doing in perpetuating and increasing a deeply emotional attachment to the Union.

––––––––––

Everett's ongoing sway over the public and embrace of the war paved the way for the most surprising development of the Civil War years: an eventual rapprochement with the Republicans. Personal connections to key Republican leaders aided policy agreement in furthering the first, fumbling movements toward this entente. A reinvigoration of Everett's antislavery streak also promoted this process. His suspicion of partisanship first restrained but eventually enabled his public support of the Republican Party. That support was substantial when it reached its full flowering.

Everett cultivated relationships with two powerful Republicans in particular in Secretary of State William Seward and Massachusetts governor John A. Andrew, and they cultivated him. When Lincoln took power, Everett dismissed him and his entire cabinet as too sectional in orientation to accomplish the task of preserving the Union. But on a visit to Washington about a month later, somewhat to his surprise he interacted amicably with both Lincoln and Seward. He was even more pleased in May 1861 to learn that Seward valued Everett's foreign policy acumen enough to accept candidates for posts on his recommendation alone.[50] When the newly elected Andrew took the governor's chair amid the secession winter, Everett distrusted him as "a genuine fanatic" who stood in the way of reconciliation with the South. But Andrew reached out to the former occupant of his seat, inviting Everett to attend important addresses to the legislature. In June 1861 Andrew appointed Everett to represent the state on a committee erecting a monument to the Declaration of Independence in Philadelphia. Two years later the governor placed Everett at the head of a commission to consider founding a state military academy. Everett went to this work with his usual diligence, meeting and traveling with his fellow commissioners to do a full study of the issues.[51] This growing if limited partnership rested on increasing political agreement as well as on personal respect. For instance, Andrew's 1862 message to the legislature ended with a demand for absolute unity behind the cause, which he defined in true Republican fashion as the preservation of the Union and popular government from slavery's aggressions. Everett sent a note to Andrew lauding "your luminous & exhaustive discussion of the subject."[52] By 1864, Everett invited Andrew to join the chummy intellectual Thursday Evening Club of which he was an integral part. They also saw eye to eye on Whiggish priorities such as funding education in the state, but ultimately their accord flowed from their shared commitment to amplifying Massachusetts's contribution to the war cause.[53]

The fact that Everett was so willing to nod in assent with Andrew's message reflected important shifts in his approach to slavery during the war. The multiple connections between slavery and the war, along with his longtime interest in the issue, had Everett studying antislavery writings in earnest. In 1861 he asked a friend to help him track down an antislavery tract from the Revolutionary era. In 1863 he read antislavery English actress Fanny Kemble's journal of her residence in Georgia and concluded that "it is really inconceivable, that Christian men & women can tolerate [slavery's] existence, or wish or work for its restoration." Reading a travel account from the slave states in 1864, he similarly remarked that "how society holds together" in a state of slavery "is inconceivable."[54] These denunciations of slavery were in a way consistent with his long-standing revulsion to slavery, but their sweeping and unequivocal nature was new. He also acted privately in ways that were slightly different from before the war. In late 1861 he gave letters of recommendation to a minister who needed military sponsorship to go preach to newly liberated slaves on the Sea Islands of South Carolina. To be sure, Everett had given plenty of money over the years to men preaching the gospel to free African Americans, and in this case he gave the letters only when satisfied that this individual was "a gentleman of great respectability." But before the war a request to preach to Carolina's black population most likely would have conjured up his fear of racial disorder.[55]

Everett hardly abandoned his wrestle between humanity and order during the war,[56] and so in important ways his positions on slavery were guided by his long-held conservative antislavery beliefs. He maintained his support for the American Colonization Society, if with diminished emphasis. As late as 1864, he still could not see support for that cause as contrary to a conservative antislavery stance.[57] At a Fast Day meeting in that same year, the speaker "dwelt at considerable length on the error of our revolutionary & constitutional fathers, in tolerating" and compromising with slavery. God, this man had preached, "made no compromise, but sooner or later, next year if not this, in the next generation if not this, in the next century if not this, gave the triumph to truth & justice." Everett rightly pointed out that this preacher did not seem to recognize "that, thus enunciated, the divine government was precisely one of compromise; if truth & justice cannot triumph this year, this generation, this century, they must wait till the next, & this under the rule of Omnipotence & omniscience."[58] Everett had always believed that what he meant by compromise with slavery had been misunderstood by abolitionists like this preacher.

But Everett felt the distance between himself and the Republicans collapsing, largely because they stood together as cheering spectators while the war worked out God's long-awaited antislavery Providence in North America. This idea that wartime emancipation was bringing to fruition his dream rather than his nightmare scenario was clearest in an open letter he wrote celebrating Missouri's ordinance of emancipation in 1863. That statute enacted gradual emancipation, but Everett enthused that he had "no doubt that, like the apprenticeship system in the British colonies, the ordinance will" soon "give way to another of immediate emancipation. But whether it does or not, Missouri is, from this time forward, substantially a free State." Viewing this development in context of the importance of slavery in Missouri in national politics from 1820 forward, Everett was "awe struck with the visible tokens of an overruling and an interposing Providence."[59] Rather remarkably, in the midst of the chaos and conflict of wartime abolition, Everett chose to accentuate the parts of that process that reminded him of British emancipation. He thereby fitted that whole process into his worldview of emancipation on Providence's timetable and via Providence's chosen means. Seen in this way, he saw it as an unmitigated blessing rather than the process he had once imagined with trepidation.[60]

This mindset manifested itself in his reactions to evolving Republican policies toward slavery. As of February 1862, with Republicans' policy of military emancipation still forming and rumors abounding about their intentions, he cautioned that any mass emancipation would raise "terrible questions" about the future of Southern labor and race relations. But he also believed that a vigorous war against Southern slavery—while "wholly extra-constitutional"—"might perhaps be justified considering the existence of Rebellion in most of the Slaveholding states." Later in 1862 he noted without protest the Republicans' abolition of slavery in the District of Columbia and approved of Lincoln's call in a message to Congress for "compensated emancipation" of border state slaves.[61]

As someone of undoubted conservative credentials who was nevertheless open-minded about changing emancipation policies, Everett represented a key target audience for the Lincoln administration. That became clear in August 1862, when Treasury secretary Salmon P. Chase reached out to Everett. About three weeks previous, Lincoln had announced to his cabinet his determination to issue what became the Emancipation Proclamation, expanding the aggressiveness of the Union's military emancipation efforts. Stunned cabinet members persuaded Lincoln to wait until a more propitious military moment so as to give the proclamation the best possible public hearing. Having just read one of Everett's patriotic speeches, Chase determined to sound him out (without revealing precisely what Lincoln was contemplating) as part of this prerelease public pulse-taking. "Have you considered," Chase inquired, "whether it will not soon be necessary to terminate Slavery at least in South Carolina & the Gulf States by a military order proceeding from the President"? Chase claimed to have "resisted the conviction of this necessity a long time, hoping the war might be successfully terminated & Slavery left to the disposition of the State authorities." But recent military events had convinced him of the necessity of bolder new measures. This was a bit misleading in that Chase had long been the most radical member of the cabinet. But his first reaction to Lincoln's cabinet announcement was that the public might perceive Lincoln's plan as inadvisably aggressive.[62]

Everett responded on the day he received this missive. He offered no constitutional objections but did wonder about the necessity of new policies. "The question you propose to me is one of vast consequence," he observed, because of the political fallout he expected. "I have *myself* no doubt of the right 'to terminate slavery in the rebel states' by an act of the war power," he stipulated, "but many persons entertaining what are called conservative opinions doubt or deny the right, and in the border states its assertion gives the government great trouble." He therefore thought the current policy of the armed forces receiving and employing "all the slaves who choose to come" would be safer politically than and of no real practical difference from a more open assault on slavery. One big change Chase had hinted at was recruiting and arming black soldiers, and Everett's response to this explosive proposition was much the same as his general reaction. "Here again I have no constitutional scruples," he averred, and in the growing chaos of the war it might be seen as "even an act of mercy toward the South, as an alternative for a *guerilla warfare of the slaves against their masters.*" But once again, Everett thought that the current policy of using black recruits for the "oppressive tasks" of logistical support was just right.[63] It was evidence of a real change that Everett failed to recoil on sight from a policy expanding military emancipation and even arming former slaves. But these were private responses to Chase's polling, and those who knew Everett's fear of race war from his knapsack and other speeches surely expected him to line up against the Emancipation Proclamation when it went into effect on 1 January 1863.

They would have been disappointed. Once he read the proclamation he unwaveringly supported it in private and public. He deemed objections to the measure, and subsequently criticisms of the performance of African American troops, factious, unfair, and beside the real issues of the war.[64] In a speech in April 1863, Everett vigorously defended the use of black troops against those who decried it as unconstitutional and revolutionary. This policy was not only legal under the laws of war, he pled, but actually would prevent rather than encourage a revival of the Haitian Revolution in the United States. "Deprecating as I do beyond the power of words to express the heart-sickening horrors of a servile insurrection, nothing has seemed to me so likely to prevent its occurrence, as to subject" the slave population of the South "to the restraints of military discipline and the control of responsible authority." In essays for the *Ledger* in late 1864, he repeated the idea that the proclamation had been a step to prevent rather than precipitate race war.[65] In this way he framed this departure from his previous stances as wholly consistent with them.

With Everett cutting such a figure on questions surrounding slavery and emancipation, some of his formerly harshest critics publicly applauded him. In a New York newspaper, Henry Ward Beecher lauded Everett for losing some of his aristocratic aloofness in recent years by writing for the *Ledger* and his labors on the lecture circuit. "His utterances on the slavery question," moreover, "are now orthodox and patriotic. The prayer which we used to hear for the aged has been answered in him, 'May his last days be his best days.'" In his diary, Everett protested against this hoary caricature of him as aristocratic but did not contest this picture of his ideas on slavery migrating.[66] In 1862, Bonner showed Everett an advance copy of Horace Greeley's sketch of Everett's career for the *Ledger*. In it, he praised Everett as the antithesis of the demagoguery of the day and an advocate of "a genial and sunny conservatism, tender and loving toward the old, yet not absolutely hopeless of the new." Everett was bemused to see this former abuser eulogizing him. He sent Greeley a gracious note acceding to his assessment of himself as a conservative but not a reactionary.[67]

But while the policy ground between Everett and the Republicans kept shrinking midwar, at first Everett's anti-party reflex kept him from fully entering their ranks. To be sure, in an 1862 Faneuil Hall rally for new troops, he praised Lincoln as a war leader. By August 1862 he was even ready to speak in the first person of the Republican majority of the North. In November 1860, he recounted, "a constitutional majority of the people thought fit" to elect Lincoln president. "For this high crime and misdemeanor on our part eleven

Southern States" seceded.[68] But even reading the ideal of a united North back onto the divisive election of 1860 was not the same as fully embracing the Republican Party. And it was that ideal of a united wartime North, combined with Everett's standard antipartisanship, that nurtured his hopes of floating above party politics. The Republicans' own failure to transcend party, he lectured a Constitutional Unionist colleague in 1861, was no excuse for trying to pursue their own "separate party action. We have no separate issue to go upon. We go with the entire North, for the vigorous prosecution of the war." As the war ground on he was confident that partisan sniping at generals like McClellan would "be the ruin of the Union cause."[69]

Everett had hardly left politics, but he would do what might seem partisan on the surface only if it were nonpartisan at its core. So in October 1862, when a group of local Republicans urged him to accept their nomination for Congress, he "intimated to them that I could not possibly accept such an invitation unless it came from *all*" the factions of the party. And in his letter officially rejecting any such nomination, he argued that he could "best serve the country and its holy cause" by staying out of the running, "especially at a moment when we are threatened with a new struggle of parties, from which I am determined to stand aloof."[70] Two months later the organizers of a Boston reception for the dismissed general and Democratic darling McClellan knew their man when they invited him to join and thus help protect McClellan from "those who would be disposed to make political capital out of his visit." Accordingly, when McClellan did visit Boston in February 1863, Everett invited people from across the political spectrum to the social events he hosted. Both during and after the visit, Everett scrutinized the public reaction to McClellan for any taint of partisanship. He was particularly offended by a report by the Republican-dominated Congressional Committee on the Conduct of the War that savaged McClellan's leadership and offered McClellan his help in defending himself. But he kept himself aloof from McClellan's most ardent backers. In response to one, he agreed—based on past personal experience—that some Republican papers' course of "stigmatizing all who differ from them as traitors" was unjust and impolitic. But he also chided that "there is some provocation given by journals" on the Democratic side.[71]

As this rebuke suggested, it was ultimately the Democrats' own pugnacious partisanship that pushed Everett out of neutrality and into the Republican coalition. His hopes for McClellan in particular centered on him pursuing a truly moderate course through the increasingly polarized Northern political landscape. In 1863, in one of his many letters of advice to McClellan, Everett offered the hope that "you may continue to pursue that wise & moderate course, which has gained you the affection of the patriotic masses," rather than fall into "the extremes of opposition" to which the peace Democrats (aka Copperheads) were leaning by that time. Both to McClellan and on other occasions, he likened the Copperheads to the Federalists whose opposition to Jefferson and Madison led them to factiousness that bordered on the treasonous even during the War of 1812. Everett felt the sting of these party hacks himself, particularly in editorial attacks by George Lunt, the anti-abolitionist firebrand from his gubernatorial days turned hardcore antiwar Democrat.[72]

Everett increasingly became convinced that key Democratic leaders had come to occupy unequivocally treasonous ground. Receiving news of the spectacular draft riots in New York City in July 1863, Everett set this disturbance down as "a disgrace to the peace democracy" whose leaders had stoked the flames of discontent. He even held these malcontents responsible for a Union defeat at Chattanooga, on the logic that the loss of the soldiers sent to put down the riots in New York allowed the Confederates to reinforce their armies in Tennessee.[73] In no meaningful way could such men be called either conservative or loyal.

Everett like so many other Northerners believed that the stakes involved and the extraordinary circumstance of domestic conflict in the Civil War robbed opposition of any claim to loyalty. Charges of treason and calls for repression of traitors thus proliferated from both soldiers and civilians in the Union states. What may seem in retrospect to be an overreaction to an overstated threat must be explained by "the tension created by 'normal' partisan conflict amid a yearning for consensus," as historian Adam Smith has put it.[74] Thus, Everett privately advocated jailing Copperhead leaders.[75] In public, he exhorted that "no one who has a drop of patriotic blood in his veins can hesitate" to support the Union cause. He declared extreme party spirit in the midst of the national crisis to be treasonable. In an 1863 public letter to a Union rally in Illinois, Everett lamented as an evil "of tremendous magnitude" the partisanship that hindered the administration "in all its measures, however patriotic and beneficent their tendency, by indiscriminate opposition." For "every blow struck at the measures of the Government, though designed only to effect a change of administration, really affords aid and comfort to the enemy" by paralyzing "the vigorous prosecution of the war." The fact that the CSA welcomed such divisions was "a pretty safe test" of their legitimacy. Everett admitted to having (unnamed) serious disagreements with some of the Lincoln administration's policies, but "I cannot but think it unpatriotic to attempt . . . to make political capital out of the difficulties, or, if you please, the errors, unavoidably incident to the conduct of a war of such gigantic dimensions."[76]

Perhaps in part in reaction against such deficient patriotism in others, over time Everett only increased his personal commitment to waging the war to the bitter end. In the summer of 1863, he paid the considerable fee required to exempt his sons Henry Sidney (age twenty-eight) and William (age twenty-three) from the new federal draft. While he granted that "they might both have been exempted for cause"—Sidney for poor health and Will for extreme nearsightedness—"I preferred to have them pay their commutation" as the patriotic thing to do. As for himself, when the War Department called in the summer of 1864 for men of "ample means" but "not liable to conscription" to "procure recruits at their own expense and present them for enlistment in the service," Everett was one of only 1,292 men to pay $125 to furnish a bounty for these "representative recruits." Toward the end of 1864, he gave his "decided approval & encouragement" to Sidney's enlistment as a major in the U.S. Army. Although personally saddened by Sidney's departure, his father "felt it my duty to encourage him in going" to give his "fair share of military service."[77]

Ready to give his money and his son to the war effort, by the fall of 1863 Everett had decided to give his votes and his voice for the Republican Party. The first major step in this process was joining and agreeing to head the Boston Union Club. Boston's elites had long had a thriving culture of clubs that gathered men of like political minds in a sociality facilitated by their restaurants and reading rooms. Much of the Copperhead sentiment during the war had clustered in Democratic clubs. Elite Republicans in the city decided they needed a club of their own, so in 1863 they followed their counterparts in other major Union cities who had created Union Leagues and Union Clubs. These organizations would act as pro-administration watchdogs and support groups, but the Boston club's charter proclaimed its nonpartisan character. So its founders created an adjunct, the New England Loyal Publication Society, to publish openly partisan propaganda by and for club members.[78]

Everett entered into this murky mix of nationalist partisan nonpartisanship, in true Everett fashion, to counter the Union Club's partisan potential. Fully aware that Republicans of all stripes predominated among the founders of this group, he had no illusions about why they approached him to be president in late February 1863. "I presume I was invited to preside over the [Union] Club," he confided in a friend, "to prevent its assuming a partizan character in public opinion, if not in reality." Although he was "almost the only person, of what are called rather vaguely 'conservative' associations who has joined the club," he hoped that with himself at the head, "we shall bring in many others, who are unconditionally loyal to the Union, and in favor of the most vigorous possible prosecution of the war."[79] Seeing the war through to the end, he proclaimed in his inaugural address, should not be a party issue but should gather "the fellow-ship of all good and true men." Although one of Lincoln's opponents in 1860, he repeated, "shall I, because I am not a political supporter of the administration, sit quietly by and see the government overturned and the country dismem-bered?" All who did not think so, of whatever party, should join the Union Club.[80] So he agreed to serve and devoted his energies to staving off attempts by radical Republicans to turn the Union Club into a blatantly partisan vehicle. He supported the club's purchase of a portrait of Washington, for instance, but fought radical Republican members' attempt to convert a holiday dinner into a thinly veiled political rally.[81]

For all these balancing acts, however, Everett was moving inexorably into the Republican camp. In the local and state elections of 1863, Everett cast his vote for the full Republican slate. He did so, he was careful to note in his diary, not because of his complete agreement with the state's Republican Party platform that year but because that platform more closely reflected "old Whig principles" than did the Democrats'. Although this was a telling assertion of old loyalties, another deciding factor was quite specific to 1863: "the success of the Republican ticket was favorable to a vigorous prosecution of the war, the only hope of the restoration of peace." Then in early 1864, he gave a hundred copies of his Union Club inaugural address to the Loyal Publication Society to distribute.[82]

During the run-up to the crucial presidential election of 1864, Everett made clear that he fully supported Lincoln's reelection. When Bonner and others circulated desultory suggestions that Everett might be a candidate for the presi-dency should the Republican Party divide into conservative and radical factions, he promptly squashed them.[83] As the leading issues of the campaign became whether to persevere in a hard war against the Confederacy and pass a consti-tutional amendment abolishing slavery throughout the United States, Everett lined up behind the Republican positions on both. The Democrats' platform supporting peace at any price, Everett determined, rendered meaningless their nomination of the War Democrat McClellan for the presidency. His "great personal regard for Genl. McClellan," he informed more than one friend, meant that "it has cost me an effort to withold [sic] from him my support. But the times are too serious to allow us to govern our conduct by personal partialities."[84] Everett evinced no qualms with the Republicans' 1864 platform, which historian James Oakes has described as "forthrightly endorsing the unconditional and immediate abolition of slavery everywhere in the United States." He did decline to sign a petition for the antislavery amendment in the spring of 1864, but his only objection was that "while the slaveholding states are waging war upon the Government it is absurd to pretend that they are entitled to the privileges which the constitution secures."[85] Everett had traveled some distance when he favored a harsher treatment of the South and slavery than the supporters of this Thirteenth Amendment.

As the election drew nigh Everett offered much more than private writings on the issues at hand. He wrote to Governor Andrew with a suggestion for how to facilitate the pro-Republican vote from the state's naval personnel. In June 1864 he shared the stage with Lincoln at a Philadelphia Sanitary Fair and spoke against "swapping horses when crossing a stream."[86] In September delegates of the state Republican Party—rechristened the Union Party for this contest—met in Worcester to nominate candidates, and they arrived having secured Everett's consent to be named as one of the party's presidential electors. Though he claimed "this was entirely unexpected," he accepted after only a very brief hesitation. Neither did the party delegates hesitate, nominating him by acclamation.[87] In early October, when party operatives plied him to speak at a rally at Faneuil Hall, he considered it "my duty to the public" to accept. He showed a draft to staunch Republican Charles Loring, who "highly approved" it, in particular a passage fully articulating the Republican position that slavery could receive no constitutional sanction as a result of the rebellion.[88]

The speech he delivered, titled "The Duty of Supporting the Government," was an impassioned appeal especially to Northern conservatives. The issues involved in this election, he avowed, were hardly mere party questions. His claim to "cherish a warm personal regard" for his Constitutional Unionist friends who were fighting for the Democracy in this contest paired uneasily with his assertion that they were much like the traitorous plotters against Washington during the Revolution. He implored his former Whig brethren to consider their past antipathy to the Democracy and argued that the current iteration thereof was worse than the one they had fought decades prior. At least "the patriotic instincts" of the Jacksonians "habitually got the better of their anti-national theories." The Civil War, he assured them, remained essentially a war for Union, given that Southern independence, not emancipation, was the prime sticking point in negotiations with the Confederates. But that said, he offered a detailed, vigorous defense of the Emancipation Proclamation on military, diplomatic, and constitutional grounds. It was, moreover, far better in keeping with the original intent of "the fathers of the Republic" than the newfangled "idea that the foundations of the Union rest on slavery." In short, the president's policies, not the Democrats' scheme of an armistice secured by "new guaranties and compromises on the subject of slavery," occupied the true conservative ground.[89]

In stark contrast to 1860, Everett experienced Lincoln's decisive reelection as a political and personal victory. In an interesting impromptu speech in mid-November, Everett argued that Lincoln deserved great respect not only for his office but also for his many noble qualities. He did add the proviso, however, "that I belong to 'the President's opposition.'"[90] But that caveat revealed just how stubborn a feature of Everett's self-image the idea of remaining aloof from parties was, for he had fully embraced the Republican cause. "One breathes freer than" when the election was still in doubt, he confided to Sumner a few days after the result became certain. "I should have considered every thing lost with the loss of the election." "The great event of the year 1864," he wrote in the *Ledger*, was the "great civic triumph" of Lincoln's reelection. For "graver" questions "were never submitted to a People, nor with a more auspicious result."[91] The meeting of the state's electoral college in early December was a particular triumph. He presided over that meeting, and in reply to a vote of thanks he framed completing the war as that generation's way of upholding "the rich legacy of our Fathers." After these ceremonies, Everett hosted a group of fellow electors and other guests, including Lincoln's son Robert, for a lavish formal celebratory dinner at his home.[92]

Everett's steadfast support for the Lincoln administration severely strained some of his cherished personal relationships. Close friends such as Robert C. Winthrop, George Ticknor, and George S. Hillard watched Everett's rapprochement with the Republicans with alarm. Repulsed by the Republicans' emancipation policies and Lincoln's expansion of executive powers, they believed conservatism dictated support for McClellan and the Democrats. Winthrop in particular stood publicly at odds with his old friend and mentor Everett. Throughout the war he refused to budge from the position that "it is the Union, and nothing more nor less nor other than the Union, for which we are contending." In 1864 he stumped for McClellan at the head of McClellan's electoral college slate in Massachusetts. One campaign speech wrapping McClellan's candidacy in the mantle of Clay and Webster sold more than 200,000 copies nationwide.[93] This divergence led to many testy interchanges whose number increased with time. In February 1863, for instance, after a Boston Public Library Trustees meeting, Ticknor warned Everett that conservative men regarded the emerging Union Club "as an abolition concern." Everett countered that "the truth is that the 'Conservatives' here & elsewhere are about as far gone in one extreme as the radicals in the other." During 1864, as these friends continued to mingle at dinner parties, Everett recorded in his diary that "we had pretty warm discussions" about politics. As the election drew closer, both Ticknor and Winthrop declined Everett's invitation to a dinner in honor of a Union general, pointedly intimating that they did so "on account of my own political 'condition.'" Everett was offended that Hillard presided at a Democratic rally and offered no protest when a speaker abused Everett. No wonder Everett believed that "the course I have pursued since the war began has cost me some friends."[94] Everett had been in this territory before, however, such as when he nurtured his personal friendship with Sumner during periods of political disagreement. In the aftermath of the bruising electoral contest of 1864, therefore, he invited Hillard to a family dinner and made sure there were "no politics talked." Winthrop also regretted their political quarrel and agreed with Everett that their public dispute must not be allowed to "disturb those personal relations which have so long existed between us."[95]

One group with which there could be no such personal adjustment was Everett's erstwhile Southern allies, whose feelings of betrayal crescendoed alongside Everett's support for their nemesis Lincoln. A Richmond editor raged that Everett had shown "himself a more implacable enemy of the South, and a more determined adversary of all compromise, than some of the rankest Abolitionists." This and other editors never tired of quoting Everett's prewar appeals for sectional conciliation. "He has an oratorical tongue," they granted, but such insensibility to his own previous pleadings indicated "a deaf and dumb heart." How Everett "ever came to see enough in the character of the slaveholding Washington, to make him the subject of eloquent and stereotyped eulogy," another editor marveled in 1863, "is a matter of some astonishment." For "the limits of earth do not contain a human being who hates anything more intensely than Edward Everett hates the South and her institutions." Even after the war, the defeated President Davis went after Everett, among other prewar Unionists such as Webster, in his defense of the right of secession.[96] Everett touchily responded that these slurs betrayed ingratitude for all that he had done for Mount Vernon.[97] Ingratitude or no, the bitterness of these Southern outbursts bore unintentional witness to Everett's perceived clout.

Aggrieved Southerners were not alone in this sense that Everett had swayed opinion in favor of the administration. Everett himself indulged in no false modesty on this score. His new political friends, whether in Boston or in Washington, repeatedly told him that his support—particularly his Faneuil Hall election address—had been crucial. A Union general stationed in Arkansas assured Everett of "the profound gratification your wise and patriotic remarks have afforded me." Everett reckoned that he had received such letters "from greater numbers of persons, & of greater varieties of position & character than on any former occasion." Among other evidence of his waxing influence, he heard "every day of persons who were led," by his election speech alone, "to vote for the re-election of Mr. Lincoln."[98] Thus he concluded that "there was a very large number of waverers here & throughout the Country, who, I verily believe, found in it, a word in season." That number was large enough, he estimated, to have swung "at least 5 States, among them" New York and Pennsylvania, against Lincoln had he joined the likes of Winthrop in supporting McClellan.[99]

There is evidence well beyond Everett's inbox to suggest that his assessment of his influence was neither fictitious nor much inflated. More than one Republican crowed shamelessly about having Everett in their column in 1864. His prominent presence in the fold strengthened the broad patriotic appeal that party leaders sought to achieve by changing the official name of the party to the Union Party. The fact that he had long "held a leading place among the conservative statesmen of this country," one Republican editor boasted, "added a hundred-fold to the weight of the judgment which at this crisis Mr. Everett gives in favor of Mr. Lincoln's reelection." At the Faneuil election meeting, Loring asserted that Everett's mere presence was but the latest and clearest evidence that Republicans were "in sympathy and association with nearly all the leading intellectual, spiritual and military lights of the age."[100] Being able to make such triumphant claims surely explains why when Everett attended a Republican celebration on election night, he "was greeted with most tumultuous and exciting cheers, which were again and again repeated, and by waving of hats." Everett reported himself "quite overcome" by this "scene such as I have never witnessed before."[101]

When less partisan observers saw former Bell-Everett men voting for Lincoln, they also ascribed that to Everett's influence. Well before the election of 1864, one of Everett's strongest critics felt compelled to admit that his speeches were "doing good in Boston" among the conservatives.[102] Other less grudging commentators granted that what Everett had brought to the Republican cause in 1864 was his reputation as an unrivaled historian and as a statesman far above the level of party hacks. Accounts of his orations, particularly the Faneuil Hall election speech, thus described an overwhelming popular interest in hearing what he had to say.[103] When a lifelong Democrat and stern anti-abolitionist heard one of Everett's speeches in Albany, New York, it convinced him to vote the Union ticket. As a result of such testimony, subsequent historians have adjudged Everett as widely persuasive in the election of 1864. They have found that his argument that the Peace Democrats' platform did not represent true conservatism swayed many Northern conservatives and that Lincoln's surprising overall strength in the border South came from converted Constitutional Unionists.[104]

In keeping with the general thrust of his wartime career, Everett pursued three endeavors that fused key themes from his overall career. These three targeted contributions included his engagement with the foreign relations of the Union, his performance as the featured speaker at Gettysburg, and his work as a fundraiser and advocate for Southern Unionists. In these activities he was able to synthesize his decades-long concerns for harmony within and the international standing of the Union and his sense of that Union's place within the larger scheme of world history. Though these contributions stood in continuity with his past sentiments and teachings, he had adapted them to the radically changed circumstances of the Civil War.

Union patriots anxious about the world standing of the torn nation—and of the would-be independent Confederacy—approached Everett to help sway foreign opinion, and Everett readily agreed. As usual, the British government's stance toward the United States mattered most, and it had taken a menacing posture even before the Lincoln administration's new minister—Everett's brother-in-law Charles Francis Adams—had arrived in London. While European governments and opinion leaders were deeply divided on how to respond in policy to the Civil War, their predominant response throughout the conflict was to think of ways to help end it. Convinced that the Union would never be able to coerce the Confederacy back into allegiance, it seemed a horrible waste of human life that also harmed the Atlantic economy. Recognized international law was vague on whether foreign nations had a right to intervene in what the Lincoln administration insisted was a domestic conflict. The British government tried to walk this tightrope by Queen Victoria's May 1861 proclamation of neutrality between the sides, recognizing both as belligerents. This fell short of recognizing Confederate independence, but it would allow the would-be nation to purchase military supplies abroad. While the British had recognized as real the Union's practically dubious blockade of Confederate ports, Union officials were outraged by the nature and hastiness of the proclamation. By June France had followed the British lead. These powers had somehow underestimated how sensitive Union men would be to this perceived encroachment on American sovereignty. Even the Emancipation Proclamation failed to fundamentally reorder British policymakers' priorities. Their primary reaction was fear that this violent form of emancipation (in contrast to their peaceful, gradual method in the 1830s) would open the door to Haitian-style race war that would prolong and worsen the vicious violence in North America.[105]

All hands were needed on deck in this crisis, and Everett's deep background in foreign policy made him an especially valuable one. As early as May 1861, Massachusetts's new attorney general reached out to him in hopes that he would find a way "to influence opinion in England." He was sure that Everett's views "would have much greater weight" than special pleading from Republicans in power. He was surely right, not only because of Everett's past positions in the diplomatic corps but also because Everett had kept up his friendly correspondence with scores of influential Britons beginning with Victoria and Prince Albert. Adams certainly found his way smoothed in the social and diplomatic circles in London by his acquaintance with, and a letter of introduction from, Everett.[106]

Everett eagerly joined this crew. He was disturbed and perplexed by the coolness of the British government and the hostility of the British press toward the Union's war cause. In addition to other evidence, he had the testimony of his son William, who was finishing up his studies at Cambridge University when the war broke out. He found it "torture being in England the first year of the war," due to "the unkindness of English opinion" toward Americans and their cause. His formerly Anglophilic father's suspicion of the motives of the British press and government thus grew until he saw their attitude as amounting to "simple bullying." He became more prone to indulge in the opinion that the Old World's hostility to the American Republic was a function of tyrants' hostility to the democratic principles that it represented. "I fear I shall never love England again, as I did before," he confided in his daughter.[107]

Everett's first action in this theater was to write an involved letter to Lord John Russell, Britain's foreign secretary and Everett's longtime friend. Everett assured Russell of the Union's prospects in the war by giving him a minute rundown of the military advantages of the Union states and their almost unanimous support for the war effort. He also asserted that "the real struggle is for the perpetuity and extension of Slavery" on the Confederates' part, the fruit of a conspiracy lasting "several years." "The controlling principle of the contest," he reiterated, "is the antagonism between Slavery and anti-Slavery; the North striving however not to interfere with it, where it is established, but to prevent its extension and its undue predominance in the general government, which is the real foundation of our repugnance to co-operate vigorously in the suppression of the African slave-trade." Given the antislavery tone of most British criticisms of the United States before the war, the queen's recent proclamation and the general "coldness and want of sympathy" from Britons for the Union cause were disappointing. Trying to bring the Union men's nationalist concerns home to Russell, Everett pursued the argument that the Confederacy's constitutional pretensions for the right of secession were as strong as Scotland's or Ireland's would be within Britain's United Kingdom. A few months later, Everett followed up with another missive repeating the argument that while this war may not be an abolitionist one on the Union's part due to constitutional restraints, it was a proslavery one on the Confederacy's part.[108] Everett had painted with boldly antislavery colors not only the war's causes this early in the conflict but also how Southern influence had misshapen American foreign policy for decades past. More than simply expedient arguments to an antislavery foreign court, on both scores this letter featured Everett reverting to his sentiments during his time as minister to Britain.

Lincoln and Seward were among those impressed when they read Everett's letters to Russell. These and Everett's overall diplomatic acumen encouraged Seward to include him in his own scheme to counteract popular and official European hostility to the Union war.[109] In the fall of 1861, he summoned Everett to Washington and told him of his wish to send a group of patriotic gentlemen "as volunteers to Europe, for the purpose as far as possible through social channels of counteracting the Confederate influence." Although the government would pay their way, Seward "wished their mission to be unofficial and as far as possible confidential." Everett would be one of five, along with Winthrop, staunch Baltimore Unionist John P. Kennedy, and two religious figures—Catholic archbishop John Hughes of New York and Episcopal bishop John McIlvane from Ohio. Seward then took Everett with him on some diplomatic rounds, including a visit to the president, who greeted their guest and would-be agent "with great cordiality." After pondering Seward's unusual offer and discussing it with friends and family members, Everett remained unsure. While vacillating, the tragic death of his thirty-one-year-old son Edward Brooks Everett convinced him to decline the position. In the fall of 1862 Seward invited Everett to Washington to repeat the request, and Everett took this reinvitation seriously enough to converse about it with Lincoln, among others. It was tempting to return to Europe and have such public usefulness to the government (Seward's scheme being an open secret in Washington's diplomatic circles). But he found it strange and borderline insulting that he would have no official title or recognition, and he remembered how he had resented President Tyler sending Duff Green on just such a mission when he was the official U.S. representative in London. His qualms won out and at the end of September he wrote to Seward "definitively excusing myself from going abroad." In the end only the two clergymen went on this rather curious errand to Europe. As late as January 1865, Seward was still contemplating sending Everett on a confidential mission to all the great powers of Europe, but nothing came of that, either.[110]

Everett did, however, employ his voice and his pen in an effort to sway European opinion. He addressed many of his wartime speeches to an international as well as a domestic audience. When speaking to banquets for foreign visitors, he did unofficial diplomacy by celebrating their nations' long friendships with the United States. In less obviously diplomatic speeches, he repeatedly placed the significance of the war in a global context. It involved "consequences vital, not merely to the permanence of the Union, but to the existence of the government, I may say of all governments." As such it was of the highest interest to "the civilized world."[111] He implored friends in Britain to see the war as one "between Freedom & Slavery" and to stop their government's "sympathy & aid" for the rebels. He forwarded copies of his speeches to European friends, and to Adams, in hopes that his demolition of the claims of the secessionists would prove persuasive abroad. He even sent packages of scientific tracts to the British Museum through the auspices of the Department of State, apparently in hopes that that would foster goodwill for the Union. During multiple visits to Washington, he spent almost all his time conferring with Seward and visiting with foreign dignitaries and ambassadors. He cultivated the friendly acquaintance of as many British visitors as possible, scrutinizing them for their sympathies in the present American conflict.[112]

Everett also used the *Ledger* as a venue for rebutting secessionists and their foreign sympathizers. He devoted a strong plurality of his monthly articles in that periodical to this theme. In them he refuted British critics' claims that the United States had always been overbearing toward Britain; his authoritative review of Anglo-American relations argued that it was vice versa. He insisted that the American Civil War "surely is a 'domestic question,' if ever there was one," and thus not the proper subject of European intervention according to those powers' own traditional foreign policy. He resented the ongoing British reproach against the United States for its long refusal to grant a right of search to suppress the slave trade, again ascribing that to the influence of slavocrats over antebellum American foreign policy. Such a barb was especially inappropriate from Confederate sympathizers, he added, given evidence (and he presented as much of it as he could) that leading Confederates advocated reopening the African slave trade to the South. Particularly effective articles skewered the Confederates for inconsistency in arguing before the world that secession was the exercise of the natural right of self-government while treating organized dissent within the Confederacy as treason. He dismissed European interventionists' late-war proposals to arbitrate the conflict as inevitably leading to a "Sham Union" that would be "*really* disunion." Rising in the full measure of his wrath, he lambasted softheaded Europeans who asked the Union government to reward the Confederates for their treasonous abandonment of all the dictates of patriotism and of that God who had preserved American sovereignty and union from the American Revolution forward.[113]

Unionists at home and Union sympathizers abroad greatly valued Everett's speeches and writings. His European correspondents professed themselves convinced (though they were more often confirmed in their beliefs) by Everett's letters and speeches. Adams thought Everett's arguments bound to "do great good at home as well as in Europe," and the previously cold brothers-in-law carried on an intermittent correspondence through the war that Adams obviously prized.[114] The Loyal Publication Society reprinted at least one of Everett's *Ledger* essays. Sumner sent his Russell letter to British correspondents and late in the war recommended Everett's appointment as minister to France. American newspapers reprinted and appreciated his foreign policy arguments. At various points of crisis for the Lincoln cabinet, rumors of Seward's resignation came accompanied by Everett's name among the supposed candidates to replace him.[115] The highest-placed admirers of Everett's international writings were the nation's chief diplomats. Seward was so taken with one of his *Ledger* articles on supposed Confederate plots to reopen the slave trade that he sent a copy to Adams in London. In 1863, Sumner told Everett that on a recent visit to the president, "I found him at his table with Bonner's Ledger in his hand. Said he — 'I am reading Mr. Everett's article.'" Lincoln read some aloud for Sumner's benefit, "making occasional observations on its felicity & its aptitude."[116]

———————

Another Everett effort that Lincoln and many others appreciated was his oration at the dedication of the cemetery for the Union dead at the Gettysburg battlefield. In late September 1863, Boston's mayor approached Everett to gauge his willingness to speak at the event. Everett told him straightaway that "I thought I could not refuse" and immediately got to work researching and writing what he knew would be a momentous speech. Everett's stature as an orator and statesman, and in particular his association with commemorations at vital American historical sites, meant he was the unanimous choice of all seventeen Union state governors whom the organizing committee consulted. They also knew that those in attendance would greatly desire the sort of detailed oration he promised to deliver. So they did everything they could to keep him on board, including setting the date for 19 November. Everett had insisted that he would need time not only for research in his library but also to extensively tour the battlefield, so they moved the event back to November rather than October. After they had secured Everett, they invited Lincoln to join and address the occasion.[117]

Everett arrived in Gettysburg on 17 November and promptly toured the battlefield with the guidance of a local professor. They were driven to the sites, symbolically enough, by a freed slave. Everett was clearly impressed by the evidences of the battle in the landscape, and in standard fashion some of his hosts gave him relics from those July days. Despite all his preparation and his long experience as an orator, "nervousness about tomorrow" kept him awake until late on the eighteenth. After riding to the ceremony ground with various dignitaries and fussing a bit about a tent he had asked organizers to erect for his private use before speaking, he sat on the stand for the long proceedings. The two hymns and strongly Unionist prayer before Everett spoke all set an emotional and patriotic tone. Many of the spectators had been standing for four hours before Everett even started, and he spoke for about two hours, from memory. But as far as he could observe, "the great multitude" all "listened without apparent weariness."[118]

What they listened to was a tour de force of Everett's art. Its main thrust was to elevate the Battle of Gettysburg's significance to at least parity with that of the ancient Battle of Marathon, framing the former by the struggle to save the sacred Union. Everett proclaimed 1–3 July 1863 as "three of those all-important days which decide a nation's history, — days on whose issue it depended whether this august republican Union, founded by some of the wisest statesmen that ever lived, cemented with the blood of some of the purest patriots that ever died, should perish or endure." Thus Americans' mourning for the Union's "martyrs" on this field was mingled with "the ascriptions of praise that rose to Heaven from twenty millions of freemen" upon receiving news of the Union victory. As he reviewed the battle's events he commented on "the providential inaction of the Rebel army" on 2 July. That "so decisive a triumph" was won by Union forces facing more numerous Confederate troops who could choose the place of their attack "I would ascribe, under Providence, to the spirit of exalted patriotism that animated them, and a consciousness that they were fighting in a righteous cause." "God bless the Union," he cried, adding that "it is dearer to us for the blood of brave men which has been shed in its defence," "these martyr-heroes" buried at Gettysburg.[119] Everett's previous career and long-held convictions had more than prepared him for this powerful argument for the significance of American history within the Providential history of freedom. He himself thought this one of the more significant aspects of his speech. These "Historical parallels" between celebrated ancient battles and Gettysburg, he told one admirer, "form by far the most original and in my judgment the most valuable portion of the address."[120]

The stakes involved in the war, he pressed, called for "the vigorous prosecution of the war." Devoting extensive space in the speech to tearing down Southern arguments for the legitimacy of secession, he castigated this rebellion as a Satan-like apostasy from the Revolutionary Fathers. In addition to this moral wrong, "the Federal Constitution . . . nowhere recognizes the States as 'sovereign.'" In fact, when those states ratified the Constitution, "they renounced all the most important prerogatives of independent States for peace and for war." For this and other reasons, "the logic of secession is on a par with its loyalty and patriotism," comprising "simple nonsense," "obvious absurdity," and "wretched sophistries." Everett disputed the accuracy of the growing Peace Democrat prediction that pressing on with the war would lead to a remorseless revolutionary struggle. "No man," he protested, "can deplore more than I do the miseries of every kind unavoidably incident to war." Indeed, before the war "a sad foreboding of what would ensue, if war should break out between North and South . . . led me, perhaps too long, to tread in the path of hopeless compromise, in the fond endeavor to conciliate those who were predetermined not to be conciliated." Those still in that naive condition should recognize that conciliation could not come without victory on the battlefield.[121]

But crucially, Everett insisted that conciliation was possible after said victory, resting this faith on Southern Unionists. He ended his discourse in classic Everett style, by appealing to "the bonds that unite us as one People," including "a common history; a common pride in a glorious ancestry." "These bonds of union are of perennial force and energy," he submitted, "while the causes of alienation are imaginary, factitious, and transient. The heart of the People, North and South, is for the Union." Even in the Confederacy, "the weary masses of the people are yearning to see the dear old flag again floating upon their capitols, and they sigh for the return of the peace, prosperity, and happiness which they enjoyed under a government whose power was felt only in its blessings."[122] Everett was also gratified whenever commentators appreciated the significance of this part of his speech. He developed this argument in a piece for the *Ledger*, proving from the history of Whigs and Tories during and after the American Revolution that, as the title of the piece said, "The Feuds Produced by Civil War [were] Not Permanent."[123]

This was vintage Everett in many ways. Among them was how he spoke for the Union of the Fathers, which he had ever seen as holy rather than fundamentally flawed. Lincoln's brief gem of a speech gave meaning to the Battle of Gettysburg by talk of a "new birth of freedom" made necessary by the Founders' compromises with slavery. Everett hardly ignored slavery as a cause of the war, but he emphasized how the Confederacy (not the prewar Union of sectional compromise) was at odds with the original intent of the sainted Founders. They would have loathed to witness the "ambitious men" of the South's attempt "to establish an oligarchy 'founded on the corner-stone of slavery.'" George Forgie, in his perceptive analysis of how those of the Civil War generation related to their Revolutionary Fathers, argued that "the Whigs had presented themselves as the party of preservation. The Republicans presented themselves as the party of restoration," undoing the damage that the Slave Power had wrought since the Founding. While Lincoln offered a variant of this Republican view with his talk of renewal, Everett (unsurprisingly) spoke definitively in that Whig tradition.[124]

Though they spoke in different political accents, the president and the orator admired each other's efforts that day and emphasized the great deal of common ground they occupied. "After I had done," Everett's account of the day reads, "the President pressed my hand with great fervor, & said 'I am more than gratified, I am grateful to you.'" The two men rode the train together from Gettysburg to Washington that night, and their conversation cemented their growing personal bond.[125] The next day, both of them back in Washington, Lincoln sent Everett a note with more specifics as to why he was "grateful" to him for his speech. "In our respective parts yesterday," he rightly noted, "you could not have been excused to make a short address, nor I a long one." He "knew Mr. Everett would not fail; and yet, while the whole discourse was eminently satisfactory, and will be of great value, there were passages in it which transcended my expectation. The point made against the theory of the general government being only an agency, whose principals are the States, was new to me, and, as I think, is one of the best arguments for the national supremacy." Lincoln astutely judged that as a known conservative and deep thinker on the nature of the Union, Everett argued from a strong position when demolishing the claims of secessionists. Lincoln also singled out another passage right from Everett's wheelhouse, in which Everett praised the work of women nurses in the war. Everett clearly prized this letter; at the top of the extant copy, he wrote: "The President of the United States. Rec[eived] 21 Nov. 1863." He boasted of it to friends near and far and even displayed it at church the next Sunday.[126]

Everett sent Lincoln his own appreciative letter on the same day. Along with thanks for the president's kindnesses toward Everett's children who had traveled with their entourage, his letter emphasized the vital issues on which the two speakers agreed. Everett penned "my great admiration of the thoughts expressed by you, with such eloquent simplicity & appropriateness," in Lincoln's brief remarks. "I should be glad," he continued, "if I could flatter myself, that I came as near to the central idea of the occasion in two hours, as you did in two minutes." Surely Everett's phrase "the central idea" referred to Lincoln's succinct articulation of the notion that the war was about whether the republican government embodied in the Union would "perish from the earth." That, rather than the idea of "a new birth of freedom," perfectly aligned with Everett's decades-long argument as well as with his own Gettysburg address. Lincoln was so pleased with Everett's letter that he mentioned and read it aloud to friends and family. Looking back months later, the president told one friend "that he had never received a compliment he prized more highly." Both men also later gave permission for these letters, along with manuscript copies of their speeches, to be sold at a fair organized by patriotic ladies (naturally) in New York for the benefit of soldiers. Everett assured the president that he parted with that letter only "with much reluctance," as a patriotic duty.[127]

Others' reactions to Everett's address were largely glowing, although that depended on political affiliation and to some degree on whether one heard rather than read it. It had a powerful emotional effect on the faithful gathered at the consecration ceremony. One of the dignitaries on the stand pronounced it "one of the greatest, most eloquent, elegant, and appropriate orations to which I ever listened." And he testified that all else present listened to the discourse "with breathless silence" and that "he had his audience in tears many times during his masterly effort."[128]

The prominence of the occasion, together with the fact that Everett grudgingly provided an advance copy of his address for the press, meant that newspaper coverage and comment on both speeches at Gettysburg was voluminous. Everett scholar Ronald Reid's survey of 260 newspapers throughout the Union states showed that editorial comments emphasized Everett's speech over Lincoln's. Both positive (almost always from pro-administration papers) and negative (from Copperhead editors) evaluations focused on his demolition of secession and hope for reconciliation after the war. He also found that metropolitan daily papers consistently devoted more column inches to Everett's speech than to Lincoln's. That may have been not only because he was the featured orator but also because he had become better known in those cities. Everett similarly overshadowed Lincoln in London newspapers, although their editors did not come to praise Everett.[129] Many Northern editors offered surpassing praise for the address's eloquence and added that its substance meant all the more coming from a statesman with his conservative background. His old antagonist Horace Greeley praised the speech with superlatives, which took Everett a bit by surprise. The U.S. consul in the German city of Oldenburg thought it masterful and useful enough that he had it translated into German and published there.[130] But others who read it shrugged it off as "long but commonplace." "It lacks the fire and spirit of true eloquence," panned one editor, "and fails to stir the blood and absorb the feelings, as one had reason to expect on such an occasion."[131] Clearly one's experience with the speech was substantially different when reading Everett's advance copy, bereft as it was of the local color and battle details he added afterward, as well as of his oratorical delivery. It was the opposite with Lincoln's speech at Gettysburg: those who heard it were divided on the merits of this short piece, while those who have read it have rarely failed to be impressed.[132]

————————

Everett did far more to raise awareness of and relieve suffering Southern Unionists than mention them in his Gettysburg oration. His own concern for their plight grew over time, spurred by conversations with exiles from Unionist bastions such as East Tennessee and western Virginia. In 1863 he learned with deep regret of the death of South Carolina Unionist James L. Petigru and cooperated with others to raise a fund for the relief of his impoverished family. He also worked to prepare a memoir of Petigru as a vehicle for traducing their shared political enemy Calhoun.[133] Beginning in July 1862, his speeches called increasing attention to "that reign of terror that palsies the Union sentiment of the South." "I greatly differ," he averred, "from those who believe this unhallowed conspiracy to be the work of the mass of the Southern people." Instead, he believed Southern Unionism to be both genuine and widespread, albeit horribly repressed by the secessionist conspirators who had maneuvered the South out of the Union in evasion of that majority's wishes. "Will you," he implored his audiences, "deliver up your Union brethren in the border States and through the South to exile, imprisonment, the scourge, and the halter?" He even applied religious rhetoric to these "faithful Union men" in a speech for aid to East Tennessee at Faneuil Hall in February 1864. The very geography of their region, he argued, suggested that Providence and nature had preordained Union in North America. Support for their cause would vindicate the idea that "if the Union means anything, it means not merely political connection and commercial intercourse, but to bear each other's burdens, and to share each other's sacrifices; it means active sympathy and mutual love."[134]

Everett's most sustained work on this theme came at the head of an intense fund-raising campaign for Unionists in East Tennessee. Some of that group's leading men went to Boston in early 1864 to ask in parlors and public rallies for monetary aid for those whom Tennessee Confederates had driven from their homes and otherwise abused. Everett could never be far down any group's list to help a fund-raiser, and he acceded to their request to preside at a meeting at Faneuil Hall. Immediately after this gathering, donations started coming to Everett personally. It had all happened so fast that he wryly described himself to Charlotte as "a sort of self constituted treasurer" of the nascent organization. He joined with friends such as Winthrop to render the effort more organized and hosted committee meetings at his house. Although the Massachusetts legislature did provide $100,000 to this cause, its main thrust would always be the sort of private fund-raising effort at which no one was better than Everett. As the other organizers knew, donors implicitly trusted Everett with their money.[135]

He threw himself into it with skill as well as an energy that belied his advanced years and failing health. Having learned from the MVLAU days, he aimed appeals for money in particular to the "Ladies of the Loyal States."[136] He devoted large percentages of his waking hours in 1864 just to receiving and dispensing of the donations flooding his office. Additionally, he penned not only repeated open letters appealing urgently for aid but also detailed lists of who had donated what in order to encourage donors who might respond to getting credit.[137] The funds came to him in amounts ranging up to $40,000 at a time, not only from individuals but also from other states' and cities' own relief associations. Furthermore, leaders of those efforts asked Everett for advice and materials that would be helpful. One Southern woman sent him a poem depicting East Tennessee Unionists' travails, hoping that its "pathos and patriotism" would enable Everett to sell it in mass quantities to benefit the cause. Other young ladies who staged a benefit play asked Everett's help in selling tickets. Everett also worked with the War Department in Washington to facilitate and expedite the delivery of supplies to the afflicted region. Everett was functioning as something of a one-man headquarters for a national movement. Much as the MVLAU had been, this relief effort was organized enough that people knew where to send donations, yet decentralized enough that a wide range of people could pursue their own initiatives and feel a rewarding personal connection to the cause.[138]

While his sympathy for Southern Unionists' sufferings was very real, placing his attentions on them seems always to have been welcome for Everett. This focus nurtured his hopes that most Southerners really were Unionists at heart and thus that the reconstruction of a Union of sentiment would be a distinct possibility following Northern victory. The idea of a suppressed Unionist majority also aided his ongoing arguments against the democratic legitimacy of secession. Aiding Southern Unionists thus combined Christian charity with impeccable Unionist politics. This subcause within the larger war cause thus provided continuity with his previous concerns and arguments.[139] He surely also reveled in the gratitude of the beneficiaries, one group of whom declared that he had "built a monument to his name amongst this people more enduring than marble." Another grateful recipient noted that "4 years ago we done what we could to Honor you; we yet Honor your principles . . . , and for those, principles, we suffer this persecution." Everett could not have known that his personal efforts had also come to the disapproving attention of Confederate officials as high as President Davis, but that would have only increased his delight. Even without that knowledge, he willingly did the considerable labor involved especially in the East Tennessee cause, recording in his diary that "I never did any thing with greater satisfaction."[140]

Such was that satisfaction that another fund-raising appeal for another group of suffering (presumed) Unionists of the South constituted Everett's final public act. In early January 1865, he met with a number of leading Bostonians to get up a Faneuil Hall meeting for the benefit of residents of Savannah, Georgia, who had been left destitute as a result of recent sustained military operations. They appointed the meeting for Monday, 9 January, and Everett stayed home from church on Sunday to prepare his speech, "deeming the Savannah affair a work of more than ordinary importance as a question of moral & religious duty." He also gave $100 of the more than $34,000 raised for these sufferers.[141]

Everett's speech at this rally in that familiar venue allowed him to issue his own anticipation of and counterpart to Lincoln's Second Inaugural's appeal for reconstruction of the Union "with malice toward none." "The main body of the inhabitants," Everett maintained, had "joyfully welcomed" William Tecumseh Sherman's conquest of Savannah. That happy fact "proves what I have always asserted, because I have always known, that there was a wide-spread Union sentiment at the South." Nothing would encourage the reemergence and spread of that sentiment better than the "benevolent work" of sending food to Savannah "without money and without price." This was good politics as well as magnanimity, for he cited Sherman himself as saying "that 'the timely relief of the suffering citizens of Savannah will be worth more to the Union cause than ten battles.' For Heaven's sake, my friends, let us hasten to win these bloodless victories." He pled for this to be done "not in the spirit of almsgiving, but as a pledge of fraternal feeling and an earnest of our disposition to resume all the kind offices of fellow-citizenship with our returning brethren." This would constitute "an act of obedience to the great law of love, which, paramount to the Constitution and the laws of the land, lays its sacred obligation on every rational creature."[142] The committee's letter transmitting the funds raised to the mayor of Savannah also dwelt at some length on the Revolutionary history that tied them together. "The annals of the South and the North," they gushed, "engraven together upon the tablets of memory, still live; and we believe that neither the South nor the North will permit them to die."[143]

It was supremely fitting that Everett would close his long public career with this ringing appeal for benevolence in the name of affective Union. As Everett got older he had become increasingly self-reflective, as illustrated by a mantra at the end of every year in his diary. Beginning in 1843 as he neared the age of fifty, he ended his last diary entry for almost every year with a reflection on his spiritual and moral performance and state. Commonly in these entries, he invoked a phrase from the Psalms: "so teach us, O God, to number our days as to apply our hearts unto wisdom." For this Victorian American gentleman who cared deeply about wrapping up every year with a bow in this way, it was clearly gratifying to be able to do the same with his life in early 1865.[144]

The Savannah appeal was Everett's final curtain because he died less than a week later. The mental and physical fatigue of 9 January, including not only speaking for Savannah but also two stints in a courtroom as part of an ongoing real estate dispute in which he was embroiled, prostrated him. Concerned that he might be "threatened with inflammation of the lungs" on top of his chronic kidney problems and neuralgia in his shoulder, he sent for the doctor and went to bed early. Thinking he had "escaped a severe attack of pneumonia" by 12 January, he was ready to get back to work and wrote the wholly typical line in his journal: "what a waste of time is not sickness!" But this was his last of forty years' worth of diary entries. In the early morning of Sunday, 15 January 1865, Edward Everett breathed his last.[145]

Conclusion

Everett's death touched off mourning throughout the Union. The legislatures of Maine, New York and Michigan passed resolutions of grief. So did the boards of colleges and historical societies in places including New York City, Philadelphia, Chicago, and St. Louis. Union Clubs from New York to San Francisco also marked his passing.[1] High federal officials greeted his death as a national event. Secretary of State William Seward wrote to Ambassador Charles Francis Adams to inform him of the death, noting that "his earnest and well directed labors in support of the Government, during the civil war, won for him the unanimous confidence and affection of the American people."[2] Henry A. Wise broke the news of Everett's death personally to President Lincoln on 15 January. The next day, at Lincoln's direction, Seward sent a proclamation to all executive offices at home and abroad directing them to render "appropriate honors" to the memory of the distinguished patriot. The secretary of war did the same for military posts.[3] Newspapers throughout the country printed these or their own obituary notices. Fittingly enough, given Everett's own collection of Washington's domestic relics, many newspapers also reverently printed Everett's last letter to his daughter Charlotte.[4]

The mourning in Boston was particularly prolonged, widespread, and intense. The mayor ordered all city churches to ring their bells, and the aldermen convened an official memorial service at Faneuil Hall on 19 January. Both houses of the state legislature passed resolutions in his honor. Institutions with which Everett's history was intertwined, such as the Mercantile Library Association, the Bunker Hill Monument Association, the Boston Public Library, and Harvard College, held special meetings, joined the Faneuil Hall assemblage, and/or made sure to memorialize Everett in their next annual meetings. A dizzying array of historical societies, individual congregations, and city councils and town meetings in suburbs of Boston followed suit. One observer posited that no death since Daniel Webster's had caused "so much public demonstration of sorrow."[5] Much as their subject was in life, the more prominent funeral services were a hot ticket. Marveling at the number and crowdedness of all these services, George S. Hillard remarked that "Boston is certainly of all places, the place to die in." Bostonians testified that all this public mourning occupied much of their thoughts in late January 1865.[6] Nor did Everett fade from their consciousness quickly after these ceremonies. In October 1865, a reporter at the public auction of Everett's house and some of his furniture wrote that many of those in attendance carried "the same spirit of sorrow and reverence" they felt at his death. Those at the 19 January Faneuil Hall gathering had resolved to raise funds for a statue of the fallen orator to be placed in that venue. That fund-raising went forward throughout that spring and helped keep Everett's memory green. The success of their efforts is represented in a bust that still resides in Faneuil Hall. And in 1894, residents of the Boston suburb named after Everett gathered—with his son, Congressman William Everett, as the guest of honor—for festivities celebrating the centennial of his birth.[7]

But how Bostonians and Americans should remember Everett became, fittingly, a matter of contestation. Unlike when Webster died, outright criticism of Everett was exceedingly rare. George Templeton Strong begged off eulogizing Everett for the Union Club in New York City, suggesting old Whig Hamilton Fish for the job. He confided to his diary that this was because "Fish is just the weak-backed, timid man of expedients and plausibilities who ought to pronounce Everett's eulogy." Even in this passage, however, Strong had to admit that "Everett has sustained the government as manfully as his organization allowed him to support anything for the last four years." Along the same lines as this mixed verdict, William Lloyd Garrison in the *Liberator* asked that eulogists remember both Everett's "highly patriotic" course during the Civil War and his "servile 'bowing of the knee to the dark spirit of slavery'" before the war "in order to preserve a Union not based upon justice and equal rights." In short, "there will be an immense amount of eulogy bestowed upon his memory; but let it be discriminating as well as generous."[8]

Speakers differed over what it would mean to treat his entire career in this "discriminating" way. Many, typically of the abolitionist and Republican stamp, read his Civil War career as redemption for his dubious antebellum exploits. George William Curtis, writing in the national magazine *Harper's Weekly*, offered that "his death is doubly happy that it occurs when his lofty fidelity to the country has disarmed" the criticisms of those—including himself—"who had been long estranged by the timidity of his political course at a time when timidity seemed almost treachery."[9] Curtis found an echo in New York Republican William Cullen Bryant, who vowed that while he had derogated Everett when "he did not resist, with becoming spirit, the aggressions of wrong, I now, looking back upon his noble record of the last four years, retract it at his grave." Adams also stated that "to me his last four years appear worth more than all the rest of his life."[10]

Many such men rated Everett's wartime phase highest for his willingness to admit he had been wrong about sectional compromise. Everett, enthused John Greenleaf Whittier, had offered more sacrifice than most Northerners during the Civil War, for "he laid on that altar not only his time, talents, and culture, but his pride of opinion, his long-cherished views of policy, his personal and political predilections and prejudices, his constitutional fastidiousness of conservatism, and the carefully elaborated symmetry of his public reputation." That was "a rare and noble magnanimity." Even before Everett had died, celebrating his support for the Republican Party in 1864, Wendell Phillips had branded his old antagonist "the cap-sheaf of American magnanimity for the last three years." It was a rare and noble figure "who, at near seventy years of age, with such a career behind him, had the loftiness of spirit to stand before twenty millions of his countrymen and say 'I was mistaken.'"[11] Phillips was not one to intimate that he might have been mistaken about Everett; he had intimated such in 1861 and that was enough for him. But others did. Whittier confessed to the Massachusetts Historical Society's memorial service that his intense antislavery conviction sometimes led him to do "injustice to the motives of those with whom I differed. As respects Edward Everett, it seems to me that only within the last four years I have truly known him." "God forgive us!" cried another poet's contribution to the same service, for slandering "the heart we might have known" in the patriot hero Everett. A Massachusetts Republican editor granted that "there have been times when we thought him timid and foolishly fearful." But "events have proved, that he calculated better, and foresaw more clearly, the dangers of disunion and the terrible character of its results, than those of us who laughed at his fears, and laughed at him for taking counsel of them." This editor was thus unsure whether Everett's antebellum course of conciliation was wise, but his wartime career had removed any doubt "that his motives were of the purest."[12]

The radical Republican man of letters Richard Henry Dana Jr. presented Cambridge's ceremony with a brilliantly nuanced assessment that took Everett's prewar conservatism seriously while maintaining some distance from it. Dana still counted himself one "of the number of those who disapprove, nay, who condemn, the course of concession and compromise to which Mr. Everett inclined." But that made him "feel the more bound to render to Mr. Everett, on this point, the justice that I think his due" by looking "at the subject from his point of view, as the phrase is, but from his interior state." Everett's devotion to the Union, Dana posited, flowed from nothing less than "a solemn conviction that it was the one great experiment . . . for the widest and highest moral and intellectual development of human nature." "Those who did not value the Union as he did," he continued, "can hardly judge him in the price he would pay for its ransom" or understand how difficult it was for this antislavery man to pay it. His seriousness about what he gave up with compromise distinguished him from the Democrats, who embraced sectional compromise "with alacrity" rather than reluctance. After having "done what he could" to preserve the peace with his MVLAU campaign, when the Slave Power began the war, he threw himself into the Union cause at all hazards, including "life-long friendships." Defending Everett from charges of inconsistency, Dana analogized that "the surgeon who sees that a capital operation may be necessary, but fears that it may be fatal to life, may put it off too long, and dally with palliatives worse than unavailing; but it would be a mistake of terms to call him inconsistent for using the knife resolutely when he sees it unavoidable." And "whatever else the war had emancipated, it had emancipated him. He was no longer bound by obligations of compact, or law, or policy, to the slave-power."[13]

The bulk of Everett eulogizers, however, portrayed Everett's wartime years as fully consistent with his career as a whole rather than as some kind of atonement for it. Different lionizers discerned different themes in that career, however. Many submitted that his ardent patriotism tied together all his efforts from the Paper War through the Civil War. The Mount Vernon and Civil War chapters might well have crowned his life, but they were just part of his decades-long effort to build the nation, at home and abroad, in good times and bad. And they agreed with Everett himself that his antebellum Unionism added persuasiveness to his wartime speeches. In short, intoned one speaker, "I can see no necessary conflict between Mr. Everett the conservative statesman, the life-long defender of the Union and the Constitution, and Mr. Everett the ardent supporter of a war to secure from destruction that Union and Constitution." Another argued that what made Everett's course consistent was his determination "to be a patriot in face of all opposition," whether it came from aristocratic Britons, abolitionists, or Southern secessionists. "First pro-slavery, then anti-slavery, not, apparently, from ideal or philosophical grounds, but from patriotism, he died an abolitionist" because he "died as a patriot."[14]

A subtheme within this emphasis on Everett as consistent Unionist would have been particularly welcome to the eulogized: reminders of his linkage to George Washington. In published eulogies, the portrait of Everett "as he appeared in delivering his oration on Washington" was the preferred portrayal.[15]

Residents of Everett's natal town gushed that "his sorrowing country weeps as for none since the immortal Washington, the majestic symmetry of whose life he best portrayed in words and works of life and love." Citizens of Cambridge, Massachusetts, pointedly met on Washington's birthday to commemorate Everett. The Mercantile Library Association of Boston, which had kicked off his MVLAU career, "resolved, that while we contemplate the noble portrait of the Father of his Country, which he presented to us, and endeavor to hold dear the memory and revere the name and character of Washington, we will ever associate with that name that of our late distinguished benefactor."[16] A Boston preacher rhapsodized that after Everett's burial at Mount Auburn Cemetery in Cambridge, there were "*two* spots now where the traveller may stand and drop a tear of admiration, gratitude, and sorrow, over the remains of *combined* greatness and goodness." One was "among the solitudes of Mt. Vernon," the other "among the multitudes of Mt. Auburn." Actually, visitors to the latter would be able to contemplate both icons of Union. For while it took until the 1850s, thanks in part to Everett's suggestion the managers of Mount Auburn had rendered the cemetery's imposing observatory tower a monument to Washington. In exquisite harmony with his life, therefore, Everett's final resting place would be at the feet of a monument to Washington.[17]

Other sketchers of Everett's life, mostly those who knew him privately, employed conciliation as their dominant color. His efforts to bind the Union together with love were characteristic of this version of the man. One of his Thursday Evening Club friends remembered that Everett had "instinctively shunned what was coarse, discordant, uncomely, unbecoming." That served him well as an orator and patriot as well as in his private dealings, for it led him to hone his gift for convincing rather than assaulting his fellow citizens. Certainly the MVLAU and East Tennessee fund-raisers "attest that his greatest triumphs were those of persuasion." No one offered a more compelling assessment of this kind than nephew and rising religious and literary star Edward Everett Hale. In a sermon for his Boston congregation on the Sunday after Everett's death, Hale argued that his uncle's life's "whole work had been one work," a "ministry of reconciliation." He had begun that ministry as an ordained minister and taken it into the dark, contentious heart of American political life. From this point of view, his Union-saving efforts were driven by his consuming "desire to sustain and establish the equal rights of men, and to work out, not a temporary truce, but a step towards lasting reconciliation" between contending—and even warring—Americans. Perhaps under Hale's influence, Everett's headstone at Mount Auburn states that "placed in many public trusts," he "remained faithful in all of them to his original calling[,] THE MINISTRY OF RECONCILIATION."[18]

Everett's grave and Washington monument tower, Mount Auburn Cemetery. The photograph of the grave is oriented toward the tower, which would be visible were it not for the foliage. Photographs by author.

Other speakers gave up the struggle to identify one overarching theme and eulogized Everett as he probably would have most wished to be remembered: as a man of multiple commitments and priorities. Curtis did this simply by cataloging Everett's range of roles in private and public life. An orator at a school named for Everett in Dorchester remembered him for "his deep interest in public education," his industrious pursuit of benevolent works, and "his Nationality." Robert C. Winthrop aptly asked: "What cause of education or literature, what cause of art or industry, what cause of science or history, what cause of religion or charity, what cause of philanthropy or patriotism, has not been a debtor . . . beyond the power of payment—. . . to his voice or to his pen!"[19]

———

How should twenty-first-century scholars and students of history conceptualize the significance of Edward Everett's long political career? It is useful to stand alongside Curtis and Winthrop and contemplate his stances on slavery and nation in connection with the full range of his political concerns. That keeps us from extracting his Unionism or his expressions on slavery from their context and thus becoming baffled at the variety of the latter. Likewise, tracking the setting of those expressions—whether international, national, or state-level— across time further contextualizes Everett's (and by extension a large subset of the nation's) career on slavery.

Appreciating how representative Everett's tortured trajectory of competing commitments was for mid-nineteenth-century America can also help us craft a more inclusive narrative of the sectional conflict that culminated in the Civil War. The script for that drama even at its most simplistic would feature three, not two, protagonists.[20] In the climactic scenes set in the 1850s and 1860s, to be sure, the two sectionalists would become the leads. But in no way could they ignore the now-supporting actor, the moderate Unionist. For the language of this character would still set the terms of the contentious dialogue, and many audience members still cheered for him or her. This character would not fade into the status of a mere extra even when the guns and swords came out in 1861. In fact, much of the clash between the leads in this era should be staged as a recruiting effort for the loyalty of the Unionist, given the strength that both sectionalists hoped to gain by bringing him or her to their side.

An outpouring of recent scholarship features strong disagreement as to how much progress nation-builders like Everett made before the Civil War. A few dissenters have marveled that "Americans managed to construct a national identity and nationalist ideology quite rapidly" by world standards in the years between the Revolution and the Civil War.[21] But the majority of scholars have argued that American national identity was incomplete and embattled before the Civil War. Indeed, the real antebellum story is how "Southerners and Northerners had come to see themselves as members of two distinct and hostile nations."[22] It is very hard to deny that secession and the Civil War represented the abject miscarriage of the ideal of a consensual Union held together by heartstrings rather than military coercion.[23]

That we should consider Everett-style antebellum American nationalism a failure overall, however, is far less clear. The fact that it was contested by sectionalism and other competing loyalties before and into the Civil War does not clinch the argument that it was weak. Indeed, the big-tent vagueness of the ideas and symbols of the Union was part of their appeal. The fact that Americans also held local and regional loyalties and expressed these situationally either alongside or in contrast to national loyalty does not refute the sincerity of their displays of patriotic emotion for national symbols such as Washington. The national ditty "Yankee Doodle" provides an instructive analogy for this flexible

Unionism. While the tune remained standard through the decades, variations in the text developed in particular places and times to express pointed partisan or sectional messages. When concert performers stoked audiences' national pride by playing instrumental versions of "Yankee Doodle," the hearers were free to let their own particular lyrics run through their heads.[24]

The Union war effort benefited from a powerful symbiosis of sectional hatred and love of nation. Students of the coming of the Civil War often forget that force was only one possible answer to secession from the rest of the Union. Russell McClintock's study of that response lays out the question of Civil War causation with useful care. "What if the North had let the South go?" he asks straightforwardly. "No war." So understanding the refusal to let secession stand is necessary to grasping the "final, most direct cause" of the Civil War.[25] While the election of 1860 that had precipitated secession showed how few Northerners were willing to vote for Unionism pure and simple, the decision to oppose secession by force showed how few of them were actuated by pure and simple sectionalism. For the undiluted sectionalist responses to secession would have been either an abolitionist war or letting the cancerous South cut itself loose from the nation. The fact that neither was the majority viewpoint indicates that antebellum Unionism powerfully shaped the behavior of the masses in the Union states.[26]

Sectionalist leaders had to shape their arguments and policies to this reality. In waging a war that demanded broad public support, even radical Republicans had to adjust their rhetoric in describing their antislavery measures. So while James Oakes has persuasively argued that Republican civilian officials more than any other group drove emancipation policy during the war, he has also shown how they had to account for moderates in the larger population. They insisted, for instance, that they understood "that emancipation would be the *effect*—even the desirable effect—of a war whose *purpose* was to restore the Union."[27] Salmon Chase gauging Everett's opinion of the would-be Emancipation Proclamation was also symptomatic of their grasp of this political reality.

As multiple Everett eulogizers bore witness, his wartime influence embodied the carryover effect of antebellum Unionism. The author of the city of Boston's official life sketch asserted that his MVLAU labors remained "fresh in the minds of all." A Cambridge minister remembered that "no person who came under the influence of" his "Character of Washington" oration "can imagine that he failed in rekindling the fire of patriotism on a thousand, thousand altars; that he failed in . . . preparing many noble hearts to offer themselves in generous sacrifice for its preservation and perpetuity." Everett's prewar Unionism, Dana held, "gave him a peculiar influence with that large class on the middle ground, not intrenched within the party lines, upon whose action the result so largely depended."[28] With all due allowance for eulogistic hyperbole, these speakers captured an essential truth about how Everett's mobilization of the memory of Washington impacted the Union population.

At first blush, antebellum American nationalism's influence on the South would seem to have been minimal. At the most basic level, it failed to stave off the secession of eleven states. Everett experienced that failure personally when erstwhile MVLAU and CUP colleagues sided with the Confederacy. He would have been even more discouraged had he lived to see Southern women marshaling the MVLAU style of apolitical gender politics to further the Lost Cause interpretation of the Civil War in its aftermath.[29]

But antebellum American nationalism nurtured the loyalties of the hundreds of thousands of white Southerners who maintained their allegiance to the Union during the Civil War. After western Virginia seceded from the rest of the state to become West Virginia, the border states numbered five, and they were populous. Pockets of Unionism within nominally Confederate states were also not inconsiderable, as Everett's East Tennessee friends could testify. Roughly two hundred thousand men from the border states and one hundred thousand from other Southern states fought for the Union army during the Civil War, some citing their unwillingness to fight against "the flag of our fathers." Elizabeth Varon's research on Elizabeth Van Lew uncovered a wide underground network of black and white Virginians whose passionate devotion to the Union cause led them to audacious spying and other resistance work in Confederate Richmond. Even in the quintessentially Confederate state of Alabama, one historian has conservatively estimated the unconditional Unionist population as fluctuating between 10 and 15 percent of the overall white population during the war. At the core of this diehard Southern Unionist political culture was a reverence for the Union of the Fathers. The fluctuations in numbers were closely correlated with the emboldening or suppressive power of the fortunes of war. Beginning in 1863 with Confederate military decline, erstwhile Whig Unionists began to prosper again in CSA politics. At the end of the war these men came out even more openly to say, as did one Georgian, "Well, you see all the evils of secession that we prophesied have become true; now we suppose the people will believe us, and not believe the old secession democrats." And this message resonated across the South, as shown by former Whigs' extreme dominance in 1865 gubernatorial, congressional, state constitutional, and state legislative elections.[30] Historians have fought their own conflict over whether losses to Confederate manpower from within the white—let alone the black—population of the South doomed the new nation.[31] But either way, persistent

Southern Unionism through the war indicates that any picture of a resistless secessionist wave even after Fort Sumter would be greatly overdrawn.

Moreover, antebellum fire-eaters did not see the persistent political power of Southern Unionist sentiment as a minor obstacle. In 1844, for instance, long-time secessionist Langdon Cheves lamented that "as often as the tongue lisps resistance" to Yankee tyranny, "you are met by the eternal cry of the Union! the Union! the danger of the Union! and you are subdued by it." A Georgia Unionist editor taunted that this was still true in 1860, judging by how secessionists "go into a sort of hysterical spasm whenever the name of the *Union* is mentioned." That was because "Unionism has been taught as a sort of religion," a Richmond editor cautioned. A secessionist Georgia editor thus felt it necessary to respond that "we love this Union sincerely; it is a sentiment with us, that has grown with us from our youth, and strengthened with our manhood. But we love justice" too, which only a Southern Rights stance could deliver. It was just this sort of Southern-friendly spin on Union sentiment that William Lowndes Yancey was seeking to achieve by his MVLAU speaking tours in the late 1850s.[32]

Throughout their late antebellum drive for disunion, fire-eaters had to reckon with the large mass of Southern moderates, especially but not exclusively in the Upper South. It was a measure of secessionists' political skill that they were able to set the Southern agenda in the 1850s although outnumbered (vastly so considering the entire South). But it was in fact their many "thwarted crusades" that "honed an angrier edge on a frustrated slavocracy," as William Freehling has put it. Southern moderates fought on the defensive after 1854, but secession was never a foregone conclusion and happened in many stages contingent on particular events. "Union savers" probably could have hoped only to "have hung in there, until the next slavery crisis," but they were decisive in explaining timing and the multiple stages (Freehling details five after Lincoln's election alone) needed to achieve secession. As historian Michael Woods has shown, secessionist leaders genuflected to the power of Unionist attachments in encouraging Southerners reluctant to join the Confederacy to mourn for the departed Union. Mourning the death of the Union was an ironic bridge to Confederate allegiance, but it aimed to convince reluctant Confederates that reconstruction of that Union was impossible. Also, secessionist leaders insisted that the Union had been murdered, rather than died a natural death, in order to lay the crime at the feet of antislavery agitators.[33]

But it also seems highly unlikely that, except from the most hardcore secessionists, white Southerners' protests of love for the Union were cynical. Jefferson Davis, for his part, developed an attachment to the Union very early in his military career, and it led him to embrace at least the concept of sectional compromise in the face of state rights zealots' assaults. Even after Lincoln's election he protested his willingness to work to save the Union of equals, until he lost all hope of compromise during the secession winter. Davis long remembered 21 January 1861, the day he resigned his Senate seat, as "the saddest day of my life." His grief was both for the loss of personal relationships in Washington (including with Everett's relatives the Wises) and for "the Union of 'our Fathers.'" Only the stern conviction that with Lincoln's election "we are to be deprived in the Union of the rights which our Fathers have bequeathed to us" impelled his decision to join Mississippi in seceding. He was far from the only one weeping during this wrenching time in the South. Indeed, part of Davis's appeal as Confederate president was that he had political clout with Unionists and—like Everett in the Union—a certain moral authority from having striven for peace for so long.[34]

As a raft of excellent scholarship building on the insights of David Potter has revealed, we can accept both these white Southerners' prewar American nationalism and their wartime Confederate nationalism as sincere because loyalty is always complex and situational. Zealous nationalists—like Everett—seek total allegiance. But for most people, as Paul Quigley has written, nationalism is "a variable and multidimensional concept that people relate to in different ways within changing contexts" rather than "a rigid container which any given individual is either wholly inside or wholly outside." The Civil War era forced on white Southerners torturous questions of how to "balance different layers of identity and loyalty when they came into conflict." This scholarship has strongly suggested that the generation of Southerners who came of age in the 1840s and 1850s, whose political consciousness was dominated by escalating sectional conflict, had an easier time transitioning to Confederate nationalism. But this describes a tendency rather than a unanimity among that generation, and for older generations there is no compelling reason to doubt the sincerity of their state, regional, and shifting national loyalties. That is especially true of conflicted Upper Southerners like Robert E. Lee, who as late as the secession winter was reading Everett's biography of George Washington and lamenting that the Father's "spirit would be grieved could he see the wreck of his mighty labors!"[35]

Confederate nation-builders therefore knew what they were doing when they incorporated mass quantities of the material of previous American nationalism into their rising structure. Drew Gilpin Faust's influential study of Confederate nationalism highlights how "strikingly self-conscious" Confederates were about the need to build a nationalist culture, with evidence including published and spoken pleas for "ceremonies, flags, 'relicks,' monuments, poems, and songs" led especially by ladies. Events and icons from the American Revolution, foremost Washington, being "at once American and southern," were pervasive in this nationalist culture. This helped in the vital project of reassuring Southerners that their nationalism was not a drastic departure from the past. So images of and references to Washington in particular proliferated in all the varied productions of this nascent-yet-proven political culture. And as late as 1865, William Gilmore Simms found it useful to cry foul when Federal troops destroyed a statue of Washington in Charleston. It all worked wonderfully to manage the transition in loyalties, as witnessed by the diary of the Virginian and MVLAU supporter Louisa H. A. Minor. In December 1860, hearing of South Carolina's secession, she rued that "prejudice has taken away all our patriotism." But by the time Virginia seceded, she was ready to recognize resistance to the Yankees as embodying both patriotism and the legacy of the founding. "What impudence! presumption! in the north to imagine they can force us to stay in the Union," she fulminated in her journal. "It is easy to conceive now what our forefathers felt when Old England wanted to make them drink tea and it did not agree with them."[36]

No Northerner was more troubled by such developments among such people than Everett. His outrage at the Confederates' perversion of the founding legacy set the tone he took toward them and the war once it had begun. But although he did not live to see the proposition tested during Reconstruction, his insider's sense of the power of Unionist sentiment led him to hope for a revitalized affective Union. This proved unduly sanguine, but it was not merely self-delusion. The sectionalists' escalating appropriations of the Unionist political culture he had sought for decades to sustain and expand indicated what a force it was during the antebellum decades. That all three sides in the antebellum sectional conflict shaped this malleable set of ideas and emotions to their own ends vitiated its power to influence policy. But had Everett lived a few more months he would have seen the triumph of the combined forces of the antislavery side and a large subset of the Unionist side. Both the overall size of that Unionist side and the strength it offered to the antislavery side when joined during the Civil War had a lot to do with the thoughtful and dedicated exertions of Edward Everett.

Appendix A

Everett, as was typical, kept careful track of which cities he visited, in what order, to deliver his "Character of Washington" speech. The following are the cities he visited; the parenthetical numbers are the number of separate visits he made to that city if there was more than one. I have arranged them in the chronological order he provided. The source for this information is Everett, *Orations and Speeches*, vol. 4, 4–17.

Boston, Mass. (2)	Maysville, Ky.	Hingham, Mass.
New Haven, Conn.	Buffalo, N.Y.	Norwich, Conn.
New York City, N.Y. (4)	Utica, N.Y.	Fitchburg, Mass.
Baltimore, Md. (2)	Troy, N.Y.	New Bedford, Mass.
Richmond, Va. (2)	Cambridge, Mass.	Portsmouth, N.H.
Petersburg, Va.	Hanover, N.H.	Augusta, Maine
Charlottesville, Va. (2)	Roxbury, Mass.	Wilmington, Del.
Washington, D.C.	Amherst, Mass.	Trenton, N.J.
Philadelphia, Pa. (4)	Northampton, Mass.	Harrisburg, Pa.
Princeton, N.J.	Newburyport, Mass.	Alexandria, Va.
Newark, N.J. (2)	Andover, Mass.	Fredericksburg, Va.
Brooklyn, N.Y. (2)	Lawrence, Mass.	Savannah, Ga.
Providence, R.I.	Brunswick, Maine	Augusta, Ga.
Charlestown, Mass.	Portland, Maine (2)	Charleston, S.C.
Springfield, Mass.	Bangor, Maine	Columbia, S.C.
Cambridgeport, Mass.	Newport, R.I.	Lynchburg, Va.
Worcester, Mass.	Medford, Mass.	Lexington, Va.
Salem, Mass.	Nashua, N.H.	Norfolk, Va.
Hartford, Conn.	West Cambridge, Mass.	Watertown, N.Y.
Taunton, Mass.	Woburn, Mass.	Binghamton, N.Y.
Albany, N.Y.	Charlemont, N.H.	Rome, N.Y.
St. Louis, Mo.	Fredonia, N.Y.	Waltham, Mass.
Chicago, Ill.	Ann Arbor, Mich.	East Bridgewater, Mass.
Detroit, Mich.	Cleveland, Ohio	Bridgewater, Mass.
Indianapolis, Ind.	Erie, Pa.	Burlington, Vt.
Cincinnati, Ohio	Lowell, Mass.	Montpelier, Vt.
Louisville, Ky.	Concord, N.H.	North Bridgewater, Mass.
Lexington, Ky.	Gloucester, Mass.	Haverhill, Mass.

Abington, Mass.   New Brunswick, N.J.   Chapel Hill, N.C.
Weymouth, Mass.   Elizabeth, N.J.   Staunton, Va.
Canandaigua, N.Y.   Plainfield, N.J.   Lynn, Mass.
Rochester, N.Y.   East Brooklyn, N.Y.   Dedham, Mass.
Auburn, N.Y.   Hopkinton, Mass.   Auburndale, Mass.
Plymouth, Mass.   Middleborough, Mass.   South Boston, Mass.
Barnstable, Mass.   Newton, Mass.   Marlborough, Mass.
Brookline, Mass.   Wilmington, N.C.   Keene, N.H.
Middletown, Conn.   Newbern, N.C.   Bristol, R.I.
New Britain, Conn.   Raleigh, N.C.   Lewiston, Maine

Appendix B

After Everett suggested small donations from the roughly million readers of the "Mount Vernon Papers," he received letters from these locations. They arrived in flurries in January 1858 and then especially in December 1858 and throughout 1859 (though centered in December 1858 and January–March 1859). The parenthetical numbers are the number of donations when above one. I have tabulated these from reels 16 and 17, EP.

I should state here, however, that this work is just the beginning of what could be done to explore the partisan and other loyalties of the grassroots members of this movement. Historian John Brooke has begun some such work for Massachusetts, but much more could be done to illuminate this broad-based, national movement and its ultimate political impact at the local, state, and national levels.

Massachusetts: Boston (24), Charlestown (4), Cambridge (3), Roxbury (3), Newburyport (2), Lynn (2), Andover (3), Stockbridge, Fitchburg, New Bedford, Lowell, Greenfield, Waltham, Salem, Springfield, North Scituate, Brighton, Lawrence

Maine: Portland, Bath, Hallowell

New Hampshire: Hampton Falls, West Andover

Vermont: Norwich, Windsor, Bennington

Rhode Island: Westerly, Bristol, Greenville, Providence, Summit

Connecticut: Hartford (2), Bridgeport, Southport, New Haven, Mystic, Jewett City, Berlin, South Manchester, Terryville, Mansfield Centre

New York: New York City (35), Brooklyn (7), Albany (2), Leeds Post Office (2), Baldwinsville, Cornwall, Oswego, Peekskill, Fort Plain, Watertown, Batavia, Utica, Keeseville (or Reeseville), Rockaway, Jefferson County, Westchester County, Delaware Bridge, Tarrytown, East Norwich, Oppenheim, Elmira, Waterloo, Westchester, Pittstown, Glassboro, Oyster Bay, New Lebanon, Kings County

New Jersey: Newark (3), Princeton, Hackettstown, Lambertville, Burlington, Montpelier, Fort Randall, Morristown, Trenton, Salem, Bergen, Camden, Orange

Pennsylvania: Philadelphia (9), Germantown, Hollisterville, Danville, Deerfield, Leiperville, Port Richmond, Wellsboro, Rochester

Maryland: Baltimore (12), Hagerstown (2), Cambridge, Catonsville, Princess Anne, Clearspring, Williamsport (N.C.?), Uniontown, Port Deposit, Irving College (near Manchester, Carroll County)

Virginia: Richmond, Fabers Mills, Loudoun County, Petersburg, Smithfield, Winchester, Romney, Staunton

North Carolina: Wilmington (2), Enfield (2), Asheville (Buncombe County!), New Bern, Le Noir (?), Wilson

South Carolina: Anderson Court House, Bath, Bluff Rabun Post Office

Georgia: Warrenton, Columbus, Newton Factory Post Office, Forsyth, Darien

Alabama: Montgomery, Washington City, Talladega

Mississippi: Friar's Point, Columbus, Palo Alto

Kentucky: Louisville (2), Grayson, Garriotts Landing (?)

Tennessee: Murfreesboro (2), Bell Worth Iron Works, Memphis, Rogersville, Farmville, Denmark

Louisiana: New Orleans (2), Loganport (2), New Iberia

Missouri: St. Louis (3), Warrensburg (2), Athens, High Point, Andrew County, St. Joseph, Creve Coeur, Lexington

Ohio: Cincinnati (3), Columbus (2), Crestline, Xenia, Norwalk, Henin (?)

Indiana: Milan, Fort Wayne

Illinois: Springfield (3), Quincy, Pratt County, Bloomington, Rushville, Godfrey, Galena, De Kalb

Michigan: Detroit, Jackson (2), Port Huron, Buchanan

Wisconsin: Cassville, Sioux City, Milford, Fainwater

Minnesota: St. Paul, Bloomington

Iowa: Garnerville

California: Sacramento, Onion Valley, Petaluma

Oregon: Cohasset, Roseburg (this one for the Washington Monument)

Canada: Montreal, New Castle (New Brunswick)

Washington, D.C. (3)

Florida: Alafia

Texas: Brownsville

Unknown states:

Williamsburgh	Pulaski	Worthington
Somers	Leominster	New Britain
Big Oak Flat	Burkettsville	Penola Post Office
Suggsville	Hastings	Bigfoot Prairie
Maysville Seminary	Churchville	Saco
Fort Pike	Stone Ridge	Bethel
Hydeville	Peterboro (2)	Head of Sassafras
Lochnagar	Stonington	Green Castle
Carbondale	Amherst	

And several with no place named.

Notes

Abbreviations

BPL   Boston Public Library Rare Books and Manuscripts, (cited courtesy of the Trustees of the Boston Public Library)

EP   Edward Everett Papers, 1675–1910, Microfilm Edition, Massachusetts Historical Society

EP-Exeter   Edward Everett Papers, Phillips Exeter Academy Library, Exeter, N.H.

EP-Harvard   Papers of Edward Everett, 1807–1864, Harvard University Archives

LC   Library of Congress, Washington, D.C.

MHS   Massachusetts Historical Society, Boston

NAR   *North American Review* (Boston)

Introduction

1. *Boston Courier Report of the Union Meeting*, 12, 16–17, 30.

2. *Charleston Courier*, 12, 14 Apr. 1858. I chose the title of this book not only from a quote used in chapter 8 to describe Everett's Mount Vernon campaign but also to put Everett's exertions in counterpoint with the secession commissioners described and analyzed so capably in Dew, *Apostles of Disunion*.

3. For a good sense of what they were up against, see Huston, *Calculating the Value*.

4. Daniel Webster's contribution to this persuasion arguably exceeded Everett's, although Elizabeth Varon rates Everett ahead of everyone else; see *Disunion!*, 5. The quality and impact of his nationalism have been explored usefully in Dalzell, *Daniel Webster and the Trial*.

5. This of course leaves wide open the possibility of a literary study or a full biography of Edward Everett. But prospective biographers should be warned that his private life does not provide much of the conflict that heightens drama. Portraying the well-adjusted family and personal life of Everett would be more like writing of J. S. Bach than of Ludwig van Beethoven.

6. Christian, "The Mind of Edward Everett"; Gill, "Edward Everett, Minister"; Horn, "Edward Everett and American Nationalism"; Geiger, "Scholar Meets John Bull"; T. Brown, "Edward Everett and the Constitutional Union Party"; Yanikoski, "Edward Everett and the Advancement of Higher Education"; Reid, *Edward Everett*; Varg, *Edward Everett*; Katula, *Eloquence of Edward Everett*; Stripp, "Other Gettysburg Address." The filiopietistic and otherwise old-fashioned Frothingham, *Edward Everett*, remains the most comprehensive biography.

7. Loring, *Hundred Boston Orators*, 421–22, 525–46; Kneeland, *Masterpieces of American Literature*, 347–62; Stark, *Dorchester Day*, 6, 13, 43, 59, 95; E. Everett, *First Battles of the Revolution*; Hart, *Commonwealth History of Massachusetts*, 4:212. For a good secondary account of his reputation in his lifetime, see Reid, *Edward Everett*, 1–3. Interestingly enough, in 1880 a Brazilian abolitionist included Everett in his list of American heroes and advocates of human progress; see D. Davis, *Slavery and Human Progress*, 296.

8. Recent works taking moderates seriously include Ashworth, *Slavery, Capitalism, and Politics*, volumes 1 and 2; Huston, *Stephen A. Douglas*; Furstenberg, *In the Name of the Father*; Belohlavek, *Broken Glass*; McClintock, *Lincoln and the Decision for War*; Barney, *Making of a Confederate*; Durham, *Southern Moderate*; Varon, *Disunion!*; Wood, "'Sacrifice on the Altar of Slavery'"; Landis, *Northern Men*; and Woods, *Emotional and Sectional Conflict*. They build on somewhat older works, such as Baker, *Affairs of Party*; Knupfer, *Union as It Is*; Crofts, *Reluctant Confederates*; Baggett, *Scalawags*; and Morrison, *Slavery and the American West*. These works remain outnumbered and outgunned by too many studies, especially of abolitionists and antislavery politicians, to cite here. And perhaps most tellingly, even the above-named works tend to assign causal significance to the extremists on slavery.

9. Mathews, "Fallen Angel"; Filler, *Crusade against Slavery*, 95, 190; Stange, *British Unitarians*, esp. 117; Nagel, *John Quincy Adams*, 332; Forbes, *Missouri Compromise*, 279–81.

10. Bartlett, "Edward Everett Reconsidered," quotation on 435; Frothingham, *Edward Everett*, x, 94, 121–25, 341, 349; Streeter, "Hawthorne's Misfit Politician"; Reid, *Edward Everett*, 12–21, 39–40, 59–60; Foletta, *Coming to Terms*, 207–20; Tyack, *George Ticknor*.

11. George Mifflin Dallas Diaries, vol. 1, p. 21, Kislak Center for Special Collections, Rare Books and Manuscripts, University of Pennsylvania; Ford, "February Meeting," 388–91.

12. Everett to Robert Bonner, 30 Nov. 1858, Edward Everett Papers, LC; Everett to Robert Gilmer, 14 Feb. 1840, Edward Everett Papers, New York Public Library, N.Y.; Everett to Miss Legare, 12 Apr. 1844, Edward Everett Letters, New-York Historical Society, N.Y.; Everett to Robert Gilmor, 11 Mar. 1840, Everett to Dolley Madison, 23 May 1848, and Everett to Mrs. M. P. Walcott, 14 Apr. 1856, EP-Exeter.

13. Forgie, *Patricide in the House Divided*, 159–99, 255–56, 271. For a similar argument, see Horn, "Edward Everett and American Nationalism," 332–35, 342.

14. An excellent example of the growing collaboration between political, social, and cultural history is Pasley et al., *Beyond the Founders*. For a concise overview linking recent literatures on the politics of memory and on nationalism, see McDonnell et al., *Remembering the Revolution*, introduction. Michael Kammen's influential book argues that nationalist tradition "is, inevitably, a political phenomenon"; see *Mystic Chords of Memory*, 5. Furstenberg, *In the Name of the Father*, shows what insights are possible when exploring similar ground to Forgie's with the tools of recent political and cultural history.

15. Bartlett, "Edward Everett Reconsidered," 427. For a similar call, see Forgie, *Patricide in the House Divided*, 162n6. Bartlett was at work on a biography of Everett when he died in 2006; for his preliminary notes from Everett's diary, see "Selections from Edward Everett's Diaries," MHS.

16. Ayers et al., *All Over the Map*; Murrin, "Roof without Walls"; McCoy, "James Madison"; Zelinsky, *Nation into State*; Yokota, *Unbecoming British*; Haynes, *Unfinished Revolution*.

17. Bellah, "Civil Religion in America"; Purcell, *Sealed with Blood*; Foletta, *Coming to Terms*, esp. 45–100; Neem, *Creating a Nation of Joiners*; Cheng, *Plain and Noble Garb*; Matthews, "'Whig History'"; Furstenberg, *In the Name of the Father*; Travers, *Celebrating the Fourth*; Dennis, *Red, White, and Blue Letter Days*; Mayo, *War Memorials*; McDonnell et al., *Remembering the Revolution*,

162–78; Gibbons, "'Yankee Doodle' and Nationalism"; Zelinsky, *Nation into State*; Yokota, *Unbecoming British*; Haynes, *Unfinished Revolution*; Smith-Rosenberg, *This Violent Empire*.

18. Anderson, *Imagined Communities*; Kammen, *Mystic Chords of Memory*, esp. 10; Hobsbawm and Ranger, *Invention of Tradition*; Gillis, *Commemorations*; Connerton, *How Societies Remember*; Halbswachs, *On Collective Memory*.

19. Howe, *Political Culture*, 25–36, 214–37; Buell, *New England Literary Culture*, 137–65; S. Gustafson, *Eloquence Is Power*; Dalzell, *Daniel Webster and the Trial*, esp. ix; Wilentz, *Rise of American Democracy*, 490; Peterson, *Great Triumvirate*, 383; Katula, *Eloquence of Edward Everett*, 31–136.

20. For an especially good exploration of this dynamic, see Morrison, *Slavery and the American West*. This paragraph's last point follows Kammen's axiom that "memory is more likely to be activated by contestation, and amnesia is more likely to be induced by the desire for reconciliation"; see *Mystic Chords of Memory*, 13. Furstenberg has quantified this phenomenon by showing that the largest number of new editions of Washington's Farewell Address came out during times of national crisis; see *In the Name of the Father*, 43. For a good corrective to seeing doughfaces and their allies as "moderates," see Grimsted, *American Mobbing*.

21. T. Smith, *Ethics of Compromise*; Pennock and Chapman, *Compromise in Ethics*; Morley, *On Compromise*. For valuable reflections on the importance of both agitation and compromise in antislavery politics, see Oakes, *Radical and the Republican*, esp. 27–28, 136, 169–70.

22. McDaniel, "Bonds and Boundaries," quotation on 89. Anthony Page's exploration of moderate antislavery London preacher Richard Price concluded that "owing to age, location and other priorities," Price's life shows "how antislavery thought did not translate easily into abolitionist action"; see "'A Species of Slavery,'" quotation on 67.

23. Potter, *Impending Crisis*, 43–48.

24. E. Foner, *Fiery Trial*, quotation on xxi; Feller, "Brother in Arms"; Ross, "Lincoln and the Ethics of Emancipation"; Guasco, *Confronting Slavery*; M. Mason, "John Quincy Adams"; Mason and Waldstreicher, *John Quincy Adams*; Fredrickson, *Big Enough to Be Inconsistent*; McKirdy, *Lincoln Apostate*; Potter, *Impending Crisis*, 338–55; Donald, *Charles Sumner*, esp. 62, 101, 109–12, 191–92.

25. In a recent book review, Andrew Shankman argues perceptively that "we need to ask how meaningful most claims to oppose slavery were prior to the Civil War." See Shankman, review of *Colonization and Its Discontents*, 603. This thought about limits beyond which the likes of Everett could not go is my beginning of an answer to that challenge.

26. E. Everett, *Orations and Speeches*, vol. 3, 120 (quotation); Abzug, *Cosmos Crumbling*; Trent, *Manliest Man*; Griffin, *Their Brothers' Keepers*. I therefore dissent from Michael F. Conlin's otherwise useful article demonstrating broad agreement among conservatives both north and south that modernity was a threat. Only in his rare crankiest moments did Everett fit Conlin's schema, and since I read Everett as a mainstream Northern Whig on questions of progress and modernity, I believe his career offers a serious qualification to Conlin's argument that his brand of conservatives was a major force in both Northern parties. See "Dangerous *Isms*."

27. Calhoon, *Political Moderation*; Greenberg, *Manifest Manhood*. Their proud sacrifices for the Union mean that they would be astonished to read Melinda Lawson's assertion that antebellum elites had never sacrificed for the nation; see *Patriot Fires*, 1–2, 98–128. For the most direct statements of how doughfaces helped slaveholders dominate the federal government and of why that mattered deeply to slaveholders, see Richards, *Slave Power*; and Ericson, *Slavery in the American Republic*.

28. Earle, *John Brown's Raid*, 65–69, quotations on 69; Varon, *Disunion!*, 9–11, 128, 151, 174, 208–9, 227–28, 263–64, 273–87, 327–28, 344.

29. Gallagher, *Union War*, quotation on 5.

30. Ibid., quotations on 3–4, 40; Gallagher, *Causes Won*, quotation on 13; Oakes, *Freedom National*, quotations on xv–xvi; Nagel, *One Nation Indivisible*, 145. For the touchstone of this thrust in the scholarship of the memory of the Civil War, see Blight, *Race and Reunion*.

31. Lawson, *Patriot Fires*, entirely overstates the novelty of wartime Union nationalism and its trappings.

32. This is a point expressed well for Webster in C. Smith, *Daniel Webster*.

Chapter 1

1. Frothingham, *Edward Everett*, 1–5; Orcutt, *Good Old Dorchester*, 323.

2. Orcutt, *Good Old Dorchester*, 241, 289–335; E. Everett, *Orations and Speeches*, vol. 2, 235.

3. Kahler, *Long Farewell*, esp. chs. 1, 3, and 4; quotation on 68.

4. Tyack, *George Ticknor*, 18–19 (quotation); Hillard, *George Ticknor*, 1:21; Formisano, *Transformation of Political Culture*, 4, 57–83, 86–88; Peterson, *Great Triumvirate*, 34; James Brewer Stewart, "Boston, Abolition, and the Atlantic World, 1820–1861," in Jacobs, *Courage and Conscience*, 101–25.

5. E. Everett, *Orations and Speeches*, vol. 3, 347, 621–22; *Illustrated Mount Vernon Record*, 2:137; diary, 19 Dec. 1850, 24 Jan. 1856, EP.

6. O. Everett, *Eulogy on General George Washington*.

7. E. Everett, "Edward Everett's College Life"; Frothingham, *Edward Everett*, 6–14. Those who wish to understand Everett's notions of the proper role and attributes of an orator would do well to study J. Adams, *Lectures on Rhetoric and Oratory*; most of these lectures were delivered while Everett was at Harvard. For an intensive analysis of Adams's impact on Everett's oratorical career, see Katula, *Eloquence of Edward Everett*, 45–63.

8. *Harvard Lyceum*, 14, 28 July, 20 Oct. 1810.

9. Ibid., 28 July, 11 Aug. 1810.

10. Ibid., 11 Aug. 1810, 26 Jan. 1811.

11. E. Everett, "Edward Everett's College Life," 194–95; Houston, *Benjamin Franklin*, quotations on 12, 15. Bartlett, "Edward Everett Reconsidered," 429–30, makes much of Everett selecting Franklin as a role model.

12. E. Everett, "Edward Everett's College Life," 27, 198; Simpson, *Man of Letters*, 2–31; Tyack, *George Ticknor*, 23–36; Frothingham, *Edward Everett*, 15; E. Lee, *Memoirs of Rev. Joseph Buckminster*, 391–92. Three decades later, when serving as a U.S. ambassador in London, Everett read Buckminster's sermons aloud to his family almost every Sunday evening, reasoning that "if Mr. Buckminster's Sermons will not" stoke his family's interest in spiritual things, "I know not what sermons will." See diary, 11 Sept. 1842, EP.

13. *Sermons by the Late Rev. Joseph S. Buckminster*, 297–310; Tyack, *George Ticknor*, 23–36.

14. *Sermons by the Late Rev. Joseph S. Buckminster*, 135–53, 213–27.

15. Ibid., 78–92. See also Papers of Joseph Stevens Buckminster, reel 3, Harvard Depository, Harvard University, Cambridge, Mass.; and Howe, *Unitarian Conscience*, 272.

16. Howe, *Unitarian Conscience*, esp. 270–300; quotations on 12, 276.

17. Harvard Phi Beta Kappa Poem of 1812, reel 47A, EP; Field, "Birth of Secular High Culture"; Frothingham, *Edward Everett*, 14–24.

18. Sermons 42 and 47, reel 48B, EP. For wartime Federalist preachers, see M. Mason, *Slavery and Politics*, ch. 2; Cleves, *Reign of Terror*, esp. chs. 3–4; and Rachel Hope Cleves, "'Hurt-

ful to the State': The Political Morality of Federalist Antislavery," in Hammond and Mason, *Contesting Slavery*, 207–26.

19. E. Everett, *Defence of Christianity*. For the controversy and the effects of Everett's book, see B. Kime, "American Unitarians."

20. Frothingham, *Edward Everett*, 30–34.

21. Washington Journal, 19, 20 Nov. 1814, EP.

22. Ibid., 24 Nov. 1814; Everett to Lucy Everett, 14 Jan. 1819, Everett to Alexander Everett, 12 Feb. 1819, Edward Everett Letterbook, Houghton Library, Harvard University, Cambridge, Mass.

23. Washington Journal, 19 Nov. 1814, EP.

24. Ibid., 18 Nov. 1814.

25. Frothingham, *Edward Everett*, 34–60; Long, *Literary Pioneers*, 63–76; Morison, *Three Centuries*, 224–27.

26. Tyack, *George Ticknor*, 43–83; W. Taylor, *Cavalier and Yankee*, 14–27; Bartlett, "Edward Everett Reconsidered," 434ff; Donald, *Charles Sumner*, 37–58.

27. Journal of England and Holland, 1815, 2 July 1815; Journal of England, Scotland . . . , 21 July 1818; Scrapbook, 1815–1818, all in EP; Everett to Alexander Everett, 7 Oct. 1819, Edward Everett Letterbook, Houghton Library.

28. Everett to Lucy Everett, 17 Feb. 1819, Everett to J. P. B. Storer, 25 Nov. 1818, Everett to Alexander H. Everett, 6 Feb. 1819, Edward Everett Letterbook, Houghton Library.

29. Hillard, *George Ticknor*, 1:297; Journal of Paris and England, pp. 107, 152, 391–97, EP.

30. Everett to President Kirkland, 30 Nov., 1 Dec. 1818, Everett to Alexander H. Everett, 27 Feb. 1819, Edward Everett Letterbook, Houghton Library; Journey from Amsterdam to Gottingen and Life in Gottingen, Journey to Holland, Journey from Gottingen to Dresden and Berlin, Journey to the Harz, Journey from Gottingen to Paris, EP.

31. Everett to Alexander H. Everett, 12 Feb. 1819, Edward Everett Letterbook, Houghton Library.

32. Richard, *Golden Age of the Classics*, esp. 10–15, 36, 38, 48.

33. Loring, *Hundred Boston Orators*, 549; Morison, *Three Centuries*, 190–227; "Everett's Lectures" notebook, Tayloe Family Papers, Albert and Shirley Small Special Collections Library, University of Virginia, Charlottesville; R. Emerson, *Complete Works*, 10:330–35.

34. Sermon on Psalm 16:6, EP.

35. Sermon on Romans 2:11, EP.

36. Wilbur, *History of Unitarianism: Socinianism*; Wilbur, *History of Unitarianism in Transylvania*, esp. 99–485; Stange, *British Unitarians*, 13–47; Wright, ed., *American Unitarianism*, esp. 181–206; O'Connor, *Athens of America*, 8–18.

37. Everett to Mrs. Nathan Hale, 5 Feb. 1820, Everett-Hopkins Papers, MHS; C. Adams, *Memoirs of John Quincy Adams*, 4:525; Faux, *Memorable Days*, 384–85; *Daily National Intelligencer*, 18, 20 Nov. 1820.

38. Frothingham, *Edward Everett*, 67–68; Mott, *History of American Magazines*, 2:226–32; Everett to Theophilus Parsons, 30 Nov. 1822, 15 Feb. 1823, BPL.

39. C. Adams, *Memoirs of John Quincy Adams*, 4:526; John Lowell to Everett, 15 Dec. 1819, BPL; Harrison Gray Otis to Everett, 15 Mar. 1820, EP.

40. King, *Life and Correspondence of Rufus King*, 6:330; Wiltse et al., *Papers of Daniel Webster*, 1:59–60, 180–82, 274–75; Sheidley, *Sectional Nationalism*, 72–85.

41. *NAR* 10 (Jan. 1820): 137–68. For Shaw's authorship, see Cushing, *Index to the "North*

American Review." For a profile of Shaw, see Malone and Johnson, *Dictionary of American Biography*, 17:42–43.

42. *Boston Daily Advertiser*, 20, 23, 26 Nov., 1, 9, 28 Dec. 1819, 3 Mar. 1820.

43. Ibid., 2 Mar. 1820. For evidence of Everett's authorship of this essay, see W. Story, *Life and Letters of Joseph Story*, 1:367.

44. *NAR* 11 (July 1820): 16–17, 14 (Jan. 1822): 5. See also 12 (Apr. 1821): 438.

45. Everett to Cushing, 27 Oct. 1820, 18 June 1823, Caleb Cushing Papers, LC.

46. Eaton, *Anglo-American Paper War*; Cairns, *British Criticisms*, 7–57; Mott, *History of American Magazines*, 1:183–211; Lease, *Anglo-American Encounters*, xi–12; N. Mason, "*Blackwood's Magazine*"; Reid, *Edward Everett*, 22–24; *Blackwood's Edinburgh Magazine* 4 (Feb. 1819): 546–63, 4 (Mar. 1819): 641–49, 6 (Feb. 1820): 554–61, 16 (Nov. 1824): 570–71, 18 (Sept. 1825): 332–34; *Edinburgh Review* 33 (Jan. 1820): 69–80, 34 (Aug. 1820): 161.

47. Haynes, *Unfinished Revolution*, esp. 12–22, 27–43, 49–76. See also Eaton, *Anglo-American Paper War*; and Howe, *Unitarian Conscience*, 183–85.

48. *Quarterly Review* 26 (Oct. 1821): 77–81, 27 (Apr. 1822), 83–85, 28 (Oct. 1822): 173–74; *Edinburgh Review* 33 (Jan. 1820): 80, 33 (May 1820): 395–431, 40 (July 1824): 427–42; *Blackwood's Edinburgh Magazine* 9 (Aug. 1821): 516–31, 16 (July 1824): 91–97, 16 (Dec. 1824): 617–52, 18 (Sept. 1825): 355–69. For more on slavery in the Paper War, see M. Mason, "Battle of the Slaveholding Liberators."

49. *NAR* 10 (Apr. 1820): 334–71.

50. See ibid., 13 (July 1821): 161–65, where he revealed his skepticism of the proslavery men's standing charge that Spanish cleric Las Casas was the original author of the African slave trade because of his desire to protect Amerindians.

51. Ibid., 11 (July 1820): 68–103.

52. Ibid., 13 (July 1821): 20–47.

53. Ibid., 17 (July 1823): 98–99.

54. Ibid., 14 (Jan. 1822): 18–19.

55. E. Everett, *Orations and Speeches*, vol. 1, viii–xi. For this spirit in his orations from these years, see ibid., 9–44.

56. *Quarterly Review* 29 (July 1823): 338–70; *Westminster Review* 1 (Jan. 1824): 101–20.

57. Samuel Gilman to Everett, 27 Apr. 1820, BPL; Robert Y. Hayne to Everett, 13, 14 Apr., 5, 30 May 1824, EP.

58. *NAR* 19 (July 1824): 92–125.

59. *Blackwood's Edinburgh Magazine* 16 (Oct. 1824): 474–82.

60. Faux, *Memorable Days*, 384–85. I could find no such passages on America, England, or slavery in manuscript versions of this sermon.

61. *Westminster Review* 29 (July 1823): 353–54. The same magazine attacked later Everett orations on the same grounds; see 5 (Jan. 1826): 173–201.

62. O'Connor, *Lords of the Loom*, 16–41; A. Schlesinger, *Veritas*, 73–75; Field, "Birth of Secular High Culture," 588.

63. Wiltse, *Papers of Daniel Webster*, 1:313–14; *Niles' Weekly Register* 23 (21 Sept. 1822): 39–40; Belohlavek, *Broken Glass*, 13–14, 51–52.

64. Hopkins et al., *Papers of Henry Clay*, 3:737–38, 792–93, 827.

65. *Aurora*, 14 Apr., 11 May 1824.

66. Tyack, *George Ticknor*, 18–23; Foletta, *Coming to Terms*, 45–100, 184–92, 207–8; O'Connor, *Athens of America*, 39–125.

67. E. Everett, *Orations and Speeches*, vol. 1, 32–39.

68. Forgie, *Patricide in the House Divided*; Purcell, *Sealed with Blood*, 171–209; Haynes, *Unfinished Revolution*, 109–12; Burstein, *America's Jubilee*, 8–83.

69. See, e.g., Frothingham, *Edward Everett*, 81–86; *Boston Patriot*, 23 Sept. 1824; *Daily National Intelligencer*, 20 Sept. 1824; *Daily National Journal*, 20 Sept., 21 Oct. 1824; *Raleigh Register*, 2, 5 Nov. 1824; *Illinois Gazette*, 18 Dec. 1824; Thomas Jefferson to Everett, 15 Oct. 1824, Thomas Jefferson Papers, LC, accessed online at http://memory.loc.gov.

70. Bunker Hill Monument Association, *Circular*. The monument was completed and dedicated in 1843. For the drive for public funds, see Everett to Nathan Appleton, 22 Feb. 1825, Appleton Family Papers, MHS. For more on the history and lofty motives of this organization, see G. Warren, *History of the Bunker Hill Monument Association*; and Purcell, *Sealed with Blood*, 171–209.

71. Martis, *Historical Atlas*, 68; Formisano, *Transformation of Political Culture*, 150–68.

72. Everett to Jefferson, 6 July 1825, Thomas Jefferson Papers, http://memory.loc.gov.

73. *American Statesman and City Register*, July 1824–Jan. 1825, esp. 25, 30 Sept. 1824, 9, 20 Nov. 1824, 25 Jan. 1825; Darling, *Political Changes in Massachusetts*, 42–46, 59–60.

74. *Boston Patriot and Daily Mercantile Advertiser*, Sept.–Nov. 1824, esp. 29 Oct. 1824.

75. Frothingham, *Edward Everett*, 89, is the source for the final total, given that the newspapers bothered only to report interim results and the final election of Everett rather than the final tally; see *American Statesman and City Register*, 4, 6, 9 Nov. 1824; and *Boston Patriot and Daily Mercantile Advertiser*, 4 Nov. 1824.

76. W. Taylor, *Cavalier and Yankee*, 13–14, 19–20, 29–30.

Chapter 2

1. For the speech, see E. Everett, *Orations and Speeches*, vol. 1, 45–72. For reactions then and since, see Wiltse et al., *Papers of Daniel Webster*, 2:32–33; Seelye, *Memory's Nation*, 60–100; and Abrams, *The Pilgrims and Pocahontas*, 105–7. Such was the reputation of this oration that one publisher translated it into Spanish; see diary, 11 Apr., 24 Sept. 1827, EP.

2. Poore, *Perley's Reminiscences*, 1:80 (first quotation); *American Statesman and City Register*, 9 Mar. 1826 (second quotation).

3. Finkelman and Kennon, *Congress and the Emergence of Sectionalism*, 91; [Holland], *Refutation of the Calumnies*, 13. For Vesey's plot and King's implication therein, see Egerton, *He Shall Go Out Free*, esp. 130–31.

4. Ames, *State Documents*, 203–9, quotations on 204, 208; see also Hamer, "Great Britain."

5. Ames, *State Documents*, 206.

6. Seabrook, *Concise View of the Critical Situation*, quotation on 16; [Turnbull], *Crisis*, quotations on 14, 115–16, 126, 131.

7. C. Adams, *Memoirs of John Quincy Adams*, 5:206, 6:313, 500, 7:53–57, 98. For a fuller discussion, see M. Mason, "John Quincy Adams"; and Mason and Waldstreicher, *John Quincy Adams*, esp. ch. 4.

8. Benton, *Thirty Years' View*, 1:65–69 (quotation on 65); Charles Hammond to Henry Clay, 7 Apr. 1826, in Hopkins, *Papers of Henry Clay*, 5:220 (second quotation); *Register of Debates*, 19th Cong., 1st Sess., 2180 (Buchanan quotations). For especially good examples of how Southerners injected slavery into this debate in the Senate, see ibid., 112–32, 207–8, 284–86, 289–91, 329–32. For the record of the meat of this debate in the House between February and April 1826, see ibid., 1208–1302, 2009–98, 2135–2514. For more on this conference, its

context, and the opposition to it, see Cayton, "Debate over the Panama Congress"; Lewis, *American Union*, 190–214; and Forbes, *Missouri Compromise*, 203–9.

9. Diary, 25 Nov. 1825, EP; Edward Everett to "My dear Sir," 8 Feb. 1826, EP-Exeter; *Massachusetts Journal*, which began in Jan. 1826.

10. C. Adams, *Memoirs of John Quincy Adams*, 7:94–95, 102–3; *Register of Debates*, 19th Cong., 1st Sess., 1246–48, 2427–33.

11. Burstein, *America's Jubilee*, 159–80, quotation on 163; *New York National Advertiser* reprinted in *American Statesman and City Register*, 11 Mar. 1826. Thomas Hart Benton sponsored a similar amendment in the Senate and likewise characterized the 1824 election as frustrating the popular will. Despite thinking that the popular voice triumphed in 1828, he was still proposing this amendment as late as 1844; see *Thirty Years' View*, 1:37–41, 46–50, 78–80, 111–12, 121–22, 2:626–29. Burstein's is the best secondary discussion of this debate, although it does overlook the essence of Everett's retort to McDuffie and thus how slavery's linkages made the controversy about much more than, and much more complicated than, Jacksonians as democrats.

12. Story, *Life and Letters of Joseph Story*, 1:493; Everett to Sally Hale, 3 Feb. (quotation), 10 Mar. 1826, Charlotte Everett to Sally Hale, 18 Mar. 1826, Everett-Hopkins Papers, MHS; Everett to Alexander Everett, 25 Mar. 1826, EP (quotations); Remini, *The House*, 112–13.

13. *Register of Debates*, 19th Cong., 1st Sess., 1570–97, quotations on 1571, 1572, 1573, 1596. For a manuscript version of the controversial part of the speech, see Edward Everett, Manuscript: "Speech in Congress on Slavery and the 3/5 Rule"; Washington, 9 Mar. 1826, BPL. Given that Churchill Cambreleng and other critics charged Everett with changing his speech for publication, it is worth noting that this manuscript matches the published speech. There is no way of telling, however, whether this scrap—which is after all not the whole speech but just the passage dealing with slavery and slave insurrection—was the version from which Everett spoke or another version prepared for publication.

14. *Register of Debates*, 19th Cong., 1st Sess., 1578–79.

15. Howe, *What Hath God Wrought*, 208.

16. John Forsyth to George M. Dallas, 6 Apr. 1818, George Mifflin Dallas Collection, Historical Society of Pennsylvania, Philadelphia; John Forsyth to Charles Jared Ingersoll, 25 Nov. 1827, Charles Jared Ingersoll Collection, Historical Society of Pennsylvania (quotation); *Register of Debates*, 19th Cong., 1st Sess., 1174, 1246–48, 1252–53. Everett identified Forsyth only in private as the author of the "immoral and irreligious" phrase; see Everett to Thaddeus Spalding, 29 Nov. 1828, EP. I have been unable to locate the offending remark or publication from Forsyth; neither his speeches in the weeks before Everett's speech as recorded in the *Register of Debates* nor secondary sources like Cason, "Public Career," or Duckett, *John Forsyth*, offer any help on this point.

17. *Register of Debates*, 19th Cong., 1st Sess., 1579.

18. *Boston Patriot and Daily Mercantile Advertiser*, 4 Mar., 16 June, 7 July 1826. For a book-length exposition of just how mainstream Everett's fear of Haiti-style race war was, see A. White, *Encountering Revolution*.

19. *Register of Debates*, 19th Cong., 1st Sess., 1579–80, 1589.

20. Diary, 20 Dec. 1829, EP; *North American Review* 28 (Jan. 1829): 150–65. Everett offered encouraging words to Cushing on this article; see Everett to Cushing, 27 Oct., 1 Nov. 1828, Caleb Cushing Papers, LC.

21. A. Everett, *New Ideas on Population*, quotations on v, 93.

22. Diary, vol. 139, p. 166, EP. This note also referred to a passage in Adam Smith's *Wealth*

of Nations and, even more mysteriously, to "L'd Chancellors" (presumably a speech by a British lord chancellor).

23. Jackson, *Collected Works of Samuel Taylor Coleridge*, 1:311–313; Erdman, *Collected Works of Samuel Taylor Coleridge*, 1:228–32; Keane, *Coleridge's Submerged Politics*, 9, 45–86.

24. Canning, *Speech . . . May 16, 1823*, quotations on 7, 8, 11, 12; Canning, *Speech . . . 16th Day of March, 1824*, quotations on 14, 22, 31, 42. Thanks to Nicholas Mason and Seymour Drescher for helping me identify these speeches.

25. Sheidley, *Sectional Nationalism*, 24–26, 107–8, quotations on 25.

26. *Register of Debates*, 19th Cong., 1st Sess., 1625–28, 1640–42, 1651–52, 1709–11, 1721–22, 1743, 1863–64, 1883, 1933.

27. Ibid., 1914–30, quotations on 1918; see also 1653–71, 1848–49.

28. Ibid., 1828–29 (Whipple), 2180 (Buchanan).

29. Ibid., 2435–37.

30. Ibid., 2442–43.

31. *New-Hampshire Statesman and Concord Register*, 1 Apr. 1826. It even attracted the attention of a Liverpool, England, editor; see *United States Telegraph*, 26 June 1826.

32. *Carolina Observer*, 5 Apr. 1826; *Lexington (Ky.) Reporter* quoted in *Boston Patriot*, 3 May 1826. See also *Charleston Courier* quoted in *Boston Patriot*, 15 Aug. 1826; *Pensacola Gazette and West Florida Advertiser*, 8 Apr. 1826; *Augusta Chronicle*, 29 Apr. 1826; and *Norfolk (Va.) Beacon* quoted in *Daily National Intelligencer*, 1 Nov. 1834.

33. *American Statesman and City Register*, 1 June 1826. For other attacks on Everett and slavery in this sheet, see 2 June, 11 July, 5 Sept., 26 Oct. 1826.

34. *Eastern Argus*, 21 Apr. 1826.

35. *Boston Patriot*, 15 Mar., 10 Apr., 9 Sept., 8 July 1826. See also 11, 12, 25 July 1826.

36. *Gazette of Maine*, 28 Mar., 4, 26 Apr. 1826; *Vermont Watchman and State Gazette*, 11, 18 Apr. 1826.

37. Bacon, *Anti-slavery before Garrison*, 27–31.

38. *Genius of Universal Emancipation*, 25 Mar., 1, 15, 22 Apr. 1826. See also 8, 29 Apr., 6, 20 May 1826.

39. Thomas Jefferson to Everett, 8 Apr. 1826, EP (also at http://memory.loc.gov). For especially damning recent illustrations of how far Jefferson had gone in accommodating slavery, see Nash and Hodges, *Friends of Liberty*.

40. Lafayette to Everett, 23 July 1826, EP.

41. Everett to Lafayette, 6 Dec. 1826, EP.

42. Everett to Jefferson, 16 Apr. 1826, EP (also at http://memory.loc.gov).

43. Everett to Gales and Seaton, 5 Aug. 1826; Everett to Professor Williston, 11 Sept. 1827; Everett to Alexander Everett, 23 Apr. 1826, EP.

44. Charlotte Everett to Sally Hale, 18, 25 Mar., 5, 21 Apr. 1826, Everett to Sally Hale, 10 Mar. 1826, Everett-Hopkins Papers, MHS.

45. Richard Rush to Everett, 15 Apr. 1826 (first quotation), Henry Clay to Everett, 9 Mar. 1826 (second quotation), Caleb Cushing to Everett, 15 Mar. 1826, Joseph Story to Everett, 21 Mar. 1826, P. O. Thacher to Everett, 27 Mar. 1826, John Marshall to Everett, 3 Apr. 1826, James Madison to Everett, 9 Apr. 1826, David Sears to Everett, 14 Apr. 1826, all in EP. See also Joseph Story to J. Evelyn Denison, 15 Mar. 1826, in Story, *Life and Letters of Joseph Story*, 1:495.

46. Peter C. Brooks to Everett, 1 Apr. 1826, Lewis Cass to Everett, 29 Apr. 1826, Everett to Alexander Everett, 25 Mar. 1826, Grenville Mellen to Everett, 25 Apr. 1826, all in EP; Everett to Cushing, 21 Mar. 1826, Caleb Cushing Papers. For further evidence that Adams approved

his course, see Edward Everett to Lemuel Shattuck, 8 Apr. 1826, Huntington Library, Shattuck Papers, HM8325 (from the research of Nic Wood—my thanks to him).

47. Everett to Sally Hale, 7 Apr. 1826, Everett-Hopkins Papers, MHS. For an echo in Everett's newspaper of this suspicious attitude toward slavery as a mere political tool in campaigns, see *Massachusetts Journal*, 30 Sept. 1826.

48. Everett to Gales and Seaton, 5 Aug. 1826, EP; Everett to Cushing, 31 Aug. 1826, Caleb Cushing Papers.

49. Webster to John C. Wright, 12 Oct. 1826, in Wiltse et al., *Papers of Daniel Webster*, 2:134–35. Webster seems to have supported Everett's jab at the three-fifths clause but not his passage on slavery itself; see ibid., 135.

50. *American Traveller*, 24 Mar. 1826.

51. *Massachusetts Journal*, 17 Oct. 1826; *Boston Patriot*, 14, 18 Oct. 1826.

52. Diary, 7 Nov. 1826, Everett to John Keyes, 7 Nov. 1826, EP; *Yeoman's Gazette*, 18, 25 Mar., 28 Oct., 4, 11 Nov. 1826. For his growing confidence, see Everett to Dr. Watkins, 5 Sept. 1826, EP; Everett to Cushing, 6 Oct. 1826, Caleb Cushing Papers. For his sense of vindication, see diary, 5, 11–12 Oct. 1826, EP; Everett to J. E. Sprague, 13 Nov. 1826, Everett to George Bancroft, 1 Dec. 1826, Everett to Alexander Everett, 9 Dec. 1826, EP.

53. *Register of Debates*, 19th Cong., 1st Sess., 2004–5, 2659.

54. Ibid., 20th Cong., 1st Sess., 964.

55. *American Statesman and City Register*, 26 May 1827. Everett was moderately interested in the Senate seat, and this criticism attracted his attention; see Diary, 23 May 1827, EP.

56. *Lowell Journal*, 7 Nov. 1828. By contrast, the leading Adamsite paper in Boston was coolly confident of Everett's reelection and had nothing to say on this matter; see *Boston Patriot and Daily Mercantile Advertiser*, 31 Oct., 1 Nov. 1828.

57. Everett to Thaddeus Spalding, 29 Nov. 1828, EP.

58. *Register of Debates*, 20th Cong., 1st Sess., 899–925, 968–98, 1006–30, 1048–63, 1068–84, 1093–1122, 1458–86, quotation on 920; Fehrenbacher, *Slaveholding Republic*, 3–8; Akehurst, "Sectional Crises," 99–102, 107–11.

59. *Register of Debates*, 20th Cong., 1st Sess., 1048, 1057–60.

60. Ibid., 1061–63; *Louisiana Advertiser*, 2 Feb. 1828.

61. *Register of Debates*, 20th Cong., 1st Sess., 1071–79, 1458–68. Booker, *Members of Congress*, lists Miner's affiliation as Federalist.

62. *Register of Debates*, 20th Cong., 1st Sess., 1093–1112.

63. *Daily National Intelligencer*, 24 Jan. 1828.

64. *Daily National Journal*, 9 Jan. 1828; *Louisiana Advertiser*, 2 Feb. 1828. My analysis of the vote by party and section relies on Booker, *Members of Congress*.

65. *Rhode Island Republican*, 7 Feb. 1828. Thanks to Nic Wood for this source.

66. *Genius of Universal Emancipation*, 12, 26 Jan. (quotation), 9 Feb. (quotation) 1828. His final notice of the debate, on 30 Aug. 1828, recorded the names of both the Northern traitors and the Southern heroes who had broken sectional rank on the bill, hoping that the former would be punished at the polls for their "sins."

67. Everett to Samuel Whitcomb, 9, 18 Aug. 1828, EP.

68. *Massachusetts Journal*, 29 Jan. 1828.

69. *Boston Statesman*, 13, 27 Sept., 29 Nov. 1828; *Yeoman's Gazette*, 27 Sept., 1 Nov. 1828; *Massachusetts Journal*, 1 (quotation), 11, 13 Nov. 1828.

70. Donald J. Ratcliffe, "The Decline of Antislavery Politics, 1815–1840," in Hammond and Mason, *Contesting Slavery*, 267–90.

Chapter 3

1. For details on the transition between the National Republican and Whig Parties, see Holt, *Rise and Fall*, 1–32.

2. Ames, *State Documents*, 113–32; C. Adams, *Memoirs of John Quincy Adams*, vol. 7; *Register of Debates*, 20th Cong., 1st Sess., 1533–93. For recent narrative histories of Removal, see Langguth, *Driven West*; Magliocca, "Cherokee Removal," 879–914; and D. Smith, *American Betrayal*.

3. Howe, *What Hath God Wrought*, 342–57, quotations on 347; Hershberger, "Mobilizing Women," 15; Magliocca, "Cherokee Removal," 902–9.

4. *Boston Patriot and Daily Mercantile Advertiser*, 29 May 1830; *Boston Statesman*, 8, 22 May 1830; Van Buren quoted in Ashworth, *Slavery, Capitalism, and Politics*, vol. 1, 423; Finkelman and Kennon, *Congress and the Emergence of Sectionalism*, 7–8, 97–124; J. Andrew III, *From Revivals to Removal*; Mielke, *Moving Encounters*; Moniz, "Saving the Lives of Strangers."

5. Hershberger, "Mobilizing Women," 15–28, quotations on 25, 27; Portnoy, *Their Right to Speak*; Varon, *We Mean to Be Counted*; Greenberg, *Manifest Manhood*; Greenberg, *Wicked War*, 3–6, 58–59; Zaeske, *Signatures of Citizenship*, 1–28.

6. Diary, 18 Aug. 1825, 10 Feb.–3 Mar. 1827, EP; Everett to Joseph Bevan, 7 July 1825, Everett to Gales and Seaton, 4 Mar. 1827, Edward Everett Letters, New-York Historical Society; C. Adams, *Memoirs of John Quincy Adams*, 6:402, 7:223, 226–27.

7. *Register of Debates*, 19th Cong., 2nd Sess., 1035, 1534–41.

8. Ibid., 21st Cong., 1st Sess., 582, 1058–79; see also Evarts, *Speeches on . . . the Removal of the Indians*, 255–300. For his reflections elsewhere on the Indians in general, see E. Everett, *Orations and Speeches*, vol. 1, 217–18, 238–39, 539–40, 634–69; vol. 2, 70–71, 111, 145; and vol. 3, 234.

9. *Register of Debates*, 21st Cong., 1st Sess., 1061–62, 1079.

10. Timothy Walker to Everett, 10 Mar. 1832, BPL; *Daily National Journal*, 15 Feb. 1831; Langguth, *Driven West*, 171. For more lavish praise for Everett's work on this issue, see *Daily National Journal*, 9–11, 24 Mar. 1831; and *New Hampshire Statesman*, 12 Mar. 1831.

11. *Boston Patriot and Daily Mercantile Advertiser*, 21, 23 Mar. 1827; *Daily National Journal*, 25 (quotation), 26, 28, 30 June, 2, 5, 6, 8 July 1830; *Journal of the Proceedings of the National Republican Convention*, quotation on 23.

12. Timothy Flint to Everett, 28 Sept. 1830, BPL.

13. Benton, *Thirty Years' View*, 1:27–29 (quotation on 28), 58–64, 163–66, 285–86, 624–26, 689–94; *Gazette of Maine*, 6 Mar. 1827 (second quotation); Simms, *Slavery in America*, 52–56, quotations on 53; Mielke, *Moving Encounters*, 51–69.

14. Lumpkin, *Removal of the Cherokee Indians*, quotations on 1:47, 71, 99; *Register of Debates*, 21st Cong., 2nd Sess., 790–93, quotations on 792.

15. *Niles' Weekly Register* 29 (8 Oct. 1825): 83, 29 (12 Nov. 1825): 165.

16. Ibid., 38 (3 July 1830): 340 (quotation); *Register of Debates*, 21st Cong., 2nd Sess., 759–74.

17. *Register of Debates*, 22nd Cong., 1st Sess., 1706–9, 1726–32, 1748–52, 2498, quotations on 1748, 1749. Such tirades moved Edmund Pendleton of New York to complain that in this debate Everett "has been subjected to some criticisms, which are, in my judgment, extremely inapplicable" (ibid., 1746).

18. Ibid., 23rd Cong., 2nd Sess., 1445–56, quotation on 1450.

19. Everett to Gales and Seaton, 12 Dec. 1831, Edward Everett Papers, New York Public Library; Everett to S. G. Drake, 18 Jan. 1837, Edward Everett Papers, American Antiquarian Society, Worcester, Mass.; diary, 13, 15 June, 4 Aug., 28 Sept., 12 Oct. 1830, 11 Jan., 2 June 1832, 2, 15, 16 Feb., 9 Mar. 1834, 18 Jan. 1835, EP. For more on this behind-the-scenes coordination,

see J. Andrew III, *From Revivals to Removal*, chs. 8–9. For more evidence of the volume of information Everett gathered relative to the Indians, see Printed Material, 1830–1859, and Miscellaneous Papers, 1812–1865, reel 52A, EP.

20. Everett to John Sergeant, 18 Apr. 1831, Everett to Henry Clay, 21 May 1831, EP; William Ellery Channing to Everett, 25 July 1830, EP-Harvard.

21. *Register of Debates*, 21st Cong., 2nd Sess., 682–717, quotations on 686; *Daily National Journal*, 8 Feb. 1831.

22. *Register of Debates*, 22nd Cong., 1st Sess., 1676–82, 1706–9, 1726–33; 23rd Cong., 2nd Sess., 1009–10.

23. Diary, 24 May 1830, 31 Jan. (first quotation), 14 (second quotation), 28 Feb., 8 Mar. 1831, 7 July 1832, EP.

24. Everett to "My dear General," 14 Jan. 1831, Everett to "Dear General," 5 Mar. 1831, Everett to Charlotte Everett, 22 Jan., 14, 15, 19, 22, 27 Feb., 1, 2 Mar. 1831, EP. Thanks to Nic Wood for suggesting I develop this possible link between removal and slavery in Everett's psyche.

25. *Boston Patriot and Daily Mercantile Advertiser*, 4 June 1830; diary, 2 Nov. 1827, 19 Aug. 1832, 18 May, 5 July 1833, EP; Everett to Thaddeus Spaulding, 25 Feb. 1830 (first quotation), Charles Sumner and Samuel Osgood to Everett, 2 Apr. 1833, EP; E. Everett, *Orations and Speeches*, vol. 2, 75 (second quotation); *Boston Courier*, 6 Dec. 1830.

26. Logan, *Hour and the Woman*, quotation on 9; Harriet Martineau to Everett, 12 Mar. (quotation), 26 Aug., 25 Nov. 1835, 21 Mar. 1837, EP; diary, 22 Jan., 4, 6, 14 Feb., 22 Mar. 1835, EP; Logan, *Harriet Martineau*.

27. Everett to "My dear General," 14 Jan. 1831, EP.

28. Hershberger, "Mobilizing Women"; Zaeske, *Signatures of Citizenship*, 1–28; J. Andrew III, *From Revivals to Removal*, esp. 8; Guyatt, "'Outskirts of Our Happiness'"; Magliocca, "Cherokee Removal."

29. Portnoy, *Their Right to Speak*, quotations on 2.

30. Everett to Joseph Bevan, 7 July 1825, Edward Everett Letters, New-York Historical Society.

31. Diary, 23 Sept. 1825, 20 Jan. 1827, 19 Jan. 1831, 5, 8 Feb., 14 Apr. 1833, EP; *Annual Reports of the American Society*, 16th Annual Report, 43, and 18th Annual Report, 1; *Massachusetts Journal*, 2 Sept. 1826.

32. Thomas Hodgkin to Everett, 3 Mar. 1833, EP.

33. Diary, 15 Jan., 14 Feb. 1832, EP; Everett to Caleb Cushing, 27 Oct., 1 Nov. 1828, Caleb Cushing Papers, LC.

34. E. Everett, *Orations and Speeches*, vol. 1, 329–43; *Annual Reports of the American Society*, 15th Annual Report, xii–xxii. For an example of how widely reprinted his ideas of African civilization were, see *Observer and Telegraph*, 9 Aug. 1832.

35. Larkin and Sloat, *Place in My Chronicle*, 134 (quotation), 195.

36. Joseph Story to Everett, 31 May 1832, in Story, *Life and Letters of Joseph Story*, 2:94; *Annual Reports of the American Society*, 15th Annual Report, 43; Ames, *State Documents*, 209–13; printed circular to Massachusetts congressmen from Levi Lincoln, governor of Massachusetts, 16 Mar. 1831, EP.

37. Brooke, "Cultures of Nationalism," 18; Burin, *Slavery and the Peculiar Solution*, 3–4, 36, 48–49, 170–73.

38. Burin, *Slavery and the Peculiar Solution*. For an exploration of the popularity of colonization and its long-term impact on Abraham Lincoln especially as mediated by Clay's influence, see E. Foner, *Fiery Trial*, xvii, 17–22, 25, 51, 123–31, 133–34, 184–86, 204, 215, 221–26, 231–37, 244, 289.

39. See issues of the *Genius of Universal Emancipation* of this time period.

40. [Turnbull], *Crisis*, 37–38, 122–26; Ames, *State Documents*, 209–13.

41. Tomek, *Colonization and Its Discontents*, quotations on xv, xx.

42. Everett to Samuel Whitcomb, 18 Aug. 1828, EP.

43. Everett to ?, 9 Mar. 1828, speech at Faneuil Hall dinner to Webster, 5 June 1828, EP; *Boston Patriot and Daily Mercantile Advertiser*, 9 June 1828; *Indiana Journal*, 26 June 1828. For the sectionalist theme in Adamsite campaigning, see *Boston Patriot and Daily Mercantile Advertiser*, 21 Apr., 8, 14 May, 10, 14, 26 June, 3, 16, 19 July, 15, 22 Aug., 17 Oct. 1828.

44. John Quincy Adams to Everett, 11 Apr. 1827, Everett to B. F. Hunt, 12 Sept. 1827, EP.

45. Ames, *State Documents*, 133–89, quotation on 145; Freehling, *Prelude to Civil War*; Peter S. Onuf, "The Political Economy of Sectionalism: Tariff Controversies and Conflicting Conceptions of World Order," in Finkelman and Kennon, *Congress and the Emergence of Sectionalism*, 47–74.

46. Hartford, *Money, Morals, and Politics*, 32–90, quotations on 32, 51; John B. Davis to Henry Clay, 5 Apr. 1831, in Hopkins, ed., *Papers of Henry Clay*, 8:332; McCormick, *Second American Party System*, 42–49; Lakwete, *Inventing the Cotton Gin*, 97.

47. Everett to B. F. Hunt, 12 Sept. 1827, EP.

48. *Register of Debates*, 21st Cong., 1st Sess., 902–12, quotations on 906, 910, 912.

49. Ibid., 915.

50. Ibid., 22nd Cong., 1st Sess., 3737–38.

51. Ibid., 22nd Cong., 1st Sess., 3749–61, quotations on 3749, 3760.

52. C. Adams, *Memoirs of John Quincy Adams*, 8:444–48, quotations on 445, 446.

53. Diary, 16–17 Dec. 1832, 11 Feb. 1833, EP.

54. *Register of Debates*, 22nd Cong., 1st Sess., 3764–71.

55. Everett to James Madison, 11, 22 Apr., 7, 28 Sept. 1830, Madison to Everett, April 1830, 20, 28, 31 Aug., 10 Sept. 1830, EP. For the article, see *NAR* 31 (Oct. 1830): 462–546.

56. Madison to Everett, 7 Oct. 1830, 14 Nov. 1831, Everett to Madison, 23 Dec. 1831, EP. For this correspondence in context, see Brant, *James Madison*, 6:468–500; McCoy, *Last of the Fathers*, 119–70.

57. John Marshall to Everett, 30 Nov. 1830, EP; diary, 14, 15 Jan. 1833, EP; Benton, *Thirty Years' View*, 365–60; C. Adams, *Diary of Charles Francis Adams*, 3:337. Everett for some reason demurred, telling Calhoun that his brother had written the piece.

58. Remini, *Daniel Webster*, 210, 421; Bartlett, *Daniel Webster*, 106–7, 109, 145–46, 199, 206.

59. Everett to Caleb Cushing, 8 Dec. 1832, EP. For evidence that Webster was genuinely attached to Everett as well, see Webster to Cushing, 13 Aug. 1834, in Wiltse et al., *Papers of Daniel Webster*, 3:362.

60. Everett to Henry Wheaton, 17 Mar. 1821, Henry Wheaton Papers, Morgan Library, New York; Bartlett, *Daniel Webster*, 3–11, 293–95, quotations on 6, 295.

61. Webster to Joel R. Poinsett, 7 May 1833, in Wiltse et al., *Papers of Daniel Webster*, 3:248.

62. Peterson, *Great Triumvirate*, 178–80; C. Smith, *Daniel Webster*, 117–18; Sheidley, *Sectional Nationalism*, 160–68. Over two decades later, Everett remembered this speech and his interactions with Webster surrounding it in great detail and continuing awe; see Everett to Charles W. March, 3 Jan. 1850, EP.

63. *Globe*, 2 Nov. 1832; Everett to Josiah S. Johnston, 28 Aug. 1831, Josiah Stoddard Johnston Papers, Historical Society of Pennsylvania, Philadelphia; *Journal of the Proceedings of the National Republican Convention*, 27.

64. *Boston Daily Advertiser and Patriot*, 14 Nov. 1832; Everett to "My dear Sir," 25 Dec. 1832,

Edward Everett Letters, 1816–1863, MHS; Everett to Alexander Everett, 11 Dec. 1832, Everett to Andrew Jackson, 20 May 1833, EP; diary, 1–5, 10–11, 21–26 June, 15 July 1833, EP; *Boston Courier*, 1 July 1833; *Maryland Gazette*, 11 July 1833; *Virginia Free Press*, 11 July 1833. See also Cole, *Presidency of Andrew Jackson*, 183–86; and Carroll, *Origins of the Whig Party*, 89–106.

65. Everett to Johnston, 23 Dec. 1832, Josiah Stoddard Johnston Papers, Historical Society of Pennsylvania.

66. C. Adams, *Memoirs of John Quincy Adams*, 8:79–80, 82, 86, 205–6, 400, 428–48, 487, 495, 517, 533, 535, 9:11–40, 103–8; Hopkins, ed., *Papers of Henry Clay*, 6:400–401, 506–7, 536–37, 579–80, 927, 1241–42, 8:197, 202, 225–26, 254, 360–61, 374, 387–89, 592–94, 659–60; Whig Party (New Hampshire) Correspondence, Houghton Library, Harvard University, Cambridge, Mass.; Everett to Peter Force, 8 Mar. 1829, Edward Everett Papers, LC; Everett to Gales and Seaton, 4 Mar. 1827, Edward Everett Letters, New-York Historical Society; Everett to Gales and Seaton, 21 Mar., 18 Apr., 23 May, 5 Aug., 25 Dec. 1826, 7 Mar. 1827, 12 Feb., 3 Mar. 1828, Edward Everett to "My dear Sir," 17 Dec. 1832, Edward Everett Letters, 1816–1863, MHS; Everett to Samuel Whitcomb, 19 July 1828, EP; *Daily National Journal*, 23 Feb. 1828; diary, 5 Dec. 1831, EP; *Register of Debates*, 23rd Cong., 1st Sess., 2136.

67. Henry Dwight Sedgwick to Everett, 12 Nov. 1830, EP-Harvard; *Scioto Gazette*, 26 July 1827; *Columbia Telescope*, 29 June, 10 Aug. 1827; *Daily National Intelligencer*, 16 July 1828; diary, 23 Aug. 1827, EP.

68. *Register of Debates*, 22nd Cong., 2nd Sess., 1735–38, 1749–50.

69. Ibid., 19th Cong., 1st Sess., 1582; Everett to Samuel Whitcomb, 19 July 1828, diary, 13 July 1832, EP.

70. Diary, 13 July 1832, Everett to George Bancroft, 20 Nov. 1829, Everett to J. E. Sprague, 30 Nov. 1829, EP; E. Everett, *Orations and Speeches*, vol. 2, 22; Meriwether et al., *Papers of John C. Calhoun*, 11:594, 12:226, 244; Everett to Martin Van Buren, 18 Aug. 1829, Martin Van Buren Papers, MHS. For a book-length analysis of the significance of cross-party and cross-sectional friendships in Washington politics, see Shelden, *Washington Brotherhood*.

71. Edward Everett to Thomas W. White, 7 Sept. 1834, BPL; Samuel Gilman to Everett, 16 Jan. 1832, EP-Harvard; diary, 18 Sept. 1831, 20 Jan., 17 Mar. 1832, EP.

72. Diary, April–June 1829, EP; E. Everett, *Orations and Speeches*, vol. 1, 195, 199–201. See also Frothingham, *Edward Everett*, 116–19, for a nice account of this trip.

73. *Daily National Journal*, 18 June, 2 July 1829; *Daily National Intelligencer*, 12 June 1829; *Niles' Weekly Register* 36 (20 June 1829): 268, 37 (29 Aug. 1829): 14–16.

74. "Memoir of Edward Everett," 104; George Washington Owen to Everett, 15 Jan. 1830, BPL; *Daily National Intelligencer*, 2 July 1829. For other examples of the coverage, see *Daily National Intelligencer*, 12, 15 June 1829; *Daily National Journal*, 12, 18 June 1829; *Scioto Gazette*, 24 June, 8 July 1829; *Indiana Journal*, 2, 16 July 1829; *Carolina Observer*, 25 June 1829; *Columbia Telescope and South-Carolina State Journal*, 26 June, 10 July 1829; *Raleigh Register, and North-Carolina State Gazette*, 9 July 1829; *New-Hampshire Statesman and Concord Register*, 11 July 1829; *Louisville Public Advertiser*, 8, 15 July 1829; and *Macon Telegraph*, 18 July 1829.

75. Remini, *The House*, 27, 104, 154; Zagarri, "Family Factor," esp. 307; Everett to Lewis Cass, 8 Oct. 1827, Everett to Alexander Everett, 26 Nov. 1827, Everett to J. G. Palfrey, 11 Jan. 1829, Everett to Alexander Everett, 8 Feb. 1834, diary, 2 Oct. 1833, EP.

76. Garraty and Carnes, *American National Biography*, 12:157–59; Everett to William S. Johnston, 14 Sept. 1829, diary, 26 Jan. 1830, 4 May, 13 Dec. 1832, 3 Jan., 12 June 1833, EP; box 6, p. 3, EP-Harvard; Everett to Josiah Johnston, 4, 19 Sept. 1829, Everett to Eliza Johnston, 7

Aug. 1831, Josiah Stoddard Johnston Papers, Historical Society of Pennsylvania; C. Adams, *Memoirs of John Quincy Adams*, 6:466–67.

77. Diary, April–June (esp. 4 May) 1829, Everett to Alexander Everett, 18 Dec. 1832, EP. Everett's letter of 9 December has not survived, although he did note — in German — in his diary that day that he had written Brooks.

78. Peter C. Brooks to Everett, 17 Dec. 1832, EP.

79. Everett to Johnston, 23 Dec. 1832, Josiah Stoddard Johnston Papers, Historical Society of Pennsylvania; diary, vol. 139, p. 28, EP.

80. Peter C. Brooks to Everett, 9 Apr. 1833, 15 Feb., 4 May 1836, EP; C. Adams, *Diary of Charles Francis Adams*, 3:95, 8:209.

81. *American Traveller*, 4 Mar. 1826; Everett to John Keyes, 7 Nov. 1826, diary, 6 Oct. 1826, 22, 23 Feb., 4 July, 29 Oct. 1827, 17 June 1831, 17, 18 Feb., 28 Apr. 1832, EP; Bigelow, *History of the Cemetery of Mount Auburn*, 5–10, 39–47, 59–61, 133–43, quotation on 142; Edward Everett to Lemuel Blake, 20 June 1826, BPL. For the Washington Monument Association's history, see the other documents bound with this last, under call #Ms. QAm. 1100 at the BPL.

82. Bingham, *Columbian Orator*, 57–58, 102–18, 237–39, 269–72, 295–99. There are times it is difficult to see Everett's role in producing these selections — to my knowledge, for instance, he was not a playwright, but one of the selections I have cited is a play on Americans in Barbary slavery — but Bingham attributed these to "Everett" without further elaboration. Everett clearly contributed these pieces to Bingham's collection, but it is far from certain he was the author of most or all of them.

83. Diary, 1, 2 Aug. 1832, EP; *NAR* 21 (Oct. 1825): 467, 22 (Apr. 1826): 373–400 (quotation on 374); *Register of Debates*, 22nd Cong., 1st Sess., 2180.

84. *United States Telegraph*, 18 Feb. 1832; *Register of Debates*, 22nd Cong., 1st Sess., 1782–1820 (quotation on 1787); *Boston Daily Advertiser and Patriot*, 18, 20, 24, 25 Feb. 1832.

85. E. Everett, *Orations and Speeches*, vol. 1, 137, 148, 196, 202, 205, 358–62, 471, 521–22, 555, 564–96, quotations on 358, 359, 361, 573.

86. Ibid., 15, 39, 45–100, 194, 203, 206, 210, 350–65, 526–60; E. Everett, *Orations and Speeches*, vol. 2, 2, 111–12, 123, 133–34, 137, 146. Everett's speeches in this vein typify the phenomenon nicely captured in the title of Sheidley's book *Sectional Nationalism*.

87. E. Everett, *Orations and Speeches*, vol. 1, 53, 100, 128–29, 145–46, 172, 194–206, 380, 609.

88. E. Everett, *Orations and Speeches*, vol. 2, 47–66, 91–98, quotations on 52, 53, 66. For scholarly works shedding light on such reading of slaves out of the New England and American Revolutionary narratives, see Melish, *Disowning Slavery*; and Furstenberg, "Beyond Slavery and Freedom."

89. C. Adams, *Memoirs of John Quincy Adams*, 7:138; *Southern Literary Messenger*, 1 (Feb. 1835): 307–12, 2 (Dec. 1835): 66; John Marshall to Everett, 3 Aug. 1828, Martin Van Buren to Everett, 9 Sept. 1828, Everett to John Keyes, 7 Nov. 1826, EP; Burstein, *America's Jubilee*, 269–72; *American Statesman*, 26 Sept. 1826. For more praise, grudging and otherwise, of his eulogies of Adams, Jefferson, and Lafayette, see *Daily National Journal*, 28 July, 20 Sept., 4 Oct. 1826; *Constitutional Whig*, 1 Sept. 1826; *Raleigh Register, and North-Carolina Gazette*, 1, 8 Sept. 1826, 11 Nov. 1834; *New-York Spectator*, 2 Oct. 1826; and *Daily National Intelligencer*, 15, 16 Sept., 21 Nov. 1834.

90. Stewart, *Abolitionist Politics*, 35; Waldstreicher, "Nationalization and Racialization," 52–56; Ratcliffe, "Decline of Antislavery Politics," in Hammond and Mason, *Contesting Slavery*, 267–90.

91. Everett to Samuel E. Sewell, 11 Feb. 1835, EP.

92. *Register of Debates*, 23rd Cong., 2nd Sess., 1131–41.

93. Everett to Rev. Timothy Flint, 20 Oct. 1830, EP.

Chapter 4

1. Diary, 31 Aug., 27–28 Sept. 1833, 28 July, 14, 19–21 Aug., 8–9 Sept., 1, 10, 12 Oct., 19 Dec. 1834, EP; Everett to Benjamin Thompson, 15 Aug. 1834, Everett to N. Hardy, 15 Aug. 1834, Joseph Story to Everett, 23 Oct. 1834, Peter C. Brooks to Everett, 25 June 1834, EP.

2. Everett to "Dear Sir," 25 June 1835, Simon Gratz Collection, Historical Society of Pennsylvania, Philadelphia. For a very similar statement, see Everett to Cushing, 1 Feb. 1835, Caleb Cushing Papers, LC.

3. Blewett, *Constant Turmoil*, 18–101; Formisano, *Transformation of Political Culture*, 222–67; Darling, *Political Changes in Massachusetts*, 173–250; Kallenbach and Kallenbach, *American State Governors*, 266–67.

4. Everett to C. P. Huntington, 29 Oct. 1835, EP.

5. Everett to Christopher A. Hack, 28 May 1835, EP. For at least one voter who found the reminder of Everett's knapsack speech compelling, see R. Emerson, *Journals*, 3:517.

6. Goodman, *Towards a Christian Republic*; Brooke, *Heart of the Commonwealth*, 269–388; Neem, *Creating a Nation of Joiners*, 77–180; McCormick, *Second American Party System*, 42–49.

7. Darling, *Political Changes in Massachusetts*, 85–129; Formisano, *Transformation of Political Culture*, 197–221, 253–56; *Niles' Weekly Register* 44 (3 Aug. 1833): 382; *New-York Spectator*, 18 July 1833; *United States Telegraph*, 20 July 1833; *Daily National Intelligencer*, 24 July 1833; *Daily Atlas*, 6, 13 Oct. 1834, 28 Feb., 12 Mar. 1835; Dalzell, *Enterprising Elite*, 164–224; Everett to Nathan Sargent, 26 Oct. 1835, Edward Everett Papers, LC; Bartlett, *Daniel Webster*, 148; Edward Everett to Samuel H. Jenks, 26 July 1833, BPL (quotation); Goodman, *Towards a Christian Republic*, 147–92; diary, 4 Mar. 1835, EP; George Bliss to Everett, March 1835, George Bliss Papers, MHS; Kallenbach and Kallenbach, *American State Governors*, 275–77. Adams lost not only the governorship but also the Senate seat he contested with Davis in 1835, and the relative outcomes for Adams and Everett of these maneuverings did not endear Everett to the Adams family; see C. Adams, *Memoirs of John Quincy Adams*, 9:242–43; C. Adams, *Diary of Charles Francis Adams*, 6:79; and Richards, *Life and Times*, 52–54.

8. Diary, 10 Nov. 1835, 21 Aug. 1836, EP; C. Adams, *Diary of Charles Francis Adams*, 6:262; *Bridgewater Republican and Old Colony Press*, 20 Nov. 1835; Goodman, *Towards a Christian Republic*, 147–92; *Vermont Patriot*, 19 Sept. 1836; *Boston Daily Advertiser*, 26 Sept., 1, 4, 7, 11, 18, 22 Oct. 1836.

9. Wiltse et al., *Papers of Daniel Webster*, 4:12, 35–39, 42–50, 56–57, 63, 68–72, 78–79, 85–95, 154; Everett to Caleb Cushing, 4 Jan. 1836, Caleb Cushing Papers, LC; Edward Everett to ———, 4 Jan. 1836, Edward Everett Letters II, MHS (quotation).

10. Diary, 30 May 1835 (quotation), 23, 29, 31 Oct., 17–21 Dec. 1838, 26 Jan., 18 July (quotation), 13 Aug. 1839, EP.

11. Ibid., 20 Feb. 1836; broadside, Commonwealth of Massachusetts, by His Excellency Edward Everett, governor of the Commonwealth of Massachusetts, 2 Mar. 1837, EP-Exeter; E. Everett, *Address of His Excellency . . . 1837*; *Daily National Intelligencer*, 17 June 1837; Hale, *Memories*, 2:11–12.

12. Diary, 4 Apr. 1836, EP; E. Everett, "Edward Everett's College Life," 195, 199; E. Everett,

Orations and Speeches, vol. 2, 142–53, 288–324, 615 (quotation); C. Adams, *Diary of Charles Francis Adams*, 6:344.

13. E. Everett, *Address of His Excellency . . . 1836*, quotations on 9, 11, 20; E. Everett, *Address of His Excellency . . . 1837*, quotations on 16, 6, 7, 18.

14. *Resolves of the General Court*, 621–45; E. Everett, *Address of His Excellency . . . 1839*. For more on Everett's impact on education in Massachusetts, see Yanikoski, "Edward Everett and the Advancement of Higher Education." For a sample of the national attention Everett's sayings and deeds on this subject attracted, see *Milwaukee Sentinel*, 9 Oct. 1838; and *Weekly Raleigh Register*, 27 Apr. 1839.

15. Edward Everett to Epes Sargent, 24 Feb. 1835, BPL; Edgar Allan Poe to Everett, 7 June 1836, Everett to T. W. White, 20 Mar., 4 Apr. 1838, Everett to Corresponding Secretary of the Georgia Historical Society, 23 July 1839, EP; diary, 5 June 1837, 8–9 Aug. 1839, EP.

16. Young, *Shoemaker and the Tea Party*, 79–194.

17. E. Everett, *Orations and Speeches*, vol. 2, 157–59, 205, 313–14, 325–34, quotations on 326, 329, 332; *Boston Daily Advertiser*, 26 Nov. 1835.

18. E. Everett, *Orations and Speeches*, vol. 2, 268–72.

19. Diary, 8 June 1835, 26–28 Feb. 1836, 11 May 1838, EP; Everett to Madison, 9 June 1835, Everett to Alexander Everett, 9 Apr. 1838, Everett to George Washington Parke Custis, 9 July 1838 and 17 June 1839, Everett to Joseph Story, 13 Sept. 1838, Everett to George Washington Lafayette, 15 Jan. 1839, EP; Everett to W. H. Gardiner, 17, 20 June 1839, EP-Harvard. For Everett's Washington-related reviews in this period, see *NAR* 47 (Oct. 1838): 318–81, and 51 (July 1840): 69–91. The play had been staged in Philadelphia beginning 4 July 1827 and then in Baltimore and Washington. See [Custis], *Indian Prophecy*; and Quinn, *Representative American Plays*, 167–68.

20. *Boston Daily Advertiser*, 7, 26 Sept., 6 Oct., 2 Nov. 1836; C. Adams, *Memoirs of John Quincy Adams*, 9:305; *Southern Literary Messenger* 4 (Jan. 1838): 61–64, 4 (July 1838): 426–30; *NAR* 44 (Jan. 1837): 138–53; *New-York Spectator*, 10 Aug. 1835; *Scioto Gazette*, 7 Oct. 1835; *Daily National Intelligencer*, 3 Sept. 1838; *New Hampshire Statesman*, 13 July 1839; *Vermont Patriot*, 30 Sept. 1839; *Pensacola Gazette*, 27 Aug. 1836 (quotation).

21. Diary, 10 Apr., 21, 29 Aug., 28–29 Sept., 2–4 Oct. 1835, 18–19, 26–27 June, 19 July 1837, EP; Everett to T. W. White, 20 Mar., 4 Apr. 1838, EP; Martineau, *Society in America*, 1:104–6, 120–34, 146. Everett's partisan and abolitionist enemies, of course, triumphed over how Martineau "boxed his ears soundly"; *Boston Daily Advocate*, reprinted in *Liberator*, 30 June 1837.

22. Nye, *Fettered Freedom*, 41–85; Richards, *"Gentlemen of Property,"* 47–81; Grimsted, *American Mobbing*, 3–32; Stewart, *Holy Warriors*, 63–69; Laurie, *Beyond Garrison*, 84–100; *Right and Wrong in Boston*, 8, 33; Rice, "Antislavery Mission of George Thompson."

23. A. Brown, *Always Young for Liberty*, 36–37, 95, 222–41; Channing, *Slavery*, quotations on 153, 162.

24. [Higginson], *Remarks on Slavery*; Martineau, *Martyr Age*, 14–15, 20; Delbanco, *William Ellery Channing*; A. Brown, *Always Young for Liberty*, esp. 58–59, 76, 222–44; Mendelsohn, *Channing*, esp. 253–59. For Channing's influence on a veritable who's who of New England antislavery activists, see Donald, *Charles Sumner*, 84–111; Grodzins, *American Heretic*, 52–59; C. Adams, *Memoirs of John Quincy Adams*, 10:39–40; Stange, "Making of an Abolitionist Martyr"; and Rugemer, *Problem of Emancipation*, 145–79.

25. Mendelsohn, *Channing*, 254–59; Malone and Johnson, *Dictionary of American Biography*, 1:433–34; Austin, *Remarks on Dr. Channing's Slavery*.

26. *Remarks on "Slavery by William E. Channing,"* quotation on 25; Austin, *Reply to the Reviewer,* 11–12.

27. Simmons, *Review of the Remarks,* quotation on 3.

28. Richardson, *Compilation of the Messages,* 2:1394–95; Howe, *What Hath God Wrought,* 428–30; Ames, *State Documents,* 214–20, quotation on 215.

29. McDuffie reprinted in *Liberator,* 12 Dec. 1835, emphasis (of course!) in original.

30. *Boston Daily Advertiser,* 18 Aug. 1835; diary, 19 Aug., 21 Oct. 1835, EP; Wiltse et al., *Papers of Daniel Webster,* 4:48–49; Everett to Cushing, 23 Dec. 1835, Caleb Cushing Papers, LC (quotation); *Liberator,* 17 Oct. 1835 (quotation). Wiltse attests that Webster was invited to the meeting, from which I infer that Everett must have been invited as well.

31. *Boston Daily Advertiser,* July–Dec. 1835, quotation from 22 Oct. 1835; *Daily Atlas,* July–Dec. 1835, quotations from 15 Aug. 1835.

32. *Boston Statesman,* 16, 23 Jan. 1836.

33. Diary, 17 Dec. 1835–15 Jan. 1836, EP.

34. E. Everett, *Address of His Excellency . . . 1836,* 29–31.

35. Diary, 6 Dec. 1835, EP.

36. Ibid., 29 Jan. 1836; Peter C. Brooks to Everett, 1 Jan. 1836, James Madison to Everett, 30 Jan. 1836, EP; Wiltse et al., *Papers of Daniel Webster,* 4:79–80; *Bridgewater Republican and Old Colony Press,* 22 Jan. 1836; *New-York Spectator,* 28 Jan. 1836; *Vermont Patriot,* 15 Feb. 1836; Frothingham, *Edward Everett,* 131–34.

37. *Bridgewater Republican and Old Colony Press,* 12, 19 Feb. 1836; *Boston Courier,* 28 Jan. 1836.

38. *Liberator,* 23 Jan. 1836. For other jabs in the *Liberator* based on his 1826 speech, see 13, 20 Feb. 1836.

39. Ibid., 20 Feb. 1836; see also 26 Mar. and 6 Aug. 1836. For an insightful recent treatment of Garrison that reveals how conflicted he and his followers were about the Founders and the value of the American nation, see McDaniel, *Problem of Democracy.*

40. *Account of the Interviews;* Garrison, *Letters of William Lloyd Garrison,* 2:55–58, 64–66; Massachusetts General Court, Senate, *Report of the Committee;* Nye, *Fettered Freedom,* 138–44; Pease and Pease, *Bound with Them,* 288–91; Yacovone, *Samuel Joseph May,* 60–65. For more on Lunt, see Garraty and Carnes, *American National Biography,* 14:141–42; and Malone and Johnson, *Dictionary of American Biography,* 6:507–8. William Goodell's speeches in these hearings offered an especially able explication of all these arguments; see Goodell, *Full Statement.* For the original documents referred to this committee, ranging from Southern state legislative memorials to abolitionist petitions, see Senate Unpassed Legislation, Report and Resolves on the Subject of Slavery, 1836, Massachusetts Archives, Boston.

41. *Account of the Interviews;* Lunt, *Origin of the Late War,* 471–80; *Boston Daily Advertiser,* 11, 16 Mar. 1836; *Daily Atlas,* 11–12 Mar. 1836; Massachusetts General Court, Senate, *Report of the Committee.*

42. *Liberator,* 12 Mar. 1836; Garrison, *Letters of William Lloyd Garrison,* 2:64–66, 79; *Boston Statesman,* 12 Mar. 1836; *Boston Daily Advocate,* 12 Apr. 1836. For the petitions sent to this select committee and its report's fate on the legislature's floor, see House Journal, 1836, 16 Jan., 5, 10, 12, 15, 21, 25 (quotation) Mar. 1836, Massachusetts Archives; and Senate Journal, 1836, 20, 21 Jan., 15 Feb. 2, 5, 10, 11, 12, 14, 19 Mar. 1836, Massachusetts Archives, Boston.

43. [Lunt], *Union;* Lunt, *Origin of the Late War,* quotations on 96, 107–8.

44. Diary, 4, 8 Mar. 1836, 21 June 1837, EP; Senate Unpassed Legislation, Message from Governor, April 6, 1836, Massachusetts Archives, Boston; Robert C. Winthrop to Everett, 24 Apr. 1838, EP.

45. See, e.g., Child, *Appeal*, 72–139, 197–98, 203.

46. Friedman, *Gregarious Saints*, 43–67; Ashworth, *Slavery, Capitalism, and Politics*, vol. 1, 170; Garrison, *Letters of William Lloyd Garrison*, 2:13–14; *Proceedings of the New England Anti-Slavery Convention*, quotations on 27, 26; *Right and Wrong in Boston*, quotation on 35; Martineau, *Martyr Age*, 15–41. Curiously, Martineau singled out for criticism as terrorizers Presidents Jackson and Van Buren, and even Lunt and Austin, but did not mention her old friend Everett by name. It was as if she was still trying to determine whether the real Everett was he of the notorious 1826 and 1836 speeches or he of the reformist goodwill in their private conversations. For more on the transformative impact on abolitionism of the Martyr Age, see McDaniel, *Problem of Democracy*, esp. 10–11, 66–112, 116; and Stewart, *Holy Warriors*, 63–96.

47. Blassingame, *Frederick Douglass Papers*, 308; Wilson, *History of the Rise and Fall*, 1:328–38, quotation on 330; May, *Some Recollections*, 126–230, quotation on 202.

48. *Liberator*, 8 Oct.–12 Nov. 1836, quotations in 15, 29 Oct. issues; Kallenbach and Kallenbach, *American State Governors*, 276–77. For an excellent recent analysis of Garrison's thoroughgoing ambivalence toward politics, see McDaniel, *Problem of Democracy*.

49. Pease and Pease, *Bound with Them*, 28–59; Stewart, *Wendell Phillips*, 58–63; Sparks, "Abolition in Silver Slippers"; Grodzins, *American Heretic*, 52–59, 167, 172–73, 333–34; Laurie, *Beyond Garrison*, 64–83; Ames, *State Documents*, 214–20; Nye, *Fettered Freedom*, esp. 117–216; Filler, *Crusade against Slavery*, 64–107; Brooks, "Building an Antislavery House," quotation on 1; *Correspondence between the Hon. F. H. Elmore*, 43–45, quotation on 44.

50. Brauer, *Cotton versus Conscience*, 1–48; Trusty, "Massachusetts Public Opinion"; D. Emerson, *Richard Hildreth*, 42–69; Hartford, *Money, Morals, and Politics*, 91–147; Moulton, "Closing the 'Floodgate of Impurity'"; Benton, *Thirty Years' View*, 2:134–43; *Daily Atlas*, 16, 20 Sept., 20 Oct. 1836; House Journal, 1837, 24 Jan., 1 Feb. 1837, Massachusetts Archives; Webster to Benjamin Douglas Silliman, 29 Jan. 1838, in Wiltse et al., *Papers of Daniel Webster*, 4:265, also 261–62, 270–71.

51. *Boston Daily Advertiser*, 4, 13 Feb., 10, 26, 29 Nov. 1836, 3 Mar. (quotation) 1837.

52. *Daily Atlas*, 10 Apr. 1837 (quotations); *Atlas*, 4, 22 Mar. 1837; *Boston Daily Advertiser*, 6 Mar., 1 Apr. 1837.

53. Diary, 7 Mar. 1837, EP; Richardson, *Compilation of the Messages*, 2:1531–36, quotations on 1535.

54. Everett to Nathan Hale, 3 Mar. 1837 (quotations), diary, 3 Mar. 1837, EP. Hale coyly addressed the idea that he spoke for Everett in this matter by indignantly denying "that we write or publish under dictation from Gov. Everett or any other person" while also asserting that "we have a right to conjecture that Gov. Everett as well as every other man of sense, whose opinions are not swayed by violent party feelings, or blind fanaticism, concurs with" the controversial editorial. See *Boston Daily Advertiser*, 4 Apr. 1837.

55. Austin, *Speech Delivered in Faneuil Hall*; Stewart, *Wendell Phillips*, 58–63, quotation on 60; Sparks, "Abolition in Silver Slippers," 91.

56. Diary, 4 Feb. 1836, 17 Aug. 1838, EP; A. Brown, *Always Young for Liberty*, 129; Everett to Mrs. W. E. Channing, 3 Feb. 1844, Richards Manuscript Collection, Howard Gotlieb Archival Research Center, Boston University, Boston.

57. Clay, *Speech of the Hon. Henry Clay*, quotations on 23, 32, 40–41; Everett to William Ellery Channing, 24 Apr. 1839, Everett to Webster, 14 Feb. 1839 (quotation), EP; diary, 13 Feb., 19 Apr. (quotation), 27 June 1839, EP; Hopkins et al., *Papers of Henry Clay*, 9:290–96, 314–15, quotation on 291; Channing, *Remarks on the Slavery Question*; Austin, *Review of the Rev. Dr. Channing's Letter*.

58. [Everett] to Robert C. Winthrop, 30 Sept. 1837, Winthrop Family Papers, MHS.

59. House Journal, 1837, 21, 24 Jan., 8, 11, 17, 20, 21, 25 Feb., 2, 17, 21 Mar., 5, 7, 10 Apr. 1837, Massachusetts Archives; Senate Journal, 1837, 23, 27 Feb., 22, 24, 25, 29–31 Mar., 4, 5, 8, 11 Apr. 1837, Massachusetts Archives. The legislature also received a flood of petitions and passed resolutions to the same effect—adding opposition to the interstate slave trade and the annexation of Texas—by overwhelming margins in 1838; tellingly, some of these resolves passed on the very same day that bills to repeal racial discrimination in Massachusetts failed. See House Journal, 1838, esp. 26 Mar., 21 Apr. 1838, Massachusetts Archives; Senate Journal, 1838, esp. 6, 10, 17, 23 Apr. 1838, Massachusetts Archives. In 1839 the legislature received a similar flood of petitions on these subjects, but both houses approved a resigned statement that "no further or more specific action is necessary or expedient thereon"; House Journal, 1839, 6 Mar. 1839, Massachusetts Archives.

60. House Journal, 1837, pp. 561–69, Massachusetts Archives; Massachusetts General Court, House, *Report and Resolves Relating to Slavery*.

61. Silbey, *American Party Battle*, 1:161–65, quotation on 162; Everett to Cushing, 22 Feb. 1836, 8 Mar. 1838, Caleb Cushing Papers, LC.

62. Blue, *No Taint of Compromise*, 48–49; Mrs. M. W. Chapman to Anne W. Weston, n.d., BPL; Belohlavek, *Broken Glass*, 62–67, 74–81, 98–101; Reed, "Emergence of the Whig Party," 274–93, 377–400; Garrison, *Letters of William Lloyd Garrison*, 2:201; *Liberator*, 7, 14 Jan., 11, 24 Mar., 7, 21, 28 Apr., 5 May, 14 July 1837; Brooks, "Building an Antislavery House," 22–23, 28–35.

63. Diary, 31 Oct. 1837, EP; *Liberator*, 10 Nov. 1837. For contemporary expectations that Morton would benefit, see, e.g., C. Adams, *Diary of Charles Francis Adams*, 8:323. For a historian who, based on a slim familiarity with the complexity and dynamism of Everett's stand, perpetuates that interpretation, see Earle, *Jacksonian Antislavery*, 103–22, esp. 111.

64. Everett to Caleb Cushing, 8 Oct., 15 Nov. 1836, Caleb Cushing Papers, LC; diary, 13, 15, 31 Oct., 2 Nov. 1837, EP; Winthrop Jr., *Memoir of Robert C. Winthrop*, 1–26.

65. Everett to William Jackson, 31 Oct. 1837, EP; *Liberator*, 10 Nov. 1837.

66. *Atlas*, 4 Nov. 1837; *Liberator*, 10 Nov. 1837.

67. Everett to Messrs. Ezra R. Johnson and W. P. Powell, 3 Nov. 1837, Everett to S. Whitcomb, 13 Nov. 1837, EP; diary, 4 Nov. 1837, EP. Jackson had written on 14 Oct. and Atwill on 26 Oct.

68. While Everett was up for reelection in 1838, this process does not seem to have repeated itself in that election. I have no explanation for this.

69. Nathaniel B. Borden to Francis Jackson, 14, 15, 17 Oct. 1839, Nathaniel B. Borden to Everett, 18 Oct. 1839, BPL.

70. Diary, 24 Oct. 1839, EP; Edward Everett to Nathaniel B. Borden, 24 Oct. 1839, BPL and EP; *Liberator*, 1 Nov. 1839.

71. Increase S. Smith to Caroline Weston, 12 Nov. 1837, BPL; diary, 3, 22 Nov. 1837, EP; *Liberator*, 10 Nov. 1837.

72. Francis Jackson to Edward Everett, 1 Nov. 1839, BPL; diary, 1, 8 Nov. 1839, EP; *Liberator*, 8 Nov. 1839 and also 1, 29 Nov. For more on Morton's responses in 1837 and 1839, see Earle, *Jacksonian Antislavery*, 103–22. For Hale's public refusal to publish Everett's 1839 letter, see *Boston Daily Advertiser*, 5 Nov. 1839.

73. Ames, *State Documents*, 232–37; diary, 7 Feb. 1839, EP; Everett to John Phillips, 11 Feb. 1839, Everett to T. W. White, 10 Feb. 1840, EP. For examples of Everett's determination to hew to the law in such cases, see diary, 15 Aug. 1836, EP; and Everett to J. T. Austin, 7 Jan.

1839, First Corps of Cadets Collection, Howard Gotlieb Archival Research Center, Boston University, Boston.

74. A Member of the Baltimore Bar to Samuel E. Sewall, 2 Aug. 1836, William A. Clarke to Samuel E. Sewall, 9 Aug. 1836, Robie-Sewall Family Papers, MHS; *Boston Daily Advertiser*, 30 Aug. 1836; diary, 21 Feb., 12 May, 11 July 1836, EP; Everett to S. E. Sewall, 13 Feb., 18, 21 May, 9, 16 July 1836, Everett to J. T. Austin, 13 Feb. 1836, Everett to His Excellency the Governor of North Carolina, 22 Feb. 1836 (quotations), Everett to "Dear Sir," 1 Mar. 1836, EP; *Liberator*, 11 June 1836. For an account of Sewall's abolitionist lawyering, which strangely concludes that he only "received slight encouragement" from Massachusetts authorities in these efforts, see Tiffany, *Samuel E. Sewall*, 33–81, quotation on 60.

75. Diary, 27–30 Sept., 5, 16 Oct. 1839, EP; Everett to Ivers Phillips, 20 Nov. 1839, Everett to Governor David Campbell, 2 Dec. 1839, EP; Executive Papers of Governor David Campbell, Library of Virginia, Richmond, files for 11 Oct., 2 Dec. (quotation) 1839; *Liberator*, 18 Oct. 1839.

76. Rugemer, *Problem of Emancipation*, quotation on 156; Haynes, *Unfinished Revolution*; McDaniel, *Problem of Democracy*; Yokota, *Unbecoming British*.

77. Everett to Sir Robert Peel, 29 Mar., 3 Oct. 1837, EP.

78. Entry for 21 Apr. 1838, Edmund Quincy Diaries, MHS; diary, 21–22 Apr., 4, 6 May 1838, 14 Apr., 18 May 1839, EP; Winthrop to Everett, May 1838, Everett to Joseph Sturge, 20 May 1839, EP; Sparks, "Abolition in Silver Slippers"; Tolf, "Edmund Quincy."

79. Thome and Kimball, *Emancipation in the West Indies*, quotations on iii, 296, 311; Sturge and Harvey, *West Indies*.

80. "The Negro Apprenticeship System," *Edinburgh Review* 67 (Jan. 1838): 477–522.

81. Diary, 4 Dec. 1838, EP; Everett to Joseph Sturge, 20 May 1839, EP; Tolf, "Edmund Quincy," 109–10.

82. Edward Everett to Edmund Quincy, 26 Apr. 1838, EP; *Correspondence between the Hon. F. H. Elmore*, 55 (emphasis in this published version).

83. Entries for 26, 27, 28 (quotation) Apr. 1838, Edmund Quincy Diaries, MHS; diary, 28, 30 Apr. 1838, EP; Everett to Edmund Quincy, 30 Apr. 1838, EP.

84. *Boston Daily Advertiser*, 2 May 1838; Rugemer, *Problem of Emancipation*, 145–290. Haughton at the *Atlas* was manifestly among the undecided, as he did not publish or comment on Everett's letter to Quincy, as if unsure what to make of or do with it.

85. *Correspondence between the Hon. F. H. Elmore*, 55; *Liberator*, 16, 23 Feb., 4, 18 May (quotations), 8 June, 24 Aug., 5, 26 Oct., 2, 23 Nov. 1838, 18 Jan. 1839; Lewis Tappan to Clay, 5 June 1838, in Hopkins et al., *Papers of Henry Clay*, 9:199–200; *Cleveland Observer*, 31 May 1838; diary, 17 Aug. 1838, EP. On this issue Everett was more antislavery than Adams, who thought reports from the West Indies were "rose-colored as to the results of emancipation"; C. Adams, *Memoirs of John Quincy Adams*, 10:129–30.

86. Kallenbach and Kallenbach, *American State Governors*, 276–77; "Memoir of Edward Everett," 111; Brooks, "Building an Antislavery House," 28–35.

87. *Bay State Democrat*, 7 Sept. 1838, 19 July–8 Nov. 1839; *Boston Statesman*, 26 Oct., 2, 9 Nov. 1839; *Boston Daily Advocate*, 18 July, 17, 19 Sept. 1836.

88. *Daily Atlas*, 8, 14 Sept., 15, 25 (quotation) Oct. 1836, 7, 9, 11 Nov. 1837, 31 Oct., 6 Nov. 1839; *Atlas*, 1 Mar. 1837; *Boston Daily Advertiser*, 10, 14 Nov. 1836.

89. Formisano, *Transformation of Political Culture*, 298–99; Tyrrell, *Sobering Up*, 225–51.

90. Everett to "My dear friend," 18 Mar. 1834, Edward Everett Collection, Rare Books and

Special Collections, Princeton University Library, Princeton, N.J.; Everett to J. C. Warren, M.D., 11 June 1839, EP; diary, 27 July 1839, EP; Tyrrell, *Sobering Up*, 149–50.

91. Kallenbach and Kallenbach, *American State Governors*, 276–77; E. Everett, *Address of His Excellency . . . 1839*, 22–24; diary, 12 Nov., 17, 25 Dec. 1838, 31 Jan., 25 Feb., 3 Apr., 29 June 1839, EP; Robert C. Winthrop to Everett, [n.d.] 1838, Everett to Daniel Webster, 14 Feb., 3 (quotation), 26 July, 23 Sept. 1839, EP; Everett to Robert C. Winthrop, 5 Nov. 1838, Winthrop Family Papers, MHS.

92. Burns, *Selections from the Works of Edward Everett*; *Boston Daily Advertiser*, 17 Aug., 17–18, 21 Sept., 26 Oct., 2, 9, 11, 21, 25 Nov. 1839; diary, 11 Nov. 1839–9 Jan. 1840, quotation from 8 Jan. 1840, EP; Kallenbach and Kallenbach, *American State Governors*, 276–77.

93. Everett to Robert C. Winthrop, 28 Oct. 1839, Winthrop Family Papers, MHS (quotations); Everett to William Henry Harrison, 20 Jan. 1840, EP; *Daily Atlas*, 16 Nov. 1839; Formisano, *Transformation of Political Culture*, 298–99; Tyrrell, *Sobering Up*, 238.

94. Diary, 3 Mar. 1838, 14, 28 Nov. 1839, 13 Jan., 31 Dec. 1840, EP; House Journal, 1840, 16 Jan. 1840, Massachusetts Archives; Senate Journal, 1840, 3–7, 13, 15 Jan. 1840, Massachusetts Archives; Everett to Webster, 23 Sept. 1839, in Wiltse et al., *Papers of Daniel Webster*, 4:395; C. Adams, *Diary of Charles Francis Adams*, 8:326–27; Everett to Cushing, 9 Dec. 1839, 18 Jan. 1840, Caleb Cushing Papers, LC; Everett to Robert C. Winthrop, 14 Nov. 1839, 11 Jan., 20 Dec. (quotation) 1840, Winthrop Family Papers, MHS.

95. Wiltse et al., *Papers of Daniel Webster*, 4:376, 382, 396; diary, 27 Aug. 1836, 25 July 1837, 4, 9, 18 Jan., 29 Feb., 3, 6 (quotation), 8, 10 Mar. 1840, EP.

Chapter 5

1. Diary, 3 July 1840, 2 Feb. 1841, EP; Frothingham, *Edward Everett*, chs. 7–8.

2. Everett to Winthrop, 15 Nov. 1840, Winthrop Family Papers, MHS.

3. *Atlas*, 22, 26 Mar. 1841; Edward Kent to Webster, 17 Feb. 1841, in Shewmaker et al., *Papers of Daniel Webster*, 1:34–36; Winthrop to Everett, 27 June 1841, Jared Sparks to Everett, 30 June 1841, EP-Harvard; diary, 24 July 1841, EP.

4. Wiltse et al., *Papers of Daniel Webster*, 5:84–86, 112–15; Shewmaker et al., *Papers of Daniel Webster*, 1:18–19; Geiger, "Scholar Meets John Bull," 581.

5. For the record of the dates of this debate in the Senate, see *Journal of the Executive Proceedings of the Senate*, 407–8, 412, 419, 437–38. So cloaked in uncertainty was Everett's confirmation that it even entered the standard published record of Congress as a rumor; see *Congressional Globe*, 27th Cong., 1st Sess., 452. For a fuller discussion of this debate and its larger political significance, see M. Mason, "Local, National, and International Politics."

6. Winthrop to Everett, 27 June 1841, EP-Harvard; *Congressional Globe*, 26th Cong., 2nd Sess., 11–12, and 27th Cong., 1st Sess., iii, vii (see index entries "Abolition petitions").

7. *Congressional Globe*, 26th Cong., 2nd Sess., 328–32, and 27th Cong., 1st Sess., 307 (Benton quotations); *Atlas*, 25–26 Mar. 1841; *New Hampshire Statesman*, 22 May 1841; *New-York Spectator*, 2 June 1841; *Whig*, 28 Apr. 1841; *Mississippi Free Trader and Natchez Daily Gazette*, 28 June 1841; *Louisville Public Advertiser*, 10 Apr. 1841; *New York Herald*, 30 Sept. 1841; *Weekly Raleigh Register*, 26 Feb. 1841; *Fayetteville Observer*, 3 Mar., 7 July 1841; *Indiana Journal*, 13 Mar. 1841; *Virginia Free Press*, 25 Feb. 1841; Meriwether et al., *Papers of John C. Calhoun*, 15:657–68.

8. H. Jones, *To the Webster-Ashburton Treaty*, esp. 69–86; Jones and Rakestraw, *Prologue to Manifest Destiny*; Haynes, *Unfinished Revolution*, 177–261; Rugemer, *Problem of Emancipation*,

197–204; *Congressional Globe*, 27th Cong., 1st Sess., 325 (quotation). For an outstanding recent study of Britain's antislavery foreign policy, see Huzzey, *Freedom Burning*.

9. *Fayetteville Observer*, 18 Dec. 1839; Southern papers quoted in *Liberator*, 16 Feb., 23 Nov. 1838; Calhoun to A. S. Clayton and others, 5 Aug. 1836, in Meriwether et al., *Papers of John C. Calhoun*, 13:263; Ashworth, *Slavery, Capitalism, and Politics*, vol. 1, 135.

10. Abel P. Upshur to Nathaniel Beverly Tucker, 7, 28 Aug. 1841, Tucker-Coleman Papers, Special Collections Research Center, Swem Library, College of William and Mary, Williamsburg, Va.

11. *Globe*, 9, 23 Sept. 1841; *Richmond Enquirer*, 3 Aug. 1841; *Arkansas State Gazette*, 14 July 1841; Poore, *Perley's Reminiscences*, 1:274.

12. *Macon Weekly Telegraph*, 7 Sept. 1841; *Arkansas State Gazette*, 22 Sept. 1841.

13. *Richmond Whig* quoted in *Atlas*, 6 Sept. 1841; *Richmond Whig*, 31 Aug., 3 Sept. 1841; *Daily National Intelligencer*, 30–31 Aug., 6, 9 Sept. 1841; *Southern Patriot*, 2 Sept. 1841 (quotation); *Raleigh Register, and North-Carolina State Gazette*, 3 Sept. 1841.

14. *Atlas*, 8 Sept. 1841; *North American and Daily Advertiser*, 27 June 1844; Poore, *Perley's Reminiscences*, 1:275; Alexander Moseley to Alexander H. H. Stuart, 26 Aug. 1841, Papers of Alexander H. H. Stuart, Albert and Shirley Small Special Collections Library, University of Virginia.

15. *Richmond Whig* quoted in *Atlas*, 1 Sept. 1841; *Richmond Whig*, 31 Aug., 7, 10 Sept. 1841.

16. J. H. Clifford to Robert C. Winthrop, 6, 14 Aug., 5 Sept. 1841, Winthrop to Clifford, 7, 22, 30 Aug. 1841, Winthrop Family Papers, MHS.

17. Hopkins et al., *Papers of Henry Clay*, 9:604; Hone, *Diary of Philip Hone*, 2:85–86, 89.

18. *Pennsylvania Inquirer and Daily Courier*, 13 (quotation), 20, 26 Aug., 1 Sept. 1841; *North American*, 13 Aug. 1841 (quotation); *Cleveland Daily Herald*, 4 Sept. 1841; *Boston Daily Advertiser*, 21, 23, 30 Aug. 1841; *Commercial Advertiser*, 19 Aug. 1841; *Atlas*, 9, 21 Aug. 1841; *Salem Gazette*, 17, 24 Aug. 1841; *Norwich Courier*, 1 Sept. 1841; Winthrop to Everett, 28 Aug. 1841, BPL.

19. *Boston Courier*, 16, 30 (quotations) Aug. 1841; *Commercial Advertiser*, 19 Aug. 1841 (quotations); *Boston Daily Advertiser*, 21 Aug. 1841; *Atlas*, 27 Aug., 7 Sept. 1841.

20. *Bay State Democrat*, 21, 23, 30 Aug., 16 Sept. 1841; *Ohio Statesman*, 28 July 1841; *Boston Statesman*, 18 Sept. 1841; *Universal Yankee Nation*, 4 Sept. 1841.

21. *Pittsfield Sun*, 26 Aug. 1841 (quotations); *New York Herald*, 31 Aug. 1841; *Bay State Democrat*, 21, 23 Aug. 1841; *Universal Yankee Nation*, 4 Sept. 1841.

22. *Liberator*, 27 Aug., 24 Sept., 24 Dec. 1841; *Emancipator*, 19 Aug., 14 Oct. 1841; *National Anti-Slavery Standard*, 2 Sept. 1841; Evelina A. S. Smith to Caroline Weston, 9 Sept. 1841, D. L. Child to Mrs. M. W. Chapman, 13 Sept. 1843, BPL. Edmund Quincy, who in his way had contributed much to creating this controversy, shared other abolitionists' bemusement at Northern Whigs' reaction; see entry for 21 Aug. 1841, Edmund Quincy Diaries, MHS.

23. Webster to Everett, 20 Nov. 1841, EP; Winthrop to Everett, 28 Aug. 1841, BPL; Winthrop to Everett, 29 Sept. 1841, EP-Harvard; Peter C. Brooks to Everett, 1 Oct. 1841, Everett-Hopkins Papers, MHS; Neilson, *Memories of Rufus Choate*, 417; *Journal of the Executive Proceedings of the Senate*, 438.

24. Webster to Everett, 24 July 1841, in Shewmaker et al., *Papers of Daniel Webster*, 1:19–21; Peter C. Brooks to Everett, 31 July 1841, Everett-Hopkins Papers, MHS.

25. Diary, 18, 19 (quotation), 23, 26 Aug., 8, 24 Sept. 1841, EP; Charlotte Everett to Sally Hale, 5 Sept. 1841, Everett-Hopkins Papers, MHS.

26. Diary, 30 Aug. 1841, EP; Everett to Webster, 3 Sept. 1841, EP; Winthrop to Everett,

29 Sept. 1841, EP-Harvard; Peter C. Brooks to Everett, 1 Oct. 1841, Charlotte Everett to Sally Hale, 5 Sept. 1841, Everett-Hopkins Papers, MHS; Everett to Winthrop, 28 Apr. 1841, Winthrop Family Papers, MHS.

27. Diary, 12, 16 Oct. 1841, 20 May 1844, EP; Webster to Everett, 20 Nov. 1841, Everett to Webster, 15 Dec. 1841, EP; Everett to Webster, 22 Oct. 1841, in Wiltse et al., *Papers of Daniel Webster*, 5:169–70; Everett to Winthrop, 23 Nov. 1841, Winthrop Family Papers, MHS (quotations); Everett to William C. Rives, 11 Mar. 1842, William C. Rives Papers, LC.

28. Everett to Sally Hale, 18 Nov. 1844, Everett-Hopkins Papers, MHS; diary, 18 Nov. 1841, EP.

29. Diary, 20 Nov. 1841, EP; Wiltse et al., *Papers of Daniel Webster*, 5:154–55.

30. Wiltse et al., *Papers of Daniel Webster*, 5:10–11, 34 (quotation on 10); H. Jones, *To the Webster-Ashburton Treaty*, esp. 54–61; Pletcher, *Diplomacy of Annexation*, 9–27; W. Jones, *American Problem*, esp. 1–39; Evans, *Sir Robert Peel*, 54.

31. Willson, *America's Ambassadors*, 197–228; diary, 23 Dec. 1841, EP; Temperley, "O'Connell-Stevenson Contretemps," quotations on 219, 223; McDaniel, *Problem of Democracy*, 59.

32. Diary, 5 Mar. 1842, EP; Frothingham, *Edward Everett*, 189; *British Parliamentary Papers*, 21:204–43, 263–74; Stevenson's letters to Webster, 9 Mar.–22 Oct. 1841, Andrew and John White Stevenson Family Papers, LC. The vacancy from 1832 to 1836 was a result of partisan politics in the Senate, resulting in Van Buren's rejection as minister in 1832 and a delay in Stevenson's nomination between 1834 and 1836.

33. Everett to Winthrop, 20 Dec. 1840 (quotation), 3 Jan. 1843, Winthrop Family Papers, MHS; Everett to Aberdeen, 14 May 1842 (quotation), vol. 85, Lord Aberdeen Papers, British Library, London; Everett to Peter C. Brooks, 2 July 1845, Everett to "My Dear Sir," 2 Feb. 1845, diary, 16–17 Dec. 1841, 27 Apr., 22–27 Dec. 1842, EP; *Daily National Intelligencer*, 9 May 1844; Geiger, "Scholar Meets John Bull," 581–82; Willson, *America's Ambassadors*, 231; Frothingham, *Edward Everett*, ch. 8.

34. Lady Ashburton to Webster, 12 Jan. 1842 (quotation), in Shewmaker et al., *Papers of Daniel Webster*, 1:490; Wiltse et al., *Papers of Daniel Webster*, 5:219; Francis Boott to Everett, 21 July 1845, BPL; Willson, *America's Ambassadors*, 229–41; Geiger, "Scholar Meets John Bull"; Gill, "Edward Everett, Minister."

35. E. Everett, *Orations and Speeches*, vol. 1, 63–65 (quotations), 529, 544; vol. 2, 424–30 (quotations), 437, 447–48, 462–63, 466, 469, 472, 474, 478–83.

36. Macvey Napier to Everett, 10 June 1845, EP; *Niles' National Register* 62 (30 July 1842): 337, 62 (13 Aug. 1842): 371, 384.

37. *New York Herald*, 2 Apr. 1844; *Daily National Intelligencer*, 9 May 1844; *Daily Atlas*, 24 Dec. 1844; *Raleigh Register*, 4 Nov. 1842; Everett to Sally Hale, 18 June 1845, Everett-Hopkins Papers, MHS; Everett to Gales and Seaton, 17 July 1843, Edward Everett Letters, 1816–1863, MHS.

38. E. Everett, *Orations and Speeches*, vol. 2, vii, 244–45, 447–83 (quotations on vii, 245); diary, 4 Apr., 18 Aug. (quotation) 1843, 29 Apr. 1844, 16, 23 Mar., 15 Apr. (quotation) 1845, EP.

39. Diary, 15, 31 July 1844, 14 Mar. (quotation) 1845, EP; Catherine Hutton to Everett, 1, 3 July 1845, EP.

40. Diary, 2, 5 (quotation) Sept. 1840, 29 July 1841. Beaumont indeed devoted very little space to the future of slavery, and even that passage appeared in context of his pursuit of his main quarry, American racism; see *Marie*, 58–63. For an excellent scholarly treatment of the range of thought and policy within the antislavery opinion that dominated Victorian Britain, see Huzzey, *Freedom Burning*.

41. Diary, 3 Dec. 1843, 17 Mar., 6, 16 Apr., 18 Aug. 1844, EP.

42. Lord Stanley to Everett, 8 Nov. 1842, vol. 34, Lord Aberdeen Papers, British Library.

43. Memorandum, 12 Nov. 1842, vol. 34, Lord Aberdeen Papers, British Library; diary, 12, 17 Nov. 1842, EP.

44. E. Everett, "Edward Everett's College Life," 195–96; Prince Albert to Everett, 18 July 1845, EP; diary, 26–27 Aug. 1840, 9 Jan. 1841, 26 Apr. 1845, EP; Everett to Winthrop, 3 Jan. 1843, Winthrop Family Papers, MHS.

45. Everett to William C. Rives, 11 Mar. 1842, William C. Rives Papers; —— Jeffrey to Everett, 27 Feb. [1845], EP; Everett to Winthrop, 27 Feb. 1841, Winthrop Family Papers, MHS.

46. Diary, 4 Apr. 1842, 12, 26 (quotation) May, 4 (quotation), 18 Nov., 3 Dec. 1843, 13 Mar., 2 July, 3 Aug. 1844, EP.

47. Everett to Gales and Seaton, 2 Nov. 1842, Edward Everett Papers, New York Public Library; Everett to Peter C. Brooks, 18 May, 2 June 1845, EP; diary, 1 Dec. 1843 (quotation), 22 Apr. 1844, May–June 1845, EP.

48. My interpretation on this point accords with that of Frothingham, who depicts how slavery-related issues "made a 'special pleader' of a Christian gentleman and diplomat" (*Edward Everett*, 234–38, quotation on 237).

49. Huzzey, *Freedom Burning*, 70–74, 99–113, quotation on 71; Meriwether et al., ed., *Papers of John C. Calhoun*, 18:141, 21:280–81.

50. Diary, 22 June 1844, 19 Mar., 21 May, 16, 28 July 1845, EP; Everett to Aberdeen, 29 Sept. 1845 (quotation), 3 Oct. 1846, vol. 85, Lord Aberdeen Papers, British Library.

51. This variance may come as a surprise to many historians given the influential historiography, running from W. E. B. Du Bois to Don E. Fehrenbacher, painting U.S. policymakers and diplomats as united behind an obstructive, if not downright proslavery, policy on this issue; see Du Bois, *Suppression*, 108–99; and Fehrenbacher, *Slaveholding Republic*, 89–172. More nuanced is H. Jones, *To the Webster-Ashburton Treaty*, 69–78.

52. Huzzey, *Freedom Burning*, 43; H. Jones, *To the Webster-Ashburton Treaty*, 74–78; Brunsman, *Evil Necessity*; diary, 13 Apr. 1842, EP (quotations).

53. For more on the larger political and diplomatic context, see M. Mason, "Battle of the Slaveholding Liberators" and "Keeping Up Appearances."

54. Wheaton, *Enquiry into the Validity*; [Cass], *Examination of the Question*; Klunder, *Lewis Cass*, 97–118; Shewmaker et al., *Papers of Daniel Webster*, 1:710–75; *Southern Literary Messenger* 8 (Apr. 1842): 289–301, 8 (June 1842): 381–96; *Niles' National Register* 62 (26 Mar. 1842): 54–60.

55. Ashburton to Aberdeen, 25 Apr. 1842, in *British Parliamentary Papers*, 24:202–3; Webster to Everett, 26 Apr. 1842, 27 Apr. 1843, Webster to Cass, 5 Apr. 1842, in Shewmaker et al., *Papers of Daniel Webster*, 1:529–32, 543–44, 929–30.

56. Everett to Webster, 28 Dec. 1841 (quotation), 23 Mar. 1842, EP; Aberdeen to Everett, 20 Dec. 1841, Everett to Aberdeen, 23 Dec. 1841, in *British Parliamentary Papers*, 21:280–83; diary, 11 Mar., 26 May 1843, EP; Everett to Webster, 31 Dec. 1841, in Shewmaker et al., *Papers of Daniel Webster*, 1:173–77; Meriwether et al., ed., *Papers of John C. Calhoun*, 20:87.

57. Everett to Webster, 3, 21 Jan. 1842, in Shewmaker et al., *Papers of Daniel Webster*, 1:488–89, 491–96; Everett to Aberdeen, 21 Feb. 1842, in *British Parliamentary Papers*, 24:113–15 (quotations on 114). Everett also wrote to Cass urging him to dial back his Anglophobia in light of the new ministry's assurances; see Everett to Cass, 21 Feb. 1842, EP.

58. Diary, 20 Sept. 1842, EP; Everett to Webster, 16 Sept. 1842, in Shewmaker et al., *Papers of Daniel Webster*, 1:698–700; H. Jones, *To the Webster-Ashburton Treaty*, 186.

59. Shewmaker et al., *Papers of Daniel Webster*, 1:802–26; *Congressional Globe*, 27th Cong., 3rd Sess., 54, 63–64, 79–81, 85, 331–36, 377–79; Benton, *Thirty Years' View*, 2:425–26, 432–34,

447–52; Webster to Stevenson, 12 Apr., 8 June 1841, Andrew and John White Stevenson Family Papers, LC.

60. Upshur to Commander Perry, 15 Mar. 1843, forwarded by Everett to Aberdeen, 26 Apr. 1843, in *British Parliamentary Papers*, 25:60–63 (quotations on 62); diary, 21 June 1843, EP; H. Jones, *To the Webster-Ashburton Treaty*, 186.

61. Jervey and Huber, "Creole Affair," quotation on 206; H. Jones, "Peculiar Institution"; Fehrenbacher, *Slaveholding Republic*, 204–11.

62. H. Jones, *To the Webster-Ashburton Treaty*, 78–86; Shewmaker et al., *Papers of Daniel Webster*, 1:519–21 (quotations on 521); Remini, *Daniel Webster*, 541–42; *Congressional Globe*, 27th Cong., 2nd Sess., 115–16, 203–4 (quotation on 203); Benton, *Thirty Years' View*, 2:409–12; *Mobile Register and Journal*, Dec. 1841 (quotation); *Richmond Enquirer*, 21 Dec. 1841; *Camden Journal*, 23 Feb. 1842.

63. Shewmaker et al., *Papers of Daniel Webster*, 1:496–97, 658–69, 680–81, 697; Jones and Rakestraw, *Prologue to Manifest Destiny*, 71–96; W. Jones, "Influence of Slavery," 49–50; H. Jones, "Peculiar Institution," 35–46; H. Jones, *To the Webster-Ashburton Treaty*, 186–87; E. Adams, "Lord Ashburton," 773–74.

64. Webster to Everett, 29 Jan. 1842, 16 May 1842, in Shewmaker et al., *Papers of Daniel Webster*, 1:177–85, 560–61; Webster to Everett, 28 June 1842, EP.

65. C. Adams, *Memoirs of John Quincy Adams*, 11:383–84; *Congressional Globe*, 27th Cong., 2nd Sess., 342–49; Peterson, *Great Triumvirate*, 322. For an especially good overview of the domestic politics of the *Creole* case, see H. Jones, "Peculiar Institution," esp. 33–38, 45–46.

66. Samuel Joseph May to Webster, 28 Mar. 1842, Papers of Samuel Joseph May, Albert and Shirley Small Special Collections Library, University of Virginia (quotation), Charlottesville; Shewmaker et al., *Papers of Daniel Webster*, 1:528–29; Channing, *Duty of the Free States*, quotations on 8, 43; *Liberator*, 11 Mar.–6 May 1842, quotations in 11 Mar.; Jay, *Creole Case*.

67. *Raleigh Register*, 12 Apr. 1842; *Richmond Enquirer*, 26 Feb. 1842 (quotation); *Camden Journal*, 16 Mar. 1842; *Charleston Courier*, 26 Feb., 4 Mar. 1842; *Arkansas State Gazette*, 23 Mar. 1842; Benton, *Thirty Years' View*, 2:413.

68. *North American*, 8 Mar. 1842 (quotation); *New York Herald*, 25 Feb. 1842 (quotation); *New-York Spectator*, 30 Mar., 9 Apr. 1842; *Daily Atlas*, 4 June 1842; *Ohio Observer*, 10 Mar. 1842.

69. Samuel Joseph May to Webster, 28 Mar. 1842, Papers of Samuel Joseph May, University of Virginia; John A. Collins to Rev. Samuel May Jr., 28 Feb. 1842, BPL.

70. Everett to Aberdeen, 1 Mar. (quotation), 3 May 1842, EP. Aberdeen responded that the compensation to British slaveholders was meant to be a one-time thing; Aberdeen to Everett, 20 May 1842, in *British Parliamentary Papers*, 24:203–4.

71. Everett to Upshur, 27 Feb. 1844, Calhoun to Everett, 7 Aug. 1844, in Meriwether et al., ed., *Papers of John C. Calhoun*, 18:55–56, 19:528–34.

72. Diary, 27, 31 Jan., 14, 16, 17, 23 Feb., 25, 28 Apr. 1842, 24 Oct. 1844, EP; Everett to Webster, 1 Mar., 2 May 1842, EP; Everett to Henry Wheaton, 10 Feb. 1842, Henry Wheaton Papers, Morgan Library; Aberdeen to Everett, 18 Apr. 1842, in *British Parliamentary Papers*, 24:193–96 (quotation on 196).

73. Everett to Winthrop, 2 Apr. 1842, Winthrop Family Papers, MHS; diary, 22 Nov. 1844, EP.

74. Pletcher, *Diplomacy of Annexation*; Haynes, "Anglophobia"; Merk, *Slavery and the Annexation*; Freehling, *Road to Disunion*, vol.1, 353–452; Morrison, *Slavery and the American West*, 4, 13–38; Manning, *Diplomatic Correspondence*, 7:4–5, 8:586, 606–13.

75. Merk, *Slavery and the Annexation*, 218–36; Meriwether et al., ed., *Papers of John C. Calhoun*,

17:329–32, 354–57, 381–83, 395–96, 470–73, 511–12, 535, 545–49, 574–82, 18:83–85, 95, 154–57; Duff Green, *United States and England*; Karp, "Slavery and American Sea Power."

76. Diary, 2 Jan., 17 Oct. 1844, EP; E. Adams, "Correspondence from the British Archives"; Haynes, *Unfinished Revolution*, 177–261; Meriwether et al., ed., *Papers of John C. Calhoun*, 17:535 (quotation), 18:53–54 (quotation on 53), 286–88; Crapol, *John Tyler*, 47–71, 176–222. For an analysis of Britain's Texas policies that rightly deems its approach to slavery there "inconsistent," see Roeckel, "Bonds over Bondage."

77. Ames, *State Documents*, 229–32; Choate, *Addresses and Orations*, 334–56 (quotation on 352); *Proceedings of a Convention of Delegates*, quotation on 8; Wiltse et al., *Papers of Daniel Webster*, 5:321–23 (quotation on 322), 6:12–20, 37 (quotation), 41, 46, 62, 67, 69–77.

78. Manning, *Diplomatic Correspondence*, 7:6–22, 25–26, 246–51; Meriwether et al., ed., *Papers of John C. Calhoun*, 18:273–78, 348–51, 544–45.

79. Everett to Ashbel Smith, 23 Nov. 1843, Ashbel Smith Correspondence, L. Tom Perry Special Collections, Brigham Young University, Provo, Utah.

80. Diary, 1 Dec. 1843, 6, 16 Apr., 28 May, 3 July (quotation) 1844, EP. For an echo from Abraham Lincoln about annexation and slavery extension, see E. Foner, *Fiery Trial*, 42.

81. He also served under James Buchanan in the first months of the Polk administration as well as under three separate and short-lived acting secretaries of state.

82. Crapol, *John Tyler*, 71–74, 90–127; Merk, *Slavery and the Annexation*; Mitton, "Free World Confronted," 63–66, 81–83; Holt, *Rise and Fall*, 170; Shewmaker et al., *Papers of Daniel Webster*, 1:27–28.

83. Diary, 16, 18, 20, 23 May, 13, 15, 17 Nov. 1843, EP; Everett to Hugh Legare, 1 July 1843, EP; Wiltse et al., *Papers of Daniel Webster*, 5:180–81, 209–10, 254–55; Merk, *Slavery and the Annexation*, 254–55; *Boston Courier*, 25 Dec. 1843.

84. *Southern Literary Messenger* 5 (Oct. 1839): 677–87 (quotation on 687); Hall, *Abel Parker Upshur*, 73–81, 87–105, 194–213; Merk, *Slavery and the Annexation*, 219, 221–24, 231, 236.

85. Upshur to Calhoun, 8 Nov. 1843, in Meriwether et al., ed., *Papers of John C. Calhoun*, 17:535; Upshur to Tucker, 26 Oct. 1843, Tucker-Coleman Papers, College of William and Mary.

86. Upshur to Everett, 28 Sept. 1843, in Manning, *Diplomatic Correspondence*, 7:6–17.

87. Everett to Tyler, 8 Apr. 1844, Edward Everett Collection, Princeton University Library; Everett to Webster, 29 Apr. 1844, in Wiltse et al., *Papers of Daniel Webster*, 6:47; Meriwether et al., ed., *Papers of John C. Calhoun*, 18:262–64, 467–68; Gujer, "Free Trade and Slavery," esp. 193–201; Ashworth, *Slavery, Capitalism, and Politics*, vol. 1, 427–37 (quotation on 428).

88. Everett to Calhoun, 15 Apr. 1844, 2, 21 Nov. 1844, in Meriwether et al., ed., *Papers of John C. Calhoun*, 18:243–44, 20:211–12, 339–40, 351–54, 21:363–67 (quotations on 20:212, 20:339).

89. Meriwether et al., ed., *Papers of John C. Calhoun*, 19:786–90 (quotations on 789), 20:30–31 (quotation on 30), 236, 436.

90. Perhaps they thought the time remaining in Tyler's presidency robbed them of the political capital and maybe even the will to push for a replacement; after all, dating back to Van Buren's nomination in the early 1830s, the London post had never been an easy one for which to secure Senate confirmation. Moreover, Calhoun continued to receive reports of Everett's effectiveness and popularity in London; see Meriwether et al., ed., *Papers of John C. Calhoun*, 21:257–58.

91. Meriwether et al., ed., *Papers of John C. Calhoun*, 19:377–78, 528–34, 558–61, 848–51, 20:528–30, 21:217–20 (quotations on 19:377, 19:558, 21:217, 220).

92. Everett to Nathan Hale, 2 Mar. 1843, Everett-Hopkins Papers, MHS; Everett to Robert C. Winthrop, 18 June 1844, Winthrop Family Papers, MHS; diary, 3 Dec. 1845, EP.

93. Everett to Sally Hale, 18 June 1845, Everett-Hopkins Papers, MHS; Meriwether et al., ed., *Papers of John C. Calhoun*, 20:95–96; Everett to Gales and Seaton, 17 July 1843, 10 Oct. 1844, Edward Everett Letters, 1816–1863, MHS; diary, 1 July 1844, EP.

94. Everett to Rives, 16 Nov. 1842, 3 Feb., 3 Apr., 16 June 1843, 29 July 1844, William C. Rives Papers, LC; diary, 6 Nov. 1843 (quotation), 22 Apr. 1844, EP.

95. Everett to Charles Sumner, 29 June 1846, Edward Everett Letters, 1816–1863, MHS; Everett to Aberdeen, 10 Dec. 1845, vol. 85, Lord Aberdeen Papers, British Library. See also Everett to J. Bigelow, M.D., 1 Apr. 1848, Edward Everett Letters, Southern Historical Collection, Wilson Library, University of North Carolina, Chapel Hill.

96. Frothingham, *Edward Everett*, 238–41; Everett to W. H. Prescott, 31 Oct. 1843, Papers of Edward Everett, Albert and Shirley Small Special Collections Library, University of Virginia.

97. Diary, 2 Apr. 1843, EP; Shewmaker et al., *Papers of Daniel Webster*, 1:695–98, 846, 877–926; Everett to Winthrop, 3 Apr., 2 June 1843, Winthrop Family Papers, MHS. Everett asked Hale to dial back his assaults on Webster for this machination; see Everett to Nathan Hale, 18 Apr., 18 May 1843, Everett-Hopkins Papers, MHS; Remini, *Daniel Webster*, 575–78; and Peterson, *Great Triumvirate*, 334.

98. Everett to Webster, 29 Apr. 1844, in Wiltse et al., *Papers of Daniel Webster*, 6:48.

99. Diary, 30 Nov. 1844, EP; Everett to Webster, 3 Apr. 1845, in Wiltse et al., *Papers of Daniel Webster*, 6:82–83; Everett to Nathan Hale, 3 Dec. 1844, Everett-Hopkins Papers, MHS; Nathan Hale to Everett, 1 Jan. 1845, EP-Harvard.

100. Pletcher, *Diplomacy of Annexation*, 235; Wiltse et al., *Papers of Daniel Webster*, 6:67–68, 80–81; diary, 14 (quotation), 28 June 1845, EP; Everett to Webster, 3 Jan. 1845 (quotation), Everett to Thomas Sewall, 3 Jan. 1845 (quotation), EP.

101. Everett to William C. Rives, 3 Jan. 1845, William C. Rives Papers, LC; Everett to Webster, 18 Apr. 1845, EP.

Chapter 6

1. Diary, 14 May (quotation), 6 July, 30 Aug., 16 Oct. (quotation), 18 Nov. 1845, 5 Feb. 1846, EP; Everett to Peter C. Brooks, 18 July 1845, EP (quotations); Morison, *Three Centuries*, 275–76. For the national prominence of this post, see coverage of Everett's appointment in the *New-Hampshire Statesman and State Journal*, 4 Apr., 26 Sept. 1845; *North American*, 31 July 1845; *Greenville Mountaineer*, 8 Aug. 1845; and *Mississippi Free Trader and Natchez Daily Gazette*, 18 Oct. 1845. For colorful depictions of the disorder of American campus life in this era, see Nathan Appleton Jr. Scrapbooks, MHS; and Bowman and Santos, *Rot, Riot, and Rebellion*.

2. Diary, 3, 22, 27 Apr., 28 May, 7, 9 (quotation) June, 8 (quotation) July, 8 Aug. (quotation), 14 Nov. 1846, EP; Everett to Edward Everett Hale, 2 Aug. 1847 (quotation), Everett-Hopkins Papers, MHS.

3. For samplings of his interaction with parents, see College Letters, 1846–1849, boxes 4 and 5, EP-Harvard.

4. Morison, *Three Centuries*, 275–80; Frothingham, *Edward Everett*, 290–91; *Addresses at the Inauguration*, 3, 15; Mrs. M. W. Chapman to Anne W. Weston, 5 May 1846, BPL.

5. Diary, 11 May, 14 Nov. 1846, 12–14 Apr., 25 Oct. 1847, EP; Everett to Edward Everett Hale, 20 Feb. 1847 (quotation), Everett-Hopkins Papers, MHS.

6. Diary, 12–14 Apr., 16 June, 31 July 1847, 25–28 Nov., 5, 7 Dec. 1848, 11 Jan. 1849, 17 Dec.

1850 (quotation), EP; Everett to Col. Lincoln, 28 Oct. 1849, BPL; Everett to Rev. President Wayland, 14 Sept. 1846, Everett to S. A. Eliot, 13 Apr. 1847, President Everett on the duties of a Harvard president, all in College Letters, box 4, EP-Harvard. For contrasting assessments of Everett's overall effectiveness as president, see Morison, *Three Centuries*, 275–80; and Yanikoski, "Edward Everett and the Advancement of Higher Education," esp. 135.

7. Everett to Daniel Webster, 18 Apr. 1849 (quotation), 14 Oct. 1850 (quotation), EP; diary, 5 Jan., 3 Mar., 31 Dec. 1849, 1 Jan., 20 (quotation), 23–24 Sept., 25, 31 Dec. 1850, 22 Feb., 11 Apr. 1851, 5 Jan. 1852 (quotation), EP; Edward Everett to G. P. Putnam, 5, 9 July 1852, EP-Exeter.

8. Diary, 29 May 1848, 5 Jan., 3 Mar., 28 May, 31 Dec. 1849, 1 Jan., 4–15 Oct., 18 Nov. 1850, 26 May 1851, 24 May, 28 June 1852, EP; Everett to J. P. Bigelow, 7 Aug. 1850, Everett to B. Seaver, 7, 8, 11, 14 Oct. 1850, Everett to Jenny Lind, 16 Oct. 1850, EP; *North American*, 15 Aug. 1850.

9. Diary, 26 Jan., 1 Nov. 1845, 19 Aug. 1846, 29 Jan., 25 May 1849, 23 May, 4, 7 Oct. 1852, EP; Everett to Watson G. Haynes, 16 Oct. 1850, EP; Albert Gallatin to Everett, 16 Dec. 1847, Everett to Gallatin, 20 Dec. 1847, Albert Gallatin Papers, New-York Historical Society, New York; E. Everett, *Orations and Speeches*, vol. 3, 97–111.

10. Everett to George Lunt, 20 Mar. 1851, EP; [Lunt], *Dove and the Eagle*; diary, 9 Nov. 1851, 11 Oct. 1852, EP.

11. Diary, 23 Nov. 1845, 28 Jan., 11 Mar., 29 July 1847, EP; E. Everett, *Orations and Speeches*, vol. 2, 498; *Daily National Intelligencer*, 10 Apr. 1852. For coverage of Everett's inaugural and Everett as temperance man, see *Boston Daily Atlas*, 30 Apr. 1846; *North American*, 4 May 1846; *Daily National Intelligencer*, 4 May 1846; *Cleveland Herald*, 5 May 1846; *Emancipator*, 13 May 1846; *Ohio Observer*, 13 May 1846; *South-Carolina Temperance Advocate*, 12 Nov. 1846; and *Pensacola Gazette*, 20 Oct. 1849.

12. Diary, 30 Mar., 16 May, 13 Sept. 1846, 31 Jan., 9 Apr. 1847, 25 Feb. 1849, EP; E. Everett, *Orations and Speeches*, vol. 3, 43–45, 124–29; *Addresses at the Inauguration*, 29–60. Everett's longing for religious revival pervaded his Sunday diary entries between 1847 and 1852, but what he had in mind as a model was an Anglican-style liturgy rather than any of the more enthusiastic sects of the day; see, e.g., diary, 4 Oct. 1846, 7 Mar. 1847, 13 June 1852, EP.

13. Diary, 27 Oct. 1846, 8 Sept., 18–20, 30 Oct., 16 Dec. 1848, 26 Oct., 10 Dec. 1849, 22 Apr. 1850, 23 July 1851, EP; George Bancroft to Everett, 10 Mar. 1848, Everett to Bancroft, 16 June (quotation), 11 July 1848, Everett to Sir Robert Peel, 27 June 1848, 19 June 1850, Everett to H. Hallam, 25 July 1848 (quotation), Everett to Lord Palmerston, 10 Aug. 1848, Everett to Sir James Graham, 19 Dec. 1849, Everett to M. de Tocqueville, 29 Mar. 1850, Everett to Chevalier Bunsen, 26 Sept. 1850, EP; Everett to Mrs. Malcolm, 22 May 1848, Richards Manuscript Collection, Boston University; *Boston Daily Atlas*, 2 Dec. 1847; Roberts, *Distant Revolutions*, esp. ch. 5; Morrison, "American Reaction."

14. Diary, 2 June, 7 Aug. (quotation) 1848, 31 Mar., 2, 6 July 1849, 7 Jan., 2 Apr., 1 Aug. 1850, 13, 15 Mar., 19, 21 Apr., 3 (quotation), 19 Nov. 1851, 28 Feb., 22 Mar. (quotation) 1852, EP; Everett to Henry Wheaton, 14 Sept. 1847, Henry Wheaton Papers, Morgan Library; E. Everett, *Orations and Speeches*, vol. 3, 73, 83–86, 89 (quotation on 84).

15. E. Everett, *Orations and Speeches*, vol. 3, 118–21, 152–53, 219–31. Everett's Harvard classmate and longtime friend Samuel Gilman found it much harder to keep conservatism from stifling his reform commitments in the context of his Unitarian ministry in Charleston, South Carolina; see Howe, "Massachusetts Yankee."

16. Diary, 25 May 1828, 31 Oct., 2, 10 Nov. 1848, 17, 26 (quotation) Apr., 8 July 1851, EP; Everett to S. Myers, 9 Oct. [sic; Nov.] 1848, EP; Everett to Professor Greenleaf, 7 May 1849, EP-Exeter; Everett to Edward Everett Hale, 11 Jan. 1849, Everett-Hopkins Papers, MHS;

Alford, *Prince among Slaves*, ch. 6, esp. 128–29; E. Everett, *Orations and Speeches*, vol. 3, 186–94 (quotation on 193).

17. Diary, 31 July 1846, EP; box 6, p. 16, EP-Harvard; Sollors, Titcomb, and Underwood, *Blacks at Harvard*, 2, 441–42; A. Schlesinger, *Veritas*, 101; Newman, *Beverly Garnett Williams*; Biographical File, Beverly Garnett Williams, Harvard University Archives, Cambridge, Mass.

18. Wilder, *Ebony and Ivy*; A. Schlesinger, *Veritas*, 101; "From a Graduate's Window," 614–15.

19. The source of the legend is Frothingham, *Edward Everett*, 299. Down to the 1970s, Harvard University Archives' curator fielded questions about the validity of this tale, until a piece in the student newspaper debunked it by revealing that Frothingham was the only and original source; see Harley P. Holden to Harvard Bulletin, 21 Nov. 1972, in Biographical File, Beverly Garnett Williams, Harvard University Archives. On the other hand, Craig Steven Wilder is so eager to nail Harvard and other elite universities for pervasive racism that he does not mention the Beverly Williams episode, instead treating Everett as a racist serving at the behest of the lords of the loom; see *Ebony and Ivy*, 253–86.

20. J. Cowles to Everett, 5 Apr. 1847, in Biographical File, Beverly Garnett Williams, Harvard University Archives; Everett to J. Cowles, 13 Apr. 1847, EP-Harvard, and EP.

21. Diary, 30 July 1847, EP; Bartlett, "Edward Everett Reconsidered," 453; Biographical File, Beverly Garnett Williams, Harvard University Archives; Newman, *Beverly Garnett Williams*; Everett to S. Myers, 9 Oct. 1848, EP.

22. Diary, 25 Dec. 1845, 11 Dec. 1846, 7 Mar. 1847, 23 Feb., 17 Mar., 3 Apr. 1850, EP; Everett to H. Ketcham, 30 Apr. 1848, EP; Everett to C. W. Upham, 9 May 1849, EP-Exeter; Upham, *Speech*. For the mainstream Northern Whig attitude that it would be better to add no territory at all, see Morrison, *Slavery and the American West*, 66–95.

23. Lyell, *Travels in North America*; Lyell, *Second Visit*.

24. Diary, 23 Mar. 1848, 7 May, 3 (quotation), 6, 8, 11, 18–19 Oct. 1849, 30 July, 5 Dec. (quotation) 1850, EP; Everett to H. Hallam, 25 July 1848 (quotation), Everett to Charles Lyell, 8 Oct. 1849, 19 Mar. 1850, EP.

25. Diary, 7 Aug. 1846, EP; Garraty and Carnes, *American National Biography*, 23:683.

26. Diary, 1–3 Mar., 8 Apr., 1 Aug., 3 Oct. 1847, 9 Oct. 1849, 16 Feb., 11 Apr. 1850, EP; Wright, ed., *American Unitarianism*, 209–37.

27. Everett to Charles Lyell, 8 Oct. 1849, EP; diary, 24 June 1846, 19 Apr. 1847, 22 Jan., 15 Nov., 6 Dec. 1849, 15 Jan., 23 Feb., 31 July (quotation), 14 Nov. (quotation) 1850, 7 June, 23 July 1852, EP; Everett to Nathan Hale, 14 June 1849, Everett-Hopkins Papers, MHS.

28. Diary, 24–27 Feb., 12 Apr. (quotation) 1848, EP; Everett to J. T. Buckingham, 31 Mar., 10, 13 Apr. 1848, Everett to Charles Francis Adams, 9, 13, 15, 23 Mar. 1848, Adams to Everett, 9 (quotation), 13, 26 Mar. 1848, EP.

29. E. Everett, *Orations and Speeches*, vol. 2, 556–96; Zboray and Zboray, *Voices without Votes*, 156. This depiction of Adams as moderate on slavery fit the overall tone of his career better than modern narratives in which he is an abolitionist at heart; see M. Mason, "John Quincy Adams"; and Mason and Waldstreicher, *John Quincy Adams*.

30. Diary, 15, 27 Apr., 3 May 1848, 24 July 1850, EP; Everett to Mrs. Malcolm, 22 May 1848, Richards Manuscript Collection, Boston University; *New Hampshire Statesman*, 28 Apr. 1848; *Cleveland Herald*, 11, 15 May 1848; Theodore Parker to Joseph H. Allen, 22 Apr. 1848, Theodore Parker Papers, MHS.

31. Everett to D. L. Child, 17 Apr. 1848, EP; Charles Sumner to Everett, 4, 5 May 1848, Everett to Sumner, 5, 6 May 1848, Papers of Charles Sumner, Houghton Library, Harvard University, Cambridge, Mass.; diary, 3 May 1848, 24 July 1850, EP.

32. Brauer, *Cotton versus Conscience*, esp. 114–205; Hartford, *Money, Morals, and Politics*, 148–212; Gatell, "'Conscience and Judgment.'"

33. Diary, 15 June 1849, 19 May 1850, 18–19 Feb. 1851, EP; Everett to Charles Lyell, 8 Oct. 1849, Everett to Nathan Hale, 18 Feb. 1851, Everett to Winthrop, 18 Feb. 1851, EP.

34. *Boston Daily Advertiser*, 7 Sept. 1849; diary, 5 Sept. 1849, EP.

35. Diary, 12 Aug., 7 Nov. 1848, 13 Nov. 1849, 31 Jan., 3, 5, 24–25 Apr., 6 July, 31 Aug., 6 Oct. 1851, EP; Everett to H. Ketchum, 13 Nov. 1850, EP; Everett to Henry A. Wise, 29 Apr., 12 Dec. 1851, Everett to Charlotte Wise, 31 Dec. 1851, Everett-Hopkins Papers, MHS; Shapiro, "Conservative Dilemma," 208–10.

36. Diary, 17 Feb., 13 Nov. 1848, 13 Oct. 1849, 21 May 1850, EP; Palfrey, *Papers on the Slave Power*; Gatell, *John Gorham Palfrey*, 1–200; *Congressional Globe*, 30th Cong., 1st Sess., 610; LeRoy P. Graf and Ralph W. Haskins to the Harvard College Alumni Association, 10 Feb. 1965, in Biographical File, Beverly Garnett Williams, Harvard University Archives; Trent, *Manliest Man*.

37. Sumner, *Charles Sumner*, 2:233; Nathan Appleton and Charles Sumner Correspondence, BPL; see also O'Connor, *Lords of the Loom*, 88.

38. Diary, 25 Oct. 1851, 13 May, 6 July 1852, EP; Winthrop to Everett, 13 May 1852, EP; Everett to John E. Denison, 24 Mar. 1851, EP-Harvard; Donald, *Charles Sumner*, 107–8, 187.

39. Everett to Sumner, 6 Dec. 1850, Papers of Charles Sumner, Houghton Library.

40. Brauer, *Cotton versus Conscience*, 22–29, 223–45; Julian, *Political Recollections*, 55–61; Earle, *Jacksonian Antislavery*, esp. chs. 2, 6, 7 (quotation on 165); Gatell, "'Conscience and Judgment,'" 43–44; Blue, *Free Soilers*, esp. 63–65.

41. Sumner to Everett, 31 July 1848, EP.

42. Everett to Sumner, 4 Aug. 1848, Papers of Charles Sumner, Houghton Library. In his diary in early August, Everett made only a laconic note about receiving and rejecting this offer; but on his next birthday's year-in-review entry he listed it, alongside his resignation from Harvard and delivering Adams's eulogy, as among the notable events; see diary, 4 Aug. 1848, 11 Apr. 1849, EP.

43. These views epitomized respectively by Silbey, *Partisan Imperative*; Maizlish and Kushma, *Essays on American Antebellum Politics*, esp. 14–121; Holt, *Political Parties*, 26–28, 88–191, 237–90; and Altschuler and Blumin, *Rude Republic*, esp. 8–10, 105–18.

44. Wiltse et al., *Papers of Daniel Webster*, 6:67–68, 286–90, 300–301; Dalzell, *Daniel Webster and the Trial*, 149–53; diary, 11 Dec. 1845, 9 Nov. 1846, 25 Sept., 29 Oct. 1849, 16 July 1850, 3 Apr. 1851, 5–6, 9 Mar., 13 July, 2 Nov. 1852, EP; Everett to Jared Sparks, 4 Mar. 1850, Everett to J. M. Chase, 30 Sept. 1850, EP; *Boston Daily Atlas*, 3 Oct. 1850; Remini, *Daniel Webster*, 727–28, 755. Everett's letter to Sumner parroted the party line as exemplified in the state Whig document from 1846, *True Whig Sentiment*.

45. Bartlett, *Daniel Webster*, 228; Remini, *Daniel Webster*, 615; Wiltse et al., *Papers of Daniel Webster*, 6:216–17, 252–54, 267–68, 270–71, 7:191–92, 197–98, 242–43; [Everett], *Diplomatic and Official Papers*, quotation on 28.

46. Bordewich, *America's Great Debate*, quotation on 117; Remini, *The House*, 142–43; Harrold, *Border War*, esp. chs. 6–7; Ames, *State Documents*, 253–69.

47. Wiltse et al., *Papers of Daniel Webster*, 7:9–23 (quotation on 19); Everett to Webster, 18 Feb. 1850, Everett to Dr. Warren, 18 Feb. 1850, Winthrop to Everett, 3 Mar. 1850, EP.

48. Webster, *Speech of the Hon. Daniel Webster*, quotations on 3, 13, 29, 31–32. For a perceptive reading of what Webster hoped to accomplish with this speech, see Dalzell, *Daniel Webster and the Trial*, 157–277.

49. Bordewich, *America's Great Debate*, 6–7, 46, 132, 144, 160, 182–83, 287–88, 300–301, 343–49.

50. Webster, *Speech of the Hon. Daniel Webster*, 16–23, 25–27; Bordewich, *America's Great Debate*, 127, 156.

51. Peterson, *Great Triumvirate*, 428–31, 442, 464–84, 492–93; Whittier, *Complete Poetical Works*, 186–87, 312–16 (quotation on 186); Kerr-Ritchie, "Samuel Ward," 208; Mann, *Slavery*, vii, 274; Menand, *Metaphysical Club*, 21; Circular, Committee of Correspondence, 10 Mar. 1851, Julius Rockwell Letters, New-York Historical Society, New York.

52. Convers Francis to Theodore Parker, 25 Feb. 1851, Theodore Parker Papers, MHS; Finkelman, *Millard Fillmore*, quotations on 125, 75; Van Tassel, "Gentlemen of Property"; Rao, "Federal *Posse Comitatus* Doctrine"; Harrold, *Border War*, esp. ch. 7.

53. Campbell, *Slave Catchers*, vii–95; Potter, *Impending Crisis*, 137–39; Foster, "Webster's Seventh of March Speech," esp. 264–67; Wiltse et al., *Papers of Daniel Webster*, 7:24–122, 150, 182–86; Durham, *Southern Moderate*, 78–116; Ashworth, *Slavery, Capitalism, and Politics*, vol. 2, 490–91.

54. *Boston Daily Advertiser*, 26 Feb., 3, 13 Apr., 30 May, 22 June 1850; Menand, *Metaphysical Club*, 3–22; Donald, *Charles Sumner*, 157; Remini, *Daniel Webster*, 741–43 (quotations); Belohlavek, *Broken Glass*, 222, 231; *Boston Statesman*, 6 Apr., 25 May 1850.

55. Fergus Bordewich has captured the schizophrenia of this line of interpretation by writing interchangeably about Northern supporters of compromise as "establishment figures" and as a crowd of "an estimated ten thousand people" in New York City! See *America's Great Debate*, 170 (quotations), 248, 302. This is an old as well as contemporary confusion; Leonard W. Levy, writing in 1950, depicted Bostonians' divided response to the FSA, confronted as they were "with a choice among cherished alternatives: liberty or union? freedom or property?" But he proceeded to write as if cotton merchants were the only ones who cared about the second words in those couplets, which leaves unexplained how that division in Boston could have been so broad and deep. See "Sims' Case," quotation on 39.

56. Potter, *Impending Crisis*, esp. 16, 98; Morrison, "American Reaction"; Donald, *Charles Sumner*, 157; Grodzins, "'Slave Law' versus 'Lynch Law'"; Foster, "Webster's Seventh of March Speech"; Stuart, *Conscience and the Constitution*; *Boston Statesman*, 11 May 1850; *Boston Daily Advertiser*, 11, 20 Mar. 1850; *Addresses and Orations of Rufus Choate*, 407–18.

57. Mann, *Slavery*, 282–337; Charles Sumner to H. D. Gilpin, 4 Feb. 1851, Charles Sumner Correspondence, LC; John Davis to [Julius Rockwell], 22 June 1852, Julius Rockwell Letters, New-York Historical Society; Parker, *Discourse Occasioned by the Death*, 1–2, 15, 66, 74; Sweeney, "Rum," quotation on 116; Baum, *Civil War Party System*, 3–54.

58. *Emancipator and Republican*, 25 July 1850.

59. Diary, 26 Dec. 1849, 29 Jan., 17 Feb., 24 Aug., 2 (quotation), 15 Nov. 1850, 12 Feb. 1851, EP.

60. Ibid., 7 Nov. 1848, 26 Nov. 1850, 12 Feb., 4 Mar., 25, 27 June 1851, 15, 20 June 1852; Everett to Sumner, 6 Dec. 1850, Papers of Charles Sumner, Houghton Library; Everett to Robert Walsh, 3 Sept. 1850, Everett to J. E. Durwage, 21 Mar. 1851, EP.

61. Everett to Nathan Appleton, 4 Feb. 1850, Appleton Family Papers, MHS; diary, 24 Aug. 1850, EP; Everett to Webster, 9 Dec. 1850, Everett to Winthrop, 15 May 1850, EP; Everett to Henry A. Wise, 17 Dec. 1850, 7, 14 May 1851, Everett-Hopkins Papers, MHS; Everett to Winthrop, 15 Dec. 1849, 28 Feb. 1850, Winthrop Family Papers, MHS.

62. Everett to Charlotte Wise, 2 Dec. 1850, Everett-Hopkins Papers, MHS (quotation); Everett to N. W. Senior, 1 Jan. 1850 (quotation), Everett to Henry Holland, 14 Mar. (quota-

tions), 12 Nov. 1850, Everett to William Marshall, 6 Mar. 1850, Everett to Winthrop, 6 Aug. 1850, Everett to Robert Walsh, 24 Dec. 1850, EP; diary, 2 Nov. 1850, EP (quotation).

63. For all this confusion, Holman Hamilton was not completely fair to Everett when he wrote of "the vacillations of Edward Everett," who "seemed to have no purpose other than ingratiation" with his correspondents in Washington (*Prologue to Conflict*, 69). Everett was conflicted more because of the inherent vexations of the crisis than because he was a rudderless sycophant.

64. Diary, 8, 11 Mar. 1850, EP.

65. Everett to Webster, 12, 13 Mar. 1850, EP.

66. Winthrop to Everett, 17 Mar. (quotations), 7 Apr. 1850, EP; Everett to Winthrop, 14, 21 (quotations) Mar., 10 Apr. 1850, Winthrop Family Papers, MHS; see also Everett to Abbott Lawrence, 2 Apr. 1850, EP.

67. Everett to Webster, 22 Mar., 3 Apr. 1850, EP. See also Wiltse et al., *Papers of Daniel Webster*, 7:40–41, 51–52; and diary, 28 Sept. 1850, EP.

68. Everett to Webster, 9 Dec. 1850, Everett to Henry Holland, 9 Dec. 1850, Winthrop to Everett, 10 Dec. 1850, Everett to A. Lawrence, 26 Nov. 1850, Everett to M. de Beaumont, 26 Nov. 1850, EP; diary, 31 July 1851, EP. Gary Collison misidentified Everett's letter to Holland as a letter he drafted to Webster but backed away from because it denounced the FSA more vigorously. The compilers of the microfilm edition of Webster's papers reproduced Everett's letterbook and crossed out parts of letters not to Webster that appeared on the same page as letters to Webster; Collison confused this with Everett having canceled out an earlier draft. See Collison, *Shadrach Minkins*, 103–4; and Papers of Daniel Webster, Microfilm Edition, reel 23, frame 31811, University Microfilms, Ann Arbor, Mich.

69. Everett to Henry Holland, 9 Dec. 1850, Everett to Winthrop, 29 May 1850, EP; diary, 4 Mar. 1851, EP.

70. Everett to Webster, 3 Apr. 1850, Winthrop to Everett, 12 May 1850, EP.

71. Webster to Everett, 10 Mar. 1850, EP; diary, 20, 29 Mar., 2, 4, 9 May, 12 June 1850, EP; Everett to Winthrop, 8 May 1850, Winthrop Family Papers, MHS; Stuart, *Conscience and the Constitution*, 7–8. For the letter and Webster's grateful public response, see *Boston Daily Advertiser*, 2, 13 Apr. 1850. David Van Tassel identified Everett as among the signers of this letter ("'Gentlemen of Property," 313), but that is an error. Frothingham, *Edward Everett*, 315–20, captures well how overwhelming the social pressure was on Everett to back Webster.

72. Winthrop to Everett, 12, 22 May 1850, Everett to Abbott Lawrence, 29 Apr. 1850, EP; Everett to Winthrop, 10 Apr. 1850, Winthrop Family Papers, MHS.

73. Winthrop to Everett, 19 July 1850, Everett to Webster, 13 Sept., 5 Oct. 1850, EP; Webster to Everett, 26 Sept. 1850, in Wiltse et al., *Papers of Daniel Webster*, 7:154, see also 7:156–59, 241–43, 259–61, 270–72, 288.

74. Everett to Nathan Hale, 7 Nov. 1850, Everett-Hopkins Papers, MHS; diary, 10 Apr. 1851, EP; *Daily National Intelligencer*, 23 Apr. 1851.

75. Everett to Hon. George Morey, Edward Everett Papers, New York Public Library; [Everett], *Works of Daniel Webster*, 1:xiii–clx (quotation on clix), 5:325 (quotation), 373–74, 381–85, 412–38; Webster, *Speech of the Hon. Daniel Webster*, title page.

76. Wiltse et al., *Papers of Daniel Webster*, 7:297–98, 305–8, 326–27, 333–34; *New York Mirror*, quoted in *Weekly Raleigh Register*, 5 Nov. 1851; Remini, *Daniel Webster*, 727–28.

77. Everett to Henry A. Wise, 28 Jan. 1852, Everett-Hopkins Papers, MHS.

78. Diary, 7 Dec. (quotation) 1850, EP; Everett to Webster, 9 Dec. 1850 (quotation), Everett to N. W. Senior, 1 Jan. 1850, Everett to Rev. Dr. Gilman, 30 Jan. 1850, EP; Everett to Henry A.

Wise, 17 Dec. 1850, Everett-Hopkins Papers, MHS; Everett to Winthrop, 15 Dec. 1849, Winthrop Family Papers, MHS.

79. Diary, 7 Nov. 1848, 15 Nov. 1850, EP.

80. Everett to Winthrop, 25 Jan. (quotation), 4 Dec. 1850, Winthrop Family Papers, MHS; Everett to Nathan Appleton, 4 Feb. 1850 (quotation), Appleton Family Papers, MHS; Everett to H. Hallam, 25 July 1848, EP.

81. Everett to H. Ketchum, 21 Jan. 1851, EP; Everett to Henry A. Wise, 14 May 1851, Everett-Hopkins Papers, MHS.

82. Fergus Bordewich thus seems dead right when he argues that "few northerners" in 1850 "were prepared to fight a war for the Union, much less to end slavery." However, he finds the increased Northern will to fight by 1861–65 in an increased consciousness of "the moral dimension of slavery" that made them so willing to "fight and die to liberate a people who only a few years earlier they feared and despised" (*America's Great Debate*, 393–96). To my mind this misreads the change by locating it in antislavery sectionalism to the exclusion of growing Unionist commitment.

83. Diary, 26, 28 July 1848, EP; Winthrop, *Addresses*, 1:70–89 (quotation on 77); Harvey, *History of the Washington National Monument*, 13–74, 113–30; Everett to Winthrop, 28 July 1848, EP; Morrison, "American Reaction."

84. Everett to Abbott Lawrence, 5 Mar. 1850 (quotation), Everett to Dr. Warren, 14 Feb. (quotation), 18 Mar. 1850 (quotation), Everett to Winthrop, 31 Oct. 1850, Everett to H. Ketchum, 4 Dec. 1850, Everett to Rufus Choate, 4 Dec. 1850, EP; diary, 24 May (quotation), 8 June, 1 July, 15, 19 Nov. 1850, EP.

85. *Mississippian*, 28 Mar. 1851; Poe, *Essays and Reviews*, 83–84, 584, 588, 1439–42, 1470; *Southern Quarterly Review* 18 (Sept. 1850): 251–54; Calhoun, *Works of John C. Calhoun*, 4:542–73, quotations on 559, 561.

86. Minardi, *Making Slavery History*, esp. ch. 5; Levy, "Sims' Case," 70–71; Mann, *Slavery*, viii, 281; Parker, *Ten Sermons*, 66–101 (quotation on 85); Sumner, *Charles Sumner*, 3:13–23, 35–37, 46–50, 130–34, 144, 163–65, 236–37, 240–42 (quotation on 47); Sumner to H. D. Gilpin, 4 Feb. 1851, Charles Sumner Correspondence, LC; Pierce, *Memoir and Letters*, 3:332–33.

87. Everett to Henry Holland, 25 June 1850, EP. He meant here that the Democrats would make 4 July a uniformly Anglophobic holiday if they monopolized it, but this moral had relevance for sectional politics as well. See also Everett to Robert Walsh, 28 Oct. 1850, EP.

88. Everett to C. A. Stetson, 17 Dec. 1850, EP; see also Everett to J. Vincent Brown and others, 28 June 1850, ibid.

89. E. Everett, *Orations and Speeches*, vol. 2, 660–63.

90. Diary, 2, 3, 8 Feb. 1845, 13 Apr. 1849, 6 Mar. 1851 (quotation), 6, 9 Apr. 1852, EP; Everett to Lord Mahon, 28 May 1850, EP.

91. Diary, 22–23 Feb., 15–17, 23, 25 May, 8, 18 June, 10 Dec. 1849, 23, 27 Apr., 15, 29 July, 29 Aug., 16 Sept. 1850, EP.

92. Bordewich, *America's Great Debate*, 132–33, 138–39.

93. Everett to Winthrop, 31 Oct. (quotation), 4 Dec. 1850, Winthrop Family Papers, MHS; Everett to Winthrop, 26 Oct. 1850, Everett to G. W. Warren, 22 Nov. 1850, EP.

94. Everett to Hon. John Wells, 26 Nov. 1850, Everett to R. G. Shaw, 5 Dec. 1850, Everett to Samuel Appleton, 10 Dec. 1850 (quotation), Everett to William Appleton, 18 Dec. 1850 (quotation), Everett to Amos Lawrence, 14 Dec. 1850, EP.

95. Diary, 13–15, 30–31 May, 8 (quotation), 14–15, 17–20 June 1850, EP.

96. E. Everett, *Orations and Speeches*, vol. 3, 3–35.

97. See also ibid., 123, 211, 237–39.

98. *Bangor Daily Whig and Courier*, 20 June 1850; *Raleigh Register*, 6 July 1850.

99. E. Everett, *Orations and Speeches*, vol. 3, 58–71.

100. [Everett], *Works of Daniel Webster*, 6:586–90; diary, 26, 28 (quotations) Feb., 1 Mar. 1851, EP; Everett to George Lunt, 20 Mar. 1851, EP.

101. Diary, 25 Dec. 1850, 5 Sept. 1851, EP; Everett to Gales and Seaton, 26 Apr. 1850, letterbook, 6–20 June 1850, EP.

102. *Southern Literary Messenger* 16 (Sept. 1850): 591; Everett to John R. Thompson, 14 Sept. 1850, Richards Manuscript Collection, Boston University.

103. Magoon, *Living Orators*, 65–116; Everett to Rev. E. L. Magoon, 6 Sept. 1850, Everett to C. W. Upham, 21, 24, 26 Sept., 5 Oct. 1850, Everett to John R. Thompson, 21, 26 Sept., 3 Oct., 7 Nov. 1850, Everett to Dr. Sprague, 17 Oct. 1850, EP. For Upham's review, see *Southern Literary Messenger* 16 (Nov. 1850): 659–66. For the prevalence of such practices in the world of literary reviews dating back well into the eighteenth century, see N. Mason, *Literary Advertising*.

104. Diary, 29 Apr. 1850, EP; *NAR* 71 (Oct. 1850): 445–64, quotations on 446, 456.

105. Magoon, *Living Orators*, for instance, listed Everett second in his pantheon, ahead even of Clay but behind Webster.

Chapter 7

1. Ticknor to Everett, 20 Nov. 1852, in Hillard, *George Ticknor*, 2:284 (quotation); diary, 2, 6, 20, 23, 30 May, 22 June, 1 July 1853, EP; Everett to T. K. Lothrop, 1 Nov. 1852, Everett to Committee of Law School, 3 Nov. 1852, Everett to Hiram Powers, 9 May, 26 June, 12 Aug., 12 Sept. 1853, 13 May 1854, EP; Wiltse et al., *Papers of Daniel Webster*, 7:191–92, 197–98, 242–43, 370; Van Tyne, ed., *Letters of Daniel Webster*, vii–x; Remini, *Daniel Webster*, 762–64.

2. Menand, *Metaphysical Club*, 15; Charles Sumner to Mrs. Story, 15 Dec. 1852, Charles Sumner Correspondence, LC.

3. Parker, *Discourse Occasioned by the Death*, quotations on 69–71, 74, 84; Parker, *Rights of Man*, 309–10, 322.

4. Everett to Henry A. Wise, 25 Oct. 1852, Everett-Hopkins Papers, MHS.

5. Purcell, "All That Remains of Henry Clay."

6. E. Everett, *Orations and Speeches*, vol. 3, 158–66, quotation on 161; *Memorial of Daniel Webster*, esp. 47–71, 232–70.

7. *Boston Daily Atlas*, 30 Oct. 1852; *Account of the Pilgrim Celebration*, esp. 8–22, 31, 37–38, 62–77, 87–96, quotation on 77. Sumner followed Everett on this program and subtly contested the contemporary moral of the Pilgrims' story by presenting them as men persecuted by power but determined to "hold fast to Freedom and Truth!" "Better be the despised Pilgrim, a fugitive for freedom, than the halting politician, forgetful of principle," he declared (*Account of the Pilgrim Celebration*, 79–86, quotations on 84–85).

8. Everett to G. J. Abbot, 1 Nov. 1852 (quotation), Everett to William H. Trescot, 11 July 1855, EP; Fillmore to Everett, 25 Oct. 1852, Everett to Fillmore, 27, 30 Oct. 1852, in EP and Millard Fillmore Papers, LC; Bemis, *American Secretaries of State*, 6:121; Wiltse et al., *Papers of Daniel Webster*, 7:122–27. For the long-standing sense that Everett would succeed Webster, see diary, 17 Nov. 1851, 25 May 1852, EP.

9. Diary, 26 Dec. 1848 (quotation), 12 Feb., 14 Sept. 1849, 1 Oct. 1850, 6–7, 18 Jan. 1851, 23 Mar. 1852, 9 July 1853, EP; Everett to J. E. Sprague, 17 Apr. 1848, Everett to Winthrop, 25 Apr. 1848, Everett to Sir James Graham, 19 Dec. 1849, Everett to George Bancroft, 2 Jan.

1850, Everett to Sir Henry Bulwer, 3 Sept. 1850 (quotation), Everett to Henry Holland, 15 Oct. 1850, Everett to Prince Albert, 10 Dec. 1850, Everett to Burdett Coutts, 26 Nov. 1850, 17 Mar. 1851, Everett to James Buchanan, 8 May 1854 (quotation), EP; Everett to Col. Aspinwall, 27 Feb. 1846, Edward Everett Letters, New-York Historical Society; Tamarkin, *Anglophilia*, 247–329; Tyack, *George Ticknor*, 180–81; Winthrop Jr., *Memoir of Robert C. Winthrop*, 88–89; Wiltse et al., *Papers of Daniel Webster*, 6:115–16, 145–46; Pletcher, *Diplomacy of Annexation*, 303, 316, 323–24, 340.

10. Fillmore to Everett, 16 Feb., 15 May 1852, diary, 29 Sept. 1851, EP.

11. Spencer, *Louis Kossuth*; Coleman, ed., *Life of John J. Crittenden*, 2:26–36.

12. Diary, 21–24, 28 Oct., 12 Nov. 1850, 2, 4 Jan., 8 Feb, 15 Nov., 8, 19, 22 Dec. 1851, 2, 8 Jan., 17, 27 Apr., 18 May 1852 (quotations on 24 Oct., 12 Nov. 1850), EP; Everett to Webster, 24 Oct., 13 Nov. 1850, EP; Shewmaker et al., *Papers of Daniel Webster*, 2:vii–viii, xiv–xvi, 4–10, 31–120 (quotation on 64); Everett to Henry A. Wise, 15, 19 Dec. 1851, 17 Feb. 1852, Everett-Hopkins Papers, MHS; Wiltse et al., *Papers of Daniel Webster*, 7:288, 294–95, 298; Shewmaker, "Daniel Webster"; Roberts, *Distant Revolutions*, 136–38.

13. Everett to Fillmore, 26 Nov., 8, 31 Dec. 1852, Millard Fillmore Papers, LC; diary, 15, 20, 24–30 Nov. 1852, EP; Richardson, *Compilation of the Messages*, 6:2699–2718 (quotations on 2701–2, 2718).

14. Holt, *Franklin Pierce*, 45–46; Holt, *Rise and Fall*, 979; Huston, "Southerners against Secession." See *Daily Scioto Gazette*, 24 Nov. 1852, for a sample of Whig crowing at the ease of Everett's confirmation.

15. Manning, *Diplomatic Correspondence*, 11:54–64, 248, 306, 375; May, *Southern Dream*; Eyal, *Young America Movement*, 135–39; Shewmaker et al., *Papers of Daniel Webster*, 2:335–434, esp. 348; *Correspondence on the Proposed Tripartite Convention*, 13–16.

16. Diary, 10 Nov., 1, 3, 8 Dec. 1852, EP; Everett to Trescot, 11 July 1855, EP.

17. *Correspondence on the Proposed Tripartite Convention*, 28–44; also in Manning, *Diplomatic Correspondence*, 6:466–75.

18. *Correspondence on the Proposed Tripartite Convention*, 45–64; diary, 7 May 1853, EP; Everett to William Marcy, 29 Aug., 26 Sept. 1853, EP.

19. Diary, 20, 25, 29, 31 Dec. 1852, 3–9, 13–14 Jan. 1853, EP.

20. Bemis, *American Secretaries of State*, 6:124–37; [Hale], *Cuba*, esp. 3–4. For the Pierce administration's policy, which differed only in nuances (such as laying greater stress on the national security implications in the event of slave revolt in Cuba, and less on Manifest Destiny) from Everett's, see Manning, *Diplomatic Correspondence*, 7:93–95, 104, 111, 508–9, 11:170–79, 193–214, 685–95, 889–90; and J. Moore, *Works of James Buchanan*, 9:260–66.

21. *Boston Daily Atlas*, 5, 7 (quotation), 26 Jan., 25 Mar. 1853; *Southern Quarterly Review* 25 (Jan. 1854): 1–17, 219–21, 25 (Apr. 1854): 429–70 (quotation on 466); *Cleveland Herald*, 11 Jan. 1853; *Daily South Carolinian*, 13 Jan., 12 Feb. 1853; *Pensacola Gazette*, 19 Feb., 8 Oct. 1853; *Daily Scioto Gazette*, 14 Jan. 1853; *Ripley Bee*, 15 Jan. 1853; *Democratic Review* 31 (Nov./Dec. 1852 and Jan. 1853): 433–56; *United States Democratic Review* 32 (May 1853): 458–78; *Bangor Daily Whig and Courier*, 29 Mar., 23 Sept., 1, 3 Oct. 1853; *North American*, 23, 24 Sept. 1853; *Daily National Intelligencer*, 23 Sept. 1853; *Daily Cleveland Herald*, 27, 30 Sept., 4 Oct. 1853; *Weekly Raleigh Register*, 28 Sept. 1853; *Mississippian and State Gazette*, 28 Jan., 14 Oct. 1853.

22. Diary, 22, 24 Sept. 1853, Everett to Trescot, 9 Jan. 1854, EP; Everett to William C. Rives, 7, 21, 26 Feb. 1853, William C. Rives Papers, LC.

23. Diary, 14 Dec. 1852, 26 Jan., 3 Feb., 4 Mar., 6–9 June 1853, EP; Everett to Hillard, 19 Dec. 1852, George Morey to Everett, telegraph, New York, 26 Jan. 1853, Mrs. Schouler to Everett,

telegraph, New York, 26 Jan. 1853, EP; *Boston Daily Atlas*, 27 Jan., 3 Feb. 1853; *Congressional Globe*, 32nd Cong., 2nd Sess., 671; Everett to Charlotte Wise, 4 Feb., 11 Mar. (quotation) 1853, Everett-Hopkins Papers, MHS; Everett to Dr. Holland, 21 Feb. 1853, EP-Exeter. Garrison in the *Liberator*, quoting the *New York Tribune*, did grouse about the easy election of this alleged doughface; see 25 Feb. 1853.

24. Diary, 9 Apr., 14 July, 13 Dec. 1853, EP.

25. Reprinted in *Daily Cleveland Herald*, 24 Aug. 1853; *Fayetteville Observer*, 1 Sept. 1853; *Bangor Daily Whig and Courier*, 12 Oct. 1853; and *Vermont Watchman*, 3 Nov. 1853.

26. *Southern Quarterly Review* 25 (Jan. 1854): 219–21.

27. *Albany Evening Journal*, 3 Aug. 1853.

28. Diary, 5, 15, 27 Aug. 1853, EP; Everett to H. Hudson, 16 Aug. 1853, EP. Everett's and Weed's very occasional relationship had been tense since a chilly encounter in London in 1843 and Weed's consequent newspaper attack on Everett's aristocratic air as minister; see Everett to Robert C. Winthrop, 3 Jan. 1844, Winthrop Family Papers, MHS.

29. *Frederick Douglass' Paper*, 19 Aug. 1853.

30. *New York Herald*, 15 Aug. 1853.

31. Everett to James Watson Webb, 30 Dec. 1853, EP-Exeter; Everett to C. G. Baylor, 19 Oct. 1853, Everett to H. Hudson, 16 Aug. 1853, EP; diary, 11 Apr., 20 Aug., 26 Oct. 1853, EP; Everett to Henry A. Wise, 27 Sept. 1853, Everett-Hopkins Papers, MHS.

32. Quoted in *Boston Daily Atlas*, 28 Mar. 1853; and *Bangor Daily Whig and Courier*, 29 Mar. 1853. See also *Cleveland Herald*, 1 Apr. 1853; *Daily Register*, 2 Apr. 1853; *Daily Scioto Gazette*, 5 Apr. 1853; and *Vermont Watchman*, 7 Apr. 1853.

33. Diary, 7 Sept. 1853, 4 May, 8 June 1854, EP; [Edward Everett, ed.], *The Original Draft of the Hulsemann Letter* (Boston: T. R. Marvin, 1853), reel 46, vol. 232, EP.

34. Diary, 10 Jan., 16 Feb., 30 June, 19, 23 July, 4, 16, 18 Aug., 13 Sept., 20 Nov., 2, 26 Dec. 1853, 10, 14 June 1854, EP; Everett to Thomas H. Palmer, 17 Feb. 1853, Everett to P. T. Barnum, 2 May 1853, Everett to Rev. Dr. Beecher, 13 July 1853, Everett to Mrs. Charles Eames, 5 May 1854, EP; Everett to James Watson Webb, 30 Dec. 1853, EP-Exeter; *Congressional Globe*, 33rd Cong., 1st Sess., 419, 446, 607, 866, 943–44, 972. The favorable notice for "Stability and Progress" in a key Southern Democratic literary review surely reinforced his confidence; see *Southern Quarterly Review* 25 (Jan. 1854): 219–21.

35. Poore, *Perley's Reminiscences*, 1:427–29, 495; diary, 21–24, 28 Feb., 1, 9 Mar. 1853, EP; Everett to Franklin Pierce, 25 Feb. 1853, EP; Holt, *Franklin Pierce*, 43, 53 (quotation). For a bracing and important argument that personal bonds and the resulting political moderation were much stronger in Washington than the standard accounts of the polarizing 1850s suggest, see Shelden, *Washington Brotherhood*, esp. ch. 6.

36. Everett to Fillmore, 22 Feb. 1853, Millard Fillmore Papers, LC; diary, 20 Feb. 1853, EP; James Buchanan to Everett, 26 May 1854, EP; *Congressional Globe*, 33rd Cong., 1st Sess., 284–90; Pierce, *Memoir and Letters of Charles Sumner*, 3:48–49, 320, 323–24, 345n1, 353–70.

37. Shelden, *Washington Brotherhood*, ch. 6; *Congressional Globe*, 33rd Cong., 1st Sess., 20, 224; E. Everett, *Orations and Speeches*, vol. 3, 251–54, quotation on 252.

38. Diary, 3 Apr. (quotation), 7–8 July, 25 Aug. 1853, EP; Everett to Charles Stearns, 16 Sept. 1853, Edward Everett Letters, New-York Historical Society; Everett to Miss Bourdett-Coutts, 4 Feb. 1853, Everett to Sumner, 15 Oct. 1853 (quotation), EP.

39. Nicholas Gilman to Nathaniel Gilman, 19 Oct. 1853, Nathaniel Gilman Papers, David M. Rubenstein Rare Book and Manuscript Library, Duke University, Durham, N.C.; *Daily National Intelligencer*, 14 Oct. 1853; *Weekly Raleigh Register*, 6 Apr. 1853; *Boston Daily Atlas*,

19 Apr. 1853; *Vermont Watchman*, 28 Apr. 1853; *Bangor Daily Whig and Courier*, 17 Jan. 1854; *Hinds County Gazette*, 25 Jan. 1854. For more praise of his patriotic orations, see *Boston Daily Atlas*, 3 June 1853; *Daily Register*, 11 June 1853; *Weekly Raleigh Register*, 15 June 1853; *Daily Scioto Gazette*, 11 June 1853; *New Hampshire Statesman*, 16 July, 20 Aug. 1853; and *Fayetteville Observer*, 18 Aug. 1853. For abolitionist dissent, see *Liberator*, 2 Sept. 1853.

40. Diary, 15, 18 Jan. 1853, EP.

41. E. Everett, *Orations and Speeches*, vol. 3, 167–94.

42. Diary, 19 (quotation), 22 Jan., 4, 10 Feb., 20 Apr. 1853, EP; Everett to General Ralston, 18 July 1853 (quotation), EP; Everett to William C. Rives, 7, 21, 26 Feb. 1853, William C. Rives Papers, LC; Edward Everett to Nathan Appleton, 6 Feb. 1853, Appleton Family Papers, MHS; *Boston Daily Atlas*, 22, 24 Jan. 1853; *Daily National Intelligencer*, 24 Jan. 1853; *Daily Scioto Gazette*, 7 Mar. 1853; *Liberator*, 11 Feb. 1853.

43. Diary, 10 Dec. 1853 (quotation), 9 Jan. 1854, EP; *Milwaukee Daily Sentinel*, 30 Dec. 1853; Donald, *Charles Sumner*, 170–74; Nevins, *Hamilton Fish*, 45–46.

44. Diary, 7 Mar., 9, 29 Apr., 23 June, 14, 19 Oct., 22 Nov. 1853, EP; Everett to William L. Marcy, 15 July, 15 Aug. 1853, Everett to James Buchanan, 31 Oct. 1853, EP; O'Connor, *Lords of the Loom*, 90–98.

45. Johannsen, *Stephen A. Douglas*, 401–64; Johannsen, *Frontier*, 77–119; Huston, *Stephen A. Douglas*; Holt, *Franklin Pierce*, esp. 75–78; Potter, *Impending Crisis*, 161–63; Shelden, *Washington Brotherhood*, 96–119; Paulus, "America's Long Eulogy," quotations on 30, 31.

46. Diary, 4 Jan., 4 Mar. 1854, EP; Johannsen, *Frontier*, 93–119; Holt, *Rise and Fall*, 807; Everett to Nathan Appleton, 19 Jan. 1854, George Ticknor to Nathan Appleton, Apr. 1854, Appleton Family Papers, MHS; Everett to John H. Clifford, 10 Jan. 1854, John H. Clifford Papers, MHS; Everett to Millard Fillmore, 4 Feb. 1854, Millard Fillmore Papers, LC.

47. Diary, 4, 27 Mar., 15 Apr., 29 June, 4 July, 6 Sept., 22, 31 Oct. 1853, EP; Everett to W. Follett Synge, 12 Sept. 1853, EP.

48. *Boston Daily Advertiser*, 30, 31 Jan., 1, 4, 6, 22, 23, 27 Feb., 1, 4 Mar. 1854; Winthrop to Everett, 28 Jan., 6, 24 Feb., 14 Apr. 1854, Fillmore to Everett, 8 Feb. 1854, EP; John H. Clifford to Everett, 20 Jan. 1854, John H. Clifford Papers, MHS; Choate to Everett, 4 Feb. 1854, in S. Brown, *Works of Rufus Choate*, 1:190–91; diary, 18, 27 Jan. 1854, EP. For another example of opposition to the bill on conservative grounds, see Winthrop, *Addresses*, 2:175–78.

49. *Congressional Globe*, 33rd Cong., 1st Sess., 352–55; diary, 7 Feb. 1854, EP; Everett to Henry A. Wise, 12 Feb. 1854, Everett-Hopkins Papers, MHS; Everett to Winthrop, 9 Feb. 1854, Winthrop Family Papers, MHS.

50. Everett to W. Aspinwall, 6 Feb. 1854, EP.

51. Diary, 8 Feb. 1854, EP; *Congressional Globe*, 33rd Cong., 1st Sess., 378; Wilson, *History of the Rise and Fall*, 2:386.

52. *Congressional Globe*, 33rd Cong., 1st Sess., appendix, 158–60.

53. Ibid., 162–63.

54. Ibid.,158–62. See also diary, 6, 9, 16 Feb. 1854, EP.

55. *Congressional Globe*, 33rd Cong., 1st Sess., appendix, 333–34.

56. Huston, "Southerners against Secession," 289; Winthrop to Everett, 24 Jan. 1854 (quotation), EP; Clifford to Everett, 20 Jan. 1854, John H. Clifford Papers, MHS.

57. Winthrop to Everett, 13 Feb. 1854, EP; *Boston Daily Atlas*, 13, 22 Feb. 1854; *Ripley Bee*, 18 Feb. 1854; diary, 8 Feb. 1854, EP; Everett to "Dear Sir," 21 Apr. 1854, EP; Everett to Henry A. Wise, 13 Sept. 1856, Everett-Hopkins Papers, MHS; *New Hampshire Statesman*, 4 Mar. 1854; *Liberator*, 17 Feb. 1854.

58. Holt, *Franklin Pierce*, 80–81; Huston, *Stephen A. Douglas*, esp. 99–106; Johannsen, *Stephen A. Douglas*, 401–64; diary, 30, 31 Jan., 6 Apr. 1854, EP. While Michael F. Holt was terribly imprecise when he characterized Everett's speech as "quintessential doughfacism," he did capture well how Everett and his kind had lost the initiative; Holt, *Rise and Fall*, 815–17.

59. Sumner, *Charles Sumner*, 4:147–48; Everett to Winthrop, 26 Feb. 1854, Winthrop Family Papers, MHS; *Congressional Globe*, 33rd Cong., 1st Sess., appendix, 234, 236.

60. Everett to J. C. Spencer, 4 Feb. 1854 (quotation), Everett to Buchanan, 8 May 1854 (quotation), Everett to Trescot, 30 Jan., 15 Feb. 1854, EP; Fillmore to Alexander H. H. Stuart, 9 Feb. 1854, Papers of Alexander H. H. Stuart and the Related Stuart and Baldwin Families, University of Virginia; Morrison, *Slavery and the American West*, 139; O'Connor, *Lords of the Loom*, 98–143.

61. Diary, 3 Mar. 1854, EP; *Boston Daily Advertiser*, 4, 6, 7 Mar. 1854; Shelden, *Washington Brotherhood*, 19–24.

62. Diary, 3 (quotation), 5–8 Mar. 1854, EP; Everett to Nathan Hale, 4 Mar. 1854, Everett-Hopkins Papers, MHS; *Boston Daily Advertiser*, 4, 6, 7 Mar. 1854; Pierce, *Memoir and Letters*, 360n4. For another defense of Everett's non-vote, see *Cleveland Herald*, 10 Mar. 1854.

63. *Congressional Globe*, 33rd Cong., 1st Sess., 550.

64. Hale, *Man without a Country*, 113; "Memoir of Edward Everett," 115.

65. Diary, 14 Mar. 1854, EP; *Congressional Globe*, 33rd Cong., 1st Sess., 617–23. For other petitions Everett introduced, see *Congressional Globe*, 33rd Cong., 1st Sess., 406, 446, 473, 485, 493, 607, 773, 834, 845, 875. For another secondary account of this incident that overstates Everett's doughface-ism and this moment of political disaster as emblematic of his entire late career, see Forbes, *Missouri Compromise*, 279–81.

66. Salmon P. Chase to John Jay, 23 Jan. 1854, Salmon P. Chase Papers, LC.

67. Theodore Parker to Charles Sumner, 19 Mar. 1854, Sumner to Parker, 22 Mar. 1854, Theodore Parker Papers, MHS; Parker, *Rights of Man*, 159, 168, 183–84, 250–324, 425, quotations on 159, 183–84, 282.

68. Donald, *Charles Sumner*, 214; *New York Evening Post* reprinted in *Liberator*, 24 Mar. 1854. For other attacks on Everett largely but not exclusively from Free Soilers and abolitionists, see *Liberator*, 14 Apr. 1854; D. Weston to "Dear Folks," 2 June 1854, BPL; Pierce, *Memoir and Letters*, 3:353–70, 390; Frothingham, *Edward Everett*, 353–54; and Hartford, *Money, Morals, and Politics*, 198–200.

69. Diary, 9 Feb., 23 Mar. 1854, EP; William H. Seward to Everett, 19 June 1854, EP.

70. Everett to Winthrop, 12 Mar. 1854, Winthrop Family Papers, MHS; Everett to Henry A. Wise, 10 Apr. 1854, Everett-Hopkins Papers, MHS; see also Everett to Rev. R. M. Devens, 13 Mar. 1854, EP.

71. Everett to Julius Rockwell, 29 June 1854, Julius Rockwell Letters, New-York Historical Society; Everett to Miss Dix, 8 Mar. 1854 (quotation), Everett to Rev. R. M. Devens, 13 Mar. 1854, EP; diary, 9–10, 21 Feb., 17 Mar. (quotation) 1854, EP.

72. Everett to Sally Hale, 26 Apr. 1854, Everett-Hopkins Papers, MHS; diary, 28 May 1854, EP; Everett to Mrs. Charles Eames, 26 May 1854, EP (quotation).

73. Diary, 29 Jan. 1854, EP; *Daily Scioto Gazette*, 30 May 1854.

74. Everett to Henry A. Wise, 23 Dec. 1852, Everett to Charlotte Wise, 4, 28 Feb., 11 Mar., 8 May 1853, Everett-Hopkins Papers, MHS.

75. Diary, 9, 18, 20, 24, 31 Mar., 12 Apr., 3–11 May 1854, EP; Everett to "Dear Sir," 8 Apr. 1854, Everett to Trescot, 24 Apr. 1854, Everett to Mrs. Charles Eames, 5 May 1854 (quotation),

EP; Everett to Henry A. Wise, 12 Mar. (quotation), 10 Apr. 1854, Everett to Charlotte Wise, 22, 30 Mar., 22 Apr. 1854, Everett-Hopkins Papers, MHS.

76. Everett to Charlotte Wise, 7 May (quotation), 13 July 1854, Everett-Hopkins Papers, MHS; Everett to Governor Washburn, 12, 17 May 1854, EP-Exeter; diary, 12, 15–17 May 1854, EP; Winthrop to Everett, 12 May 1854, Everett to Charles Eames, 16 May 1854, EP; *Congressional Globe*, 33rd Cong., 1st Sess., 1255.

77. *Boston Daily Advertiser*, 20, 22 (quotation) May 1854; *Weekly Herald*, 27 May 1854; *Milwaukee Daily Sentinel*, 27 May 1854; *Daily Cleveland Herald*, 24 May 1854; *Boston Daily Atlas*, 22 May 1854; *Daily National Intelligencer*, 22 May 1854.

78. Everett to Charles Sumner, 22 May 1854, Papers of Charles Sumner, Houghton Library; Everett to Winthrop, 12, 13 (quotation) May 1854, Winthrop Family Papers, MHS; Everett to Asbury Dickens, 20 May 1854 (quotation), EP-Exeter; Everett to Abbott Lawrence, 12 May 1854, Everett to Mrs. Charles Eames, 12, 22 May 1854, EP; Everett to Millard Fillmore, 2 June 1854, Millard Fillmore Papers, LC; Everett to Charlotte Wise, 8, 25 June, 13 July, 15 Aug. 1854, Everett-Hopkins Papers, MHS; Edward Everett to L. D. Johnson, 27 May 1854, BPL. Sumner sent Everett a telegram assuring him that he would honor his wishes if it came to that; Sumner to Everett, 24 May 1854, EP. But there is no evidence in the congressional record that Sumner offered the explanation Everett requested. William Dawson, the senator Everett proposed "pair off" with him, voted for the final bill rather than abstained; *Congressional Globe*, 33rd Cong., 1st Sess., 1321.

79. Everett to Mrs. Charles Eames, 12 May 1854, EP. See also Everett to Charlotte Wise, 30 Mar. 1854, Everett to Henry A. Wise, 3 Oct. 1856, Everett-Hopkins Papers, MHS.

80. Diary, 30 July 1854, EP.

Chapter 8

1. Von Frank, *Trails of Anthony Burns*; Maltz, *Fugitive Slave on Trial*; Barker, *Imperfect Revolution*; Earle, "'Stark Mad Abolitionists'"; Ames, *State Documents*, 288; Mulkern, *Know-Nothing Party*; Anbinder, *Nativism and Slavery*; Stephen E. Maizlish, "The Meaning of Nativism and the Crisis of the Union," in Maizlish and Kushma, *Essays on American Antebellum Politics*, 166–98.

2. Everett to Mrs. Charles Eames, 7 June (quotation), 2 July, 14 Sept., 21 Oct., 13 Nov. 1854, 18 June 1855 (quotation), EP; see also Everett to William H. Trescot, 20 Oct. 1854, EP; diary, 27 May, 17 Aug., 3 Oct. 1854, EP; and *Boston Daily Advertiser*, 5 Oct. 1854.

3. Frothingham, *Edward Everett*, 372; Everett to Mrs. Charles Eames, 1 Aug., 9 Oct. (quotation) 1854, 16 May 1855 (quotation), EP; diary, 23 June 1854 (quotation), EP.

4. Diary, 16, 20 Nov. 1854, 16 Mar. (quotation), 11 Apr., 10 June 1855, EP; Everett to Mrs. Charles Eames, 4 Nov. 1854, EP. His sense of being mistreated relative to his Kansas-Nebraska performance proved persistent; see Everett to Hillard, 27 May 1859, EP.

5. Everett to James A. Hamilton, 10 Nov., 3, 17 Dec. 1855, 7, 21 Jan. 1856, in EP, in James A. Hamilton Papers, New York Public Library, New York, and in J. Hamilton, *Reminiscences of James A. Hamilton*, 404–8.

6. Diary, 2 May, 1 Dec. (quotation) 1855, 2 Jan. 1856, EP; *Fayetteville Observer*, 15 July 1858; M. Smith, *Enemy Within*.

7. Millard Fillmore to Everett, 13 Dec. 1854, 7 Apr. 1855, Everett to Trescot, 12 Sept., 29 Dec. 1856, EP; Everett to Henry A. Wise, 18 July, 20 Sept., 10 Oct., 7 Nov. 1856, Everett-Hopkins Papers, MHS; Everett to Fillmore, 11 Apr. 1855, 9 July 1856, Fillmore to Everett, 12 July

1856, Millard Fillmore Papers, LC. Mark E. Neely Jr. has argued that "the American Party represented the supreme attempt to establish an ethnic rather than a civic nationalism in this country" (Gallagher and Shelden, *Political Nation*, 58). As such it was antithetical to Everett's own nationalist project, never more so than in this era. For portraits of the severe indecision faced by many ex-Whigs in this era, see Hamilton Fish to Hamilton, 13, 17 June, 12 Sept. 1856, James A. Hamilton Papers, New York Public Library; and Holt, *Rise and Fall*, chs. 22–26.

8. Buchanan to Everett, 11 Dec. 1856, Everett to Buchanan, 8 Dec. 1856, 19 Jan. 1857, EP; diary, 5 Nov., 12 Dec. 1856, EP.

9. Diary, 29 Oct. (quotation), 4 Nov., 2 Dec. 1856, 3 Nov. 1857, 2 Nov. 1858, 8 Nov. 1859, EP; Everett to Caleb Cushing, 11 Oct. 1855, Caleb Cushing Papers, LC.

10. Diary, 31 May, 2, 10 June, 19 July 1854, 29 Mar., 27 Aug., 17 Oct., 1 Nov., 8 Dec. 1856, 21 June 1857, EP; Everett to James H. Thornwell, 7 Feb. 1856 (quotation), Everett to Trescot, 17 Dec. 1855 (quotation), 22 July 1857, EP; Everett to John J. Crittenden, 3 Mar. 1860, John J. Crittenden Papers, David M. Rubenstein Rare Book and Manuscript Library, Duke University, Durham, N.C.; Hale Jr., *Life and Letters*, 1:251–52. Support for the New England/ Massachusetts Emigrant Aid Association came from a wide swath of Northern political opinion; see Lawrence, *Life of Amos A. Lawrence*, 73–106.

11. Diary, 18 July 1854, 24 Jan., 6 Sept. 1856, 8, 27 Feb., 31 Mar., 20 June 1857, 29 July, 26 Nov. 1858, 2 Nov. 1859, EP; E. Everett, *Orations and Speeches*, vol. 4, 27.

12. E. Everett, *Orations and Speeches*, vol. 3, 288, 378 (quotation), 384, 451, 466–76, 486–523, 537–614; vol. 4, 54–57, 60–64, 66–73; diary, 26 Oct. 1854, 30 Oct., 15 Nov. 1856, 27 Aug. 1859, EP; Everett to Henry A. Wise, 31 Oct. 1857, Everett to Charlotte Wise, 20 Nov. 1857, Everett-Hopkins Papers, MHS; Frothingham, *Edward Everett*, 363–65; Hillard, *George Ticknor*, 2:299–400.

13. Diary, 21, 27 (quotation) Nov., 3 Dec. 1856, 28 Sept., 1, 11 (quotation), 12 Oct. 1859, EP.

14. Diary, 7 Sept. 1854, 8 Feb. 1855, EP; Everett to Henry A. Wise, 13 May 1856, Everett-Hopkins Papers, MHS; Everett to T. B. Macauley, 6 Nov. 1855, EP; *Boston Daily Advertiser*, 5, 15, 31 Aug., 5, 8, 11 Sept., 9 Oct. 1854. For a good discussion of why these agitators resorted to provocative language, see Stewart, *Wendell Phillips*, 73, 117–45. The other letters and especially diary entries complaining of the abusiveness and corruption of the Republicans and abolitionists in this era are so numerous that to cite them here would strain the patience of every last reader and editor, although I could provide them upon request. For evidence that Everett was not alone in these views, see the 1856 pamphlet *Great Fraud upon the Public Credulity*.

15. Diary, 21 Nov. 1855, 15 June 1857, EP; Bridgman, *Pilgrims of Boston*, iii, xi–xvi.

16. E. Everett, *Orations and Speeches*, vol. 3, 260–67; S. Brown, *Works of Rufus Choate*, 1:264–72; *Boston Daily Courier*, 23 July 1859; E. Everett, *Orations and Speeches*, vol. 4, 178–85. The Choate eulogy provoked a brief controversy when detractors argued that Everett was making a virtue out of necessity by crediting Choate for the unpopularity of their shared views; see *New York Daily Tribune*, 29 July 1859; *Boston Daily Courier*, 4 Aug. 1859; and John Clark to Caleb Cushing, 29, 31 July 1859, Caleb Cushing Papers, LC.

17. Diary, 26 June 1857, EP; Clay Monumental Association to Alexander R. Boteler, 20 Feb. 1860, Alexander R. Boteler Papers, David M. Rubenstein Rare Book and Manuscript Library, Duke University, Durham, N.C. For more on what Clay represented to his Unionist disciples in this period, see Paulus, "America's Long Eulogy," esp. 33.

18. Diary, 23 Jan. 1856, 21 Aug. 1858, EP; Everett to Caleb Cushing, 21 Mar. 1859, Caleb Cushing Papers, LC; Choate, *Addresses and Orations*, 517–29; Everett, *Discourse Delivered*, Houghton Library, Harvard University, Cambridge, Mass.; E. Everett, *Orations and Speeches*,

vol. 4, 186–234; *Seventy-Fourth Anniversary*, quotations on 18, 62; E. Everett, *Orations and Speeches*, vol. 3, 390–411.

19. E. Everett, *Orations and Speeches*, vol. 3, 292–354, quotation on 335. For more on this celebration, including the fulsome audience reaction, see Orcutt, *Good Old Dorchester*, 200–214; *Boston Daily Advertiser*, 6 July 1855; and *Daily National Intelligencer*, 21 July 1855.

20. Diary, 5 Oct. 1854, EP; Everett to Winthrop, 4 Oct. 1854, Winthrop Family Papers, MHS.

21. Everett to Winthrop, 8 June 1854, 17 Jan. 1855, EP; diary, 15 Apr. 1856, 26 June, 13 Aug. 1857, 16 Nov. 1858, EP; Winthrop, *Addresses*, 2:258–91; E. Everett, *Orations and Speeches*, vol. 4, 103–29 (quotation on 118), and vol. 3, 415, 482–85; *Boston Daily Advertiser*, 22 Jan. 1855; *Daily National Intelligencer*, 29 Jan. 1855; Everett to F. Plummer, 10 Sept. 1856, Edward Everett Papers, American Antiquarian Society; Edward Everett to G. Livermore, 27 June 1854, Edward Everett Letters, 1816–1863, MHS.

22. Forgie, *Patricide in the House Divided*, 159–99, 255–56, 271; Horn, "Edward Everett and American Nationalism," 332–35, 342; Seelye, *Memory's Nation*, 437.

23. Diary, 6 Apr., 11 May 1855, 24 Apr. 1856, 21 Aug. 1858, 13 Oct. 1859, EP; E. Everett, *Orations and Speeches*, vol. 4, 76–78, 257 (quotation on 77).

24. E. Everett, *Orations and Speeches*, vol. 3, 344–48, 526–36, 615–19, and vol. 4, 189–91.

25. Chambers, *Memories of War*.

26. J. Lee, *Experiencing Mount Vernon*, 21, 65, 102, 104–5, 128, 135, 139–42, 146–52, 169–74, 174–82, 186, 190–96, 203, 206–7. See also J. Lee, "Historical Memory"; Furstenberg, *In the Name of the Father*; Kahler, *Long Farewell*; and Casper, *Sarah Johnson's Mount Vernon*, 32–33.

27. J. Lee, *Experiencing Mount Vernon*, 197–98 (quotations); Thane, *Mount Vernon Is Ours*, 3–180; West, *Domesticating History*, xi–37; *Illustrated Mount Vernon Record*, vol. 1, 1; Casper, *Sarah Johnson's Mount Vernon*, 63–71; J. Lee, "Historical Memory," 299; Varon, *We Mean to Be Counted*, 10–70, 124–36, 210n58; *Boston Statesman*, 1 Apr. 1854; M. Gustafson, *Women and the Republican Party*, ch. 1. My analysis of the MVLAU as a throwback to an earlier phase of women's activism relies heavily on Lasser and Robertson, *Antebellum Women*, although the MVLAU's work of nonpartisan single-issue reform in collaboration with men fits more neatly into the mainstream described for the 1850s by Ginzburg, *Women and the Work of Benevolence*, esp. ch. 4. And given that women played significant roles in the national rituals of mourning at Washington's death, this effort was a throwback in that sense as well; see Kahler, *Long Farewell*, 73–85. The whole MVLAU episode, alongside the raft of scholarship on antebellum women and politics to which it speaks, underscores that Nina Silber overstated the novelty of women's political relevance and activism during the American Civil War; see *Gender and the Sectional Conflict*, esp. xiii, 40, 54.

28. Everett and Abbott Lawrence to Isaac H. Shepard, 12 July 1853, EP; diary, 18 Feb. 1854, EP.

20. Diary, 17, 21, 24, 31 July 1855, EP; Everett to Charles G. Chase and others, 15 Oct. 1855, EP; Everett to "Dear Charles," 11 Feb. 1856, Everett-Hopkins Papers, MHS. For Everett's characteristically precise account of his involvement in this cause, see E. Everett, *Orations and Speeches*, vol. 4, 3–17.

30. Everett to S. Austin Allibone, 11 Dec. 1855, EP; diary, 15 Dec. 1856, EP.

31. E. Everett, *Orations and Speeches*, vol. 4, 20–51.

32. Diary, 23 May, 11 Aug. (quotation), 30 Oct., 29 Dec. 1855, 18, 26 Feb. 1856, EP; Everett to Thompson, 3 Nov. 1855, Everett to Mrs. Charles Eames, 7 Nov. 1855, EP; Everett to Edward Everett Hale, 25 Feb. 1856, Everett-Hopkins Papers, MHS. For Phillips and the profitable lyceum circuit, see Stewart, *Wendell Phillips*, 54, 177–95.

33. Diary, 3 Mar.–20 Apr., 1, 5, 12 May, 5 Dec. 1856, 24 Apr., 4 Aug., 24 Dec. 1857, 25, 28, 29 Jan., 31 May 1858, EP; Everett to Henry A. Wise, 5 Mar. 1856, EP. For an example of the form letter, see Everett to L. A. Dimock, 20 Dec. 1858, Papers of Edward Everett, University of Virginia.

34. Diary, 1, 13 May, 17 Aug., 15, 19, 28 Sept., 14 Oct., 2 Dec. 1857, 8 Feb., 5 May, 20 Oct., 26 Nov. 1858, EP.

35. Diary, 10, 17 Mar., 3 Apr. 1856, EP.

36. Ibid., 23 Mar. 1856, 13, 19 Apr. 1858; Everett to Governor Wise, 4 Mar. 1856, Everett to Truman Smith, 16 Jan. 1859, EP-Exeter; Everett to William C. Rives, 28 Mar. 1856, William C. Rives Papers, LC; E. Everett, *Mount Vernon Papers*, 3–4, 6, 8.

37. Diary, 10 Oct. 1856, 3 Apr., 3 May 1857, EP; Edward Everett to Charles Deane, 7 Dec. 1858, BPL; Everett to Henry A. Wise, 31 Oct. 1857, Everett to Charlotte Wise, 23 Apr. 1860 (quotation), Everett-Hopkins Papers, MHS.

38. Washington Irving to Thomas W. Olcott et al., 14 Mar. 1857, Winthrop to Everett, 23 Feb. 1856, EP; *Southern Literary Messenger* 22 (Apr. 1856): 317 (quotation); Minor, *Southern Literary Messenger*, 188–89; *NAR* 84 (Apr. 1847): 362–63.

39. Diary, 24 May 1858, 2 July 1859, EP; Everett to Charlotte Wise, 1, 19 Nov., 4 Dec. 1855, 28 Feb., 22 Mar. 1856, Everett to Henry A. Wise, 18 Dec. 1855, Everett-Hopkins Papers, MHS; Frothingham, *Edward Everett*, 373–407. He could not get over the delight of staying in such a hotel named after him; see diary, 28 Feb., 9, 10 Apr. 1856, 1 June 1857, EP.

40. E. Everett, *Orations and Speeches*, vol. 3, 620–23; diary, 1 Aug. 1857, 22–23 Feb. 1858, EP.

41. E. Everett, *Orations and Speeches*, vol. 3, 631–47.

42. Everett to Charlotte Wise, 22 Mar. 1856 (quotation), Everett to Henry A. Wise, 13 Apr. 1856, Everett-Hopkins Papers, MHS; Everett to Mrs. Charles Eames, 19 Apr. 1856, EP; Prescott to Lady Lyell, 31 May 1858, in Ticknor, *Life of William Hickling Prescott*, 406 (quotation); diary, 26 Apr. 1859, EP (quotation); Winthrop Jr., *Memoir of Robert C. Winthrop*, 209.

43. Craven, *Legend of the Founding Fathers*, 56–182; Morrison, *Slavery and the American West*; Furstenberg, *In the Name of the Father*, 71–103; Sarah J. Purcell, "Martyred Blood and Avenging Spirits: Revolutionary Martyrs and Heroes as Inspiration for the U.S. Civil War," in McDonnell et al., *Remembering the Revolution*, 280–93; Minardi, *Making Slavery History*; Crider, "De Bow's Revolution"; Watkins, "Slavery."

44. Casper, *Sarah Johnson's Mount Vernon*, 70–75; Andrews, *Three Classic African-American Novels*, 11–69 (quotation on 68).

45. Diary, 30 June, 4 July 1855, EP; *Liberator*, 29 June (quotation), 6, 13 July 1855; *Frederick Douglass' Paper*, 20 July 1855; *Boston Daily Advertiser*, 3 July 1855; William Lloyd Garrison to Samuel J. May, 19 Sept. 1859, in Garrison, *Letters of William Lloyd Garrison*, 4:654; *Liberator*, 30 Sept. 1859.

46. Samuel May Jr. to Richard Davis Webb, 11 Mar. 1856, BPL; *Liberator*, 26 Nov. 1858 (quotation), 14 Jan. 1859.

47. Blassingame, *Frederick Douglass Papers*, 226–31.

48. *Albany Evening Journal*, 21 Mar. 1857.

49. Reprinted in *Lowell Daily Citizen and News*, 27 July 1858.

50. Stewart, *Wendell Phillips*, esp. xii, 35, 43, 57–62, 70–73, 104–5, 147–52, 177–208, quotations on 60, 189–92; W. Phillips, *Speeches, Lectures, and Letters*, 1st ser., 254–62, quotations on 256, 261.

51. Sumner, *Charles Sumner*, 5:95–96; see also 4:8, 66, 73–79, 163–71, 190, 228–29, 237–38, 5:141, 145–48, 155–58, 206–11, 234–48, 6:22–28, 70.

52. Parker, *Historic Americans*, esp. 3–9, 75–146, quotations on 77, 136, 145. He did not specifically name Everett in these lectures, but his private correspondence leaves no doubt that he was one of his prime targets. As he wrote to one friend, "Everett is a Rhetorician; his trade is to make speeches, he does this on all occasions except those where manly regard for justice is required then 'mi vocal organs' are out of tune, 'mi health is so deranged' that he can't speak a word." See Theodore Parker to Charles Ellis, 22 Sept. 1859 (quotation), Parker to Charles Sumner, 16, 21 May 1858, Theodore Parker Papers, MHS.

53. Bonner, *Mastering America*, ch. 6, esp. 194–205; Walther, *William Lowndes Yancey*, esp. 211–13 (quotation on 212). This episode in Yancey's career is consistent with William W. Freehling's portrait of him as one with an endless capacity to present his secessionist schemes behind a facade of reasonableness; see Freehling, *Road to Disunion*, vol. 2, esp. 336.

54. Diary, 10 July 1857, EP; Everett to Robert C. Winthrop, 18 Sept. 1857, Winthrop to Everett, 19 Sept. 1857, Everett to Rev. J. H. Martin, 13 July 1857, EP; *Boston Daily Advertiser*, 24 July 1857.

55. *Daily Morning News*, 14 May 1858.

56. *Weekly Raleigh Register*, 4 June 1856, 24 June 1857.

57. Diary, 23–27 May 1856, EP; Everett to Henry A. Wise, 23 May 1856, Everett-Hopkins Papers, MHS; Woods, "'Indignation'"; Woods, *Emotional and Sectional Conflict*, ch. 5, esp. 163–64.

58. Diary, 28–30 May 1856, EP; Everett to E. Huntington, 29 May 1856, EP; *Boston Daily Advertiser*, 29 May 1856.

59. Diary, 7 June 1856, EP; *Boston Daily Advertiser*, 2 June 1856. These remarks were reprinted without comment in *Daily Cleveland Herald*, 2 June 1856; *Daily National Intelligencer*, 3 June 1856; *New York Herald*, 3 June 1856; *Liberator*, 6 June 1856; *Milwaukee Daily Sentinel*, 7 June 1856; *Fayetteville Observer*, 9 June 1856; *Vermont Chronicle*, 10 June 1856; *Daily Scioto Gazette*, 10 June 1856; *Weekly Raleigh Register*, 11 June 1856; and *New Hampshire Statesman*, 14 June 1856.

60. Everett to Henry A. Wise, 2 June 1856 (quotation), Everett-Hopkins Papers, MHS; Everett to Trescot, 27 July 1856 (quotation), Everett to Mrs. Pellet, 13 June 1856, EP; Woods, "'Indignation'"; Woods, *Emotional and Sectional Conflict*, esp. chs. 4–5.

61. Diary, 7 June 1856, EP, including clipping from *New York Times*, 7 June 1856; *Lowell Daily Citizen and News*, 2, 7 June 1856; *Liberator*, 13 June 1856. Everett declined the new invitation, without deigning to tell the legislature his reason; see diary, 13 June 1856, EP; and Everett to Messrs. Orris S. Ferry et al., 13 June 1856, EP. Looking back decades later, Henry Wilson seems to have agreed with the *New York Times* estimate of the Taunton remarks; see *History of the Rise and Fall*, 2:494.

62. Horace Maynard to Everett, 19 Sept. 1857, EP; *Richmond Enquirer* reprinted in *Liberator*, 27 June 1856; *The South* reprinted in *Milwaukee Daily Sentinel*, 23 Apr. 1858; *Dadeville (Ala.) Banner* reprinted in *Liberator*, 25 June 1858.

63. *Liberator*, 14 May, 26 Nov. 1858.

64. Diary, 21 June 1856, EP; Everett to Mrs. Charles Eames, 21 June 1856, Everett to Mrs. W. F. Ritchie, 26 June 1856, EP.

65. Diary, 3–6, 20 June 1856, EP; Everett to Nathan Hale, 20 June 1856, Everett-Hopkins Papers, MHS.

66. *The South*, 11 Feb. 1858. Pryor had been working up to a full-scale attack on the MVLAU for some weeks and felt confident in launching it only with Everett as a target; see ibid., 26, 29 Jan., 1, 10 Feb. 1858.

67. Everett to Nathan Hale, 17 Feb. 1858, Everett-Hopkins Papers, MHS; *Daily National*

Intelligencer, 14 May 1858. For examples of papers reprinting this letter and reacting very differently to it, see *Weekly Raleigh Register*, 26 May 1858; and *Liberator*, 28 May 1858.

68. Theodore Parker to Charles Sumner, 16, 21 (quotations) May 1858, Theodore Parker Papers, MHS; diary, 1 Nov. 1858, EP.

69. Diary, 11 June, 26 July (quotation), 31 Aug., 2–3 Sept., 31 Oct. (quotation), 17 Nov., 22 Dec. 1856, 13, 22 Jan. 1857, EP; Everett to Trescot, 10 June 1856 (quotation), Everett to Mrs. W. F. Ritchie, 26 June 1856 (quotation), EP; Everett to Henry A. and Charlotte Wise, 6 June 1856, Everett to Charlotte Wise, 11, 12, 17 June, 20 Aug. 1856, Everett to Henry A. Wise, 28, 30 July, 20 Sept., 10 Oct. (quotation) 1856, Everett-Hopkins Papers, MHS.

70. Diary, 20 Aug. 1854, 9 July, 10 Aug. 1856, 17 Jan., 20 Sept. 1857, 31 Jan., 3 Feb., 17 Sept. 1858, 7 Feb. 1859, EP.

71. Everett to Hunter, 5 Sept. 1857 (quotations), Everett to Mrs. W. F. Ritchie, 26 June 1856, Everett to Trescot, 17 Jan. 1858, EP; Edward Everett to J. J. Maslette, 8 Sept. 1856, EP-Exeter; Everett to Henry A. Wise, 21 Dec. 1856, Everett-Hopkins Papers, MHS; Everett to Henry A. Wise, 21 Dec. 1856, Everett-Hopkins Papers, MHS; Diary, 7 Mar., 16 May, 23 Oct., 2 Nov., 15 Dec. 1858, 25 Sept., 8 Nov. 1859, EP.

72. Everett to Hillard, 10 July 1858, EP (quotation); Everett to Robert Bonner, 13 Jan. 1859, Edward Everett Papers, LC; diary, 18 Oct. 1858, EP.

73. Diary, 4 Aug., 8 Oct. 1854, 6 June 1855, 31 [*sic*; 30] May 1856, EP; *Boston Daily Advertiser*, 5 Aug. 1854.

74. Everett to Rev. Dr. Osgood, 3 Apr. 1857, Everett to Hillard, 28 Dec. 1858, EP; diary, 22 Feb. 1856, 27 Mar. 1857, EP.

75. Diary, 23 Feb. (quotation), 19 Mar. 1857, EP; Everett to Mrs. Charles Eames, 28 Feb. 1857 (quotations), Everett to Trescot, 22 July, 5 Aug. 1857, EP; Everett to Henry A. Wise, 19 Feb., 23 Mar., 25 Apr. 1857, Everett to Charlotte Wise, 25 Feb., 11 May 1857, Everett-Hopkins Papers, MHS.

76. Thane, *Mount Vernon Is Ours*, esp. 142–62; Julia Gardiner Tyler to Anna C. O. M. Ritchie, 11 Feb. 1856, Papers of Anna Cora Ogden Mowatt Ritchie, Albert and Shirley Small Special Collections Library, University of Virginia. Rounding to the nearest thousand, I calculate Everett's financial contribution to the MVLAU as around $104,000, based on his estimate that his speech and the $10,000 from Robert Bonner (see below) yielded around $90,000, and private contributions sent him as a result of the "Mount Vernon Papers" (see below) totaled around $14,000; see E. Everett, *Orations and Speeches*, vol. 4, 3–17; and diary, 10 May 1860, EP.

77. Dana, *Address Upon the Life*, 53 (quotation); Forgie, *Patricide in the House Divided*, 159–99; Everett to D. S. Dickenson, 16 Sept. 1858, EP. I calculated the number of repetitions from Everett's published account in E. Everett, *Orations and Speeches*, vol. 4, 3–17.

78. Diary, 23 Sept. 1858, 21 Mar. 1859, EP; Everett to ticket agent of the Wilmington & Baltimore Railroad, 28 Apr. 1860, Edward Everett Papers, New York Public Library; *Weekly Raleigh Register*, 6 Apr. 1859; entries for 23–29 Mar. 1856, 9–15 May 1858, Diary of Louisa H. A. Minor, Albert and Shirley Small Special Collections Library, University of Virginia.

79. For insight into such organizational work, see William McLaughlin to Alexander H. H. Stuart, 23 Nov. 1857, Papers of Alexander H. H. Stuart and the Related Stuart and Baldwin Families, University of Virginia.

80. *Illustrated Mount Vernon Record*, both volumes, quotation on 2:122.

81. *Charleston Mercury*, 14 Apr. 1858; *Daily Morning News*, 17, 19 Apr. 1858.

82. *Daily National Intelligencer*, 13 Mar., 11 Apr., 23 May 1856, 30 Jan., 17 July 1858; *Boston Daily Advertiser*, 1, 5 Mar., 14, 17, 21, 23 Apr. 1856, 24 Feb., 20 Mar., 5 May, 20 June 1857; *Vermont*

Chronicle, 15 Apr. 1856; *New York Herald*, 23 Mar., 23 Apr., 15, 27 May 1857, 13 Nov. 1858; *Newark Advocate*, 13 May 1857; *Daily Chronicle and Sentinel*, 29 May 1857; *Weekly Raleigh Register*, 3 Mar. 1858, 20 Apr., 18 May 1859; *New Hampshire Statesman*, 20 Mar. 1858. Even lukewarm critics had to concede that Everett and this oration had become very much "the fashion"; see, e.g., *Fayetteville Observer*, 2 May 1859.

83. *Daily National Intelligencer*, 22, 29 Mar. 1856, 28 July 1858; *Weekly Raleigh Register*, 30 Apr. 1856.

84. *Virginia Free Press*, 3 Apr. 1856.

85. *NAR* 84 (Apr. 1857): 334–63 (quotation on 363); *New York Herald*, 21, 23 Apr. 1858; *North American and United States Gazette*, 6 Feb. 1858.

86. *New York Herald*, 13 Nov. 1858; *Charleston Mercury*, 3 May 1856; see also *North American and United States Gazette*, 14 Mar. 1856.

87. *Weekly Raleigh Register*, 3 Sept. 1856 (quotation); *Newark Advocate*, 21 Jan. 1857; *Fayetteville Observer*, 13 Sept. 1858.

88. *New Hampshire Statesman*, 31 Oct. 1857.

89. *Life Illustrated* (New York City), reprinted in *Liberator*, 21 Mar. 1856.

90. See Scrapbook, 1833–1865, Scrapbook, 1850–1865, and especially Scrapbook, 1850s, reel 52B, EP.

91. Mott, *History of American Magazines*, 2:15–16, 23–24, 356–63 (quotation on 15); diary, 14, 28 Sept. 1858, EP; Everett to W. O. Bartlett, 6, 11 Oct. 1858, EP.

92. Diary, 23, 26 Oct., 3, 6, 25 Nov. 1858, EP; Everett to W. O. Bartlett, 1 Nov. 1858, Everett to Robert Bonner, 6 Nov. 1858, EP.

93. Everett, *Mount Vernon Papers*, 124–34, 155–62, 327–51; Everett, *Life of George Washington*, 99–103, 211–22, 262–72, quotations on 263, 222.

94. *New York Herald*, 22 Nov., 14 Dec. 1858; *NAR* 91 (July 1860): 289–90; *Daily National Intelligencer*, 11 Dec. 1858; *Charleston Mercury*, 13 Dec. 1858; *Daily Cleveland Herald*, 13 Dec. 1858; *Weekly Raleigh Register*, 15 Dec. 1858; *Kansas Herald of Freedom*, 25 Dec. 1858; *Vermont Patriot*, 17 Dec. 1858; *New Hampshire Statesman*, 18 Dec. 1858; *Milwaukee Daily Sentinel*, 12 Mar. 1859. For evidence of their mutual satisfaction including ongoing collaborations once this series was finished, see diary, 9, 15 Nov. 1858, 18 Apr., 14 Sept., 29 Nov.–1 Dec. 1859, EP; Edward Everett to Cora Ritchie, 6 Sept. 1859, BPL; and Everett to Henry A. Wise, 14 Jan. 1860, Everett-Hopkins Papers, MHS.

95. *Daily Cleveland Herald*, 11 Dec. 1858 (quotation); *Freedom's Champion*, 2 Apr. 1859; *Fayetteville Observer*, 18 Nov. 1858; *Liberator*, 26 Nov. 1858, 8 Apr. 1859; *Southern Literary Messenger* 31 (Aug. 1860): 159–60; *Milwaukee Daily Sentinel*, 12 Jan. 1861.

96. Elizabeth Cabot quoted in Zboray and Zboray, *Voices without Votes*, 202.

97. Diary, 18, 20 Nov., 4 Dec. 1858, 22 Jan., 7, 10, 13 Feb., 14 Mar. 1859, EP.

98. Everett, *Mount Vernon Papers*, 8–10.

99. Diary, 10 May 1860, EP; R. Coady & Co., Bill of Exchange, Honolulu, Sandwich Islands, 5 Jan. 1859, BPL. For an even further accounting of donations made to the MVLAU, see *Illustrated Mount Vernon Record*, both volumes. Either Everett or Frothingham seem to have thought the Hawaiian contribution notable enough that they gave it to Hale for mention in his newspaper; see *Boston Daily Advertiser*, 28 Mar. 1859.

100. Daniel Era Paris to Everett, 11 Jan. 1858, William B. Swanger to Everett, n.d., Mr. and Mrs. G. B. Smith to Everett, 14 Jan. 1859, George G. Castle to Everett, 25 Dec. 1858, EP.

101. G. M. Rushing to Everett, 29 Dec. 1858, R. G. Woodson to Everett, 7 Jan. 1859, EP. For strong suggestions from MVLAU supporters that donations to this cause were an entirely

appropriate way to mark both the Fourth of July and Christmas, see *Daily Constitutionalist*, 19 Dec. 1858, 2 July 1859.

102. Michael Curran to Everett, 9 Jan. 1859, Jacob Stone to Everett, 4 Jan. 1859, EP.

103. *Harper's Monthly Magazine* 17 (July 1858): 268–69. The secondary literature on which this paragraph draws includes Cope, *George Washington in and as Culture*; Schwartz, *George Washington*; Bryan, *George Washington in American Literature*; Furstenberg, *In the Name of the Father*; Bruggeman, *Here, George Washington Was Born*; and especially Forgie, *Patricide in the House Divided*; and Higham, *From Boundlessness to Consolidation*.

104. Lengel, *Inventing George Washington*, 118; Yablon, "Land of Unfinished Monuments."

105. Everett to Julia M. Cabell, 28 Mar. 1856, EP; Everett to ticket agent of the Wilmington & Baltimore Railroad, 28 Apr. 1860, Edward Everett Papers, New York Public Library; Edward Everett to Rev. Dr. Bellows, 14 Dec. 1857, EP-Exeter; Edward Everett to Samuel Souther, 20 July 1858, BPL; Everett to Edward W. Foster, 27 June 1857, Mercantile Library Association of Boston Collection, Howard Gotlieb Archival Research Center, Boston University, Boston; Everett to "Dear Sir," 9 Sept. 1857, Richards Manuscript Collection, Boston University; Everett to B. A. Gould, 23 Aug. 1856, Edward Everett Letters, Southern Historical Collection, University of North Carolina; diary, 16–18 Apr. 1856, 29 Apr. 1857, 27 Feb. 1859, EP.

106. *Southern Literary Messenger* 25 (July 1857): 70; see also *Illustrated Mount Vernon Record*, 1:3, 4, 6, 44, 48, 54–55, 72, 93, 117, and 2:17, 27, 40, 60, 73, 85, 124, 163, 199.

107. *Appeal for the Purchase*, 3; *Illustrated Mount Vernon Record*, 2:3–4; Lengel, *Inventing George Washington*, 118.

108. *Boston Daily Courier*, 4 Aug. 1859; Forgie, *Patricide in the House Divided*, 159–99; Howe, "Massachusetts Yankee."

109. Lengel, *Inventing George Washington*, ix–x, 13–65, 106–39, 211–14; Seth C. Bruggeman, "'More Than Ordinary Patriotism': Living History in the Memory Work of George Washington Parke Custis," in McDonnell et al., *Remembering the Revolution*, 127–43; Bruggeman, *Here, George Washington Was Born*, 24–50; Rotenstein, "Gas Man" and "Civil War"; Everett to Charlotte Wise, 6 Mar. 1859, Everett-Hopkins Papers, MHS.

110. *Illustrated Mount Vernon Record*, 1:5, 22, 2:17, 215 (quotation); *Dover Gazette and Strafford Advertiser*, 19 Nov. 1859 (quotation).

111. E. Everett, *Orations and Speeches*, vol. 3, 644 (quotation); Reid, "Edward Everett's 'The Character of Washington,'" 153; manuscripts of "Character of Washington" oration, reel 48, EP; diary, 20 July, 17 Aug. 1857, 11 Jan. 1858, 31 May 1859, EP; *Illustrated Mount Vernon Record*, 1:20; Everett to Townsend Ward, 3 Nov. 1856, clipping from *North American and United States Gazette*, 16 Apr. 1856, Edward Everett File, Society Collection, Historical Society of Pennsylvania, Philadelphia.

112. Diary, 28 Aug. 1854, 20 Feb., 1–2, 5, 8, 31 Mar., 10 Nov. 1856, 11 Jan., 4, 25 Feb., 1 Mar., 12 Nov. 1858, 20, 29–30 Jan. 1859, 21 Feb., 26 May 1860, EP; Everett to Mrs. William Eve, 2 July 1860, Edward Everett Letters, New-York Historical Society (quotation).

113. Everett, *Mount Vernon Papers*, 6, 81–97, 106–14, 124–34, 221–47, quotations on 4, 124.

Chapter 9

1. *Bangor Daily Whig and Courier*, 4 Jan. 1860; *Lowell Daily Citizen and News*, 29 Dec. 1859; *Charleston Mercury*, 19 Dec. 1859; *Fayetteville Observer*, 19 Dec. 1859; *Newark Advocate*, 16 Dec. 1859; *Daily National Intelligencer*, 24 Dec. 1859, 26 Jan., 3 Feb. 1860; *New York Herald*, 24, 29, 30

Dec. 1859, 1, 7, 8, 13 Jan. 1860; *Weekly Raleigh Register*, 28 Dec. 1859, 11 Jan. 1860; *Daily Constitu-tionalist*, 3 Nov. 1859; *The Republic and its Crisis. Speeches of Hon. Edward Everett, at the Boston Union Meeting, Dec. 8 1859; and of Ex-Gov. Thos. H. Seymour, and Prof. Samuel Eliot, of Trinity College, at the Hartford Union Meeting, Dec. 14, 1859. Published by Request of Many of the Conservative and Union Loving Men of Connecticut, 1860*, Albert and Shirley Small Special Collections Library, University of Virginia; Stabler, "History of the Constitutional Union Party," 273–300. For a window into the organization of these meetings, see William Appleton et al. to Caleb Cushing, 3 Dec. 1859, Caleb Cushing Papers, LC.

2. *Great Union Meeting*, 3–7; *Boston Courier Report of the Union Meeting*, 3–8, 10, 12, 13, 20, 22, 24–26, 30; *Official Report of the Great Union Meeting*, 3, 41, 43–44, 86–89, 93–176; *North American and United States Gazette*, 8 Dec. 1859; *Frank Leslie's Illustrated Newspaper*, 31 Dec. 1859. For examples of such mischaracterization of these meetings, see Fite, *Presidential Campaign of 1860*, 23–30; and P. Foner, *Business and Slavery*, 156–68.

3. *Great Union Meeting*, 14–21, 27, 34, 42–43, 46–47, 55–59.

4. *New York Herald*, 13 Dec. 1859. For crowd estimates, see *Daily National Intelligencer*, 21 Dec. 1859; *Fayetteville Observer*, 22 Dec. 1859; *Dover Gazette and Strafford Advertiser*, 24 Dec. 1859; and *New York Herald*, 21 Dec. 1859. Even the signatures calling for the meeting took up over eighty pages in the published account; see *Official Report of the Great Union Meeting*, 93–176.

5. *Official Report of the Great Union Meeting*, 47–48; see also 6, 14–15, 21–27, 36–39, 49, 55, 60, 62–64, 67–70, 73, 76–77.

6. Ibid., 9–10, 19, 27–28.

7. Everett to Charlotte Wise, 10 Dec. 1859, Everett-Hopkins Papers, MHS; *Boston Courier Report of the Union Meeting*, 10–17, 23–24, 28–30 (for more on the thousands calling for and in attendance at this meeting, see 3–8).

8. *Boston Courier Report of the Union Meeting*, 12–17; E. Everett, *Orations and Speeches*, vol. 4, 235–47. For an intelligent, in-depth reading of the Haitian aspect of this speech and how that resonated in the public mind in this era, see Clavin, *Toussaint Louverture*, 162–80.

9. Diary, 3, 13 Dec. 1859, EP; E. Everett, *Orations and Speeches*, vol. 4, 235–47; Everett to Henry A. Wise, 14 Nov., 3 Dec. 1859, Everett-Hopkins Papers, MHS.

10. Lawrence, *Life of Amos A. Lawrence*, 122–38 (quotation on 134); *Great Union Meeting*, 5 (quotation); *Republic and Its Crisis*, 13; *Official Report of the Great Union Meeting*, 73.

11. *Boston Courier Report of the Union Meeting*, 11; *Official Report of the Great Union Meeting*, 29–34 (quotation on 30); see also 59–61.

12. *Boston Courier Report of the Union Meeting*, 17–23; *Official Report of the Great Union Meeting*, 76. For other anti-abolitionist rants of this kind, see *Great Union Meeting*, 30, 35–36, 38, 42–43; *Official Report of the Great Union Meeting*, 24, 48–54; and *Boston Courier Report of the Union Meeting*, 11–12, 16.

13. Belohlavek, *Broken Glass*, 224, 294–96, 303, 312–13; Holt, *Franklin Pierce*, 110–11. For another harrowing look into the hard-line Democratic anti-abolitionist mindset in this era, see J. White, "Pennsylvania Judge."

14. Millard Fillmore to Saul L. M. Barlow et al., 16 Dec. 1859, Millard Fillmore Papers, LC; *Daily Constitutionalist*, 25 Dec. 1859 (quotation); *Boston Daily Advertiser*, 21, 24 Dec. 1859; *Bangor Daily Whig and Courier*, 26 Dec. 1859.

15. Everett to Charles G. Loring, 10 Dec. 1859, Charles G. Loring Papers, Houghton Li-brary, Harvard University, Cambridge, Mass.; Everett to Charlotte A. Wise, 10 Dec. 1859, Everett-Hopkins Papers, MHS; diary, 13 Dec. 1859, EP. Democrats, of course, preferred Cushing's anti-abolitionist energy to the polished restraint of Everett's speech; see, e.g.,

William Anderson to Caleb Cushing, 14 Dec. 1859, A. Sanborn et al. to Cushing, 24 Dec. 1859, Caleb Cushing Papers, LC.

16. *Liberator*, 30 Dec. 1859; W. Phillips, *Speeches, Lectures, and Letters*, 2nd ser., 294–308; Theodore Parker to Caroline C. Thayer, 10 Jan. 1860, Theodore Parker Papers, MHS; Stephen Barker to Mrs. M. W. Chapman, 24 Jan. 1860, BPL.

17. *Bangor Daily Whig and Courier*, 10 Dec. 1859, 12 Jan. 1860; Basler, *Collected Works of Abraham Lincoln*, 4:13 (quotation), 3:550, 554.

18. *New York Herald*, 16 (quotation), 20 Dec. 1859. Some otherwise distinguished and nuanced readings of the crisis of the 1850s have inordinately followed this interpretation of the Union meetings; see Potter, *Impending Crisis*, 380–81.

19. *New York Herald*, 21 Dec. 1859; *North American and United States Gazette*, 6 (quotations), 8 Dec. 1859; An Old Man to Caleb Cushing, 11 Dec. 1859, Caleb Cushing Papers, LC.

20. *Daily Morning News*, 13 Dec. 1859; *Richmond Examiner* quoted in *Boston Daily Advertiser*, 16 Dec. 1859; *Daily Mississippian*, 19 Jan 1860.

21. Everett to Henry A. Wise, 16 Dec. 1859, Everett-Hopkins Papers, MHS.

22. Sarah B. Seddon to Caleb Cushing, 17 Dec. 1859, Caleb Cushing Papers, LC; *Fayetteville Observer*, 19, 22 Dec. 1859, 23 Jan. 1860.

23. *Daily Constitutionalist*, 11 Dec. 1859; see also 29 July, 3 Aug., 16, 23 Sept., 3 Nov., 7, 8, 13, 16, 24 Dec. 1859.

24. Quotations from newspapers including *North American and United States Gazette*, 8 Dec. 1859; *Daily National Intelligencer*, 9 Dec. 1859; and *New York Herald*, 21, 23 Dec. 1859. For the organization of the CUP, see Thomas A. R. Nelson to John Bell, 10 Jan. 1851, Neill S. Brown to John Bell, 10 Aug. 1858, Papers of John Bell, LC; Nathan Sargent to Alexander H. H. Stuart, 31 Oct. 1858, Sargent to Stuart, 18, 27 Feb., 28 Aug., 17 Nov. 1859, Papers of Alexander H. H. Stuart, LC; Kirwan, *John J. Crittenden*, 342–50; Stabler, "History of the Constitutional Union Party," 349–415; Daniel W. Crofts, "The Southern Opposition and the Crisis of the Union," in Gallagher and Shelden, *Political Nation*, 85–111; and Holt, *Political Crisis of the 1850s*, 203–14. For an especially rich documentary trail of the founding of the CUP, see Alexander R. Boteler Papers, Duke University.

25. Curl, "Baltimore Convention," 256–58; Hesseltine, *Three against Lincoln*, 124–25. For hopes for peeling off conservative Republicans harbored at the very inception of the CUP, see Nathan Sargent to Alexander H. H. Stuart, 31 Oct. 1858, Sargent to Stuart, 18, 27 Feb., 28 Aug. 1859, Papers of Alexander H. H. Stuart, LC.

26. Kirwan, *John J. Crittenden*, 350–53; Parks, *John Bell*, esp. 349–55; Stabler, "History of the Constitutional Union Party," 416–40.

27. *Union Guard*, 12 July, 23, 30 Aug. 1860; Curl, "Baltimore Convention," 270–71; Hesseltine, *Three against Lincoln*, 121–22, 127, 131–40; Stabler, "History of the Constitutional Union Party," 465–68.

28. Egerton, *Year of Meteors*, 96, 189. For similar puzzlement over other politicians' appeals to women, see Fuller, *Election of 1860*, 119; and Bordewich, *America's Great Debate*, 73.

29. Curl, "Baltimore Convention," 270–71; Everett to Joseph Barbiere, 16 May 1860, Edward Everett Papers, American Antiquarian Society; Everett to Washington Hunt, 14 May 1860, Everett to Hillard, 15 May 1860, Everett to John J. Crittenden, 28 May 1860, EP; Everett to Henry A. Wise, 14 May 1860, Everett-Hopkins Papers, MHS; Everett to Crittenden, 7 May 1860, John J. Crittenden Papers, Duke University.

30. Everett to W. W. Corcoran, 6 June 1860, Edward Everett Papers, LC; Everett to Mrs. Charles Eames, 29 June 1860, EP; Everett to Charlotte Wise, 7 May 1860, Everett to Henry A.

Wise, 18, 28 May 1860, Everett to Henry A. Wise, 2 June 1860 (quotations), Everett-Hopkins Papers, MHS.

31. Everett to Hillard, 15 May 1860 (first quotation), Everett to Mrs. Charles Eames, 17 May 1860, EP; Everett to Henry A. Wise, 14 May 1860, Everett-Hopkins Papers, MHS; Everett to John J. Crittenden, 2 June 1860, John J. Crittenden Papers, Duke University; Potter, *Impending Crisis*, 417; Egerton, *Year of Meteors*, 97 (second quotation). Though Everett did not mention this in 1860, it is also true that in 1853 Bell had expressed rather severe hostility to Everett, and that reached Everett's attention; see diary, 11 Feb. 1853, EP.

32. Everett to J. P. Kennedy, 17 May 1860, EP.

33. Diary, 12, 16, 22, 24, 31 May 1860, EP.

34. *Union Guard*, 16 Aug. 1860; —— to Everett, 25 May 1860, Edward Everett Papers, American Antiquarian Society; Amos A. Lawrence to John J. Crittenden, 25 May 1860, John J. Crittenden Papers, Duke University; Everett to Henry A. Wise, 18 May 1860, Everett-Hopkins Papers, MHS; Henry A. Wise to Everett, 20 May 1860, EP; Stabler, "History of the Constitutional Union Party," 480–92, 520–25, 693–98.

35. John J. Crittenden et al. to Everett, 25 May 1860, EP.

36. *Union Guard*, 12 July 1860.

37. Egerton, *Year of Meteors*, esp. 85–101; Fuller, *Election of 1860*, 2, 103–39; Ashworth, *Slavery, Capitalism, and Politics*, vol. 2, 592–606; Peter B. Knupfer, "Aging Statesmen and the Statesmanship of an Earlier Age: The Generational Roots of the Constitutional Union Party," in Blight and Simpson, *Union and Emancipation*, 57–78; Crofts, *Reluctant Confederates*, esp. 75–81; Stabler, "History of the Constitutional Union Party"; Crenshaw, *Slave States*, esp. ch. 6.

38. For just a very few examples ranging across time and genres, see Nevins, *Ordeal of the Union*, 4:261–62; Morrison, *Slavery and the American West*, esp. 232; and Wilentz, *Rise of American Democracy*, 745–91. For a treatment in which the founding of the CUP is quite literally a footnote, see Fite, *Presidential Campaign of 1860*, 131n2. Even works focused on CUP luminaries perpetuate this caricature; see, e.g., T. Brown, "Edward Everett and the Constitutional Union Party"; and Kirwan, *John J. Crittenden*, 356.

39. Wm. B. Brock to "Dear Brothers," 1860, William Clark Doub Papers, David M. Rubenstein Rare Book and Manuscript Library, Duke University, Durham, N.C. (quotation); Ned to Joseph S. Williams, 5 Dec. 1860, Joseph S. Williams Papers, David M. Rubenstein Rare Book and Manuscript Library, Duke University, Durham, N.C.; diary, beginning of vol. 179, reel 40, EP; Nathan Appleton Jr. Scrapbooks, MHS. Thanks to Doug Egerton for suggesting I highlight this point about third parties.

40. Curl, "Baltimore Convention," 274; Strong, *Diary of the Civil War*, 59. For a fascinating window into the earnestness of CUP organizers, see Friends of Bell and Everett Association Minute Book, 1860–1862, Historical Society of Pennsylvania, Philadelphia.

41. *New York Herald*, 5 Feb., 6, 17 Sept., 7–8, 25, 28 Oct., 3 Nov. 1860; *Daily National Intelligencer*, 19 Sept., 10 Oct. 1860; *Weekly Raleigh Register*, 11 July, 26 Sept., 17, 31 Oct., 7 Nov. 1860; *Hinds County Gazette*, 21 March 1860; *Virginia Free Press*, 30 Aug. 1860.

42. See various *Union Guard* issues (quotation from 27 Sept. 1860); B. H. Magruder to Everett, 14 May 1860, E. Henderson Otis to Everett, 16 June 1860, EP; Alexander R. Boteler Papers, Duke University.

43. *Address of the National Executive Committee*, 1, 4; *Life, Speeches, and Public Service*, 97–101; Varon, *We Mean to Be Counted*, 144–46; *Union Guard*, 23, 30 Aug. 1860. For more on gendered rhetoric and the sectional crisis, see Varon, *Disunion!*, 186–91, 196, 201, 203, 221.

44. E. Everett, *Orations and Speeches*, vol. 4, 277–310, 315–16, 319, quotations on 284–85, 295.

45. Everett to George S. Hillard, 1 June 1860, EP; diary, 18, 22 (quotation), 23 June, 20 July, 3, 7, 28–29 Aug., 13, 14, 27 Sept., 1, 4–24 Oct. 1860, EP.

46. Diary, 29 June, 10 Aug., 6 Sept. 1860, EP.

47. Ibid., 22 Feb., 3 Mar. (quotation), 29–30 Aug., 2, 26 Sept. 1860.

48. Thanks to Michael Woods for encouraging me to develop this way of looking at the standard wisdom on the Republicans.

49. Strong, *Diary of the Civil War*, 8; Varon, *Disunion!*; E. Foner, *Fiery Trial*, 141; Donald, *Lincoln*, 247; Nevins, *Ordeal of the Union*, 4: 240; Wilentz, *Rise of American Democracy*, 758.

50. Basler, *Collected Works of Abraham Lincoln*, 3:333, 536–37, 550; see also 3:19, 29, 87, 93, 117, 220, 276, 307–8, 374–76, 398, 407, 414–17, 436, 439, 464–66, 484, 489, 496, 498, 502, 522–54, 4:30; E. Foner, *Fiery Trial*, 60–62, 70–72; Brookhiser, *Founders' Son*; and Ross, "Lincoln and the Ethics of Emancipation."

51. Egerton, *Year of Meteors*, 110–48, quotation on 147; Huston, *Calculating the Value*, 228–29, quotations on 229; Freehling, *Road to Disunion*, vol. 2, 329–31, quotation on 330; Nichols, *Disruption of American Democracy*, 337–47; Fuller, *Election of 1860*, 15; Mitgang, *Abraham Lincoln*, 164–67.

52. For examples from the Douglasites, see Silbey, *American Party Battle*, 2:82–113. For good secondary discussions of the CUP's opponents' strategy and tactics in this regard, see Parks, *John Bell*, 361–88; and Paulus, "America's Long Eulogy."

53. Silbey, *American Party Battle*, 2:114–50 (quotation on 119); Stewart, *Wendell Phillips*, 211 (quotation); W. Phillips, *Speeches, Lectures, and Letters*, 1st ser., 300–301; Sumner, *Charles Sumner*, 6:313–14, 330–31, 355–58, 7:7–19, 26–40, 74–75, 83, 86–87; Egerton, *Year of Meteors*, 186. They likewise hammered Douglas on this score, such as when they contrasted Founding Fathers' antislavery expressions with Douglas's notorious statement "I don't care whether slavery is voted up or down"; see Fite, *Presidential Campaign of 1860*, 161–62, 256–57.

54. Washington Hunt to John Bell, 24 May 1860, Papers of John Bell, LC.

55. *Speech of Hon. John C. Breckinridge*, 1–16. See also J. Davis, *Rise and Fall of the Confederate Government*, 1:46–47, 577–78.

56. Fite, *Presidential Campaign of 1860*, 174–87, 336–42; Crenshaw, *Slave States*, ch. 5.

57. O'Connor, *Lords of the Loom*, 141; Mitgang, *Abraham Lincoln*, 186; Blassingame, *Frederick Douglass Papers*, 3:384–86. See also *Public Record and Past History,*; *Speech of Hon. John C. Breckinridge*, 14; *Mobile Tribune* quoted in *Union Guard*, 18 Oct. 1860; Egerton, *Year of Meteors*, 191; Stabler, "History of the Constitutional Union Party," 553–55. For a good discussion of the CUP worldview in this respect, see Ashworth, *Slavery, Capitalism, and Politics*, vol. 2, 592–606.

58. Dumond, *Southern Editorials on Secession*, 191–95 (quotation); *Public Record and Past History*, 2–12, 20–26.

59. *Public Record and Past History*, 29–32; see also John M. Speed to Everett, 17 July 1860, BPL; and Fite, *Presidential Campaign of 1860*, 174–87, 336–42.

60. *Union Guard*, quotations on 184, 252; *Life, Speeches, and Public Service*, 10–32, 49–58, 65–92, 102–18; Dumond, ed., *Southern Editorials on Secession*, 159–62, 166–67, 195–98, 214–18.

61. Egerton, *Year of Meteors*, 190; Joshua J. Bell to John Bell, 20 Sept. 1860, Papers of John Bell, LC. Alabama true believer Henry W. Hilliard, however, did do an election speaking tour of Northern cities; see Durham, *Southern Moderate*, 137; and Franklin, *Southern Odyssey*, 248–53.

62. Egerton, *Year of Meteors*, 100–101.

63. John M. Speed to Everett, 17 July 1860, John H. McCue to Everett, 25 July 1860, BPL. See also T. J. Anderson to Everett, 12 June 1860, EP.

64. *Weekly Raleigh Register* and *Daily Register*, 17, 31 Oct. 1860; *Union Guard*, 19, 26 July, 23 Aug., 6 Sept., 25 Oct. 1860.

65. Andrew H. H. Dawson to Everett, 26 July 1860, BPL.

66. Everett to Hillard, 21 July 1860, EP.

67. Everett to A. H. H. Dawson, 25 Oct. 1860, EP; "Mr. Everett" [1860; a long undated document in Everett's own hand], Alexander R. Boteler Papers, Duke University. For the published version, see *Union Guard*, 4, 18 Oct. 1860. For more on his anguish over these replies, see diary, 20, 22–23, 25 Oct. 1860, EP.

68. John M. Speed to Everett, 27 July 1860, BPL; Stabler, "History of the Constitutional Union Party," 731.

69. White, ed., *Philadelphia Perspective*, 34–35, 38, 46–47, 56–57.

70. Strong, *Diary of the Civil War*, 26 (quotations), 59; Bates quoted in Curl, "Baltimore Convention," 276.

71. *Daily National Intelligencer*, 11 June 1860 (quotation); typescript of William Appleton Diary Notes, 15 Sept. 1860, Appleton Family Papers, MHS; Henry M. Fuller to Bell, 22 June 1860, Papers of John Bell, LC; Zboray and Zboray, *Voices without Votes*, 205. This was only in part due to the "insult" Hale perceived in Everett receiving the second slot on the ticket.

72. Stabler, "History of the Constitutional Union Party," 640–712; Nevins, *Ordeal of the Union*, 4:285–86, 297–98; Kirwan, *John J. Crittenden*, 356–60; Nichols, *Disruption of American Democracy*, 337–47; Baker, *Affairs of Party*, 46, 325–27; Crofts, *Reluctant Confederates*, 75–81; Strong, *Diary of the Civil War*, 42. For press coverage of fusion attempts that, even in the most enthusiastic pieces, underscore the difficulties, see *Virginia Free Press*, 27 Sept. 1860; *Weekly Raleigh Register*, 26 Sept., 17 Oct. 1860; *New York Herald*, 7–8, 25–28 Oct., 3 Nov. 1860; and *Daily National Intelligencer*, 10 Oct. 1860. The Papers of John Bell, LC, also contain a vivid account of the rise and fall of the fusion cause in 1860. For an excellent exploration of Northern Democrats' internal divisions that roots them in the late 1850s, see Guelzo, "Houses Divided." Jefferson Davis, interestingly enough, was an early proponent of fusion against the Republicans; see J. Davis, *Rise and Fall of the Confederate Government*, 1:52, 577–78.

73. For a strong statement that this was possible, see Knupfer, *Union as It Is*, 208–11. For a strong statement of doubt, together with a useful review of this historiographical debate, see Egerton, *Year of Meteors*, 335–37.

74. Freehling, *Road to Disunion*, vol. 2, 339–41.

75. Alexander C. Blount to William A. Graham, 12 July 1860, Pensacola, Fla., in Hamilton and Williams, *Papers of William Alexander Graham*, 5:168 (quotation); Nathan Sargent to Alexander H. H. Stuart, 24 Aug. 1860, Papers of Alexander H. H. Stuart, LC (quotation); Lewis McKenzie to Alexander H. H. Stuart, 31 Aug. 1860, Papers of Alexander H. H. Stuart and the Related Stuart and Baldwin Families, University of Virginia. These points about the political culture of the Upper South follow Ramage and Watkins, *Kentucky Rising*, 1–59; and Crofts, *Reluctant Confederates*. Thanks also to Michael Woods, the expert on the emotional history of the sectional crisis, for this point about the impact of fear.

76. Diary, 12 Sept. 1860, EP; William Appleton Diary Notes, 15 Sept. 1860, Appleton Family Papers, MHS; Baum, *Civil War Party System*, 49–54; Belohlavek, *Broken Glass*, xii–xiv, 312.

77. Egerton, *Year of Meteors*, 212; Burnham, *Presidential Ballots*, 71–87; E. Foner, *Fiery Trial*, 144; entry for 13 Sept. 1860, Friends of Bell and Everett Association Minute Book, 1860–1862, Historical Society of Pennsylvania; Dittenhoefer, *How We Elected Lincoln*, 33 (quotation), 40. For respectful Republican dismissals of the CUP, see *Boston Daily Advertiser*, 10, 11, 14 May, 2 June 1860; and Curl, "Baltimore Convention," 272–74.

78. Diary, 26 Oct., 2, 8, 12 Nov. 1860, EP.

79. See, e.g., Everett to Charlotte Wise, 20 Nov. 1860, 16 Mar. 1861, Everett-Hopkins Papers, MHS; Everett to John J. Crittenden, 23 Dec. 1860, John J. Crittenden Papers, Duke University.

80. Diary, 21 Dec. 1860, EP; Everett to Mrs. Charles Eames, 31 Dec. 1860, EP; Everett to Richard Keith Call, 31 Dec. 1860, Richard Keith Call Correspondence, State Archives of Florida, Tallahassee (thanks to Miriam Gan Spalding for sending me a copy of this letter). While his proposed solution was a bit wild, Everett was far from alone in his frustration over the haplessness of Congress in particular; see, e.g., H. Adams, "Great Secession Winter," 661–62, 666, 682–83.

81. Diary, 19 Jan., 2 Feb. 1861, EP; Everett to Trescot, 23 Mar. 1861, EP. For a good exploration of the long debate over coercion versus consent in maintaining the Union and of the stances various public figures took on that question during the secession crisis, see Steele, "Thomas Jefferson."

82. Everett to Trescot, 23 Mar. 1861, EP.

83. Diary, 4 Dec. 1860, EP; Everett to Charlotte Wise, 22 Dec. 1860, Everett-Hopkins Papers, MHS.

84. Everett to Millard Fillmore, 30 Jan. 1861, Everett to Robert C. Winthrop, 5 Jan. 1861, EP; Edward Everett to Townsend Ward, 20 Dec. 1860, EP-Exeter; Everett to Benson J. Lossing, 8 Dec. 1860, Edward Everett Letters, 1816–1863, MHS; diary, 6 Feb. 1861, EP. For other examples of his passivity and hopelessness, see Everett to John J. Crittenden, 23 Dec. 1860, John J. Crittenden Papers, Duke University; and Everett to Charlotte Wise, 6 Dec. 1860, Everett-Hopkins Papers, MHS.

85. Diary, 31 Dec. 1860, EP; J. Bradish et al. to Everett, 25 Jan. 1861, George Bancroft to Everett, 20 Feb. 1861, Fillmore to Everett, 6 Feb. 1861, EP.

86. Everett to Crittenden, 16 Feb. 1861, Board of Aldermen, City of Boston, 11 Feb. 1861, John J. Crittenden Papers, Duke University.

87. *Memorial of Edward Everett*; diary, 21 Jan. 1861, EP. For other accounts of this petition, see McClintock, *Lincoln and the Decision for War*, 152–55, 163–64; and O'Connor, *Lords of the Loom*, 146–49. For insightful studies of the compromise efforts, see Crofts, *Reluctant Confederates*, 195–255; and Kirwan, *John J. Crittenden*, 366–421.

88. This narrative relies heavily on, and quotes from, the vivid and detailed account left by Winthrop in "Memorandum, January 1861," in Winthrop Family Papers, reel 29, MHS. For other sources on this mission, see Stegmaier, *Henry Adams in the Secession Crisis*, 165–76.

89. Diary, 30 Jan., 4, 7 Feb. 1861, EP. For more on the Peace Conference, see Gunderson, *Old Gentlemen's Convention*.

90. Stegmaier, *Henry Adams in the Secession Crisis*, 97; Sumner, *Charles Sumner*, 7:180 (quotation).

91. Stampp, *And the War Came*, 123–78; McClintock, *Lincoln and the Decision for War*, 2–5, 66–84, 105–225, 254–80; Cooper, *We Have the War upon Us*; Potter, *Impending Crisis*, 523; Ware, *Political Opinion in Massachusetts*, 40–66; Freehling and Simpson, *Showdown in Virginia*; Strong, *Diary of the Civil War*, 64, 70–115; Coleman, *Life of John J. Crittenden*, 2:240–60; F. Moore, *Rebellion Record*, 1:18; Dumond, *Southern Editorials on Secession*, 334–36, 344–46, 351–52, 371–79. All this evidence of popular enthusiasm for Union-saving compromise, especially when added to Goldschmidt, "Northeastern Businessmen," refutes the dismissive characterizations of compromise sentiment in this era, including by excellent historians such as Eric Foner, who has presented "northern business leaders, especially those with commercial ties to the

South," as the only ones who "bombarded Lincoln with calls for compromise" in the secession winter; *Fiery Trial*, 146–47. For an intriguing argument that helps account for Northern policy confusion in the secession winter, see James L. Huston's essay in Fuller, *Election of 1860*, 29–67.

Chapter 10

1. Diary, 13, 17 Apr. 1861, EP.

2. Ibid., 19 Apr. 1861, 22 Jan. 1857; Everett to E. J. Wilson, 19 Apr. 1861, Edward Everett Letters, 1816–1863, MHS.

3. Everett to Robert Bonner, 14 May 1861, Edward Everett Papers, LC; Everett to George S. Hillard, 6 May 1861, EP (quotation).

4. Everett to D. N. Haskell, 29 Apr. 1861, EP-Exeter; Frothingham, *Edward Everett*, 416–17, 420–22, quotation on 416.

5. Lincoln quoted in E. Foner, *Fiery Trial*, 149; Stampp, *And the War Came*, 212, 292; Belohlavek, *Broken Glass*, 315–32; O'Connor, *Civil War Boston*, 50–61; Ware, *Political Opinion in Massachusetts*, 67–82; Strong, *Diary of the Civil War*, 119–29; Weber, *Copperheads*, 13–17.

6. Johannsen, *Frontier*, 186–87, quotation on 187; Egerton, *Year of Meteors*, 2–3, 321–30, quotation on 328; McClintock, *Lincoln and the Decision for War*, 268–69; McDaniel, *Problem of Democracy*, 210–31, quotation on 221; W. Phillips, *Speeches, Lectures, and Letters*, 1st ser., 464–65, quotation on 465; Freidel, *Union Pamphlets*, 296, 304, 317; Stewart, *Wendell Philips*, 218–25; Mason, Viens, and Wright, eds., *Massachusetts and the Civil War*, esp. introduction and chs. 1, 3, and 4.

7. E. Everett, *Orations and Speeches*, vol. 4, 326–27, 337–38, 397–400, 433. For other, later iterations of this idea, see ibid., 473–77, 586–87, 724–75.

8. Ibid., 330, 399, 448, 480, 500, 510, 522.

9. John A. Andrew to Caleb Cushing, 27 Apr. 1861, Caleb Cushing Papers, LC.

10. Garraty and Carnes, *American National Biography*, 23:684; Kime, "'Troublous Times'"; A. Taylor, *Divided Family*, 91–122; Strong, *Diary of the Civil War*, 134–38.

11. Everett to Charlotte Wise, 6 Mar., 20, 24, 26, 30 Apr. 1861, Everett to Henry A. Wise, 18, 29 Apr., 4 May 1861, Everett-Hopkins Papers, MHS. The government chose instead to rent his house; see diary, 4 May 1861, EP. Everett ultimately forbore publicly crowing about Wise's Norfolk participation; see Everett to Charlotte Wise, 6 May 1861, Everett-Hopkins Papers, MHS.

12. Bonner, *Mastering America*, xx–xxi, 219, quotation on xxi; Crofts, *Reluctant Confederates*, 104–29, 134, 153, 289–352; A. Taylor, *Divided Family*, 13–34; Don Green, "Constitutional Unionists," 238–39; Parks, *John Bell*, 389–407; Durham, *Southern Moderate*, 139–50; Kirwan, *John J. Crittenden*, 422–76.

13. Dumond, *Southern Editorials on Secession*, 505, 381.

14. L. P. McDowell to Everett, 10 Apr. 1861, Everett to Ann Pamela Cunningham, 8 Aug. 1861, EP.

15. Diary, 25 May 1861, EP; Bernath, *Confederate Minds*.

16. Kate Bonyer to Everett, 3 June 1861, EP.

17. Lettie Burwell to Everett, 3 June 1861, EP.

18. Everett to Charlotte Wise, 19 May 1862, Everett-Hopkins Papers, MHS; Everett to Winthrop, 14 June 1861, Winthrop Family Papers, MHS.

19. Everett to Henry A. Wise, 10 May 1861 (quotations), Everett-Hopkins Papers, MHS; *Letters of the Hon. Joseph Holt*, 35–40, quotations on 36, 37; Everett to Virginia Lewis, 17 May

1861 (quotations), Everett to Ann Pamela Cunningham, 8 Aug. 1861, EP. In addition to the above pamphlet, Everett's 15 May 1861 letter to a Southern friend was printed in the *Boston Daily Advertiser*, 7 June 1861; *Daily Cleveland Herald*, 10 June 1861; *Bangor Daily Whig and Courier*, 11 June 1861; *Daily National Intelligencer*, 11 June 1861; *Liberator*, 14 June 1861; and *Vermont Chronicle*, 11 June 1861. For other Northern conservatives who felt betrayed by the defection of their former CUP allies, see O'Connor, *Lords of the Loom*, 156–68.

20. Everett to Hillard, 14 Apr. 1861, EP; diary, 22 July 1861, EP. See also Everett to Charlotte Wise, 6 Jan., 26 Apr. 1861, Everett-Hopkins Papers, MHS. He was incredulous at how long the short-war theory persisted in William Seward's mind; see diary, 25 June 1862, EP.

21. While James McPherson's influential narrative of the Civil War recognizes diversity on this point, his most quotable characters and overall narrative thrust uphold the idea that eager sectionalists rushed naively to war; see *Battle Cry of Freedom*, 238, ch. 10. For just one recent iteration of this interpretation, see M. Adams, *Living Hell*, ch. 1. For examples of other prewar moderates who warned of a long and disruptive war, see Varon, *Disunion!*; Freehling and Simpson, *Showdown in Virginia*, 36, 174, 185; and Cooper, *Jefferson Davis*, 360.

22. Diary, 24 May 1861 (quotations), 12 Dec. 1862, 10 July 1863, EP; Everett to Winthrop, 23 Apr. 1861, EP (quotations). Scott issued just such an order on 31 July 1861; see Sarah E. Tracy to Everett, 7 Aug. 1861, EP.

23. E. Everett, *Orations and Speeches*, vol. 4, 464 (quotation); *Addresses by His Excellency*, 6, 12–13 (quotation on 12); Mitgang, *Abraham Lincoln*, 358.

24. Grant, "'How a Free People Conduct a Long War'"; Freidel, *Union Pamphlets*; Hess, *Liberty, Virtue, and Progress*; Parish, *North and the Nation*, 149–226; Richard Carwardine, "Abraham Lincoln, the Presidency, and the Mobilization of Union Sentiment," in Grant and Reid, *American Civil War*, 68–97.

25. Diary, 25 July 1861, 15 Dec. 1864, EP; Everett to Charlotte Wise, 2 Aug. 1861, Everett to Winthrop, 15 Oct. 1861, EP; Everett to Charlotte Wise, 17 Nov. 1861, Everett-Hopkins Papers, MHS.

26. Reid, *Edward Everett*, 89–103, offers an illuminating discussion of these continuities.

27. Everett to Hillard, 6 May 1861, EP; Everett to Winthrop, 5 June 1861, Winthrop Family Papers, MHS.

28. E. Everett, *Orations and Speeches*, vol. 4, 335–36, 345–411, 464–90, 553–95, 600–601, quotations on 335, 372, 348, 483, 484.

29. This based on my reading of Freidel, *Union Pamphlets*.

30. E. Everett, *Orations and Speeches*, vol. 4, 583. For just a few other examples, see *New York Ledger*, 19 Mar., 9 Apr., 14 May, 18 June, 2 July, 10 Sept. 1864; and Everett to Charles W. Slack, 5 Sept. 1864, BPL.

31. Diary, 6 May, 27 June 1862, EP; Everett to Henry A. Wise, 20 Apr. 1862, Papers of George B. McClellan Sr., LC; Everett to Henry A. Wise, 19 July 1862, Everett-Hopkins Papers, MHS; *North American and United States Gazette*, 20 Oct. 1864.

32. E. Everett, *Orations and Speeches*, vol. 4, 329, 331, 399, 405–6, 432–34, 445–46, 476–77, 488, 519, 529–35, 539, 563–70, 587–88, 595, 668, 712–13, 726, quotations on 331, 405, 529, 566.

33. F. Moore, *Rebellion Record*, 1:5–46, 161–62, 205–8, 2:388–91; diary, 17 May 1861, EP.

34. Diary, 14 Nov., 23 Dec. (quotation) 1861, 15 Aug. 1863, EP; William H. Seward to Everett, 23 May 1861, John Jay to Everett, 24 July 1861, John Andrew to Everett, 22 Aug. 1861, EP.

35. *Boston Daily Advertiser*, 20 Apr., 7 June, 16 Sept., 17 Oct. 1861; *Bangor Daily Whig and Courier*, 11 May, 11 June 1861; *Liberator*, 14 June 1861; *Vermont Chronicle*, 11 June 1861; *Frank Leslie's Illustrated Newspaper*, 30 Apr. 1861; *Lowell Daily Citizen and News*, 14 May, 21, 26 Aug.

1861; *North American and United States Gazette*, 14 May 1861; *Milwaukee Morning Sentinel*, 14 May 1861; *Daily National Intelligencer*, 21 May, 11 June, 30 Aug., 26 Sept. 1861; *Liberator*, 12, 19, 26 July, 2 Aug., 6 Sept., 18 Oct. 1861; *Daily Cleveland Herald*, 10 June, 8 July, 24 Aug., 29 Nov. 1861, 5 June 1862; *Scioto Gazette*, 23 July, 10 Sept. 1861; *Daily Evening Bulletin*, 27 July, 13 Nov. 1861; *Freedom's Champion*, 27 July 1861; *New York Herald*, 21 Oct. 1861.

36. Everett to Bonner, 10 July, 21 Aug. (quotations) 1861, Edward Everett Papers, LC; diary, 4 July, 18 Nov. 1861, 30 Nov. 1863, EP.

37. E. Everett, *Orations and Speeches*, vol. 4, 464, 489–90; Everett to Bonner, 22 Jan., 11 Apr. 1863, Edward Everett Papers, LC. He delivered it nineteen times in New York; nine times each in Massachusetts and Connecticut; five times in Pennsylvania; thrice in Illinois, Wisconsin, and Michigan; twice in Ohio and Iowa; and once in Maine, Rhode Island, New Jersey, Missouri, and Minnesota.

38. Diary, 24 Mar. 1862 (quotation), 1–2, 6, 13–15, 18–19 Jan. 1864, EP; Everett to Bonner, 21 June 1861, Edward Everett Papers, LC; Everett to N. A. and R. A. Moore, 11 Jan. 1865, in both Edward Everett Papers, American Antiquarian Society, and Edward Everett Collection, Princeton University Library.

39. Diary, 21 Mar., 29 Apr. 1862, 9 Jan. 1863, EP; Remini, *The House*, 178–79; Scott, *Visitation of God*.

40. F. Moore, *Rebellion Record*, 1:145 (quotations); Freidel, *Union Pamphlets*, 29–101, 381–449, 551–606.

41. Lengel, *Inventing George Washington*, 93–98; [Alexander], *Washington's Vision*, title page.

42. Hale, *Man without a Country*, quotations on 3, 5, 23, 26, 22.

43. Basler, *Collected Works of Abraham Lincoln*, 4:195, 235–36, 239–44, 266, 269, 271. Amy Taylor has demonstrated how common it was among a multitude of speakers and writers in the nineteenth century to employ this metaphor of family for the Union; see *Divided Family*, 8–12, 123–41, 178–89, 209–13. Thus I am not claiming a direct influence for Everett or the Union meetings but rather that their rhetoric resonated broadly and deeply in the political culture of the era.

44. E. Foner, *Fiery Trial*, 159. See ch. 3 for how Everett shaped these speeches.

45. Henry A. Wise to Everett, 28 Apr. 1861, EP.

46. J. Lee, *Experiencing Mount Vernon*, 216–23.

47. McPherson, *For Cause and Comrades*, quotation on 13.

48. McWhirter, *Battle Hymns*, esp. 32–58, quotation on 32; *Patriotic Song Book*, 1–2, 16–17, 27, 29, 35, 62–63, quotations on 1, 2; W. Smith, *Grand Army War Songs*, 3–7, 13–17, 20–25, 36–41, 47–53, 56–59, 70–85, 90–91, 106–7, 126–27, 156–57; Glass, *Singing Soldiers*, 12–14, 28–29; *War Songs*, 1–31; Silber, *Gender and the Sectional Conflict*, 21.

49. Gallagher, *Union War*, esp. 39, 57–61, 67.

50. Diary, 15 Feb., 4, 6 Mar., 3, 7 Apr., 10 May 1861, EP.

51. Ibid., 5 Jan. (quotation), 15 Feb., 19 Apr., 14–15 May, 14 June 1861, 11–13, 16, 21, 27, 29 Aug., 17 Sept., 6–9, 27, 29 Oct. 1863, 5 Jan. 1864; Commission of Governor Andrew, 12 June 1861, EP.

52. J. Andrew, *Address of His Excellency . . . January 3, 1862*, 69–73; Everett to John A. Andrew, 14 Apr. 1862, John A. Andrew Papers, MHS.

53. Everett to Andrew, 9, 14 Jan. 1863, 6, 9 Jan., 5 May 1864, John A. Andrew Papers, MHS; J. Andrew, *Address of His Excellency . . . January 8, 1864*, 49–69.

54. Diary, 17 July 1863, 5 Oct. 1864, EP (quotations); Everett to Townsend Ward, 25 May 1861, Edward Everett File, Society Collection, Historical Society of Pennsylvania; Everett to

J. P. Thompson, 3 Dec. 1864, Edward Everett Letters, Beinecke Rare Book and Manuscript Library, Yale University, New Haven, Conn.

55. Diary, 19 Nov. 1861, EP. He also contributed money for the relief of suffering freed slaves in the Southwest, which was no great change from his previous donations to such causes; see Everett to Charles G. Loring, 30 Dec. 1863, Charles G. Loring Papers, Houghton Library.

56. As perhaps illustrated best by his diary entries for 23 Feb. 1862 ("the longer I live the more deeply I feel the importance of order") and 25 June 1864 ("I have some doubt of the humanity" of various fishing practices he observed), EP.

57. Diary, 16 Dec. 1864, EP; John Caldwell to Everett, 12 June 1864, EP.

58. Diary, 7 Apr. 1864, EP.

59. Everett to Dr. W. G. Eliot, 24 July 1863, EP; *North American and United States Gazette*, 20 Aug. 1863; *Liberator*, 11 Sept. 1863. For more on the Missouri law, see Oakes, *Freedom National*, 468–69. For another expression of the idea that wartime emancipation was providential, see E. Everett, *Orations and Speeches*, vol. 4, 728.

60. See *New York Ledger*, 10, 24 Dec. 1864.

61. Diary, 21 Feb. (quotation), 17 Apr., 2 Dec. 1862, EP. For an excellent narrative and analysis of Republicans' emancipation policies, see Oakes, *Freedom National*.

62. Chase to Everett, 12 Aug. 1862, EP; E. Foner, *Fiery Trial*, 219; Chase to William Cullen Bryant, 4 Aug. 1862, Chase to Caleb B. Smith, 5 Aug. 1862, Salmon P. Chase Papers, LC.

63. Everett to Chase, 14 Aug. 1862, EP.

64. Everett to S. G. Ward, 5 Aug. 1863, EP; Everett to Bonner, 29 Dec. 1862, Edward Everett Papers, LC; diary, 2 Jan., 2, 4 Aug. 1863, EP

65. E. Everett, *Orations and Speeches*, vol. 4, 585 (quotations), 726–28; *New York Ledger*, 10, 24 Dec. 1864.

66. Diary, 8 May 1862, EP.

67. *New York Ledger*, 26 Apr. 1862; diary, 30 Mar. 1862, EP; Everett to Bonner, 30 Mar. 1862, Edward Everett Papers, LC; Everett to Horace Greeley, 15 Apr. 1862, MA 174, Greeley–Edward Everett, Morgan Library, New York.

68. E. Everett, *Orations and Speeches*, vol. 4, 499, 504, 532 (quotation on 532).

69. Everett to Hillard, 10 Sept. 1861, EP (quotation); diary, 15 (quotation), 27 Sept., 9, 10 Nov. 1862, 6, 11 May 1863 EP.

70. Diary, 22 (quotation), 24 Oct. 1862, EP; *Daily National Intelligencer*, 27 Oct. 1862 (quotation). The idea of Everett as a consensus candidate did gain some traction in the press; see *Lowell Daily Citizen and News*, 22 Oct. 1862; and *New Hampshire Statesman*, 25 Oct. 1862.

71. Everett to W. H. Gardiner, 21 Apr. 1863, EP-Harvard (quotation); diary, 8 Dec. 1862, EP; Everett to Rev. R. C. Waterton, 3 Feb. 1863, Edward Everett Letters, New-York Historical Society; Everett to McClellan, 18 Feb., 25 July 1863, Papers of George B. McClellan Sr., LC.

72. Everett to McClellan, 23 Feb. (quotation), 25 July 1863, Papers of George B. McClellan Sr., LC; diary, 23 Feb., 20 Apr., 9 Sept. 1863, 26 Oct., 10, 28 Dec. 1864, EP; McClellan, *Civil War Papers*, 437–38, 550–51, 554–55, 566.

73. Diary, 17 July, 20 Aug. (quotation), 27 Sept. 1863, EP. Everett's logic was shared by many at the time and also by Jennifer Weber, historian of the Copperheads; see *Copperheads*, esp. 2, 114.

74. A. Smith, *No Party Now*, quotation on vii; Blair, *With Malice toward Some*; Ramold, *Across the Divide*; White, "'To Aid Their Rebel Friends.'" For the most persuasive, sustained argument that the Copperhead threat to the Union war was real, see Weber, *Copperheads*.

75. Everett to Henry A. Wise, 22 July 1862, Everett-Hopkins Papers, MHS. A friend of Everett's was sure that Everett would want to know that one of his house servants might be "a rebel in disguise"; see A. J. Wright to Everett, 7 Oct. 1864, BPL.

76. E. Everett, *Orations and Speeches*, vol. 4, 489–99, 553, 580–85, quotation on 498; *War Policy of the Administration*, 6–8.

77. Everett to Henry A. Wise, 30 July 1863, Everett-Hopkins Papers, MHS; *War of the Rebellion*, ser. 3, vol. 5, 649–50, 917, quotations on 649; Andrew to Everett, 28 July 1864, EP; O'Connor, *Civil War Boston*, 160; diary, 31 Dec. 1864, 1 Jan. 1865, EP.

78. O'Connor, *Civil War Boston*, 141–42; Ware, *Political Opinion in Massachusetts*, 122–26; Blair, *With Malice toward Some*, 202–5; A. Smith, *No Party Now*, 67–84. For a good window into the practical workings of such clubs, see diary, 17 Dec. 1864, EP.

79. Everett to Rev. Dr. Bellows, 6 Mar. 1863, EP (quotation); Everett to Charlotte Wise, 8 Mar. 1863, Everett-Hopkins Papers, MHS.

80. Everett, *Address Delivered at the Inauguration*, 3, 46.

81. Diary, 28 Feb., 6 Mar., 26 Oct., 14 Dec. 1863, EP.

82. Ibid., 3 Nov. 1863 (quotations), 6 Jan. 1864.

83. Ibid., 25 Mar. 1864; Everett to Bonner, 25 Mar. 1864, Edward Everett Papers, LC.

84. Everett to Charles G. Loring, 16 Sept. 1864 (quotations), Charles G. Loring Papers, Houghton Library; diary, 18 July, 31 Aug. 1864, EP; Everett to George Bancroft, 17 Oct. 1864, George Bancroft Papers, MHS. Everett's reaction confirms and extends Weber's conclusion that "mainstream Democrats had made a terrible mistake in ceding such control to the peace wing at the convention"; see *Copperheads*, 170–203, quotation on 183.

85. Oakes, *Freedom National*, 471; diary, 18 Apr. 1864, EP.

86. Everett to Andrew, 11 Oct. 1864, John A. Andrew Papers, MHS; *Boston Daily Advertiser*, 18 June 1864; *Daily Cleveland Herald*, 18 June 1864.

87. Diary, 14 (quotation), 15 Sept. 1864, EP; *Lowell Daily Citizen and News*, 20 Sept. 1864.

88. Diary, 6, 17 (quotation) Oct. 1864, EP. For an excellent exploration of this consistent Republican position, see Oakes, *Freedom National*.

89. E. Everett, *Orations and Speeches*, vol. 4, 698–728.

90. Ibid., 741–46, quotation on 743.

91. Everett to Sumner, 10 Nov. 1864, Papers of Charles Sumner, Houghton Library (quotations); *New York Ledger*, 14 Jan. 1865; Everett to Henry A. Wise, 17 Nov. 1864, Everett-Hopkins Papers, MHS.

92. E. Everett, *Orations and Speeches*, vol. 4, 747–52, quotation on 752; Everett to Henry A. Wise, 3, 9 Dec. 1864, Everett to Charlotte Wise, 10 Dec. 1864, Everett-Hopkins Papers, MHS; diary, 6–7 Dec. 1864, EP.

93. *Addresses by His Excellency*, 16 (quotation); Harris, "Conservative Unionists," 313–15; Winthrop Jr., *Memoir of Robert C. Winthrop*, 258, 261–62; Hillard, *George Ticknor*, 2:440–70; Frothingham, *Edward Everett*, 416, 450, 459, 463, 466; Winthrop to McClellan, 29 Oct., 14 Nov. 1864, Papers of George B. McClellan Sr., LC. Millard Fillmore likewise invested his political capital in McClellan; see Fillmore to Mrs. McClellan, 24 Mar. 1864, Fillmore to Hiram Ketcham, 16 Sept. 1864, Papers of George B. McClellan Sr., LC. For Winthrop's speech, see Freidel, *Union Pamphlets*, 1076–1118.

94. Diary, 13 Nov. 1861, 5 July, 19 Oct. 1862, 17 Feb. (quotations), 24 Mar. 1863, 21 May (quotation), 22 (quotation) Sept., 26 [sic; 24] Oct. 1864, EP; Everett to Loring, 16 Sept. 1864, Charles G. Loring Papers, Houghton Library (quotation); Tyack, *George Ticknor*, 234–35.

95. Diary, 24 Dec. 1864, EP; Winthrop Jr., *Memoir of Robert C. Winthrop*, 248.

96. *Fayetteville Observer*, 18 July 1861 (quotations); *Daily Morning News*, 8 Apr., 10 Nov. (quotations) 1863; *Daily Mississippian*, 27 June 1862; *Weekly Mississippian*, 19 Nov. 1862; *Semi-Weekly Raleigh Register*, 4 Apr. 1863; *Richmond Dispatch* quoted in *Milwaukee Daily Sentinel*, 14 Dec. 1863 and *Liberator*, 1 Jan. 1864; *Daily Richmond Examiner*, 15 Feb. 1864; *Mobile Evening Telegraph*, 3 Nov. 1864; J. Davis, *Rise and Fall of the Confederate Government*, 1:116–34, 172.

97. Everett to Wise, 4, 16, 24 Aug. 1864, Everett-Hopkins Papers, MHS.

98. General C. C. Andrews to Everett, 3 Nov. 1864 (quotation), Sumner to Everett, 16 Sept. 1864, Andrew to Everett, 5 Nov. 1864, Julia Ward Howe to Everett, 10 Nov. 1864, EP; diary, 27 Oct. (quotation), 25 Nov. (quotation), 15, 16, 30 Dec. 1864, 15 Jan. 1865, EP.

99. Everett to Henry A. Wise, 17 Nov. 1864 (quotations), Everett-Hopkins Papers, MHS; Everett to Charles Francis Adams, 18 Dec. 1864, EP; Everett to Bancroft, 25 Oct. 1864, George Bancroft Papers, MHS.

100. Seward to Everett, 17 Sept. 1864, EP; *Boston Daily Advertiser*, 20 Oct. 1864 (quotations); *Bangor Daily Whig and Courier*, 22 Oct. 1864; *Lowell Daily Citizen and News*, 21 Dec. 1864; *Vermont Chronicle*, 14 Jan. 1865; A. Smith, *No Party Now*, 155.

101. *Liberator*, 18 Nov. 1864; diary, 8 Nov. 1864, EP.

102. Charles Eliot Norton to George William Curtis, 16 Apr. 1863, [Charles Eliot Norton] Letters, Houghton Library, Harvard University, Cambridge, Mass. My thanks to George Forgie for this citation. One wartime English traveler encountered several abolitionists who remained unconvinced by Everett's change of heart; see Chancellor, *Englishman*, 42, 61, 63, 66, 68.

103. *Boston Daily Advertiser*, 14 Apr. 1863, 20 Oct. 1864; *New Hampshire Statesman*, 8 May 1863, 11 Nov. 1864.

104. Vorenberg, *Final Freedom*, 174–75; Frothingham, *Edward Everett*, 412, 465–67; Harris, "Conservative Unionists," esp. 313; Smith, *No Party Now*, 155, 218n10.

105. Jones, *Blue and Gray Diplomacy*, esp. 4, 38–81, 113–284; Huzzey, *Freedom Burning*, 21–39.

106. Diary, 17 May 1861, EP (quotations); Prince Albert to Everett, 9 May 1860, Duke of Newcastle to Everett, 7 Oct. 1860, Earl of Aberdeen to Everett, 30 Mar. 1861, Charles Francis Adams to Everett, 14 June 1861, EP. See also List of recipients, 1850s, vol. 225, reel 43, EP.

107. Chancellor, *Englishman in the American*, 38 (quotations); Everett to Charlotte Wise, 30 Dec. 1861, 5 Jan. 1862 (quotations), Everett to Henry A. Wise, 20 Apr. 1863, Everett-Hopkins Papers, MHS, diary, 6 June 1861, 18 Feb., 22, 26 Mar., 14 Apr. 1862, 28 Apr., 22 June, 14 Oct. 1863, EP; Edward Everett to Charles W. Slack, 5 Sept. 1864, BPL.

108. Everett to Lord John Russell, 28 May (quotations), 19 Aug. 1861, EP. For background to this letter and the private expression of similar thoughts, see diary, 28 May 1861, 10 May 1864, EP; Everett to Sumner, 27 Sept. 1861, Papers of Charles Sumner, Houghton Library.

109. William H. Seward to Everett, 5, 6 Aug., 12 Sept. 1861, EP. Seward first enlisted Everett as a commissioner to an international industrial fair in London; see Seward to Everett, 14 Sept. 1861, EP. The idea was not unique to the Union government; in April 1862 the Confederate government sent its own quasi-official, secret agent to Europe with government funds for commissioning pro-Confederate articles in the European press. See H. Jones, *Blue and Gray Diplomacy*, 152–60.

110. Diary, 1 (quotations), 4, 6, 9 Nov. 1861, 21–25, 30 (quotation) Sept. 1862, EP; Seward to Everett, 17 Oct. 1861, 8, 17 Sept. 1862, Everett to Seward, 30 Sept. 1862, Everett to Frank P. Blair, 3, 18 Oct. 1862, EP; Everett to Henry A. Wise, 19 Nov. 1861, 1 Oct. 1862, 5 Jan. 1865, Everett-Hopkins Papers, MHS; Everett to Winthrop, 3 Nov. 1861, Winthrop Family Papers,

MHS; Winthrop Jr., *Memoir of Robert C. Winthrop*, 220–22; Crawford, *Russell's Civil War*, 162–65; Lord Lyons to Earl Russell, 11 Nov. 1861, in Barnes and Barnes, eds., *American Civil War through British Eyes*, 1:210. Unsurprisingly, Adams agreed with Everett's decision to decline; see diary, 5 Nov. 1862, EP.

111. E. Everett, *Orations and Speeches*, vol. 4, 363–65, 420, 457–63, 465 (quotations), 487–88, 540–46, 674–83, 726. For some of the recent scholarly books that have helped us understand—as Everett and so many others in his generation did—the international frame of reference in which the USA and CSA waged the Civil War, see Doyle, *Cause of All Nations*; and Fleche, *Revolution of 1861*.

112. Edward Everett, autograph letter signed to Lady Belper, 22 June 1863, Gilder Lehrman Collection (quotations); Everett to Dean Milman, 3 Mar. 1862, EP-Exeter; Sir John T. Coleridge to Everett, 15 June 1861, Karl Friedrich Neumann to Everett, 18 Sept. 1864, Lord Overstone to Everett, 15 Oct. 1861, Adams to Everett, 28 July 1861, 29 Apr. 1863, EP; diary, 6 Nov. 1862, 19–29 Nov. 1863, 8 Sept., 6 Oct. 1864, EP; Everett to Mrs. Anne Smyth, 13 May 1861, Edward Everett Collection, Princeton University Library.

113. *New York Ledger*, 18 Jan., 1, 29 Mar., 19 Apr., 19 July (quotation) 1862, 24 Jan., 21, 28 Feb., 28 Mar., 11 Apr., 16 May, 6 June 1863, 14 May, 18 June, 2 July, 10 Sept., 5 Nov. (quotation) 1864.

114. Sir John T. Coleridge to Everett, 15 June 1861, Karl Friedrich Neumann to Everett, 18 Sept. 1864, Lord Overstone to Everett, 15 Oct. 1861, Adams to Everett, 28 July 1861 (quotation), 23 Jan., 13, 27 Feb., 29 Apr. 1863, EP.

115. E. Everett, *Monroe Doctrine*; Crawford, *Russell's Civil War*, 140; Pierce, *Memoir and Letters*, 4:255, 260; Henry A. Wise to Everett, 22 Dec. 1862, Everett-Hopkins Papers, MHS; Strong, *Diary of the Civil War*, 282; *Boston Daily Advertiser*, 25 Nov., 20 Dec. 1861; *Daily Cleveland Herald*, 25 Nov. 1861; *New Hampshire Statesman*, 30 Nov. 1861.

116. Seward to Everett, 8 June 1863, Sumner to Everett, 4 Apr. 1863, EP.

117. Diary, 23 (quotation), 24, 25 Sept., 13, 22–23, 28–30 Oct., 2, 6–7, 9, 11–14 Nov. 1863, EP; Everett to Mrs. Charles Eames, 3 Nov. 1863, EP; Everett to Charlotte Wise, 10 Nov. 1863, Everett to Henry A. Wise, 12 Nov. 1863, Everett to C. Hale, 13, 15 Nov. 1863, Everett-Hopkins Papers, MHS; Wills, *Lincoln at Gettysburg*, 21–25, 42–52; Stripp, "Other Gettysburg Address," 162, 165. When a newspaper piece from a soldier charged Everett with errors in his account of the battle, Everett stood behind his research; diary, 26 Dec. 1863, EP.

118. Diary, 17–19 Nov. 1863, EP; LaFantasie, "Paradox of the Gettysburg Addresses," 82–85; French, *Witness to the Young Republic*, 24, 431–38.

119. E. Everett, *Orations and Speeches*, vol. 4, 622–59, quotations on 624, 626, 637, 640, 658–59. At his Union Club inaugural address, Everett had offered an early version of this argument that American history, especially the Civil War, equaled or even exceeded in significance the more celebrated events of European history; see ibid., 554–57. For a nice discussion of Everett as well positioned to make this argument, see Stripp, "Other Gettysburg Address," 167–68.

120. Everett to W. S. Wait, 17 Dec. 1863, EP.

121. E. Everett, *Orations and Speeches*, vol. 4, 640–52, quotations on 648–50, 652.

122. Ibid., 657–58.

123. Everett to Rev. Dr. Thomas Sewall, 25 Nov. 1863, EP; *New York Ledger*, 6 Feb. 1864.

124. E. Everett, *Orations and Speeches*, vol. 4, 646; Forgie, *Patricide in the House Divided*, 243–93, quotation on 252.

125. Diary, 19 (quotation), 20 Nov. 1863, EP.

126. Lincoln to Everett, 20 Nov. 1863, Letters to Edward Everett, 1863–1864, Loose Mss.

Lincoln, MHS; Barton, *Lincoln at Gettysburg*, 105; Johnson, *Writing the Gettysburg Address*, 14–17, 185; Petersen, *Gettysburg Addresses*, 40, 165.

127. Everett to Lincoln, 20 Nov. 1863 (quotations), 30 Jan. 1864 (quotations), Lincoln to Everett, 4 Feb. 1864, EP; Everett to Bonner, 25 Nov. 1863, Edward Everett Papers, LC.

128. French, *Witness to the Young Republic*, 435 (quotations); Wills, *Lincoln at Gettysburg*, 33–36, 50–51.

129. Reid, "Newspaper Responses"; Mitgang, *Abraham Lincoln*, 361–63.

130. *Daily National Intelligencer*, 20 Nov. 1863; *Vermont Watchman and State Journal*, 27 Nov. 1863; *Boston Daily Advertiser*, 12 Dec. 1863; Everett to Bonner, 25 Nov. 1863, Edward Everett Papers, LC; Seward to Everett, 8 July 1864, EP.

131. White, *Philadelphia Perspective*, 208; *Milwaukee Daily Sentinel*, 26 Nov. 1863; Poore, *Perley's Reminiscences*, 2:146.

132. Insights suggested by Johnson, *Writing the Gettysburg Address*, 180–85. See also Stripp, "Other Gettysburg Address," 166.

133. Diary, 5 Apr., 27 Aug. 1862, 8, 10, 23 June, 26 July, 26, 28, 30 Aug., 23 Sept., 11 Dec. 1863, EP.

134. E. Everett, *Orations and Speeches*, vol. 4, 501–3, 519–23, 529, 536–38, 560–62, 660–65, quotations on 501, 529, 660, 665; *Liberator*, 14 Oct. 1864; *Boston Daily Advertiser*, 17 Oct. 1864; *Lowell Daily Citizen and News*, 19 Oct. 1864.

135. Diary, 3, 9–12, 15, 17, 20–21, 25 Feb. 1864, EP; N. G. Taylor to Everett, 17 Mar. 1864, Amos A. Lawrence to Everett, 16 Feb. 1864, EP; Everett to Charlotte Wise, 27 Feb. 1864, Everett-Hopkins Papers, MHS (quotation). They also solicited the federal government for funds; see *War of the Rebellion*, ser. 1, vol. 52, pt. 1, 143–44.

136. "To the People of Massachusetts," Miscellaneous Papers, 1812–1865, reel 52A, EP (quotation).

137. Diary, 1 Mar., 14 Aug., 27–29 Dec. 1864, 3 Jan. 1865, EP; Everett to Edward Everett Hale, 2 Mar. 1864, Everett-Hopkins Papers, MHS; Everett to Andrew, 5 May 1864, John A. Andrew Papers, MHS; *Boston Daily Advertiser*, 13, 15–17, 22, 25–27, 29 Feb., 1 Mar.–30 June, 27 July, 9 Aug. 1864.

138. Anna H. Dorsey to Everett, 5 Apr. 1864 (quotation), Lloyd P. Smith to Everett, 3 Mar. 1864, N. G. Taylor to Everett, 3, 19 Mar., 18 Apr. 1864, F. C. Moody to Everett, 5 Mar. 1864, Alonzo Hill to Everett, 18 Mar. 1864, Albert W. Paine to Everett, 9 Apr. 1864, William J. Bacon to Everett, 23 Apr. 1864, J. Lowell to Everett, 29 June 1864, Elizabeth P. Peabody to Everett, 7, 13, 19 May 1864, Everett to Edwin M. Stanton, 24 Apr. 1864, Brigadier General Canby to Everett, 4 May 1864, EP.

139. For private expressions of these hopes, see, e.g., Everett to Winthrop, 23 Feb. 1862, Winthrop Family Papers, MHS; and diary, 4–5 July 1864, EP.

140. *Boston Daily Advertiser*, 20 Oct. 1864 (quotation); John Caldwell to Everett, 12 June 1864, EP (quotation); J. G. M. Ramsay to Jefferson Davis, 13 Apr. 1864, in *War of the Rebellion*, ser. 1, vol. 52, pt. 2, 655–56; diary, 12 Nov., 28 Dec. (quotation) 1864, EP. For similar encomiums on Everett from recipients of his later efforts for Savannah, see Office of the Mayor, Boston, *Savannah and Boston*, 8, 10, 32.

141. Diary, 5, 7, 8 (quotation) Jan. 1865, EP; Office of the Mayor, Boston, *Savannah and Boston*, 43, 45.

142. E. Everett, *Orations and Speeches*, vol. 4, 753–59.

143. Office of the Mayor, Boston, *Savannah and Boston*, 14–15.

144. Diary, 31 Dec. 1843 (and etc. until 31 Dec. 1863, the last time he included this refer-

ence), EP. The biblical reference is Psalm 90:12. Thanks to Jim Stewart for a conversation that encouraged me to develop this insight.

145. Diary, 9, 11, 12 (quotation) Jan. 1865, EP; Frothingham, *Edward Everett*, 468–70.

Conclusion

1. Reel 19, EP; *Lowell Daily Citizen and News*, 17 Jan. 1865.

2. Seward to Adams, 16 Jan. 1865, EP.

3. Henry A. Wise to William Everett, 15 Jan. 1865, Everett-Hopkins Papers, MHS; United States War Department, *General Orders*, Order No. 4.

4. *Lowell Daily Citizen and News*, 16, 20 Jan., 15 Apr. 1865; *Boston Daily Advertiser*, 16, 18–21, 23, 31 Jan., 1, 24 Feb., 10 Mar. 1865; *Daily Cleveland Herald*, 16, 20 Jan. 1865; *Daily National Intelligencer*, 16, 30 Jan. 1865; *North American and United States Gazette*, 16 Jan., 14 Mar. 1865; *Bangor Daily Whig and Courier*, 17, 20 Jan. 1865; *New Hampshire Statesman*, 20 Jan., 3 Feb. 1865; *Vermont Watchman and State Journal*, 20 Jan. 1865; *Vermont Chronicle*, 21, 28 Jan., 25 Mar. 1865; *Milwaukee Daily Sentinel*, 26 Jan., 4, 6, 10 Feb. 1865; *Liberator*, 27 Jan., 17 Feb., 10 Mar., 9 June 1865; *Frank Leslie's Illustrated Newspaper*, 28 Jan., 29 Apr. 1865. For even more press coverage, see vol. 247 on reel 49B, EP.

5. *Memorial of Edward Everett*, esp. 79–81; reel 19, EP; *Boston Investigator*, 25 Jan. 1865.

6. Richard Henry Dana to C. F. Choate, 15, 20 Feb. 1865, Letters to C. F. Choate, Albert and Shirley Small Special Collections Library, University of Virginia, Charlottesville; George S. Hillard to J. Francis Fisher, 18 Jan. 1865 (quotation), Francis T. Hart Collection, Historical Society of Pennsylvania, Philadelphia; "Mother" to Nathan Appleton, 23 Jan. 1865, Appleton Family Papers, MHS.

7. *Memorial of Edward Everett*, 40, 53, 66–67, 108–9; *Boston Daily Advertiser*, 27 Jan., 3, 7, 23 Mar., 19 Oct. 1865; William Amory to Caleb Cushing, 27 Jan. 1865, Cushing to Amory, 28 Jan. 1865, Caleb Cushing Papers, LC; "Everett's Great Day" (newspaper file), Everett-Hopkins Papers, MHS.

8. Strong, *Diary of the Civil War*, 544–45; *Liberator*, 20 Jan. 1865.

9. *Harper's Weekly*, 28 Jan. 1865; Curtis, *Orations and Addresses*, 1:74–81, 3:225. Thanks to George Forgie for referring me to this obituary.

10. *Boston Daily Advertiser*, 21 Jan. 1865; C. Adams, *Diary of Charles Francis Adams*, 3:10. See also Bartol, *Memorial of Virtue*, 11–12.

11. *Tribute of the Massachusetts Historical Society*, 89; *Lowell Daily Citizen and News*, 21 Dec. 1864; *Vermont Chronicle*, 14 Jan. 1865.

12. *Tribute of the Massachusetts Historical Society*, 67, 88; *Springfield Republican* quoted in *New Hampshire Statesman*, 11 Nov. 1864. For a similar sentiment, see *Memorial of Edward Everett*, 64.

13. Dana, *Address upon the Life*, 46–56.

14. *Tribute of the Massachusetts Historical Society*, 32–33, 56–57, 74–75 (quotation on 75); Osgood, *Our Patriot Scholar*, 9–10 (quotations); *NAR* 100 (Apr. 1865): 563; *Tribute to the Memory of Edward Everett*, 3–6, 66, 72–74, 82–83; N. Hall, *Memorial of Edward Everett*, 10–12; Ellis, *Life, Services, and Character*, 13–16; Hedge, *Discourse on Edward Everett*, 12–21; Manuscript of Boston Athenaeum Memorial Service, Edward Everett Papers, LC; *Daily Evening Bulletin*, 16 Jan. 1865.

15. See, e.g.., *Memorial of Edward Everett*.

16. Mayor of Cambridge to the City Council, Meeting of the Resident Members of the Dorchester Antiquarian and Historical Society (quotation), Special Meeting of the Mercan-

tile Library Association of Boston, reel 49, EP; *Memorial of Edward Everett*, 304 (quotation); Dana, *Address upon the Life*, 11; *Boston Daily Advertiser*, 25 Feb. 1865.

17. Todd, *Death in the Palace*, 19; Bigelow, *History of the Cemetery of Mount Auburn*, 39–47, 59–61, 142.

18. Whipple, *Character*, 243–52, quotations on 244, 251; Hale, *Edward Everett in the Ministry of Reconciliation*, quotations on 4, 8, 11; Hale, *Sketches of the Lives*, 2–7; Putnam, *Edward Everett*; *Proceedings of the Bunker Hill Monument Association*, 43–44; *Tribute of the Massachusetts Historical Society*, 31.

19. *Harper's Weekly*, 28 Jan. 1865; *Services at the Everett School*, 19–22; *Memorial of Edward Everett*, 49. See also Hale, *Sketches of the Lives*, 2–7.

20. Loyalties get even more complicated when one casts the African American population in this drama, of course. And Kenneth Noe's study of late-joining Confederate troops—who made up 22.5% of the Confederate army—provides one example of how this drama can be complicated even further. He found that his subjects were largely apolitical, neither hardcore Confederates nor coerced Unionists at heart. He thus rightly notes that narratives that attend almost exclusively to the most committed on both sides are misleading. See *Reluctant Rebels*, esp. 2–3, 6–7, 26, 37.

21. Kramer, *Nationalism in Europe and America*, quotation on 126; Bercovitch, *Rites of Assent*; Donald Ratcliffe, "The State of the Union, 1776–1860," in Grant and Reid, *American Civil War*, 3–38.

22. Onuf and Onuf, *Nations, Markets, and War*, quotation on 174; R. Warren, *Legacy of the Civil War*, 3–13; Stampp, "Concept of a Perpetual Union"; Nagel, *This Sacred Trust*, vii–193; Curti, *Roots of American Loyalty*; Kermes, *Creating an American Identity*; Lawson, *Patriot Fires*; Guyatt, *Providence*; Abrams, *Pilgrims and Pocahontas*; Sheidley, *Sectional Nationalism*; Seelye, *Memory's Nation*; Bonner, *Mastering America*; Grant, *North over South*; Wilentz, *Rise of American Democracy*, 745–91; Woods, *Emotional and Sectional Conflict*; Brooke, "Cultures of Nationalism."

23. Nagel, *One Nation Indivisible*, 281–88; Lawson, *Patriot Fires*, xiii–13; Peterson, *Great Triumvirate*, 495–99. For an especially good, nuanced exploration of the strength and weakness of the affective theory of Union in this era, see Woods, *Emotional and Sectional Conflict*, esp. the prologue and epilogue.

24. Waldstreicher, *In the Midst of Perpetual Fetes*; Nagel, *One Nation Indivisible*; Ayers et al, *All Over the Map*; Kersh, *Dreams of a More Perfect Union*; Travers, *Celebrating the Fourth*; Purcell, *Sealed with Blood*; Gibbons, "'Yankee Doodle' and Nationalism"; Ostendorf, *Sounds American*. For a seminal essay that suggested the complexities of American nationalism in the early Republic, see Potter, "Historian's Use of Nationalism."

25. McClintock, *Lincoln and the Decision for War*, x.

26. For an argument relative to the impact of Webster's nationalism that is similar to mine for Everett, see Peterson, *Great Triumvirate*, 495–99.

27. Oakes, *Freedom National*, 129; see also 136, 310.

28. *Memorial of Edward Everett*, 16–17, 65; *Tribute to the Memory of Edward Everett*, 95; Dana, *Address upon the Life*, 59.

29. Silber, *Gender and the Sectional Conflict*, 73–74.

30. Alexander, "Persistent Whiggery," quotation on 311; Freehling, *South vs. the South*, 61; Baggett, *Scalwags*, 9, 79–80 (quotation on 79); Varon, *Southern Lady*; Storey, *Loyalty and Loss*, esp. 4–55; Hamilton and Williams, *Papers of William Alexander Graham*, 7:47–51, 173–75, 262–63.

31. For representative recent entries, see Gallagher, *Confederate War*; and Freehling, *South vs. the South*.

32. Peterson, *Great Triumvirate*, 349; Dumond, *Southern Editorials on Secession*, 27, 32–35; Robinson, *Bitter Fruits of Bondage*, 77.

33. Freehling, *Road to Disunion*, vol. 2, quotations on 59, 425; Woods, *Emotional and Sectional Conflict*, ch. 7; Bonner, *Mastering America*, 149–83; Huston, "Southerners against Secession."

34. Cooper, *Jefferson Davis*, 3–9, 44, 116, 120, 184, 204–6, 217–22, 230, 237, 296, 281–82, 309, 312–17, 338–47 351, 412, 524 (quotations on 3, 7, 9); Shelden, "Messmates' Union," 471–72; Shelden, *Washington Brotherhood*, 116–17; Woods, *Emotional and Sectional Conflict*, ch. 7; Remini, *The House*, 166.

35. Quigley, *Shifting Grounds*, quotations on 5, 214; Gallagher, *Becoming Confederates*, quotation on 17; A. Taylor, *Divided Family*; Ruminski, "'Tradyville'"; Ayers, "Loyalty and America's Civil War." For Potter's influential ruminations on these questions, see Potter, *Impending Crisis*, ch. 17; and Potter, "Historian's Use of Nationalism."

36. Faust, *Creation of Confederate Nationalism*, 7–21 (quotations on 7, 8, 14, 21); Gallagher, *Becoming Confederates*, 3, 8–9, 12–17, 27–31, 87; Glass, ed., *Singing Soldiers*, 30–31; Furstenberg, *In the Name of the Father*; Simms, *City Laid Waste*, 107; McCoy, *Last of the Fathers*, 323–69; Diary of Louisa H. A. Minor, University of Virginia, quotations on 23–29 Dec. 1860 and 27 January–2 February 1861.

Bibliography

Archival Sources

Ann Arbor, Michigan
  University Microfilms
    Papers of Daniel Webster, Microfilm Edition, 41 reels, 1971
Boston, Massachusetts
  Boston Public Library Rare Books and Manuscripts
    Francis H. Appleton Scrapbook
    Nathan Appleton Autobiographical Sketch
    Nathan Appleton and Charles Sumner Correspondence, July–September 1848
    Edward Everett, Manuscript: "Speech in Congress on Slavery and the ⅗ Rule"
    Edward Everett Manuscripts
    Josiah Stoddard Johnston Manuscripts
    Letters Written to Nathan Appleton, Thomas Gold Appleton, and Others
  Howard Gotlieb Archival Research Center, Boston University
    First Corps of Cadets Collection
    Mercantile Library Association of Boston Collection
    Richards Manuscript Collection
  Massachusetts Archives
    House Journal, 1836, 1837, 1838, 1839, 1840, SC1/series 532
    Senate Journal, 1836, 1837, 1838, 1839, SC1/series 531
    Senate Unpassed Legislation, Message from Governor, April 6, 1836, SC1/series 231
    Senate Unpassed Legislation, Report and Resolves on the Subject of Slavery, 1836,
      SC1/series 231
  Massachusetts Historical Society
    John A. Andrew Papers, 1772–1895
    Appleton Family Papers, 1539–1941
    Nathan Appleton Jr. Scrapbooks
    George Bancroft Papers, 1816–1890
    George Bliss Papers, 1797–1914
    John H. Clifford Papers, 1634–1967
    Edward Everett Letters, 1816–1863
    Edward Everett Letters II, 1830–1865

Edward Everett Papers, 1675–1910, Microfilm Edition

Everett-Hopkins Papers, 1813–1921

Letters to Edward Everett, 1863–1864, Loose Mss. Lincoln

Memorial of Edward Everett, Lemuel Shaw, Robert C. Winthrop . . ., 23 January 1861, broadside (Boston, n.p., 1861)

Theodore Parker Papers, 1826–1865

Photostats

Edmund Quincy Diaries, 1824–1850, in Quincy, Wendell, Holmes, and Upham Papers, Microfilm Edition

Robie-Sewall Family Papers, 1611–1905

Saltonstall Papers

"Selections from Edward Everett's Diaries, 1825–1865," edited by Irving H. Bartlett

Martin Van Buren Papers

Vaughan Family Papers, 1768–1950

Winthrop Family Papers, Microfilm Edition

Cambridge, Massachusetts

Harvard Depository, Harvard University

Papers of Joseph Stevens Buckminster, Microfilm Edition

Harvard University Archives

Biographical Files, Call Number HUG 300

Papers of Edward Everett, 1807–1864

Houghton Library, Harvard University

Edward Everett, *A Discourse Delivered at the Dedication of the Statue of Daniel Webster in the State House Grounds in Boston, on the 17th of September, 1859,* MS Am 1415

Edward Everett Letterbook, 1818–1819

Charles G. Loring Papers

[Charles Eliot Norton] Letters, ca. 1830–1908, MS Am 1088.2

Papers of Charles Sumner, Microfilm Edition

Whig Party (New Hampshire) Correspondence, 1820–1838

Chapel Hill, North Carolina

Southern Historical Collection, Wilson Library, University of North Carolina

Edward Everett Letters, 1830–1862

Charlottesville, Virginia

Albert and Shirley Small Special Collections Library, University of Virginia

Papers of Edward Everett, 1811–1864

Jefferson Papers of the University of Virginia, 1732–1828, Main Series III, Microfilm Edition

Letters to C. F. Choate

Papers of Samuel Joseph May

Diary of Louisa H. A. Minor

Randolph-Meikleham Family Papers

Papers of Anna Cora Ogden Mowatt Ritchie

Papers of Alexander H. H. Stuart and the Related Stuart and Baldwin Families, 1776–1878

Tayloe Family Papers

Durham, North Carolina
  David M. Rubenstein Rare Book and Manuscript Library,
      Duke University
    Alexander R. Boteler Papers, 1729–1924
    Alexander Brown Papers, 1814–1878
    John J. Crittenden Papers, 1786–1932
    William Clark Doub Papers, 1778–1899
    John W. Dudley Papers
    Nathaniel Gilman Papers, 1830–1895
    Hanson A. Risley Papers, 1774–1908
    Joseph S. Williams Papers, 1857–1882
Exeter, New Hampshire
  Phillips Exeter Academy Library
    Edward Everett Papers
London, United Kingdom
  British Library
    Lord Aberdeen Papers, vols. 34, 85, Additional Manuscripts
New Haven, Connecticut
  Beinecke Rare Book and Manuscript Library, Yale University
    Edward Everett Letters, Za Letter File
New York City, New York
  The Gilder Lehrman Institute of American History
    The Gilder Lehrman Collection
  Morgan Library
    MA 174, Greeley–Edward Everett
    Henry Wheaton Papers
  New-York Historical Society
    S. R. Anderson Papers
    Edward Everett Letters
    Albert Gallatin Papers (microfilm edition)
    Julius Rockwell Letters
  New York Public Library
    Edward Everett Papers
    James A. Hamilton Papers
Philadelphia, Pennsylvania
  Historical Society of Pennsylvania
    George Mifflin Dallas Collection
    Edward Everett File, Society Collection
    Friends of Bell and Everett Association Minute Book, 1860–1862
    Simon Gratz Collection
    Francis T. Hart Collection
    Charles Jared Ingersoll Collection
    Josiah Stoddard Johnston Papers, 1821–1839
    Peters Papers
  Kislak Center for Special Collections, Rare Books and Manuscripts,
      University of Pennsylvania
    George Mifflin Dallas Diaries, 1837–1860

Princeton, New Jersey
  Rare Books and Special Collections, Princeton University Library
    Edward Everett Collection, 1828–1865
Provo, Utah
  L. Tom Perry Special Collections, Brigham Young University
    Ashbel Smith Correspondence, 1843–1851
Richmond, Virginia
  Library of Virginia
    Executive Papers of Governor David Campbell, 1837–1840
Tallahassee, Florida
  State Archives of Florida
    Richard Keith Call Correspondence, 1820–1860
Washington, D.C.
  Library of Congress
    Papers of John Bell
    Salmon P. Chase Papers, University Publications of America
      Microfilm Edition
    Caleb Cushing Papers, 1785–1906
    Edward Everett Papers, 1857–1865
    Millard Fillmore Papers, 1809–1874, Microfilm Edition
    Thomas Jefferson Papers, accessed online at http://memory.loc.gov
    Library of Congress Archives, Receipts for Books
    Papers of George B. McClellan Sr., 1823–1898
    William C. Rives Papers
    Andrew and John White Stevenson Family Papers
    Papers of Alexander H. H. Stuart, 1790–1868
    Charles Sumner Correspondence, 1841–1874
Williamsburg, Virginia
  Special Collections Research Center, Swem Library, College of
      William and Mary
    Tucker-Coleman Papers
Worcester, Massachusetts
  American Antiquarian Society
    Edward Everett Papers, 1832–1865
    George Washington Papers, 1754–1958

Published Government Documents

British Parliamentary Papers: Slave Trade. 95 vols. Shannon, Ireland: Irish University Press, 1968–.
Congressional Globe. Washington, D.C.: Blair and Rives, 1834–73.
Journal of the Executive Proceedings of the Senate of the United States of America from March 4, 1837, to September 13, 1841, Inclusive. Vol. 5. Washington, D.C.
Massachusetts General Court, House of Representatives. Report and Resolves Relating to Slavery in the District of Columbia. Boston, 1837.
Massachusetts General Court, Senate. Report of the Committee to Whom Was Referred the Memorial of the Anti-Slavery Society. Senate Document no. 57.

Register of Debates in Congress. Washington, D.C.: Gales and Seaton, 1825–37.

Resolves of the General Court of the Commonwealth of Massachusetts. Boston: Dutton and Wentworth, 1838.

Richardson, James D., ed. A Compilation of the Messages and Papers of the Presidents. 11 vols. Washington, D.C.: Bureau of National Literature, 1911.

United States War Department. General Orders. Washington, D.C.: War Department, 1865.

The War of the Rebellion: A Compilation of the Official Records of the Union and Confederate Armies. 70 vols. Washington, D.C.: Government Printing Office, 1880–1901.

Newspapers and Magazines

Albany Evening Journal

American Statesman and City Register

American Traveller (Boston)

Arkansas State Gazette (Little Rock)

Augusta (Ga.) Chronicle / Daily Chronicle and Sentinel

Aurora (Philadelphia)

Bangor (Maine) Daily Whig and Courier

Bay State Democrat (Boston)

Blackwood's Edinburgh (U.K.) Magazine

Boston Courier

Boston Daily Advertiser

Boston Daily Advertiser and Patriot

Boston Daily Advocate

Boston Investigator

Boston Patriot and Daily Mercantile Advertiser

Boston Statesman

Bridgewater (Mass.) Republican and Old Colony Press

Camden (S.C.) Journal

Carolina Observer (Fayetteville, N.C.) / Fayetteville Observer

Charleston Courier / Charleston Daily Courier

Charleston Mercury

Cleveland (Ohio) Daily Herald / Cleveland Herald / Daily Cleveland Herald

Cleveland Observer (Hudson, Ohio)

Columbia Telescope and South-Carolina State Journal

Commercial Advertiser (New York)

Constitutional Whig (Richmond, Va.)

Daily Atlas / Atlas / Boston Daily Atlas (Boston)

Daily Constitutionalist (Augusta, Ga.)

Daily Evening Bulletin (San Francisco)

Daily Madisonian (Washington, D.C.)

Daily Morning News (Savannah, Ga.)

Daily National Intelligencer (Washington, D.C.)

Daily National Journal (Washington, D.C.)

Daily Richmond (Va.) Examiner

Daily South Carolinian (Columbia)

Democratic Review (Washington, D.C.)

Dover (N.H.) Gazette and Strafford Advertiser

Eastern Argus (Portland, Maine)

Edinburgh (U.K.) Review

Emancipator (New York)

Emancipator and Free American / Emancipator and Republican (Boston)

Frank Leslie's Illustrated Newspaper (New York)

Frederick Douglass' Paper (Rochester, N.Y.)

Freedom's Champion (Atchison, Kans.)

Gazette of Maine (Portland)

Genius of Universal Emancipation (Baltimore)

Globe (Washington, D.C.)

Greenville (S.C.) Mountaineer

Hampshire Gazette (Northampton, Mass.)

Harper's Weekly / Harper's Monthly Magazine (New York)

Harvard Lyceum (Cambridge, Mass.)

Hinds County Gazette (Raymond, Miss.)

Illinois Gazette (Shawneetown)

Indiana Journal (Indianapolis)

Kansas Herald of Freedom (Wakarusa)

Liberator (Boston)

Louisiana Advertiser (New Orleans)

Louisville (Ky.) Public Advertiser

Lowell (Mass.) Daily Citizen and News

Lowell (Mass.) Journal

Macon (Ga.) Telegraph / Macon Weekly Telegraph

Maryland Gazette (Annapolis)
Massachusetts Journal (Boston)
Milwaukee Sentinel / Milwaukee Daily
    Sentinel / Milwaukee Morning Sentinel
Mississippian and State Gazette / Weekly
    Mississippian / Daily Mississippian (Jackson)
Mississippi Free Trader and Natchez Daily
    Gazette
Mobile (Ala.) Evening Telegraph
Mobile (Ala.) Register and Journal
National Anti-Slavery Standard (New York)
Newark (Ohio) Advocate
New Hampshire Sentinel (Keene)
New-Hampshire Statesman and Concord
    Register / New-Hampshire Statesman and
    State Journal / New Hampshire Statesman
    (Concord)
New Haven (Conn.) Daily Palladium
New York Daily Tribune
New York Herald / Weekly Herald
New York Ledger
New-York Spectator
Niles' Weekly Register (Baltimore, Md.)
North American and Daily Advertiser /
    North American and United States Gazette
    (Philadelphia)
North American Review (Boston)
Norwich (Conn.) Courier
Observer and Telegraph / Ohio Observer
    (Hudson)
Ohio Statesman (Columbus)
Pennsylvania Inquirer and Daily Courier
    (Philadelphia)
Pensacola Gazette and West Florida Advertiser /
    Pensacola Gazette (Tallahassee, Fla.)

Philadelphia Inquirer
Pittsfield (Mass.) Sun
Quarterly Review (London)
Raleigh Register, and North-Carolina State
    Gazette / Daily Register / Weekly Raleigh
    Register / Semi-Weekly Raleigh Register
Rhode Island Republican (Newport)
Richmond Enquirer
Richmond Whig
Ripley (Ohio) Bee
Salem (Mass.) Gazette
Scioto Gazette / Daily Scioto Gazette
    (Chillicothe, Ohio)
The South (Richmond, Va.)
South-Carolina Temperance Advocate
    (Columbia)
Southern Literary Messenger (Richmond)
Southern Patriot (Charleston, S.C.)
Southern Quarterly Review (New Orleans)
Union Guard (Washington, D.C.)
United States Democratic Review (New York)
United States Telegraph (Washington, D.C.)
Universal Yankee Nation (Boston)
Vermont Chronicle (Bellows Falls)
Vermont Patriot and State Gazette / Vermont
    Patriot (Montpelier)
Vermont Watchman / Vermont Watchman and
    State Gazette / Vermont Watchman and State
    Journal (Montpelier)
Virginia Free Press and Farmers' Repository /
    Virginia Free Press (Charlestown)
Westminster Review (London)
The Whig (Jonesborough, Tenn.)
Yeoman's Gazette (Concord, Mass.)

Published Primary Sources

An Account of the Interviews Which Took Place on the Fourth and Eighth of March between a
    Committee of the Massachusetts Anti-Slavery Society, and the Committee of the Legislature.
    Boston: Isaac Knapp, 1836.
An Account of the Pilgrim Celebration at Plymouth, August 1, 1853, Containing a List of the
    Decorations in the Town, and Correct Copies of the Speeches Made at the Dinner-Table. Revised by
    the Pilgrim Society. Boston: Crosby, Nichols, and Co., 1853.
Adams, Charles Francis. Diary of Charles Francis Adams. 8 vols. Edited by by Aida DiPace
    Donald, David Donald, et al. Cambridge, Mass.: Belknap Press of Harvard University
    Press, 1964–86.

————, ed. *Memoirs of John Quincy Adams, Comprising Portions of His Diary from 1795 to 1848.* 12 vols. Philadelphia, 1874–77; repr., Freeport, N.Y.: Books for Libraries Press, 1969.

Adams, Ephraim Douglass, ed. "Correspondence from the British Archives Concerning Texas, 1837–1846, III." *Southwestern Historical Quarterly* 16 (July 1912): 75–98.

Adams, John Quincy. *Lectures on Rhetoric and Oratory.* 2 vols. Edited by J. Jeffery Auer and Jerald L. Banninga. 1810; repr., New York: Russell and Russell, 1962.

Addresses at the Inauguration of the Hon. Edward Everett, LL.D., as President of the University at Cambridge, Thursday, April 30, 1846. Boston: C. C. Little and J. Brown, 1846.

Addresses by His Excellency Governor John A. Andrew, Hon. Edward Everett, Hon. B. F. Thomas, and Hon. Robert C. Winthrop, Delivered at the Mass Meeting in Aid of Recruiting, Held on the Common under the Auspices of the Committee of One Hundred and Fifty, on Wednesday, August 27, 1862. Boston: J. E. Farwell and Co., 1862.

Address of the National Executive Committee of the Constitutional Union Party to the People of the United States. N.p., [1860].

[Alexander, Charles Wesley]. *Washington's Vision: The First Union Story Ever Written.* Philadelphia: C. W. Alexander and Co., 1864.

Ames, Herman V., ed. *State Documents on Federal Relations: The States and the United States.* 1906; repr., New York: Da Capo Press, 1970.

An Appeal for the Purchase and Future Preservation of the Home and Grave of Washington. March, 1857. By the Ladies' Mount Vernon Association of the Union, Organized by a Southern Matron in April 1854. Charleston: A. J. Burke, 1857.

Andrew, John A. *Address of His Excellency John A. Andrew, to the Two Branches of the Legislature of Massachusetts, January 3, 1862.* Boston: William White, 1862.

————. *Address of His Excellency John A. Andrew, to the Two Branches of the Legislature of Massachusetts, January 8, 1864.* Boston: Wright and Potter, 1864.

Andrews, William L., ed. *Three Classic African-American Novels.* New York: Mentor, 1990.

Annual Reports of the American Society for Colonizing the Free People of Colour of the United States: Volumes 11–20. 1818–1910; repr., New York: Negro Universities Press, 1969.

Austin, James Trecothick. *Remarks on Dr. Channing's Slavery.* Boston: Russell, Shattuck and Co., 1835.

————. *Reply to the Reviewer of the Remarks on Dr. Channing's Slavery.* Boston: John H. Eastburn, 1836.

————. *Review of the Rev. Dr. Channing's Letter to Jonathan Phillips, Esq. on the Slavery Question.* Boston: John H. Eastburn, 1839.

————. *Speech Delivered in Faneuil Hall, December 8, 1837, at a Meeting of Citizens Called on the Petition of William E. Channing and Others.* Boston: John H. Eastburn, 1837.

Bacon, Leonard Woolsey. *Anti-slavery before Garrison.* New Haven, Conn.: Tuttle, Morehouse and Taylor, 1903.

Barnes, James J., and Patience P. Barnes. *The American Civil War through British Eyes: Dispatches from British Diplomats.* 3 vols. Kent, Ohio: Kent State University Press, 2003–5.

Bartol, C. A. *The Memorial of Virtue: A Sermon Preached in the West Church, Jan. 22, 1865, after the Death of Edward Everett.* Boston: Walker, Wise, and Co., 1865.

Basler, Roy P., ed. *The Collected Works of Abraham Lincoln.* 10 vols. New Brunswick, N.J.: Rutgers University Press, 1953–74.

Beaumont, Gustave de. *Marie; or, Slavery in the United States.* Translated by Barbara Chapman, introduction by Alvis L. Tinnin. 1835; repr., Stanford: Stanford University Press, 1958.

Benton, Thomas Hart. *Thirty Years' View; or, A History of the Working of the American Government for Thirty Years, from 1820 to 1850*. 2 vols. New York: D. Appleton and Co., 1854.

Bingham, Caleb. *The Columbian Orator: Containing a Variety of Original and Selected Pieces, Together with Rules; Calculated to Improve Youth and Others in the Ornamental and Useful Art of Eloquence*. Boston: J. H. A. Frost et al., 1832.

Blassingame, John W., ed. *The Frederick Douglass Papers, Series One: Speeches, Debates, and Interviews*. Vol. 3, *1855–1863*. New Haven: Yale University Press, 1985.

Booker, Mary Ames, ed. *Members of Congress since 1789*. 3rd ed. Washington, D.C.: Congressional Quarterly, 1985.

Boston Courier Report of the Union Meeting in Faneuil Hall, Thursday, Dec. 8th, 1859. Boston: Clark, Fellows, and Company, 1859.

Bridgman, Thomas. *The Pilgrims of Boston and Their Descendants: With an Introduction by Edward Everett; Also, Inscriptions from the Monuments in the Granary Burial Ground, Tremont Street*. New York: D. Appleton and Co.; Boston: Phillips, Sampson and Co., 1856.

Brown, Samuel Gilman. *The Works of Rufus Choate with a Memoir of His Life*. 2 vols. Boston: Little, Brown and Co., 1862.

Bunker Hill Monument Association. *Circular*. Boston, 1824.

Burns, James. *Selections from the Works of Edward Everett, with a Sketch of His Life*. Boston: J. Burns, 1839.

Calhoun, John C. *The Works of John C. Calhoun*. Edited by Richard K. Cralle. 6 vols. New York: D. Appleton and Co., 1854–58.

Canning, George. *The Speech of the Right Hon. George Canning, in the House of Commons, on the Motion of Thomas Fowell Buxton, Esq. as Printed in the "Times" and "Morning Chronicle" of Friday, May 16, 1823*. London: W. Marchant, 1823.

———. *The Speech of the Rt. Hon. George Canning, in the House of Commons, on the 16th Day of March, 1824, on Laying before the House the "Papers in Explanation of the Measures Adopted by His Majesty's Government, for the Amelioration of the Condition of the Slave Population in His Majesty's Dominions in the West Indies."* London: John Murray, 1824.

[Cass, Lewis]. *An Examination of the Question, Now in Discussion, between the American and British Governments, Concerning the Right of Search. By an American*. Baltimore: N. Hickman, 1842.

Chancellor, Christopher, ed. *An Englishman in the American Civil War: The Diaries of Henry Yates Thompson, 1863*. London: Sidgwick and Jackson, 1971.

Channing, William Ellery. *The Duty of the Free States, or Remarks Suggested by the Case of the "Creole."* Boston: William Crosby and Co., 1842.

———. *Remarks on the Slavery Question, in a Letter to Jonathan Phillips, Esq*. London: J. Green, 1839.

———. *Slavery*. 1836; repr., New York: Negro Universities Press, 1968.

Child, Lydia Maria. *An Appeal in Favor of That Class of Americans Called Africans*. 1833; repr., Amherst: University of Massachusetts Press, 1996.

Choate, Rufus. *Addresses and Orations of Rufus Choate*. Boston: Little, Brown, and Co., 1878.

Clay, Henry. *Speech of the Hon. Henry Clay, in the Senate of the United States, on the Subject of Abolition Petitions, February 7, 1839*. Boston: James Munroe and Co., 1839.

Correspondence between the Hon. F. H. Elmore, One of the South Carolina Delegation in Congress and James G. Birney, one of the Secretaries of the American Anti-Slavery Society. New York: American Anti-Slavery Society, 1838; repr., New York: Arno Press and the New York Times, 1969.

Correspondence on the Proposed Tripartite Convention Relative to Cuba. Boston: Little, Brown and Co., 1853.

Crawford, Martin, ed. *William Howard Russell's Civil War: Private Diary and Letters, 1861–1862.* Athens: University of Georgia Press, 1992.

Curtis, George William. *Orations and Addresses.* Edited by Charles Eliot Norton. 3 vols. New York: Harper and Brothers, 1894.

Cushing, William. *Index to the "North American Review."* Cambridge, Mass.: John Wilson and Son, 1898.

[Custis, George Washington Parke]. *The Indian Prophecy, a National Drama in Two Acts.* Georgetown, D.C.: James Thomas, 1828.

Dana, Richard Henry, Jr. *An Address upon the Life and Services of Edward Everett; Delivered before the Municipal Authorities and Citizens of Cambridge, February 22, 1865.* Cambridge, Mass.: Dakin and Metcalf (also Sever and Francis), 1865.

Davis, Jefferson. *The Rise and Fall of the Confederate Government.* 2 vols. New York: D. Appleton and Co., 1881.

Deese, Helen R., ed. *Daughter of Boston: The Extraordinary Diary of a Nineteenth-Century Woman, Caroline Healey Dall.* Boston: Beacon Press, 2005.

Dittenhoefer, Abram J. *How We Elected Lincoln: Personal Recollections.* 1916; repr., Philadelphia: University of Pennsylvania Press, 2005.

Doggett, Simeon. *Two Discourses on the Subject of Slavery.* Boston: Minot Pratt, 1835.

Dumond, Dwight L., ed. *Southern Editorials on Secession.* 1931; repr., Gloucester, Mass.: Peter Smith, 1964.

Duyckinck, Edward A. *Cyclopaedia of American Literature: Embracing Personal and Critical Notices of Authors, and Selections from Their Writings; From the Earliest Period to the Present Day; With Portraits, Autographs, and Other Illustrations.* 2 vols. New York: Charles Scribner, 1855.

Earle, Jonathan. *John Brown's Raid on Harpers Ferry: A Brief History with Documents.* Boston and New York: Bedford/St. Martin's, 2008.

Ellis, Rufus. *The Life, Services, and Character of Edward Everett: A Sermon Preached in the First Church, January 22, 1865.* Boston: John Wilson and Son, 1865.

Emerson, Ralph Waldo. *The Complete Works of Ralph Waldo Emerson.* 12 vols. in 6. New York: William H. Wise, 1926.

———. *The Journals of Ralph Waldo Emerson, 1820–1872.* 10 vols. Edited by Edward Waldo Emerson and Waldo Emerson Forbes. Boston: Houghton Mifflin, 1909–14.

Erdman, David V., ed. *The Collected Works of Samuel Taylor Coleridge: Essays on His Times.* 3 vols. Princeton: Princeton University Press, 1978.

Evarts, Jeremiah, ed. *Speeches on the Passage of the Bill for the Removal of the Indians: Delivered in the Congress of the United States, April and May, 1830.* Boston: Perkins and Marvin, 1830.

Everett, Alexander H. *America; or, A General Survey of the Political Situation of the Several Powers of the Western Continent, with Conjectures on Their Future Prospects. . . .* Philadelphia: H. C. Carey and I. Lea, 1827.

———. *New Ideas on Population, with Remarks on the Theories of Malthus and Godwin.* 1826; repr., New York: Augustus M. Kelley, 1970.

Everett, Edward. *An Address Delivered at the Inauguration of the Union Club, 9 April 1863.* Boston: Little, Brown, and Co., 1863.

———. *Address of His Excellency Edward Everett, to the Two Branches of the Legislature, . . . January 6, 1836.* Boston: Dutton and Wentworth, 1836.

——. *Address of His Excellency Edward Everett, to the Two Branches of the Legislature,* . . . *January 4, 1837*. Boston: Dutton and Wentworth, 1837.

——. *Address of His Excellency Edward Everett, to the Two Branches of the Legislature,* . . . *January 2, 1839*. Boston: Dutton and Wentworth, 1839.

——. *A Defence of Christianity: Against the Work of George B. English, a.m., Entitled The Grounds of Christianity Examined, by Comparing the New Testament with the Old*. Boston: Cummings and Hilliard, 1814.

——. "Edward Everett's College Life." *Old and New* 4 (July/August 1871): 18–27, 194–201.

——. *First Battles of the Revolution*. New York: E. Maynard and Co., 1890.

——. *The Life of George Washington*. New York: Sheldon and Co., 1860.

——. *The Monroe Doctrine*. . . . Loyal Publication Society Pamphlets no. 34. New York: Wm. C. Bryant and Co., 1863.

——. *The Mount Vernon Papers*. New York: D. Appleton and Co., 1860.

——. *Orations and Speeches on Various Occasions*. Vol. 1. 1836; 8th ed., Boston: Little, Brown, and Co., 1870.

——. *Orations and Speeches on Various Occasions*. Vol. 2. 1850; 9th ed., Boston: Little, Brown, and Co., 1878.

——. *Orations and Speeches on Various Occasions*. Vol. 3. 1859; repr., Boston: Little, Brown, and Co., 1870.

——. *Orations and Speeches on Various Occasions*. Vol. 4. Boston: Little, Brown, and Co., 1868.

[Everett, Edward, ed.]. *The Diplomatic and Official Papers of Daniel Webster, While Secretary of State*. New York: Harper and Brothers, 1848.

[——]. *The Works of Daniel Webster*. 6 vols. Boston: Little, Brown, and Co., 1851.

Everett, Oliver. *An Eulogy on General George Washington,* . . . *Pronounced at Dorchester, February 22, 1800*. Charlestown, Mass.: Samuel Etheridge, 1800.

Faux, William. *Memorable Days in America: Being a Journal of a Tour to the United States*. . . . London: W. Simpkin and R. Marshall, 1823.

Ford, Worthington C., ed. "February Meeting, 1908." *Proceedings of the Massachusetts Historical Society*, 3rd ser., 1 (1907–8): 315–93.

——. *Writings of John Quincy Adams*. 7 vols. New York: Macmillan Company, 1913–17.

Freehling, William W., and Craig M. Simpson, eds. *Showdown in Virginia: The 1861 Convention and the Fate of the Union*. Charlottesville: University of Virginia Press, 2010.

French, Benjamin Brown. *Witness to the Young Republic: A Yankee's Journal, 1828–1870*. Edited by Donald B. Cole. Hanover, N.H.: University Press of New England, 1989.

Freidel, Frank, ed. *Union Pamphlets of the Civil War, 1861–1865*. 2 vols. Cambridge, Mass.: Belknap Press of Harvard University Press, 1967.

"From a Graduate's Window." *Harvard Graduates' Magazine* 17 (June 1908): 612–18.

Garrison, William Lloyd. *The Letters of William Lloyd Garrison*. 6 vols. Edited by Walter M. Merrill and Louis Ruchames. Cambridge, Mass.: Belknap Press of Harvard University Press, 1971–81.

Glass, Paul, ed. *Singing Soldiers: A History of the Civil War in Song*. New York: Da Capo Press, 1964.

Goodell, William. *A Full Statement of the Reasons Which Were in Part Offered to the Committee of the Legislature of Massachusetts, on the Fourth and Eighth of March, Showing Why There Should Be No Penal Laws Enacted,* . . . *Respecting Abolitionists and Anti-Slavery Societies*. Boston: Isaac Knapp, 1836.

The Great Fraud upon the Public Credulity in the Organization of the Republican Party: An Address to the Old-Line Whigs of the Union. Washington, D.C.: Union Office, 1856.

Great Union Meeting, Philadelphia, December 7, 1859: Fanaticism Rebuked. Philadelphia: Crissy and Markley, 1859.

Green, Duff. *The United States and England. By an American.* London, 1842.

Hale, Edward Everett. *Edward Everett in the Ministry of Reconciliation: A Sermon Preached in the South Congregational Church, Boston, Jan. 22, 1865.* Boston: Alfred Mudge and Son, 1865.

——. *The Man without a Country and Other Stories.* Ware, U.K.: Wordsworth Editions Limited, 1995.

——. *Memories of a Hundred Years.* 2 vols. New York: Macmillan Co., 1902.

——. *Sketches of the Lives of the Brothers Everett.* Boston: Little, Brown, and Co., 1878.

[Hale, Edward Everett, ed.]. *Cuba: The Everett Letters on Cuba.* Boston: George H. Ellis, 1897.

Hall, Nathaniel. *A Memorial of Edward Everett: A Discourse Preached in the First Church, Dorchester, Sunday, Jan. 22, 1865.* Boston: Walker, Wise, and Co.; Ebenezer Clapp, 1865.

Hamilton, J. G. de Roulhac, and Max R. Williams, eds. *The Papers of William Alexander Graham.* 7 vols. Raleigh, N.C.: State Department of Archives and History, 1957–84.

Hamilton, James A. *Reminiscences of James A. Hamilton; or, Men and Events, at Home and Abroad, during Three Quarters of a Century.* New York: Charles Scribner and Co., 1869.

Harvey, Peter. *Reminiscences and Anecdotes of Daniel Webster.* Boston: Little, Brown, and Co., 1877.

Hedge, Frederic Henry. *Discourse on Edward Everett, Delivered in the Church of the First Parish, Brookline, on the Twenty-Second January.* Boston: Geo. C. Rand and Avery, 1865.

Hesseltine, William B., ed. *Three against Lincoln: Murat Halstead Reports the Caucuses of 1860.* Baton Rouge: Louisiana State University Press, 1960.

[Higginson, Francis John]. *Remarks on Slavery and Emancipation.* Boston: Hilliard, Gray, and Co., 1834.

Hillard, George, ed. *Life, Letters, and Journals of George Ticknor.* 2 vols. Boston: James R. Osgood and Co., 1877.

[Holland, Edwin Clifford]. *A Refutation of the Calumnies Circulated against the Southern and Western States, Respecting the Institution and Existence of Slavery among Them.* Charleston: A. E. Miller, 1822; repr., New York: Negro Universities Press, 1969.

Hone, Philip. *The Diary of Philip Hone, 1828–1851.* 2 vols. Edited by Bayard Tuckerman. New York: Dodd, Mead and Company, 1889.

Hopkins, James F., et al., eds. *The Papers of Henry Clay: Selections.* 10 vols. and a supplement. Lexington: University of Kentucky Press, 1959–92.

The Illustrated Mount Vernon Record, The Organ of the Mount Vernon Ladies' Association of the Union. Vol. 1, July 1858 to June 1859. Philadelphia: Devereux and Co., 1859.

The Illustrated Mount Vernon Record, The Organ of the Mount Vernon Ladies' Association of the Union. Vol. 2, July 1859 to June 1860. Philadelphia: Devereux and Co., 1860.

Jackson, J. R. de J., ed. *The Collected Works of Samuel Taylor Coleridge: Lectures 1818–1819 on the History of Philosophy.* 2 vols. Princeton: Princeton University Press, 2000.

Jay, William. *The Creole Case and Mr. Webster's Despatch.* New York: Office of the New York American, 1842.

Journal of the Proceedings of the National Republican Convention, Held at Worcester, October 11, 1832. Boston: Stimpson and Clapp, 1832.

Julian, George. *Political Recollections, 1840 to 1872*. 1884; repr., New York: Negro Universities Press, 1970.

Keyes, Erasmus. *Fifty Years' Observations of Men and Events Civil and Military*. New York: Scribner, 1884.

Kime, Wayne R., ed. "The 'Troublous Times' of 1860–1861: A Memoir by Colonel Richard Irving Dodge, U.S. Army." *Civil War History* 59 (June 2013): 206–34.

King, Charles R., ed. *The Life and Correspondence of Rufus King*. 6 vols. New York: G. P. Putnam's Sons, 1894–1900.

Larkin, Jack, and Caroline Sloat, eds. *A Place in My Chronicle: A New Edition of the Diary of Christopher Columbus Baldwin, 1829–1835*. Worcester, Mass.: American Antiquarian Society, 2010.

Lee, Eliza Buckminster. *Memoirs of Rev. Joseph Buckminster, D.D., and of His Son, Rev. Joseph Stevens Buckminster*. Boston: Wm. Crosby and H. P. Nichols, 1849.

Lee, Jean B., ed. *Experiencing Mount Vernon: Eyewitness Accounts, 1784–1865*. Charlottesville: University of Virginia Press, 2006.

Letters of the Hon. Joseph Holt, the Hon. Edward Everett, and Commodore Charles Stewart, on the Present Crisis. Philadelphia: William S. and Alfred Martien, 1861.

The Life, Speeches, and Public Service, of John Bell, Together with a Sketch of the Life of Edward Everett, Union Candidates for the Office of President and Vice-President of the United States. New York: Rudd and Carleton, 1860.

Lumpkin, Wilson. *The Removal of the Cherokee Indians from Georgia*. 2 vols. 1907; repr., New York: Arno Press, 1969.

[Lunt, George]. *The Dove and the Eagle*. Boston: Ticknor, Reed, and Fields, 1851.

Lunt, George. *The Origin of the Late War: Traced from the Beginning of the Constitution to the Revolt of the Southern States*. New York: Appleton, 1866.

[———]. *The Union*. Boston: Crocker and Brewster, 1860.

Lyell, Charles. *A Second Visit to the United States of North America*. 2 vols. New York: Harper and Brothers; London: John Murray, 1849.

———. *Travels in North America, in the Years 1841–2*. 2 vols. New York: Wiley and Putnam, 1845.

Magoon, Elias Lyman. *Living Orators in America*. New York: Baker and Scribner, 1849.

Mann, Horace. *Slavery: Letters and Speeches*. 1851; repr., New York: Negro Universities Press, 1969.

Manning, William R., ed. *Diplomatic Correspondence of the United States: Inter-American Affairs, 1831–1860*. 12 vols. Washington, D.C.: Carnegie Endowment for International Peace, 1932–39.

Martineau, Harriet. *The Martyr Age of the United States of America, with an Appeal on Behalf of the Oberlin Institute in Aid of the Abolition of Slavery*. Newcastle upon Tyne, U.K.: Finlay and Charlton, 1840.

———. *Society in America*. 3 vols. London: Saunders and Otley, 1837.

May, Samuel J. *Some Recollections of Our Antislavery Conflict*. 1869; repr., New York: Arno Press, 1968.

McClellan, George B. *The Civil War Papers of George B. McClellan: Selected Correspondence, 1860–1865*. Edited by Stephen W. Sears. New York: Ticknor and Fields, 1989.

"Memoir of Edward Everett. Communicated by William Everett." *Proceedings of the Massachusetts Historical Society* 18 (December 1903): 91–117.

A Memorial of Daniel Webster, from the City of Boston. Boston: Little, Brown and Co., 1853.

A Memorial of Edward Everett, from the City of Boston. Boston: Printed by Order of the City Council, 1865.

Meriwether, Robert L., Clyde N. Wilson, W. Edwin Hemphill, and Shirley B. Cook, eds. *The Papers of John C. Calhoun*. 28 vols. Columbia: University of South Carolina Press, 1959–2003.

Mitgang, Herbert, ed. *Abraham Lincoln: A Press Portrait*. 1956; repr., Athens: University of Georgia Press, 1989.

Moore, Frank, ed. *The Rebellion Record: A Diary of American Events, with Documents, Narratives, Illustrative Incidents, Poetry, Etc*. 11 vols. New York: G. P. Putnam and D. Van Nostrand, 1862–69.

Moore, John Bassett, ed. *The Works of James Buchanan: Comprising His Speeches, State Papers, and Private Correspondence*. 12 vols. Philadelphia: Lippincott, 1908-11; repr., New York: Antiquarian Press, 1960.

Morse, John T., Jr. *Life and Letters of Oliver Wendell Holmes*. 2 vols. London: Sampson Low, Marston and Co., 1896.

Neilson, Joseph. *Memories of Rufus Choate*. Boston: Houghton, Mifflin, and Co., 1884.

Office of the Mayor, Boston. *Savannah and Boston: Account of the Supplies sent to Savannah; With the Last Appeal of Edward Everett in Faneuil Hall, the Letter to the Mayor of Savannah, and the Proceedings of the Citizens, and Letter of the Mayor of Savannah, by the Executive Committee*. Boston: John Wilson and Son, 1865.

Official Report of the Great Union Meeting Held at the Academy of Music, New York, December 19, 1859. New York: Davies and Kent, 1859.

Osgood, Samuel. *Our Patriot Scholar: Discourse in Memory of Edward Everett, at Vespers, in the Church of the Messiah [New York], Sunday, January 22*. New York: James Miller, 1865.

Ouseley, William Gore, Sir. *Reply to an "American's Examination" of the "Right of Search": With Observations on Some of the Questions at Issue between Great Britain and the United States and on Certain Positions Assumed by the North American Government*. London: John Rodwell, 1842.

Palfrey, John G. *Papers on the Slave Power, First Published in the "Boston Whig" in July, August, and September, 1846*. Boston: Merrill, Cobb and Co., 1846.

Parker, Theodore. *A Discourse Occasioned by the Death of Daniel Webster, Preached at the Melodeon on Sunday, October 31, 1852*. Boston: Benjamin B. Mussey and Co., 1853.

———. *Historic Americans*. Boston: Horace B. Fuller, 1878.

———. *The Rights of Man in America*. Edited by Franklin B. Sanborn. 1911; repr., New York: Negro Universities Press, 1969.

———. *Ten Sermons of Religion*. 2nd ed. Boston: Little, Brown and Co., 1855.

The Patriotic Song Book: A Superior Collection of Choice Tunes and Hymns, Written and Composed for the Times, to Be Sung during the War by the Uprising Millions of Men, Women, and Children, Who Stand by the Flag of Our Country, and Despise Traitors. New York: Horace Waters, 1861.

Phillips, Ulrich B., ed. *The Correspondence of Robert Toombs, Alexander H. Stephens, and Howell Cobb: Annual Report of the American Historical Association, 1911*. New York: Da Capo Press, 1970.

Phillips, Wendell. *Speeches, Lectures, and Letters*. 1st ser. N.p., 1863.

———. *Speeches, Lectures, and Letters*. 2nd ser. Boston: Lothrop, Lee and Shepard Co., 1891.

Pierce, Edward L. *Memoir and Letters of Charles Sumner*. 4 vols. Boston: Roberts Brothers, 1893–94.

Poe, Edgar Allan. *Essays and Reviews*. Edited by G. R. Thompson. New York: Library of
America, 1984.

Poore, Benjamin Perley. *Perley's Reminiscences of Sixty Years in the National Metropolis*. 2 vols.
Philadelphia: Hubbard Brothers, 1886.

Pratt, Minot. *A Friend of the South in Answer to Remarks on Dr. Channing's Slavery*. Boston:
Otis, Broaders and Co., 1836.

*Proceedings of a Convention of Delegates Chosen by the People of Massachusetts, without Distinction
of Party, and Assembled at Faneuil Hall, in the City of Boston, . . . to Take into Consideration the
Proposed Annexation of Texas to the United States*. Boston: Eastburn's Press, 1845.

Proceedings of the Bunker Hill Monument Association at the Annual Meeting, June 17, 1865. Boston:
Bunker Hill Monument Association, 1865.

*Proceedings of the First Annual Meeting of the New-York State Anti-slavery Society: Convened at
Utica, October 19, 1836*. Utica, N.Y.: Published for the Society, 1836.

Proceedings of the New England Anti-Slavery Convention: Held in Boston, May 24, 25, 26, 1836.
Boston: Isaac Knapp, 1836.

The Public Record and Past History of John Bell and Edward Everett. Washington, D.C.: National
Democratic Executive Committee, 1860.

Putnam, A. P. *Edward Everett: A Sermon Occasioned by the Death of Edward Everett, Preached at
the Church of the Saviour, Brooklyn, NY, January 22, 1865*. New York: George F. Nesbitt and
Co., 1865.

Remarks on "Slavery by William E. Channing." Boston: John H. Eastburn, 1836.

*Right and Wrong in Boston: Report of the Boston Female Anti Slavery Society; With a Concise
Statement of Events, Previous and Subsequent to the Annual Meeting of 1835*. Boston: Boston
Female Anti Slavery Society, 1836.

Seabrook, Whitemarsh B. *A Concise View of the Critical Situation, and Future Prospects of the
Slave-holding States, in Relation to Their Coloured Population*. 2nd ed. Charleston: A. E.
Miller, 1825.

Sermons by the Late Rev. Joseph S. Buckminster, with a Memoir of His Life and Character. 2nd ed.
Boston: Wells and Lilly, 1815.

Services at the Everett School in Boston, on the Death of Edward Everett. Boston: J. E. Farwell
and Co., 1865.

*The Seventy-Fourth Anniversary of the Birth-day of Daniel Webster: Celebrated at the Revere
House—Boston, January 18, 1856*. Boston: Office of the Daily Courier, 1856.

Shanks, Henry Thomas, ed. *The Papers of Willie Person Mangum*. 5 vols. Raleigh: State
Department of Archives and History, 1950–56.

Shewmaker, Kenneth E., et al., eds. *The Papers of Daniel Webster: Diplomatic Papers*. 2 vols.
Hanover, N.H.: University Press of New England, 1983–87.

Silbey, Joel H., ed. *The American Party Battle: Election Campaign Pamphlets, 1828–1876*. 2 vols.
Cambridge, Mass.: Harvard University Press, 1999.

Simmons, George F. *Review of the Remarks on Dr. Channing's Slavery, by a Citizen of
Massachusetts*. Boston: James Munroe and Co., 1836.

Simms, William Gilmore. *A City Laid Waste: The Capture, Sack, and Destruction of the City of
Columbia*. Edited by David Aiken. Columbia: University of South Carolina Press, 2005.

———. *Slavery in America: Being a Brief Review of Miss Martineau on that Subject. By a South
Carolinian*. Richmond: Thomas W. White, 1838.

Smith, Wilson G., ed. *Grand Army War Songs: A Collection of War Songs, Battle Songs, Camp*

Songs, National Songs, Marching Songs, Etc. . . . Cleveland and Chicago: S. Brainard's Sons, 1886.

Sollors, Werner, Caldwell Titcomb, and Thomas A. Underwood, eds. *Blacks at Harvard: A Documentary History of African-American Experience at Harvard and Radcliffe.* New York: New York University Press, 1993.

Speech of Hon. J. C. Breckinridge, Vice-President of the United States, at Ashland, Kentucky, Sept. 5, 1860, Repelling the Charge of Disunion and Vindicating the National Democracy. Washington, D.C.: National Democratic Executive Committee, 1860.

Stegmaier, Mark J., ed. *Henry Adams in the Secession Crisis: Dispatches to the Boston Daily Advertiser, December 1860–March 1861.* Baton Rouge: Louisiana State University Press, 2012.

Story, William W. *Life and Letters of Joseph Story, Associate Justice of the Supreme Court of the United States, and Dane Professor of Law at Harvard University.* 2 vols. 1851; repr., Freeport, N.Y.: Books for Libraries Press, 1971.

Strong, George Templeton. *Diary of the Civil War, 1860–1865.* Edited by Allen Nevins. New York: Macmillan, 1962.

Stuart, Moses. *Conscience and the Constitution, with Remarks on the Recent Speech of the Hon. Daniel Webster in the Senate of the United States on the Subject of Slavery.* Boston: Crocker and Brewster, 1850.

Sturge, Joseph, and Thomas Harvey. *The West Indies in 1837: Being the Journal of a Visit to Antigua, Montserrat, Dominica, St. Lucia, Barbados, and Jamaica; Undertaken for the Purpose of Ascertaining the Actual Condition of the Negro Population of Those Islands.* London: Hamilton, Adams, and Co., 1838.

Sumner, Charles. *Charles Sumner: His Complete Works.* 20 vols. Boston: Lee and Shepherd, 1900; repr., New York: Negro Universities Press, 1969.

Thome, James A., and J. Horace Kimball. *Emancipation in the West Indies: A Six Months' Tour in Antigua, Barbodoes, and Jamaica, in the Year 1837.* New York: American Anti-Slavery Society, 1838.

Ticknor, George. *Life of William Hickling Prescott.* Philadelphia: J. P. Lippincott, 1863.

Todd, John E. *Death in the Palace: A Sermon in Memory of Edward Everett, Central Congregational Society, Boston, January 22, 1865.* Boston: Dakin and Metcalf, 1865.

Tribute of the Massachusetts Historical Society, to the Memory of Edward Everett, January 30, 1865. Boston: Massachusetts Historical Society, 1865.

Tribute to the Memory of Edward Everett, by the New-England Historic-Genealogical Society, at Boston, Mass., January 17 and Feb. 1, 1865. Boston: New-England Historic-Genealogical Society, 1865.

The True Whig Sentiment of Massachusetts. Boston, 1846.

[Turnbull, Robert]. *The Crisis; or, Essays on the Usurpations of the Federal Government. By Brutus.* Charleston: A. E. Miller, 1827.

Upham, Charles Wentworth. *Speech of Charles W. Upham of Salem, in the House of Representatives of Massachusetts, on the Compromises of the Constitution.* Salem, Mass.: Tri-Weekly Gazette Office, 1849.

Upshur, A. P., and John A. Upshur. "Letter of A. P. Upshur to J. C. Calhoun." *William and Mary Quarterly*, 2nd ser., 16 (October 1936): 554–57.

Van Tyne, C. H., ed. *The Letters of Daniel Webster: From Documents Owned Principally by the New Hampshire Historical Society.* 1902; repr., New York: Greenwood Press, 1968.

Vindication of John Bell from Misrepresentations of the Breckinridge Executive Committee, as Contained in Their Campaign Document, no. 5. N.p.: Bell and Everett National Executive Committee, 1860.

The War Policy of the Administration: Letter of the President to the Union Mass Convention in Springfield, Illinois. Albany: Albany Journal, 1863.

War Songs: A Collection of the Songs of the Nation, Songs of Patriotism, Songs of the Flag . . . Boston: O. Ditson Co., 1906.

Webster, Daniel. *Speech of the Hon. Daniel Webster, upon the Subject of Slavery: Delivered in the United States Senate on Thursday, March 7, 1850. As Revised and Corrected by Himself. . . .* Boston: Redding and Co., 1850.

Wheaton, Henry. *Enquiry into the Validity of the British Claim to a Right of Visitation and Search of American Vessels Suspected to Be Engaged in the African Slave-Trade.* 1842; repr., New York: Negro Universities Press, 1969.

White, Jonathan W., ed. "A Pennsylvania Judge Views the Rebellion: The Civil War Letters of George Washington Woodward." *Pennsylvania Magazine of History and Biography* 129 (April 2005): 195–225.

———. *A Philadelphia Perspective: The Civil War Diary of Sidney George Fisher.* New York: Fordham University Press, 2007.

Whittier, John Greenleaf. *The Complete Poetical Works of John Greenleaf Whittier: Cambridge Edition.* Boston: Houghton, Mifflin and Company, 1894.

Wilson, Henry. *History of the Rise and Fall of the Slave Power in America.* 3 vols. Boston: James R. Osgood and Co., 1872–77.

Wiltse, Charles M., et al., eds. *The Papers of Daniel Webster: Correspondence.* 7 vols. Hanover, N.H.: University Press of New England, 1974–86.

Winthrop, Robert C. *Addresses and Speeches on Various Occasions.* 4 vols. Boston, 1852–86.

Secondary Sources

Abrams, Ann Uhry. *The Pilgrims and Pocahontas: Rival Myths of American Origin.* Boulder, Colo.: Westview Press, 1999.

Abzug, Robert H. *Cosmos Crumbling: American Reform and the Religious Imagination.* New York: Oxford University Press, 1994.

Adams, Ephraim Douglass. "Lord Ashburton and the Treaty of Washington." *American Historical Review* 17 (July 1912): 764–82.

Adams, Henry. "The Great Secession Winter of 1860–61." *Proceedings of the Massachusetts Historical Society* 43 (1910): 656–87.

Adams, Michael C. C. *Living Hell: The Dark Side of the Civil War.* Baltimore: Johns Hopkins University Press, 2014.

Akehurst, Hazel. "Sectional Crises and the Fate of Africans Illegally Imported into the United States, 1806–1860." *American Nineteenth Century History* 9 (June 2008): 97–122.

Alexander, Thomas B. "Persistent Whiggery in the Confederate South, 1860–1877." *Journal of Southern History* 27 (August 1961): 305–29.

Alford, Terry. *Prince among Slaves: The True Story of an African Prince Sold into Slavery in the American South.* 30th anniversary ed. New York: Oxford University Press, 2007.

Altschuler, Glenn C., and Stuart M. Blumin. *Rude Republic: Americans and Their Politics in the Nineteenth Century.* Princeton: Princeton University Press, 2000.

Anbinder, Tyler. *Nativism and Slavery: The Northern Know Nothings and the Politics of the 1850s.* New York: Oxford University Press, 1992.

Anderson, Benedict. *Imagined Communities: Reflections on the Origin and Spread of Nationalism.* 1983; rev. ed., London and New York: Verso, 1991.

Andrew, John A., III. *From Revivals to Removal: Jeremiah Evarts, the Cherokee Nation, and the Search for the Soul of America.* Athens: University of Georgia Press, 1992.

Ashworth, John. *Slavery, Capitalism, and Politics in the Antebellum Republic.* Volume 1, *Commerce and Compromise, 1820–1850.* Cambridge: Cambridge University Press, 1995.

——— . *Slavery, Capitalism, and Politics in the Antebellum Republic.* Volume 2, *The Coming of the Civil War, 1850–1861.* Cambridge: Cambridge University Press, 2007.

Ayers, Edward L. "Loyalty and America's Civil War." 49th Annual Robert Fortenbaugh Memorial Lecture, Gettysburg College, Gettysburg, Penn., 2010.

Ayers, Edward L., et al. *All Over the Map: Rethinking American Regions.* Baltimore: Johns Hopkins University Press, 1996.

Baggett, James Alex. *The Scalawags: Southern Dissenters in the Civil War and Reconstruction.* Baton Rouge: Louisiana State University Press, 2003.

Baker, Jean H. *Affairs of Party: The Political Culture of Northern Democrats in the Mid-nineteenth Century.* 1983; repr., New York: Fordham University Press, 1998.

Barker, Gordon S. *The Imperfect Revolution: Anthony Burns and the Landscape of Race in Antebellum America.* Kent, Ohio: Kent State University Press, 2010.

Barney, William L. *The Making of a Confederate: Walter Lenoir's Civil War.* New York: Oxford University Press, 2008.

Bartlett, Irving H. *Daniel Webster.* New York: W. W. Norton, 1978.

——— . "Edward Everett Reconsidered." *New England Quarterly* 69 (September 1996): 426–60.

Barton, William E. *Lincoln at Gettysburg: What He Intended to Say; What He Said; What He Was Reported to Have Said; What He Wished He Had Said.* Indianapolis: Bobbs-Merrill, 1930.

Baum, Dale. *The Civil War Party System: The Case of Massachusetts, 1848–1876.* Chapel Hill: University of North Carolina Press, 1984.

Bellah, Robert N. "Civil Religion in America." In *Beyond Belief: Essays on Religion in a Post-Traditional World,* 168–91. New York: Harper and Row, 1970.

Belohlavek, John M. *Broken Glass: Caleb Cushing and the Shattering of the Union.* Kent, Ohio: Kent State University Press, 2005.

Bemis, Samuel Flagg, ed. *The American Secretaries of State and their Diplomacy.* 10 vols. New York: Pageant Book Company, 1928.

Bercovitch, Sacvan. *The Puritan Origins of the American Self.* New Haven, Conn.: Yale University Press, 1975.

——— . *The Rites of Assent: Transformations in the Symbolic Construction of America.* New York: Routledge, 1993.

Bernath, Michael T. *Confederate Minds: The Struggle for Intellectual Independence in the Civil War South.* Chapel Hill: University of North Carolina Press, 2010.

Bigelow, Jacob. *A History of the Cemetery of Mount Auburn.* Boston: James Munroe and Co., 1859.

Blair, William A. *With Malice toward Some: Treason and Loyalty in the Civil War Era.* Chapel Hill: University of North Carolina Press, 2014.

Blewett, Mary. *Constant Turmoil: The Politics of Industrial Life in Nineteenth-Century New England.* Amherst: University of Massachusetts Press, 2000.

Blight, David W. *Race and Reunion: The Civil War in American Memory*. Cambridge, Mass.: Belknap Press of Harvard University Press, 2001.

Blight, David W., and Brooks D. Simpson, eds. *Union and Emancipation: Essays on Politics and Race in the Civil War Era*. Kent, Ohio: Kent State University Press, 1997.

Blue, Frederick J. *The Free Soilers: Third Party Politics, 1848–54*. Urbana: University of Illinois Press, 1973.

———. *No Taint of Compromise: Crusaders in Antislavery Politics*. Baton Rouge: Louisiana State University Press, 2005.

Bonner, Robert E. *Mastering America: Southern Slaveholders and the Crisis of American Nationhood*. Cambridge: Cambridge University Press, 2009.

Bordewich, Fergus M. *America's Great Debate: Henry Clay, Stephen A. Douglas, and the Compromise that Preserved the Union*. New York: Simon and Schuster, 2012.

Bowman, Rex, and Carlos Santos. *Rot, Riot, and Rebellion: Mr. Jefferson's Struggle to Save the University That Changed America*. Charlottesville: University of Virginia Press, 2013.

Brant, Irving. *James Madison*. 6 vols. Indianapolis: Bobbs-Merrill, 1948–61.

Brauer, Kinley J. *Cotton versus Conscience: Massachusetts Whig Politics and Southwestern Expansion, 1843–1848*. Lexington: University of Kentucky Press, 1967.

Brooke, John L. "Cultures of Nationalism, Movements of Reform, and the Composite-Federal Polity: From Revolutionary Settlement to Antebellum Crisis." *Journal of the Early Republic* 29 (Spring 2009): 1–33.

———. *The Heart of the Commonwealth: Society and Political Culture in Worcester County, Massachusetts, 1713–1861*. New York: Cambridge University Press, 1989.

Brookhiser, Richard. *Founders' Son: A Life of Abraham Lincoln*. New York: Basic Books, 2014.

Brown, Arthur W. *Always Young for Liberty: A Biography of William Ellery Channing*. Syracuse, N.Y.: Syracuse University Press, 1956.

Brown, David. "William Lloyd Garrison, Transatlantic Abolitionism and Colonisation in the Mid Nineteenth Century: The Revival of the Peculiar Solution?" *Slavery and Abolition* 33 (June 2012): 233–50.

Brown, Thomas. "Edward Everett and the Constitutional Union Party." *Historical Journal of Massachusetts* 2 (1983): 69–81.

Bruggeman, Seth C. *Here, George Washington Was Born: Memory, Material Culture, and the Public History of a National Monument*. Athens: University of Georgia Press, 2008.

Brunsman, Denver. *The Evil Necessity: British Naval Impressment in the Eighteenth-Century Atlantic World*. Charlottesville: University of Virginia Press, 2013.

Bryan, William Alfred. *George Washington in American Literature, 1775–1865*. New York: Columbia University Press, 1952.

Buell, Lawrence. *New England Literary Culture: From Revolution through Renaissance*. Cambridge: Cambridge University Press, 1986.

Burin, Eric. *Slavery and the Peculiar Solution: A History of the American Colonization Society*. Gainesville: University Press of Florida, 2005.

Burnham, Walter Dean. *Presidential Ballots, 1836–1892*. Baltimore: Johns Hopkins Press, 1955.

Burstein, Andrew. *America's Jubilee*. New York: Alfred A. Knopf, 2001.

Cairns, William B. *British Criticisms of American Writings, 1815–1833: A Contribution to the Study of Anglo-American Literary Relationships*. Madison: University of Wisconsin Press, 1922.

Calhoon, Robert McCluer. *Political Moderation in America's First Two Centuries*. New York: Cambridge University Press, 2009.

Campbell, Stanley W. *The Slave Catchers: Enforcement of the Fugitive Slave Law, 1850–1860.* Chapel Hill: University of North Carolina Press, 1968.

Carlson, Leonard A., and Mark A. Roberts. "Indian Lands, 'Squatterism' and Slavery: Economic Interests and the Passage of the Indian Removal Act of 1830." *Explorations in Economic History* 43 (July 2006): 486–504.

Carroll, E. Malcolm. *Origins of the Whig Party.* Durham, N.C.: Duke University Press, 1925.

Casper, Scott E. *Sarah Johnson's Mount Vernon: The Forgotten History of an American Shrine.* New York: Hill and Wang, 2008.

Cayton, Andrew R. L. "The Debate over the Panama Congress and the Origins of the Second American Party System." *Historian* 47 (February 1985): 219–38.

Chambers, Thomas A. *Memories of War: Visiting Battlegrounds and Bonefields in the Early American Republic.* Ithaca: Cornell University Press, 2012.

Cheng, Eileen Ka-May. *The Plain and Noble Garb of Truth: Nationalism and Impartiality in American Historical Writing, 1784–1860.* Athens: University of Georgia Press, 2008.

Clavin, Matthew J. *Toussaint Louverture and the American Civil War: The Promise and Peril of a Second Haitian Revolution.* Philadelphia: University of Pennsylvania Press, 2010.

Cleves, Rachel Hope. *The Reign of Terror in America: Visions of Violence from Anti-Jacobinism to Antislavery.* Cambridge: Cambridge University Press, 2009.

Cole, Donald B. *The Presidency of Andrew Jackson.* Lawrence: University Press of Kansas, 1993.

Coleman, Mrs. Chapman. *The Life of John J. Crittenden.* 2 vols. Philadelphia: J. B. Lippincott and Co., 1871.

Collison, Gary. *Shadrach Minkins: From Fugitive Slave to Citizen.* Cambridge, Mass.: Harvard University Press, 1997.

Conlin, Michael F. "The Dangerous *Isms* and the Fanatical *Ists*: Antebellum Conservatives in the South and the North Confront the Modernity Conspiracy." *Journal of the Civil War Era* 4 (June 2014): 205–33.

Connerton, Paul. *How Societies Remember.* Cambridge: Cambridge University Press, 1989.

Cooper, William J., Jr. *Jefferson Davis, American.* New York: Vintage, 2000.

——. *The South and the Politics of Slavery, 1828–1856.* Baton Rouge: Louisiana State University Press, 1978.

——. *We Have the War upon Us: The Onset of the Civil War, November 1860 -April 1861.* New York: Alfred A. Knopf, 2012.

Cope, Kevin L., ed. *George Washington in and as Culture.* New York: AMS Press, 2001.

Crapol, Edward. *John Tyler, the Accidental President.* Chapel Hill: University of North Carolina Press, 2006.

Craven, Wesley Frank. *The Legend of the Founding Fathers.* New York: New York University Press, 1956.

Crenshaw, Ollinger. *The Slave States in the Presidential Election of 1860.* Baltimore: Johns Hopkins Press, 1945.

Crider, Jonathan B. "De Bow's Revolution: The Memory of the American Revolution in the Politics of the Sectional Crisis, 1850–1861." *American Nineteenth Century History* 10 (September 2009): 317–32.

Crofts, Daniel W. *Reluctant Confederates: Upper South Unionists in the Secession Crisis.* Chapel Hill: University of North Carolina Press, 1989.

Curl, Donald Walter. "The Baltimore Convention of the Constitutional Union Party." *Maryland Historical Magazine* 67 (Fall 1972): 254–77.

Curti, Merle. *Roots of American Loyalty*. New York: Columbia University Press, 1946.

Cushing, William. *Index to the North American Review, Volumes I–CXXV, 1815–1877*. Cambridge, Mass.: John Wilson and Son, 1878.

Dalzell, Robert F., Jr. *Daniel Webster and the Trial of American Nationalism, 1843–1852*. Boston: Houghton Mifflin, 1973.

———. *Enterprising Elite: The Boston Associates and the World They Made*. Cambridge, Mass.: Harvard University Press, 1987.

Darling, Arthur B. *Political Changes in Massachusetts, 1824–1848*. New Haven, Conn.: Yale University Press, 1925.

Davis, David Brion. *Slavery and Human Progress*. New York: Oxford University Press, 1984.

Delbanco, Andrew. *William Ellery Channing: An Essay on the Liberal Spirit in America*. Cambridge, Mass.: Harvard University Press, 1981.

Dennis, Matthew. *Red, White, and Blue Letter Days: An American Calendar*. Ithaca: Cornell University Press, 2002.

Dew, Charles B. *Apostles of Disunion: Southern Secession Commissioners and the Causes of the Civil War*. Charlottesville: University Press of Virginia, 2001.

Donald, David Herbert. *Charles Sumner and the Coming of the Civil War*. 1960; rev. ed., Naperville, Ill.: Sourcebooks, 2009.

———. *Lincoln*. New York: Simon and Schuster, 1995.

Doyle, Don H. *The Cause of All Nations: An International History of the American Civil War*. New York: Basic Books, 2014.

Du Bois, W. E. B. *The Suppression of the African Slave-Trade to the United States of America, 1638–1870*. Cambridge, Mass.: Harvard University Press, 1896.

Duckett, Alvin Laroy. *John Forsyth, Political Tactician*. Athens: University of Georgia Press, 1962.

Durham, David I. *A Southern Moderate in Radical Times: Henry Washington Hilliard, 1808–1892*. Baton Rouge: Louisiana State University Press, 2008.

Earle, Jonathan H. *Jacksonian Antislavery and the Politics of Free Soil, 1824–1854*. Chapel Hill: University of North Carolina Press, 2004.

———. "The Making of the North's 'Stark Mad Abolitionists': Antislavery Conversion in the United States, 1824–1854." *Slavery and Abolition* 25 (December 2004): 59–75.

Eaton, Joseph. *The Anglo-American Paper War: Debates about the New Republic, 1800–1825*. New York: Palgrave Macmillan, 2012.

Egerton, Douglas R. *He Shall Go Out Free: The Lives of Denmark Vesey*. Madison, Wisc.: Madison House, 1999.

———. *Year of Meteors: Stephen Douglas, Abraham Lincoln, and the Election That Brought on the Civil War*. New York: Bloomsbury Press, 2010.

Emerson, Donald E. *Richard Hildreth*. Baltimore: Johns Hopkins Press, 1946.

Ericson, David F. *Slavery in the American Republic: Developing the Federal Government, 1791–1861*. Lawrence: University Press of Kansas, 2011.

Evans, Eric J. *Sir Robert Peel: Statesmanship, Power and Party*. 2nd ed. New York: Routledge, 2006.

Eyal, Yonatan. *The Young America Movement and the Transformation of the Democratic Party, 1828–1861*. Cambridge: Cambridge University Press, 2007.

Faust, Drew Gilpin. *The Creation of Confederate Nationalism: Ideology and Identity in the Civil War South*. Baton Rouge: Louisiana State University Press, 1988.

Fehrenbacher, Don E. *The Slaveholding Republic: An Account of the United States Government's*

Relations to Slavery. Edited by Ward M. McAfee. New York: Oxford University Press, 2001.

Feller, Daniel. "A Brother in Arms: Benjamin Tappan and the Antislavery Democracy." *Journal of American History* 88 (June 2001): 48–74.

Field, Peter. "The Birth of Secular High Culture: The *Monthly Anthology and Boston Review* and Its Critics." *Journal of the Early Republic* 17 (Winter 1997): 575–609.

Filler, Louis. *The Crusade against Slavery, 1830–1860*. New York: Harper and Row, 1960.

Finkelman, Paul. *Millard Fillmore*. New York: Henry Holt, 2011.

Finkelman, Paul, and Donald R. Kennon, eds. *Congress and the Emergence of Sectionalism from the Missouri Compromise to the Age of Jackson*. Athens, Ohio: Ohio University Press for the United States Capitol Historical Society, 2008.

Fite, Emerson Davis. *The Presidential Campaign of 1860*. 1911; repr., Port Washington, N.Y.: Kennikat Press, 1967.

Fleche, Andre M. *The Revolution of 1861: The American Civil War in the Age of Nationalist Conflict*. Chapel Hill: University of North Carolina Press, 2012.

Foletta, Marshall. *Coming to Terms with Democracy: Federalist Intellectuals and the Shaping of an American Culture*. Charlottesville: University Press of Virginia, 2001.

Foner, Eric. *The Fiery Trial: Abraham Lincoln and American Slavery*. New York: W. W. Norton, 2010.

Foner, Philip S. *Business and Slavery: The New York Merchants and the Irrepressible Conflict*. Chapel Hill: University of North Carolina Press, 1941.

Forbes, Robert Pierce. *The Missouri Compromise and Its Aftermath: Slavery and the Meaning of America*. Chapel Hill: University of North Carolina Press, 2007.

Forgie, George. *Patricide in the House Divided: A Psychological Interpretation of Lincoln and His Age*. New York: W. W. Norton, 1979.

Formisano, Ronald P. *The Transformation of Political Culture: Massachusetts Parties, 1790s–1840s*. New York: Oxford University Press, 1983.

Foster, Herbert Darling. "Webster's Seventh of March Speech and the Secession Movement, 1850." *American Historical Review* 27 (January 1922): 245–70.

Franklin, John Hope. *A Southern Odyssey: Travelers in the Antebellum North*. Baton Rouge: Louisiana State University Press, 1976.

Fredrickson, George M. *Big Enough to Be Inconsistent: Abraham Lincoln Confronts Slavery and Race*. Cambridge, Mass.: Harvard University Press, 2008.

Freehling, William W. *Prelude to Civil War: The Nullification Controversy in South Carolina, 1816–1836*. New York: Oxford University Press, 1965.

———. *The Road to Disunion*. Volume 1, *Secessionists at Bay, 1776–1854*. New York: Oxford University Press, 1990.

———. *The Road to Disunion*. Volume 2, *Secessionists Triumphant, 1854–1861*. New York: Oxford University Press, 2007.

———. *The South vs. the South: How Anti-Confederate Southerners Shaped the Course of the Civil War*. New York: Oxford University Press, 2001.

Friedman, Lawrence J. *Gregarious Saints: Self and Community in American Abolitionism, 1830–1870*. New York: Cambridge University Press, 1982.

Frothingham, Paul Revere. *Edward Everett, Orator and Statesman*. Boston: Houghton Mifflin Company, 1925.

Fuller, A. James. *The Election of 1860 Reconsidered*. Kent, Ohio: Kent State University Press, 2013.

Furstenberg, François. "Beyond Slavery and Freedom: Autonomy, Agency, and Resistance in Early American Political Discourse." *Journal of American History* 89 (March 2003): 1295–1330.

———. *In the Name of the Father: Washington's Legacy, Slavery, and the Making of a Nation.* New York: Penguin, 2006.

Gallagher, Gary W. *Becoming Confederates: Paths to a New National Loyalty.* Athens: University of Georgia Press, 2013.

———. *Causes Won, Lost, and Forgotten: How Hollywood and Popular Art Shape What We Know about the Civil War.* Chapel Hill: University of North Carolina Press, 2008.

———. *The Confederate War.* Cambridge, Mass.: Harvard University Press, 1999.

———. *The Union War.* Cambridge, Mass.: Harvard University Press, 2011.

Gallagher, Gary W., and Rachel A. Shelden, eds. *A Political Nation: New Directions in Mid-Nineteenth-Century American Political History.* Charlottesville: University of Virginia Press, 2012.

Garraty, John A., and Mark C. Carnes, eds. *American National Biography.* 24 vols. New York: Oxford University Press, 1999.

Garrison, Tim Alan. "United States Indian Policy in Sectional Crisis: Georgia's Exploitation of the Compact of 1802." In *Congress and the Emergence of Sectionalism: From the Missouri Compromise to the Age of Jackson*, edited by Paul Finkelman and Donald R. Kennon, 97–124. Athens: Ohio University Press, 2008.

Gatell, Frank Otto. "'Conscience and Judgment': The Bolt of the Massachusetts Conscience Whigs." *Historian* 21 (November 1958): 18–45.

———. *John Gorham Palfrey and the New England Conscience.* Cambridge, Mass.: Harvard University Press, 1963.

Geiger, John O. "A Scholar Meets John Bull: Edward Everett as United States Minister to England, 1841–1845." *New England Quarterly* 49 (December 1976): 577–95.

Gibbons, William. "'Yankee Doodle' and Nationalism, 1780–1920." *American Music* 26 (Summer 2008): 246–74.

Gillis, John, ed. *Commemorations: The Politics of National Identity.* Princeton: Princeton University Press, 1994.

Ginzburg, Lori D. *Women and the Work of Benevolence: Morality, Politics, and Class in the Nineteenth-Century United States.* New Haven: Yale University Press, 1990.

Goodman, Paul. *Towards a Christian Republic: Antimasonry and the Great Transition in New England, 1826–1836.* New York: Oxford University Press, 1988.

Grant, Susan-Mary. "'How a Free People Conduct a Long War': Sustaining Opposition to Secession in the American Civil War." In *Secession as an International Phenomenon: From America's Civil War to Contemporary Separatist Movements*, edited by Don H. Doyle, 132–50. Athens: University of Georgia Press, 2010.

———. *North over South: Northern Nationalism and American Identity in the Antebellum Era.* Lawrence: University Press of Kansas, 2000.

Grant, Susan-Mary, and Brian Holden Reid, eds. *The American Civil War: Explorations and Reconsiderations.* New York: Longman, 2000.

Green, Don. "Constitutional Unionists: The Party That Tried to Stop Lincoln and Save the Union." *Historian* 69 (Spring 2007): 231–53.

Greenberg, Amy S. *Manifest Manhood and the Antebellum American Empire.* Cambridge: Cambridge University Press, 2005.

————. *A Wicked War: Polk, Clay, Lincoln, and the 1846 U.S. Invasion of Mexico*. New York: Alfred A. Knopf, 2012.

Griffin, Clifford S. *Their Brothers' Keepers: Moral Stewardship in the United States, 1800–1865*. New Brunswick, N.J.: Rutgers University Press, 1960.

Grimsted, David. *American Mobbing, 1828–1861: Toward Civil War*. New York: Oxford University Press, 1998.

Grodzins, Dean. *American Heretic: Theodore Parker and Transcendentalism*. Chapel Hill: University of North Carolina Press, 2002.

————. "'Slave Law' versus 'Lynch Law' in Boston: Benjamin Robbins Curtis, Theodore Parker, and the Fugitive Slave Crisis, 1850–1855." *Massachusetts Historical Review* 12 (2010): 1–33.

Guasco, Suzanne Cooper. *Confronting Slavery: Edward Coles and the Rise of Antislavery Politics in Nineteenth-Century America*. DeKalb: Northern Illinois University Press, 2013.

Guelzo, Allen C. "Houses Divided: Lincoln, Douglas, and the Political Landscape of 1858." *Journal of American History* 94 (September 2007): 391–417.

Gunderson, Robert Gray. *Old Gentlemen's Convention: The Washington Peace Conference of 1861*. Madison: University of Wisconsin Press, 1961.

Gustafson, Melanie Susan. *Women and the Republican Party, 1854–1924*. Urbana: University of Illinois Press, 2001.

Gustafson, Sandra M. *Eloquence Is Power: Oratory and Performance in Early America*. Chapel Hill: University of North Carolina Press for the Omohundro Institute of Early American History and Culture, 2000.

Guyatt, Nicholas. "'The Outskirts of Our Happiness': Race and the Lure of Colonization in the Early Republic." *Journal of American History* 95 (March 2009): 986–1011.

————. *Providence and the Invention of the United States, 1607–1876*. Cambridge: Cambridge University Press, 2007.

Halbswachs, Maurice. *On Collective Memory*. Translated and edited by Lewis A. Coser. Chicago: University of Chicago Press, 1992.

Hale, Edward E., Jr. *The Life and Letters of Edward Everett Hale*. 2 vols. Boston: Little, Brown, and Co., 1917.

Hall, Claude H. *Abel Parker Upshur: Conservative Virginian, 1790–1844*. Madison: State Historical Society of Wisconsin, 1964.

Hamer, Philip M. "Great Britain, the United States, and the Negro Seamen Acts, 1822–1848." *Journal of Southern History* 1 (February 1935): 3–28.

Hamilton, Holman. *Prologue to Conflict: The Crisis and Compromise of 1850*. Lexington: University of Kentucky Press, 1964.

Hammond, John Craig, and Matthew Mason, eds. *Contesting Slavery: The Politics of Bondage and Freedom in the New American Nation*. Charlottesville: University of Virginia Press, 2011.

Harris, William C. "Conservative Unionists and the Presidential Election of 1864." *Civil War History* 38 (December 1992): 298–318.

Harrold, Stanley. *Border War: Fighting over Slavery before the Civil War*. Chapel Hill: University of North Carolina Press, 2010.

Hart, Albert Bushnell, ed. *Commonwealth History of Massachusetts*. 5 vols. New York: States History Company, 1927–30.

Hartford, William F. *Money, Morals, and Politics: Massachusetts in the Age of the Boston Associates*. Boston: Northeastern University Press, 2001.

Harvey, Frederick L. *History of the Washington National Monument and Washington National Monument Society*. Washington, D.C.: Government Printing Office, 1903.

Haynes, Sam W. "Anglophobia and the Annexation of Texas: The Quest for National Security." In *Manifest Destiny and Empire: Antebellum American Expansion*, edited by Sam W. Haynes and Christopher Morris, 115–45. College Station: Texas A&M University Press, 1997.

——. *Unfinished Revolution: The Early American Republic in a British World*. Charlottesville: University of Virginia Press, 2010.

Hershberger, Mary. "Mobilizing Women, Anticipating Abolition: The Struggle against Indian Removal in the 1830s." *Journal of American History* 86 (June 1999): 15–40.

Hess, Earl J. *Liberty, Virtue, and Progress: Northerners and Their War for the Union*. 1988; 2nd ed., New York: New York University Press, 1997.

Higham, John. *From Boundlessness to Consolidation: The Transformation of American Culture, 1848–1860*. Ann Arbor, Mich.: William L. Clements Library, 1969.

Hobsbawm, Eric, and Terence Ranger, eds. *The Invention of Tradition*. Cambridge: Cambridge University Press, 1983.

Holt, Michael F. *Franklin Pierce*. New York: Henry Holt, 2010.

——. *The Political Crisis of the 1850s*. New York: W. W. Norton, 1978.

——. *Political Parties and American Political Development from the Age of Jackson to the Age of Lincoln*. Baton Rouge: Louisiana State University Press, 1992.

——. *The Rise and Fall of the American Whig Party: Jacksonian Politics and the Onset of the Civil War*. New York: Oxford University Press, 1999.

Houston, Alan. *Benjamin Franklin and the Politics of Improvement*. New Haven: Yale University Press, 2008.

Howe, Daniel Walker. "A Massachusetts Yankee in Senator Calhoun's Court: Samuel Gilman in South Carolina." *New England Quarterly* 44 (June 1971): 197–220.

——. *The Political Culture of the American Whigs*. Chicago: University of Chicago Press, 1979.

——. *The Unitarian Conscience: Harvard Moral Philosophy, 1805–1865*. Cambridge, Mass.: Harvard University Press, 1970.

——. *What Hath God Wrought: The Transformation of America, 1815–1848*. New York: Oxford University Press, 2007.

Huston, James L. *Calculating the Value of the Union: Slavery, Property Rights, and the Economic Origins of the Civil War*. Chapel Hill: University of North Carolina Press, 2003.

——. "Southerners against Secession: The Arguments of the Constitutional Unionists in 1850–51." *Civil War History* 46 (December 2000): 281–99.

——. *Stephen A. Douglas and the Dilemmas of Democratic Equality*. Lanham, Md.: Rowman and Littlefield, 2007.

Huzzey, Richard. *Freedom Burning: Anti-Slavery and Empire in Victorian Britain*. Ithaca, N.Y.: Cornell University Press, 2012.

Jacobs, Donald M., ed. *Courage and Conscience: Black and White Abolitionists in Boston*. Bloomington: Indiana University Press for the Boston Athenaeum, 1993.

Jervey, Edward D., and C. Harold Huber. "The Creole Affair." *Journal of Negro History* 65 (Summer 1980): 196–211.

Johannsen, Robert W. *The Frontier, the Union, and Stephen A. Douglas*. Urbana: University of Illinois Press, 1989.

——. *Stephen A. Douglas*. New York: Oxford University Press, 1973.

Johnson, Martin P. *Writing the Gettysburg Address*. Lawrence: University Press of Kansas, 2013.

Jones, Howard. *Blue and Gray Diplomacy: A History of Union and Confederate Foreign Relations*. Chapel Hill: University of North Carolina Press, 2010.

———. "The Peculiar Institution and National Honor: The Case of the *Creole* Slave Revolt." *Civil War History* 21 (1975): 28–50.

———. *To the Webster-Ashburton Treaty: A Study in Anglo-American Relations, 1783–1843*. Chapel Hill: University of North Carolina Press, 1977.

Jones, Howard, and Donald A. Rakestraw. *Prologue to Manifest Destiny: Anglo-American Relations in the 1840s*. Wilmington, Del.: Scholarly Resources, 1997.

Jones, Wilbur Devereux. *The American Problem in British Diplomacy, 1841–1861*. Athens: University of Georgia Press, 1974.

———. "The Influence of Slavery on the Webster-Ashburton Negotiations." *Journal of Southern History* 22 (February 1956): 48–58.

Kahler, Gerald E. *The Long Farewell: Americans Mourn the Death of George Washington*. Charlottesville: University of Virginia Press, 2008.

Kallenbach, Joseph E., and Jessamine S. Kallenbach, eds. *American State Governors, 1776–1976: Volume I (Electoral and Personal Data)*. Dobbs Ferry, N.Y.: Oceana Publications, 1977.

Kammen, Michael. *Mystic Chords of Memory: The Transformation of Tradition in American Culture*. New York: Alfred A. Knopf, 1991.

Karp, Matthew J. "Slavery and American Sea Power: The Navalist Impulse in the Antebellum South." *Journal of Southern History* 2 (May 2011): 283–324.

Katula, Richard A. *The Eloquence of Edward Everett: America's Greatest Orator*. New York: Peter Lang, 2010.

Keane, Patrick J. *Coleridge's Submerged Politics: The Ancient Mariner and Robinson Crusoe*. Columbia: University of Missouri Press, 1994.

Kermes, Stephanie. *Creating an American Identity: New England, 1789–1825*. New York: Palgrave Macmillan, 2008.

Kerr-Ritchie, Jeffrey R. "Samuel Ward and the Making of an Imperial Subject." *Slavery and Abolition* 33 (June 2012): 205–19.

Kersh, Rogan. *Dreams of a More Perfect Union*. Ithaca, N.Y.: Cornell University Press, 2001.

Kirwan, Albert D. *John J. Crittenden: The Struggle for the Union*. Lexington: University of Kentucky Press, 1962.

Klunder, Willard Carl. *Lewis Cass and the Politics of Moderation*. Kent, Ohio: Kent State University Press, 1996.

Kneeland, John. *Masterpieces of American Literature: Franklin: Irving: Bryant: Webster: Everett: Longfellow: Hawthorne: Whittier: Emerson: Holmes: Lowe*. Boston: Houghton Mifflin and Co., 1891.

Knupfer, Peter B. *The Union as It Is: Constitutional Unionism and Sectional Compromise, 1787–1861*. Chapel Hill: University of North Carolina Press, 1991.

Kramer, Lloyd. *Nationalism in Europe and America: Politics, Cultures, and Identities since 1775*. Chapel Hill: University of North Carolina Press, 2011.

LaFantasie, Glenn W. "The Paradox of the Gettysburg Addresses." *Civil War Monitor* 3 (Summer 2013): 78–102.

Lakwete, Angela. *Inventing the Cotton Gin: Machine and Myth in Antebellum America*. Baltimore: Johns Hopkins University Press, 2003.

Landis, Michael Todd. *Northern Men with Southern Loyalties: The Democratic Party and the Sectional Crisis*. Ithaca, N.Y.: Cornell University Press, 2014.

Langguth, A. J. *Driven West: Andrew Jackson and the Trail of Tears to the Civil War*. New York: Simon and Schuster, 2010.

Lasser, Carol, and Stacey Robertson. *Antebellum Women: Private, Public, Partisan*. Lanham, Md.: Rowman and Littlefield, 2010.

Laurie, Bruce. *Beyond Garrison: Antislavery and Social Reform*. New York: Cambridge University Press, 2005.

Lawrence, William. *Life of Amos A. Lawrence, with Extracts from His Diary and Correspondence*. Boston: Houghton, Mifflin, and Co., 1888.

Lawson, Melinda. *Patriot Fires: Forging a New American Nationalism in the Civil War North*. Lawrence: University Press of Kansas, 2002.

Lease, Benjamin. *Anglo-American Encounters: England and the Rise of American Literature*. Cambridge: Cambridge University Press, 1981.

Lee, Jean B. "Historical Memory, Sectional Strife, and the American Mecca: Mount Vernon, 1783–1853." *Virginia Magazine of History and Biography* 109 (2001): 255–300.

Lengel, Edward G. *Inventing George Washington: America's Founder, in Myth and Memory*. New York: HarperCollins, 2011.

Levy, Leonard W. "Sims' Case: The Fugitive Slave Law in Boston in 1851." *Journal of Negro History* 35 (January 1950): 39–74.

Lewis, James E., Jr. *The American Union and the Problem of Neighborhood: The United States and the Collapse of the Spanish Empire, 1783–1829*. Chapel Hill: University of North Carolina Press, 1998.

Logan, Deborah A. *Harriet Martineau, Victorian Imperialism, and the Civilizing Mission*. Farnham, U.K.: Ashgate, 2010.

———. *The Hour and the Woman: Harriet Martineau's "Somewhat Remarkable" Life*. Dekalb: Northern Illinois University Press, 2002.

Long, Orie Williams. *Literary Pioneers: Early American Explorers of European Culture*. Cambridge, Mass.: Harvard University Press, 1935.

Loring, James Spear. *The Hundred Boston Orators Appointed by the Municipal Authorities and Other Public Bodies, from 1770 to 1852; Comprising Historical Gleanings, Illustrating the Principles and Progress of Our Republican Institutions*. Boston: John P. Jewett and Co.; Cleveland: Jewett, Proctor, & Worthington, 1852.

Lothrop, Samuel Kirkland. *Memoir of Hon. Nathan Hale, LL.D*. Cambridge, Mass.: John Wilson and Son, 1881.

Magliocca, Gerard N. "The Cherokee Removal and the Fourteenth Amendment." *Duke Law Journal* 53 (December 2003): 873–991.

Maizlish, Stephen E., and John J. Kushma, eds. *Essays on American Antebellum Politics, 1840–1860*. College Station: Texas A&M University Press, 1982.

Malone, Dumas, and Allen Johnson, eds. *Dictionary of American Biography*. 11 vols. New York: Charles Scribner's Sons, 1927–36.

Maltz, Earl M. *Fugitive Slave on Trial: The Anthony Burns Case and Abolitionist Outrage*. Lawrence: University Press of Kansas, 2010.

Martis, Kenneth C. *The Historical Atlas of United States Congressional Districts, 1789–1983*. New York: Free Press, 1982.

Mason, Matthew. "The Battle of the Slaveholding Liberators: Great Britain, the United States, and Slavery in the Early Nineteenth Century." *William and Mary Quarterly*, 3rd ser., 59 (July 2002): 665–96.

———. "John Quincy Adams and the Tangled Politics of Slavery." In *A Companion to*

John Adams and John Quincy Adams, edited by David Waldstreicher, 402–21. Hoboken, N.J.: Wiley-Blackwell, 2013.

——— . "Keeping Up Appearances: The International Politics of Slave Trade Abolition in the Nineteenth-Century Atlantic World." *William and Mary Quarterly*, 3rd ser., 66 (October 2009): 809–32.

——— . "The Local, National, and International Politics of Slavery: Edward Everett's Nomination as U.S. Minister to Great Britain." *Journal of the Civil War Era*, forthcoming.

——— . *Slavery and Politics in the Early American Republic*. Chapel Hill: University of North Carolina Press, 2006.

Mason, Matthew, Katheryn P. Viens, and Conrad Edick Wright, eds. *Massachusetts and the Civil War: The Commonwealth and National Disunion*. Amherst: University of Massachusetts Press, 2015.

Mason, Matthew, and David Waldstreicher, eds. *John Quincy Adams and the Politics of Slavery: Selections from the Diary*. New York: Oxford University Press, forthcoming.

Mason, Nicholas. "*Blackwood's Magazine*, Anti-Americanism, and the Beginnings of Transatlantic Literary Studies." *Symbiosis: A Journal of Anglo-American Literary Relations* 14 (October 2010): 142–57.

——— . *Literary Advertising and the Shaping of British Romanticism*. Baltimore: Johns Hopkins University Press, 2013.

Mathews, James W. "Fallen Angel: Emerson and the Apostasy of Edward Everett." *Studies in the American Renaissance* (1990): 23–32.

Matthews, J. V. "'Whig History': The New England Whigs and a Usable Past." *New England Quarterly* 51 (June 1978): 193–208.

May, Robert E. *The Southern Dream of a Caribbean Empire, 1854–1861*. Baton Rouge: Louisiana State University Press, 1973.

Mayo, James M. *War Memorials as Political Landscape: The American Experience and Beyond*. New York: Praeger, 1988.

McClintock, Russell. *Lincoln and the Decision for War: The Northern Response to Secession*. Chapel Hill: University of North Carolina Press, 2008.

McCormick, Richard Patrick. *The Second American Party System: Party Formation in the Jacksonian Era*. Chapel Hill: University of North Carolina Press, 1966.

McCoy, Drew R. "James Madison and Visions of American Nationality in the Confederation Period: A Regional Perspective." In *Beyond Confederation: Origins of the Constitution and American National Identity*, edited by Richard Beeman et al., 226–59. Chapel Hill: University of North Carolina Press for the Institute of Early American History and Culture, 1987.

——— . *The Last of the Fathers: James Madison and the Republican Legacy*. New York: Cambridge University Press, 1989.

McDaniel, W. Caleb. "The Bonds and Boundaries of Antislavery." *Journal of the Civil War Era* 4 (March 2014): 84–105.

——— . *The Problem of Democracy in the Age of Slavery: Garrisonian Abolitionists and Transatlantic Reform*. Baton Rouge: Louisiana State University Press, 2013.

McDonnell, Michael A., et al., eds. *Remembering the Revolution: Memory, History, and Nation Making from Independence to the Civil War*. Amherst: University of Massachusetts Press, 2013.

McKirdy, Charles. *Lincoln Apostate: The Matson Slave Case*. Oxford: University Press of Mississippi, 2011.

McPherson, James M. *Battle Cry of Freedom: The Civil War Era*. New York: Oxford University Press, 1988.

———. *For Cause and Comrades: Why Men Fought in the Civil War*. New York: Oxford University Press, 1997.

McWhirter, Christian. *Battle Hymns: The Power and Popularity of Music in the Civil War*. Chapel Hill: University of North Carolina Press, 2012.

Melish, Joanne Pope. *Disowning Slavery: Gradual Emancipation and "Race" in New England, 1780–1860*. Ithaca, N.Y.: Cornell University Press, 1998.

Menand, Louis. *The Metaphysical Club: A Story of Ideas in America*. New York: Farrar, Straus and Giroux, 2001.

Mendelsohn, Jack. *Channing the Reluctant Radical*. Boston: Little, Brown, 1971.

Merk, Frederick. *Slavery and the Annexation of Texas*. New York: Alfred A. Knopf, 1972.

Mielke, Laura L. *Moving Encounters: Sympathy and the Indian Question in Antebellum Literature*. Amherst: University of Massachusetts Press, 2008.

Miller, Perry. *Errand into the Wilderness*. Cambridge, Mass.: Belknap Press of Harvard University Press, 1956.

Minardi, Margot. *Making Slavery History: Abolitionism and the Politics of Memory in Massachusetts*. New York: Oxford University Press, 2010.

Minor, Benjamin B. *The Southern Literary Messenger, 1834–1864*. New York: Neale Pub. Co., 1905.

Moniz, Amanda Bowie. "Saving the Lives of Strangers: Humane Societies and the Cosmopolitan Provision of Charitable Aid." *Journal of the Early Republic* 29 (Winter 2009): 607–40.

Morison, Samuel Eliot. *Three Centuries of Harvard, 1636–1936*. Cambridge, Mass.: Harvard University Press, 1937.

Morley, John Viscount. *On Compromise*. 1886; repr., London : Macmillan, 1908.

Morrison, Michael A. "American Reaction to European Revolutions, 1848–1852." *Civil War History* 49 (June 2003): 111–32.

———. *Slavery and the American West: The Eclipse of Manifest Destiny and the Coming of the Civil War*. Chapel Hill: University of North Carolina Press, 1997.

Mott, Frank Luther. *A History of American Magazines*. 5 vols. Cambridge, Mass.: Harvard University Press, 1938–68.

Moulton, Amber D. "Closing the 'Floodgate of Impurity': Moral Reform, Antislavery, and Interracial Marriage in Antebellum Massachusetts." *Journal of the Civil War Era* 3 (March 2013): 2–34.

Mulkern, John R. *The Know-Nothing Party in Massachusetts: The Rise and Fall of a People's Movement*. Boston: Northeastern University Press, 1990.

Murrin, John M. "A Roof without Walls: The Dilemma of American National Identity." In *Beyond Confederation: Origins of the Constitution and American National Identity*, edited by Richard Beeman et al., 333–47. Chapel Hill: University of North Carolina Press for the Institute of Early American History and Culture, 1987.

Nagel, Paul C. *John Quincy Adams: A Public Life, a Private Life*. New York: Alfred A. Knopf, 1997.

———. *One Nation Indivisible: The Union in American Thought, 1776–1861*. New York: Oxford University Press, 1964.

———. *This Sacred Trust: American Nationality, 1798–1898*. New York: Oxford University Press, 1971.

Nash, Gary B., and Graham Russell Gao Hodges. *Friends of Liberty: Thomas Jefferson, Tadeusz Kosciuszko, and Agrippa Hull: A Tale of Three Patriots, Two Revolutions, and a Tragic Betrayal of Freedom in the New Nation*. New York: Basic Books, 2008.

Neem, Johann N. *Creating a Nation of Joiners: Democracy and Civil Society in Early National Massachusetts*. Cambridge, Mass.: Harvard University Press, 2008.

Nevins, Allan. *Hamilton Fish: The Inner History of the Grant Administration*. New York: Dodd, Mead, 1936.

——. *Ordeal of the Union*. 8 vols. New York: Charles Scribner's Sons, 1947–71.

Newman, Richard. *Beverly Garnett Williams: First African American Student Admitted to Harvard*. Cambridge: printed by author, 2002.

Nichols, Roy Franklin. *The Disruption of American Democracy*. 1948; repr., New York: Collier Books, 1962.

Noe, Kenneth W. *Reluctant Rebels: The Confederates Who Joined the Army after 1861*. Chapel Hill: University of North Carolina Press, 2010.

Nye, Russell B. *Fettered Freedom: Civil Liberties and the Slavery Controversy, 1830–1860*. East Lansing: Michigan State University Press, 1963.

Oakes, James. *Freedom National: The Destruction of Slavery in the United States, 1861–1865*. New York: W. W. Norton, 2013.

——. *The Radical and the Republican: Frederick Douglass, Abraham Lincoln, and the Triumph of Antislavery Politics*. New York: W. W. Norton, 2007.

O'Connor, Thomas H. *The Athens of America: Boston, 1825–1845*. Amherst: University of Massachusetts Press, 2006.

——. *Civil War Boston: Home Front and Battlefield*. Boston: Northeastern University Press, 1997.

——. *Lords of the Loom: The Cotton Whigs and the Coming of the Civil War*. New York: Charles Scribner's Sons, 1968.

Onuf, Nicholas, and Peter Onuf. *Nations, Markets, and War: Modern History and the American Civil War*. Charlottesville: University of Virginia Press, 2006.

Onuf, Peter S. *Jefferson's Empire: The Language of American Nationhood*. Charlottesville: University Press of Virginia, 2000.

Orcutt, William Dana. *Good Old Dorchester: A Narrative History of the Town, 1630–1893*. 2nd ed. Cambridge, Mass.: University Press, 1908.

Ostendorf, Ann. *Sounds American: National Identity and the Music Cultures of the Lower Mississippi River Valley, 1800–1860*. Athens: University of Georgia Press, 2011.

Page, Anthony. "'A Species of Slavery': Richard Price's Rational Dissent and Antislavery." *Slavery and Abolition* 32:1 (2011): 53–73.

Parish, Peter J. *The North and the Nation in the Era of the Civil War*. Edited by Adam I. P. Smith and Susan-Mary Grant. New York: Fordham University Press, 2003.

Parks, Joseph H. *John Bell of Tennessee*. Baton Rouge: Louisiana State University Press, 1950.

Pasley, Jeffrey L., et al., eds. *Beyond the Founders: New Approaches to the Political History of the Early American Republic*. Chapel Hill: University of North Carolina Press, 2004.

Paulus, Sarah Bischoff. "America's Long Eulogy for Compromise: Henry Clay and American Politics, 1854–58." *Journal of the Civil War Era* 4 (March 2014): 28–52.

Pease, Jane H., and William H. Pease. *Bound with Them in Chains: A Biographical History of the Antislavery Movement*. Westport, Conn.: Greenwood Press, 1972.

Pennock, J. Roland, and John W. Chapman, eds. *Compromise in Ethics, Law, and Politics*. Nomos 21. New York: New York University Press, 1979.

Petersen, Svend. *The Gettysburg Addresses: The Story of Two Orations*. New York: Frederick Ungar, 1963.

Peterson, Merrill D. *The Great Triumvirate: Webster, Clay, and Calhoun*. New York: Oxford University Press, 1987.

Pletcher, David M. *The Diplomacy of Annexation: Texas, Oregon, and the Mexican War*. Columbia: University of Missouri Press, 1973.

Portnoy, Alisse. *Their Right to Speak: Women's Activism in the Indian and Slave Debates*. Cambridge, Mass.: Harvard University Press, 2005.

Potter, David M. "The Historian's Use of Nationalism and Vice Versa." *American Historical Review* 67 (July 1962): 924–50.

———. *The Impending Crisis, 1848–1861*. New York: Harper and Row, 1976.

Purcell, Sarah J. "All That Remains of Henry Clay: Political Funerals and the Tour of Henry Clay's Corpse." *Common-Place* 12 (April 2012), at www.common-place.org.

———. *Sealed with Blood: War, Sacrifice, and Memory in Revolutionary America*. Philadelphia: University of Pennsylvania Press, 2002.

Quigley, Paul. *Shifting Grounds: Nationalism and the American South, 1848–1865*. New York: Oxford University Press, 2011.

Quinn, Arthur Hobson. *Representative American Plays, from 1767 to the Present Day*. 7th ed. New York: Appleton-Century-Crofts, 1953.

Ramage, James A., and Andrea S. Watkins. *Kentucky Rising: Democracy, Slavery, and Culture from the Early Republic to the Civil War*. Lexington: University Press of Kentucky, 2011.

Ramold, Steven J. *Across the Divide: Union Soldiers View the Northern Home Front*. New York: New York University Press, 2013.

Rao, Gautham. "The Federal *Posse Comitatus* Doctrine: Slavery, Compulsion, and Statecraft in Mid-Nineteenth-Century America." *Law and History Review* 26 (Spring 2008): 1–56.

Reid, Ronald F. "Edward Everett's 'The Character of Washington.'" *Southern Speech Journal* 22 (1957): 144–56.

———. *Edward Everett: Unionist Orator*. New York: Greenwood Press, 1990.

———. "Newspaper Responses to the Gettysburg Addresses." *Quarterly Journal of Speech* 53 (1967): 50–60.

Remini, Robert V. *The House: The History of the House of Representatives*. New York: Smithsonian Books, 2006.

———. *Daniel Webster: The Man and His Time*. New York: W. W. Norton, 1997.

Rice, C. Duncan. "The Antislavery Mission of George Thompson to the United States, 1834–35." *Journal of American Studies* 2 (April 1968): 13–31.

Richard, Carl J. *The Golden Age of the Classics in America: Greece, Rome, and the Antebellum United States*. Cambridge, Mass.: Harvard University Press, 2009.

Richards, Leonard L. *"Gentlemen of Property and Standing": Anti-Abolition Mobs in Jacksonian America*. New York: Oxford University Press, 1970.

———. *The Life and Times of Congressman John Quincy Adams*. New York: Oxford University Press, 1986.

———. *The Slave Power: The Free North and Southern Domination, 1780–1860*. Baton Rouge: Louisiana State University Press, 2000.

Roberts, Timothy Mason. *Distant Revolutions: 1848 and the Challenge to American Exceptionalism*. Charlottesville: University of Virginia Press, 2009.

Robinson, Armstead L. *Bitter Fruits of Bondage: The Demise of Slavery and the Collapse of the Confederacy*. Charlottesville: University of Virginia Press, 2005.

Rocckell, Lelia M. "Bonds over Bondage: British Opposition to the Annexation of Texas." *Journal of the Early Republic* 19 (Summer 1999): 257–78.

Ross, Dorothy. "Lincoln and the Ethics of Emancipation: Universalism, Nationalism, Exceptionalism." *Journal of American History* 96 (September 2009): 379–99.

Rotenstein, David S. "The Civil War, George Washington, and the Mount Vernon Factory." Post at blog.historian4hire.net.

——. "The Gas Man, George Washington, and a Magic Lantern." Post at blog.historian 4hire.net.

Rugemer, Edward Bartlett. *The Problem of Emancipation: The Caribbean Roots of the American Civil War.* Baton Rouge: Louisiana State University Press, 2008.

Ruminski, Jarret. "'Tradyville': The Contraband Trade and the Problem of Loyalty in Civil War Mississippi." *Journal of the Civil War Era* 2 (December 2012): 511–37.

Schlesinger, Andrew. *Veritas: Harvard College and the American Experience.* Chicago: Ivan R. Dee, 2005.

Schlesinger, Arthur M., Jr., ed. *History of American Presidential Elections, 1789–1968.* 2 vols. New York: Chelsea House, 1971.

Schwartz, Barry. *George Washington: The Making of an American Symbol.* New York: Free Press, 1987.

Scott, Sean A. *A Visitation of God: Northern Civilians Interpret the Civil War.* New York: Oxford University Press, 2011.

Seelye, John D. *Memory's Nation: The Place of Plymouth Rock.* Chapel Hill: University of North Carolina Press, 1998.

Shankman, Andrew. Review of *Colonization and Its Discontents*, by Beverly C. Tomek. *Journal of the Civil War Era* 2 (December 2012): 602–5.

Shapiro, Samuel. "The Conservative Dilemma: The Massachusetts Constitutional Convention of 1853." *New England Quarterly* 33 (June 1960): 207–24.

Sheidley, Harlow W. *Sectional Nationalism: Massachusetts Conservative Leaders and the Transformation of America, 1815–1836.* Boston: Northeastern University Press, 1998.

Shelden, Rachel A. "Messmates' Union: Friendship, Politics, and Living Arrangements in the Capital City, 1845–1861." *Journal of the Civil War Era* 1 (December 2011): 453–80.

——. *Washington Brotherhood: Politics, Social Life, and the Coming of the Civil War.* Chapel Hill: University of North Carolina Press, 2013.

Shewmaker, Kenneth. "Daniel Webster and the Politics of Foreign Policy, 1850–1852." *Journal of American History* 63 (September 1976): 303–15.

Silber, Nina. *Gender and the Sectional Conflict.* Chapel Hill: University of North Carolina Press, 2008.

Silbey, Joel H. *The Partisan Imperative: The Dynamics of American Politics before the Civil War.* New York: Oxford University Press, 1985.

Simpson, Lewis. *The Man of Letters in New England and the South: Essays on the History of the Literary Vocation in America.* Baton Rouge: Louisiana State University Press, 1973.

Sinha, Manisha. *The Counter-Revolution of Slavery: Politics and Ideology in Antebellum South Carolina.* Chapel Hill: University of North Carolina Press, 2000.

Smith, Adam I. P. *No Party Now: Politics in the Civil War North.* New York: Oxford University Press, 2006.

Smith, Craig R. *Daniel Webster and the Oratory of Civil Religion.* Columbia: University of Missouri Press, 2005.

Smith, Daniel Blake. *An American Betrayal: Cherokee Patriots and the Trail of Tears*. New York: Henry Holt, 2011.

Smith, Michael Thomas. *The Enemy Within: Fears of Corruption in the Civil War North*. Charlottesville: University of Virginia Press, 2011.

Smith, Thomas V. *The Ethics of Compromise and the Art of Containment*. Boston: Starr King Press, 1956.

Smith-Rosenberg, Carroll. *This Violent Empire: The Birth of an American National Identity*. Chapel Hill: University of North Carolina Press for the Omohundro Institute of Early American History and Culture, 2010.

Spencer, Donald S. *Louis Kossuth and Young America: A Study of Sectionalism and Foreign Policy, 1848–1852*. Columbia: University of Missouri Press, 1977.

Stampp, Kenneth M. *And the War Came: The North and the Secession Crisis, 1860–1861*. 1950; paperback ed., Baton Rouge: Louisiana State University Press, 1970.

——. "The Concept of a Perpetual Union." In *The Imperiled Union: Essays on the Background of the Civil War*, 3–36. New York: Oxford University Press, 1980.

Stange, Douglas Charles. "Abolition as Treason: The Unitarian Elite Defends Law, Order, and the Union." *Harvard Library Bulletin* 28 (April 1980): 152–70.

——. *British Unitarians against American Slavery, 1833–65*. Rutherford, N.J.: Fairleigh Dickinson University Press, 1984.

——. "The Making of an Abolitionist Martyr: Harvard Professor Charles Theodore Christian Follen (1795–1840)." *Harvard Library Bulletin* 24 (January 1976): 17–24.

Stark, James A. *Dorchester Day Celebration of the 277th Anniversary of the Settlement of Dorchester (Mass.)*. Boston: Municipal Printing Office, 1907.

Steele, Brian. "Thomas Jefferson, Coercion, and the Limits of Harmonious Union." *Journal of Southern History* 74 (November 2008): 823–54.

Stewart, James Brewer. *Abolitionist Politics and the Coming of the Civil War*. Amherst: University of Massachusetts Press, 2008.

——. "Abolitionists, Insurgents, and Third Parties: Sectionalism and Partisan Politics in Northern Whiggery, 1836–1844." In *Crusaders and Compromisers: Essays on the Relationship of the Antislavery Struggle to the Antebellum Party System*, edited by Alan M. Kraut, 25–43. Westport, Conn.: Greenwood Press, 1983.

——. *Holy Warriors: The Abolitionists and American Slavery*. Rev. ed. New York: Hill and Wang, 1996.

——. *Wendell Phillips: Liberty's Hero*. Baton Rouge: Louisiana State University Press, 1986.

Storey, Margaret M. *Loyalty and Loss: Alabama's Unionists in the Civil War and Reconstruction*. Baton Rouge: Louisiana State University Press, 2004.

Story, Ronald. *The Forging of an Aristocracy: Harvard and the Boston Upper Class, 1800–1970*. Middletown, Conn.: Wesleyan University Press, 1980.

Streeter, Robert E. "Hawthorne's Misfit Politician and Edward Everett." *American Literature* 16 (1944): 26–28.

Stripp, Fred. "The Other Gettysburg Address." *Civil War History* 1 (June 1955): 161–73.

Sweeney, Kevin. "Rum, Romanism, Representation, and Reform: Coalitional Politics in Massachusetts, 1847–1853." *Civil War History* 22 (June 1976): 116–37.

Tamarkin, Elisa. *Anglophilia: Deference, Devotion, and Antebellum America*. Chicago: University of Chicago Press, 2008.

Taylor, Amy Murrell. *The Divided Family in Civil War America*. Chapel Hill: University of North Carolina Press, 2005.

Taylor, William R. *Cavalier and Yankee: The Old South and American National Character.* 1957; repr., New York: Garden City Books, 1963.

Temperley, Howard. "The O'Connell-Stevenson Contretemps: A Reflection of the Anglo-American Slavery Issue." *Journal of Negro History* 47 (October 1962): 217–33.

Thane, Elswyth. *Mount Vernon Is Ours: The Story of Its Preservation.* New York: Duell, Sloan and Pearce, 1966.

Tiffany, Nina Moore. *Samuel E. Sewall: A Memoir.* Boston: Houghton, Mifflin, 1898.

Tise, Larry E. *Proslavery: A History of the Defense of Slavery in America, 1701–1840.* Athens: University of Georgia Press, 1987.

Tomek, Beverly C. *Colonization and Its Discontents: Emancipation, Emigration, and Antislavery in Antebellum Pennsylvania.* New York: New York University Press, 2011.

Travers, Len. *Celebrating the Fourth: Independence Day and the Rites of Nationalism in the Early Republic.* Amherst: University of Massachusetts Press, 1997.

Trent, James W., Jr. *The Manliest Man: Samuel G. Howe and the Contours of Nineteenth-Century American Reform.* Amherst: University of Massachusetts Press, 2012.

Tyack, David B. *George Ticknor and the Boston Brahmins.* Cambridge, Mass.: Harvard University Press, 1967.

Tyrrell, Ian R. *Sobering Up: From Temperance to Prohibition in Antebellum America, 1800–1860.* Westport, Conn.: Greenwood Press, 1979.

Van Tassel, David D. "Gentlemen of Property and Standing: Compromise Sentiment in Boston in 1850." *New England Quarterly* 23 (September 1950): 307–19.

Varg, Paul A. *Edward Everett: The Intellectual in the Turmoil of Politics.* Selinsgrove, Penn.: Susquehanna University Press, 1992.

Varon, Elizabeth. *Disunion! The Coming of the American Civil War, 1789–1859.* Chapel Hill: University of North Carolina Press, 2008.

———. *Southern Lady, Yankee Spy: The True Story of Elizabeth Van Lew, a Union Agent in the Heart of the Confederacy.* New York: Oxford University Press, 2003.

———. *We Mean to Be Counted: White Women and Politics in Antebellum Virginia.* Chapel Hill: University of North Carolina Press, 1998.

Von Frank, Albert J. *The Trials of Anthony Burns: Freedom and Slavery in Emerson's Boston.* Cambridge, Mass.: Harvard University Press, 1998.

Vorenberg, Michael. *Final Freedom: The Civil War, the Abolition of Slavery, and the Thirteenth Amendment.* Cambridge: Cambridge University Press, 2001.

Waldstreicher, David. *In the Midst of Perpetual Fetes: The Making of American Nationalism, 1776–1820.* Chapel Hill: University of North Carolina Press for the Omohundro Institute of Early American History and Culture, 1997.

———. "The Nationalization and Racialization of American Politics: Before, beneath, and between Parties, 1790–1840." In *Contesting Democracy: Substance and Structure in American Political History, 1775–2000,* edited by Byron E. Shafer and Anthony J. Badger, 37–64. Lawrence: University Press of Kansas, 2001.

Walther, Eric H. *William Lowndes Yancey and the Coming of the Civil War.* Chapel Hill: University of North Carolina Press, 2006.

Ware, Edith Ellen. *Political Opinion in Massachusetts during the Civil War and Reconstruction.* New York: Columbia University Press, 1916.

Warren, George Washington. *The History of the Bunker Hill Monument Association.* Boston: James R. Osgood, 1877.

Warren, Robert Penn. *The Legacy of the Civil War: Meditations on the Centennial*. New York: Random House, 1961.

Weber, Jennifer L. *Copperheads: The Rise and Fall of Lincoln's Opponents in the North*. New York: Oxford University Press, 2006.

West, Patricia. *Domesticating History: The Political Origins of America's House Museums*. Washington, D.C.: Smithsonian Institution Press, 1999.

Whipple, Edwin P. *Character and Characteristic Men*. Boston: Houghton, Mifflin, 1886.

White, Ashli. *Encountering Revolution: Haiti and the Making of the Early Republic*. Baltimore: Johns Hopkins University Press, 2010.

Wilbur, Earl Morse. *A History of Unitarianism in Transylvania, England, and America*. Cambridge, Mass.: Harvard University Press, 1952.

———. *A History of Unitarianism: Socinianism and Its Antecedents*. Cambridge, Mass.: Harvard University Press, 1947.

Wilder, Craig Steven. *Ebony and Ivy: Race, Slavery, and the Troubled History of America's Universities*. New York: Bloomsbury, 2013.

Wilentz, Sean. *The Rise of American Democracy: Jefferson to Lincoln*. New York: W.W. Norton, 2005.

Wills, Garry. *Lincoln at Gettysburg: The Words That Remade America*. New York: Touchstone, 1992.

Willson, Beckles. *America's Ambassadors to England, 1785–1928*. London: John Murray, 1928.

Winthrop, Robert C., Jr. *A Memoir of Robert C. Winthrop, Prepared for the Massachusetts Historical Society*. Boston: Little, Brown, 1897.

Wood, Nicholas. "'A Sacrifice on the Altar of Slavery': Doughface Politics and Black Disenfranchisement in Pennsylvania, 1837–1838." *Journal of the Early Republic* 31 (Spring 2011): 75–106.

Woods, Michael E. *Emotional and Sectional Conflict in the Antebellum United States*. Cambridge: Cambridge University Press, 2014.

———. "'The Indignation of Freedom-Loving People': The Caning of Charles Sumner and Emotion in Antebellum Politics." *Journal of Social History* 44 (Spring 2011): 689–705.

Wright, Conrad Edick, ed. *American Unitarianism, 1805–1865*. Boston: Massachusetts Historical Society and Northeastern University Press, 1989.

Wunder, John R., and Joann M. Ross, eds. *The Nebraska-Kansas Act of 1854*. Lincoln: University of Nebraska Press, 2008.

Yablon, Nick. "'Land of Unfinished Monuments': The Ruins-in-Reverse of Nineteenth-Century America." *American Nineteenth Century History* 13 (June 2012): 153–97.

Yacovone, Donald. *Samuel Joseph May and the Dilemmas of the Liberal Persuasion, 1797–1871*. Philadelphia: Temple University Press, 1991.

Yokota, Kariann Akemi. *Unbecoming British: How Revolutionary America Became a Postcolonial Nation*. New York: Oxford University Press, 2011.

Young, Alfred F. *The Shoemaker and the Tea Party: Memory and the American Revolution*. Boston: Beacon Press, 1999.

Zaeske, Susan. *Signatures of Citizenship: Petitioning, Antislavery, and Women's Political Identity*. Chapel Hill: University of North Carolina Press, 2003.

Zagarri, Rosemarie. "The Family Factor: Congressmen, Turnover, and the Burden of Public Service in the Early American Republic." *Journal of the Early Republic* 33 (Summer 2013): 283–316.

Zboray, Ronald J., and Mary Saracino Zboray. *Voices without Votes: Women and Politics in Antebellum New England*. Durham, N.H.: University of New Hampshire Press, 2010.

Zelinsky, Wilbur. *Nation into State: The Shifting Symbolic Foundations of American Nationalism*. Chapel Hill: University of North Carolina Press, 1988.

Dissertations, Theses, and Unpublished Sources

Brooks, Corey. "Building an Antislavery House: Political Abolitionists and the U.S. Congress." Ph.D. diss., University of California–Berkeley, 2010.

Cason, Robert Florence. "The Public Career of John Forsyth, 1813–1834." M.A. thesis, Emory University, 1935.

Christian, William Kenneth. "The Mind of Edward Everett." Ph.D. diss., Michigan State College, 1952.

Gill, George J. "Edward Everett, Minister to the Court of St. James, 1841–1845." Ph.D. diss., Fordham University, 1959.

Goldschmidt, Eli. "Northeastern Businessmen and the Secession Crisis." Ph.D. diss., New York University, 1972.

Gujer, Bruno. "Free Trade and Slavery: Calhoun's Defense of Southern Interests against British Interference, 1811–1848." Ph.D. diss., University of Zurich, 1971.

Horn, Stuart J. "Edward Everett and American Nationalism." Ph.D. diss., City University of New York, 1973.

Kime, Bradley. "American Unitarians and the George B. English Controversy." Unpublished paper.

Mitton, Steven Heath. "The Free World Confronted: The Problem of Slavery and Progress in American Foreign Relations, 1833–1844." Ph.D. diss., Louisiana State University, 2005.

Reed, John J. "The Emergence of the Whig Party in the North: Massachusetts, New York, Pennsylvania, and Ohio." Ph.D. diss., University of Pennsylvania, 1953.

Sparks, Robert V. "Abolition in Silver Slippers: A Biography of Edmund Quincy." Ph.D. diss., Boston University, 1978.

Stabler, John B. "A History of the Constitutional Union Party: A Tragic Failure." Ph.D. diss., Columbia University, 1954.

Tolf, Robert W. "Edmund Quincy: Aristocrat Abolitionist." Ph.D. diss., University of Rochester, 1957.

Trusty, Norman Lance. "Massachusetts Public Opinion and the Annexation of Texas, 1835–1845." Ph.D. diss., Boston University, 1964.

Watkins, Jordan Tuttle. "Slavery, Sacred Texts, and the Antebellum Confrontation with History." Ph.D. diss., University of Nevada–Las Vegas, 2014.

White, Jonathan W. "'To Aid Their Rebel Friends': Politics and Treason in the Civil War North." Ph.D. diss., University of Maryland, 2008.

Yanikoski, Richard Alan. "Edward Everett and the Advancement of Higher Education and Adult Learning in Antebellum Massachusetts." Ph.D. diss., University of Chicago, 1987.

Index

Stanley, Lord, 135–36
Stanton, Elizabeth Cady, 222
Stevenson, Andrew, 131–32, 134, 147, 350 (n. 32)
Stewart, James Brewer, 223
Strong, George Templeton, 254, 256, 261–62, 311
Stuart, Moses, 170
Sturge, Joseph, 116–17
Sumner, Charles, 149–50, 162, 164–66, 170–71, 179, 186, 195–99, 202–3, 206, 209, 218, 223–31, 256, 267–68, 269, 294, 295, 301, 361 (n. 7), 366 (n. 78)
Sumter, Fort, 267, 269–73, 275–76, 319

Tariffs, 43, 71–79, 137–38, 162
Taylor, Zachary, 164–65, 168, 175, 187
Temperance, 66, 119–21, 155, 166
Texas, annexation of, 106, 109–12, 144–46, 169, 173, 190
Thome, James, 116–18
Thompson, George, 97
Thompson, John R., 183, 219
Thursday Evening Club, 285, 314
Ticknor, George, 13, 16, 21, 185, 188, 294
Tobey, Edward S., 267
Tomek, Beverly, 70
Tories, British, 46, 115, 156
Trescot, William H., 212
Tucker, Nathaniel Beverley, 147
Turnbull, Robert, 39, 69
Turner, Nat, 80
Tyler, John, 124–31, 137–51, 299

Union: Americans' commitment to, 3–5, 7–11, 35, 76–77, 88, 96, 128, 168–71, 177, 182, 186, 189, 195, 210, 219–326 passim, 379–80 (n. 91); opinions on the meaning and nature of, 2, 33, 65, 72, 75–78, 80–81, 89, 215, 235, 244–45, 253, 264–70, 273–75, 277–78, 282–84, 302–4, 306, 321
Union Clubs, 291–92, 294, 310, 311
Unionist party fusion attempts, 77–78, 176,

235, 293, 296. See also Constitutional Union Party
Union meetings, 243–49, 263, 267, 282, 382 (n. 43)
Unitarianism, 16–17, 23–24, 67
University of Virginia, 35, 232, 274
Upham, Charles Wentworth, 183
Upshur, Abel P., 126, 140, 143–51

Van Buren, Martin, 61, 80, 105–6, 107, 112–13, 165, 189, 350 (n. 32)
Van Lew, Elizabeth, 318
Varon, Elizabeth, 9, 61, 318
Vesey, Denmark, 38, 159
Victoria, Queen, 131–32, 136, 153, 188, 297–98
Vinton, Samuel, 79

Wales, Prince of, 255
Walsh, Robert, 28–29
Ward, Samuel Ringgold, 169
War of 1812, 17–18, 20, 44, 55, 77, 290
Warren, Joseph, 103, 180–81
Washburn, Emory, 208
Washington, Bushrod, 20
Washington, George, 1, 4–5, 12–14, 34, 45, 177–79, 254, 257, 259, 273–75, 281–84, 316, 320–21; Everett and, 1, 5, 12–14, 19–20, 21, 34, 84–85, 95–96, 136, 161, 180–82, 186, 196, 210, 214–42 passim, 244–45, 250–51, 254–55, 258, 264, 266, 270, 273–83, 292, 293, 295, 310, 313–15, 317–18, 320; Farewell Address of, 5, 179–80, 182, 188, 190, 218, 231, 237, 241, 244–45, 254, 257
Washington, John A., Jr., 216, 232
Washington, Martha, 217
Webster, Daniel, 3, 5, 34, 37, 53, 69, 71, 74, 76–77, 79, 90, 92, 94, 99, 102, 107, 108, 120, 122, 126, 130–31, 138–46, 148–49, 154, 159, 162, 167–76, 181–82, 184–85, 187–89, 194, 196, 206, 214, 222–24, 271, 283, 294, 295, 310–11; relationship with Everett, 14, 25, 32, 76–77, 93, 110, 124, 150, 167–76,